MAGNÚS EIRÍKSSON
A FORGOTTEN CONTEMPORARY OF KIERKEGAARD

Magnús Eiríksson
A Forgotten Contemporary of Kierkegaard

Edited by Gerhard Schreiber and Jon Stewart

Museum Tusculanum Press
2017

Gerhard Schreiber and Jon Stewart (eds.)
Magnús Eiríksson
A Forgotten Contemporary of Kierkegaard

Layout and cover design by Katalin Nun Stewart, Denmark
Printed in Denmark by Tarm Bogtryk
ISBN 978 87 635 4390 3
ISSN 1903 3338

Danish Golden Age Studies
vol. 10

Cover illustration:
Frederik Theodor Kloss, *Reykjavik.*
Illustration from *Prospecter af Island* (1835)
Public domain image. www.heimskringla.no

This volume is published with financial support from
Lillian og Dan Finks Fond
Jens Nørregaard & Hal Kochs Mindefond
Aksel Tovborg Jensens Legat
Landsdommer V. Gieses Legat

Museum Tusculanum Press
Birketinget 6
DK-2300 Copenhagen S
Denmark
order@mtp.dk
www.mtp.dk

Magnús Eiríksson (1806-81)
(Photo by Carl Peter Herman Most, around 1863.
Private collection. Courtesy of Aðalsteinn Garðarsson.)

Table of Contents

List of Contributors

Vilhjálmur Árnason, University of Iceland, Department of Philosophy, Gimli, IS-101 Reykjavík, Iceland.

Roe Fremstedal, University of Tromsø, Department of Philosophy, NO-9037 Tromsø, Norway.

Friedrich Hauschildt, Händelstr. 17, 29223 Celle, Germany.

Stefan M. Jonasson, 9 Rowand Avenue, Winnipeg, Manitoba R3J 2N4, Canada.

Carl Henrik Koch, Department of Media, Cognition and Communication, University of Copenhagen, Njalsgade 80, 2300 Copenhagen S, Denmark.

Jón Bragi Pálsson, University of Iceland, Department of Philosophy, Gimli, IS-101 Reykjavík, Iceland.

Gerhard Schreiber, Goethe University Frankfurt, Department of Protestant Theology, Norbert-Wollheim-Platz 1, 60629 Frankfurt am Main/Institute for Theology and Social Ethics, Technical University of Darmstadt, Dolivostr. 15, 64293 Darmstadt, Germany.

Jon Stewart, Søren Kierkegaard Research Centre at the University of Copenhagen, Farvergade 27D, 1463 Copenhagen K, Denmark.

Curtis L. Thompson, Thiel College, Department of Religion, 75 College Avenue, Greenville, PA 16125-2181, USA.

Gudmundur Bjorn Thorbjornsson, Vrije Universiteit Brussel, Philosophy and Moral Sciences, Pleinlaan 2, B-1050 Brussels, Belgium.

Sigridur Thorgeirsdottir, University of Iceland, Department of Philosophy, Gimli, IS-101 Reykjavík, Iceland.

Abbreviations of Kierkegaard's Primary Texts

BA = *The Book on Adler*, trans. by Howard V. Hong and Edna H. Hong, Princeton: Princeton University Press 1998.

CD = *Christian Discourses*, trans. by Howard V. Hong and Edna H. Hong, Princeton: Princeton University Press 1997.

CUP1 = *Concluding Unscientific Postscript*, vol. 1, trans. by Howard V. Hong and Edna H. Hong, Princeton: Princeton University Press 1982.

CUP2 = *Concluding Unscientific Postscript*, vol. 2, trans. by Howard V. Hong and Edna H. Hong, Princeton: Princeton University Press 1982.

EO1 = *Either/Or*, Part I, trans. by Howard V. Hong and Edna H. Hong, Princeton: Princeton University Press 1987.

EO2 = *Either/Or*, Part II, trans. by Howard V. Hong and Edna H. Hong, Princeton: Princeton University Press 1987.

FT = *Fear and Trembling*, trans. by Howard V. Hong and Edna H. Hong, Princeton: Princeton University Press 1983.

JP = *Søren Kierkegaard's Journals and Papers*, ed. and trans. by Howard V. Hong and Edna H. Hong, assisted by Gregor Malantschuk, vols. 1–6, vol. 7 Index and Composite Collation, Bloomington and London: Indiana University Press 1967-78.

KJN = *Kierkegaard's Journals and Notebooks*, vols. 1–11, ed. by Niels Jørgen Cappelørn, Alastair Hannay, David Kangas, Bruce H. Kirmmse, George Pattison, Vanessa Rumble, and K. Brian Söderquist, Princeton and Oxford: Princeton University Press 2007-.

LD = *Letters and Documents*, trans. by Henrik Rosenmeier, Princeton: Princeton University Press 1978.

M = *The Moment and Late Writings*, trans. by Howard V. Hong and Edna H. Hong, Princeton: Princeton University Press 1998.

Pap. = *Søren Kierkegaards Papirer*, vols. I to XI–3, ed. by Peter Andreas Heiberg, Victor Kuhr and Einer Torsting, Copenhagen: Gyldendalske Boghandel, Nordisk Forlag 1909–48; second, expanded ed., vols. I to XI–3, by Niels Thulstrup, vols. XII–XIII supplementary volumes, ed. by Niels Thulstrup, vols. XIV–XVI index by Niels Jørgen Cappelørn, Copenhagen: Gyldendal 1968-78.

PC = *Practice in Christianity*, trans. by Howard V. Hong and Edna H. Hong, Princeton: Princeton University Press 1991.

PF = *Philosophical Fragments*, trans. by Howard V. Hong and Edna H. Hong, Princeton: Princeton University Press 1985.

PV = *The Point of View including On My Work as an Author, The Point of View for My Work as an Author, and Armed Neutrality*, trans. by Howard V. Hong and Edna H. Hong, Princeton: Princeton University Press 1998.

SKS = *Søren Kierkegaards Skrifter*, vols. 1–28, K1–K28, ed. by Niels Jørgen Cappelørn, Joakim Garff, Jette Knudsen, Johnny Kondrup, Alastair McKinnon and Finn Hauberg Mortensen, Copenhagen: Gad 1997-2013.

WL = *Works of Love*, trans. by Howard V. Hong and Edna H. Hong, Princeton: Princeton University Press 1995.

Acknowledgements

The present volume is the first anthology devoted to the Icelandic theologian and religious author Magnús Eiríksson, a forgotten contemporary of Søren Kierkegaard. Such a project would never have been realized without the support of numerous people and institutions. First and foremost we would like to thank all of the contributing authors for their willingness and diligent efforts to venture into uncharted scholarly terrain. Their outstanding articles can without hesitation be regarded as pioneering work, which fruitfully goes beyond the many predominant generalizations and oversimplifications in the limited scholarship on this fascinating Icelandic thinker.

The nucleus of this anthology goes back to a special session about Magnús Eiríksson at a conference of The Nordic Network of Kierkegaard Research (NordForsk) on "Kierkegaard's Philosophical Psychology" at the University of Iceland on May 24, 2013. This session was organized by Vilhjálmur Árnason (University of Iceland) in cooperation with Jon Stewart from The Søren Kierkegaard Research Centre (University of Copenhagen). Short presentations and a panel discussion by the Icelandic scholars Pétur Pétursson, Páll Valsson and Kristian Guttesen were followed by a lecture by Gerhard Schreiber (Goethe University Frankfurt) on "Eiríksson's Relation to Kierkegaard Reconsidered." The subsequent lively discussion was testimony to a clear interest in Eiríksson's ideas and at the same time revealed how regrettable it was that there had been so little by way of serious scholarly study of this thinker. From this event arose the plan of making Magnús Eiríksson the sole object of an anthology, and when this was made known it proved relatively easy to find qualified scholars interested in contributing articles.

A further intermediary stage in this project is found in the seminar "Criticisms of Kierkegaard: Magnús Eiríksson," which was organized by Jon Stewart under the auspices of NordForsk and The Søren

Kierkegaard Research Centre. This seminar took place at the University of Copenhagen on August 27, 2014, and the featured speakers were Roe Fremstedal (University of Tromsø), who presented his paper "Magnus Eiríksson's Critique of Kierkegaard and Kierkegaard's Response" and Gerhard Schreiber whose lecture was entitled "Eiríksson, Kierkegaard and the Immediacy of Faith."

Many individuals have been helpful in creating this work. Aðalsteinn Garðarsson, Hólmfríður Kolbrún Gunnarsdóttir, Ævar Kjartansson and Pétur Pétursson provided us many important and interesting information about the familial background of Magnús Eiríksson and the Icelandic reception of his works and ideas. Finn Gredal Jensen helped with the proofreading of the final text. We would like to thank Jón Bragi Pálsson and Silvia Vignati for their tremendous help with preparing the auction catalogue of Eiríksson's library. In this respect our thanks also goes to Hans Larsson from The Swedish Labour Movement's Archives and Library (Arbetarrörelsens arkiv och bibliotek), Huddinge, Sweden, as well as to Jeanette Schindler and Johnson Srigiri for their help in translating. We are especially grateful to Poul Houe for his meticulous corrections and astute critical comments, which improved the manuscript considerably. Last, not least, we would like to thank Katalin Nun Stewart for her most conscientious efforts in taking care of the layouting, typesetting, and cover design.

We are extremely thankful to everyone involved for their kind cooperation, without which this volume would never have been possible.

Generous financial support for this work has been provided by Lillian og Dan Finks Fond, Jens Nørregaard & Hal Kochs Mindefond, Aksel Tovborg Jensens Legat, and Landsdommer V. Gieses Legat.

Introduction

Magnús Eiríksson was born on June 21, 1806,[1] the eldest of the five children of Eiríkur Grímsson (1770-1813), a farmer, and Þorbjörg Stephánsdóttir (1786-1841), a pastor's daughter, on the northernmost farm of Iceland in Skinnalón on the peninsula Melrakkaslétta, county of Norður-Þingeyjarsýsla.[2] After graduating from the Bessastaðir Latin School in 1829 with top marks, Eiríksson worked in Reykjavík as a clerk for Lorentz Angel Krieger (1797-1838), the then governor of Iceland (1829-37), who soon became favorably disposed towards Eiríksson and assisted him with money to enable him to study theology at the University of Copenhagen. With financial help provided by his stepfather Björn Sigurðsson (1778-1852) and Krieger, Eiríksson embarked on a ship to sail to Denmark in the summer of 1831, on the very day that he had broken his engagement with Guðríður Magnúsdóttir Bergmann (1807-80)—an event which caused considerable stir in Reykjavík.[3]

Eiríksson entered the University of Copenhagen in the winter semester of 1831-32, one year after Søren Kierkegaard (1813-55), and began his studies of theology after passing the second exam in October

[1] Contrary to the prevailing opinion, Eiríksson was *not* born on June 22, but on June 21, as indicated in the parish records (see Ágúst Hákonarson Bjarnason, "Um Magnús Eiríksson," *Skírnir. Tímarit hins íslenska bókmenntafélags*, vol. 98, 1924, pp. 39-73, here p. 42 (note 1)) and also, for example, in the certificate from Bessastaðir Latin School in the Department of Manuscripts at The National and University Library of Iceland, Lbs. 387, fol. (ID 7954).

[2] At that time Iceland was a part of the Kingdom of Denmark. After having been under the control of the Danish Crown since 1380, Iceland became a sovereign state in a personal union with Denmark in 1918 (when it was the Kingdom of Iceland), before the Republic of Iceland was established on June 17, 1944.

[3] See Jón Helgason, *Vér Íslands börn*, vols. 1-3, Reykjavík: Iðunn 1968-70; vol. 3, *Heimur á við hálft kálfskinn*, pp. 7ff.

of 1831.[1] Eiríksson focused mainly on the study and interpretation of the Bible and soon made a name for himself as a devoted exegete. After passing his theological exam on April 28, 1837, again with top marks, Eiríksson made a short summer trip to Iceland to visit his relatives and friends on the East Fjords. Disappointing their hope that he would settle in Iceland and become a pastor, Eiríksson returned to Copenhagen, where he spent the years from 1838 to 1847 as a *manuduktør*, a tutor assisting younger students to prepare for the official exams in theology.

For a time Eiríksson enjoyed being in great demand, particularly in the fields of Old and New Testament exegesis. Yet his unyielding and relentless opposition to the fashionable speculative theology of Hans Lassen Martensen (1808-84), "the rising star of the Faculty,"[2] steadily damaged his reputation,[3] and sharply reduced the demand for his services. This led to serious financial difficulties, which was made more acute by the fact that Eiríksson had willingly assisted other friends and acquaintances with money[4] and had to publish many of his works at his own expense.[5] In his hour of need, Eiríksson even appealed to Kierkegaard directly for material support, but this request was refused.[6]

---

1 At this time students usually took their matriculation exam (*examen artium*) in October and around a year later completed the second exam (*examen philologico-philosophicum*), after which they could begin their studies in their area of expertise. See Julia Watkin, "Copenhagen University," in her *Historical Dictionary of Kierkegaard's Philosophy*, Lanham and London: Scarecrow Press 2001, pp. 57f. In his *examen artium* in October 1831, Eiríksson obtained the first grade (*laudabilis*), see the certificate in Lbs. 387, fol. (ID 7954).

2 Niels Thulstrup, "The University," in *Kierkegaard as a Person*, Copenhagen: C.A. Reitzel 1983 (*Bibliotheca Kierkegaardiana*, vol. 12), pp. 50-62, here p. 58.

3 In 1847, Eiríksson even went so far as to sue Martensen for his teachings in a letter to King Christian VIII himself; see Magnús Eiríksson, *Speculativ Rettroenhed, fremstillet efter Dr. Martensens "christelige Dogmatik", og Geistlig Retfærdighed, belyst ved en Biskops Deeltagelse i en Generalfiskal-Sag*, Copenhagen: Salomon 1849, p. II. As to the "Public Prosecutor's Action" against Eiríksson in the aftermath of this letter, see the texts and extracts reproduced in *Speculativ Rettroenhed*, pp. 87-134.

4 See Hermann Heinrich Louis Schwanenflügel, "Magnus Eirikson," [sic!] *Det nittende Aarhundrede. Maanedskrift for Literatur og Kritik*, vols. 1-6, ed. by Georg Brandes and Edvard Brandes, Copenhagen: Gyldendal 1875-77; vol. 6, 1877, pp. 266-294, here p. 284 and p. 294.

5 All of Eiríksson's works between 1870 and 1874 were published by Eiríksson himself.

6 See Eiríksson's letter to Kierkegaard of October 14, 1847, and Kierkegaard's frigid response (probably) on the very same day in *SKS* 28, 370-372, Brev 245 / *LD*, 228-230, Letter 163 and *SKS* 28, 372, Brev 246 / *LD*, 231, Letter 164, respectively.

In 1856, Eiríksson's tight financial situation, which was a consistent feature of his life from the 1840s onward, could have easily taken a turn for the better, when he, thanks to the efforts and persuasiveness of the Icelandic bishop Helgi Guðmundsson Thordersen (1794-1867), agreed to apply for a pastoral appointment on Iceland.[1] He needed persuading since he was critical of the church's doctrine.[2] Soon after his application for this appointment was granted, however, Eiríksson tendered his resignation—a fact that can be traced to the drastic changes that his theology, above all his understanding of the Bible, underwent during the period of his literary silence (1851-63), when he published almost only occasional articles in magazines and newspapers.[3]

From 1863 on, Eiríksson's writings exhibit a radical and ever-intensifying critique of both the Bible and the Church doctrine, especially the doctrines of the Trinity and the divinity of Christ. Eiríksson's self-understanding, as it appears ever more clearly in his late writings, is that of a reformer of the prevailing faith of the Christian Church. With perfect clarity and unsurpassable polemics he writes in *Paul and Christ* (1871):

> The Christian world needs a religious Reformation; the sad religious state of things among the Christian peoples make this clear. Therefore, it will not be possible to avoid such a reformation for long; it will and must come.... For the true religious simplicity, the childlike piety and inwardness, which is the main thing in the Christian-religious relation to God, is missing among all the well-known German scholars and free-thinking progressive theologians in the present, and the same thing is also true of the other Christian countries. This lies in the irreligious spirit of the age....For since the simple and rational religious truth, which we here seek to put forth instead of the ecclesiastical confusions—in order thereby to rescue people

---

1 According to Schwanenflügel, already in 1841 "a family member" ("Magnus Eirikson," p. 285)—probably Eiríksson's brother Jón—successfully applied for a good parish in East Iceland, unbeknown to Eiríksson, who refused to take this offer.

2 See Gerhard Schreiber, " 'Like a Voice in the Wilderness': Magnús Eiríksson's Tenacious Critique of Martensen—and Martensen's 'Lofty Silence,' " in *Hans Lassen Martensen. Theologian, Philosopher and Social Critic*, ed. by Jon Stewart, Copenhagen: Museum Tusculanum Press 2012 (*Danish Golden Age Studies*, vol. 6), pp. 155-191, here pp. 158-167.

3 See the bibliography on Magnús Eiríksson by Gerhard Schreiber in the present volume.

> from the stream of irreligiosity, which now carries away the majority and which the church cannot stop—is either straightforwardly the teaching of Christ or in agreement with it and its spirit, then to deny this salvific truth, which is now brought forth anew after it has for such a long time been garbled and repressed by the church, would amount to crucifying Christ anew: and those who now do this, will, note well, not be any less guilty than those who did it the first time, but their sin and guilt will in fact be much greater.[1]

In contrast to the deification of humanity, as expressed for him in the doctrine of the divinity of Christ, Eiríksson stressed the essential *unity* of God and the role of Jesus as (merely) a prophet and a teacher. The aim of Eiríksson's "reform" was to be a new, "rational religion," marked through and through by freedom of thought and conscience in matters of religion and by a positively understood "simple-mindedness" and "love of one's neighbor."[2]

In Denmark, on the whole, Eiríksson's writings provoked a wide spectrum of reactions, mainly in the form of anonymous or pseudonymous reviews and articles. These ranged in tone from radical rejection at one extreme, to a broad middle of more or less positively-disposed reviews, to open professions of sympathy for Eiríksson and his message at the other end. The main Church figures and theologians in Copenhagen, however, constantly took care to avoid engaging Eiríksson or his ideas in public debate and met his critique of the Church with "lofty silence."[3] Contrary to the ambiguous reception in Denmark, in his

---

[1] Magnús Eiríksson, *Paulus og Christus eller Pauli Lære om Retfærdiggjørelsen sammenlignet med Christi Lære om Syndsforladelsen, tilligemed nogle Bemærkninger om andre paulinske Lærdomme m. M.*, Copenhagen: Magnús Eiríksson 1871, pp. XXIX-XXX (emphases removed).

[2] See Gerhard Schreiber, "Magnús Eiríksson: An Opponent of Martensen and an Unwelcome Ally of Kierkegaard," in *Kierkegaard and His Danish Contemporaries*, Tome II, *Theology*, ed. by Jon Stewart, Aldershot: Ashgate 2009 (*Kierkegaard Research: Sources, Reception and Resources*, vol. 7), pp. 49-94, here pp. 68-70, as well as the article by Friedrich Hauschildt in the present volume.

[3] Magnús Eiríksson, *Dr. Martensens trykte moralske Paragrapher, eller det saakaldte "Grundrids til Moralphilosophiens System af Dr. Hans Martensen," i dets forvirrede, idealistisk-metaphysiske og phantastisk-speculative, Religion og Christendom undergravende, fatalistiske, pantheistiske og selvforguderiske Væsen*, Copenhagen: H.C. Klein 1846, p. II. See also Eiríksson's retrospective account in "My Activity as an

native Iceland, Eiríksson's reception was almost uniformly harsh,[1] often being accompanied by threatening and abusive language.[2] In Sweden, by contrast, Eiríksson's thought found more fertile soil—thanks above all to the freethinking pastor Nils Johan Ekdahl (1799-1870),[3] who translated two of Eiríksson's books into Swedish.

In 1878, Eiríksson was even provided with funds to make a brief return to Iceland—the homeland that he had not seen since that summer

---

Author" ("Min Forfattervirksomhed," in *Flyvende Blade for Literatur, Kunst, og Samfundsspørgsmaal*, vols. 1-3, ed. by Vilhelm Møller, Copenhagen: Peter Bjørnbaks Forlag 1874-75, vol. 3, no. 11 (June 12, 1875), pp. 81-83, no. 12 (June 19, 1875), pp. 90-93, and no. 13 (June 26, 1875), pp. 100-104), where he states that his "opponents who have always seemed to be afraid of my writings, always tried to hush them up" (p. 81). This continuing silence of "the competent ones" (as stated in an anonymous review of Eiríksson's book *Jøder og Christne* (1873) in *Dagens Nyheder*, 1873, no. 113, April 28) was criticized by Eiríksson's advocates and opponents alike. As soon as in the draft "Self-Defense against Unauthorized Acknowledgment" from mid-November 1846, by means of which Kierkegaard sought to counter Eiríksson's praise (in his 1846 book *Dr. Martensens trykte moralske Paragrapher*) of Kierkegaard's *Postscript* as an excellent critique of Martensen's speculative theology, Kierkegaard talked of "a misuse of the polemics of silence," by means of which "the elite...have wanted to destroy him [sc. Eiríksson]" (*Pap.* VII-1 B 88, pp. 287–98 / *CUP2*, 127–37, here *Pap.* VII-1 B 88, p. 294 / *CUP2*, 134). On Kierkegaard's deep discomfort with Eiríksson's "unauthorized" praise see Schreiber, "Magnús Eiríksson: An Opponent of Martensen and an Unwelcome Ally of Kierkegaard," pp. 71-81 and pp. 86-90.

1 See sections I and II of the article on the Icelandic reception of Eiríksson by Vilhjálmur Árnason and Jón Bragi Pálsson in the present volume.

2 See, for example, Stephen Hole Fritchman, *Men of Liberty. Ten Unitarian Pioneers*, Boston: Beacon Press 1944, pp. 163-180, here p. 171: Eiríksson "was called by his detractors 'Magnus, the serpent's tongue.' One minister from Iceland [sc. Jón Þórðarson Thoroddsen (1818-68)] cried: 'The devil possess[es] this anti-Christ. Where are the authorities that they do not burn this modern Arius as the men at Geneva burned Servetus?' Then, thinking he may have been too violent, or perhaps impolitic, he added: 'At least his books could be burned and he himself banished for life' "; compare "J. Þ. Th." [Jón Þórðarson Thoroddsen], "NOKKUR ORÐ um Magnús Eiríksson og stóru bókina," *Íslendingur*, vol. 4, 1865, no. 12 (June 22), pp. 89-90, here p. 90. See also the article by Gudmundur Bjorn Thorbjornsson on Eiríksson's quarrel with the Catholic priests on Iceland in the present volume.

3 See Harald Ossian Wieselgren, "*Ekdahl, Nils Johan*," in *Nordisk familjebok. Konversationslexikon och realencyklopedi*, vols. 1-20, ed. by Nils Lindner, Stockholm: Gernandts boktryckeri-aktiebolag 1876-99; vol. 4, 1881, columns 294f. For an example of Eiríksson's often repeated praise of Ekdahl and his "love to the truth," see the preface of Magnús Eiríksson, *Gud og Reformatoren. En religiøs Idee. Samt nogle Bemærkninger om de kirkelige Tilstande, Dr. S. Kierkegaard og Forfatteren*, Copenhagen: J.H. Schubothe 1866, pp. III-XXXII, here especially pp. V-VI.

trip in 1837, and which he had been forced to postpone visiting until, in the end, his failing health made such a visit impossible. After his death on July 3, 1881, at Frederik's Hospital in Copenhagen, Eiríksson's friends set up a mounted bust—which has since been dismantled—on his grave in Garnison's Cemetery.[1]

In general, Eiríksson was characterized by those who knew him as an extraordinarily congenial and helpful person, and he was generally addressed as "Frater (brother)."[2] However, in theological questions he was relentless[3] and so completely convinced of the correctness of his position and the truth of his belief that he preferred to accept the social position of an outsider and consequently live with personal deprivations than sacrifice his conviction. "It speaks for his extraordinary moral strength that he could never give up what he regarded as truth and justice. For this his nature was too simple, his soul too full of honesty."[4] To subordinate himself or go along with what was in the existing Christianity in his eyes contrary to the testimony of the Bible or was rejected for clear reasons based on rationality was out of the question for Eiríksson.

With his criticism of society, politics and religion Eiríksson admittedly never really gained a hearing. Also his much discussed and generally positively received treatise *On Baptists and Infant Baptism* (1844),[5] in which he sought to protest publicly against the repression

---

1 See the picture of the bust in Bjarnason, "Um Magnús Eiríksson," as insertion between p. 40 and p. 41.

2 For example, no less than Jón Sigurðsson, *Bréf Jóns Sigurðssonar. Úrval*, ed. by Jón Jensson and Þorleifur H. Bjarnason, Reykjavík: Hið íslenska bókmenntafélag 1911, p. 231, p. 252 and p. 374. See further Eiríkur Albertsson, *Magnús Eiríksson. Guðfræði hans og trúarlíf*, Doctoral Dissertation, Háskóli Íslands, Reykjavik 1938, p. 39. Also various letters to Magnús Eiríksson from his friends and acquaintances were using simply "Frater" (brother) as form of address, see Lbs. 302-305, fol. (ID 282-285) and Lbs. 1238, 4to (ID 1561), Department of Manuscripts at The National and University Library of Iceland.

3 On the conflict with Grundtvig see the article by Carl Henrik Koch in the present volume; on the conflict with Martensen see the article by Gerhard Schreiber together with Martensen's post-mortem defense by Curtis Thompson.

4 Schwanenflügel, "Magnus Eirikson," pp. 283f. (emphases removed).

5 Magnús Eiríksson, *Om Baptister og Barnedaab, samt flere Momenter af Den kirkelige og speculative Christendom*, Copenhagen: P.G. Philipsen 1844. See the mainly positive reviews by Carl Emil Scharling and Christian Thorning Engelstoft in *Theologisk Tidsskrift*, vol. 8, 1844, pp. 399-404; by Anonymous in *Fædrelandet*, 1844, no. 1572 and nos 1590-1591; by "Th. G. R." in *Kjøbenhavnsposten*, 1844, no. 92 (April 20); by "En Lægmand i den angrebne danske Statskirke" in *Kjøbenhavnsposten*, 1844, no. 104 (May

of the Baptist free-church movement in the 1840s by Danish state and church, and the practice of forced baptism,[1] failed to set off a *theological* discussion. Testimony to his wholly humble success as a religious author, who later had to sell his own books at his front door,[2] can also be found in the fact that, with a single exception,[3] none of his works were ever sold out in his lifetime; after his death, in his own personal library at the time it was auctioned off at the end of September 1881 there were still a quite large number of copies of his works remaining.[4]

One must maintain "that he, who labored all his life so strictly and honestly and with such unbending conviction, nonetheless had such a small effect, indeed, here at home [sc. in Denmark] almost none at all!"[5] Toward the end of Eiríksson's lifetime, 1877, the literary historian Hermann Heinrich Louis Schwanenflügel (1844-1921) concludes, not without a tinge of regret: "We have to realize that Magnus Eiríksson's

---

6); by Anonymous in *Allgemeine Literatur-Zeitung*, 1845, vol. 2, no. 246 (November), columns 777-784; no. 247 (November), columns 785-792; no. 248 (November), columns 795-800; and by Anonymous in *Aarhuus Stifts-Tidende*, 1844, no. 89 (May 21); for a more critical review see Ludvig Nicolaus Helveg in *For Literatur og Kritik*, vol. 2, 1844, pp. 305-314.

1 See Schreiber, "'Like a Voice in the Wilderness,'" pp. 158-167.

2 See Schwanenflügel, "Magnus Eirikson," p. 294.

3 That is, the work *Hvem har Ret: Grundtvigianerne eller deres Modstandere? og Hvad har Christus befalet om Daaben? Nogle orienterende Bemærkninger*, Copenhagen: E.L. Thaarup 1863, which saw a second printing in the same year.

4 According to the auction catalogue of Eiríksson's library, *Fortegnelse over endel forskjellige gode og velconditionerede Bogsamlinger...tilhørende Boerne efter afdøde Overlærer Poul Chr. Nielsen, Districtslæge Wilhjelm, Pastor Krogh, Cand. theol. Magn. Eiriksson, Krigsraad Juul m.fl.*, Copenhagen: J.D. Qvist 1881, pp. 138-170, it still contained, for example, 553 copies of *Er Johannes-Evangeliet et apostolisk og ægte Evangelium og er dets Lære om Guds Menneskevorden en sand og christelig Lære?* (1864), 93 copies of *Kunne vi elske Næsten som os selv?* (1870), 78 copies of *Om Bønnens Virkning og dens Forhold til Guds Uforanderlighed* (1870), 74 copies of *Paulus og Christus eller Pauli Lære om Retfærdiggjørelsen* (1871), 81 copies of *Jøder og Christne* (1873) and 387 copies of *Herr A. Pedrin og Christendommen* (1874). Even of Eiríksson's debut book *Om Baptister og Barnedaab* (1844) there were 84 copies left in his own library, and as late as his "Min Forfattervirksomhed" (1875), Eiríksson notes that the remaining copies can be purchased at a reduced price (see no. 11, p. 83, note 1). Moreover, there are reports that Eiríksson's books were burned due to the radicality of his thought; see for example Fritchman, *Men of Liberty*, p. 172: "evidence exists that some pious parents in Iceland and Denmark burned his books."

5 Hans Sofus Vodskov, "Magnus Eiriksson," in his *Spredte Studier*, Copenhagen: Gyldendalske Boghandels Forlag (F. Hegel & Søn) 1884, pp. 31-40; here p. 31.

time has not yet arrived."[1] When Eiríksson died a few years later, "it was as a theologically insignificant figure."[2] In sharp contrast to the writings of other poets and thinkers in Golden Age Denmark, above all to the writings of Kierkegaard, the extensive works of Eiríksson—amounting to over 4,200 pages—would soon be forgotten after his death: "his fate was to be unheard and then quickly forgotten."[3]

In a certain sense Eiríksson himself can be seen as responsible for this sad fate. The exaggerated stridency and polemical character of his writings not only interfered with the substance and efficacy of their argumentation, but also eclipsed their nobler goals and motives. We can see this clearly, for example, in *On Baptists and Infant Baptism* (1844), where Eiríksson's larger aim—to speak up on behalf of the persecuted Baptists and against intolerance in matters of religion or belief as a demonstration of one's spiritual weakness—is easily overshadowed by his polemic against, above all, Martensen. The literary critic and historian of religion Hans Sofus Vodskov (1846-1910) in his obituary for Eiríksson, concludes not without a certain justice:

> He did not admire the witty and excellent in Kierkegaard, but this was rather an offense to him; in his writings there is no sign that an enthusiastic poetic word, a great historical or scientific thought ever gripped his mind; religion seems literally to have been his one and all. His form corresponded to this; even where the content was the most erudite and demanded a high degree of education to be understood, his style nonetheless still bore the stamp of the common man: even, colorless exposition, lengthy tiresome repetitions and childlike resources to make things clear, such as boldface type of different sizes, used on every page, or even an addition under the line: "NB. This point is very important."[4]

---

[1] Schwanenflügel, "Magnus Eirikson," p. 294.

[2] Julia Watkin, "Eiríksson, Magnus," in her *Historical Dictionary of Kierkegaard's Philosophy*, Lanham and London: Scarecrow Press 2001, pp. 69-72, here p. 70.

[3] Carl Henrik Koch, "En ihærdig kritiker: Magnús Eiríksson," in his *Den danske idealisme. 1800-1880*, Copenhagen: Gyldendal 2004, pp. 292-298; here p. 298.

[4] Vodskov, "Magnus Eiriksson," p. 36. Regarding the addition, Vodskov probably refers to the table of contents of Eiríksson's work *On Baptists and Infant Baptism* (1844), see *Om Baptister og Barnedaab*, p. CX.

The radicalization of Eiríksson's position that took place starting in 1851, as the above quoted passage from *Paul and Christ* clearly shows, soon made any reasoned (public) debate with Eiríksson for the Church authorities utterly impossible.

Eiríksson's bitter polemics and provocative invectives against the theology and church of his time often conceal his consistent effort to emphasize over and over again in his writings the rational, practical and tolerant side of Christianity and make a plea for liberty and fraternity also in the field of religion. It is all too easy to overlook the fact that Eiríksson in many respects expressed truly remarkable and noteworthy views, thoughts and ideas and took on a pioneering role in quite different contexts.

Eiríksson's book *Is Faith a Paradox and "By Virtue of the Absurd"?* (1850),[1] published under the pseudonym Theophilus Nicolaus, is the first monograph ever written on Søren Kierkegaard. Substantially deepening and expanding his general, abstract critique of Kierkegaard's understanding of faith in *Fear and Trembling* (1843) in his treatise *Faith, Superstition, and Unbelief* from 1846,[2] Eiríksson offered a detailed response to the account of Abraham in *Fear and Trembling* (Chapter 1) and an alternative interpretation of Johannes de silentio's parable of the "knight of faith" and the "princess" (Chapter 2). Moreover, he drew Kierkegaard's Climacus writings *Philosophical Fragments* (1844) and *Concluding Unscientific Postscript* (1846) into his argument as well, claiming that they also present Christian faith as "by virtue of the absurd"—inasmuch as Climacus identifies "the absurd," by virtue of which faith exists, with "the paradox": God's incarnation in Jesus Christ (Chapter 3).

In Kierkegaard's (drafted) replies to Eiríksson's critique,[3] we encounter several important and noteworthy statements: not only

---

1 [Theophilus Nicolaus], *Er Troen et Paradox og "i Kraft af det Absurde"? et Spørgsmaal foranlediget ved "Frygt og Bæven, af Johannes de silentio", besvaret ved Hjelp af en Troes-Ridders fortrolige Meddelelser, til fælles Opbyggelse for Jøder, Christne og Muhamedanere, af bemeldte Troes-Ridders Broder*, Copenhagen: Chr. Steen & Søn 1850.

2 Magnús Eiríksson, *Tro, Overtro og Vantro, i deres Forhold til Fornuft og Forstand, samt til hinanden indbyrdes*, Copenhagen: H.C. Klein 1846.

3 See *SKS* 23, 176f., NB17:19 / *KJN* 7, 178f.; *SKS* 23, 177f., NB17:21 / *KJN* 7, 180; *SKS* 23, 182f., NB17:28 / *KJN* 7, 185; *SKS* 23, 197f., NB17:50 / *KJN* 7, 200f.; *Pap.* X-6 B 68-69 / *JP* 6, 6598-6599; *Pap.* X-6 B 70-71; *Pap.* X-6 B 72-76; *Pap.* X-6 B 77 / *JP* 6,

about the meaning of "the absurd" and "the paradox," but also about the *perspectival* and to this extent *relative* qualities of the utterances of Johannes de silentio and Johannes Climacus, since both pseudonyms remain outside faith.[1] The importance of Eiríksson's treatise was first recognized by Michael Theunissen and Wilfried Greve, who made it accessible in their *Materialien zur Philosophie Søren Kierkegaards* (1979), where they presented certain parts of Eiríksson's treatise in a German translation along with explanatory notes.[2]

But Kierkegaard was not the only figure in Golden Age Denmark to have been the target of the Icelander's critical pen. Eiríksson also issued serious attacks on important theological leaders such as Martensen and Grundtvig. Understanding Eiríksson's polemics with these figures on some of the main theological issues of the day sheds light on the period as a whole and provides a new perspective on the complex and diverse discussions concerning religion in the Golden Age.

Eiríksson's later writing *Can We Love Our Neighbor As Ourselves?* (1870)[3] can, furthermore, be considered the first commentary on

---

6600; *Pap.* X-6 B 78-81 / *JP* 1, 9-12; *Pap.* X-6 B 82 / *JP* 6, 6601; *Pap.* X-6 B 128, pp. 170f. / *CUP2*, 161-163 (*JP* 6, 6596); *Pap.* X-6 B 129, pp. 171f.

[1] See Cornelio Fabro, "Faith and Reason in Kierkegaard's Dialectic," in *A Kierkegaard Critique: An International Selection of Essays Interpreting Kierkegaard*, ed. by Howard Albert Johnson and Niels Thulstrup, New York: Harper and Brothers 1962, pp. 156-206; here pp. 174-185; Olivier Cauly, "La foi est-elle un paradoxe ou 'une vertu de l'absurde'? À propos d'une critique de Magnus Eiriksson (Theophilus Nicolaus)," *Kairos. Revue de la Faculté de Philosophie de l'Université de Toulouse*, vol. 10, 1997, pp. 99-114; Jóhanna Þráinsdóttir, "Er trúin þverstæða? Gagnrýni Magnúsar Eiríkssonar á trúarskoðunum Kierkegaards í 'Ugg og ótta,'" *Tímarit Máls og menningar*, vol. 61, 2000, pp. 35-45; Gerhard Schreiber, "Ist der Glaube ein Paradox und 'kraft des Absurden'? – Kierkegaards Auseinandersetzung mit Magnús Eiríksson," in *Kierkegaard and Faith*, ed. by Roman Králik et al., Šaľa and Mexico City: Sociedad Iberoamericana de Estudios Kierkegaardianos 2008, pp. 34-47; Schreiber, "Magnús Eiríksson: An Opponent of Martensen and an Unwelcome Ally of Kierkegaard," pp. 75-86; see the article by Roe Fremstedal in the present volume.

[2] Magnús Eiríksson, "Ist der Glaube ein Paradox oder 'in kraft des Absurden'?," trans. by Wilfried Greve, in *Materialien zur Philosophie Søren Kierkegaards*, ed. by Michael Theunissen and Wilfried Greve, Frankfurt: Suhrkamp 1979 (*suhrkamp taschenbuch wissenschaft*, vol. 241), pp. 147-160.

[3] Magnús Eiríksson, *Kunne vi elske Næsten som os selv? Nogle tildeels nye Tanker om Kjærligheden samt flere derhen hørende Skriftsteder*, Copenhagen: Paa Forfatterens Forlag 1870. Already Tonny Aagaard Olesen, "The Obscure Kierkegaard. One Hundred Years of *Postscript* Commentary," *Kierkegaard Studies Yearbook*, 2005, pp. 314-338, pointed to

Kierkegaard's ethics as it is presented in *Works of Love* (1847).[1] In a critical encounter with Kierkegaard's concept of love, Eiríksson deploys his own interpretation of the Christian idea of love in a way that anticipates certain aspects of the later interpretations of Kierkegaard's writings by Theodor W. Adorno (1903-69) and Knud Ejler Løgstrup (1905-81).[2]

In the political sphere, by contrast, one finds remarkably progressive statements in Eiríksson's *Letters to Clara Raphael* (1851).[3] In this epistolary novel, published under the pseudonym Theodor Immanuel, Eiríksson entered the so-called Clara Raphael feud[4] and produced arguments in defense of women's rights and emancipation similar to those that John Stuart Mill (1806-73) used almost two decades later in his *The Subjection of Women* (1869).[5]

It would be interesting, from the perspective of the history of theology, to make an investigation of Eiríksson's delineation of the development of the Church in the post-Apostolic age in his later writings not as a process of the "self-revelation" of Christian truth, but precisely as a process of alienation from and renunciation of Christianity—and here one is reminded of the description by Franz Camille Overbeck (1837-1905) of the descent from "original Christianity" into "historical Christianity," or of the later account by Adolf von Harnack (1851-1930) of "non-dogmatic Christianity." A thorough investigation of this subject as well as of Eiríksson's later theological position and biblical exegesis is still wanting.

---

the book by Eiríksson as, however, "another example of an uncomprehending reader" (p. 318).

1 Søren Kierkegaard, *Kjerlighedens Gjerninger. Nogle christelige Overveielser i Talers Form*, vols. 1-2, Copenhagen: C.A. Reitzel 1847.

2 See the article by Friedrich Hauschildt in the present volume.

3 Magnús Eiríksson [Theodor Immanuel], *Breve til Clara Raphael*, Copenhagen: C.A. Reitzel 1851.

4 See Katalin Nun, *Women of the Danish Golden Age: Literature, Theater and the Emancipation of Women*, Copenhagen: Museum Tusculanum Press 2013 (*Danish Golden Age Studies*, vol. 8), pp. 85-129.

5 John Stuart Mill, *The Subjection of Women*, London: Longmans, Green, Reader, and Dyer 1869. To this see Bjarnason, "Um Magnús Eiríksson," pp. 55-58; Albertsson, *Magnús Eiríksson*, pp. 105-120; Jóhanna Þráinsdóttir, "Gleymdur liðsmaður kvenna. Um Magnús Eiríksson, guðfræðing og rithöfund, og framlag hans til frelsisbaráttu kvenna", *Menningarblað. Lesbók Morgunblaðsins*, May 10, 1997, pp. 4f. See the article by Sigrídur Thorgeirsdóttir in the present volume.

The same thing is true for a detailed investigation of the reception of Eiríksson's later writings. Given, on the one hand, Eiríksson's critical attitude toward the doctrines of the Trinity and the Divinity of Christ, in contrast to which he stressed the essential *unity* of God and the role of Jesus as (merely) a prophet and a teacher; and given, on the other hand, Eiríksson's further insistence on the rationality of Christian faith, and on freedom of thought and conscience in matters of religion—it is no surprise to find that Eiríksson is often labeled a "pioneer" or "precursor" to the Unitarian movement in Denmark.[1] Ágúst Hákonarson Bjarnason (1875-1952), Professor of Philosophy at the University of Iceland when it was founded in 1911 and rector of the University of Iceland between 1918 and 1928, even stated in an address delivered at Harvard University in May of 1923 that Magnús Eiríksson was "the very first Icelandic Unitarian, perhaps the first determined Unitarian in all Scandinavia."[2]

These few examples must suffice to illustrate how regrettable it is that there is still no detailed study of Eiríksson. The silence that accompanied Eiríksson in his lifetime, has—a few exceptions notwithstanding[3]—continued after his death.[4] It seems to us to be time to end this silence and make the beginning of a sustained encounter with and discussion of

1 See Schreiber, " 'Like a Voice in the Wilderness,' " pp. 190f.

2 Ágúst H. Bjarnason, "Magnús Eiríksson: The First Icelandic Unitarian," transcribed from the original manuscript, edited and introduced by Stefan M. Jonasson, p. 298 in the present volume. Furthermore see—more cautious than in the Harvard lecture—Bjarnason, "Um Magnús Eiríksson," p. 42 and pp. 50f.

3 See the international bibliography on Magnús Eiríksson in the present volume.

4 To date only a single monograph on Eiríksson has been published: the 384-page-long doctoral thesis by Eiríkur Albertsson (1887-1972) entitled *Magnús Eiríksson. Guðfræði hans og trúarlíf* [Magnús Eiríksson. His Theology and Religious Life] (1938), which was the first dissertation to be defended at The Faculty of Theology at the University of Iceland. However, after this highly learned and thorough investigation (see the review by Ágúst Hákonarson Bjarnason in *Skírnir*, vol. 113, 1939, pp. 211-217) there followed, contrary to expectation, a roughly 60-year period of silence about Eiríksson in Iceland. See sections VI and VII of the article on the Icelandic reception of Eiríksson by Vilhjálmur Árnason and Jón Bragi Pálsson in the present volume. See, however, Jón Helgason, *Vér Íslands börn*, vols. 1-3, Reykjavík: Iðunn 1968-70; vol. 3, *Heimur á við hálft kálfskinn*, pp. 7-123 and Arnór Sigurjónsson, *Einars saga Ásmundssonar*, vols. 1-3, Reykjavík: Bókaútg. Menningarsjóðs 1957-70; vol. 1, *Bóndinn í nesi*, pp. 37-38 and pp. 258-316 (Section XIII). We thank Hólmfríður Kolbrún Gunnarsdóttir and Ævar Kjartansson for this information.

Eiríksson's works and ideas. The present anthology is to be understood as a first step in this direction.

Gerhard Schreiber, Frankfurt am Main
Jon Stewart, Copenhagen
June 21, 2015

Copenhagen. The Old Stock Exchange
(Engraving by Albert Henry Payne, ca. 1850.
Public domain picture, https://commons.wikimedia.org.)

I. Historical Background and Context

Magnús Eiríksson and Philosophy

Carl Henrik Koch

Magnús Eiríksson (1806-81) was first and foremost an extremely knowledgeable Bible scholar specializing in exegesis and characterized by a deep and heartfelt, but unorthodox Christianity. His knowledge of philosophy seems to have been extremely limited, and only the contemporary Danish philosophers who moved in the area between theology and philosophy could claim his interest. It was also in this field that he found his main object of criticism: the Hegel-inspired speculative theology as it was taught by the leading figure in 19th-century Danish theology, Hans Lassen Martensen (1808-84), whom he constantly and stubbornly attacked, without being given a reply.[1]

The following analysis is divided into two sections. The first investigates both the list of books in the collection which Eiríksson left behind and references in his writings for clues about his relationship to contemporary international and Danish philosophy. From this account it can be concluded that both foreign and Danish philosophy are only of peripheral importance to Eiríksson's philosophical project and are mentioned primarily for the sake of criticism. The second section is

1 On Eiríksson's attack on Martensen, see Gerhard Schreiber's "Magnús Eiríksson: An Opponent of Martensen and an Unwelcome Ally of Kierkegaard" in *Kierkegaard and His Danish Contemporaries*, Tome II, *Theology*, ed. by Jon Stewart, Aldershot: Ashgate 2009 (*Kierkegaard Research: Sources, Reception and Resources*, vol. 7), pp. 49-94. See also the same author's " 'Like a Voice in the Wilderness': Magnús Eiríksson's Tenacious Critique of Martensen—and Martensen's 'Lofty Silence,' " in *Hans Lassen Martensen: Theologian, Philosopher and Social Critic*, ed. by Jon Stewart, Copenhagen: Museum Tusculanum 2012 (*Danish Golden Age Studies*, vol. 6), pp. 155-89.

concerned with Eiríksson's criticism of Martensen and Søren Kierkegaard and with his assertion that faith is a matter of reason—an assertion which depends on the somewhat idiosyncratic meaning he ascribes to the concepts of "reason" and "understanding." This understanding formed the basis for his philosophical thought. Since it is apparent from the first section that the contemporary philosophical literature hardly affected him to any significant degree, the task in the second section is to trace the source of these definitions. Surprisingly, this source seems to be one of the lectures of his main enemy Martensen.

I. Eiríksson and the Contemporary Philosophical Literature

If one looks at thc list of the book collection of around 1200 numbers, which was sold at auction in 1881 upon Eiríksson's death,[1] it seems that his interest in philosophy was extremely limited. If one wishes to be generous, one can say that at most 5% of the books can be described as philosophical, whereas Icelandic literature, including Icelandic theological literature, Icelandic translations and books related to Iceland, constitute just over a third. Of the almost 600 works on philosophy and theology, philosophy represents approximately 10% and seems to be a bit arbitrary. As in other cases, one cannot infer from the content of the auction catalogue to the owner's actual reading. Some of Eiríksson's friends could have taken interesting works for themselves before the auction took place. For example, it is evident that key works are missing, such as Martensen's *Christian Dogmatics* from 1849, which Eiríksson attacked repeatedly, and Kierkegaard's *Philosophical Fragments* from 1844 and the *Concluding Unscientific Postscript* from 1846, which are also mentioned by Eiríksson.[2] The Reading Association of Regensen College, the Reading Association Athenaeum and the Students' Association had,

---

1 *Fortegnelse over endel forskjellige gode og velconditionerede Bogsamlinger, bestaaende af theologiske, juridiske, medicinske, historiske, æsthetiske, sprog- og naturvidenskabelige Værker samt Restoplagene af forskjellige theologiske Bøger, tilhørende Boerne efter afdøde Overlærer Nielsen, Districtslæge Wilhjelm, Pastor Krogh, Cand. theol. Magnús Eiríksson, Krigsraad Juul m.fl.*, ed. by Christian Hee, Copenhagen: J.D. Quist 1881, pp. 138-70.

2 See, for example, Magnús Eiríksson, *Tro, Overtro og Vantro, i deres Forhold til Fornuft og Forstand, samt til hinanden indbyrdes*, Copenhagen: H.C. Klein 1846, pp. 106-9 (note).

like the Royal Library, large, accessible libraries, that Eiríksson could have used. Furthermore, Eiríksson might have owned books that he later got rid of. Although it is not possible to draw any conclusions regarding the works that could have been in his collection, but which are not, one can nevertheless say something about its owner's interests based on the works that are there, even though the date of their acquisition is unknown, and even though it is impossible to know whether they were ever read if he did not refer to them or quote from them in his publications.

With the exception of a handful of minor Swedish works, only six foreign philosophers are represented in the collection. On finds in Eiríksson's library *Theoretisches System der gesunden Vernunft, ein akademisches Lehrbuch* from 1765 (no. 416),[1] a hastily composed work by the controversial philosopher and later celebrated educator Johann Bernard Basedow (1723-90). From 1753 to 1761 Basedow was professor of eloquence and moral philosophy at the Knight Academy in the Danish provincial town Sorø, but was dismissed because of his unorthodox religious views. His work does not seem to have left any traces in Eiríksson's thought.[2] There is likewise no mention in Eiríksson's publications of the second edition of Johann Friedrich Herbart's (1776-1841) *Kurze Enzyklopädie der Philosophie* (1831) from 1841 (no. 560), which was a standard reference work. Eiríksson had two Danish translations of Kant (1724-1804), his anthropology from 1802 (no. 585) and his lectures on logic from 1803 (no. 586), but none of his more central works. Nor is Kant ever mentioned in Eiríksson's writings. A Danish translation from 1870 of some lectures by the English psychologist Henry Maudsley (1835-1918) on the mind-body problem from a physiological perspective (*Om Forholdet mellem Sjæl og Legeme samt mellem Sindssygdomme og andre Lidelser af Nervesystemet. Tre Foredrag*, no. 638) was published too late to be able to leave its mark on Eiríksson's home-made philosophy, which seems to have been framed in the mid-1840s.

---

1 The listed numbers refer to the numbers in the catalogue of Eiríksson's book collection.

2 On Basedow and Danmark, see Olaf Carlsen, *Über J.B. Basedows Entlassung von der Ritterakademie zu Sorö*, Copenhagen: Lewin og Munksgaard 1937 and Carl Henrik Koch, *Dansk oplysningsfilosofi 1700-1800*, Copenhagen: Gyldendal 2003, pp. 197-206.

Eiríksson owned a single work by the Kant-inspired German philosopher Ernst Reinhold (1793-1855), who developed a kind of speculative theism, namely, the second edition from 1839 of his *Lehrbuch der Geschichte der Philosophie* (no. 735), which was originally published in 1836. There is likewise no reference to this work in Eiríksson's writings. This short list of foreign philosophical literature in Eiríksson's collection of books is completed with Friedrich Schleiermacher's (1768-1834) posthumously published *Dialektik* from 1839 (no. 772), from which Eiríksson quotes in his book against Martensen's *Christian Dogmatics*.[1] Eiríksson also owned poet Christian Winther's (1796-1876) translation of some of Schleiermacher's sermons (no. 773).[2]

Eiríksson had great respect for Schleiermacher and protested strongly when the priest Jens Paludan-Müller (1813-99), in a short work, turned against Martensen's dogmatics, which he compared with Schleiermacher's. Paludan-Müller found in Martensen Schleiermacher's assertion of the absolute validity of religious subjectivity for religious life in the form of the feeling of absolute dependence on the divine.[3] Eiríksson argued that there is a difference of opinion between Martensen and Schleiermacher, who is, Eiríksson writes, "the religious hero who appreciates the absolute feeling of dependence which is religion's true essence; Martensen puts religion's innermost being in a relation of identity, in the unity of being of God and Man and Man's consciousness of it."[4] Next, Schleiermacher, Eiríksson said, "insofar as he is considered a critical theologian, is an excellent penetrating, profound and scientific theologian; Martensen has not much to do with criticism, and when he criticizes or contradicts, it is based more on mere assertions than scientific grounds...."[5] Finally, Schleiermacher is "considered as a philosopher or

---

1 Magnús Eiríksson, *Den nydanske Theologies Cardinaldyder belyste ved Hjelp af Dr. Martensens Skrifter samt Modskrifterne, tilligemed 75 theologiske Spørgsmaal, rettede til Dr. H. Martensen*, Copenhagen: Chr. Steen & Søn 1850, p. 80 (note).

2 *Dr. Friedrich Schleiermachers Prædikener om det christelige Huusliv*, trans. by Christian Winther, Copenhagen: P.G. Philipsen 1839.

3 See Jens Paludan-Müller, *Om Dr. Martensens christelige Dogmatik*, Copenhagen: C.A. Reitzel 1850, pp. 5ff.

4 Eiríksson, *Den nydanske Theologies Cardinaldyder*, p. 78. The many forms used to indicate emphasis such as italics, the spacing of letters and the use of bold type have been omitted in the quotations from the printed works. Some of the quotations from Eiríksson have been modified to make them more intelligible.

5 Ibid., pp. 78f.

philosophical theologian, a deep thinker," whereas Martensen does not really think much but has "visions."[1] In connection with this Eiríksson claims that "Dr. Martensen knows a good deal about God before the Created (the World) existed; by contrast, Schleiermacher knows nothing about the existence of God outside the World or in and for itself."[2] As evidence, he quotes Schleiermacher from his *Dialectics* to the effect that, irrespective of the world, we know nothing about God or about God in itself.[3] Eiríksson believes, however, that Martensen has such knowledge based on his assumption of an essential unity between God and man. In connection with this, several things may be remarked. First, man's knowledge of himself, his self-consciousness, can hardly be considered *a priori* knowledge. Secondly, Eiríksson's claim seems to be contrary to what Martensen says in the *Christian Dogmatics*, where he writes, "there is no divine quality which, when it is thought in a living manner, is not transitive, not expressing a relation to the world,"[4] and here he repeats the Hegelian thesis that "without the world God is not God,"[5] which runs counter to the view that Eiríksson ascribes to Martensen.

The small and random selection of foreign philosophical books, none of which can be called major philosophical works, seems to suggest that Eiríksson's interest in philosophy was extremely limited. The collection contains, for example, no work by Hegel, although he is the foreign philosopher most often mentioned by Eiríksson. By contrast, Eiríksson's main interest, biblical exegesis, is well represented. For example, he owned seven works by the Tübingen School's main figure Ferdinand Christian Baur (1792-1860) and six by the exegetical writer Wilhelm Martin Leberecht de Wette (1780-1849).

Unlike foreign philosophy, contemporary Danish philosophy was richly represented in Eiríksson's book collection. However, not all the Danish philosophical works in Eiríksson's collection of books and their authors will be discussed below, but only those that played a role in the debates of the age. None of the four who have been disregarded here

---

1 Ibid., p. 79.
2 Ibid., pp. 79f.
3 See *Friedrich Schleiermacher's literarischer Nachlaß. Zur Philosophie*, vol. 2.2 (*Dialektik*, ed. by Ludwig Jonas), Berlin: G. Reimer 1839, p. 154 (§ 216).
4 Hans Lassen Martensen, *Den christelige Dogmatik*, Copenhagen: C.A. Reitzel 1849, p. 111 (§ 47).
5 Ibid., p. 139 (§ 59).

(Frederik Clemens Bendtsen Dahl (1822-1920), Poul Sophus Vilhelm Heegaard (1835-84), Gabriel Sibbern (1824-1903) and Frederik Ludvig Bang Zeuthen (1805-74)) left traces in Eiríksson's writings.

Eiríksson owned five books (nos. 398-402) by Søren Kierkegaard's school friend, the philosopher and theologian Adolph Peter Adler (1812-69), including Adler's master's thesis, *The Isolated Subjectivity in its Main Forms* from 1840. This is a right-Hegelian work in which Hegel's "abstract subjectivity" ("*die abstrakte Subjektivität*") or "infinite subjectivity" ("*die unendliche Subjektivität*") is analyzed as "the isolated subjectivity."[1] The isolated subjectivity is a subjectivity deprived of substantiality. It has not co-opted the objective in itself and is therefore a subjectivity that persists in a completed moment in human development, that is, representing the culture not of its own day but of the past. The objective, that is, thc historical development, realizes itself in individuals, but if they become detached from the development, they are maintained in an isolated mode. On the basis of Hegel's history and philosophy of religion, Adler describes in his thesis the isolated subjectivity's historical appearance as a moment in the individual's development from nature to spirit.

Some years after the publication of the dissertation Adler allegedly received a revelation in which Christ commanded him to burn his Hegelian manuscripts and in the future to adhere to the Bible. Since he, as pastor, Sunday after Sunday preached about his revelation, he was dismissed from his post. He wrote numerous books and treatises in which he expounded his revelation, and the other four books of Adler that were in Eiríksson's collection are all from this period in his life. There can be no doubt that a figure like Adler interested Eiríksson, but there does not seem to be references to either him or his books in Eiríksson's own writings.

Eiríksson owned two copies of the *magnum opus* of left Hegelian Hans Brøchner (1820-75), professor of philosophy at the University of

---

[1] See G.W.F. Hegel, *Sämtliche Werke. Jubiläumsausgabe in zwanzig Bänden*, vols. 1-22, ed. by Hermann Glockner, 4th ed., Stuttgart and Bad Cannstatt: Frommann-Holzboog 1965; vol. 8, pp. 334f. On Adler see Carl Henrik Koch, *En flue på Hegels udødelige næse eller Om Adolph Peter Adler og om Søren Kierkegaards forhold til ham*, Copenhagen: C.A. Reitzel 1990, as well as Carl Henrik Koch, *Den danske Idealisme*, Copenhagen: Gyldendal 2004, pp. 463-71.

Copenhagen from 1860 to his death. Brøchner was related to Kierkegaard and in many ways inspired by him. In his *magnum opus*, entitled *About the Religious in its Unity with the Humane* from 1869 (nos. 461-62),[1] he argued against Kierkegaard. Kierkegaard had set a dividing line between ethics and religion and an absolute distinction between the religious and the human. On the contrary, Brøchner had argued for the unity of the ethical and the human, which included the ethical. Brøchner's book was an original contribution to the philosophy of religion, and he remains one of the leading Danish philosophers of religion.[2]

Brøchner studied theology, but, after the study of the critical writings of the left Hegelians David Friedrich Strauss (1808-74) and Ludwig Feuerbach (1804-72), he rejected Christianity's central tenets. When he stated his position, in 1841, in his application to take the qualifying examination in theology, his petition was rejected. Instead, he took a master's degree in Semitic philology with Greek, Latin and philosophy as minor subjects. The case attracted much attention and was featured in both the metropolitan and provincial press.

There seems to be no references in Eiríksson's writings to Brøchner's masterpiece, but he does refer to two of his other books, namely, a small booklet (*Some Notes on Baptism, on Occasion of Professor Martensen's Work "Christian Baptism"*) from 1843,[3] in which Brøchner criticized Martensen's conception of baptism in his pièce d'occasion *Christian Baptism* from the same year, and the book, *The Problem of Faith and Knowledge* from 1868.[4] In the former piece Brøchner attacked Martensen for at the same time believing that baptism—with Martensen's words—is "the mother of faith,"[5] and that baptism cannot fail; if faith is a condition of salvation, this implies the view of baptism that everyone who is baptized is saved, a consequence, which Martensen, however, would not want to accept. In

---

1 Hans Brøchner, *Om det Religiøse i dets Enhed med det Humane. Et positivt Supplement til "Problemet om Tro og Viden,"* Copenhagen: P.G. Philipsen 1869.

2 On Brøchner, see Koch, *Den danske Idealisme*, pp. 497-522 and S.V. Rasmussen, *Den unge Brøchner*, Copenhagen: Gyldendal 1966.

3 Hans Brøchner, *Nogle Bemærkninger om Daaben, foranledigede ved Professor Martensens Skrift: "Den christelige Daab,"* Copenhagen: P.G. Philipsen 1843.

4 Hans Brøchner, *Problemet om Tro og Viden. En historisk-kritisk Afhandling*, Copenhagen: P.G. Philipsen 1868.

5 Hans Martensen, *Den christelige Daab betragtet med Hensyn paa det baptistiske Spørgsmaal*, Copenhagen: C.A. Reitzel 1843, p. 58.

the latter piece, Brøchner also aimed a sharp attack at speculative theology and its attempt to bridge the gap between faith and reason in order to develop a scholarly theology. Eiríksson referred to Brøchner's pamphlet in his great defense of the Baptists. He was particularly interested in using Brøchner as an example of how speculative philosophy can bring a person who was preoccupied with it, "over into the domain of infidelity."[1] However, at the same time he praises Brøchner for having had courage and shown sincerity.

In the mid-1860s, a dispute about the relationship between faith and knowledge broke out in Danish intellectual life. The dispute lasted over five years and produced more than 25 pamphlets and books and almost 100 articles in the daily press and magazines.[2] In 1868 Brøchner issued his main contribution in the dispute, *The Problem of Faith and Knowledge*, in which he countered arguments by Martensen and his colleague Rasmus Nielsen (1809-84). In his contribution to the debate Martensen had argued that the will and thus faith is superior to reason and knowledge, whereas Nielsen's position, which was the occasion for the dispute, was that faith and knowledge are based on principles which are not in conflict and therefore can be united in the same consciousness.

In a couple of works from the 1870s, Eiríksson discussed some of the views that Brøchner had presented in his polemical booklet. In *About Prayer and its Relation to God's Immutability*, he criticized very respectfully Brøchner's conception of prayer. The concept of prayer, Brøchner writes, includes two factors, namely, "1) The prayer is made to the personal God, whose will is determined by prayer; 2) The object of prayer is the miracle."[3] But, Brøchner believes, it is irrational to pray to an immutable will, which, according to the Christian view, wants the best for man. It would be an expression of disbelief to want to change the will of God through prayer and ask for something that is contrary to what He had previously decided, and which therefore arises under the laws of life, that is, to ask for a miracle. Against this Eiríksson argues that Brøchner conceived of the matter

---

[1] Magnús Eiríksson, *Om Baptister og Barnedaab, samt flere Momenter af Den kirkelige og speculative Christendom*, Copenhagen: P.G. Philipsen 1844, pp. XXXIX-XL.

[2] See Koch, *Den danske idealisme*, pp. 435-61.

[3] Hans Brøchner, *Problemet om Tro og Viden. En historisk-kritisk Afhandling*, Copenhagen: P.G. Philipsen 1868, p. 95.

> in a far too one-sided manner, since in his evaluation of prayer, its efficacy and relationship to God's nature and attributes he seems to have stuck too much to the logical-metaphysical side of things, which is not of the same kind as the religious side, and in the light of which "the phenomenon, which is the religious consciousness' *Urphänomen* and penetrates everything, even the lowest forms of religion, namely, prayer,"[1] therefore cannot be judged well.[2]

The true source of prayer, Eiríksson believes, is not the suppliant's desire to change the deity's will because

> when it [that is, the source] is to be truly resigned and pious, then it will be only the religious piety and resignation to God's will, and this piety must be either a permanent mental nature, a lasting and living relation to God, or a repentant and humble frame of mind, which exists beforehand, and which is independent of belief in a certain number of dogmas.[3]

In the same year that Eiríksson published his book on prayer, he wrote a short essay titled *Could We Love Our Neighbor as Ourselves?* In the preface he, among other things, portrayed his relationship to and his criticism of Kierkegaard. In his treatment of Christian love Eiríksson refers to Kierkegaard's book *Works of Love* from 1847 (no. 593) and a number of his articles in the journal *The Moment* from 1855. Here he writes:

> It might perhaps seem strange that I have so much against him [that is, Kierkegaard], or rather, his views, but this is a natural consequence of the contrast between his and my conception of religion and Christianity, with all that they entail, and the contrast between our whole spiritual being. The natural, simple-minded, spiritually healthy thinking cannot possibly be in agreement with someone, who is unnatural, paradoxical and overwrought, brilliantly witty and in some respects a genius. From the beginning, I had a degree of sympathy for Dr. S.K., which can be seen on several places in

---

[1] Quoted with a few minor deviations from Brøchner's *Problemet om Tro og Viden*, p. 95.

[2] Magnús Eiríksson, *Om Bønnens Virkning og dens Forhold til Guds Uforanderlighed. Nogle Oplysninger og Bemærkninger, nærmest byggede paa andelig Erfaring og et umiddelbart Gudsforhold*, Copenhagen: Magnús Eiríksson 1870, pp. 9f.

[3] Ibid., p. 14.

> my previous writings. Beside what is good and is worthy of recognition, which I have always found in him, I have also always found much that has offended me and that I could not approve of, either because it struck me as too artificial and unnatural, or because it conflicted with what I saw as truth, or because it conflicted with other doctrines and assertions in his works.[1]

In a footnote to the description of Kierkegaard as "in some respects a genius" Eiríksson emphasizes that Kierkegaard's genius is not religious genius In addition, there are too many "delusions, contradictions and paradoxes" in Kierkegaard, and where the genius finds new truths, which he communicates, Kierkegaard as a religious author has only "brought division and confusion into the religious."[2]

Brøchner is also touched upon in this short work. In his work on the dispute about faith and knowledge Martensen had asserted that will, which among other things serves to maintain faith, is superior to reason, and that faith, therefore, has primacy in relation to knowledge, which in turn must submit to faith. By contrast, Brøchner in his book about faith and knowledge had argued that reason has primacy and therefore the decision of what is to be willed. On this point Eiríksson was in agreement with Martensen and could only regret that Martensen had not tried to counter Brøchner. For example, Eiríksson writes in his response to Brøchner:

> The man of will, whom we might also call the man of love (it is the man whose will, prior to being engaged by thirst of knowledge or vain curiosity, is aiming at the good and at that which bears the stamps of humanity), is first of all preoccupied with that which in general can be applied. He appreciates only knowledge so far as he can obtain something good, which bears the stamp of humanity, that which makes his fellow-creatures better and happier and himself a better and happier man.[3]

---

1 Magnús Eiríksson, *Kunne vi elske Næsten som os selv? Nogle tildeels nye Tanker om Kjærligheden samt flere derhen hørende Skriftsteder*, Copenhagen: Magnús Eiríksson 1870, pp. VIII-IX.

2 Ibid., p. IX.

3 Ibid., p. 88. The discussion of Brøchner and the reference to his book on faith and knowledge is found in the long footnote on pp. 89ff.

Eiríksson also owned Frederik Dreier's (1827-53) little book *The Faith of Ghosts and Free Thinking* (no. 489)[1] even in two copies.[2] Although often referred to as Denmark's first socialist, Dreier was rather an anarchist. Eiríksson and Dreier knew each other since they were both members of The Society of Handworkers' Education, which was founded in 1847.[3] Dreier seems to have admired Eiríksson for his energetic attack on Martensen and wrote about him in a manuscript that "His point of view, a cloudy, rationalist feeling-based religiosity in Christian form, is utterly untenable, but vis-à-vis Martensen's empty mysticism and exclusiveness, he represents respectively reason and unconditional heroism."[4] In his book on the faith of ghosts Dreier in the style of the French Enlightenment attacked Christianity and the church. He was a declared atheist and rejected the idealist philosophy that characterized Danish intellectual life through the middle of the 19th century. Instead of the idealist dualism between soul and body or spirit and matter, he maintained a materialism, and instead of the Hegelians' conceptual manipulation, he espoused empiricism or rather sensuality and a positivistic anti-metaphysical conception of science. Dreier regarded the world soul or objective reason and God as members of a metaphysical ghost cabinet, and he denied that there is a meaning in history different from that which man creates through his actions. "God is a spirit," wrote Dreier and continued:

> But this very concept, which denotes something absolutely different from matter, has...only arisen by unscientific speculations. Spirits were airy and yet human-like beings, which were made redundant by the true scientific classification and knowledge of the phenomena that they were intended to explain. Anything that is outside us is material, and everything that is within us, in our body or in our consciousness is also material in certain specific compounds, forms and activities.[5]

---

1 Frederik Dreier, *Aandetroen og den frie Tænkning*, Copenhagen: J.D. Qvist 1852.

2 On Dreier, see Koch, *Den danske Idealisme*, pp. 539-49.

3 Svend Erik Stybe, *Frederik Dreier. Hans liv, hans samtid og hans sociale tænkning*, Copenhagen: Munksgaard 1959, p. 89.

4 Ibid., p. 125.

5 Frederik Dreier, *Aandetroen og den frie Tænkning*, Copenhagen: J.D. Quist 1852, p. 41.

We can only guess what Eiríksson thought of such a view. Presumably he considered Dreier to be a lost soul.

Eiríksson owned the first volume of the journal *Perseus* from 1837 (no. 557) by the period's aesthetic arbiter of taste and one of its most prominent figures, Johan Ludvig Heiberg (1791-1860). This work contained Heiberg's long review of a book by the speculative theologian Valdemar Henrik Rothe (1777-1857), namely, *The Doctrine of the Trinity and Reconciliation* from 1836.[1]

Heiberg was more than any other the personification of the Danish Hegelianism. As a young man he had been seized by the Hegelian philosophy and published in 1830-31, as professor at the Royal Military College in Copenhagen, the masterpiece of Danish Hegelianism, *Outline of the Lectures on the Philosophy of Philosophy or Speculative Logic.*[2] Eiríksson described Heiberg as the "Danish scholar who with the greatest energy has acquired, and with the greatest results used, the Hegelian speculation."[3] Eiríksson further called Heiberg and Martensen "the Danish speculative officers" as opposed to Martensen's advanced students, whom he called "the speculative-commissioned officers or sergeants."[4]

To far greater extent than Hegel himself, Heiberg stressed that the Hegelian system includes everything, that is, that everything can be determined by concepts and developed within the framework of the system, and that it is a rational system in which the components can be

---

1 An English translation of the review can be found in *Heiberg's* Perseus *and Other Texts*, ed. and trans. by Jon Stewart, Copenhagen: Museum Tusculanum 2011 (*Texts from Golden Age Denmark*, vol. 6), pp. 83-180. On Heiberg as a philosopher, see Koch, *Den danske idealisme*, pp. 225-48. The Hegel reception in Denmark from 1824 to 1842 has been meticulously and exhaustively described by Jon Stewart in *A History of Hegelianism in Golden Age Denmark*, Tome I, *The Heiberg Period: 1824-1836*; Tome II, *The Martensen Period: 1837-1842*, Copenhagen: C.A. Reitzel 2007 (*Danish Golden Age Studies*, vol. 3).

2 An English translation of the treatise can be found in *Heiberg's Speculative Logic and Other Texts*, ed. and trans. by Jon Stewart, Copenhagen: Reitzel 2006 (*Texts from Golden Age Denmark*, vol. 2), pp. 39-213.

3 Eiríksson, *Tro, Overtro og Vantro*, p. 30 (note).

4 Magnús Eiríksson, *Dr. Martensens trykte moralske Paragrapher, eller det saakaldte "Grundrids til Moralphilosophiens System af Dr. Hans Martensen", i dets forvirrede, idealistisk-metaphysiske og phantastisk-speculative, Religion og Christendom undergravende, fatalistiske, pantheistiske og selvforguderske Væsen*, Copenhagen: H.C. Klein 1846, p. 104 (note).

developed with strict logical necessity. The logic which constitutes the system's structure is also the logic of existence. Heiberg was apparently captivated by this rationalist view of Hegel as panlogist, that is, as a philosopher who fully identifies thinking and being or reality and reason, and only ascribed to the inexplicable, evil and irrational a limited and self-eliminating existence. The age's Danish Hegelian understanding and hence its critique of Hegelian philosophy, which can be found, for example, in Kierkegaard, was in full compliance with Heiberg.

In addition to the above logic Heiberg also published some minor treatises of Hegelian character, but neither these, the review of Rothe nor the *Logic* was mentioned by Eiríksson. As will be discussed in Section II, both in *Faith, Superstition and Unbelief* and in *Is Faith a Paradox and "By Virtue of the Absurd"?*, published in 1850, in which he criticized Kierkegaard's *Fear and Trembling*, Eiríksson only referred to a treatise by Heiberg in the journal *Intelligentsblade*.

Martensen's speculative theology was the main target of Eiríksson's criticism, but also Hegel (and Hegelianism) and Kierkegaard came under fire. Eiríksson seems to have studied Martensen and Kierkegaard extensively. He had 10 books and pamphlets by Martensen, including *Outline for a System of Moral Philosophy* from 1841 (no. 634), *Christian Baptism* from 1843 (no. 636), *Dogmatic Elucidations* (no. 636) from 1850, which is Martensen's response to critics of the *Christian Dogmatics*, *On Faith and Knowledge* from 1867 (no. 635)—all of which were the subject of Eiríksson's criticism. There are four works by Kierkegaard included on the list, *Fear and Trembling* from 1843 (no. 594), *Works of Love* (1847) in an edition of 1862 (no. 593), P.C. Kierkegaard's edition of *The Point of View for my Work as an Author* from 1857 (no. 595), and the first volume from the same year of the posthumous papers (no. 596). Eiríksson's relationships with Martensen and Kierkegaard are issues for other articles in this volume and will not be dealt with systematically here.

The extremely eloquent philosophy professor Rasmus Nielsen (1809-84), who was the same age as Eiríksson and one of the age's celebrated cultural figures, is, with a total of 16 volumes, the best represented author in Eiríksson's book collection (no. 690-700). In 1841-42, Nielsen had given a series of lectures about the speculative logic, the beginning of which Eiríksson had attended. About his experiences in the Nielsen's auditorium Eiríksson wrote somewhat humorously in 1846:

> These lectures, which were attended by 20-30 selected speculators of the city, from which the speculative process took place with such energy that some of them almost continuously kept both hands on their head. I endured it for 5 to 6 lessons when I began to feel dizzy, because I have never been so high up. Then I absented myself from greater danger, perhaps a violent death….Now I am…not only convinced that all the basic features of Hegel's speculative logic are utterly false, and I comfort myself with trying to prove it, and shall, with God's help, do so, if the speculative professors continue to lecture on this doctrine and thereby ruin the students.[1]

Despite this harangue Eiríksson seems originally to have had a certain respect for Nielsen and to have nurtured some expectations for his development. For in a discussion of Nielsen's book *Paul's Letter to the Romans* from 1841,[2] when Eiríksson notes that Nielsen found much of the speculative dogmatism in the Letter to the Romans, he writes:

> It is not a little sad when those who by nature are equipped with glorious gifts, with a liveliness and mettle in the spirit, which stands above the mediocre and pedestrian, and thus with a healthy and sensible education of these gifts, and could become spirited men—which I for my part have had reason to suppose about Professor Nielsen according to the acquaintance I have with him from our student years—are entangled in such a dangerous, terrible and intellectually confusing labyrinth as the speculative logic.[3]

Years later, he seems to have completely given up hope that Nielsen would develop in the positive direction. After Denmark's defeat in 1864 to Prussia and Austria, with the subsequent loss of the duchies of Schleswig and Holstein there were many who wanted the Danish people to be awakened to spiritual strength, and some people had pointed to Rasmus Nielsen—somewhat ironically by Eiríksson called the Danish Plato—as the man who was to meet this challenge. But from this

---

1 Eiríksson, *Tro, Overtro og Vantro*, p. 82 (note).
2 Rasmus Nielsen, *Pauli Brev til Romerne*, Copenhagen: Forfatterens Forlag 1841.
3 Eiríksson, *Om Baptister og Barnedaab*, pp. X-XI (note).

quarter, Eiríksson feels, such efforts are not to be expected. This requires a genius—and especially in Denmark such persons are rare.[1]

Nielsen was already as a young man gripped by the Hegelian dialectic and had a close relationship with Martensen, whose textbook on dogmatics he discussed in detail with the author before the book's release. But when the book was published, Nielsen was a disciple of Kierkegaard and wrote against the speculative attempt at a scientific approach in theology, which Martensen stood for. In one of his works from this period he repeated again and again that "Christianity is higher than science, and the Gospel faith is different in kind from theology."[2] Kierkegaard thought that Nielsen had plundered his pseudonymous writings and broke with him. Later Eiríksson named Nielsen as "Kierkegaard's enthusiastic, but dependent supporter."[3]

In the early 1850s Nielsen changed tracks again and threw himself into a rather comprehensive study of the sciences, especially mathematics, chemistry, physiology and biology. Hegel's philosophy of nature had been a mistake, Nielsen thought, which was due to the fact that Hegel had underestimated the independence of sensuous reality in relation to thought. In order to implement the Hegelian project—which was also Heiberg's and Nielsen's project—to unite the Idea and reality, that is, to see reality as a whole that develops towards a goal, philosophy must ally itself with the sciences and explore what each of them can contribute to the realization of the project. Nielsen presented his studies in a series of philosophical textbooks, published from the late 1850s up to the '60s. But the relationship between faith and knowledge also preoccupied him. Where Kierkegaard's assertion that subjectivity is truth applies to the sphere of faith, science declares objectivity to be truth. But with these statements faith has lost all influence on science, and science has in turn lost all influence on the faith. The spheres of faith and science are thus different. From this it follows, Nielsen felt that "faith and knowledge could then without contradiction be united in one consciousness; their

---

1 See Magnús Eiríksson, *Gud og Reformatoren. En religiøs Idee. Samt nogle Bemærkninger om de kirkelige Tilstande, Dr. S. Kierkegaard og Forfatteren*, Copenhagen: J.H. Schubothe 1866, p. IX.

2 Rasmus Nielsen, *Evangelietroen og Theologien*, Copenhagen: C.A. Reitzel 1850, p. 37 (et passim).

3 Eiríksson, *Gud og Reformatoren*, p. 104 (note).

mutual strife is not derived from anything essential. The strife between them is only psychological; it is human frailty that, on the one hand, has not enough resignation to live with the objectivity of science and, on the other, not enough inwardness to maintain faith."[1] Faith and knowledge are not contradictory, and the problem with uniting them in one consciousness is, Nielsen believed, only a psychological problem. It was this view that ushered in the previously mentioned controversy about the relationship between faith and knowledge that took place in Danish cultural life in the 1860s. Despite fierce criticism, Nielsen maintained his position, but came weakened out of the dispute, which contributed to the fact that theology was deprived of its once-dominant role. The interest in Hegel and his thinking died out, empiricism and positivism took hold, and the natural sciences and medicine took the place of theology, psychology, and philosophy. The controversy therefore ushered in an almost complete reorientation in Danish culture.

None of this seems to have influenced Eiríksson. He noted that Nielsen agreed with Kierkegaard, and while the controversy about the relationship between faith and knowledge raged around him, he was, concerned with countering Nielsen's perception of Kierkegaard. Nielsen writes in an article on Kierkegaard's mental state, fully consistent with the understanding of his work that Kierkegaard himself had presented in *The Point of View for My Work as an Author*: "it belongs just to the peculiar in Kierkegaard's being that he from the beginning is so in agreement with himself, so internally perfect....Kierkegaard is to such a degree an *a priori* nature that he is just short of the perfect."[2] In other words, Kierkegaard had from the outset been so completely aware of what he would do with his life that the possibility of development was almost excluded. To this claim Eiríksson says, "We would now seek to demonstrate that Dr. S. Kjerkegaard, in spite of his rare talent, was as perfectible as other imperfect mortals, and as a consequence of this, the 'internal compliance' with himself 'from first to last' that R. Nielsen attaches to Kjerkegaard, is a rather splendid misunderstanding."[3] Eiríksson rejects as mistakes

---

1 Rasmus Nielsen, *Philosophisk Propædeutik i Grundtræk*, Copenhagen: Gyldendal 1857, p. 77.

2 Rasmus Nielsen, "Om S. Kierkegaards 'mentale Tilstand,' " *Nordisk Universitets-Tidskrift*, vol. 4, no. 1, 1858, pp. 1-29; here p. 7.

3 Eiríksson, *Gud og Reformatoren,* p. 81.

the view of *Fear and Trembling* that Abraham had faith "in virtue of the absurd" and the *Postscript*'s talk about the paradoxical nature of the religious. Furthermore, Kierkegaard's critique of the Church and its men is inconsistent because he accepts the teachings of the fundamental church dogmas (for example, the Trinity and the dogma of Christ's divine nature). It is also inconsistent, Eiríksson believes, that Kierkegaard emphasizes a vivid inwardness as the essence of man's relation to God, while he retains the dogmas. In addition, the contradiction, which, according to Kierkegaard, exists between the Christian and the human is wrong because "Christianity in its essence is precisely the truly human."[1] Kierkegaard was, Eiríksson believed, greatly perfectible.

We find only three books by the philosophy professor Frederik Christian Sibbern (1785-1872) in Eiríksson's surviving collection of books: a textbook of psychology from 1843 (no. 782), which Eiríksson refers to a couple of times, but only to criticize; the little chief work *Speculative Cosmology as the Basis for Speculative Theology* from 1846 (no. 784), which Eiríksson does not refer to; and the posthumously published *Moral Philosophy as a Theory of Righteousness and Inclination* from 1878 (no. 783).[2]

Sibbern was, if anyone, the main philosopher of the Danish Golden Age and Danish Romanticism. He covered all the main areas of philosophy, including psychology and aesthetics, and wrote, on the basis of an unhappy love affair, two of the age's beloved literary masterpieces *Posthumous Letters of Gabrielis* (1826) and *From Gabrielis' Letters to and from Home* (1850). In his youth he was influenced by the Romantic philosophy of nature and especially by the fiery Henrich Steffens (1773-1845). In 1813 he was called home from his grand tour to Germany to take a professorship in philosophy in Copenhagen. In Berlin, he had met the elder Fichte, Schleiermacher and Solger (1780-1819) and attended their lectures, in Weimar he had spoken with Goethe, who had enraptured him, and in Munich he had associated with Schelling. Only after 58 years of service as a professor did he retire.

Sibbern wrote much during his many years as professor. Textbooks, systematic works—for example, an aesthetics in three volumes, in

[1] Ibid., p. 103.
[2] On Sibbern see Koch, *Den danske idealisme*, pp. 87-160.

which he expounded the Danish Golden Age aesthetics—and political pamphlets flowed from his pen. He was not a distant observer of daily events, but attempted throughout his long life, albeit unsuccessfully, to influence political opinion in Denmark. Søren Kierkegaard described him as both "the lovable, peculiar thinker, State Councilor Sibbern" and "the political fool—Sibbern."[1]

In several places in his large authorship Sibbern distinguishes between explicative philosophy or reflective philosophy, on the one hand, and the actual or speculative philosophy, on the other. Explicative philosophy uses as its point of departure the actually given statements, such as the Christian faith's dogmas or the principles of mental life, which psychology presents, analyzes and clarifies, and then they are combined into a systematic whole. Then it is the task of speculative philosophy to justify or prove the validity of the thus prepared material.

There is no reason to believe that Eiríksson worked his way through Sibbern's philosophy. As will be seen later, he only mentions Sibbern in a few places in his writings, and when he does, it is only to criticize him. Perhaps the reason for Eiríksson's somewhat negative disposition towards Sibbern is that the philosopher throughout his long life increasingly expressed opinions which were considered to be contrary to orthodox Christianity. For example, he believed that one could be a good Christian, even if one had no knowledge of Christ's life and teachings. It is clear that Sibbern was not a man for Eiríksson.

Sibbern's predecessor was the eclectic Kant critic Niels Treschow (1751-1833), who was called to the professorship of philosophy when the first university in Norway was founded in 1813. There were in Eiríksson's book collection six books by Treschow, including several of his major works (nos. 929-34).[2] Treschow's very straightforward thinking seems to have been attractive to Eiríksson, characterized as it was by the views that are consistent with common sense. Treschow's philosophy was a modified version of the Leibniz-Wolffian monadology, in which he, like both Leibniz and Wolff, made the law of identity the foundation of philosophy. Like Wolff, he paid tribute to a form of empiricism, which he, however, combined with Spinozism and with Locke's doctrine of

---

1 *SKS* 27, 493f., Papir 416 / *JP* 6, 6196.

2 On Treschow, see Koch, *Dansk Oplysningsfilosofi*, pp. 121-70.

ideas. In addition, he was inspired by Plato, Plotinus and the 17th-century Christian English Platonists. The eclectic result of all these sources of inspiration was a philosophy, which can be characterized as individualism or personalism, as identity philosophy and as Christian philosophy.

Among the books by Treschow that Eiríksson owned was *On Human Nature in General, Especially its Spiritual Side* from 1812 (no. 930), a textbook in psychology, which Eiríksson quoted once in his showdown with Martensen's moral philosophy without, however, worrying about specifying a page reference.

Martensen began his moral philosophy by establishing that moral philosophy presupposes man's free will, which may be thought, he writes, "as the principle of absolute independence from all alien causality" and "unconditioned self-subsistence, infinite self-determination."[1] Freedom is also determined as possibility, that is, as a potentiality, "which with inner necessity brings along with it its actuality."[2] Eiríksson gives three quotations and continues saying that a philosopher would write about this concept of freedom if he

> thought like an earth resident, like a human being...: "There may even be the question of whether this freedom is an object of experience." In any case, it is true that such freedom is not given to restricted, reasonable beings, but must be regarded as something abstract, or freedom in its abstraction, but we doubt much that freedom, with its peculiarity is given as an abstraction.[3]

1 Hans Lassen Martensen, *Grundrids til Moralphilosophiens System. Udgivet til Brug ved academiske Forelæsninger*, Copenhagen: C.A. Reitzel 1841, § 7, p. 8. (H.L. Martensen, *Outline to a System of Moral Philosophy*, in *Between Hegel and Kierkegaard: Hans L. Martensen's Philosophy of Religion*, trans. by Curtis L. Thompson and David J. Kangas, Atlanta: Scholars Press 1997, p. 258.)

2 Martensen, *Grundrids*, § 9, p. 9. (*Outline*, p. 258.)

3 Magnús Eiríksson, *Dr. Martensens trykte moralske Paragrapher, eller det saakaldte "Grundrids til Moralphilosophiens System af Dr. Hans Martensen", i dets forvirrede, idealistisk-metaphysiske og phantastisk-speculative, Religion og Christendom undergravende, fatalistiske, pantheistiske og selvforguderske Væsen*, Copenhagen: H.C. Klein 1846, p. 52. The quotation in Eiríksson's statement is from Treschow's *Om den menneskelige Natur i Almindelighed, især dens aandelige Side*, Copenhagen: Fr. Brummer 1812, p. 287.

Treschow is one of the few philosophical writers whom Eiríksson—and hardly rightly so—cites in support of his views.

The review here of Eiríksson's use of contemporary philosophical literature on the basis of the list of his book collection shows all too clearly that he mainly referred to the other people to distance himself from them. The discussions that took place in the contemporary intellectual contexts, such as those for or against the Hegelian philosophy, do not seem to have held his interest. He contributed just as little to the two great debates about the relationship between faith and knowledge that took place in Denmark around 1850 and into the mid-1860s.[1] In fact, there is only one philosopher whose thoughts Eiríksson could have cited as a major source of inspiration—but did not—namely Jacobi—and this despite the fact that he knew that his own concepts about reason and understanding were derived from him. It cannot be determined whether this reflects Eiríksson's desire to appear as an original thinker or is just due to the fact that he was so focused on his own agenda, namely, trying to promote the idea that contemporary philosophy and theology—indeed, his Danish contemporaries as a whole—had a misconception of Christianity, but it is probably most reasonable to assume the latter. If this is the case, then he was similar to Kierkegaard despite the differences that separated them with regard to both literary skills and philosophical abilities.

Also some philosophical writers whose books do not appear in Eiríksson's book collection found favor in his eyes. In connection with a note in which he praises a theological work of the Irish theologian, economist and logician Richard Whately (1787-1863), who from 1832 served as Archbishop of Dublin, he mentions the same author's *Elements of Logic*, the first edition of which appeared in 1826 and was reprinted several times during the century.[2] If Eiríksson had become acquainted with the book, he might have been attracted to what the author says in his preface, where he argues that theologians also will benefit from a textbook in logic:

---

1 See Koch, *Den danske Idealisme*, pp. 361-78 and pp. 435-61.

2 Eiríksson, *Om Baptister og Barnedaab*, p. 205 (note).

> The cause of Truth universally, and not least, of religious Truth, is benefited by everything that tends to promote sound reasoning, and facilitate the detection of fallacy.…Among the enemies of the Gospel now, are to be found men not only of learning and ingenuity, but of cultivated argumentative powers, and not unversed in the principles of Logic. If the advocate of our Religion think proper to disregard this help, they will find, on careful inquiry, that their opponents do not.[1]

Eiríksson's reasoning does not testify that he ever dealt with logic. His books abound with examples of the type of fallacy known as *ad hominem* arguments, that is, arguments where one attacks the person instead of concerning oneself with the issue.

Only one philosophical writer seems entirely to have attracted Eiríksson, namely, the Danish natural scientist Hans Christian Ørsted (1777-1851), who in 1850 published the first volume of a collection of his treatises on popular aesthetics, philosophy of religion and philosophy of science under the collective title *The Spirit in Nature*.[2] The book does not appear on the list of Eiríksson's book collection. In an appendix to his book *Is Faith a Paradox and "By Virtue of the Absurd"?* from the same year as *The Spirit in Nature*,[3] Eiríksson gave an enthusiastic discussion of Ørsted's view on the philosophy of religion, which he thought was, in the main points, in agreement with his own. He therefore found both confirmation and support in Ørsted, who was one of the most revered Danish cultural figures.[4]

For Ørsted, the whole of reality, both its physical and its spiritual side, was a great realm of reason that human reason can penetrate because it is part of it. The essence of human reason, Ørsted thought, is to think consistently, that is, in accordance with itself. The laws, which reason is subject to, are the laws of logic, which require consistency of human

---

1 Richard Whately, *Elements of Logic*, 8th ed., London: Fellowes 1844 [1826], pp. XXXIV-XXXV.

2 Hans Christian Ørsted, *Aanden i Naturen*, Copenhagen: Høst 1850.

3 Magnús Eiríksson [Theophilus Nicolaus], *Er Troen et Paradox og "i Kraft af det Absurde"? et Spørgsmaal foranlediget ved "Frygt og Bæven, af Johannes de silentio", besvaret ved Hjelp af en Troes-Ridders fortrolige Meddelelser, til fælles Opbyggelse for Jøder, Christne og Muhamedanere, af bemeldte Troes-Ridders Broder*, Copenhagen: Chr. Steen & Søn 1850.

4 See Koch, *Den danske idealisme*, pp. 57-85.

thought. A similar consistency must be assumed between the forces of nature and the laws, which nature is subject to, since without such consistency no nature would exist. Therefore, there must be a correlation between human or subjective reason and the reason in the world or objective reason. The laws of nature are rational laws, and therefore they can be known *a priori*. Ørsted called them the thoughts of nature or God thoughts since he identified the reason of the world with the divine. Therefore, there was no contradiction between faith, understood as rational faith, and knowledge, and science was, according to Ørsted, in its essence worship. Although Eiríksson was aware that he did not agree with Ørsted about everything, he believed that he had a spiritual kinship with him and that they were in agreement in asserting the role of reason in relation to religious beliefs.

But Eiríksson seems generally to have read his own beliefs into Ørsted. One example is Ørsted's concept of infidelity in a paper entitled "Superstition and Unbelief in their Relation to Natural Science," which, with its 45 pages, is the second longest in *The Spirit in Nature*. Here Ørsted characterized infidelity as "a tendency to reject that which human beings usually assume about spiritual things, so far as one only acquires this by an immediate internal sense and does not prove it by thinking."[1] After quoting this passage in Ørsted, Eiríksson continues:

> The author disapproves of this infidelity when he just assumes that man, as rational being, by this inner spiritual sense can receive, and spiritually perceive the spiritual, which he is not able to comprehend by thinking, just as he, by means of the outward, physical senses, perceives what is corporeal. This is also our view....[2]

Eiríksson seems to have found his own teachings on reason as the sense of the eternal and infinite (see below) in Ørsted. But Ørsted's point is just the opposite. Infidelity, Ørsted thinks, is particularly the case if a person's relation to the spiritual is one of feeling and not one of reason. The inner sense that Ørsted discusses is not, in his opinion, like the sense

---

1 Hans Christian Ørsted, *Aanden i Naturen*, Copenhagen: Høst 1850, p. 105.
2 Eiríksson, *Er Troen et Paradox og "i Kraft af det Absurde"?*, p. 192.

of reason that Eiríksson is talking about, a true and reliable source of religious beliefs.

II. Characteristics of Eiríksson's Philosophy

In his brief *Outline to a System of Moral Philosophy* from 1841 Martensen wrote:

> In the Christian view of life God is not only life's creative beginning but also its result, its final all-embracing end. As such or as the highest Good, God is to be realized by human freedom. The divine end is nothing different from the very self of God and the meaning of all God's demands on the human is that the very self of God will be, all in all, that God will gain personal shape in the human individual....Consequently, God or the highest Good wants to become human and thus requires a God-Human of every individual. But this demand would be empty and meaningless if it did not presuppose as its possibility that originally existing unity of the divine nature and human nature.[1]

It is only possible for a man to want the good if it is possible to achieve an agreement of his will with God's will. But "God's will cannot be separated from God's essence, and it becomes unattainable in all eternity for the human to carry out God's will if God is not permitted essentially in the human soul."[2] Here Martensen, according to Eiríksson, has identified human nature and the nature of God, and he considered this identification to be "The basic idea of the Martensenian theology"[3] and its fundamental and fatal mistake. Eiríksson found its roots in the Hegelian and Hegel-inspired philosophy. Somewhat bombastically he satirized this basic assumption:

> The doctrine that man by Christ and in him has been essentially and personally one with God, and that the baptized Christians thus have become gods just as God became man, as well as the doctrine that the

[1] Martensen, *Grundrids*, § 48, pp. 50f. (*Outline*, pp. 281f.)
[2] Martensen, *Grundrids*, § 49, p. 51. (*Outline*, p. 282.)
[3] Eiríksson, *Dr. Martensens trykte moralske Paragrapher*, p. 60 (note).

> Atonement is objectively accomplished by the fact that God became man, has such a glorious appearance, such a radiant splendor as hardly any other doctrine. Therefore it is to be hoped that the Danish Christians, a large number of which seem to have the life-task to chase after appearances, by Mr. Martensen's efforts and the work of his pupils, will be so happy to acquire faith such that they not only are objectively (!) reconciled, but are also themselves godlike humans or human gods. Consequently, those doctrines would contribute to glorify him, as Doctor and Professor Theologiae, court preacher and above all as the Danish theologian who first taught "God and man's essential unity," and still always will be the first among many brethren.[1]

In his confrontation with the theologians and philosophers, whom he disagreed with, Eiríksson often made use of highly polemical language, as the quotation illustrates. For example, he talks about Martensen's "speculative superiority or misery" and calls him an "unfair and dishonest teacher."[2] In one passage he speaks of "the speculative General Superintendent [sc. Bishop] Hegel."[3] When he argued against people who thought differently, he often did so—especially in his early works—by demonstrating an alleged conflict with the words of the Bible or by deriving consequences from the discussed views that were contrary to his own view of Christianity. But his own views were far from orthodox. For example, he rejected both the Trinity and the dogma that Jesus had a divine nature, that is, Eiríksson rejected the dogma of the Incarnation. Moreover, he regarded the story of the Fall as a myth, and he rejected the doctrine of original sin as being in direct conflict with Christianity. After the completion of his theology degree in 1837 Eiríksson had a fruitful business as a private tutor of theology. This dried up and disappeared completely in step with his unorthodox view of Christianity becoming known among the students, and the result was that he lived in abject poverty from the mid-1840s until the end of his life. Still, he managed

[1] Ibid., p. 106.
[2] Magnús Eiríksson, *Speculativ Rettroenhed, fremstillet efter Dr. Martensens "christelige Dogmatik", og Geistlig Retfærdighed, belyst ved en Biskops Deeltagelse i en Generalfiskal-Sag*, Copenhagen: Trykt hos J.S. Salomon 1849, p. 92.
[3] Eiríksson, *Dr. Martensens trykte moralske Paragrapher*, p. 54.

to publish a wide range of longer and shorter works, which he financed himself and published with his own imprimatur.

Eiríksson lived in a time that may be described as the flowering period of Danish philosophy, or—with Johannes de silentio's somewhat more negative and satirical description—in a period when "Theology sits all rouged and powdered in the window and offers to philosophy its beauty for sale."[1] Eiríksson adds to this his own description of the situation in contemporary Danish theology: "The so-called orthodox, half- or quarter-orthodox theologians could...not catch sight of the monster [sc. speculative philosophy]; they fraternized with speculation and the speculators, and welcomed the intelligent assistance, which was granted them."[2]

Like Søren Kierkegaard, Eiríksson turned passionately against all attempts to put faith in conceptual form, that is, to formulate a scholarly theology and make the conditions of existence and subjective life the object of an objective and thus scholarly study. Eiríksson wrote, it is about

> light and peace being prevalent within man. Light and peace are inseparable. But light does not consist of a bunch of skills or philosophical and speculative doctrines, but rather of the fact that the one simple truth stands clear before the spirit's eye and that the simple, but clear and rational knowledge of truth is narrowly united with a living trust and faith in God.[3]

For Eiríksson, as for Kierkegaard, the pure and simple faith was a matter of salvation. But the quotation also shows the points on which he was fundamentally in disagreement with Kierkegaard. Where faith, for Eiríksson, implied light and peace, for Kierkegaard, it meant renouncing the world and suffering, which, Eiríksson thought, was contrary to God's love.[4] In one of his critical encounters with Kierkegaard, he quoted the following from *The Moment*:

---

1 *SKS* 4, 128 / *FT*, 32.
2 Eiríksson, *Gud og Reformatoren*, p. 64.
3 Ibid., p. 79.
4 See, for example, ibid., pp. 67ff. (note).

> The truth is: to become a Christian is to become, humanly speaking, unhappy for this life; the proportion is: the more you involve yourself with God and the more he loves you, the more you will become, humanly speaking, unhappy for this life, the more you will come to suffer in this life.[1]

On this Eiríksson remarked:

> How does K. come…to present the matter in this way? He has come to this by making Christianity on the whole as absurd or paradoxical and unnatural, so unnatural that one neither would have thought that it was meant for man nor that man was receptive to it. God hates man, whom He Himself created, and whom He Himself maintains by His eternal power and His eternal love, because He from the beginning has given man the capacities and powers, which man is in possession of; these capacities and powers could well be abused and, unfortunately, have been abused, but can never be destroyed and, used in the right way, make it possible for man to seek God.[2]

But most striking is that Eiríksson, unlike Kierkegaard, says that faith is related to the "rational knowledge of truth." In his criticism of Kierkegaard he rejected his talk about "the absurd" in *Fear and Trembling* and "the religious paradox" in the *Concluding Unscientific Postscript*.[3] In one passage he writes:

> It is not because of the doctrine that the Christian, or rather the true religious faith, is "in virtue of the absurd," that man must come to knowledge of religious truth. When the so-called Christian faith "in virtue of the absurd" and "indignation" is a condition of true Christianity, then Christ has not brought men light and peace, but on the contrary, caused and created an insoluble contrast, an enmity, a fragmentation of man's mind and not an opposition between the bad and good in man, but a decidedly hostile opposition between the good intellectual powers in man.[4]

---

1 *SKS* 13, 266 / *M*, 212.

2 Eiríksson, *Om Bønnens Virkning*, p. 38.

3 See, for example, Eiríksson, *Er Troen et Paradox og "i Kraft af det Absurde"?*, pp. 53ff. and pp. 149ff.

4 Eiríksson, *Gud og Reformatoren*, pp. 75f.

It is already implied in Eiríksson's rejection of the dogma of Christ's divine nature that he must reject "the religious paradox."

Kierkegaard, who knew Eiríksson from his time as a university student, responded to his complaints just as little as Martensen did.[1] However, a slightly annoyed journal entry in connection with the publication in 1850 of *Is Faith a Paradox and "By Virtue of the Absurd"?* shows that he took note of Eiríksson's attack and found that it was based on a misunderstanding. He begins with the observation: "You see, this is what happens when clumsiness intervenes in opposition to an artistic design."[2] He goes on to point out that Eiríksson has completely failed to notice that the pseudonym Johannes Climacus declares that he is not a believer. The entry ends with a sigh:

> What has cost me days of diligence, enormous effort, an almost sleepless dialectical persistence in keeping the threads properly arranged in this delicate construction—this simply does not exist for others. I am simply identified with my pseudonyms, and then some nonsense gets patched together that—of course—is understood by many more: yes, of course![3]

The background of Eiríksson's understanding of faith as reason's concern is his somewhat idiosyncratic concepts of reason and understanding, which constitute the foundation for what might be called his epistemology and philosophy of religion. Kierkegaard never used the word "reason" (*fornuft*) in any technical sense, and the word is rare in his writings. Presumably he believed that in the past too many illegitimate associations were linked to it. By contrast, the word "understanding" (*forstand*) in both a technical and a non-technical meaning appears numerous times in his writings. Specifically Kierkegaard states that the religious paradox, which lies in the "the sphere of faith," is a faith against understanding,[4] and that faith's martyrdom is to "crucify the understanding."[5] But Kierkegaard—or

---

[1] A brief account of the relation between Eiríksson and Kierkegaard can be found in Svend Aage Nielsen, *Kierkegaard og Regensen*, Copenhagen: Gråbrødre Torv's Forlag 1965, pp. 70-75.

[2] *SKS* 23, 182, NB17:28 / *KJN* 7, 185.

[3] *SKS* 23, 183, NB17:28 / *KJN* 7, 185.

[4] *SKS* 7, 527 / *CUP1*, 579f.

[5] *SKS* 7, 508 / *CUP1*, 559.

ather his pseudonym Johannes Climacus—also explains carefully that faith does not imply a denial of the understanding:

> Consequently the believing Christian both has and uses his understanding, respects the universally human, does not explain someone's not becoming a Christian as a lack of understanding, but believes Christianity against the understanding and here uses the understanding—in order to see to it that he believes against the understanding.[1]

As will become apparent, Eiríksson was in a certain sense in agreement with Kierkegaard in that faith is conceived to be contrary to the intellect, but this is only true if the understanding—which Eiríksson perceived as a lower faculty—does not submit to or allow itself to be guided by the higher reason.

Eiríksson presented his conceptual determinations of reason and understanding and the fixing of the limits of their application in the only work on the philosophy of religion, or rather epistemology, that he ever published, and which is actually a kind of critical philosophy in the Kantian sense—although it does not contain any references to Kant or other epistemologists. There is a single reference to Hegel's philosophical propaedeutic. This work came from Hegel's time as school superintendent in Nuremberg and was edited posthumously by Karl Rosenkranz and published in 1840 as volume 18 of Hegel's works.

Eiríksson's short work appeared in 1846 under the title *Faith, Superstition and Unbelief, in Their Relation to Reason and Understanding, as well as to Each Other* and has the stated goal to explain "the principle for the acquisition, perception, assessment and preparation of religion and Christianity with the dogmas which must be assumed to belong to this,"[2] and in connection with this to explain faith compared to human reason, since faith "in its deepest foundation is reasonable," and reason is the human ability, "in which faith rests."[3] Eiríksson understands "reason" here in the subjective sense and not as the reason that prevails in the world.

---

1 *SKS* 7, 516 / *CUP1*, 568.

2 Magnús Eiríksson, *Tro, Overtro og Vantro, i deres Forhold til Fornuft og Forstand, samt til hinanden indbyrdes*, Copenhagen: H.C. Klein 1846, p. IV.

3 Ibid., p. 22 and p. 24.

Eiríksson defines "reason" as the sense of the infinite and eternal. It is receptive, like the external senses which receive impressions from the outside world; it does not judge or reflect—that is the business of the understanding—but immediately detects or perceives, and where the understanding isolates man from the divine and therefore can be an enemy of reason, we perceive God and his revelation immediately with the faculty of reason:

> When we then, with deep and clear-thinking theologians and philosophers say that reason (*die Vernunft* from *vernehmen*, to perceive, that is, in a spiritual way) is the sense for the infinite and eternal, the sense for the higher ideas, the sense for the universal—or something more determinate—the sense with which we perceive God and His revelations both inside and outside of us, then we believe that we have specified in a preliminary manner the nature of reason in its true essence and activity.[1]

Reason detects or senses that something spiritual is the case, that God exists and that He has revealed Himself both in nature and in the human mind. At the same time man also experiences immediately why the Godhead reveals Himself to man, that is, what benefit and joy man will have from what is revealed, for example, to act or not to act in certain ways. In the sense that the presence of the "that" of faith is immediately explained on the basis of the "why," it is "justified" in it. Also if the deity is silent, that is, if the "that-not" exists, its reason and explanation lies in the "why" of faith. Reason's judgment "is limited to a 'that or a that-not,' which is grounded on a mere common and immediate 'why,' but reason does not assert anything about the exact and rational specification of the thing's 'why' or 'how.'"[2] It is the task of the understanding to answer questions about the nature of the revealed, the "what" and the "how."[3]

After determining "reason" and "understanding" Eiríksson can in relation to these determinations characterize "infidelity," "faith" and

---

[1] Ibid., p. 27.

[2] Ibid., p. 36.

[3] In *Gud og Reformatoren*, pp. 76-78 (note), Eiríksson gave a brief account of his use of the concepts "reason" and "understanding."

"superstition." The infidels accept only what is justified by concrete and tangible grounds of understanding, and it is therefore based on a lower understanding, which is isolated from reason. If the scientist stops with knowledge of the understanding and ignores the sense of reason, and consequently rejects the existence of the infinite and eternal, he is a non-believer. But if he includes religious ideas in his science, his theories will lose their scientific character. Science is, Eiríksson writes, "as such unbelieving, and therefore abandons its concept by becoming orthodox."[1] Faith and knowledge must not be mixed. Faith is based on the sense of reason, on the logical "that" and the rational "why," but does not exclude the understanding. Superstition is based either on the imagination and irrationality or on something external, which is given authority. It excludes both reason and understanding, not least because it mixes them up and confuses them with each other.[2] Merely formally the conceptual distinctions are formulated as follows:

> Unbelief, which stands at the ground of the mere understanding does not demand alone the "that" and the "why" of things [sc. the "rational" "that" = the tangible existence, and the "understandable" "why" = the empirically substantiated explanation], but also the "what" and the "how." Faith is satisfied by the first two (that is, the rational "that" and the rational and immediate "why"). Superstition is not based on the rational "that" or "why" (since it seems to assume that faith, to be genuine, must be blind) but usually indicates a false "why," etc.[3]

It is worth noting that, for Eiríksson, there is no animosity between reason and understanding, or between faith and knowledge. The believer can—or rather must—both try to determine conceptually his religious beliefs and reflect on them, although the primeval cause of existence is inscrutable. Eiríksson's entire *oeuvre* can be seen as a concern for the understanding, that is, as an explanation of the consequences resulting from his underlying religious beliefs.

As mentioned above, Eiríksson refers in the book to Hegel's introductory courses, a reference which seems to be the only specific

---

1 Eiríksson, *Tro, Overtro og Vantro*, p. 68.
2 Ibid., p. 50.
3 Ibid., p. 68.

reference to Hegel in his *oeuvre*. Eiríksson can hardly have read anything else by Hegel and seems to base the sharp criticism, which he aims at Hegelianism, on what he heard or read about Hegel. His knowledge of both foreign and domestic philosophy seems, as mentioned, very limited. Positively described, his philosophy can be characterized as homespun, and negatively as unclear and postulating.

In addition to Hegel, who appears five times in the book, Eiríksson cites Sibbern twice and Heiberg once in connection with Hegel. In addition, there are a handful of philosophical theologians, among them his main enemy Martensen and the, for Eiríksson at the time when he published the book, much more acceptable Jacob Peter Mynster (1775-1854), the primate of the Danish Church. Later—after Mynster had entered the fray on Martensen's side—Eiríksson came to doubt the nature of Mynster's understanding of Christianity and his personal qualities.[1] For example, he concludes, after having shown that Mynster denied the divinity of Christ on the cross and thus, according to Eiríksson's view, repealed and destroyed the Church's teaching about Christ's atonement of sins, because in that case it was not God, but a man who suffered, that "Mr. Bishop turns his mantle to the wind," that is, is opportunistic or dishonest.[2]

In most of the places where Eiríksson criticizes Hegel and the Hegelians it often happens by means of satirical descriptions and criticisms of the juxtaposition of opposites and their mediation. In *Faith, Superstition and Unbelief* there is a lengthy footnote of a more substantial, although somewhat primitive nature, where he begins by calling Hegel "the great builder of castles in the air."[3]

In the footnote Eiríksson contrasts Hegel's idealism with his own realism. Hegel and the Hegelians claim that their thinking is without presuppositions since the system begins with the abstraction "being," but pure being is without characteristics and therefore equal to "nothing." Anyone who, unlike Hegel, truly wants to begin without presuppositions,

---

1 See Eiríksson, *Speculativ Rettroenhed*, pp. 94ff.
2 Ibid., p. 97.
3 Eiríksson, *Tro, Overtro og Vantro*, p. 30 (note). The footnote runs from p. 30 to p. 32. The following quotations are from this footnote.

> finds it the most in agreement with and the most satisfying for reason, understanding and the heart to determine the relationship between man's subjective acquaintance and knowledge and the existing objects for human knowing, which in their objective actuality exist independently of man.

Objective reality, the created world including social and cultural conditions, are the given presupposition for human knowledge and are its objects. The same applies to a number of ideas, such as the ideas of the good, the righteous and the holy, which, like all other existing things, have their origin in the Creator.

With Hegel and his followers this is different. Man is endowed with reason, subjective reason, and actuality, which man is a part of, is a rationally ordered whole, that is, a product of objective reason. But since man is a part of the world—including society and culture—there is no qualitative difference between objective reason and subjective reason. The historical development is the actualization of objective reason or the spirit of the world, and it is the constant task of subjective reason to appropriate this development, to become aware of it. Since the individual's being is a product of it, he acquires himself, that is, obtains a real self-awareness, in that he achieves awareness of the steps that the development has reached.

The outlined relationship between objective and subjective reason, or what Eiríksson called "the confusion of God's and of man's nature" leads to a claim that

> God would be nothing but a product of human knowledge, wisdom and knowledge, or at least in all cases—for that we should not make this doctrine too one-sided—God is gradually produced jointly by nature, which develops in time, and humanity. But it is God, who has produced both; He is the eternal and, for us human beings, incomprehensible cause and ground, both for the existence, the development and the conservation of nature and humanity.[1]

According to Hegel, God's self-consciousness—and hence the nature of God—is man's consciousness of God.

---

[1] Ibid., pp. 31f. (note).

In support of his view of Hegel's philosophy of religion Eiríksson quotes from an article from 1842 by Heiberg, who distinguishes between the physical objects, which are what they are, independent of our knowledge of them, and spiritual things, such as the state, religion and science, about which one can say:

> Just as they are objects of our knowledge, so our knowledge is again an object of them, and at any new step of our knowledge we change their existence and make it into something else. You will readily perceive that the God who is known and loved is not the same as the one who is merely feared as an unknown creature, and that the degrees in our knowing and love exert a change on God's existence, because his dominion in man's mind and heart is dependent on this whole development in man.[1]

It is obvious that such a view clearly must be contrary to Eiríksson's perception of Christianity. "The arch master of arbitrariness Hegel...has confused, poisoned, and, insofar as he could, destroyed the true concept of God."[2]

In connection with the criticism of the Hegelians' view of the relationship between objective and the subjective reason Eiríksson also argues that Hegel has turned upside down man's spiritual abilities and, as evidence to support it, refers to §§ 163-172 in the *Philosophische Propädeutik*. This section is entitled "*Das Denken*" and consists of three subsections: "*Verstand*," "*Urtheilen*" and "*Vernünftiges Denken*,"[3] where Eiríksson's disapproval is aroused especially by Hegel's characterization of reason as negative or dialectical and the division of it into reflective reason and inferential reason with the subdivision between formal reason and teleological reason. By seeing reason as the ability to reason, that is, to reflect, and the ability to infer, Hegel has, according to Eiríksson, confused reason with understanding and has therefore—which is the fundamental flaw in his thought—not perceived reason as the sense of the infinite. Since he, furthermore, according to Eiríksson, has put on a par understanding and judgment and has not realized that the understanding can be enriched by reason, Hegel has conceived the

---

[1] Johan Ludvig Heiberg, "Autoritet," *Intelligensblade*, no. 7, 1842, pp. 162f.
[2] Eiríksson, *Tro, Overtro og Vantro*, p. 35 (note).
[3] Hegel, *Sämtliche Werke. Jubiläumsausgabe*, vol. 3, pp. 212-15.

understanding as "the cold, flat understanding, which fears reason and therefore is misled and limited."[1]

Although Sibbern is judged somewhat more mildly than Hegel, he also is criticized for ambiguity regarding the distinction between understanding and reason. That Sibbern distinguishes between objective and subjective understanding, Eiríksson can accept, but not the corresponding distinction between objective and subjective reason. Eiríksson refers here to Sibbern's textbook on psychology from 1843.[2] Moreover, Eiríksson seems not to know much about Sibbern's thought. For example, he writes that Sibbern "with more firmness and energy should have opposed the stream of false thinking emerging here at the University in recent years, the philosophy that confuses and undermines all sound thinking, and any Christian and true religious world-view—if he were only able to be so."[3] Eiríksson apparently overlooked the fact that Sibbern had criticized Hegelian philosophy as early as 1838 in a long review of the first volume of Heiberg's journal *Perseus*.[4] In the same year a part of this review appeared in book form, and this also included the critique of Hegel's philosophy.[5]

By contrast, Eiríksson has nothing but praise for Mynster, who, in a paper in 1821 in accordance with Friedrich Heinrich Jacobi (1743-1819), defines reason as man's ability to provide "immediate ideas of transcendent objects,"[6] that is, as "receptivity, the sense for the supersensible."[7] In connection with this characterization of reason Mynster refers to Jacobi's *Von den Göttlichen Dingen und ihrer Offenbarung* from 1811, where Jacobi

---

1 Eiríksson, *Tro, Overtro og Vantro*, p. 39 (note).

2 Frederik Christian Sibbern, *Psychologie, indledet ved almindelig Biologi, i sammentrængt Fremstilling. Ny Udarbeidelse*, Copenhagen: Paa eget forlag 1843, pp. 262f.

3 Eiríksson, *Tro, Overtro og Vantro*, p. 34 (note).

4 Johan Ludvig Heiberg, *Perseus, Journal for den speculative Idee*, vol. 1, 1837. Sibbern's review appeared in *Maanedsskrift for Litteratur*, vol. 19, 1838, pp. 283-360, pp. 424-60, pp. 546-82; vol. 19, 1838, pp. 20-60, pp. 103-36, pp. 193-244 and pp. 405-49.

5 Frederik Christian Sibbern, *Bemærkninger og Undersøgelser, fornemmelig betreffende Hegels Philosophie, betragtet i Forhold til vor Tid*, Copenhagen: C.A. Reitzel 1838.

6 Jacob Peter Mynster, "Udvikling af Begrebet Tro," *Det Kongelige Danske Videnskabernes Selskabs philosophiske og historiske Afhandlinger*, vol. 1, Copenhagen: Kongelige Danske Videnskabernes Selskab 1821, pp. 200-36, here quoted from J.P. Mynster, *Blandede Skrivter*, vols. 1-3, Copenhagen: Gyldendal 1852-53 [vols. 4-6, posthumously ed. by Just Henrik Paulli, Copenhagen: Gyldendal 1855-57]; vol. 1, p. 27.

7 Ibid., p. 31.

writes that "*Es ist in jedem endlichen oder sinnlichen Wesen (denn jedes endliche Wesen ist nothwendig ein sinnliches) die Vernunft nichts andres als der Sinn für das Uebersinnliche.*"[1] Jacobi distinguishes between reason and understanding, in that the latter is thought to receive its material from the sensory world.

Although the same distinction between reason and understanding, and the expression of their characteristics is found in Eiríksson, he has hardly taken his concepts of reason and understanding directly from Jacobi, whom he does not mention. Gerhard Schreiber has suggested that Mynster could be the source,[2] but on the face of it this is less likely since Mynster, in agreement with Jacobi, defines reason as the sense of the transcendent, whereas Eiríksson, as quoted above, defines it as the sense of the infinite and eternal,[3] although he also says that "the supersensible, the higher spiritual…is mostly the object of reason."[4]

However, in the book of faith, superstition and unbelief Eiríksson indirectly indicated his source. In connection with an explanation of how rational faith can be shocked by the irrational, he explains in a footnote where his knowledge of philosophy for the most part comes from:

> When, in 1839, I had the desire to acquire a more complete knowledge of the systems of the most outstanding recent philosophers, I, although a graduate for two years, attended Professor Martensen's lectures on the history of modern philosophy. I was, naturally, on account of my interest, an attentive auditor, and I also followed the lecture quite well, which was pretty clear and interesting, and I was able more or less to put myself in the

---

1 Friedrich Heinrich Jacobi, *[V]on den Göttlichen Dingen und ihrer Offenbarung*, Leipzig: Gerhard Fleischer 1811, p. 199; here quoted from *Friedrich Heinrich Jacobi's Werke*, vols. 1-6, ed. by Friedrich Roth und Friedrich Köppen, Leipzig: Gerhard Fleischer 1812-25; vol. 3, p. 436. The most detailed explanation of the distinction between reason and sense, and their characteristics can be found in the preface to the reissue of Jacobi's *David Hume über den Glauben, oder Idealismus und Realismus. Ein Gespräch* (1786) in volume 2 of his *Werke*, which is simultaneously also intended as an introduction to Jacobi's collected works. Here it is said that reason "senses" the transcendent (p. 9), where the mind is nothing but the ability to reflect on the sensual, that is, subordinating the sensuous beliefs to concepts (p. 65).

2 Gerhard Schreiber, "Magnús Eiríksson: An Opponent of Martensen and an Unwelcome Ally of Kierkegaard" (see p. 17 above, note 1), p. 61 (note 77).

3 Eiríksson, *Tro, Overtro og Vantro*, p. 27.

4 Ibid., p. 42.

> different systems, for there was always something in them that appealed to reason. But when we got to Hegel and the instructor began to present his doctrine of being and nothing, etc., oh, what a feeling! It was like when you give a healthy animal something, which it rebels against without knowing whether it is harmful or not, and meets it with involuntary disgust and vomit if it eats a bit of it. When the lesson was over, I was, like the ancient Hebrews, on the verge of tearing my clothes to pieces.[1]

The lecture course in the winter semester of 1838-39, which is referred to here, was announced under the title: "*Historia philosophiae recentioris (inde a Kantio ad Hegelium usque) ejusque ad theologicam relatio*" (The History of the More Recent Philosophy (From Kant to Hegel) and its Relation to Theology). Years later Martensen wrote in his memoirs that to introduce the students to the speculative dogma, which was his real concern, he had to lead them through modern philosophy and its relationship to theology:

> I decided therefore to give a separate lecture on the more recent history of philosophy and its relation to theology from Kant to Hegel. Even before my appointment I had, in winter 1837-38, given this lecture for a mixed group, which had specially requested me to do so, and each time it was repeated, the most numerous auditors came from different faculties, indeed even men who had positions in government.[2]

The lecture course was later repeated five times, the last time in the winter semester 1850.[3]

At the Royal Library in Copenhagen there are two sets of notes to the lectures, which Martensen, according to the above, gave privately in 1837-38 and later repeated. One of these and the largest, which fills three notebooks and is written by two hands, is the most interesting because it contains individual corrections from Martensen's hand and

---

1 Ibid., p. 81 (note).

2 Hans Lassen Martensen, *Af mit Levned*, vols. 1-3, Copenhagen: Gyldendal 1882-83; vol. 2, pp. 3f.

3 See the overview of Martensen's lectures in Skat Arildsen, *Biskop Hans Lassen Martensen. Hans Liv, Udvikling og Arbejde*, vol. 1, *Studier i det 19. Aarhundredes Aandsliv*, Copenhagen: Gad 1932, pp. 156-58.

comes from Martensen's archives, from where it was given to the library. There is no fundamental difference between the two sets of notes, and both contain the same key phrases and passages and roughly the same quotations,[1] but the larger manuscript seems more professionally executed. Since the name of the person doing the transcribing appears on the title page in the vast majority of the student transcriptions from the period, whereas this is not the case for the longer set of notes, it must be assumed that this was one of the sets of notes, which were offered for sale and purchased by more affluent students. It is well known that in Søren Kierkegaard's and Peter Christian Kierkegaard's archives there are sets of notes to Martensen's lectures on speculative dogmatics from the winter semester of 1838-39, which are also likely to have been made professionally with the goal of selling them.

After an introduction, including an explanation of the sources, the lectures examine Kant, the elder Fichte, Jacobi, de Wette, Schleiermacher, Schelling, Hegel and the Hegelian school. Here it is primarily the lectures on Jacobi that are of interest. In the 15th lecture from January 23, 1838 Martensen refers to Jacobi, who is said to think that "truth is not a systematic thinking, it is a matter of the heart, of life beyond all systems."[2] Then Jacobi's distinction between reason and understanding is introduced, "because this ties together everything for J[acobi]." Martensen is said to have continued:

> What then is the organ with which I believe? ...To this J[acobi] answers: reason, it is the sense of the infinite and eternal. The word "*Vernunft*" comes from "*vernehmen*," to sense, to be receptive, to perceive the given. In this sense it can be said that God has reason for he is productivity, but human reason, by contrast, does not produce, it only senses the given. However, this should not be understood as if it were a *tabula rasa*, an absolute passivity; no! it proves to be active, but it is a negative activity, which only appears in

---

1 The shorter set of notes bears the title, "*Forelæsninger over Philosophiens Historie*" and has the call number NKS 577, 8°; the larger one has the title "*Lic. Martensens Indledningsforedrag til den nyere Philosophies Studium 1837-38*" and has the call number NKS 3434, 4°. Both give an account of 33 lectures covering the period from November 14, 1837 to March 27, 1838. From the repetition of the same lecture course in 1838-39 there is in Søren Kierkegaard's papers a concise and expertly executed set of notes. It is printed in *Pap.* II C 25 (in vol. XII), pp. 280-331.

2 NKS 3434, 4°, hefte 2, p. 165.

> the perception of the given, just as the eye perceives colors, the ear tones.... reason determines—*that* something is, not *how* it is—this is a matter for the understanding—it determined the existence of the object.[1]

As is apparent from the information given above, Eiríksson also operated with the "that" of reason and the "how" of the understanding. Nothing like this can be found in Mynster. There is so much consistency between Martensen's statement of Jacobi's philosophy and Eiríksson's view that it is reasonable to consider Martensen's lectures to be Eiríksson's immediate source.

After his death in 1881 Eiríksson was quickly forgotten, and the Danish church historians who have dealt with Martensen, with only a few exceptions, have largely ignored him. Eiríksson was literally a fighter for the Lord and was one of the critics of the Danish Hegelianism and the Martensenian speculative theology, who was rightly overshadowed by Kierkegaard.

Translated by Jon Stewart

[1] NKS 3434, 4°, hefte 2, pp. 168f. (emphasis mine).

The Courtyard of Residential College Regensen with the Round Tower
(Litograph, ca. 1840.
Public domain picture, https://commons.wikimedia.org.)

II. Eiríksson and His Contemporaries

Eiríksson, Martensen, and the Deification of Humanity

Gerhard Schreiber

Magnús Eiríksson's dispute with the Danish theologian Hans Lassen Martensen (1808-84) can be divided, like his writings generally, into two phases. The first phase consists of the period of Eiríksson's dispute with Martensen *sensu stricto*, from 1844 until 1851, during which a fierce opposition to Martensen served as the impetus that sparked almost all of Eiríksson's literary activity. Later, there came a period—lasting from 1863 to 1874—characterized by a radical and ever-intensifying critique of both the Bible specifically and of Church doctrine generally, particularly the doctrine that Jesus of Nazareth is the Son of God. In this latter period, Eiríksson's references to Martensen are mostly peripheral to his writings. The intervening years may be characterized as a period of literary silence, since during this time Eiríksson published only occasional articles in

This article is a revised and enlarged version of parts of my two articles "Magnús Eiríksson: An Opponent of Martensen and an Unwelcome Ally of Kierkegaard," in *Kierkegaard and His Danish Contemporaries*, Tome II, *Theology*, ed. by Jon Stewart, Aldershot: Ashgate 2009 (*Kierkegaard Research: Sources, Reception and Resources*, vol. 7), pp. 49-94, especially pp. 55-66, and " 'Like a Voice in the Wilderness': Magnús Eiríksson's Tenacious Critique of Martensen—and Martensen's 'Lofty Silence,' " in *Hans Lassen Martensen: Theologian, Philosopher and Social Critic*, ed. by Jon Stewart, Copenhagen: Museum Tusculanum Press 2012 (*Danish Golden Age Studies*, vol. 6), pp. 155-91. I thank Ashgate Publishing and Museum Tusculanum Press for granting permission to use the texts of these publications in the present article.

newspapers, magazines or periodicals,[1] possibly along with one or two brief, and seemingly quite whimsical, pseudonymous pamphlets.[2]

In the two main phases of his career, Eiríksson's main allegation against Martensen, which may be regarded as his critique's *basso ostinato*, remained essentially the same: Martensen's speculative theology leads to the *deification of humanity*. It should be noted, however, that this allegation underwent a tiny, though consequential, change from the first

[1] See Magnús Eiríksson, "Brigham Joung," *Illustreret Magazin*, vol. 2, 1854, no. 36 (September 2), pp. 281-83 and no. 37 (September 9), pp. 290-92; "Wartburg," *Illustreret Magazin*, vol. 2, 1854, no. 36 (September 2), pp. 283f. and no. 38 (September 16), p. 301; "Endnu et Indlæg i Sagen: Dr. S. Kierkegaard contra Biskop Martensen m. Fl.," *Kongeriget Danmarks Avertissements-Tidende*, 1855, no. 82 (April 10), columns 16f.; no. 83 (April 11), columns 16f.; no. 84 (April 12), columns 16f.; no. 85 (April 13), columns 16f.; no. 86 (April 14), column 16; no. 89 (April 18), column 16; no. 91 (April 20), columns 16f.; no. 92 (April 21), column 16; no. 93 (April 23), column 16; (trans.), "Brudstykker af den islandske Elucidarius," *Annaler for nordisk Oldkyndighed og Historie*, 1857, pp. 238-308; "Til Íslendínga," *Þjóðólfur*, vol. 9, 1857, nos. 34-35 (September 14), p. 140.

[2] On various occasions, the pamphlet (8 pages) *En liden Epistel til Hvidtølsbrygger Hans Mikkelsen, i Kallundborg, indeholdende en chemisk Undersøgelse af hans "Hvidtøl,"* Copenhagen: Møllers Boghandel 1852 (2nd edition, 1852), published under the pseudonym (or name) "Lars Maagensen," is ascribed to Eiríksson; see Edvard Collin, *Anonymer og Pseudonymer i den danske, norske og islandske Literatur samt i fremmede Literaturer, forsaavidt disse omhandle nordiske Forhold, fra de ældste Tider indtil Aaret 1860*, Copenhagen: J. Lund 1869, p. 135; Emil Ottokar Weller, *Lexicon Pseudonymorum. Wörterbuch der Pseudonymen aller Zeiten und Völker, oder Verzeichniss jener Autoren, die sich falscher Namen bedienten*, 2nd revised and enlarged edition, Regensburg: Coppenrath 1886, p. 336; Balder Vermund Aage Erichsen and Alfred Krarup, *Dansk historisk bibliografi. Systematisk fortegnelse over bidrag til Danmarks historie til udgangen af 1912*, vols. 1-3, Copenhagen: Gad 1917-27; vol. 1, p. 266 (no. 4569); *Index bio-bibliographicus notorum hominum*, ed. by Jean-Pierre Lobies et al., Pars C, Corpus alphabeticum, I. Sectio generalis, Supplementum vol. 99,7, ed. by Susanna Wand, Osnabrück: Biblio-Verlag 2003, p. 618. The same applies to the pamphlet (16 pages) *Epistel eller Sendebrev til Den Herre "Intrepidus" (?) angaaende H. M. Kongens Ægteskab og Reise i Jydernes Land*, Copenhagen: Zuschlags Boghandling 1852 (16 pages), which is published under the pseudonym "Adam Homo," see Weller, *Lexicon Pseudonymorum*, 2nd edition, p. 4; Erichsen and Krarup, *Dansk historisk bibliografi*, vol. 1, p. 265 (no. 4546); *Index bio-bibliographicus notorum hominum*, vol. 99,7, p. 618. It should be mentioned, however, that in the auction catalogue of Eiríksson's library that is included in *Fortegnelse over endel forskjellige gode og velconditionerede Bogsamlinger, bestaaende af theologiske, juridiske, medicinske, historiske, æsthetiske, sprog- og naturvidenskabelige Værker samt Restoplagene af forskjellige theologiske Bøger, tilhørende Boerne efter afdøde Overlærer Nielsen, Districtslæge Wilhjelm, Pastor Krogh, Cand. theol. Magnús Eiríksson, Krigsraad Juul m.fl.*, ed. by Christian Peter Hee, Copenhagen: J.D. Quist 1881, pp. 138-70, neither of the pamphlets is listed, unlike all of Eiríksson's (other) writings; see ibid., pp. 149f. (nos. 494-511) and pp. 168f. (nos. 1178-1214).

phase to the second. Whereas the deification of humanity was understood in the first phase as referring specifically to humanity's *self*-deification, in the second phase Eiríksson extended his critique to *all* deification of humanity, even including the deification of the human being Jesus of Nazareth. Here Eiríksson claims that, by his very activity of advancing and advocating the idea of the incarnation of God in Christ, Martensen has blasphemed the *one* true God.

In what follows, I will offer an outline of the course and progress of Eiríksson's critique, focusing mainly on the period of Eiríksson's early writings from 1844 until 1851 (Sections I to IV). After presenting important examples of Eiríksson's dispute with Martensen in his later writings (Section V), I will comment briefly, in my final Section (VI), on Martensen's constant reaction towards Eiríksson's critic: to maintain a "lofty silence."[1]

I. The Starting Point of Eiríksson's Critique

After passing his candidate's examination in April 1837, Eiríksson spent the next few years as a *manuduktør*, a tutor assisting younger students to prepare for the official exams in theology. From the start of his student years, Eiríksson had felt drawn to the rational theology and Biblical exegesis of Henrik Nicolai Clausen (1793-1877).[2] At the same time, he felt a deep distrust toward Nikolai Frederik Severin Grundtvig (1783-1872) and his followers, whom he condescendingly labeled "the Catholicizing theologians,"[3] since "Grundtvig is no Evangelical theologian. In fact he belongs to the Papist realm, and would fit better in

1 Magnús Eiríksson, *Dr. Martensens trykte moralske Paragrapher, eller det saakaldte "Grundrids til Moralphilosophiens System af Dr. Hans Martensen", i dets forvirrede, idealistisk-metaphysiske og phantastisk-speculative, Religion og Christendom undergravende, fatalistiske, pantheistiske og selvforguderske Væsen*, Copenhagen: H.C. Klein 1846, p. II. Eiríksson's excessive use of italics and other forms of emphasis have not been reproduced in the quotations.

2 See, for example, Magnús Eiríksson, *Om Baptister og Barnedaab, samt flere Momenter af Den kirkelige og speculative Christendom*, Copenhagen: P.G. Philipsen 1844, p. VI, where Eiríksson describes Clausen as an excellent representative of the "*Evangelical party*," whose understanding of Christianity "stood nearest to the Christian truth."

3 Ibid.

the Papal State than in an Evangelical-Protestant church."[1] Eiríksson felt an even stronger antipathy, meanwhile, toward the speculative theology of Martensen, whose rise at the university coincided with Eiríksson's period of employment as a *manuduktør* from 1838 to 1847. By the late 1830s, Martensen's widely popular lectures on dogmatics had provoked sharp disapproval in Eiríksson: he regarded Martensen's Biblical exegesis as not only without Scriptural warrant, but as "completely arbitrary" as well.[2] Eiríksson was even more disturbed by the extreme excitement with which Martensen's fashionable theology was greeted by its student audience. As the students at Copenhagen grew ever more enthusiastic about speculative dogmatics, they spent less and less time on exegesis. They were thus on the road, Eiríksson lamented, to "becoming freethinkers, conscious or unconscious pantheists and self-glorifiers."[3]

For a time Eiríksson was in great demand, particularly in the fields of Old and New Testament exegesis. Yet his unyielding opposition to the fashionable speculative theology of Martensen, steadily harmed Eiríksson's reputation, and sharply reduced the demand for his services. This led to serious financial difficulties, particularly since Eiríksson was forced to publish many of his works at his own expense. In his hour of need, Eiríksson even asked Kierkegaard directly for material support. In a letter to Kierkegaard from October 14, 1847 Eiríksson writes:

> Mr. Kierkegaard!
> It is true I applied to you last year for financial support I greatly needed, without succeeding in winning your sympathy, and accordingly you were probably not expecting to hear from me again. But as I am still in the same financial difficulty, if not greater—for I do not even know myself when it has been greatest during these past two years, even though I have always, often in a totally unexpected manner, been helped for the time being—I have decided to make another attempt with you, for after all, it is written, "Ask, and ye shall be given."...I have often mused on what the reason might be why you have earlier been unwilling to support me, for you must have realized that I am one of the few who strive in the same or a similar direction as you yourself, quite aside from the fact that several people

---

1 Ibid., p. 107.
2 Ibid., p. XI.
3 Ibid., p. XXXIX.

> must have found it so natural that they have spread this rumor, which I happened to hear even as recently as this summer; for it seems most natural to me to explain it in this way, since I cannot very well assume that you yourself would ever have been the cause of it. If you should be afraid it might become generally known that you had supported me against Mr. Martensen and other even more powerful people, then it shall, if you so desire, remain a secret. Honorable Sir!...If you want to do anything for me, then I need it right now. In any case, I ask you to notify me in a few words, which may either be left where I live or with the porter at [the college residence] Regensen, *before next Sunday.*[1]

Shortly afterward, probably on the same day,[2] Kierkegaard replied to Eiríksson's request in the following manner:

> You yourself request, and I find that quite natural, that I reply "in a few words" to your detailed letter. That is to say, you request without reasons *pro* and *contra* that I be brief, a "Yes" or a "No." Here is my reply: I cannot comply with your request.
>
> Respectfully
> S. K.[3]

What is interesting in this context, is the fact that Eiríksson not only indicates that he had sought and failed to win Kierkegaard's financial support during the previous year as well[4] (no other letter from Eiríksson to Kierkegaard is preserved), contrary to a rumor then circulating in Copenhagen to the effect that Kierkegaard had been supporting Eiríksson financially,[5] but also he describes himself as "one of the few

1 *SKS* 28, 370-372, Brev 245 / *LD*, 228-230, Letter 163 (translation slightly altered).
2 See Svend Aage Nielsen, *Kierkegaard og Regensen. Kierkegaards forhold til F. C. Petersen, Poul Martin Møller, D. G. Monrad, Magnus Eiriksson, Carl Ploug, P. L. Møller, Hans Brøchner og J. C. Hostrup*, Copenhagen: Graabrødre Torv's Forlag V. Severin Petersen 1965, p. 72.
3 *SKS* 28, 372, Brev 246 / *LD*, 231, Letter 164 (translation slightly altered).
4 See, on the contrary, Nielsen, *Kierkegaard og Regensen*, p. 144.
5 See Kierkegaard`s drafts of an article entitled "A Little Explanation" (*Pap.* VIII-2 B 175-176, pp. 274-278), which can be found among Kierkegaard's papers from 1847. The purpose of this "Explanation" was to expunge a rumor to the effect that Kierkegaard had "provided Mag. E. with the monies necessary for the publication of his book [sc. *Dr. Martensens trykte moralske Paragrapher* (1846)]" (*Pap.* VIII-2 B 175, p. 275).

who strive in the same or a similar direction" as Kierkegaard. What is this *point of agreement* that Eiríksson invokes in his search for financial support?

This point of agreement between Eiríksson and Kierkegaard was primarily their shared opposition to Martensen—which may also be considered, in a way, the main cause of Kierkegaard's dismissive attitude toward Eiríksson.[1] Unlike Kierkegaard, who took care to veil his own (no less unrelenting) critique of Martensen under the cloak of pseudonymity and by means of allusions and "code words,"[2] Eiríksson did not hesitate to voice publicly, and without qualification, his opposition to Martensen's teachings. When he even drew Kierkegaard into his own dispute with Martensen by publicly interpreting Kierkegaard's pseudonymously authored writings as *Kierkegaard's* excellent critique of Martensen's speculative theology,[3] Kierkegaard repeatedly felt compelled to express a kind of "self-defense" against this "unauthorized acknowledgment."[4]

Although Eiríksson, as mentioned above, had felt a strong antipathy toward Martensen's speculative theology right from the start, he hesitated at first to condemn Martensen publicly for his teachings. This changed, however, in the early 1840s, when Eiríksson grew alarmed at the Church's mounting repression of the Baptist free-church movement.[5]

---

[1] See Schreiber, "Magnús Eiríksson: An Opponent of Martensen and an Unwelcome Ally of Kierkegaard," pp. 86-89.

[2] Jon Stewart, *Kierkegaard's Relations to Hegel Reconsidered*, New York: Cambridge University Press 2003, p. 278; see also p. 454 and pp. 465f.

[3] See, for example, Eiríksson, *Dr. Martensens trykte moralske Paragrapher*, p. IV (note): "For although he [sc. Kierkegaard] has gone further than I in his opposition to the Church dogma, the tradition, the so-called objective, and although our concepts of faith are greatly dissimilar...we are clearly in essential agreement about the character of the speculative, particularly the Martensenian theology, to which he plainly refers in many places. I can therefore please Mr. Martensen by informing him that this book [sc. Kierkegaard's *Concluding Unscientific Postscript*] has freed him of a group of his followers, namely, among the candidates and advanced students, whom he will scarcely be in a position to convert again, as some of them have informed me directly."

[4] See *Pap.* VII-1 B 88, pp. 287-298 / *CUP2*, 127-137; see also *Pap.* VII-1 B 87, pp. 284-286 / *CUP2*, 125-127; *Pap.* VII-1 B 89-91; *Pap.* VIII-2 B 175-176. As to Kierkegaard's reaction to Eiríksson's praise, see Schreiber, "Magnús Eiríksson: An Opponent of Martensen and an Unwelcome Ally of Kierkegaard," pp. 71-75.

[5] On the persecution of the Baptist movement, see Hal Koch, *Den Danske Kirkes Historie*, vol. 6, Copenhagen: Gyldendal 1954, pp. 305-10 and Kaj Baagø, *Vækkelse og*

On December 27, 1842, the Baptists' practice of adult baptism was challenged by a royal decree, proclaimed by means of a Chancellery Bill (*Kancelliplakat*) that required Baptist parents to baptize their children in infancy. At first Church authorities were asked to proceed with caution, and refrained from leveling the fines that the edict dictated. Yet when this caution failed to bring the Baptists into line, Bishop Jacob Peter Mynster (1775-1854) declared himself in favor of forced baptism, and a number of pastors soon put that policy into practice.[1] After Nicolai Faber (1789-1848), Bishop of Odense, published a treatise on the Baptist controversy,[2] Martensen followed suit with a book of his own: *Christian Baptism, Considered with Reference to the Baptist Question* (1843).[3]

As had previously been the case in his April 1842 article "The Present Religious Crisis,"[4] in which he had addressed the Baptist controversy for the first time, Martensen's actual position on forced baptisms remained obscure in his new book. *Christian Baptism* focuses on the systematic-theological justification for the practical-theological legitimacy of infant baptism; it thus involves a radical critique of the Baptist outlook and practice of adult baptism. Yet neither in "The Present Religious Crisis" nor in *Christian Baptism* do we find any statements on the issue of forced baptism. In his memoirs *From My Life* (1882-83), Martensen recalled that, although he did not mean to support Mynster's practice of forced baptism, he "could very well understand his [Mynster's] standpoint."[5] It should be noted, however, that Martensen does remark in "The Present Religious Crisis" that the state church, in its efforts to protect its unity

---

kirkeliv i København og omegn i første halvdel af det 19. århundrede, Copenhagen: Gad 1960, pp. 118-43.

1 For Mynster's position, see the text, likely from this period, published posthumously as *Om Giendaab og Giendøbernes statsret[s]lige Forhold i Danmark*, in Jacob Peter Mynster, *Blandede Skrivter*, vols. 1-3, Copenhagen: Gyldendal 1852-53 [vols. 4-6, posthumously ed. by Just Henrik Paulli, Copenhagen: Gyldendal 1855-57]; vol. 5, pp. 333-370, especially pp. 353ff.

2 Nicolai Faber, *De anabaptistiske Bevægelser i Danmark betragtede fra det christelige og kirkelige Standpunct*, Odense: G. Hempels Forlag 1842.

3 Hans Lassen Martensen, *Den christelige Daab betragtet med Hensyn paa det baptistiske Spørgsmaal*, Copenhagen: C.A. Reitzel 1843.

4 Hans Lassen Martensen, "Nutidens religiøse Crisis," *Intelligensblade*, vol. 1, 1842, no. 3 (April 15), pp. 53-73; see especially pp. 57-61, p. 67 and pp. 71-73.

5 Hans Lassen Martensen, *Af mit Levnet*, vols. 1-3, Copenhagen: Gyldendal 1882-83, vol. 2, p. 72.

against the threat of "religious fanaticism," should avoid any "all too powerful intrusion" by the state, since "this battle must be fought in the purely spiritual realm."[1]

Nevertheless, Martensen's entry into the discussion did suffice to give Eiríksson an opportunity to speak up on behalf of the persecuted Baptists—and also to voice publicly his opposition to Martensen's account of baptism and to his speculative theology in general. Eiríksson articulated his views in *On Baptists and Infant Baptism* (1844), [2] his first (and mainly positively received[3]) publication: a 750-page-long book devoted to exposing the un-Christian character of the persecution of the Baptists by the Danish Church and state:

> To use any weapons other than intellectual ones in the intellectual and particularly Christian domain demonstrates that the Christian-spiritual life is more or less falsified and counterfeit in those who do or exhort such things. No doubt, an aggressive spiritual battle can be consistent with the supreme law of love; but external constraint, oppression, and deprivation of property, liberty or life can in no way be compatible with it. Therefore, he who fights according to the principles of Christian charity will never, can never deprive anybody of such things, not even those against whom he has

---

1 Interestingly, this argumentation is not dissimilar to that of Eiríksson in *Om Baptister og Barnedaab*, p. XIX (see the quotation belonging to p. 67 below, note 1).

2 Magnús Eiríksson, *Om Baptister og Barnedaab, samt flere Momenter af den kirkelige og speculative Christendom*, Copenhagen: P.G. Philipsen 1844.

3 The reviews by Carl Emil Scharling and Christian Thorning Engelstoft in *Theologisk Tidsskrift*, vol. 8, 1844, pp. 399-404; by Anonymous in *Fædrelandet*, 1844, no. 1572 and nos 1590-1591; by "Th. G. R." in *Kjøbenhavnsposten*, 1844, no. 92 (April 20); by "En Lægmand i den angrebne danske Statskirke" in *Kjøbenhavnsposten*, 1844, no. 104 (May 6); by Anonymous in *Allgemeine Literatur-Zeitung*, 1845, vol. 2, no. 246 (November), columns 777-784; no. 247 (November), columns 785-792; no. 248 (November), columns 795-800 and by Anonymous in *Aarhuus Stifts-Tidende*, 1844, no. 89 (May 21) were mainly positive, whereas Ludvig Nicolaus Helveg's review in *For Literatur og Kritik*, vol. 2, 1844, pp. 305-314 was more critical. Also worthy of mention are two anonymously published pamphlets prompted by *Om Baptister og Barnedaab*: the wholly critical *Epistola eller Sende-Brev til Sr. Magnus Eiriksson fra en anden gammel Landsbypræst. Til Publici videre Nytte og Fornøielse nu til Trykken befordret*, Copenhagen: H.C. Klein 1844, which parodied Eiríksson's polemical style, and a pamphlet anonymously published by the Icelandic poet Grímur Thomsen (1820-96) in response to it: *En Privatskrivelse til den anden gamle Landsbypræst, fra hans gamle Ven, den første gamle Candidat, som Commentar over Herr Pastors Epistola til Sr. Magnus Eiriksson*, Copenhagen: P.G. Philipsen 1844.

> most vehemently fought or will fight with his intellectual weapons. But what a Christian individual will not and cannot do without breaking the fundamental law of Christianity, neither the church nor a whole community will be able to do without committing the same transgression....When, therefore, the Church transgresses and annihilates as far as possible—in order to be Christian—the law of charity that is the very essence and foundation of Christianity, then, I say, it manifestly works its own destruction as a Christian Commonwealth; and the more it has been able to establish th[is] principle of intolerance and unfriendliness, the more it already has proven that it is no longer a Christian commonwealth, except in name.[1]

Appealing to the Bible as the "basis" for his argument, and emphasizing that he was himself no member of the Baptist movement,[2] Eiríksson defended the right of Baptist parents to postpone their children's baptism. He attempted to document historically, moreover, that the practice of infant baptism was neither commanded by Jesus nor of apostolic origin, but was introduced much later into the Church.[3] The modern—and to that extent "un-Christian"—practice of infant baptism should therefore be abandoned, Eiríksson argued; it should be replaced with a purely formal "church induction ceremony" or "upbuilding ceremony."[4]

Turning away from the *practice* of infant baptism, Eiríksson sought at the same time to expose and refute its theological underpinnings,

---

1 Eiríksson, *Om Baptister og Barnedaab*, p. XIX; see also pp. 287-89 and pp. 562-672. Compare, however, Curtis L. Thompson, *Following the Cultured Public's Chosen One. Why Martensen Mattered to Kierkegaard*, Copenhagen: Museum Tusculanum Press 2008 (*Danish Golden Age Studies*, vol. 4), p. 46: "a book written by the Baptist-oriented theological candidate Magnús Eiríksson."

2 See ibid., pp. 551-562. In his book *Tro, Overtro og Vantro, i deres Forhold til Fornuft og Forstand, samt til hinanden indbyrdes*, Copenhagen: H.C. Klein 1846, pp. XIIf., Eiríksson defends himself once more against the charge of being a Baptist himself. He had never been entirely satisfied, he writes, with the Baptists' views on religion or efforts at reform; and the more he reflected on them, the less satisfied he became. In saying this, Eiríksson did not mean that the Baptists' departures from Church doctrine were unfounded. On the contrary, he thought that their case against the Church was airtight, but their "modifications *were not sufficient* or *fundamental enough*" (ibid., p. XIII).

3 See Eiríksson, *Om Baptister og Barnedaab*, pp. 467-538.

4 Ibid., p. 540.

as they appear in the "Faberian-Martensenian account of baptism."[1] In particular, we will now see, Eiríksson leveled two criticisms against Martensen's account of baptism in *Christian Baptism* (1843),[2] which he derided as grounded in a "boundlessly arbitrary exegesis"[3] of the relevant sources in Scripture. First, Eiríksson attacked Martensen's claim that the infant is baptized not *because* it has faith, but *so that it may* have faith, for which reason "faith is the fruit of baptism" and "baptism is necessary for blessedness."[4] Such a view, Eiríksson wrote, must be regarded as wholly unjustified and false, for the teachings of Christ and the Apostles univocally insist that baptism presupposes faith.[5] Moreover, Eiríksson added, Martensen has contradicted his own prior words in propounding the above view, since in his lectures on "Speculative Dogmatics" (1838-39)[6] he had claimed that justifying faith can and should *precede* baptism. But this implies that baptism is *not* necessary for blessedness.[7]

Eiríksson's second fundamental criticism was directed against the "magical" or "miraculous effects" that Martensen in his view ascribes to baptism. He here refers to Martensen's claims that "Christ gives himself and

---

[1] See ibid., pp. 316-433, especially pp. 317-320.

[2] When he refers to Martensen's 1842 article "Nutidens religiøse Crisis" on the other hand, Eiríksson attacks above all the "intolerance" with which that article treats the local Baptists, inasmuch as it conflates them with the Anabaptists (*Schwarmgeister*) of the Reformation period. This conflation, Eiríksson charges, is inaccurate both as an historical matter and in terms of the beliefs at issue, which is why he seeks to distinguish the Baptist movement from the Anabaptist movement on both historical (pp. 3-31) and dogmatic (pp. 69-84) terms, and so to prove the illegitimacy of applying to the Baptists the laws once used to suppress the Anabaptists. See also Eiríksson, *Om Baptister og Barnedaab*, pp. 38-42, p. 48 and p. 68; see further Martensen, "Nutidens religiøse Crisis," p. 60.

[3] Eiríksson, *Om Baptister og Barnedaab*, p. XIII; see, for example, pp. 237-240 and pp. 262-269.

[4] Martensen, *Den christelige Daab*, p. 3 and p. 66.

[5] See Eiríksson, *Om Baptister og Barnedaab*, pp. 237-273.

[6] See p. 69 below, note 4.

[7] Here Eiríksson refers especially to the following dictated passage in his own notes to § 89 (on Baptism) of Martensen's lectures: "From the subjective side, a candid confession of the common faith of the Church is needed before the eyes of God and the congregation—which presupposes, in the case of an adult, that the rebirth has already taken place before the baptism. Since justifying faith can take place before baptism, baptism is not absolutely necessary for blessedness" (ibid., p. 230; see pp. 230-232 (note)); compare the almost identical lecture transcription (from an unknown hand) found among Kierkegaard's papers in *Pap.* II C 28 (in *Pap.* XIII, pp. 44-116), pp. 98f. (§ 89).

the Spirit wholly and undivided to the baptized,"[1] and that baptism brings the infant—even if not via a transformation of human nature—into "an organic relation to Christ," thus rendering the infant an "*organ* of Christ."[2]

We mentioned earlier that Eiríksson's critique of Martensen in *On Baptists and Infant Baptism* addressed itself not only to Martensen's account of baptism, but also to his speculative theology as such. In particular, Eiríksson charged that Martensen's speculative theology leads to the "self-deification" of humanity.[3] Eiríksson supported this charge by reproducing a number of passages from his own notes to Martensen's as yet unpublished lectures on "Speculative Dogmatics" (1838-39),[4] which he had personally attended, focusing on Martensen's commentary on the doctrine of the Trinity.[5] The latter action prompted Martensen, at the end of April 1844, to pen a newspaper article entitled "Literary

---

1 Eiríksson, *Om Baptister og Barnedaab*, p. 317 (§ 1); see Martensen, *Den christelige Daab*, p. 59: "just as Christ in baptism gives himself wholly and undivided to each individual, so too he gives the Spirit wholly to each individual."

2 Martensen, *Den christelige Daab*, p. 58 and p. 57. For Eiríksson's critique of this "magical" conception of baptism, which is found most prominently in Martensen's *Den christelige Daab*, pp. 55-59, see Eiríksson, *Om Baptister og Barnedaab*, pp. 225ff.; pp. 321-334, pp. 347f. and pp. 368f.

3 See Eiríksson, *Om Baptister og Barnedaab*, pp. XXVI-XLI (especially p. XXXIX), pp. 234f. and pp. 281f.; see also Eiríksson, *Tro, Overtro og Vantro*, pp. 86-88.

4 The 1838 summer semester course covered §§ 1-59; its continuation in winter semester, 1838-1839 covered §§ 60-99. On this see Jon Stewart, *A History of Hegelianism in Golden Age Denmark,* Tome II, *The Martensen Period: 1837-1842*, Copenhagen: C.A. Reitzel 2007 (*Danish Golden Age Studies*, vol. 3), pp. 238-245 and pp. 284-287. Among Kierkegaard's papers (see KA, C pk. 3 læg 5), there exists a contemporary lecture transcription (from an unknown hand) of §§ 1-23; see *Pap.* II C 26 and 27 (in *Pap.* XIII, pp. 3-43; see also *SKS* 18, 374-386, KK:11 / *KJN* 2, 342-352, which contains Kierkegaard's incomplete resume of Martensen's introductory remarks and of §§ 1-23, based on this lecture transcription) and of §§ 60–99, see *Pap.* II C 28 (in *Pap.* XIII, pp. 44-116). A third volume covering §§ 24-59, made by the same unknown auditor, can be found in the Peter Christian Kierkegaard Archive at the Royal Library in Copenhagen, see *NKS* 3005, 4° VI.

5 See Eiríksson, *Om Baptister og Barnedaab*, pp. 336-345, where Eiríksson cites from his notes to §§ 37-39 (on the Trinity) and § 40 (on Creation) of Martensen's lectures on "Speculative Dogmatics" (1838-39). The passages reproduced by Eiríksson derive exclusively from paragraphs that Martensen dictated, and which constituted the basis of his analysis. In the classroom, Martensen first read these paragraphs aloud; then he explained their key points further and illustrated them with examples. Moreover, as he states in the first note to p. 336, Eiríksson had compared his own notes to other notes from the same lecture. In point of fact, a comparison of the passages reproduced by Eiríksson with the lecture transcription found in the Peter Christian

Abuse,"[1] in which—without responding to the substance of Eiríksson's accusations[2]—Martensen fiercely condemned Eiríksson's "preprinting" of his lectures as "a violation of intellectual copyright." By publishing those lectures from 1839, Eiríksson had in a sense beaten Martensen to the punch. Yet in another sense it may be said that it was Martensen who had beaten Eiríksson to the punch, inasmuch as it was he who had first published, in *Christian Baptism* (1843), a revision of his prior account of the doctrine of baptism. This forced Eiríksson to come from behind, so to speak, with his transcript of the 1839 lectures, in order to show that Martensen's earlier statements did not conform to his later views.

In "Literary Abuse," Martensen reveals that in point of fact he had *himself* considered making his account of the doctrine of the *Trinity* accessible to an expert audience, after that account had attained the requisite "maturity." Yet the paragraphs cited by Eiríksson had been formulated only "in an incomplete and rough state"; they were not intended for a "scholarly readership."[3] They were "only a kind of mnemonic device," Martensen insisted; "they attain their value only by way of the freely spoken word and the personal interaction between the lecturer and his listeners."[4] Taken outside that context, the dictated paragraphs can furnish only "an incomplete, not even half-true impression"[5] of their meaning.

Unsurprisingly, a biting response from Eiríksson to this rather strange line of argument was not a long time coming. It can be found a few days later in a newspaper article entitled "Academic Usage."[6] Here Eiríksson points out that, in this first and (as Martensen indicates) final

---

Kierkegaard Archive (see previous note) reveals some small discrepancies, but no decisive differences in content.

1 Hans Lassen Martensen, "Litterairt Uvæsen," *Berlingske politiske og Avertissements-Tidende*, 1844, no. 115 (April 29), 1844, p. [1], columns [1]-[3].

2 An *indirect* reference to Eiríksson's critique, however, can be found in Martensen's foreword to the second edition of his *Den christelige Daab*, Copenhagen: C.A. Reitzel 1847, p. [III], where he writes that "multiple readers have found that the doctrine of baptism presented here leads into the realm of the magical." Yet this criticism indubitably depends on a conflation of the concepts of "the magical" and "the mysterious."

3 Martensen, "Litterairt Uvæsen," p. [1], column [2].

4 Ibid.

5 Ibid.

6 Magnús Eiríksson, "Academisk Væsen," *Berlingske politiske og Avertissements-Tidende*, 1844, no. 124 (May 9), p. [1], column [4]; p. 2, columns [1]-[3].

contribution to the debate, Martensen did not attempt to refute even a single point of criticism, nor to defend a single one of his assertions, but sought to "evade the reality of the matter with a show of learned gentility."[1] As to Martensen's suggestion that the paragraphs in question "attain their value only by way of the freely spoken word,"[2] Eiríksson points out that Martensen had published similar draft paragraphs in his *Outline to a System of Moral Philosophy* (1841),[3] often rendering them "even more obscure and opaque"[4] than those unpublished paragraphs in his 1838-1839 lecture course. Eiríksson was happy to agree that the paragraphs here at issue offered only "an incomplete, not even half-true impression"[5] of things—but only in the sense that the paragraphs were *essentially* incomplete and untrue. In contrast to his fluency in moral philosophy, Martensen clearly seemed to be on unsure footing in the realm of dogmatics, as Martensen himself admitted when he claimed that the dogmatic paragraphs in his lectures lacked the requisite "maturity."[6] Indeed, Eiríksson wrote, this very statement—by which Martensen notified his audience that his own dogmatic teachings, which he had by then been promulgating for years, were immature—proves conclusively that it is both useful and necessary to investigate these teachings further, and bring them to the light of day.

II. A Hidden Influence

As Eiríksson anticipated, Martensen offered no further comments on the matter, and did not respond to Eiríksson's critique of his account of baptism either.[7] Eiríksson, however, did not join in this silence. In

---

1 Ibid., p. [1], column [4].

2 Martensen, "Litterairt Uvæsen," p. [1], column [2].

3 Hans Lassen Martensen, *Grundrids til Moralphilosophiens System*, Copenhagen: C.A. Reitzel 1841 (English translation: *Outline to a System of Moral Philosophy*, in *Between Hegel and Kierkegaard. Hans L. Martensen's Philosophy of Religion*, trans. by Curtis L. Thompson and David J. Kangas, Atlanta, Georgia: Scholars Press 1997, pp. 245-313). For Eiríksson's critique of this work, see Section III of this article.

4 Eiríksson, "Academisk Væsen," p. [2], column [2].

5 Martensen, "Litterairt Uvæsen," p. [1], column [2].

6 Ibid.; compare Eiríksson, "Academisk Væsen," p. [2], column [2].

7 Martensen extended his silence to other attacks on his account of baptism as well; an example is Hans Brøchner's *Nogle Bemærkninger om Daaben, foranledigede ved Professor*

his treatise *Faith, Superstition, and Unbelief in their Relation to Reason and the Understanding and to One Another* (1846)[1]—a propaedeutic analysis of the fundamental notions and presuppositions of Christian faith, which would later serve as the foundation for Eiríksson's attack on Kierkegaard's account of faith as a "paradox" and as "by virtue of the absurd"[2]—Eiríksson once again criticizes Martensen's account of baptism. Insofar as faith in the subjective sense (that is, understood as conviction and trust) always has an object, and thus always is faith in something, it is subject to certain preconditions. Unlike Martensen and "others who are similarly spiritually deranged"[3]—who posit "that baptism

---

Martensens Skrift: "Den christelige Daab," Copenhagen: P.G. Philipsen 1843, which concurs with Eiríksson's critique on certain points and is similarly bound up in opposition to Martensen's speculative theology in general. It was first in the aforementioned foreword to the second edition of his *Den christelige Daab* (1847) that Martensen responded briefly to his critics (see p. 70 above, note 2). Aside from this preface and the newspaper article against Eiríksson, Martensen produced no further writings between his 1843 essay on "The Church Year" ("Kirke-Aaret," in *Urania. Aarbog for 1844*, ed. by Johan Ludvig Heiberg, Copenhagen: H.I. Bing 1843, pp. 161-188) and his *magnum opus* of July 1849, *Den christelige Dogmatik*. Regarding Martensen's "literary silence," see Thompson, *Following the Cultured Public's Chosen One*, pp. 45-48.

[1] Magnús Eiríksson, *Tro, Overtro og Vantro, i deres Forhold til Fornuft og Forstand, samt til hinanden indbyrdes*, Copenhagen: H.C. Klein 1846.

[2] See Magnús Eiríksson [Theophilus Nicolaus], *Er Troen et Paradox og "i Kraft af det Absurde"? et Spørgsmaal foranlediget ved "Frygt og Bæven, af Johannes de silentio", besvaret ved Hjelp af en Troes-Ridders fortrolige Meddelelser, til fælles Opbyggelse for Jøder, Christne og Muhamedanere, af bemeldte Troes-Ridders Broder*, Copenhagen: Chr. Steen & Søn 1850 as well as *SKS* 23, 176f., NB17:19 / *KJN* 7, 178f.; *SKS* 23, 177f., NB17:21 / *KJN* 7, 180; *SKS* 23, 182f., NB17:28 / *KJN* 7, 185; *SKS* 23, 197f., NB17:50 / *KJN* 7, 200f.; *Pap.* X-6 B 68-69 / *JP* 6, 6598-6599; *Pap.* X-6 B 70-71; *Pap.* X-6 B 72-76; *Pap.* X-6 B 77 / *JP* 6, 6600; *Pap.* X-6 B 78-81 / *JP* 1, 9-12; *Pap.* X-6 B 82 / *JP* 6, 6601; *Pap.* X-6 B 128, pp. 170f. / *CUP2*, 161-163 (*JP* 6, 6596); *Pap.* X-6 B 129, pp. 171f. On Eiríksson's critique of Kierkegaard's account of faith, see Olivier Cauly, "La foi est-elle un paradoxe ou 'une vertu de l'absurde'? À propos d'une critique de Magnus Eiriksson (Theophilus Nicolaus)," *Kairos. Revue de la Faculté de Philosophie de l'Université de Toulouse*, vol. 10, 1997, pp. 99-114; Jóhanna Þráinsdóttir, "Er trúin þverstæða? Gagnrýni Magnúsar Eiríkssonar á trúarskoðunum Kierkegaards í 'Ugg og ótta,'" *Tímarit Máls og menningar*, vol. 61, 2000, pp. 35-45; Gerhard Schreiber, "Ist der Glaube ein Paradox und 'kraft des Absurden'?—Kierkegaards Auseinandersetzung mit Magnús Eiríksson," in *Kierkegaard and Faith*, ed. by Roman Králik et al., Mexico City et al., Sociedad Iberoamericana de Estudios Kierkegaardianos 2008, pp. 34-47 and "Magnús Eiríksson: An Opponent of Martensen and an Unwelcome Ally of Kierkegaard," pp. 75-86; see also the article by Roe Fremstedal in the present volume.

[3] Eiríksson, *Tro, Overtro og Vantro*, pp. 7f.

is the necessary condition and precondition of faith"[1]—Eiríksson asserts that faith presupposes "acquaintance" and "education." It presupposes acquaintance, inasmuch as all those who have faith have faith in something that they must be acquainted with indirectly or directly; and it presupposes education, inasmuch as these faithful must be made acquainted with the object of their faith.[2] These two preconditions for faith are not, however, available to small children; and for this reason, the Church has "cultivated a superstition" when it has taught that infants can and truly do have faith.[3] Worse still, the speculative theologians have brought this "deceptive superstition" to its "peak" in their efforts to defend and exalt infant baptism. For they have claimed that infants are baptized "to make them able to believe," as though a "seed of faith" could be "grafted onto" them by means of baptism.[4]

On the basis of his conviction that true faith must "absolutely be a rational faith"[5]—reason is no "enemy of faith," but is instead "its closest and most natural ally, its organ and its necessary condition"[6]—Eiríksson diagnoses Martensen's account of baptism as an impressive example of a fatal mixture of "superstition" and "unbelief." In order to understand both Eiríksson's position and his critique adequately, we need to take a closer look at his conception of "reason" in this context. In keeping with the German etymology of "reason"—*Vernunft* from *vernehmen* (to apprehend, to sense, to feel)—reason is for Eiríksson an essentially "receptive faculty." Reason is "the sense for the infinite and eternal; the sense for the higher Ideas...the sense with which we apprehend God

---

1 Ibid., p. 8.

2 See ibid., pp. 8f. and pp. 11f., where Eiríksson refers to Romans 10:14-17 as justification for his account; see also his extensive argumentation in his *Om Baptister og Barnedaab*, pp. 221-87. To preempt the objection that it must be possible for faith to exist even without these preconditions—as in the case of Abraham—Eiríksson insists that faith nonetheless "necessarily presupposes so much maturity or development of the human understanding and reason" (Eiríksson, *Tro, Overtro og Vantro*, p. 11) that it is possible to understand the human speech or higher hints and messages through which God reveals himself to humanity. With regard to Abraham in particular, Eiríksson was concerned precisely to demonstrate the *exceptional* character of Abraham's situation, which makes "Abraham's faith *unusable* as a model for later or present-day believers" (p. 15, emphasis mine).

3 Ibid., p. 16.

4 Ibid., p. 17.

5 Ibid., p. 93; compare p. X and pp. 10f.

6 Ibid., p. XI.

and his revelations both within and without us."[1] Reason is thus not only "the medium, the connecting link," *by which* free and rational individuals unite themselves with "the higher spiritual essence";[2] the "sense of reason" is similarly "that *through which* [*hvorigjennem*] the human being receives the workings and revelations of God."[3] In contrast to this essentially receptive-passive and immediate activity of reason, the "subjective understanding" represents the essentially active faculty, by which we conceive or understand the "immediately received objective" objects of understanding that reach us via reason or sensory perception.[4] If the understanding is in this sense already "a superior faculty," it can become "still more superior" when it makes itself subservient to reason as regards what is higher and spiritual. When the understanding thereby "heeds the voice of reason," it may "be lifted up into a higher region, and be transformed into a higher understanding, an understanding of and insight into matters divine."[5]

Whereas in "unbelief" the "mere understanding" is dominant, and presumes to be the "judge" of faith (and hence "unbelief" in essence represents only "an assuming and knowing" grounded in "proofs of the understanding"), in "superstition" the understanding is, by contrast, "judged and excluded." Yet reason, too, is "not given appropriate regard" in superstition,[6] for here faith refuses to recognize that its own relation to reason constitutes the "limit"[7] that it cannot pass beyond without becoming *eo ipso* a "limitless" superstition. Only in "rational faith" are the rational sense and the understanding met with due respect, and positioned in appropriate relation to one another. For "rational faith" apprehends its objects via the medium of reason: "either...indirectly along the historical path, or by means of an immediate revelation of divine matters to the single individuals."[8] The understanding is not thereby (as in superstition) excluded or disparaged; yet *insofar* as "rational faith" requires no "grounds of understanding," it can assume and believe something that it is not capable

[1] Ibid., p. 27.
[2] Ibid., p. 39.
[3] Ibid., p. 85 (emphasis added).
[4] Ibid., p. 40.
[5] Ibid., p. 47; compare p. 95.
[6] Ibid., pp. 49f.
[7] Ibid., p. 24; compare p. 58 and p. 93.
[8] Ibid., p. 93.

of understanding.[1] The object of "rational faith" is thus "that of which we, strictly speaking, have no immediate positive acquaintance, but which along a purely spiritual path makes itself present to the rational sense."[2] To summarize, the "rationality" that Eiríksson demands of Christianity and of all true faiths requires that reason become the medium *through which* a human being receives the objects of his faith: "Reason is the passage, the channel, along which the spiritual, the divine comes to us."[3] Hence the criterion whereby an object can be judged an object of the true faith is precisely this: that the object in question "must address the uncorrupted rational sense according to its essence."[4] Nothing that contradicts the "rational sense" can "belong to the region of faith."[5]

This peculiar conception of reason[6] should be enough to warn us away from all unreserved characterizations of Eiríksson's theological stance (at least after 1830)[7] as "rationalism" or "neo-rationalism." The rationalist label was attached to Eiríksson already during his lifetime,[8] and was destined to become a recurring motif in the secondary

---

1 Ibid.; compare pp. 93f.
2 Ibid., p. 58.
3 This is Eiríksson's formulation in "Min Forfattervirksomhed," (see p. 76 below, note 2), p. 90. In *Tro, Overtro og Vantro*, Eiríksson adds "that God has given humanity a lodestar, an inner light" (p. 84).
4 Eiríksson, *Tro, Overtro og Vantro*, p. 59.
5 Ibid.
6 Eiríksson was well aware of the peculiarity of his conception of reason, as he indicates for example in *Gud og Reformatoren. En religiøs Idee. Samt nogle Bemærkninger om de kirkelige Tilstande, Dr. S. Kierkegaard og Forfatteren*, Copenhagen: J.H. Schubothe 1866, pp. 76-8 (note). In a note to his definition of "reason" as "the sense for the higher, spiritual, and eternal" (p. 76; compare *Tro, Overtro og Vantro*, p. 27), Eiríksson explains: "I can assume that the vast majority of this book's readers possess a very different conception of the human faculty that we have called 'reason' than the one we have offered" (p. 76).
7 See Eiríksson, *Om Baptister og Barnedaab*, p. 18.
8 On this see the Preface to *Tro, Overtro og Vantro*, pp. V-VII, where Eiríksson protests against others' assessment of his "direction and religious outlook" (in their reactions to *Om Baptister og Barnedaab*) to the effect "that I am fundamentally unbelieving, a notion that they express with the label 'rationalist' or the like," and that his "unbelief (rationalism)" has now simply appeared with great "enthusiasm" and "in a new shape." See also, in Kierkegaard's drafts of a reply to Theophilus Nicolaus (see p. 72 above, note 2), Climacus' astonishment that Theophilus Nicolaus, "a declared rationalist," has explicitly countenanced "direct communications from God, higher intimations, visions, revelations" (*Pap.* X-6 B 68, pp. 73f.).

literature.[1] That this is in fact an oversimplification can also be seen in his "My Activity as an Author" (1875), a retrospective account of Eiríksson's authorship.[2] Here Eiríksson simply supposes, regarding the basic idea of *Faith, Superstition, and Unbelief*—and thereby expanding on what is written there—that reason is perfectible through faith inasmuch as true faith "comes to the aid" of reason, and so "completes" a human being's "acceptance" of the higher spiritual things that are received by the rational sense:

> for the higher spiritual things, which we receive by means of the rational sense, are conceived or understood, strictly speaking, either not at all or only quite imperfectly....Hence faith is so far from being superfluous, or from standing in hostile opposition to reason, that it in fact comes to reason's aid, supplies its lack, completes our acceptance of and conviction about the higher spiritual essence, which at first presented itself to the rational sense and was immediately understood or received by it, and then was taken up

1 As, for example, in Rasmus Tønder Nissen, *De nordiske Kirkers Historie*, ed. by Thor Georg Bernhard Odland, Kristiania: Steen 1884, p. 540; Frederik Nielsen, "Eiriksson, Magnus," in *Kirke-Leksikon for Norden*, vols. 1-4, ed. by Frederik Nielsen, Aarhus: Jydsk Forlags-Forretning 1900-29; vol. 1, p. 733; Hal Koch and Bjørn Kornerup (eds.), *Den Danske Kirkes Historie*, vols. 1-8, Copenhagen: Gyldendalske Boghandel, Nordisk Forlag 1950-66; vol. 6, *Tiden 1800-1848*, by Hal Koch, 1954, p. 322; Julia Watkin, *Historical Dictionary of Kierkegaard's Philosophy*, Lanham, Md. and London: Scarecrow Press 2001, pp. 69-77, here p. 69; Niels Thulstrup, "Martensen's *Dogmatics* and its Reception," in *Kierkegaard and His Contemporaries. The Culture of Golden Age Denmark*, ed. by Jon Stewart, Berlin and New York 2003 (*Kierkegaard Studies Monograph Series*, vol. 10), pp. 181-202; here p. 194 ("he was an extreme rationalist.") See also Emanuel Hirsch's characterization of Eiríksson in Søren Kierkegaard, *Gesammelte Werke*, Section 35, *Briefe*, Düsseldorf and Cologne: Diederichs 1950, p. 170. Three exceptions to this trend are (1) Hafsteinn Pjetursson, "Magnús Eiríksson," *Teologisk Tidsskrift for den danske Folkekirke*, Ny Række, vol. 3, 1901-1902, pp. 116-143; pp. 120-123; (2) Hans Sofus Vodskov, *Spredte Studier*, Copenhagen: Gyldendalske Boghandels Forlag (F. Hegel & Søn) 1884, pp. 31-40; pp. 31f. (reprinted in Hans Sofus Vodskov, *Litteraturkritik i udvalg*, ed. by Erik Reitzel-Nielsen, vol. 1, Copenhagen: C.A. Reitzel 1992, pp. 204-209; p. 205); and (3) Carl Henrik Koch, *Den danske idealisme. 1800-1880*, Copenhagen: Gyldendal 2004, pp. 294-296.

2 Eiríksson, "Min Forfattervirksomhed," *Flyvende Blade for Literatur, Kunst og Samfundsspørgsmaal*, ed. by Vilhelm Møller, vol. 3, no. 11 (June 12, 1875), pp. 81-83; no. 12 (June 19, 1875), pp. 90-93, and no. 13 (June 26, 1875), pp. 100-104.

by reason's sister and ally, faith, by means of which the object's acceptance grew firm and unshakable.[1]

As a possible source for Eiríksson's account, Carl Henrik Koch points to Friedrich Heinrich Jacobi's (1743-1819) definition of reason (*Vernunft*) as "the apprehension [*Vernehmung*] of the suprasensible."[2] This conjecture deserves careful consideration, since there are in fact several points of agreement between Eiríksson's and the later Jacobi's conceptions of reason.

Jacobi's theory of knowledge is grounded in the difference between the faculties of sensible and supersensible perception. Jacobi writes: "Much as there exists a sensible intuition, an intuition by means of *sense*, so too there exists a rational intuition by means of *reason*," that is, a "reasoning intuition" (*Vernunftanschauung*), which is no more in need of proof than the "sensible intuition."[3] Jacobi describes reason as "the organ of the apprehension [*Vernehmung*] of the supersensible,"[4] or as "the sense for the supersensible;"[5] and in so doing he, like Eiríksson, stresses the primacy of reason's *receptivity*. As Jacobi explains, it is not the *self-activity* of reason, but rather reason's *receptivity*, that makes it count as reason: "The root of reason [*Vernunft*] is *apprehending* [*Vernehmen*]."[6] Reason thus always already refers to an object of apprehension that it (literally) "perceives" (in the sense of "to take as true"; German "*wahr-nehmen*," from *Wahrnehmung*, "perception").

A further point of agreement between Jacobi and Eiríksson concerns the distinction between reason and understanding: both argue that reason and the understanding should be neither confused with one another nor detached from one another.[7] In contrast to the understanding—insofar as

---

1 Ibid., p. 90; see also *Tro, Overtro og Vantro*, p. 21, pp. 42f., p. 58, and the conclusion on pp. 92-95.

2 See Koch, *Den danske idealisme. 1800-1880*, pp. 294-296.

3 Friedrich Heinrich Jacobi, *Werke. Gesamtausgabe*, vols. 1-7.2, ed. by Klaus Hammacher and Walter Jaeschke, Hamburg: Meiner and Stuttgart-Bad Cannstatt: Frommann-Holzboog 1998ff.; vol. 2, p. 402; see also pp. 409f.

4 Jacobi, *Werke. Gesamtausgabe*, vol. 2, p. 377; see also p. 401

5 Jacobi, *Werke. Gesamtausgabe*, vol. 3, p. 123.

6 Jacobi, *Werke. Gesamtausgabe*, vol. 2, p. 201; see also p. 208.

7 For Eiríksson's version of this claim, see *Tro, Overtro og Vantro*, pp. 25-34 and p. 36. Jacobi's theory of knowledge similarly implies a correlation, rather than a separation, of reason and the understanding; on this see Günther Baum, *Vernunft und Erkenntnis. Die Philosophie F.H. Jacobis*, Bonn: Bouvier 1969, pp. 113-123.

this refers to the human faculty of discursive reflection and abstraction—Jacobi, like Eiríksson, considers reason "a higher faculty."[1] Reason alone can give philosophy its *content*; whereas the understanding constitutes a faculty of abstraction that is capable only of *formal* determinations, that is, of delineating the concepts through which philosophy acquires its *form*. Reason, for its part, does not produce any concepts: it "builds no systems, nor makes any judgments, but simply is, like the outer senses, merely revelatory, positively proclamatory."[2] Much as the "sensory intuition" reveals the actuality of things, the "reasoning intuition" reveals the actuality of ideas; although for Jacobi this does *not* mean (as it does for Eiríksson) that a human being can receive otherworldly directives through his reason (despite the fact that, for Jacobi as for Eiríksson, God is assuredly the final object that he has in mind when he writes of the "reasoning intuition").

With this we arrive at the manifest differences between Jacobi's and Eiríksson's accounts of reason: differences that make it rather unlikely, despite the undeniable points of agreement just listed, that Jacobi *himself* could have been the direct source of Eiríksson's account. Neither Eiríksson nor Jacobi ascribes complete passivity to reason, as one would find in naïve realism; much as Jacobi detects the union of spontaneity and receptivity in every act of the "reasoning intuition," Eiríksson holds that reason, albeit predominantly a receptive faculty, necessarily involves a moment of activity ("judgment") as well. In contrast to Eiríksson, however, Jacobi attributes a dual structure to reason *itself*, inasmuch as reason concerns itself in fact with both an inside and an outside, with both "subjective" and "objective reason," that is, with two sides whose correspondence alone yields the single entity "reason."[3] Eiríksson, however, attempts to define reason purely subjectively as "the human faculty within which faith reposes."[4] He rejects all talk of "objective reason" as "inappropriate, confusing, and inauthentic."[5] Meanwhile the "correspondence" structure

---

[1] Jacobi, *Werke. Gesamtausgabe*, vol. 2, pp. 409f.; see also p. 387

[2] Ibid., p. 402; see also pp. 403f. Eiríksson, by contrast, does ascribe an (immediate) "moment of judgment" to reason as well; see *Tro, Overtro og Vantro*, pp. 36f., p. 42.

[3] See Jacobi, *Werke. Gesamtausgabe*, vol. 1, pp. 259f. and vol. 2, p. 87.

[4] Eiríksson, *Tro, Overtro og Vantro*, p. 24; see also pp. 28f.

[5] Ibid., p. 28; see also pp. 27-34.

inherent in Jacobi's account of reason[1] may be detected not only in his *later* distinction between "nominal" [*substantivisch*] and "adjectival [*adjektivisch*] reason," that is, the difference "between a reason that belongs to man and a reason to which man belongs,"[2] but can also already be seen in Jacobi's conception of reason as "apprehension."

Apart from his reprise of Jacobi's derivation of reason (*Vernunft*) from apprehending (*Vernehmen*)—a derivation that had become common enough by the beginning of the 19th century—we find in Eiríksson's thought no other major elements of the Jacobi's theory of knowledge, for example, "feeling" or the "reasoning intuition." Moreover, at the decisive moment in *Faith, Superstition, and Unbelief* where Eiríksson first introduces his definition of reason as "the sense for the infinite and eternal"—a definition to which he later returns time and again—Eiríksson attributes this definition only to "certain deep and clear-thinking theologians and philosophers" in general.[3] It is noteworthy that this last definition, with its strong echoes of Schleiermacher's definition of "religion" as "the sensibility and taste for the infinite"[4] and "intuition of the universe"[5] in the second of his speeches *On Religion* (1799), is nowhere to be found in Jacobi's own writings.

All in all, it is unlikely that Eiríksson developed his account of reason in the course of a *direct* encounter with Jacobi's thought. Jacobi is not mentioned even once by name in Eiríksson's writings; and the 1881 auction catalogue of Eiríksson's library contained not a single one of Jacobi's books.[6] A far more plausible direct influence on Eiríksson's

---

[1] On this see Walter Jaeschke, "Eine Vernunft, welche nicht die Vernunft ist. Jacobis Kritik der Aufklärung," in *Friedrich Heinrich Jacobi. Ein Wendepunkt der geistigen Bildung der Zeit*, ed. by Walter Jaeschke and Birgit Sandkaulen, Hamburg: Meiner 2004, pp. 199-216, especially pp. 208-216.

[2] Jacobi, *Werke. Gesamtausgabe*, vol. 2, p. 370; compare vol. 1, pp. 259f.

[3] Eiríksson, *Tro, Overtro og Vantro*, p. 27

[4] Friedrich Schleiermacher, *On Religion: Speeches to its Cultured Despisers*, trans. from the 1st German edition (1799) and ed. by Richard Crouter, Cambridge and New York: Cambridge University Press 1988, p. 23.

[5] Ibid., p. 24.

[6] See *Fortegnelse over endel forskjellige gode og velconditionerede Bogsamlinger, bestaaende af theologiske, juridiske, medicinske, historiske, æsthetiske, sprog- og naturvidenskabelige Værker samt Restoplagene af forskjellige theologiske Bøger, tilhørende Boerne efter afdøde Overlærer Nielsen, Districtslæge Wilhjelm, Pastor Krogh, Cand. theol. Magnús Eiríksson, Krigsraad Juul m.fl.*, ed. by Chr. Hee, Copenhagen: J.D. Quist 1881, pp. 138-70.

account of reason was Mynster: particularly the final chapter in Mynster's article "Development of the Notion of Faith" (1821),[1] which Eiríksson cites repeatedly, and praises explicitly, in *Faith, Superstition, and Unbelief.*[2] In this article, Mynster defines reason—with repeated reference to Jacobi (!)—as the receptive faculty that endows human beings with the capacity for faith, inasmuch as it is the faculty "by means of which the human being receives immediate impressions of supersensible objects."[3] The understanding, meanwhile, is not an "immediate faculty of knowledge" of this sort; for what we wish to understand must already have been *given* to us by other means: "the sensible things must already be given to us: the sensible things must already have been present in the sense, the higher things in reason."[4] Through reason, finally, "we apprehend [*fornemme*] God and his voice, as much as in the inward as in the outward revelations"; and in saying this Mynster assents to the view of other "careful thinkers," who "understand reason in its subjective meaning as receptivity, as a sense for the supersensible."[5]

This considerable agreement between Eiríksson and Mynster as regards *content* notwithstanding, it must be conceded though, that the exact *formulation* of the definition of reason as "the sense for the infinite and eternal"[6] cannot be found in Mynster's 1821 article. It *can*, however, be found in Martensen's (!) remarks *about* Jacobi in his lecture course in the winter semester 1838-39, which was announced under the title: "*Historia philosophiæ recentioris (inde a Kantio ad Hegelium usque) ejusque ad theologiam relatio*" (The History of Modern Philosophy (from Kant to Hegel) and its Relation to Theology)[7]—the very same course of lectures that Eiríksson had, as he himself wrote in *Faith, Superstition, and Unbelief,*

1 Jacob Peter Mynster, "Udvikling af Begrebet Tro," in *Det Kongelige Danske Videnskabernes Selskabs philosophiske og historiske Afhandlinger*, vol. 1, Copenhagen 1821, pp. 200-36 The citations that follow use the pagination in J. P. Mynster, *Blandede Skrivter* (see p. 65 above, note 1), vol. 1, pp. 3-35.

2 See Eiríksson, *Tro, Overtro og Vantro*, pp. 41f. (note) and p. 46.

3 Mynster, "Udvikling af Begrebet Tro," p. 27.

4 Ibid., p. 33.

5 Ibid., pp. 30f.

6 Ibid., p. 27.

7 For an account of this lecture course, which was a (revised) repetition of Martensen's well-attended private lectures given in the preceding winter semester 1837-38, see Stewart, *The Martensen Period: 1837-1842*, pp. 277-84.

"followed quite well" as an "attentive listener."[1] A set of subscription notes (*kollegieabonnement*) of Martensen's lecture,[2] which is preserved in Kierkegaard's *Nachlass*,[3] contains the following passage: "The difference between understanding and reason is present throughout J.'s [Jacobi's] entire system. 'Reason is [a] sense for the infinite and eternal,' it is thus nothing productive, but receptive, and thus cannot be ascribed to God; it is only a sense."[4] Thus, it can be assumed that the immediate source of Eiríksson's peculiar, and in a way Jacobian, conception of reason was not only Mynster, but also Eiríksson's *bête noire* Martensen.[5]

This "productive reception"[6] of Martensen with regard to Eiríksson's understanding of "reason" as an essentially receptive faculty notwithstanding, Eiríksson did criticize Martensen's account of baptism harshly, in *Faith, Superstition, and Unbelief*, as a fatal amalgamation of "superstition" and "unbelief." As he had done in *On Baptists and Infant Baptism* (1844), Eiríksson once again focuses his criticism on two particular Martensenian claims, each of which he now associates with one of these two deformations of the true "rational faith." Eiríksson locates *unbelief*—in which, as we have seen, the "mere understanding" is dominant and presumes to be the "judge" of faith—in Martensen's account

---

1 Eiríksson, *Tro, Overtro og Vantro*, p. 81 (note).

2 For this practice see the "Critical Account of the Text" of *Journal KK* in *KJN* 2, 587-596; here 593-596.

3 It is printed in *Pap.* II C 25 (in vol. XII), pp. 280-331.

4 *Pap.* II C 25 (in vol. XII), p. 302.

5 For a somewhat different account of this matter, see the last section of the article "Magnús Eiríksson and Philosophy" by Carl Henrik Koch in the present volume.

6 For the "productive reception" as a type and/or attitude of reception as well as its differentiation from an "unproductive reception," see Heiko Schulz, "Marheineke: The Volatilization of Christian Doctrine," in *Kierkegaard and his German Contemporaries*, Tome II, *Theology*, ed. by Jon Stewart, Aldershot: Ashgate 2007 (*Kierkegaard Research: Sources, Reception and Resources*, vol. 6), pp. 117-142; p. 127f.: "A reception is unproductive, if and only if, although author A has evidently been taken note of by author B (be it ever so sporadically or briefly), this reception leaves no or only marginal (explicit and/or implicit) traces in B's writings. A genuinely productive reception is distinguished by the central role that author A's work takes on in author B's work *vis-à-vis* type, content and genesis, even when traces of the former are only recognizable in isolated passages of the latter." See also Schulz, "Die Welt bleibt immer dieselbe. Typologisch orientierende Bemerkungen zur Rezeptionsgeschichte Søren Kierkegaards," in his *Aneignung und Reflexion*, vol. 1, *Studien zur Rezeption Søren Kierkegaards*, Berlin and Boston: Walter de Gruyter 2011 (*Kierkegaard Studies Monograph Series*, vol. 24), pp. 3-24; especially pp. 8-15.

of faith as "the fruit of baptism."[1] By contrast, *superstition*—in which the understanding by contrast is "judged and excluded," and reason, too, is not given appropriate regard, inasmuch as faith refuses to recognize that its own relation to reason constitutes the "limit" beyond which it cannot pass without becoming *eo ipso* a "limitless" superstition—is to be found in Martensen's assumption that "just as Christ in baptism gives himself wholly and undivided to each individual, so too does he also give the Spirit wholly to each individual."[2] In a further echo of *On Baptists and Infant Baptism*,[3] and again with reference to Martensen's lectures on "Speculative Dogmatics" (1838-39), Eiríksson takes the latter sentence as proof that speculative theology leads to "*self-deification*,"[4] since it implies that "all who are baptized become new versions [*Udgaver*] of Christ, and therefore all become Gods."[5] But if there are as many Gods as baptized Christians, then one must *either* abandon the notion of the *one* God, *or* one must assume that all of these (baptized) individuals-*cum*-God are reducible to the *one* true God, and are wholly absorbed in His personality—meaning not only that their personalities as such disappear, but also that personal immortality itself is lost.

In contrast to superstition, with its fatal consequences, true faith regards God as "an invisible, incorporeal, eternal, self-conscious Spirit, who…is both within the world and elevated above it."[6] The limited personality of one of God's rational and free creatures can never be identical with God's own eternal and unlimited personality. Yet this is precisely what Martensen's Hegelian speculation presumes. Eiríksson demonstrates this, without dwelling on the details, by referring to §§ 49-50 of Martensen's *Outline to a System of Moral Philosophy* (1841). Here, at the beginning of the second part of his system ("The Good as Ideal"), Martensen presents his doctrine of "the personal unity of God and humanity" as distinguished from the mere "mystical" or "moral" unity of

---

1 Martensen, *Den christelige Daab*, p. 3; see Eiríksson, *Tro, Overtro og Vantro*, pp. 10f. and p. 67.

2 Martensen, *Den christelige Daab*, p. 59; see Eiríksson, *Tro, Overtro og Vantro*, p. 18; pp. 66f.; pp. 72f.; and p. 100 (note).

3 See Eiríksson, *Om Baptister og Barnedaab*, pp. 234f.

4 Eiríksson, *Tro, Overtro og Vantro*, p. 86; see also pp. 86-88.

5 Ibid., pp. 87f.

6 Ibid., p. 90.

God and humanity.[1] It is this doctrine of "the personal unity of God and humanity" that came to be the main focus of Eiríksson's criticism in his next polemical work, directed at Martensen's *Outline to a System of Moral Philosophy*.

III. The Criticism of Martensen's Moral Philosophy and the "Public Prosecutor's Action"

As the title makes unmistakably clear, Eiríksson's goal in *Dr. Martensen's Published Moral Paragraphs, or the So-called "Outline to a System of Moral Philosophy," in its Confused, Idealistic-Metaphysical and Fantastic-Speculative, Religion and Christianity Destroying, Fatalistic, Pantheistic and Self-Deifying Essence* (1846),[2] is to bring to light "the un-Christian, irreligious, fatalistic, pantheistic or atheistic and self- and humanity-deifying element"[3] in Martensen's moral philosophy. Here Eiríksson's accusation of "deifying humanity" refers above all to Martensen's doctrine of "the personal unity of God and humanity"[4] (rather than a "mystical" or "moral" unity) as the absolute realization of the religious ideal by God's personal incarnation in Christ, as Martensen explains in the aforementioned §§ 49-50 of his *Outline to a System of Moral Philosophy*. According to Martensen, "God or the highest good"[5] is to be realized by human freedom, and so "will gain personal shape in the human individual."[6] For this reason, God—who *is* precisely that which

---

1 See Martensen, *Grundrids til Moralphilosophiens System*, pp. 51-55 (§§ 49-50); (*Outline to a System of Moral Philosophy*, pp. 282f.) to Eiríksson's *Tro, Overtro og Vantro*, pp. 90f. (note).

2 Magnús Eiríksson, *Dr. Martensens trykte moralske Paragrapher, eller det saakaldte "Grundrids til Moralphilosophiens System af Dr. Hans Martensen", i dets forvirrede, idealistisk-metaphysiske og phantastisk-speculative, Religion og Christendom undergravende, fatalistiske, pantheistiske og selvforguderske Væsen*, Copenhagen: H.C. Klein 1846.

3 Ibid., p. VI.

4 Martensen, *Grundrids til Moralphilosophiens System*, p. 53 (§ 50); (*Outline to a System of Moral Philosophy*, p. 283; translation slightly modified.) See also ibid., pp. 51-55 (§§ 49-50) to Eiríksson's *Dr. Martensens trykte moralske Paragrapher*, pp. 95-106.

5 Ibid., p. 51 (§ 48); (*Outline to a System of Moral Philosophy*, p. 282; translation slightly modified.)

6 Ibid. (*Outline to a System of Moral Philosophy*, p. 281.)

he commands—demands "a *God-human* of every individual."[1] To be sure, this demand of God would necessarily be an empty one, a demand that could not be fulfilled by human freedom, if "the originally *existing* unity of the divine and human nature"[2] were not already present; or, as Martensen elsewhere writes, "if God is not *essentially* present in the human soul."[3] On Eiríksson's reading, Martensen here proposes the apotheosis of humanity itself. Eiríksson makes this clear by adding the following gloss: "that is, if we do not have God's essence within us, if we are mere human beings and not gods as well."[4] By means of this "deification of humanity," not only the opposition between God and man—religion's necessary condition—but also "all religion" is *eo ipso* "nullified and annihilated."[5]

Martensen's criticism of the mystical-pantheistic "abstract-*essential* unity"[6] of God and man makes clear, however, that he in no way supported the leveling of the difference between God and humanity that Eiríksson here accuses him of promulgating. This can also be seen in Martensen's critique of Johann Gottlieb Fichte's (1762-1814) "moral world-view," insofar as this world-view ultimately collapses into precisely the same mystical notion of an "essential unity of God and humanity" that is mentioned above, and so "nullifies the fundamental difference [between God and humanity], and annihilates the concept of a *com*munity and a *co*operation of God and humanity."[7] Turning away from Martensen's moral philosophy—and recalling Martensen's declaration, in his account of baptism, that "in baptism Christ gives himself and the Spirit wholly and undivided to everyone"[8]—Eiríksson goes on to argue that Martensen considers that "all those who are baptized, and indeed

1 Ibid. (*Outline to a System of Moral Philosophy*, p. 282.)
2 Ibid. (*Outline to a System of Moral Philosophy*, p. 282; translation slightly modified.)
3 Ibid., p. 51 (§ 49); (*Outline to a System of Moral Philosophy*, p. 282; translation slightly modified.)
4 Eiríksson, *Dr. Martensens trykte moralske Paragrapher*, p. 96.
5 Ibid., pp. 95f.
6 Martensen, *Grundrids til Moralphilosophiens System*, p. 51 (§ 49); (*Outline to a System of Moral Philosophy*, p. 282).
7 Ibid., p. 53 (§ 49, note); (*Outline to a System of Moral Philosophy*, p. 282; translation slightly modified).
8 Eiríksson, *Dr. Martensens trykte moralske Paragrapher*, p. 97; see Martensen, *Den christelige Daab*, p. 59.

only these, are essentially and personally one with God,"[1] and so are capable of fulfilling God's will. By sublating the difference between God and humanity, Martensen's doctrine annihilates not only the fundamental basis of all religion, but nullifies specifically the ecclesiastical doctrine of the reconciliation of man with God through Christ, since according to the Martensenian reconciliation as a "physical-metaphysical act" the human being and God are "essentially and personally one."[2]

At the end of his book, Eiríksson capped his polemic against Martensen with the threat of a public lawsuit. For given the fact that Martensen's moral philosophy "actually sublates everything that deserves the name of religion," one ought nonetheless to ask how it could be possible "that a teacher of this kind could hold a public professorial chair and, moreover, exercise the Church office of preacher?"[3] If Martensen should not himself see fit to resign, or if his superiors did not dismiss him, Eiríksson wished to reserve the right to sue Martensen

> as a fraudulent and dishonest teacher who does not teach the doctrine that he pretends to teach, which in his capacity as a teacher of the church he ought to teach, and which he has tacitly committed himself to teach; as a man who through his teaching undermines and annihilates all true faith and religion at their innermost core and deepest root.[4]

When even these words elicited no response from Martensen—a fact that Eiríksson attributed to the influence of Bishop Mynster, who had no doubt "advised [Martensen] to be silent"[5]—Eiríksson carried out the above open threat. In June 1847, Eiríksson presented the matter in a letter to King Christian VIII himself, in which he, moreover, "complained about the principles and conduct of the government in many other matters, which belong more properly or solely to the realm of politics."[6] Because of the latter complaints, expressed so frankly—Eiríksson himself concedes

---

1 Ibid.
2 Ibid., p. 100.
3 Ibid., pp. 151f.
4 Ibid., pp. 158f.
5 Magnús Eiríksson, *Speculativ Rettroenhed, fremstillet efter Dr. Martensens "christelige Dogmatik", og Geistlig Retfærdighed, belyst ved en Biskops Deeltagelse i en Generalfiskal-Sag*, Copenhagen: Salomon 1849, p. II.
6 Ibid.

that his letter "indeed" contained "unusually rough and inconsiderate remarks"[1]—Eiríksson found himself charged with *lèse-majesté* in the form of a so-called *Generalfiskalsag*, a "Public Prosecutor's Action."[2] This charge, however, was soon dropped: for on January 20, 1848, immediately after Frederik VII acceded to the throne, a general amnesty was proclaimed. Eiríksson was by no means pleased with this outcome, since he was thoroughly convinced both of the validity of his case against Martensen and "that here the court was on my side."[3] Ultimately, however, Eiríksson came to see the annulment of the *Generalfiskalsag* as "a sign of God's sagacious Governance," and came to believe still more strongly that God wished to deploy him "to promote the good."[4]

IV. Martensen's Christian Dogmatics

Eiríksson's critical response to Martensen's *Christian Dogmatics* (1849)[5] is found in his book *Speculative Orthodoxy, Presented in Accordance with Dr. Martensen's 'Christian Dogmatics,' and Ecclesiastical Justice, Illustrated by a Bishop's Involvement in a Public Prosecutor's Action* (1849).[6]

---

[1] Ibid., p. III. Because Eiríksson held that the heart of his complaint, which pertained to the political sphere and in part to the question of religious freedom as well, had been rendered obsolete by the new king's promises at his coronation, Eiríksson declined—not least also out of pious regard for the deceased king—to publish his letter to Christian VIII. Eiríksson behaved quite differently, however, in his quarrel with Martensen and (now also) Mynster as well. In particular, it was "Bishop Mynster's inconceivable alliance with Prof. Martensen, which is a scandal to every earnest and candid expert on the matter," that roused Eiríksson's anger, coupled with the fact that Martensen's "teaching is so infinitely far apart from his [Mynster's]" (p. 134, emphases removed; see also p. 119 and pp. 139f. As regards Eiríksson's letter to King Christian VIII, see also Anonymous, "Danmark," *Den Norske Rigstidende*, 1847, no. 157 (July 28), as well as Anonymous, "Udenlandske Efterretninger," *Morgenbladet*, 1847, no. 209 (July 28).

[2] On this charge against Eiríksson, see the texts and extracts reproduced in *Speculativ Rettroenhed*, pp. 87-134; see also Anonymous, *Nyt Aftenblad*, 1848, no. 36; *Berlingske politiske og Avertissements-Tidende*, 1848, no. 37, as well as Pjetursson, "Magnús Eiríksson," pp. 125f.

[3] Eiríksson, *Speculativ Rettroenhed*, p. III; see also p. V.

[4] Ibid., pp. 135f.

[5] Hans Lassen Martensen, *Den christelige Dogmatik*, Copenhagen: C.A. Reitzel 1849.

[6] Magnús Eiríksson, *Speculativ Rettroenhed, fremstillet efter Dr. Martensens "christelige Dogmatik" og geistlig Retfærdighed, belyst ved en Biskops Deeltagelse I en Generalfiskal-Sag*, Copenhagen: Salomon 1849.

With regard to Martensen's *Christian Dogmatics* in general, Eiríksson here notes that its "basic outlook, standpoint, and method" exhibit no fundamental changes when compared to those of Martensen's earlier lectures on dogmatics: "the most important basic teachings are, in all essential aspects, the same."[1] Contrary to the expectations of many, Martensen has merely "re-baptized" the dogmatics that he once called "speculative";[2] yet this indicates only, Eiríksson adds (in a wry allusion to the Baptism controversy), that Martensen would appear "to belong to the Anabaptists" himself.[3] At certain points in *Christian Dogmatics*, an element of "un-Christian speculation and unrestrained fantasy" proves to be so greatly in the ascendant that one might say that "his caprice and confusion" are now much deeper than before. Eiríksson concludes that, despite all of his intellectual exertions, Martensen has continued to fail to grasp the Christian truth "in its most essential character."[4]

If one asks what "main outlook or principle" may be ascribed to Martensen's *Christian Dogmatics*—that is, whether it should be labeled Biblical, ecclesiastical, rationalistic, or speculative-philosophical, Eiríksson responds that one can only call it a potpourri, a "confused mass"[5] of many different, mutually contradictory elements:

> It should be clear from the foregoing that, however many fully or half-Christian particulars are to be found in the work—and no matter how appealing or interesting those particulars might be—it is nonetheless a monstrosity when regarded as a whole. It is neither one thing nor another, but an agglomeration of everything possible: Biblical elements, Church orthodoxy, rationalism, Hegelian speculation, Gnostic fantasies, and other errors. For this reason, when judged specifically as a "scholarly presentation"

---

1 Ibid., p. IV; see also p. 2.

2 Compare also Kierkegaard's comment on Martensen's freshly published *Christian Dogmatics* in a journal entry from November 1849: "It consists of the lectures that had been titled 'Speculative Dogmatics,' but this adjective had indeed been removed (a difference rather like the one Peer Degn [sc. the half-literate in Ludvig Holberg's comedy *Erasmus Montanus eller Rasmus Berg* (1731)] makes in reference to the same book, one copy half-bound in vellum, the other in full leather binding)" (*SKS* 22, 327, NB13:86 / *KJN* 6, 330).

3 Eiríksson, *Speculativ Rettroenhed*, p. [1]; compare ibid., pp. 2f. with Martensen, *Den christelige Dogmatik*, p. [I].

4 Eiríksson, *Speculativ Rettroenhed*, pp. IV-V; see also pp. 65-67.

5 Ibid., p. 68; see also p. 66.

> of the doctrines of Christianity and the Church, it is surely a monstrosity with no equal.[1]

With its numerous contradictions and arbitrary use of Scripture, Martensen's *Dogmatics* is "equally despicable whether it be regarded from the theoretical or the practical point of view," for which reason it will be unable to satisfy "any party or faction at all within Christendom."[2]

Eiríksson's goal is not so much to offer a comprehensive critique of Martensen's work as it is to draw attention to certain main claims and theses, found predominantly in "the first sections" following Martensen's introduction,[3] that can give the reader a reasonably clear glimpse of the gist of Martensen's teachings. Eiríksson's critique centers on Martensen's doctrine of the Trinity, which serves as the basis for all of his further utterances about the individual Persons of the Godhead.[4] Above all, Eiríksson criticizes Martensen's distinction between an "essential Trinity"—God's relation and inner reciprocal relationship to *Himself* (*ad intra*) as a Trinitarian God—and an "economic Trinity"—God's relationship to *the World* (*ad extra*) as a Trinitarian God—which Martensen inherits from the dogmatic-theological tradition.[5] In truth, Eiríksson notes, Martensen is thereby proposing "a double Trinity"[6] within which the Trinitarian Persons are doubled. As regards Martensen's doctrine of the "essential Trinity," Eiríksson's primary objection is that it makes God the Father into an entity whose original state is merely that of a "natural ground,"[7] lacking in self-consciousness and freedom,

1 Ibid., p. 74. As far as the form of presentation was concerned, Martensen had attempted to follow the Hegelian method, though this led merely to caricature—"since Hegel was, as is well known, no theologian *ex professo*, but a philosopher, and therefore had no need to bring ecclesiastical dogmatics or to apply his method to the individual dogmas of the Church. Yet Mr. Martensen has done this and in so doing has confounded the whole" (p. 68).

2 Ibid., pp. 76f.

3 See ibid., p. 4. In practice, Eiríksson refers mainly to Martensen, *Den christelige Dogmatik*, pp. 64-70 (§§ 27-28); pp. 123-136 (§§ 52-58); pp. 139-142 (§§ 59-61); pp. 219-234 (§§ 99-105); pp. 312-318 (§§ 132-135); pp. 395-401 (§§ 181-184) and pp. 404-411 (§§ 186-189).

4 Compare Eiríksson, *Speculativ Rettroenhed*, pp. 4-24, and pp. 37-44 together with the diagram on p. 49, to Martensen, *Den christelige Dogmatik*, pp. 123-136 (§§ 52-58).

5 See Martensen, *Den christelige Dogmatik*, pp. 127f. (§ 54, Addition).

6 Eiríksson, *Speculativ Rettroenhed*, p. 20; see also p. 4.

7 Compare ibid., p. 9 to Martensen, *Den christelige Dogmatik*, p. 130 (§ 56).

who comes to consciousness only by way of begetting God-the-Son: "Without the Son, the Father could not say to Himself 'I'; for the form of the Ego, without an objective something different from the Ego (a not-I, a Thou), in relation to which it can grasp itself as Ego, is inconceivable."[1] As Father, God cannot be conscious of himself, cannot say "I" to himself, until he has distinguished himself from himself as Father from Son, and has objectified himself in the Son (as the "not-I" to whom he can say "Thou"). And even further: this God who becomes conscious of himself (as Father) both *in* and *through* the Son is *still* not yet free or "freely acting." For Father and Son first become free when the Holy Spirit "proceeds" from them both:

> But if the inner revelation were terminated in the Son, God would be manifest to Himself merely according to the *necessity* of His nature and thought, not according to the *freedom* of His will....If then the "birth" of the Son out of the essence of the Father denotes the momentum of necessity, the "procession" of the Holy Spirit from the Father and the Son denotes the momentum of freedom in the inner revelation.[2]

For Eiríksson, this Martensenian doctrine of the "essential Trinity," which dictates that God the Father first comes to self-consciousness and freedom in the Son and the Holy Spirit, is "certainly a *non plus ultra* of a product of speculative fantasy," involving a tangled mass of problems and contradictions.[3] For even apart from the fact that "there is not even a tittle" of such a doctrine in either the Bible or the confessional documents of the Church,[4] Martensen has also failed to grasp that God's self-consciousness is wholly independent of the concept of his Fatherhood, for indeed the latter presupposes the former—for "is it possible to think of a rational being as a father without first thinking of it as conscious?"[5]

A still worse misconception, according to Eiríksson, is one that arises in Martensen's account as a consequence of his doctrine of the Trinity, a consequence that is not articulated explicitly but is "expressed against

---

1 Martensen, *Den christelige Dogmatik*, p. 131 (§ 56); see also p. 129 (§ 55).
2 Ibid., p. 132 (§ 56).
3 Eiríksson, *Speculativ Rettroenhed*, p. 10.
4 Ibid., p. 11.
5 Ibid., p. 7.

his will,"[1] namely, in the sense that God is not to be regarded as *one* God in *three* Persons, but as one *single* Person who takes part in *three relations*. For even though Martensen does himself speak of God's "threefold personality," or even of "one God in three Persons,"[2] he nonetheless gravitates toward the expression "moment" in his efforts to describe the individual "persons" of the Trinity; and he writes that "God in Himself is a merely impersonal deity, who first in Christ says 'I' to Himself, and first in the congregation knows Himself as Spirit."[3] As Eiríksson reasons (adducing two further citations to support his inference),[4] it follows that in the first "moment" of the essential Trinity, God cannot yet be regarded as a Person, since God's Personhood requires that all three "moments" be integrated into a *single* Person.

At the same time, Eiríksson also discerns a countervailing, and indeed capricious, claim on Martensen's part, to the effect that each of the three "moments of the divine essence" manifests "the entirety of God," God's "entire essence,"[5] in itself—though each does so in a different way: "There are therefore three eternal acts of consciousness, and the entire divine Ego is in each of these three acts. Each hypostasis has being solely through the other two. Here there is no temporal first or last. The entire Trinity stands in one present Now."[6] Eiríksson points out, however, that if the entire essence of the Godhead is contained in each of its three "moments" (Father, Son, and Spirit), then God's attribute of omniscience, for example (which Martensen describes as part of God's perfection in his section on "Divine Attributes"[7]), must

1 Ibid., p. 14; see also pp. 14-17.
2 See Martensen, *Den christelige Dogmatik*, pp. 123f. (§ 52).
3 Ibid., p. 127 (§ 54).
4 For one, see Eiríksson's *Speculativ Rettroenhed*, p. 15, where he cites Martensen, *Den christelige Dogmatik*, pp. 128f. (§ 55), albeit with marked discrepancies from the original wording: "God's personality and self-consciousness are *unthinkable* unless the 3 moments are thought as inextricably united with one other." Martensen's actual wording read as follows: "to have an ontological conception of the essential Trinity is thus to have a conception of the necessary *fundamental form* of the personal life of God; is to have a conception of those moments in the essence of God, without which personality and self-consciousness are *unthinkable*." Eiríksson's second reference, which is consistent with Martensen's wording, is to the passage referred to on p. 89 above, note 2, namely, Martensen, *Den christelige Dogmatik*, p. 132 (§ 56).
5 Martensen, *Den christelige Dogmatik*, p. 123 (§ 52).
6 Ibid., p. 133 (§ 56).
7 See ibid., p. 114 (§ 49).

necessarily belong to *all three* "moments" of God. In "The Doctrine of the Son"—that is, within the presentation of the economic Trinity, in which what "stands in one present Now[1]" in God's inner self-revelation manifests itself *economically* in the forms of time and history as creation, recreation, and sanctification—Martensen writes, in a reference to Mark 13:32 ("But about that day or hour no one knows, neither the angels in heaven, nor the Son, but only the Father"), that "Christ's knowledge is not universal knowledge, but a limited knowledge."[2] Yet if God the Son, as the second "moment" of the *essential* Trinity, as "Logos," cannot be equated with the second "moment" of the *economic* Trinity, with "Christ," then in reality we are dealing with "two Sons of God"[3] in two different Trinities.

It would seem, then, that Martensen had good reason to bring both of these Trinities into his system. In Eiríksson's words, this is a maneuver that is "just as clever as it is convenient."[4] It is *clever* because one can simultaneously use the doctrine of the first (essential) Trinity to demonstrate one's orthodoxy in comparison to all unbelieving rationalists, and the doctrine of the second (economic) Trinity to show one's agreement with Scripture. It is *convenient* chiefly because one may thereby abrogate the challenge, with all its arduousness, of uniting the opposites in a rational way—and after that "one simply speculates (fantasizes)."[5]

At the very end of *Speculative Orthodoxy*, Eiríksson writes that this book would remain his "final attack on Prof. Martensen"—unless, that is, Martensen or one of his "stooges" (*Haandlangere*) were to make further steps necessary.[6] When, however, Martensen published his *Dogmatic*

---

1 Ibid., p. 133 (§ 56).

2 Ibid., p. 354 (§ 153). Martensen then goes on to try to explain the difference between the unlimited and the limited in Christ's knowledge by means of the concept of "the *central*, the fundamentally typical [*grundbilledlige*] knowledge," by virtue of which Christ's knowledge "is nevertheless the perfect knowledge" (ibid.).

3 Eiríksson, *Speculativ Rettroenhed*, p. 21; see especially ibid., p. 49, as well as Martensen, *Den christelige Dogmatik*, p. 316 (§ 134): "Still there are not two Sons of God, but one Son of God; Christ did not add a new second Son to the Trinity; the entire movement takes place within the circle of the Trinity itself."

4 Eiríksson, *Speculativ Rettroenhed*, p. 22.

5 Ibid.

6 Ibid., p. 140.

Elucidations (1850),[1] in which he responded in detail to criticisms of his *Christian Dogmatics* by Rasmus Nielsen (1809-84) and Jens Paludan-Müller (1813-88),[2] and then took note in his Preface—and only in his Preface—of Eiríksson's critique as well, Eiríksson felt compelled to produce one final treatise against Martensen: *Cardinal Virtues of the New Danish Theology, Illustrated by Means of Dr. Martensen's Writings, Along with the Refutations, Together with 75 Theological Questions Addressed to Dr. H. Martensen* (1850).[3] At the beginning of his book,[4] Eiríksson professes surprise that Martensen never addressed his criticisms directly, even though in his Preface he had singled out Eiríksson for mention as one "who had wanted to test the doctrines himself"[5] (whereas his other critics had restricted themselves to the Introduction of his *Christian Dogmatics*, allegedly neglecting "what the *Dogmatics* chiefly inquires into, namely, the dogmas themselves"[6]). To Eiríksson, the fact that Martensen subsequently responded *only* to the criticisms of Nielsen and Paludan-Müller, and disregarded Eiríksson's own allegations "with lofty silence," signified that Martensen was incapable of refuting Eiríksson's critique, and chose silence because this strategy "was most convenient."[7]

In *Cardinal Virtues of the New Danish Theology*, Eiríksson sought to contrast his own critique of Martensen with that of Nielsen and Paludan-Müller. Here the measured tone of his polemic is noticeable.[8] Against Nielsen's consciously Kierkegaardian description of Christian

---

1 Hans Lassen Martensen, *Dogmatiske Oplysninger. Et Leilighedsskrift*, Copenhagen: C.A. Reitzel 1850.

2 Rasmus Nielsen, *Mag. S. Kierkegaards "Johannes Climacus" og Dr. H. Martensens "Christelige Dogmatik". En undersøgende Anmeldelse*, Copenhagen: C.A. Reitzel 1849; Jens Paludan-Müller, *Om Dr. Martensens christelige Dogmatik*, Copenhagen: C.A. Reitzel 1850.

3 Magnús Eiríksson, *Den nydanske Theologies Cardinaldyder belyste ved Hjelp af Dr. Martensens Skrifter samt Modskrifterne, tilligemed 75 theologiske Spørgsmaal, rettede til Dr. H. Martensen*, Copenhagen: Chr. Steen & Søn 1850.

4 See ibid., pp. 5-9.

5 Martensen, *Dogmatiske Oplysninger*, p. 4. However, Martensen goes on to declare that everyone would admit that Eiríksson has fallen prey to "severe misunderstandings" (ibid.).

6 Ibid., p. 5.

7 Eiríksson, *Den nydanske Theologies Cardinaldyder*, p. 9; see also p. 6 and pp. 9f.

8 See, for example, ibid., p. 13, where Eiríksson writes that "a notable self-awareness, refinement, and spiritual maturity" was in evidence in "many places" in Martensen's *Dogmatiske Oplysninger*.

faith as "the paradox" or "the absurdity principle,"[1] Eiríksson describes himself as agreeing with Martensen on this matter of *principle*—that is, with the principle that Christian faith cannot possibly be grounded in absurdity. However, Eiríksson criticizes Martensen's *application* of this principle as "bad and completely false," even if the principle itself is "in and of itself correct."[2] To substantiate this charge, Eiríksson cites several passages in which faith and reason part company for Martensen. In an echo of his position in *Speculative Orthodoxy*, Eiríksson closes *Cardinal Virtues of the New Danish Theology* by arriving at a similarly negative overall appraisal of Martensen's *Christian Dogmatics*.[3] This is clear from the "75 theological questions" for Martensen that Eiríksson poses in his book's final section, questions that refer specifically to "the peculiar doctrine" set forth in *Christian Dogmatics*.[4]

V. Eiríksson's Critique of Martensen in His Late Work

Cardinal Virtues of the New Danish Theology (1850) ultimately came to be Eiríksson's last written salvo against Martensen. Once again, Martensen chose not to respond.[5] In his subsequent writings, Eiríksson mentions

1 See Nielsen, *Mag. S. Kierkegaards "Johannes Climacus,"* pp. 27-33.

2 Eiríksson, *Den nydanske Theologies Cardinaldyder*, p. 50; see also pp. 15-47 and pp. 50-59 with Martensen, *Dogmatiske Oplysninger*, pp. 17-26. In "Min Forfattervirksomhed," p. 92, Eiríksson refers again to this "principled" agreement between himself and Martensen, and writes that Martensen could have inferred from this agreement that Eiríksson was not one of those "who have dedicated themselves exclusively to being nothing but opponents." This last line is a sly word play on the final sentence of Martensen's *Dogmatiske Oplysninger*, p. 104.

3 Compare Eiríksson, *Den nydanske Theologies Cardinaldyder*, p. 55 and pp. 124-132 to his *Speculativ Rettroenhed*, pp. 67-78.

4 See Eiríksson, *Den nydanske Theologies Cardinaldyder*, pp. 132-158. For Eiríksson's critique of Martensen's doctrine of the Trinity (which is, in fact, a brief extract of his critique in his *Speculativ Rettroenhed*, pp. 4-24 and pp. 37-44) see pp. 133-135 (Questions 4-10) and pp. 138-142 (Questions 20-26). For a fascinating account of how Martensen might have responded to Eiríksson's "75 theological questions," see the article by Curtis Thompson in the present volume.

5 See Martensen's letter to Ludvig Jacob Mendel Gude on November 26, 1850, in *Biskop H. Martensens Breve*, ed. by Selskabet for Danmarks Kirkehistorie ved Bjørn Kornerup, vols. 1-3, Copenhagen: Gad 1955-1957, vol. 1, pp. 14-16 (no. 10), here: p. 14: "Eiriksen [sic!] has already written and published a new book attacking me—which I, however, have already put aside."

Martensen only incidentally and, for the most part, peripherally. It would almost seem that Eiríksson had finally come to terms with Martensen's dogged silence and the resulting impossibility of true dialogue between them. Yet a far more important factor, in all likelihood, is the fact that after 1851, Eiríksson's *own* theological standpoint underwent a decisive intensification and radicalization.

Following a period of relative literary silence between 1851 until 1863,[1] Eiríksson came out with a series of writings that differed markedly from those that had come before. The essential difference here concerns his understanding of the Bible. At no point had Eiríksson ever been a proponent of the doctrine of the Divine inspiration of Scripture; but it had been the Bible to which he had consistently appealed, throughout his confrontation with Martensen, as the final authority for both his own position and for his critique of others' standpoints. In his writings from 1863 onwards, however, Eiríksson progressed to an increasingly radical critique of both the Bible specifically and of Church doctrine generally, including and especially the doctrine that Jesus is the Son of God—until at last Eiríksson broke with Church dogma completely. It had become more and more clear to him, that the very idea of the (self-)deification of humanity (including even the human being Jesus of Nazareth), which he had so radically rejected, and had criticized so harshly, in Martensen's theology, was in fact already contained in the Bible itself, above all in John and in St. Paul's Epistles. As a result, Eiríksson felt increasingly compelled not to defend his position as *in line with* the Bible, but to defend it *against* the Bible *itself* and its claims to integrity and authenticity, since he had now come to regard the Bible itself as "a book in which the chaff must be separated from the wheat."[2]

Even in those writings of Eiríksson that preceded his period of literary silence, it is possible to detect signs of his later, radical approach to Church dogma[3]—even if Eiríksson had then refrained from exploring

[1] See Eiríksson's own explanation of his literary silence in his *Gud og Reformatoren*, p. III; see also p. 60 above, note 2.

[2] Eiríksson, "Min Forfattervirksomhed," p. 100.

[3] See, for example, Eiríksson's anonymously published essay "Nogle Bemærkninger til Orientering i de nærværende kirkelige Tilstande," *Den Nordiske Folkeskole*, vol. 10, 1849, no. 5 (February 9), columns 65-72; no. 8 (March 2), columns 113-119; no. 22 (June 8), columns 337-344; no. 47 (December 21), columns 681-691, particularly the fourth section ("Vor Tids religiøse Tilstande"). See also *Er Troen et Paradox og "i Kraft*

the full theological or personal implications of his views. As Eiríksson recounts in hindsight in "My Activity as an Author" (1875), his earlier relation to the Bible was "responsible" for the fact that he did not pursue further his critique of "the system of Church dogma, and above all the doctrines of the Trinity and the divinity of Christ."[1] He was at that point still "a one-sided Scriptural theologian, who held firm to everything that was contained in Scripture."[2] As late as in his pseudonymously published *Letters to Clara Raphael* (1851),[3] Eiríksson offers a detailed account of why he cannot believe in the doctrine of the Triune God as well as in the doctrine of God's incarnation in Jesus of Nazareth,[4] which, as he attempts to show, is contained nowhere in the New Testament, *without* casting aspersions on the integrity and authenticity of the Bible itself.

Eiríksson's critical attitude toward the Church's dogmatic teachings, and his unshakable conviction that he was acting in the service of "the love of truth,"[5] are perhaps best epitomized in his public appearance at

---

af det Absurde"?, pp. 120-125 and 168-175, where Theophilus Nicolaus prefers the "pre-Christian" position to that of dogmatic-ecclesiastical Christianity. Already in *Tro, Overtro og Vantro* (1846), Eiríksson criticized the notion of the divinity of Jesus Christ and the characterization of Jesus as a "God-man" as part of his attack on the "Faberian-Martensenian account of baptism" (see pp. 87f. and pp. 99-101), and took care to speak of Jesus Christ exclusively as "the Savior" (*Frelseren*) (see p. 70, p. 84 and pp. 95-101).

1 Eiríksson, "Min Forfattervirksomhed," p. 100.

2 Ibid., p. 90.

3 Magnús Eiríksson [Theodor Immanuel], *Breve til Clara Raphael*, Copenhagen: C.A. Reitzel 1851. For an interpretation of Eiríksson's *Letters to Clara Raphael*, see Vilborg Sigurðardóttir, *Um kvenréttindi á Íslandi til 1915*, Unpublished BA Thesis, University of Iceland 1967 (National and University Library of Iceland); Auður Styrkársdóttir, "Forspjall," in John Stuart Mill, *Kúgun kvenna*, trans. by Sigurð Jónasson, ed. by Vilhjálmur Árnason, Reykjavik: Hið íslenska bókmenntafélag 1997, pp. 9-65, here pp. 37f.; Jóhanna Þráinsdóttir, "Gleymdur liðsmaður kvenna. Um Magnús Eiríksson, guðfræðing og rithöfund, og framlag hans til frelsisbaráttu kvenna," *Menningarblað. Lesbók Morgunblaðsins*, 1997 (May 10), pp. 4f., as well as the article by Sigríður Þorgeirsdóttir in the present volume. On the so-called "Clara Raphael feud," see, moreover, Katalin Nun, *Women of the Danish Golden Age: Literature, Theater and the Emancipation of Women*, Copenhagen: Museum Tusculanum Press 2013 (*Danish Golden Age Studies*, vol. 8), pp. 85-111.

4 See Eiríksson, *Breve til Clara Raphael*, pp. 50-89, especially pp. 78-81.

5 See the subtitle of Eiríksson's book *Jøder og Christne eller Hvorledes blev Jesus fra Nazareth betragtet i den ældste Kirke og hvorledes blev han senere betragtet? En populær, historisk-kritisk Undersøgelse, tilegnet de Sandhedskjærlige*, Copenhagen: Magnús Eiríksson 1873.

the Fourth Nordic Church Conference in Copenhagen on September 5-7, 1871, where he addressed "The Relation of Neo-Rationalism to the Christian Faith," the conference's first theme. Unlike the speakers before him, who had sought to establish what "neo-rationalism" means, Eiríksson argued that it was far more important to ask what is meant by "Christian faith"—and whether the faith proclaimed by the Church truly coincides with the teachings and faith of Jesus Christ himself. After his talk was repeatedly interrupted by both the audience and the moderators, Eiríksson at last appealed directly, before all present, to "the Lord of Heaven and Earth," finishing his prayer with the following words: "Help me and all who seek Your truth to find it, and to spread it among the people in order to bring them to You, You who are the light and the life, the eternal source of truth and bliss; for the people are so distant from you. Father, forgive my sins, be gracious to me and hear my prayer!"[1]

In the effort to explain this fundamental change in Eiríksson's theological stance, both a theological and a personal reason can be

---

[1] Thus reads the official shorthand report of Eiríksson's speech in *Forhandlingerne paa Det Fjerde Nordiske Kirkemöde i Kjøbenhavn den 5., 6. og 7. September 1871*, ed. by Kr. Madsen, Copenhagen: Gyldendal 1871, pp. 46-51; here p. 51. This resolute and unbending challenge to the leaders of the Church brought Eiríksson numerous expressions of respect and sympathy, and contributed to the formation of a circle of sponsors, who—without necessarily subscribing to Eiríksson's "religious views" (as they expressly declared in their *Indbydelse til at bidrage til at understøtte Magn. Eiriksson, Kbh. d. 11. Nov. 1872*, Copenhagen: no publisher given 1872)—sought to remedy his difficult financial situation. On Eiríksson's appearance and behavior at "*Det Fjerde Nordiske Kirkemøde*," see the anonymous articles in *Berlingske politiske og Avertissements-Tidende*, 1871, no. 212 (September 6); *Dagbladet*, 1871, no. 215 (September 6); *Bergens Adressecontoirs Efterretninger*, 1871, no. 220 (September 18); *Dagbladet*, 1871, no. 232 (September 26); *Dagbladet*, 1871, no. 233 (September 27); *Dagbladet*, 1871, no. 233 (September 27); *Dagbladet*, 1871, no. 234 (September 28); *Folkets Avis*, 1871, no. 234 (September 28). See also Hans Friedrich Helveg, "Om Ankerne over det Nordiske Kirkemøde," *Dansk Kirketidende*, 1871, no. 42 (October 15), columns 659-666; "Gammel- og Ny-Rationalisme," *Dansk Kirketidende*, 1876, no. 37 (September 17), columns 601-610; Niels Lindberg, [On Eiríksson at the "Nordiske Kirkemøde" (1871)], *Dansk Kirketidende*, 1871, no. 36 (September 10), columns 565-576 (No. 36) and nos. 38-39 (September 24), columns 593-624; M. Chr. Levinssøn, *Magnus Eirikssons "Restancer" i "Folkets Avis" og paa det nordiske Kirkemøde*, Copenhagen: no publisher given 1872; as well as the tendentious and quite dramatized report of Eiríksson's speech and the audience's reaction by Matthías Jochumsson, "Dvöl mín í Danmörku 1871-1872," *Iðunn*, vol. 1, 1916, no. 3 (January), pp. 258-265.

adduced. Eiríksson's intensive preoccupation not least with the works of the leading figures of the (new) Tübingen school of theology—particularly its founder and doyen Ferdinand Christian Baur (1792-1860) and Baur's radical follower, David Friedrich Strauss (1808-74)—as well as with the "the epoch-making pioneer of historical criticism"[1] in the field of Pentateuchal studies, Wilhelm Martin Leberecht de Wette (1780-1849), no doubt had a catalytic influence on this decisive change in Eiríksson's understanding of the Bible.[2] (It should be noted, however, that these figures' various motivations and outlooks were by no means simply congruent with Eiríksson's own effort, in his late work, to undertake his own "historical-critical" approach to the Biblical writings.)[3] Eiríksson's consistent self-understanding, as he expressed it ever more clearly in his later writings, is that of a reformer. "A reformation of the church must begin," he wrote, "a thorough reform of the prevailing religious ideas."[4] The aim of this reform should be a new, "rational religion," marked

---

1 As acknowledged by Julius Wellhausen, *Prolegomena to the History of Israel*, trans. by J. Sutherland Black and Allan Menzies, Edinburgh: Adam & Charles Black 1885, p. 4.

2 See "Min Forfattervirksomhed," p. 100, where Eiríksson writes about his period of literary silence as follows: "During this period I came to know many important things—partly through my own efforts and thought, and partly through certain books, that I had previously had neither the time or nor the motivation to become acquainted with." See also *Om Baptister og Barnedaab*, p. VII, as well as *Jøder og Christne*, p. [II]. According to the auction catalogue of Eiríksson's library (see *Fortegnelse over endel forskjellige gode og velconditionerede Bogsamlinger*, pp. 138-170), Eiríksson's library contained works by Ferdinand Christian Baur (1792-1860; see catalogue nos. 432-438); Wilhelm Martin Leberecht de Wette (1780-1849, nos. 944-952 as well as *Tro, Overtro og Vantro*, p. 48 (note)); David Friedrich Strauss (1808-74; nos. 798-803); Eduard Gottlob Zeller (1814-1908; no. 960); Carl Franz Albert Schwegler (1819-57; nos. 778-779) and Adolf Hilgenfeld (1823-1907; no. 564).

3 Hermann Heinrich Louis Schwanenflügel, "Magnus Eirikson," [sic!] *Det nittende Aarhundrede. Maanedskrift for Literatur og Kritik*, vols. 1-6, ed. by Georg Brandes and Edvard Brandes, Copenhagen: Gyldendal 1875-77; vol. 6, 1877, pp. 266-294, emphasizes the following main differences between Eiríksson and the Tübingen school: first, Eiríksson "lacked almost all of the Tübingen thinkers' historical apparatus"; second, whereas the Tübingen thinkers undertook "the *scholarly* task" of detecting the various phases of development in the early Christian Church, Eiríksson sought to dispatch "the *religious* task" of excising everything from the New Testament "that conflicted with his understanding of God and Christ" (p. 287).

4 Eiríksson, *Gud og Reformatoren*, p. XV and p. III; see also pp. III-VIII, pp. XII-XIV and pp. XXIX-XXXII.

through and through by a positively understood "simple-mindedness" and "love of one's neighbor."[1]

On the other hand, Hafsteinn Pjetursson (1858-1929) emphasizes the (literally) "fundamental" significance of Eiríksson's dream visions for the development of his religious outlook. As early as July 1844, Eiríksson had a dream that he reported in an unpublished manuscript on dream visions[2] as follows:

> It seemed to me that I was in *Frue Kirke* [Our Lady's Church] (where I saw only a few people). I was near the altar, facing it. Then I became aware of an enormous pillar to the left of the altar...[which] reached to the church's dome and seemed to abut it. I gazed at the pillar in greatest astonishment, for I remembered quite clearly that I had never seen it before. While I stood there, gazing at the pillar, it became detached from the dome, sank lower and lower, and—when it was no more than 3½ to 4 ells [7 to 8 ft.] in height—it became transformed into a human figure. Then I saw that this human figure was the same image of Christ as the one that stands above the altar in *Frue Kirke* (and at the same time I observed that the image was not there)....Now this white marble figure moved, walked a few paces along the floor, and then turned round to face the altar...and laid down, face forward, at 3 to 4 ells' [6 to 8 ft.] distance from the altar.[3]

---

1 See Magnús Eiríksson, *Kunne vi elske Næsten som os selv? Nogle tildeels nye Tanker om Kjærligheden samt flere derhen hørende Skriftsteder*, Copenhagen: Magnús Eiríksson 1870, pp. 45-48 and pp. 114f.; *Gud og Reformatoren*, p. XVI (note), p. XIX (note), p. 26, p. 59, pp. 70-72, p. 79, pp. 102-104, p. 111 and p. 134; *Paulus og Christus eller Pauli Lære om Retfærdiggjørelsen sammenlignet med Christi Lære om Syndsforladelsen, tilligemed nogle Bemærkninger om andre paulinske Lærdomme m. M.*, Copenhagen: Magnús Eiríksson 1871, pp. XXIX-XXX; *Jøder og Christne eller Hvorledes blev Jesus fra Nazareth betragtet i den ældste Kirke og hvorledes blev han senere betragtet? En populær, historisk-kritisk Undersøgelse, tilegnet de Sandhedskjærlige*, Copenhagen: Magnús Eiríksson 1873, p. 88, p. 93, p. 95, p. 105, p. 251, p. 255, p. 261, pp. 268f., pp. 299-302 and p. 309.

2 Department of Manuscripts at The National and University Library of Iceland, ÍB. 479, 4to (ID 6627). See the extracts from the 4th of the 13 dream visions in Hafsteinn Pjetursson, "Magnús Eiríksson," *Teologisk Tidsskrift for den danske Folkekirke*, Ny Række, vol. 3, 1901-1902, pp. 116-143; here pp. 129f. (compare also Hafsteinn Pjetursson, "Magnús Eiríksson," *Tímarit hins íslenska bókmenntafjélags*, vol. 8, 1887, pp. 1-33; here pp. 16-18).

3 ÍB. 479, 4to, Leaf 8, pp. [2-3]; compare Pjetursson, "Magnús Eiríksson" (1901-02), pp. 129f.

Around thirteen months later, on August 1, 1845, Eiríksson dreamed the same dream again, with the following crucial addition: "As the figure of Christ walked along the floor and turned round to the altar and laid down, I heard a voice (but saw no one) saying to me: 'The pillar, you see, denotes the disfiguration [*Vanskabning*] that the Church has made of Christ; he himself wants to show you that he worships God; *but no one who worships God is God*.'"[1]

At this point, a detailed analysis of the reasons and factors for this fundamental change in Eiríksson's theological stance would lead too far afield. What is crucial here is that it cannot truly be said that Eiríksson (first) underwent "his major, spiritual crisis" during his period of literary silence.[2] It is rather the case that Eiríksson's understanding of the Bible changed decisively during this period; and *this* change now made it possible for him to continue to intensify his preexisting critical stance, already long-hardened, toward (certain elements of) the Church's dogmatic teachings, and finally to break with them completely. This change of his own standpoint led Eiríksson to change the focus of his attention as well, turning not only to other problem areas in theology, but to other theological opponents as well.[3] As we remarked at

---

1 ÍB. 479, 4to, Leaf 9, p. [1] (the words reproduced in italics are double underlined in the original manuscript); compare Pjetursson, "Magnús Eiríksson" (1901-02), p. 130.

2 Vodskov, *Spredte Studier*, p. 37; see also Emanuel Skjoldager, "An Unwanted Ally: Magnus Eiriksson," in *Kierkegaaard as a Person*, ed. by Niels Thulstrup and Marie Mikulová Thulstrup, Copenhagen: C.A. Reitzel 1983 (*Bibliotheca Kierkegaardiana*, vol. 12), pp. 102-108, here p. 104: "In these years [1850-63] he went through a spiritual crisis, in the course of which he claimed to have received a special revelation. This made him claim subsequently that some of the supremely important truths about the major doctrines of Christianity he had got not from any man, but by the gracious aid of God and his spirit." Julia Watkin, "Eiríksson, Magnus," in her *Historical Dictionary of Kierkegaard's Philosophy*, Lanham and London: Scarecrow Press 2001, pp. 69-72, even states that "[t]he years 1850-63 were a period of spiritual crisis for him [sc. Eiríksson], and it is in this period that he claimed to have experienced visions in which *God* directly revealed to him the *truth* concerning major Christian doctrines" (p. 70). See, contrary to these interpretations, Pjetursson, "Magnús Eiríksson," p. 128.

3 To name three examples: (1) Eiríksson's pamphlet *Nokkrar athugasemdir um Sannanir "katólsku prestanna í Reykjavík" fyrir guðdómi Jesú Krists*, Copenhagen: Louis Klein 1868 was directed primarily against the French Catholic priest Jean-Baptiste Baudoin (1831-75), who was—together with Bernard Bernard (1821-95)—the first Catholic priest to serve in Iceland after the Reformation. Specifically, it is a reply to Baudoin's accusations against Eiríksson (sparked by the latter's denial that Jesus Christ was God) in the anonymously published pamphlet *Jesús Kristr er Guð. Þrátt fyrir mótmæli*

the beginning of this section, after 1851 Eiríksson refers to Martensen mostly peripherally. Yet there are *three important exceptions*:

1. In the midst of his period of "literary silence," Eiríksson published an article entitled "Yet Another Contribution to the Debate: Dr. S. Kierkegaard *contra* Bishop Martensen" (1855).[1] The occasion for and focus of this article was Martensen's momentous address at the memorial service for Bishop Mynster, held in Christiansborg Slotskirke on February 5, 1854, during which Martensen referred to Mynster as a "witness to the truth."[2] This declaration elicited a vigorous protest from

---

herra Magnúsar Eiríkssonar, Reykjavík: Hinir katólsku prestar í Reykjavík 1867. To this dispute between Eiríksson and Baudoin see also the intervention made by Jónas Guðmundsson, *Hvaða trú hafa hinir svo nefndu kath. prestar, eptir því sem þeir koma fram í riti sínu, Jesús Kristur er guð, þrátt fyrir mótmæli hr. Magnúsar Eiríkssonar?*, Reykjavík: Einar Þórðarson 1867, which prompted Baudoin, in turn, to publish anonymously a pamphlet entitled *Er það satt eðr ósatt, sem hra Jónas Guðmundsson segir um bækling vorn: "Jesús Kristr er Guð" o. s. frv.?*, Reykjavík: Einar Þórðarson 1867. For a more detailed account of this quarrel, see the articles by Gudmundur Bjorn Thorbjornsson as well as by Vilhjálmur Árnason and Jón Bragi Pálsson in the present volume. (2) Eiríksson's treatise *Om Bønnens Virkning og dens Forhold til Guds Uforanderlighed. Nogle Oplysninger og Bemærkninger, nærmest byggede paa andelig Erfaring og et umiddelbart Gudsforhold*, Copenhagen: Magnús Eiríksson 1870, was prompted by and addressed to the left-Hegelian philosopher Hans Brøchner (1820-75) and his book *Problemet om Tro og Viden. En historisk-kritisk Afhandling*, Copenhagen: P.G. Philipsen 1868. (3) Eiríksson's pamphlet *Herr A. Pedrin og Christendommen. Nogle Oplysninger om hans Skrift: "Vor Herres og Frelsers Jesu Christi nye Testament og Magnus Eirikssons reformeerte Jødedom,"* Copenhagen: no publisher given 1874—his last independent publication—was provoked by and directed against the religious author Andreas Daniel Pedrin (1823-91) and his pamphlet *Vor Herres og Frelsers Jesu Christi nye Testament og Magnus Eirikssons reformeerte Jødedom*, Copenhagen: no publisher given 1874.

[1] Magnús Eiríksson, "Endnu et Indlæg i Sagen: Dr. S. Kierkegaard contra Biskop Martensen m. Fl.," *Kongeriget Danmarks Avertissements-Tidende*, 1855, no. 82 (April 10), columns 16f.; no. 83 (April 11), columns 16f.; no. 84 (April 12), columns 16f.; no. 85 (April 13), columns 16f.; no. 86 (April 14), column 16; no. 89 (April 18), column 16; no. 91 (April 20), columns 16f.; no. 92 (April 21), column 16; no. 93 (April 23), column 16.

[2] Hans Lassen Martensen, *Prædiken holdt i Christiansborg Slotskirke paa 5te Søndag efter Hellig Tre Konger, Søndagen før Biskop Mynsters Jordefærd*, Copenhagen: C.A. Reitzel 1854, see especially pp. 5f. See also Martensen's explanation of his use of the phrase "witness to the truth" as applied to Mynster in his memoirs *From My Life*: "I do not intend to make the least excuse for this term—as though it were less than proper, or something that ought to be retracted. I would use the same term today. When taken in the right sense—that is, in context—my expression was completely proper. But S. Kierkegaard had the dishonesty and the effrontery to tear it out of context, to take it to an extreme, and to assign to the term 'witness to the truth' the meaning 'blood witness'

Kierkegaard, which marked the opening of Kierkegaard's vitriolic attack on the Danish State Church during the last year of his life.[1]

Eiríksson's response to this opens by harshly criticizing Martensen's eulogy. He goes so far as to compare Martensen to the Jewish high priest Caiaphas, who according to the Gospels of Matthew and John was involved in the trial of Jesus. On Eiríksson's account, both Martensen and Caiaphas misunderstood the needs and demands of their times. Both tried to shore up and glorify the existing state of things—Caiaphas, by seeking to shunt Jesus aside and nullify his actions; and Martensen, in exalting Mynster and dubbing him a "witness to the truth." Yet just as Caiaphas' actions led only to the opposite of what he had planned, so too Martensen's efforts to maintain the *status quo* served only to demonstrate that "the existing religious situation" was necessarily in need of change.[2]

In order to be a witness to the truth and to deserve that title rightfully, one must—according to Eiríksson—"(1)…seek the truth with sincerity and candor, without regard for earthly advantages, and only in this manner come to awareness of the truth; (2) pronounce, promulgate, and preach the truth that one has come to know…; (3) practice [this]

---

or 'martyr.' Naturally, neither I nor anyone else had had this in mind. I had included Mynster among the Christian witnesses to the truth because my sermon emphasized his importance to our fatherland, the desolate times in which he appeared, his battle against unbelief and rationalism, and how he had reintroduced the Gospel into many hearts. Anyone who carefully considers the concept of a witness to the truth must come to the realization that the main thing is that a person so characterized must have witnesses to *the truth*, but that suffering and persecution are in no way a sure sign of a witness to the truth, because fanatics and false teachers have also often been subjected to great suffering and have become martyrs. Furthermore, external suffering and martyrdom belong to certain historical epochs and presuppose particular social conditions and circumstances; they cannot appear during all epochs, while witnesses to the truth may be found at all times and under all social conditions" (Martensen, *Af mit Levnet*, vol. 3, pp. 14f.; quoted in translation by Thompson, *Following the Cultured Public's Chosen One*, p. 82).

1 Kierkegaard's initial article in *Fædrelandet* 1854, no. 295 (December 18) was entitled: "Var Biskop Mynster et 'Sandhedsvidne,' et af 'de rette Sandhedsvidner'—er *dette Sandhed*?" ("Was Bishop Mynster a 'Witness to the Truth,' One of 'the Proper Witnesses to the Truth'—Is *This the truth*?"), see *SKS* 14, 123-126 / *M*, 3-8. Apart from one initial reply to Kierkegaard in the newspaper *Berlingske Tidende*, 1854, December 28, Martensen, who had been appointed to the Bishop of Zealand on April 15, 1854, remained silent throughout Kierkegaard's attack.

2 Eiríksson, "Endnu et Indlæg," no. 82 (April 10, 1855), column 16.

truth in one's life."[1] Following a detailed effort to substantiate and elaborate these "essential requirements" for a witness to the truth, and to consider their applicability to the case of Mynster, Eiríksson arrives at the conclusion that Mynster cannot possibly have been a witness to the truth. It follows that Kierkegaard, in his conflict with Martensen, had "the truth on his side," even if he had carried "the matter to extremes."[2] At the end of his article, Eiríksson adds a personal note making it clear that he has "never" stood in any "relation of duty to or dependence on" Kierkegaard.[3] His reason for writing this article is impersonal in every way and is essentially as follows: "Dr. theol. Bishop Martensen had brutally assaulted the Christian truth, but Dr. S. Kierkegaard had protested against this; and now I felt myself summoned, obligated, and justified in supporting Kierkegaard's protest, and showing that it was justified, in my own way and from my own standpoint."[4]

2. The second important locus in Eiríksson's late writings in which he engaged in an extensive polemic against Martensen is found in the book *Who is Right—the Grundtvigians or Their Opponents? And What Did Christ Command About Baptism?* (1863).[5] The backdrop to this book is the opposition between N.F.S. Grundtvig and his followers, on the one hand, and the "Scriptural theologians"—chiefly H.N. Clausen and Martensen as well—on the other, an opposition that had been smoldering since the mid-1850s, and came to open blows in 1863.[6] The real core of this debate was the question of the origin of the Apostles' Creed. Whereas according to Grundtvig's so-called "ecclesiastical view" (in its mature form),[7] "the living word" of the *Symbolum Apostolicum* as

---

1 Ibid., no. 83 (April 11, 1855), column 16.

2 Ibid., no. 86 (April 14, 1855), column 16.

3 Ibid., no. 93 (April 23, 1855), column 16.

4 Ibid.

5 Magnús Eiríksson, *Hvem har Ret: Grundtvigianerne eller deres Modstandere? og Hvad har Christus befalet om Daaben? Nogle orienterende Bemærkninger*, Copenhagen: E.L. Thaarup 1863.

6 For a more detailed illustration of Martensen's role in this discussion, see Arildsen, *Biskop Hans Lassen Martensen*, pp. 302-324, especially pp. 307-316.

7 For an account of the development of Grundtvig's "ecclesiastical view" with regard to his idea of "the living word," which underwent several modifications or enhancements, see the commentaries (to Kierkegaard's journal entries NB15:53 and NB26:109) written by Niels Jørgen Cappelørn in *SKS* K23, 80f., and *SKS* K25, 118-120. The concrete occasion for Martensen's critical statement against Grundtvig's "ecclesiastical

the *articulus stantis et cadentis* of Grundtvig's ecclesiology was conveyed to the Apostles entirely and completely by Christ *himself*, Martensen sought to show, in his *In Defense of the So-called Grundtvigianism* (1863),[1] that Grundtvig's position is not only controversial on dogmatic and practical-theological grounds, but is also *historically* problematic. It has no historical evidence to rely on, Martensen wrote, and is instead a postulatory "*a priori* construction" with no real presence in the history of the Church.[2]

Like Martensen, Eiríksson similarly dismisses Grundtvig's idea of "the living word" as "pure fantasy,"[3] since the Apostles' Creed could never have originated in Christ himself. Yet the same holds also for the Trinitarian command of baptism at Matthew 28:19, which means in turn that baptism itself, as not instituted by Christ, also cannot be a sacrament.[4] However, with regard to the relation between Apostolic Christianity and subsequent developments in the history of the Church,

---

view" (see the following note) was the latter's article "Lys-Ordet og Livs-Ordet i Vorherre Jesu Christi Menighed," *Dansk Kirketidende*, 1863, no. 22 (May 24), columns 347-358, which was published together with Grundtvig's poem "Guds-Ordet til os," ibid., columns 345f. On this see also Gerhard Schreiber, *Apriorische Gewissheit. Das Glaubensverständnis des jungen Kierkegaard und seine philosophisch-theologischen Voraussetzungen*, Berlin and Boston: De Gruyter 2014 (*Kierkegaard Studies Monograph Series*, vol. 30), pp. 47-49.

1 Hans Lassen Martensen, *Til Forsvar mod den saakaldte Grundtvigianisme*, Copenhagen: Gyldendal 1863, especially pp. 7ff.; see also "Uklare Forsøg paa at omdanne Reformationen" in Martensen's *Katholicisme og Protestantisme. Et Leilighedsskrift*, Copenhagen: Gyldendal 1874, pp. 161-187, especially pp. 164ff., where he offers a brief summary of his thoughts. Grundtvig's reaction to Martensen's 1863 book, which marks the latter's ultimate break with Grundtvig's "ecclesiastical view," consists of his three poems "Livet og Dogmatiken," *Dansk Kirketidende*, no. 44, October 25, 1863, columns 701-703; "Guds 'Hvad' og 'Hvorledes,' " ibid., columns 703f.; and "Livs-Ordet til os af Jesu Mund," ibid., columns 705f.

2 Martensen, *Til Forsvar mod den saakaldte Grundtvigianisme*, p. 47.

3 Eiríksson, *Hvem har Ret: Grundtvigianerne eller deres Modstandere?*, p. 19.

4 Here it is plainly visible just how significantly changed and radicalized the later Eiríksson's position has become. See, for example, Eiríksson, *Om Baptister og Barnedaab*, from 1844 (see Section I), where Jesus' command of baptism at Matthew 28:18-20 is construed simply as indicating that the practice of *infant* baptism was neither commanded by Jesus nor of apostolic origin; see ibid., p. 237, p. 290 (no. 3) and pp. 443-445. Thus *infant* baptism is not to be considered as a sacrament and—since it was introduced much later into the Church and possesses only "ecclesiastical authority" (p. 539)—should be replaced with a purely formal "church induction ceremony" or "upbuilding ceremony" (p. 540; see also pp. 307f.).

as they were given dogmatic expression in the Nicene Creed (325 AD) and the Chalcedonian Creed (451 AD), Eiríksson finds himself in full agreement with the critical attitude of Grundtvig and his followers toward those later articulations of Christianity. Yet the Grundtvigians quickly fall into self-contradiction, Eiríksson writes, when they nonetheless seek to retain teachings contained in the later creeds that they themselves criticize. In Eiríksson's view, this is because they have failed to recognize the "main reason" *why* these later creeds deserve rejection. In sharp opposition to Martensen's claim that both the Nicene Creed and the Chalcedonian Creed "are merely interpretations and more precisely explanations" of the earlier Apostles' Creed,[1] Eiríksson points out that the later Creeds "contain...entirely different teachings about the essence and the person of Jesus Christ than the Apostles' Creed,"[2] inasmuch as they transform the human being Jesus of Nazareth, the Messiah, into an eternal divine Person. Whereas Martensen treats Church history in the manner of a good Hegelian speculative thinker, namely, as "the great process of appropriation of Christian revelation,"[3] Eiríksson treats the development of the Church in the post-Apostolic age not as a process of the "self-revelation" of Christian truth, but precisely—and here one is reminded of the description by Franz Camille Overbeck (1837-1905) of the descent from "original Christianity" into "historical Christianity"; or of the later account by Adolf von Harnack (1851-1930) of "non-dogmatic Christianity"—as a process of alienation from and renunciation of Christianity.

3. That the latter process of alienation and renunciation represents a fatal aberration, as a result of which the true religion—that is, faith in the *single* true God—was increasingly falsified, is the thesis of Eiríksson's book *God and the Reformer: A Religious Idea* (1866).[4] This text marks the third and last noteworthy polemic against Martensen in Eiríksson's later writings. According to *God and the Reformer*, the falsification of the true belief in God took place in *three steps*. First, impressions of a certain *human*

1 Martensen, *Til Forsvar mod den saakaldte Grundtvigianisme*, p. 48.
2 Eiríksson, *Hvem har Ret: Grundtvigianerne eller deres Modstandere?*, p. 26.
3 Martensen, *Til Forsvar mod den saakaldte Grundtvigianisme*, p. 79.
4 Magnús Eiríksson, *Gud og Reformatoren. En religiøs Idee. Samt nogle Bemærkninger om de kirkelige Tilstande, Dr. S. Kierkegaard og Forfatteren*, Copenhagen: J.H. Schubothe 1866.

being, who was simply a "founder of a religion" or "reformer," came to be commingled with impressions of *God*. Next, the manifold impressions of this "founder" led to numerous discussions and disputes, which detracted attention from God and from the inner, immediate relation to him.[1] In the third and final step, the falsification of religion became complete as the "founder" or "reformer" came to be seen as "the incarnation" of God Himself. In this process, the one true God promulgated by the "founder" or "reformer" is suppressed; in its place, "a poisonous seed is planted in the field of religion," a seed which will sooner or later grow to destroy the religion utterly.[2] According to Eiríksson, as the doctrine of the Incarnation came to be the central constitutive element of the Church's edifice of teachings, the authentic and true religion was transformed into a "poisonous snake."[3] Yet whereas the snake in the Biblical Garden of Eden corrupted the first human beings by promising that they would become like God *merely* in the sense of gaining the *knowledge* of good and evil, Church theologians like Martensen have gone further than the snake, Eiríksson charged, inasmuch as, "by means of the Incarnation of God," they have proclaimed and established "the *essential* unity of God and humanity."[4]

Inasmuch as recent theological speculation has carried this "snake theology" to its utmost extreme, Eiríksson continues, it has unwittingly "unmask[ed]" the "poisonous snake" that had concealed itself for centuries under religion's surface.[5] By introducing theological speculation to Denmark, Martensen has done "an important service" to the religion, particularly inasmuch as Martensenian speculative theology led straightforwardly to the "deification of humanity," and indeed embodied this deification "in its innermost essence."[6] Yet this last fact was simply overlooked, or ignored, in Denmark. Even Kierkegaard failed to acknowledge the falsifications of Church doctrine in the later creeds. In fact, Eiríksson argues, Kierkegaard cited the doctrine of the Incarnation as the basis for his entirely false notion of faith as "by virtue

1 See ibid., pp. 30-33 and pp. 44-48.
2 Ibid., p. 56; see also pp. 54-59 and pp. 147-150.
3 Ibid., p. 59.
4 Ibid., p. 61 (emphases removed and emphasis added); see also pp. 60f., where Eiríksson refers to Martensen's *Grundrids til Moralphilosophiens System*, pp. 51-55 (§§ 49-50).
5 Ibid., pp. 62f.
6 Ibid., p. 65; see also pp. 65f. (note) as well as p. 34 (note) and p. 52 (note).

of the absurd."[1] Yet just as the main concern of Eiríksson's treatise was the relation between God as religion's object and the "founder of the religion" or "reformer," Eiríksson sought to show that the words of the "founder" are to be used with "judiciousness and caution," for the authenticity of these words can be established only "spiritually."[2] We thus arrive at the result "that a founder of a religion or reformer must, as much as possible, be confined outside the religious relationship that arises between God and the individual human being." Thus religion, if it is not to perish with the passage of time—must "be freed...from this all-consuming and slowly fatal poison that is the Incarnation and the doctrine of the Incarnation."[3]

With this last statement—to the effect that religion must be freed not only from the *doctrine* of the Incarnation, but from the Incarnation *itself*—the path was cleared for the increasing radicalization of Eiríksson's critique, both of the Bible and of the Church's dogmatic tradition. This process reached its climax in his book *Jews and Christians, or How Was Jesus of Nazareth Regarded in the Oldest Church, and How Was He Regarded Later? A Popular, Historical-Critical Investigation, Dedicated to the Lovers of Truth* (1873).[4] Here Eiríksson attempts to provide "historical-critical" grounding for a view that he had presented as a mere "religious idea" in *God and the Reformer*, namely, that Jesus of Nazareth was in reality not

---

1 For further critical remarks on Kierkegaard, see Eiríksson, *Gud og Reformatoren*, pp. 66-112, especially pp. 80-104. After he once more criticizes Kierkegaard's "dialectical tumbling with concepts," his conceptual exaggerations at the expense of the truth, Eiríksson adds the following note: "The late Dr. *S. Kierkegaard* once admitted as much to me in a private conversation, after I had expressed my opposition to his conception of faith as 'by virtue of the absurd,' that he had indeed pushed the point to extremes" (p. 102 (note)). Although Eiríksson seeks to show the radical contradictions and errors of Kierkegaard's account, he by no means wishes to "belittle Dr. S. Kierkegaard's real merits" (p. 107). This same criticism of Kierkegaard's conception of faith is found in *Er Troen et Paradox og "i Kraft af det Absurde"?*, pp. 175-80.

2 Eiríksson, *Gud og Reformatoren*, pp. 112f. Just as he had already done in his *Hvem har Ret: Grundtvigianerne eller deres Modstandere?*, Eiríksson subsequently offers a thorough account of why the Trinitarian command of baptism at Matthew 28:19 cannot have been issued by Christ himself, and hence that baptism cannot be a sacrament. See Eiríksson, *Gud og Reformatoren*, pp. 114-27.

3 Ibid., pp. 146f.

4 Magnús Eiríksson, *Jøder og Christne eller Hvorledes blev Jesus fra Nazareth betragtet i den ældste Kirke og hvorledes blev han senere betragtet? En populær, historisk-kritisk Undersøgelse, tilegnet de Sandhedskjærlige*, Copenhagen: Magnús Eiríksson 1873.

God, but only a reformer of Old Testament Judaism. In Eiríksson's view, Jesus understood himself as "God's servant and the Jews' reformer."[1] It never occurred to him to represent himself as God:

> Jesus Christ did not appear in order to teach a new religion or to discover multiple divine persons in the single, eternal, infinitely divine being. He appeared only in order to give the Jewish religion...a greater inwardness and spirituality. He came in order to teach human beings to worship God in spirit and in truth.[2]

Inasmuch as Jesus' followers considered him only to be "the Messiah," their "Christianity" was in reality only a "reformed Judaism."[3] Echoing *God and the Reformer*, Eiríksson here similarly claims that a ruthless process of falsifying the "original Apostolic doctrine" of Jesus commenced at the end of the second century, reaching its climax in 325 AD, when the Council of Nicaea confirmed the divinity of Christ as Church dogma.[4]

When Eiríksson sent a copy of *Jews and Christians* (1873) to Martensen, he attached an imploring letter soliciting an appraisal of the book. Martensen responded with a cool rebuff. At the close of his letter of reply, Martensen expressed his wish, "in all sincerity," that "the Lord enlighten you and lead you to recognize the Truth!"[5]

---

1 Ibid., p. 24; see also pp. 24-32.
2 Ibid., p. 254.
3 Ibid., p. 249.
4 See ibid., pp. 249-57.
5 This letter from Martensen to Eiríksson is reprinted in Pjetursson, "Magnús Eiríksson," pp. 137f. See also Martensen's letter to Gude of April 21, 1873, in *Biskop H. Martensens Breve*, vol. 3, p. 75 (no. 360): "Now M. Eiriksen [sic!] has sent me a new book, *Jews and Christians*, along with a long letter in which he adjures me, by the judgment seat of God and the Truth, to enter into a debate with him. I am at present engaged in formulating a discouraging answer. And yet it would be even less appropriate to let his letter rest entirely unanswered."

VI. On the Utility and Futility of Any Theological Discussion with Eiríksson

In his late retrospective account of his work, "My Activity as an Author" (1875), Eiríksson assesses the curious behavior—the effort to "hush up" his writings—exhibited by his theological adversaries. Eiríksson ascribes this behavior to a "fear" of those writings.[1] Whether this interpretation is justified or not, Martensen's continuing silence in the face of Eiríksson's attacks is certainly regrettable. Martensen thereby lost the opportunity not only for any possible dialogue with Eiríksson, but also for any further specification and clarification of his own position against a line of criticism that was in part fully comprehensible and justified. In the words of Skat Arildsen:

> After all, Martensen's work offers rich materials for an eager critic and vicious polemicist to work with, especially one after Eiríksson's mold. Eiríksson rightly protests against Martensen's terminology, which was often indefinite, unclear, and not infrequently self-contradictory, and against his thoroughgoing but all too easily achieved mediations—however dexterous Martensen's dialectical game made itself seem, and however strong an impression his eloquent style made.[2]

Martensen's refusal to participate in *any* substantive debate with Eiríksson became explicit in both of the two sole points in his writings at which Eiríksson is addressed. In Martensen's 1844 newspaper article "Literary Abuse," which Eiríksson later ridiculed as "pitiable,"[3] Martensen merely condemned Eiríksson's "preprinting" of his lectures on "Speculative Dogmatics" (1838-39). He did not reply to Eiríksson's critique of his account of baptism—not even to the charge, by all accounts justified, of an inconsistency between Martensen's university lectures and his 1843 book *Christian Baptism* on the relation between faith and baptism. Nor did he respond in any way to Eiríksson's accusation—his most central allegation—that speculative theology as such leads to the "self-deification" of humanity.

---

1 Eiríksson, "Min Forfattervirksomhed," p. 81.
2 Arildsen, *Biskop Hans Lassen Martensen*, p. 210.
3 Eiríksson, *Dr. Martensens trykte moralske Paragrapher*, p. [I].

Martensen's reaction to Eiríksson's unauthorized preprint of parts of his dogmatic lectures can arguably be explained by appeal to Martensen's own intellectual development.[1] Without going into details,[2] it can be concluded that a decisive turning-point in Martensen's theological development—Stewart even speaks of "a crisis"[3]—took place in the years after 1842. The reason for this was the rising strength of Left-Hegelianism in Denmark, in light of which Martensen felt compelled to modify his position in order to distance himself publicly from Hegelianism.[4] At the latest in the wake of the so-called "examination scandal,"[5] caused by the left-Hegelian philosopher Hans Brøchner (1820-75)[6]—the translator of D.F. Strauss' *The Christian Doctrine Depicted in Its Historical Development and in Its Struggle with Modern Science* (1840-41)[7] into Danish[8]—Martensen had started revising his earlier lectures on dogmatics. The (revised) lectures never appeared in print as such; instead, it was only in 1849 that they were absorbed into, and published in the form of, Martensen's *Christian Dogmatics*. His sharp condemnation of Eiríksson's

---

1 As stated above (see pp. 71f. above, note 7), aside from the foreword to the second edition of his *Den christelige Daab* (1847) and the newspaper article against Eiríksson (1844, see p. 70 above, note 1), Martensen produced no further writings between late 1843 and the middle of 1849.

2 On this see Curtis L. Thompson, "Introduction," in *Between Hegel and Kierkegaard*, pp. 22-40; Jon Stewart, "Kierkegaard and Hegelianism in Golden Age Denmark," in *Kierkegaard and His Contemporaries: The Culture of Golden Age Denmark*, pp. 106-45, here pp. 119-23; Stewart, *Kierkegaard's Relations to Hegel Reconsidered*, pp. 61f.; Stewart, *The Martensen Period: 1837-1842*, pp. 705-10.

3 Stewart, *Kierkegaard's Relations to Hegel Reconsidered*, p. 61.

4 See especially Martensen, "Nutidens religiøse Crisis," pp. 55ff., together with Stewart, *Kierkegaard's Relations to Hegel Reconsidered*, pp. 140f.

5 Jens Holger Schjørring, "Martensen," in *Kierkegaard's Teachers*, ed. by Niels Thulstrup and Marie Mikulová Thulstrup (*Bibliotheca Kierkegaardiana*, vol. 10), Copenhagen: C.A. Reitzel 1982, pp. 177-207; here p. 192. See also Stewart, *Kierkegaard's Relations to Hegel Reconsidered*, pp. 140f.

6 See Harald Høffding, "Hans Brøchner," in his *Danske Filosofer*, Copenhagen: Gyldendalske Boghandel, Nordisk Forlag 1909, pp. 196-206; Svend Valdemar Rasmussen, *Den unge Brøchner*, Copenhagen: Gyldendal 1966, pp. 16-31; Schjørring, "Martensen," pp. 191-95.

7 David Friedrich Strauss, *Die christliche Glaubenslehre in ihrer geschichtlichen Entwicklung und im Kampfe mit der modernen Wissenschaft dargestellt*, vols. 1-2, Tübingen: C.F. Osiander and Stuttgart: F.H. Köhler 1840-41.

8 David Friedrich Strauss, *Fremstilling af den christelige Troeslære i dens historiske Udvikling og i dens Kamp med den moderne Videnskab*, trans. by Hans Brøchner, vols. 1-2, Copenhagen: H.C. Klein 1842-43.

preprinting of these lectures can thus (also) be traced back to the fact that, ever since delivering these lectures, Martensen's dogmatic-theological stance had been in constant flux, and indeed had transcended his earlier position.

Still more marked is the reluctance to engage in theological debate with Eiríksson that Martensen exhibited in his 1850 book *Dogmatic Elucidations*. Here Martensen, in his Preface, had singled out Eiríksson for mention as one who, unlike his other critics, had "wanted to test the doctrines himself."[1] But then he went on to respond exclusively to the criticisms of Nielsen and Paludan-Müller. Martensen justified this approach by claiming that it was Nielsen and Paludan-Müller who "have roused the most attention, relatively speaking, in the public interested in [the] present issue."[2] Here again Martensen lost an opportunity to clarify his doctrine of the Trinity by demonstrating that the distinction it draws between an "essential Trinity" and an "economic Trinity" does not lead, as Eiríksson claims, to a reduplication of the persons of the Trinity, that is, to "a double Trinity."

If Martensen's dismissal of the very possibility of a debate with Eiríksson is regrettable,[3] and if Eiríksson's annoyance and displeasure with Martensen's "lofty silence" is quite understandable, we should nonetheless ask whether it would actually have made sense for Martensen to involve himself directly in a quarrel with Eiríksson. Could such involvement have led to a fruitful and productive dialogue? Would a genuine exchange of views have been possible in this case? I see reason for skepticism on this point. For the same polemical intensity with which Eiríksson—the

---

1 Martensen, *Dogmatiske Oplysninger*, p. 4.

2 Ibid., p. 8.

3 On this see Kierkegaard's draft, entitled "Self-Defense Against Unauthorized Acknowledgment" (*Pap.* VII-1 B 88, pp. 287-298 / *CUP2*, 127-137) in which he (as Climacus) protests vehemently against Eiríksson's praise of Kierkegaard's writings as an excellent critique of Martensen's theology. Climacus grants that Eiríksson's effort to remove Martensen from his post was indubitably "well intentioned," and that Eiríksson exhibited the necessary "passion," which now, however, has risen to a "fanatic bad temper" (*Pap.* VII-1 B 88, p. 290 / *CUP2*, 130). Alluding to Martensen's continuing silence in spite of Eiríksson's attacks, Climacus notes mockingly that the one thing Eiríksson needs is an opponent. One person *alone* is not enough for a dispute between *two*. And so it makes no sense for Eiríksson to attempt to draw Climacus over to his side, for even "a hundred *on one side* are not enough for a dispute" (ibid.).

"raging Roland,"[1] as Kierkegaard called him in his journals—sets forth his criticism (and even sought to *sue* Martensen) would have made an unemotional and objective discussion impossible.[2] From the beginning, Eiríksson read Martensen's writings with a hermeneutic of mistrust and suspicion, rooted in his presumption that Martensen's speculative theology leads inexorably to the deification of humanity. Eiríksson's stubborn insistence on taking every utterance of Martensen's literally,[3] and his determination to use every imprecision in Martensen's writings as a warrant for questioning his entire theological standpoint as such, force us at many points to draw the conclusion that Eiríksson simply did not *want* to understand Martensen. The exaggerated stridency and polemical character of Eiríksson's writings not only interfered with the substance and efficacy of their argumentation, but also eclipsed their nobler goals and motives. We can see this clearly, for example, in *On Baptists and Infant Baptism* (1844), where Eiríksson's larger aim—to protest publicly the repression of the Baptist free-church movement, and the "un-Christian" practice of forced baptism—is easily overshadowed by his polemic against Martensen.

Even though a more measured tone is detectable in Eiríksson's last book-length polemic against Martensen, *Cardinal Virtues of the New Danish Theology*, the radicalization of Eiríksson's position that took place starting in 1851 soon made any reasoned debate with Martensen utterly impossible. Whereas Martensen, with his appointment as Bishop of Zealand on April 15, 1854, was to hold the office of Primate of the Danish State Church for the next three decades until his death in 1884, Eiríksson grew more and more estranged—estranged not only from academic theology, but also from the Church (doctrine) and all official Christianity as such, until he finally broke with it completely. In the

---

1 *Pap.* VII-1 B 88, p. 287 / *CUP2*, 128.

2 That Eiríksson himself was well aware of his writings' polemical vehemence, but took it on board approvingly anyway, is evident in his *Dr. Martensens trykte moralske Paragrapher*, pp. 161f. To the objections of others that he was attacking Martensen too ferociously, Eiríksson retorted: "But why not?" (p. 161). Whatever one might wish to say about his manner of proceeding—"it does not affect me" (p. 162).

3 On this characterization of Eiríksson's criticism see, for example, Paul Victor Rubow, *Kierkegaard og hans Samtidige*, Copenhagen: Gyldendalske Boghandel, Nordisk Forlag 1950, pp. 23-29; here p. 23, as well as Arildsen, *Biskop Hans Lassen Martensen*, p. 210.

face of the continuing silence of "the competent ones"[1] in theology and church—a silence criticized by Eiríksson's advocates and opponents alike, and which Eiríksson himself increasingly read as a validation of the truth of his critique of the Church and its doctrine—a number of laypeople with religious interests, such as the religious author Andreas Daniel Pedrin (1823-91)[2] and the postal supervisor and author Jørgen Christian Theodor Faber (1824-86),[3] felt called upon to take a public stand against Eiríksson's views. In Sweden, by contrast, Eiríksson's thought found more fertile soil, thanks above all to the freethinking pastor Nils Johan Ekdahl (1799-1870), who translated two of Eiríksson's books into Swedish.[4] It is not by chance that, in 1877-80, Eiríksson's final publications appeared in *Swedish* newspapers and journals—most prominently in the journal *Sanningsökaren* or "The Truth-Seeker."[5]

---

1 Anonymous, *Dagens Nyheder*, 1873, no. 113.

2 For Eiríksson's dispute with Pedrin, see pp. 99f. above, note 3.

3 See Jørgen Christian Theodor Faber, *Aabent Brev til Danmarks Theologer om Nyrationalismens Forhold til den kristne Tro*, Copenhagen: Gad 1871, which offers an open-minded assessment of Eiríksson's position; see also the reviews of Faber's book by Niels Lindberg in *Dansk Kirketidende*, 1871, no. 50 (December 10), columns 794-799, as well as by Anonymous ("R.") in *Dagbladet*, 1872, no. 13.

4 Magnús Eiríksson, *Johannis Evangelium. Är det en äkta apostolisk Bok och är dess Lära: att Gud är vorden Menniska, en sann och kristlig Lära? En Religiös-Dogmatisk Historisk-Kritisk Undersökning*, trans. by Nils Johan Ekdahl, Stockholm: L.J. Hiertas Forläg 1864 as well as *Läran om dopet* [a translation of *Hvem har Ret: Grundtvigianerne eller deres Modstandere? og Hvad har Christus befalet om Daaben? Nogle orienterende Bemærkninger*, Copenhagen: E.L. Thaarup 1863], trans. by Nils Johan Ekdahl, Stockholm: L.J. Hiertas Forläg 1865. For an example of Eiríksson's often repeated praise of Ekdahl and his "love to the truth," see the preface of *Gud og Reformatoren*, especially pp. V-VI.

5 See Magnús Eiríksson, "Förnuftstro och kyrkolära," *Sanningsökaren. Nordisk månadskrift för förnuftstro och praktisk kristendom*, vol. 1, 1877, no. 2, pp. 41-47; "Förtröstan på Gud," *Sanningsökaren. Nordisk månadskrift för förnuftstro och praktisk kristendom*, vol. 1, 1877, no. 4, pp. 113-121; "Kierkegaard och kristendomen," *Sanningsökaren. Nordisk månadskrift för förnuftstro och praktisk kristendom*, vol. 1, 1877, nos. 7-8, pp. 203-239; "Ortodoxe teologer och kritiske filosofer," *Sanningsökaren. Nordisk månadskrift för förnuftstro och praktisk kristendom*, vol. 1, 1877, nos. 9-10, pp. 289-305; "Kristi religion och kristna religionen. Svar till Robinson," *Sanningsökaren. Nordisk månadskrift för förnuftstro och praktisk kristendom*, vol. 2, 1878, nos. 1-2, pp. 11-34; "Död och odödlighet," *Sanningsökaren. Nordisk månadskrift för förnuftstro och praktisk kristendom*, vol. 2, 1878, no. 9, pp. 259-267; "Om Johannesevangeliets Kristus," *Sanningsökaren. Nordisk månadskrift för förnuftstro och praktisk kristendom*, vol. 3, 1879, no. 4, pp. 104-121; "Striden om Johannesevangeliet," *Sanningsökaren. Nordisk månadskrift för förnuftstro och praktisk kristendom*, vol. 4, 1880, nos. 1-2, pp. 39-49.

In the face of Eiríksson's ever-intensifying critique of both the Bible and of all Church doctrine in his later writings, which reached its culmination in his 1873 book *Jews and Christians*, Martensen's wish to Eiríksson in his response to that book, despite its evident arrogance—"the Lord enlighten you and lead you to recognize the Truth!"[1]—also deserves to be taken seriously. Given, on the one hand, Eiríksson's critical attitude toward Church dogma, particularly toward the doctrines of the Trinity and the divinity of Christ, in contrast to which he stressed (at least in his late work) the essential *unity* of God and the role of Jesus as (merely) a prophet and a teacher; and given, on the other hand, Eiríksson's further insistence on the rationality of Christian faith, and on freedom of thought and conscience in matters of religion—it should not surprise us to find that Eiríksson is often labeled a "pioneer" or "precursor," in a broad spiritual sense, to the Unitarian movement,[2] which found its way to Denmark in 1900. It is an irony of fate that Garnison's Cemetery in Copenhagen, where Eiríksson was buried, lies only a stone's throw away from the "Unitarians' House" erected there in 1927—and which is now the official seat of Denmark's Unitarian Church Society.

---

1 See Pjetursson, "Magnús Eiríksson," p. 138, where Martensen's letter is reprinted (see also p. 107 above, note 5). Martensen's three-volume autobiography *Af mit Levnet* makes no mention of Eiríksson at all.

2 See, for example, Ágúst Hákonarson Bjarnason, "Magnus Eiriksson, the first Icelandic Unitarian" (handwritten manuscript, address at Harvard Divinity School, May 21, 1923), Andover-Harvard Theological Library, Cambridge, Massachusetts (bMS 103/5-15); subsequently published in Icelandic as "Um Magnús Eiríksson," *Skírnir*, vol. 98, 1924, pp. 39-73; see the transcription of the original manuscript by Stefan M. Jonasson in this volume. See also Stephen Hole Fritchman, *Men of Liberty: Ten Unitarian Pioneers*, Boston: Beacon Press 1944, pp. 163-180; Thorvald Kierkegaard, *Magnus Eiriksson og Mary B. Westenholz. To Forkæmpere for Unitarismen i Danmark*, Copenhagen: no publisher given 1958 (an offprint from *Protestantisk Tidende*, 1957), pp. 3-9 ("Magnus Eiriksson. Den første Forkynder af Unitarisme i Danmark"); Valtýr Emil Gudmundson, *The Icelandic Unitarian Connection: Beginnings of Icelandic Unitarianism in North America, 1885-1900*, completed posthumously by Barbara J.R. Gudmundson, with a foreword by Conrad Wright, Winnipeg, Manitoba: Wheatfield Press 1984, pp. 6-10 ("The Soul of Icelandic Religious Liberalism—Magnús Eiríksson").

Martensen and Eiríksson's Accusations: A Post-Mortem Defense

Curtis L. Thompson

Magnús Eiríksson was a significant theologian who hailed from Iceland but attended school and spent his career in Copenhagen. His critical spirit led him to adopt a distinctive theology that affirmed the absolute unity of God and that negated the doctrines of the Trinity and the essential unity of God and the human in Christ. His later teachings were formative for what became the Unitarian religious tradition in Denmark. This essay's first part introduces the issues before us. The discussion is broadened by the second section's treatment of three notions from David Friedrich Strauss. The third part presents my best sense for how Martensen might have responded to the theological questions directed to him by Eiríksson. The essay closes with an enumeration of some of the essential differences between Martensen and Eiríksson.

I. Introduction

In our work as scholars we quite frequently speak on behalf of others. We summarize their positions and arguments, cite their ideas, quote their words, and do the best job we can to empathize with them, to stand in their shoes, so that we are able accurately to interpret their spoken or written words or creative works. It is a bit different, though, when one attempts, as I am doing, to declare how a person who is now dead would have responded to a critic to whom he had very self-consciously chosen not to respond. Hans L. Martensen maintained his posture of "lofty silence"[1] in relation to Magnús Eiríksson's criticisms of him. Even as the critical books published by Eiríksson against him from 1844 to 1850 came to number four, Martensen still did not budge from his silent stance.

A question to ask is why someone would consent to the request to write a post-mortem defense on behalf of another. I agreed to attempt such a defense for Martensen because I think I have gotten to know him fairly well and believe that offering a response from his perspective to Eiríksson's accusations could contribute something to the fresh work that is now being done on Eiríksson. The task is appealing also in that, in light of the special circumstances, I am being afforded considerable creative license in articulating the defense.

When one turns to the mountain of material that Eiríksson published in criticizing Martensen, the task of responding to it is intimidating simply because of the sheer number of pages to be considered. One can imagine that Martensen, had he changed his mind and decided to reply to Eiríksson, might have hesitated to go through with it because of the difficulty of responding to such a voluminous attack. The person writing a post-mortem defense of Martensen is faced with the same problem. To alleviate this issue, I have decided to whittle down the material by following Eiríksson's own suggestion in that regard. The "cantankerous Icelander," as Skat Arildsen called him,[2] in 1844 published the first of the four books contra-Martensen, *On Baptists and Infant Baptism*,[3] which included accusations against Martensen's speculative theology as expressed in the latter's 1843 book on Christian baptism.[4] Eiríksson's

---

1 Magnús Eiríksson, *Dr. Martensens trykte moralske Paragrapher, eller det saakaldte "Grundrids til Moralphilosophiens System af Dr. Hans Martensen," i dets forvirrede, idealistisk-metaphysiske og phantastisk-speculative, Religion og Christendom undergravende, fatalistiske, pantheistiske og selvforguderiske Væsen*, Copenhagen: H.C. Klein 1846, p. II.

2 Skat Arildsen, *Biskop Hans Lassen Martensen. Hans Liv, Udvikling og Arbejde*, vol. 1, *Studier i det 19. Aarhundredes Aandsliv*, Copenhagen: Gad 1932, p. 288.

3 Magnús Eiríksson, *Om Baptister og Barnedaab, samt flere Momenter af Den kirkelige og speculative Christendom*, Copenhagen: P.G. Philipsen 1844.

4 Hans Lassen Martensen, *Den christelige Daab betragtet med Hensyn paa det baptistiske Spørgsmaal*, Copenhagen: C.A. Reitzel 1843.

second book *Dr. Martensen's Published Moral Paragraphs* (1846)[1] focused on Martensen's *Outline to a System of Moral Philosophy* (1841)[2] and the third book *Speculative Orthodoxy* (1849)[3] on Martensen's *Christian Dogmatics* (1849).[4] Eiríksson's fourth book, *Cardinal Virtues of the New Danish Theology*,[5] was published in 1850 because in his *Dogmatic Elucidations* (1850),[6] Martensen had mentioned Eiríksson's critique but had not responded to any details of the criticism. This fourth book, then, presented critical comments against Martensen's *Christian Dogmatics* and his *Dogmatic Elucidations*, "together with 75 theological questions, addressed to Dr. H. Martensen."[7] Eiríksson compressed his critique into this list of questions for the convenience of answering. Eiríksson too was aware of the capacious nature of his critical writings, and so he was considerately making the task of responding a manageable one for Martensen. Obviously, Martensen never responded. I, however, will take up Eiríksson's invitation and will utilize the 75 theological questions as a somewhat manageable means of access to Eiríksson's most important criticisms of Martensen.

II. David Friedrich Strauss

Helpful for getting a feeling for the contours of Martensen's intellectual landscape and for setting the stage for the exchange between Eiríksson

[1] Magnús Eiríksson, *Dr. Martensens trykte moralske Paragrapher, eller det saakaldte "Grundrids til Moralphilosophiens System af Dr. Hans Martensen", i dets forvirrede, idealistisk-metaphysiske og phantastisk-speculative, Religion og Christendom undergravende, fatalistiske, pantheistiske og selvforguderske Væsen*, Copenhagen: H.C. Klein 1846.

[2] Hans Lassen Martensen, *Grundrids til Moralphilosophiens System. Udgivet til Brug ved academiske Forelæsninger*, Copenhagen: C.A. Reitzel 1841.

[3] Magnús Eiríksson, *Speculativ Rettroenhed, fremstillet efter Dr. Martensens "christelige Dogmatik", og Geistlig Retfærdighed, belyst ved en Biskops Deeltagelse i en Generalfiskal-Sag*, Copenhagen: Trykt hos J.S. Salomon 1849.

[4] Hans Lassen Martensen, *Den christelige Dogmatik*, Copenhagen: C.A. Reitzel 1849.

[5] Magnús Eiríksson, *Den nydanske Theologies Cardinaldyder belyste ved Hjelp af Dr. Martensens Skrifter samt Modskrifterne, tilligemed 75 theologiske Spørgsmaal, rettede til Dr. H. Martensen*, Copenhagen: Chr. Steen & Søn 1850.

[6] Hans Lassen Martensen, *Dogmatiske Oplysninger. Et Leilighedsskrift*, Copenhagen: C.A. Reitzel 1850.

[7] See note 5 above.

and Martensen is examining a few thoughts of the left-wing Hegelian David Friedrich Strauss, who was born in the same year as Martensen (1808) and died in 1874, ten years before him.

In the fall of 1834 Martensen left on a two-year study trip. In 1835, while on his trip, Strauss published a book. Martensen recollects in his memoirs: "During my stay in Heidelberg an incident occurred that contributed much to the tremor in the Hegelian school...the publication of David Strauss' *The Life of Jesus*. This writing created an enormous sensation, one can say, in the whole of Christendom."[8] Strauss' huge book closely scrutinizes the four Gospels of the New Testament. It begins with a long Introduction and ends with an extensive "Concluding Dissertation" on "The Dogmatic Import of the Life of Jesus."[9] Our interest lies especially in his closing reflections. Strauss states that the results of his inquiry are apparently to have "annihilated the greatest and most valuable part of that which the Christian has been wont to believe concerning his Saviour Jesus."[10] The question becomes, then, what is to be the response to this "act of desecration"[11] that has been perpetrated by Strauss' inquiry? The purpose of his conclusion is "to re-establish dogmatically that which has been destroyed critically."[12]

Strauss' concluding remarks provide a good summary of many different Christological positions on the theological scene at that time, from the orthodox, to that of rationalism, Schleiermacher, the symbolical views including those of Kant and De Wette, and the speculative. Eiríksson would normally be identified most closely with the rationalist Christological position and Martensen with the speculative. From Strauss' discussion, three areas of consideration can be lifted out as especially relevant to painting a portrait of the intellectual landscape that was influencing Martensen. Three important ideas from Strauss instigate provocative thoughts respectively about

---

[8] Hans Lassen Martensen, *Af mit Levned*, vols. 1-3, Copenhagen: Gyldendal 1882-83, vol. 1, p. 122.

[9] David Friedrich Strauss, *The Life of Jesus Critically Examined*, trans. by George Eliot, ed. by Peter C. Hodgson, Ramsey, New Jersey: Sigler Press 1994 [1972], pp. 757-84.

[10] Strauss, *The Life of Jesus*, p. 757.

[11] Ibid.

[12] Ibid.

spirit, myth, and race. Investing a little time in these notions will be useful in preparing the way for the Eiríksson-Martensen encounter.

The first idea is on spirit and is from Strauss' deliberations on speculative Christology. He writes: "It is the essential property of a spirit, in the distribution of itself into distinct personalities, to remain identical with itself, to possess itself in another than itself.[1] This is quite a good summary of Hegel's central concept of spirit. Martensen likely would have largely agreed with Strauss' view of spirit. This statement on spiritual identity has huge implications for Martensen's understanding of the relations among the three subsistences of the Trinity. This is one of the major disagreements, it seems, between Martensen and Eiríksson, because Eiríksson does not appear to find room in his thinking for this notion of spirit and the understanding of identity associated with it.

The second idea is that of myth, which is included in Strauss' discussion of the symbolical view of Christology. Here Strauss points to the Protestant critical biblical scholar Georg Konrad Horst (1769-1832) who, at an earlier period, presented this symbolical view of the history of Jesus with singular clearness. The provocative idea is: "The history of the gospel is in fact the history of human nature conceived ideally, and exhibits to us in the life of an individual, what man ought to be, and, united with him by following his doctrine and example, can actually become."[2] In his *Christian Dogmatics* Martensen addresses this position, which he characterizes as "modern Docetism,"[3] at some length. The general gist of his position is also stated in his memoirs, where he claims that Strauss' book *The Life of Jesus* aimed to show Christ's life as a myth rather than an actual history, so that the New Testament is no longer trustworthy because its recounted event did not happen.[4] Martensen's main criticism of Strauss' view of myth is that the timeframe is not long enough from the death of Jesus to the writing of the gospels for robust cycles of myth to have developed. As a follower of Hegel and Schelling, however, Martensen does fully

1 Strauss, *The Life of Jesus*, p. 777.
2 Ibid., p. 776.
3 Martensen, *Den christelige Dogmatik*, p. 291, see pp. 291-306 (*Christian Dogmatics*, p. 244, see pp. 244-58).
4 Martensen, *Af mit Levned*, vol. 1, pp. 122f.

recognize the place of imagination in religious expression and in theological formulation; this is obvious in his claim that the human's need for an incarnation would have led to humanity inventing it if it had not occurred in the Christ.[1]

The third provocative idea of Strauss centers on the human race. In Strauss' rather harsh understanding of the Hegelian transition from *Vorstellungen* or representations to *Begriffe* or concepts, he tends to leave behind much of the richness of religion in making the interpretive move to the philosophical idea. Christologically, the major issue that arises centers on whether the focal point of the incarnation is on Jesus the individual or on the human race. Strauss makes clear his preference for the human race. Strauss acknowledges that the rational is the real, and "the idea of the unity of the divine and human nature…must have an historical existence."[2] Thus comes Strauss' primary claim that the key to Christology is replacing the individual, the Christ, to which the church assigns its predicates and properties, with an idea, "the idea of the race."[3] With such critically speculative views of spirit, myth, and race prevailing within cutting edge theological reflection winning the day, how is the theologian of the church to proceed? Martensen sets forth his answer to Strauss in his *Christian Dogmatics.*

---

1 Hans Lassen Martensen, *Den menneskelige Selvbevidstheds Autonomie i vor Tids dogmatiske Theologie*, trans. and ed. by Lauritz Vilhelm Petersen, Copenhagen: C.A. Reitzel 1841, p. 32 (*The Autonomy of Human Self-Consciousness in Modern Dogmatic Theology*, in *Between Hegel and Kierkegaard: Hans L. Martensen's Philosophy of Religion*, trans. by Curtis L. Thompson and David J. Kangas, Atlanta: Scholars Press 1997, p. 95).

2 Strauss, *The Life of Jesus* p. 779.

3 Strauss, *The Life of Jesus* pp. 779f. He clarifies (p. 780) that "Humanity" is the real unity of the two natures—God and the human, because human history discloses the Spirit as ever more completely subjugating nature; while sinfulness can be attributed to individual humans, such pollution cannot touch the race or its history; Humanity dies, rises, and ascends to the heavens as its mortality as a personal, national, and terrestrial spirit arises in unity with the infinite spirit of the heavens; the race is the true Christ and faith in this reality kindles within individuals the idea of Humanity, by which the individual human being participates in the divinely human life of the species; at the heart of this idea is the spiritual negating of the natural, the Spirit's negation of the negation, which is the only way to true spiritual life.

III. A Q and A Session

At the outset of posing his 75 questions in his 1850 book *Cardinal Virtues of the New Danish Theology*, Eiríksson writes that he is addressing to Dr. Martensen the following questions, as occasioned by the peculiar doctrine that is found in his *Christian Dogmatics*, and inviting him for his own sake, for the sake of others, and especially for the sake of Christian truth, to answer them and give all the explanations concerning them that he is able to give.[1] Clearly, I cannot present Martensen's precise answers in his defense. In Martensen's stead I attempt as best I am able to creatively set forth Martensenian answers to a few of Eiríksson's 75 questions.[2] It is tempting to become immersed in the detail of the questions. To prevent that from happening, I will diligently strive to keep the discourse of the encounter at a fairly general level.

A. Questions on Knowing God

The first couple of questions Eiríksson poses ask whether the human can know God and whether God is inconceivable.[3] Martensen would answer that the human mind is indeed limited and the eternal, invisible God is a mystery beyond human understanding. But the human is created for God, and therefore it would be tragic if the human could not know God. However, the human does know God because it is God's nature to love, and the divine love involves God's communicating of Godself. Through divine self-communication God establishes a relationship with God's creatures, and in the relationship with humans God is revealed. God is known through creation and a deeper knowledge of God comes through the redemptive experience. All knowledge of God, though, takes place because God first loved the world and takes the initiative to

---

1 Eiríksson, *Den nydanske Theologies Cardinaldyder*, p. 132.

2 Eiríksson's excessive use of italics and other forms of emphasis have not been reproduced in the quotations. Quotations from *Christian Dogmatics* have quite often been changed somewhat from the way they appear in the English translation: Hans Lassen Martensen, *Christian Dogmatics: A Compendium of the Doctrines of Christianity*, trans. [from the 1856 German edition] by William Urwick, Edinburgh: T.&T. Clark 1874 [1866].

3 Eiríksson, *Den nydanske Theologies Cardinaldyder*, pp. 132f.

relate to humans; human participation in that relationship carries with it knowledge, with the level of knowledge being dependent on the intensity of the relationship. On God's inconceivability or incomprehensibility, Martensen would suggest that one needs to distinguish between an absolute and a relative incomprehensibility.[1] The mysterious and majestic reality of God transcends the human's ability to capture it conceptually, and in this sense God is inconceivable. This view, though, sells short the ability humans have to imagine and think about the divine things and to arrive at better or worse conceptions of the divine reality. Martensen holds that the Christian can have a true but not an adequate knowledge of the nature of God.[2]

For Martensen, human knowledge of God is possible because of the human relationship with God. Martensen views religion as "a *life* in God": "the religious relation to God is an existential relation, a consciousness of the God-relation that is one with the personal life and being in this relation."[3] This personal relation to God finds its universal expression in the conscience, which has a side directed to the world that becomes the basis of morality and a side directed to God insofar as the conscience [*Samvittigheden* or *con-scientia*] "is the human's original co-knowledge with God of its personal existential relation to God, an immediate, a perceptible co-knowledge with God."[4] It should be stated that, for Martensen, the relation to God is not limited to the conscience. The fundamental religious relation Martensen identifies as "a feeling of unbounded awe," which involves thinking as well as feeling and thus allows the religious relation to be free.[5] Martensen understands the

---

1 Martensen, *Dogmatiske Oplysninger*, pp. 20-21.

2 Martensen, *Den christelige Dogmatik*, p. 109 (*Christian Dogmatics*, p. 91). Absolute inconceivability claims that God cannot be conceived pure and simple. Relative inconceivability claims that an exhaustive conceiving of God is definitely impossible, but a partial yet significant conceiving of God is possible and can bear forth a conception of God that can be refined through further scrutiny that judges the adequacy of the concept in terms of the degree to which it expresses the reality of God as experienced in the living relationship with God. Martensen affirmed such a relatively adequate conceiving of God.

3 Martensen, *Den christelige Dogmatik*, p. 8 (*Christian Dogmatics*, p. 5).

4 Martensen, *Den christelige Dogmatik*, p. 9 (*Christian Dogmatics*, p. 6). This holy point of contact between the divine and the human is the ground of the God-human unity that will be much discussed in answering these questions.

5 Martensen, *Den christelige Dogmatik*, p. 12 (*Christian Dogmatics*, p. 8).

religious knowledge of God as culminating not merely in a "knowledge in the form of abstract thought" but "in a comprehensive view of the world and the human in its relation to God"; this is because religious knowledge is not confined to the thoughts originating from the conscience, but extends as well to the symbolic, imaginative representations originating from that source.[1] This is to say that it is not only reason (*Fornuften*) but also the imagination (*Phantasie*) that must be denominated as the originating organ of religious knowledge: without the imagination and an imaginative view, religion will not make its appearance in the world.[2]

B. Questions on the Trinity

Of Eiríksson's 75 questions, more than half of them (Qq. 3-47) concern the doctrine of the Trinity.[3] The next few paragraphs will answer some of the concerns that Eiríksson has about Martensen's treatment of this central Christian dogma. First, he questions Martensen's distinction between the eternal and economic Trinity, seemingly unaware that this is a classic distinction in the Christian tradition. Eiríksson appears to be unable to affirm the distinctive character of each of the three Trinitarian "moments" as presented in what he calls an "imaginative view."[4] For Martensen, revelation, from the divine side, is religion, from the human side. In examining the human side of the matter, the distinction between analysis and dialectic can be introduced.[5]

---

1 Martensen, *Den christelige Dogmatik*, p. 13 (*Christian Dogmatics*, p. 9).

2 Ibid. These intellectual and imaginative deliverances of the conscience comprise the human's religious knowledge that emerges from the religious relation to God demarcated especially by the conscience. Within the context of Christianity, such religious contents of human self-consciousness are at the same time God's revelation.

3 Eiríksson, *Den nydanske Theologies Cardinaldyder*, pp. 133-150.

4 Ibid., pp. 133-135.

5 The first half of Kant's *Critique of Pure Reason* was devoted to analysis that breaks down and the second half to dialectic that puts back together. The imaginative thinking in which one engages in reflecting on the Triune God necessitates doing analysis that breaks down the reality under consideration into its parts. The Triune God is a dialectical whole whose parts can be analytically broken down but in reality are dialectically together. Conceptual distinguishing can be differentiated from chronological distinguishing. So a rational human being can without question imagine a particular divine hypostasis such as the Father as distinct from Son and Spirit, but it must be remembered that this is the workings of the analytical understanding. While

Eiríksson wonders if imagining the Father as a "moment," in particular as "a primal ground of nature," is a worthy representation.[1] Martensen thinks that analytical imaging of the Father as an independent "moment" or "point" can be helpful in serving the dialectical imagery of the completeness of the Father's "moment" as coming in relation to the other two "moments."[2] But, Eiríksson asks, if the Trinitarian God is one, how can there be three moments? Are not Father, Son, and Spirit one essence in one person, and isn't it heretical to disagree with this orthodox view?[3] On Martensen's view, at the heart of the divine life is relationship, and three is the number of relationship. The Lover, the Beloved, and the Loving are the three essential elements of a relationship of love, as Augustine and others have pointed out. For the Christian doctrine of the Trinity one also encounters the number three in the religious experience of Jesus the Christ in unity with God the Father through the workings of the Holy Spirit. The threeness of this economic Trinity is matched by the threeness of Father, Son, and Spirit of the essential Trinity. The necessity of threeness is grounded in the threefold nature of Christian experience and in the threefold nature of love. These internal and external expressions of threeness mirror one another and mutually support one another.[4]

---

the result might well be helpful for thought, it must be recognized as the skewed view that it is, since it does not provide the complete picture. For the full picture, one must also call on dialectical reason which affirms the truth that this hypostasis is in intimate interrelationship with the other two hypostases. The narrative of the Trinity requires insight from both the understanding's analysis and reason's dialectic.

1 Eiríksson, *Den nydanske Theologies Cardinaldyder*, pp. 133f.

2 One can identify analytically "the eternal Father" as a "primal ground of nature" without self-consciousness and freedom, apart from making the claim that there was once a time when this "part" existed with no relationship with the Son and the Spirit. Again, the whole matter of identity is at stake. Is the identity located in the discrete oneness of a "moment" or are these "moments" indissolubly connected with one another and creating their identities as participating in the others? The latter reality involves an identity that is relational. If the three moments or hypostases are discrete, separate realities, each with non-relational identities, then it makes no sense to think of relation as making a difference for identity. But if the moment is an image produced by the analytical understanding that is transcended by an image produced by dialectical reason, then it is another story. Self-consciousness and freedom are complex relational realities that cannot be accounted for apart from dynamic relating.

3 Eiríksson, *Den nydanske Teologies Cardinaldyder*, p. 135.

4 Martensen, *Den christelige Dogmatik*, pp. 128f. (*Christian Dogmatics*, p. 107).

Christianity has never wanted to claim nonsensically in relation to the doctrine of the Trinity that 1 = 3. "Three persons in one essence" has been the traditional Christian claim, but Martensen never explicitly affirms this formulation, so the question Eiríksson raises is surely an appropriate one. For Martensen the central concept of revelation is personality, and this notion is linked to that of love; so for him God must be thought of in terms of a single personality of love. On the other hand, he wants to take seriously what had traditionally been designated the three persons of Father, Son, and Spirit. So he speaks of Christianity teaching that the God of love "reveals itself in a threefold personality as Father, Son, and Holy Spirit."[1] He also writes of Christianity directing human beings to the one God in a threefold direction.[2] He explains that these three are hypostases, each expressing for itself the whole essence and each for itself revealing the whole God in different ways.[3]

Eiríksson construes Martensen's claim that the Father creates the world by the Son as implying that the Father is therefore not involved in creating.[4] Martensen's response to this, in short, would be that the Father creates through possibilities, which are in the Son, so the Father creates through the Son.[5] Eiríksson's questions show that he does not hold that the three hypostases of the Trinity are spiritual realities. As Strauss indicated, spirit remains identical with itself while possessing itself in another than itself. Father and Son (and Spirit as well) remain identical with themselves while possessing themselves in the others. All the divine attributes are in the Father, in the Son, and in the Holy Spirit;[6] therefore, all three are equal. That each of these three by itself reveals the whole of God does not mean that particular areas of divine activity, such

---

1 Martensen, *Den christelige Dogmatik*, p. 123 (*Christian Dogmatics*, p. 102).

2 Ibid.

3 Ibid. Martensen's preferred designations for these three hypostases are "modes of subsistence," the same term Karl Barth settles on as his preferred usage in treating the Trinity. This change is made by Martensen because he thinks it allows for a clearer dogmatic formulation of the Christian doctrine of the triune God as a God of love. I do not think that Martensen would agree that the Church has for all times considered this preferable view of his as heretical; and, if that were the case, he would recognize that any time one is engaged in the creative task of constructive theology, one runs the risk of having one's formulations judged as heretical.

4 Eiríksson, *Den nydanske Theologies Cardinaldyder*, p. 136.

5 Martensen, *Den christelige Dogmatik*, p. 141 (*Christian Dogmatics*, p. 116).

6 Martensen, *Den christelige Dogmatik*, pp. 123f. (*Christian Dogmatics*, pp. 102f.).

as creating, redeeming, and sanctifying, cannot be associated with one or another particular mode of subsistence, so long as one remembers that the whole God is active in each activity.[1]

Eriksson asks whether Martensen's claim that God the Father conceiving Godself as an other, the Son, means that the Father is no longer actual.[2] Martensen would answer by making a distinctive point in his Trinitarian doctrine. The Old Testament represents God becoming manifest to Godself in Wisdom, but this was not yet the Son.[3] In the Son God thinks Godself as an other and is thus able to know himself as the Father of the thinking Logos.[4] The act of the Father conceiving himself as the Son is an eternal act, an act in which the Father is always engaged, and without this activity God would not be God. The Son and the objectivity of the world are a condition for God's eternal I-ness.[5] The Son is a necessary condition for the Father's Ego, but since the Son is eternally begotten by the Father, there never is a time when the Father does not benefit from the otherness of the Son.

Eiríksson charges Martensen with endorsing a "successive Trinity," that is, one in which the Trinitarian moments succeed each other, for instance, as the Father passes over into the Son, and the Son passes over into the Spirit.[6] Martensen does not affirm such a succession in reference to either the economic or the essential Trinity. The "successive Trinity"

---

1 The Christian tradition has declared that God's life in itself or the essential Trinity is divisible or threefold. The tradition has declared that the saving work of God in history or the economic Trinity is indivisible, for the whole Godhead is at work in every divine activity. The divine divisibility means that the hypostases are distinct, not that they are separate. Eiríksson seems to have the view that the Father and the Son are separate realities. Martensen would say that God the Father has created and is creating the world. God the Father creates the world through the Son or Logos and sustains and governs the world through the Son or Logos as well. And to the question of whether God the Father exists, Martensen responds that the begetting of the Son by the Father is in eternity, which means that it is activity taking place in the eternal now. Therefore, the Father is always begetting and the Son is always being begotten. The Father also creates through the Son, and this is not a one-time activity at the beginning of time but an ongoing activity as the Father through the Son engages in continuing creation. God the Father exists.

2 Eiríksson, *Den nydanske Theologies Cardinaldyder*, p. 138.

3 Martensen, *Den christelige Dogmatik*, p. 131 (*Christian Dogmatics*, p. 109).

4 Ibid.

5 Martensen, *Den christelige Dogmatik*, pp. 131f. (*Christian Dogmatics*, p. 109).

6 Eiríksson, *Den nydanske Theologies Cardinaldyder*, pp. 138f.

that Eiríksson finds in Martensen's dogmatics appears to be nothing other than the modalistic heresy of Sabellianism that Martensen explicitly addresses as an unworthy viewpoint that is to be rejected.[1] Such a view's impersonal deity cannot support talk of a revelation of love, and it denies the Triune God's independence from the world; one needs to "distinguish between the internal or essential and the external or economic revelation of God."[2]

Eiríksson raises questions about the nature of the transformation that the divine undergoes with the procession from the Father to the Son and then to the Spirit.[3] While Martensen claims that the living God of love does undergo transformation in relation to the God-human or Christ, he in no sense is claiming that the divine is progressing from non-existence to existence. On the question of God's transformation, Martensen would have stood in agreement with Kierkegaard's distinction between God being unchanged and yet eminently moved.[4] For both thinkers God is love. Love is always there, it is unchanging; yet the nature of love is to relate intimately to the beloved, and intimate relating means being continually moved. Martensen held that created nature attains its culminating point in humanity, which is the point of unity for God and the creature.[5] On Martensen's view, the unity of divine and human nature is not most pointedly the focus of the Incarnation, since that unity is already present in the human as created in God's image; the

---

1 Martensen, *Den christelige Dogmatik*, p. 126 (*Christian Dogmatics*, pp. 104f.).

2 Martensen, *Den christelige Dogmatik*, p. 127 (*Christian Dogmatics*, pp. 105f.). Eiríksson's critique might be referring to the essential Trinity. He speaks of God the Father being completely absorbed or swallowed up by the Son, so that consequently the Father is sublated or annihilated. The Danish verb is a form of *ophæve*, which is comparable to the German *aufheben*, a critically important term of Hegel. It appears that Eiríksson is translating *ophæves* as meaning *is annihilated*. This sense of *annihilating, destroying, canceling, overcoming*, of course, is one meaning of *aufheben*, but there is also the meaning of *preserving* that is conveyed by this verb. This makes a difference in how the relations between Father and Son and between Son and Spirit are understood. Eiríksson seems to have understood the sublating merely as an annihilating and does not acknowledge the preserving aspect of the sublating. The same issue is raised in relation to the Son being sublated or *ophæves* by the Spirit. The same point of interpretation applies: sublating of the Son in the Spirit involves a preserving of the Son's actuality in the Spirit.

3 Eiríksson, *Den nydanske Theologies Cardinaldyder*, pp. 140 ff.

4 See, for example, *SKS* 24, 358, NB24:56 / *JP* 4, 4891.

5 Martensen, *Den christelige Dogmatik*, p. 153 (*Christian Dogmatics*, p. 127).

new is rather in the union of an earthly human "as the self-revelation of the divine Logos."[1]

Eiríksson asks if Christ or the Holy Spirit exists outside the Church or Christendom, or if they only live in Christendom and Christians.[2] Martensen answers that the promise of the Gospel is that Christ and the Holy Spirit are really present within the Church. Martensen does not subscribe to the converse, that Christ and the Holy Spirit are not present outside the Church. He does not want to place a limit on God's workings in the world. Thus, in his writing on *Christian Baptism*, he affirms the proposition that "baptism is necessary for salvation," while allowing for the possibility that in some circumstances God might possess resources for accomplishing an action outside of the established structures.[3] The Spirit is the living efficacious energy of God returning upon Godself, thus making God free, and the Spirit is the means by which the creation is moved into the new creation. Inspiration plays an important role in facilitating that movement.

Martensen distinguishes between the Logos that operates creatively and the Christ who operates redemptively. The efficacy of Christ is real; however, those who are not counted within the Christian community are surely not without the supporting active presence of the divine Logos in their lives. The divine activity in the creation and in the new creation serves the same goal.[4]

Eiríksson wonders what is the nature of this contrast between the Logos and the Christ, and inquires whether Martensen does not endorse two Sons, one in the kingdom of nature and the other in the kingdom of grace, one outside the Church and the other inside (and does not Martensen even affirm a third Son of the Devil identified as

---

[1] Martensen, *Den christelige Dogmatik*, p. 287 (*Christian Dogmatics*, p. 240). Martensen cites New Testament self-designations by Jesus in which he declares himself to be the Son of God and the Son of Humanity. Most 21st-century New Testament scholars would identify those claims as originating with the early church community rather than with Jesus himself, while others would be willing to attribute them to the post-Easter Jesus working through the early church community, and thus interpret them as what might be called self-designations at second-hand.

[2] Eiríksson, *Den nydanske Theologies Cardinaldyder*, p. 144.

[3] Martensen, *Den christelige Daab betragtet med Hensyn paa det baptistiske Spørgmaal*, Copenhagen: C.A. Reitzel 1843, pp. 68f.

[4] Martensen, *Den christelige Dogmatik*, p. 311 (*Christian Dogmatics*, p. 262).

the Christ's brother?). Is not the knowledge held by the Logos and the Christ different? And he wonders if one is not left with two beginnings, one of cosmogony and another of creation.[1]

Martensen's response is that the double mediating activity taking place in the revelation of the Logos (world-creating) and in the revelation of the Christ (world-perfecting) need not lead to a separation. There is a perduring distinction between *exitus* and *reditus*, between the outgoing, creative activity of the Godhead and the reuniting-back-to-God activity of the Christ by means of which God can be all-in-all; however, these activities are not the work of two Sons but rather one.[2] The revelation of the Logos in Christ and the eternal revelation of the Logos are described by Martensen.[3] The difference between the level of knowledge held by the Logos and that held by Christ can be mitigated somewhat by the fact that on Martensen's view God's omniscience is limited in that God knows the future as future and not as present; in this sense the omniscient God does not know all.[4] Martensen does not affirm an unconditional foreknowledge, for that view militates against human freedom, but he does affirm a conditional foreknowledge in which events are given shape by human freedom and therefore can only be known as possibilities rather than actualities.[5] Martensen thinks that Christ's knowledge is best characterized as the central knowledge that is the root metaphor of knowledge.[6] Martensen agrees that the beginning can be considered from the viewpoints of cosmogony and creation.[7] The divine Logos lies at the foundation of both of these activities that lead respectively to natural creation and spiritual creation.[8]

Martensen does speak of the metaphysical grounding of the Christ's incarnation, that had there been no sin, the Logos would have still become incarnate. That is language of a divine determination of enfleshment, and there could equally be metaphysical language of a non-

---

1 We find these queries of Eiríksson in Questions 28-42, *Den nydanske Theologies Cardinaldyder*, pp. 143-48.

2 Martensen, *Den christelige Dogmatik*, pp. 391f. (*Christian Dogmatics*, p. 329).

3 Martensen, *Den christelige Dogmatik*, pp. 316f. (*Christian Dogmatics*, pp. 266f).

4 Martensen, *Den christelige Dogmatik*, p. 114 (*Christian Dogmatics*, p. 95).

5 Martensen, *Den christelige Dogmatik*, pp. 257f. (*Christian Dogmatics*, pp. 218f.).

6 Martensen, *Den christelige Dogmatik*, p. 354 (*Christian Dogmatics*, p. 299).

7 Martensen, *Den christelige Dogmatik*, pp. 144f. (*Christian Dogmatics*, pp. 119f.).

8 Martensen, *Den christelige Dogmatik*, p. 148 (*Christian Dogmatics*, p. 122).

interrupted commitment of the Logos to the creation. If the Logos is the self-communication of God, then Martensen's claim is that there is a twofold quality to that self-communicating. Unchangeable love is God's essence,[1] but manifesting that love in the world requires two strategic ways of operating, and these ways of creation and new creation work conjointly to accomplish their goal of embracing the world in love. As to the question of the Devil as Christ's brother, Martensen comments that the Son, as the contrast from the Father, is also the true basis for the world as a reality in contrast to God. Key here is the distinction between the cosmical and the holy principles that are present within the human.[2] It is possible for these two central principles to be related in an appropriate way, which is when the cosmical serves the higher principle of holiness. But it is also possible for the cosmical to be elevated over the holiness principle; in explaining that situation, the question of the devil enters into the discussion. Martensen states that he could not call the Devil Christ's older brother, but he might call him the younger brother; for God's Son is the eternal presupposition of the world and the Devil is the metaphorical expression for the cosmical principle.[3]

C. Questions on the Unity of God and the Human

Eiríksson had inquired earlier as to how the unity of divine and human natures happens.[4] For Martensen the unity of natures is not only accomplished in Christ. Inspiration, as Eiríksson rightly notes, is key to completing what happens in the Incarnation; the two are inseparable, for "what Christ's miracle of revelation [Incarnation] is in the objective, the miracle of inspiration is in the subjective."[5] The human's unity of essence with God is established in being created in the image of God. Baptism is the Christian sacrament by means of which the process of actualizing the essential unity commences. The unity of natures occurs in creation. Martensen understands the essential unity of divine and human natures

1 Martensen, *Den christelige Dogmatik*, p. 362 (*Christian Dogmatics*, p. 305).
2 Martensen, *Den christelige Dogmatik*, p. 163 (*Christian Dogmatics*, pp. 137f).
3 Martensen, *Den christelige Dogmatik*, pp. 224f (*Christian Dogmatics*, pp. 190f.)
4 Eiríksson, *Den nydanske Theologies Cardinaldyder*, p. 143.
5 Martensen, *Den christelige Dogmatik*, p. 25 (*Christian Dogmatics*, pp. 18f.).

as a pantheistic claim that the Christian should affirm, although his final commitment is to a panentheistic view. Panentheism, the claim that all things are in God, entails endorsing the divine self-limitation,[1] but the God who limits Godself engages in saving work through the Incarnation and the means of grace by which the Christian is empowered to actualize its essential unity with God into an actual unity. The result is a *theosis* or deification, by which the human resides in God.

Eiríksson raises the question of whether the person baptized is essentially one with God.[2] For Martensen the essential unity of the human with God is a reality at birth since it is part of being created in God's image. He states very clearly that the predisposition for the uniting of the human and divine nature is granted to every creature created in the divine image.[3] For Martensen, history's ultimate purpose is the perfect union of God and the human; he believes it follows from this that this union must have been present in the beginning of history as in a fruitful seed.[4] He declares that if the image of God were not merely to remain "a gift, but a self-acquired attribute of humanity,"[5] it was necessary that human beings enter into the task of realizing the fullness of being human into which they are called. The gift/task distinction is a form of the essence/actual distinction, which Martensen applies both to the divine Logos and to the human. The divine Logos as pre-existing is "merely the essential, not the actual Mediator between God and the creature; for the contrast between the created and the uncreated is still only sublated in essence, but not in existence; the strife between God and the sinful world is still only sublated in idea, not in life and existence."[6] And the human, who is created with a human nature that has the essential capacity for becoming united with the divine nature, must nevertheless be about the

---

1 Martensen, *Den christelige Dogmatik*, pp. 97f. (*Christian Dogmatics*, pp. 80f.).

2 Eiríksson, *Den nydanske Theologies Cardinaldyder*, p. 150.

3 Martensen, *Den christelige Dogmatik*, p. 306 (*Christian Dogmatics*, p. 258).

4 Martensen, *Den christelige Dogmatik*, p. 176 (*Christian Dogmatics*, p. 149). Genesis 1:26 speaks of the human being created in the image of God and in God's likeness. Some theologians have interpreted the distinction between image and likeness in terms of gift and task: the image of God involves giving humans a gift of all that they need for God's image to become a reality within them, and it also involves being called to the task of actualizing the gift and making it a reality in human life. Martensen would count himself among those theologians.

5 Martensen, *Den christelige Dogmatik*, p. 182 (*Christian Dogmatics*, p. 155).

6 Martensen, *Den christelige Dogmatik*, pp. 283f. (*Christian Dogmatics*, pp. 237f.).

task of actualizing that essence, a task that can come about through the assistance of the creative and redemptive activities of God.

Eiríksson questions how baptism functions in this regard.[1] For Martensen, baptism is one of two sacraments regarded as critical for mediating God's redeeming activity to the human. It is a visible act by which God's invisible grace is brought to the baptized. This does not mean the divine activity works magically; rather, it functions within the relational dynamics of the Christian community. The transformation of humans occurs over time as words and actions of love give shape to a lover, to one who uses her freedom to give expression to love. Martensen acknowledges that the word "God-human" is not found in the New Testament, but he contends that the thought expressed by it lies at the basis of its Christology.[2] In the same way he might acknowledge that, while the precise language of humans being transformed into God-humans might not be found in the New Testament, the thought expressed by it lies at the basis of its Soteriology.[3] On Martensen's view, the efficacy of baptism does not presuppose a magical view of Christian baptism. For him, it might be said that baptism is very much a social or communal ritual; God's Spirit works in, with, and under the human spirits who nurture the baptized.

Eiríksson inquires into how it is that the essential human is related to the actual human; how does this transition take place, and what conditions must be in place for the essential God-human to become actual?[4] Martensen would maybe acknowledge that it is good to see Eiríksson acknowledging the conditional or contingent features of the sacrament of baptism. Not conditional or contingent is God's working to make good on the divine promise to be present with the baptized to nurture her and to guide her toward fullness of life. While there is an unconditionality about the promise, the circumstance is that the divine work is always carried out in relation to human beings who are free. To that extent, the conditionality and contingency of the situation must

---

1 Eiríksson, *Den nydanske Theologies Cardinaldyder*, p. 150f.

2 See Martensen, *Den christelige Dogmatik*, p. 287 (*Christian Dogmatics*, p. 240).

3 When years later Eiríksson later came to agree that such thoughts are in the New Testament, he turned away from more traditional Christianity to a Unitarian version of it.

4 Eiríksson, *Den nydanske Theologies Cardinaldyder*, p. 152.

be taken into account. God does all that can be done to support the transformation of the baptized from essential to actual God-human. The faithful trust in that support, but human freedom must never be counted out of the complete circumstance.

Eiríksson asks who are actual God-humans, and who are not, that is, who are the merely essential God-humans.[1] Martensen might respond, O relentless questioner Eiríksson, wouldn't it be wonderful if answers could be had to all questions? Christians are exhorted to work out their salvation in fear and trembling, and the human situation is such that uncertainty is ever part of religious experience, no matter how much faithful trust in God's grace and commitment to living a life of love can remove the focus from oneself and assuage the sting of that uncertainty. The items that Eiríksson suggests are all helpful hints for ways in which the actualization of the essential God-human might be beneficial; these and other factors can work together to good effect. There will always remain, though, a question of the extent to which one has actualized the predisposition toward becoming a God-human. That is in part because of the reality of sin and in part because it is our human nature to question the extent of our productivity. Martensen would likely counsel us, with Luther, to rely on God's grace and move beyond the self-centeredness of such scrutiny by loving the neighbor.

Eiríksson queries about what happens to grace in the human's essential nature.[2] Martensen definitely wants to affirm the place of grace in bringing about the change of state brought by the Incarnation for those who are among the faithful. I think Martensen would agree with Luther, that grace and forgiveness bring to the faithful a "transmoral conscience,"[3] by which the terrifying character of the imperative is put to rest by the consoling character of the indicative. This state would allow the relation of conscience, dependence, and obedience still to have its impact,

---

1 Ibid., pp. 151f.

2 Ibid., p. 152.

3 The notion of the transmoral conscience is found at many points in Luther's writings. It is often present in his discussion of the relation of law and gospel. Frequently when Luther affirms "justification by grace through faith," he is affirming a joyful conscience that is created by the unconditional acceptance of God in Christ; by means of this good, joyful transmoral religious conscience centered in God's loving acceptance, a person is able to accept herself because power of the divine promise overrides and shuts up the bad moral conscience that until then had been plaguing her.

which some have identified as the third use of the law that guides and leads, but the harshness of the second use of the law would be softened.

D. Questions on Inspiration in Relation to Incarnation

We have already encountered the notion of inspiration. Eiríksson's questions 56 through 66 find him asking about the relation of inspiration to the Incarnation, and how one should understand Martensen's claim that these two are inseparable. If inspiration was exclusively linked to the apostolic period, must not the incarnation be so linked to it as well?[1] For Martensen the Incarnation is about a human being in whom dwells the fullness of the Godhead bodily; it is not just about the unity of a human with God.[2] The incarnate Christ is not the first instance of a soul being united with God; rather, the Christ is the Only begotten of the Father, "the world-redeeming Mediator who must be thought of in an eternal relation to the Father and to the human race."[3] This incarnate Christ accomplishes what is needed, which is a personal, actual exposition of the union of natures.[4] Martensen views the apostolic church, the first stage in the church's historical development, as the most intensively perfect state.[5] This stage serves as the church's standard and norm for its faith and life; the apostolic age's primitive excellence and fullness resided not in any single apostle but in the sum total of the apostolic consciousness, as that apostolic revelation received expression in the New Testament.[6] The new creation made possible by the incarnate Christ unleashes forces that work to nurture that regenerated consciousness that is the basis of inspiration. Martensen would likely make the case that the apostolic age as a period of intense inspiration was due to the potent efficacy of incarnational forces at work during that time. However, to say that

---

1 Eiríksson, *Den nydanske Theologies Cardinaldyder*, pp. 52f.

2 Martensen, *Den christelige Dogmatik*, p. 307 (*Christian Dogmatics*, p. 259).

3 Martensen, *Den christelige Dogmatik*, p. 306, p. 308 (*Christian Dogmatics*, p. 258, p. 259).

4 Martensen, *Den christelige Dogmatik*, pp. 309f. (*Christian Dogmatics*, p. 261).

5 Martensen, *Den christelige Dogmatik*, p. 402 (*Christian Dogmatics*, p. 336).

6 Martensen, *Den christelige Dogmatik*, p. 403, pp. 411-413, p. 483 (*Christian Dogmatics*, p. 336, pp. 343-345, p. 417).

this age was peculiar is not to say that incarnational forces are not at work in other ages instigating instances of inspiration. He insists that while the apostolic age is spoken of as the period of inspiration, it must be necessarily assumed that there are different degrees of inspiration and granted that inspiration has been possessed in different degrees at different times.[1] Inspiration must be described, declares our Danish systematician, as the progressive communication of the Spirit, and this must be viewed as unfolding hand-in-hand with the progressive development of human consciousness and freedom.[2]

Eiríksson wonders if post-apostolic Christ-communication comes from the Church, whereas in the apostolic period it came from outside or from above.[3] Martensen would likely say that, whether in the apostolic times or in contemporary times, the Christ-communication is mediated through the activity of human beings who are a part of the community called church. This working of the Christ and the Spirit is the empowering force of this community; and this effective force is a transcendent power, but Martensen might not be totally comfortable with speaking of this as coming from outside or from above during the apostolic time. This force is incarnationally present and not far removed from the people of faith. Similarly, he would realize that church tradition

---

1 Martensen, *Den christelige Dogmatik*, p. 407 (*Christian Dogmatics*, p. 340).

2 Martensen, *Den christelige Dogmatik*, p. 409 (*Christian Dogmatics*, p. 343). Martensen maintains, as did Kierkegaard too, that there are no disciples at second hand. The contemporaneous Christ appears in the context of the church to the contemporary disciple in such a way that responding in faith is comparable to the person of the first century who encountered the Christ in person. The sacrament of baptism is one means by which the Christ communicates himself to everyone. Martin Luther speaks of the incarnation of Christ continuing its work in the preaching of the Word, by which the Christ is brought ever closer to the hearts of the faithful. I doubt that Martensen would refuse to give serious consideration to such a view. The incarnation is a living, dynamic event that continues its work in the church down through the ages. Martensen would have been less worried than Eiríksson is about establishing the rational confines of the doctrine of the Incarnation and the correlational reality of inspiration as well. The Spirit blows where it will. In Eiríksson's questions we seem to encounter a desire to confine the incarnation for the sake of rational clarity. Concepts of language are utilized to give expression to the realities of the faith. However, there is some flexibility in how that is done. While consistency is a fine virtue for theologians to strive for, there are times when other concerns are more important. We ought to seek simplicity but we also ought not be overly upset when this aspirant ideal in some measure needs to be set aside.

3 Eiríksson, *Den nydanske Cardinaldyder*, p. 154.

has validity only as long as it has vitality as en-spirited by this divine effective force. Without such grounding in the Spirit, tradition quickly is transmuted from a living passing on of experienced truth to a dead repetition of meaningless rituals. That is why the true church is always criticizing corruption and putting forth new endeavors to reform and purify herself so as to be aligned with appropriate patterns.[1] For Martensen, inspiration was not limited to the apostles.[2] He is not out to confiscate inspiration from anybody, even though he is attempting to make the case for the distinctive spiritual efficacy of the regenerate consciousness as empowered by the new creation.

Martensen was not without self-confidence. He would not have judged himself to be with utterly no inspiration. At the minimum, as a Christian he was participating in the new creation and was operating with a regenerate consciousness.[3] As a participant in regeneration, Martensen would have regarded his judgments, most likely, not as infallible, but as no less worthy of consideration as candidates for truth than those of other theologians. Inspiration is linked to the incarnation. However, the incarnation in its fullness is prepared for over a long history of events.[4]

Eiríksson's questions seem to presuppose that the Christ and the apostles should have had full knowledge of the incarnation. Martensen claims more knowledge for the historical Jesus than many New Testament scholars today would attribute to him. And yet, he strongly endorses the conception of *kenosis* or "the divine self-limitation." If the incarnation and the concept of the Mediator are to be taken seriously, then God must be understood to feel the limitations of human nature as God's own limitations, that God experiences the states of human nature as God's own states, that the Godhead must be conceived as being wrapped up or clothed in the humanity of Christ, and that the external infinitude of the divine attributes are converted into an inner infinitude,

---

1 Martensen, *Den christelige Dogmatik*, p. 420 (*Christian Dogmatics*, p. 352).

2 Martensen, *Den christelige Dogmatik*, p. 407 (*Christian Dogmatics*, p. 340).

3 Martensen, *Den christelige Dogmatik*, p. 461 (*Christian Dogmatics*, p. 385).

4 Martensen, *Den christelige Dogmatik*, p. 284 (*Christian Dogmatics*, p. 236). The announcements of Christ contained in the Old Testament were in a real sense a continual coming of the Logos, a progressively incarnational coming, we might say, that culminates in the actual incarnation itself. If inspiration and incarnation are inseparable, then such an extended view of incarnation would extend as well to the view of inspiration's presence among the prophets.

in order they it might find room within the limits of human nature.[1] This view of the limitations of Christ's knowledge and power somewhat mitigates the issue of the Christ not knowing about the doctrine of the incarnation.

E. Questions on Reconciliation

Eiríksson raised questions about the essential and actual human-divine unity, and he also raises questions about the essential and actual reconciliation. He wonders if the essential reconciliation is not quite different from the Christian reconciliation about which the New Testament speaks.[2] Martensen understands grace as operating in creation to perfect human nature so that it can reach its destiny. Key is the human's need for God, which establishes a longing that is not satisfied until it has taken on its divine nature. Because of the fall into sin, humanity needs redeeming grace as well as perfecting grace: "Nature seeks after grace like the plant that bends toward the light; for indelible in the sinful human nature is 'the longing after the kingdom of God,' which through need, pain, and aspiration leads the human towards the fullness of grace."[3] Eiríksson is sensing that Martensen is affirming a conditionality to reconciliation, and he is right on that, but he is not right in thinking this view is not present in the New Testament. The incarnation brings about an essential reconciliation, but that reconciliation has to take hold within the lives of individuals. Martensen has gone to great pains in developing a theology in which nature and grace work in harmony rather than in opposition to one another. This is talked about as cosmogony and creation, God's activity in the kingdom of nature and the kingdom of spirit, the metaphysical and the historical, etc. When it comes to dealing with the doctrine of reconciliation, he does not want to suddenly abandon this theology and reduce the process of reconciliation to a pure process of nature. The very distinction between essential and actual reconciliation is precisely for the purpose of introducing freedom and contingency into the picture so that spiritual considerations can be

---

1 Martensen, *Den christelige Dogmatik*, pp. 319f. (*Christian Dogmatics*, p. 269).
2 Eiríksson, *Den nydanske Theologies Cardinaldyder*, pp. 155f.
3 Martensen, *Den christelige Dogmatik*, p. 423 (*Christian Dogmatics*, pp. 353f.).

considered along with the natural. Martensen might well agree with Eiríksson that as his theology stresses the two themes of creation and new creation, it does emphasize the idea of incarnation in his theology over that of reconciliation.

Eiríksson charges that Martensen's Trinitarian theology, as presenting an account of a God of metamorphosis or change, is a type of denial of God.[1] Martensen's response would be that if God is an utterly unchanging reality, then his theology could be construed as a denial of God. But if God is essentially love, then it seems that God would be involved in a process of metamorphosis just as Eiríksson suggests. If God's love moves God to respond in ever new ways to the creation so that love might be won from it, then Martensen's theology can be regarded as a beautiful affirmation of God.

Lastly, Eiríksson questions whether it would be good if this theology encouraged Christians not only to know Christ's glory, but furthermore to look upon themselves as a "Christ-bearer" or "God-human."[2] Martensen and those who appreciate his overall theological vision might grant that the first order of encouragement is to know Christ's glory. Agreement might be reached by them that wise counsel would not take the form of urging the faithful to look upon themselves as "Christ-bearers." At the same time, they might realize the wisdom in taking seriously the call to imitate Christ by living lives of love that take the form, as Luther says, of being little Christs to the neighbor. If that scenario includes Christians striving to be "Christ-bearers," then there might be agreement that that would not be all bad.

IV. Conclusions of Eiríksson and of Martensen

Eiríksson concludes his book with a few culminating comments. These paragraphs are not part of the 75 questions he presents, but they do offer some interesting insights into his situation and shed some further light on why Eiríksson was motivated to carry forth his prolonged attack on Martensen. The relationship between these two individuals

---

[1] Eiríksson, *Den nydanske Theologies Cardinaldyder*, p. 157. See also his *Speculativ Rettroenhed*, pp. 70-73.

[2] Eiríksson, *Den nydanske Theologies Cardinaldyder*, p. 158.

is an interesting one, and of course we have access to precious little from Martensen on this. In his conclusions, Eiríksson continues by congratulating himself on the astuteness of his questions and pointing out that those who read his book will have to acknowledge that it and the questions he proposes have been written by a scholar of some accomplishment.[1] Eiríksson has been charged by Martensen with operating with "deep misunderstandings," and so he takes the opportunity to point out that Martensen too has been misunderstood.[2] Furthermore, Eiríksson clarifies that he has always tried to be fair in assessing Martensen's views, which he thinks he has not misunderstood. A response from Martensen could bring clarity for those trying to understand him. Eiríksson expresses frustration in being faced with the trying task of interpreting Martensen's thinking, which becomes especially difficult when one never receives the benefit of clarifications that could come with some answers to the questions he has posed.[3] Eiríksson is convinced that a judgment needs to be rendered on whether or not Martensen's theology should be allowed to be spread through the country. Obviously, his position on the matter is not left in doubt.[4] Eiríksson ends his book expressing his hope that in the future, when the matter between him and Martensen is discussed, it will be framed in appropriate fashion.[5]

The diatribe ended, Eiríksson becomes largely silent on the matter of Martensen from that point on, joining the target of his criticisms in the mode of stillness or enclosing reserve in relation to the other.

Having rehearsed some of Eiríksson's conclusions, we can turn to Martensen's conclusions. Here some imagination and creativity are called for in formulating a final statement in the post-mortem defense. We considered in David Friedrich Strauss the notions of spirit, mythical language, and race. Those notions—which spill out into pretty large areas of confusion between the Dane and the Icelander when their differences in understanding each of them are spelled out—can here be used to set forth concluding comments from Martensen's perspective on his behalf.

---

1 Ibid., pp. 159f.
2 Ibid., p. 160.
3 Ibid., pp. 161f.
4 Ibid., pp. 163f.
5 Ibid., p. 164.

Martensen would have agreed with Strauss on his view that "it is the essential property of a spirit, in the distribution of itself into distinct personalities, to remain identical with itself, to possess itself in another than itself."[1] This applies to the reality of God and to the reality of human beings. Martensen's agreement and alliance with Hegel is not unqualified, but on this central matter of spirit he stands largely in the Hegelian camp. For him, God is finally Spirit. When it comes to articulating his understanding of the hypostases of the Trinity, he therefore regards them as spiritual forms of existence, consciousness, subsistence, etc., which remain identical with themselves while possessing themselves in another than themselves. Eiríksson operates with quite a different mindset. He presupposes more of a substantialist view that emphasizes the discrete content of an entity such as a hypostasis and has great difficulty imagining and accommodating a more flexible, processive, relational view of such realities. There is a wide gap on this issue between these two men. This difference generates many questions. The Trinity is a focus of many of these questions, but there is also a concern expressed about the nature of God. On Eiríksson's view, God and the divine attributes are to be presented by a theologian of the church as they have been presented in the tradition. That means thoughts about God should give expression to an eternal reality who does not change and whose attributes such as omniscience ought not be reformulated in relation to more modern ways of thinking. This is not to say that Eiríksson himself affirms and holds such a traditional view, but he thinks it is the theologian's duty to articulate thoughts about God that are in keeping with the tradition.

Martensen disagrees with Strauss quite vigorously on his view of myth, at least as he applies it to New Testament writings. This is not to say, though, that Martensen has disdain for language of mythology and language of the imagination. In fact, many aspects of Romanticism could be identified in Martensen's interests and writings. A major theme in his reflection as a theologian is that religious faith is grounded and nurtured in religious language. He disagrees with Hegel and Strauss in the way they relegate such language to the status of picture-language that is to be transcended in the conceptual language which grasps and expresses the content of religion but does so in a form that is more

[1] Strauss, *The Life of Jesus*, p. 777.

appropriate to thinking, and in particular, to philosophical thinking. When a Romantic composer states that words are not at all up to music in the ability to arouse feelings, that a song possesses a potency that words about the song do not have a chance of communicating—then he is affirming a similar view to that of the Romantic theologian Martensen who contends that faith's language embodies a living power that can by no means be matched by more systematic formulations of it.[1] On this matter, he and Eiríksson again stand in disagreement.

Having considered spirit and imaginative language, the third Straussian notion that can shed light on the different perspectives of Eiríksson and Martensen is that of the race. Eiríksson eventually leaves traditional Christianity behind because he arrives at the conclusion that the New Testament and Christian theology actually do affirm an essential unity of God and the human that takes on actual reality in the God-human. At the time he was criticizing Martensen, Eiríksson was of the view that Martensen's arguing for this claim was setting him at odds with the Christian tradition. Eiríksson's self-understanding in making the critique of Martensen was that he, Eiríksson, was speaking on behalf of the tradition. Martensen regards the proposition that there is an essential unity between the divine and human nature as the central claim of pantheism. In arguing that Christian faith must affirm pantheism at the outset of its deliberations, it was this proposition regarding essential unity that he was especially concerned to affirm. Of course, his stance also stressed that the Christian must move beyond pantheism, but one starts with pantheism and especially this fundamental claim

---

[1] Martensen stated this well in articulating the nature of the relation between faith and knowledge (*Dogmatiske Oplysninger*, p. 48). Faith's existential knowledge finds its grounding in a religious language that is imaginative. Martensen's position appreciates the robustness of faith's imaginative language and thereby presupposes a particular understanding of the assessment of the function of reason in relation to the deliverances of the imagination. Hegel and Strauss give reason a preference over the imagination, while Martensen's position gives a privileged status to the imagination and its language. That difference is even greater when considering Martensen's view as opposed to Eiríksson. There maybe needs to be care taken in characterizing Eiríksson as a "rationalizing theologian," because good scholars have argued for the ambiguity of the matter; however, it can safely be claimed that Eiríksson is very much a rationalist when compared to Martensen. This leads him to function with presuppositions that are not shared by the more established theologian who is his target of choice for criticizing.

concerning essential unity is to be preserved even as one goes further. However, essential unity is not actual unity. There is the whole process of actualization that has to be set into place for the unity to assume a realized form in reality. Lying behind all of these claims for Martensen is the Son, the Logos, the incarnation of the Logos in the God-human, and the redeeming and perfecting work of the Christ in the church through the Spirit. There is singularity about the incarnate one, and this one provides the fundamental ground for the empowering of human beings into the fullness of life. That fullness of life, for Martensen, is a fullness that takes shape as one comes to live in God. The metaphysical reality of the Son is the reason that human beings created in God's image possess essential unity with God, and the incarnate reality of the Son is the reason human beings are able to progress toward actual unity with God. Without question, Martensen is fully aware that the situation of human beings participating in God is not one in which human beings are literally becoming God. The categorical difference between Creator and creature is not abolished with an actual unity of the natures. But the participation is real and the effects are sublime.

We remind ourselves that Strauss had wanted to replace the individual Christ with the idea of the human race: " 'Humanity' is the real unity of the two natures—God and the human."[1] Martensen does not want to dismiss this idea of the race as being an unimportant theological claim, but he does not want to set it over against the focus on an individual. The Son as the Logos working in creation makes manifest a race of human beings created in the image of God and thus possessing a nature that is essentially united with the divine nature. Furthermore, though, the Son as the incarnate Logos working in the new creation makes manifest a human being who is the God-human and thus distinctively the First-Born. The Christian affirms both of these claims. Eiríksson is simply unable to bring himself to endorse such a view. Martensen's dogmatic prose falls in this case on deaf ears because, from Martensen's perspective, Eiríksson is not able to embrace the full radical claim of the Christian incarnation in its metaphysical and historical implications. This includes the anthropological payoff of this understanding, that is,

---

1 Strauss, *The Life of Jesus*, p. 776.

the distinction between the essential and the subjective will, which never gains resonance with Eiríksson.

The fifth Danish edition of Martensen's *Christian Dogmatics* included an introductory essay by Alfred Theodor Jørgensen (1874-1953) entitled "Some Features of the History of Martensen's Dogmatics: A Segment of the History of Danish Theology."[1] He makes reference to Eiríksson's *Speculative Orthodoxy* book, and thinks that the "author's tone and understanding of dogmatics on the whole are summed up by his claim that Martensen's work theoretically is "a monstrosity with many heads" and practically "can only have detrimental effects" for those who appropriate it.[2] Jørgensen mentions Eiríksson's employment of H.N. Clausen against Martensen, and he thinks that Eiríksson's unclear positive theological stand only shows Eiríksson to be an extreme rationalist who harbors a fanatical hatred of everything that is called speculation.[3] There is some truth in Jørgensen's assessment.

The same can be said of Skat Arildsen's (1901-98) comments, when he depicts Eiríksson's polemic against Martensen's dogmatics as setting forth damning judgments that "must be described as a strange blending of the misunderstood and overdrawn with caricatured moments of truth," as he directed his criticism against some of the principal doctrines of the dogmatics but "supplied only sporadic engagement on the battlefield of the questions of principle": "The result of Eiríksson's 'critical' interrogation of *Christian Dogmatics* is disheartening. The Martensenian work [declares Eiríksson] is 'endowed' with such a 'monstrous manysidedness,' that makes it impossible to classify, it being a 'hotchpotch of everything possible,' 'a motley mass' of mutually conflicting and contradicting elements: 'ecclesial, biblical, rationalistic, mystical, Hegelian, Gnostic.'"[4] Eiríksson contends that, whether considered from the theoretical or

1 Alfred Theodor Jørgensen, "Nogle Træk af Martensens Dogmatiks Historie. Et Afsnit af den danske Teologis Historie," in Hans Lassen Martensen, *Den christelige Dogmatik*, 5th edition, ed. and introduced by Alfred Theodor Jørgensen, Copenhagen: Gad 1904, pp. I-XXII.

2 Ibid., p. XV The quotation, from Eiríksson, *Speculativ Retroenhed*, p. 76.

3 Martensen, *Den christelige Dogmatik*, 5th edition, pp. XVI-XVII.

4 Arildsen, *Biskop Hans Lassen Martensen*, p. 274, where he is quoting from Eiríksson, *Speculativ Rettroenhed*, p. 67, p. 68, p. 74.

the practical point of view, the writing is "reprehensible" and unable to "satisfy any party or movement in Christendom."[1]

Arildsen concludes "that Martensen certainly was a 'religious genius,' but definitely not a critical thinker."[2] I think it is hard to disagree on the religious genius part of the claim. However, the manner in which one engages in critical thinking is determined by many factors and commitments. Martensen held reason in check, but the case can be made that he operated very consistently in his critical thinking as that thinking was conditioned by the commitments he was making to the imaginative language of the Christian faith and to the living God over against which and in whom he was living his life. Martensen's critical thinking was commensurate with his faith commitments, and this led him to carry out his theological formulating in a quite courageous fashion. In fact, Eiríksson was frustrated with Martensen both because he wasn't following the canons of intelligibility that guided Eiríksson's deliberation and because he was being too cavalier in his theologizing, and this led him into what Eiríksson regarded as heretical views.

Martensen did not respond to Eiríksson in any significant way because he was aware of the huge divide between their world-views; he didn't sense enough common ground to be able to carry on a fruitful conversation. He also was fully aware that he was the person with the power in the situation and that to enter into a debate with one regarded by the public as possessing less power could only lead to possible loss rather than gain for him. A considered response from Martensen could have surprisingly opened the door to a conversation in which positions on both sides were clarified and an advance of one sort or another was made. However, Martensen simply could not bring himself to do it. I hope that offering this very belated post-mortem defense in Martensen's stead to Eiríksson's accusations might still at this late date have a fructifying function in deliberations on the relation between these two fascinating individuals.

---

1 Arildsen, *Biskop Hans Lassen Martensen*, p. 275, where he is quoting from Eiríksson, *Speculativ Rettroenhed*, pp. 76-77.

2 Ibid., p. 295.

Eiríksson's Critique of Kierkegaard and Kierkegaard's (drafted) Response: Religious Faith, Absurdity, and Rationality

Roe Fremstedal

I. Introduction

Magnús Eiríksson's pseudonymous work *Is Faith a Paradox and "By Virtue of the Absurd"?* (1850) is an important book for several reasons. Everything points to the fact that it is the very first monograph written and published on Kierkegaard. Although largely ignored by his contemporaries and by later Kierkegaard scholars, Eiríksson's book is accessible, clearly written, and often convincing. Eiríksson succeeds, at least to some degree, in identifying central problems in Kierkegaard's pseudonymous authorship, and Kierkegaard's drafted response to Eiríksson goes some way towards clarifying his position and sketching a solution to some of the problems. Eiríksson anticipates one of the classical controversies of Kierkegaard scholarship by arguing, at length, that Kierkegaard's pseudonyms Johannes de silentio and Johannes Climacus portray faith as irrational. Moreover, Kierkegaard's response to Eiríksson has hardly received the attention it deserves,[1] although it is clearly relevant for understanding and evaluating Kierkegaard's position. This is the case not only with regard to the (still ongoing) debate on whether or not Kierkegaard is an irrationalist,[2] but also with regard

1 See *Pap.* X-6 B 68-82, pp. 72-88 / *JP* 1, 9-12 and *JP* 6, 6598-6601.

2 For the debate on irrationalism, see, for example, Robert Herbert, "Two of Kierkegaard's Uses of 'Paradox,'" *The Philosophical Review*, vol. 70, 1961, pp. 41-55; Henry Allison, "Christianity and Nonsense," *Review of Metaphysics*, vol. 20, 1967, pp.

to Kierkegaard's much-discussed use of pseudonyms, and the relation between *Fear and Trembling* and the *Concluding Unscientific Postscript*. This means that Eiríksson's 1850 book and Kierkegaard's response is not just of historical importance, since these two texts shed light on issues that are still relevant and debated today.

Is Faith a Paradox and "By Virtue of the Absurd"? is a work that is argumentative, polemical, and full of satire. Eiríksson argues against the portrayal of religious faith as absurd in *Fear and Trembling* and the *Concluding Unscientific Postscript* by claiming that faith is rational, although it transcends human understanding. Eiríksson makes the case that Kierkegaard's pseudonyms should have said something other than what they say, given fundamental ideas about Abrahamic religious faith that are shared by the pseudonyms and Eiríksson. Eiríksson uses the *Concluding Unscientific Postscript* to criticize *Fear and Trembling*, although he deals with the latter in much more detail than the former. While Eiríksson's analysis of the *Postscript* is selective, eclectic, and relatively short,[1] the analysis of *Fear and Trembling* is much more comprehensive. In fact, Eiríksson's commentary on *Fear and Trembling* is longer than the book itself.[2]

In 1850, Kierkegaard read *Is Faith a Paradox and "By Virtue of the Absurd"?* and drafted a long, interesting response that he did not

---

432-60; J. Heywood Thomas, "Paradox," in *Concepts and Alternatives in Kierkegaard*, ed. by Niels Thulstrup and Maria Mikulová Thulstrup, Copenhagen: C.A. Reitzel 1980 (*Biblioteca Kierkegaardiana*, vol. 3), pp. 192-219; Timothy P. Jackson, "Kierkegaard's Metatheology," *Faith and Philosophy*, vol. 4, 1987, pp. 71-85; Merold Westphal, *Kierkegaard's Critique of Reason and Society*, University Park, Pennsylvania: Pennsylvania State University Press 1991, p. vii, p. 21, p. 27, p. 90, p. 125; John Lippitt and Daniel Hutto, "Making Sense of Nonsense: Kierkegaard and Wittgenstein," *Proceedings of the Aristotelian Society*, vol. 98, 1998, pp. 263-86; Ulrich Knappe, *Theory and Practice in Kant and Kierkegaard*, Berlin and New York: Walter de Gruyter 2004 (*Kierkegaard Studies Monograph Series*, vol. 9), p. 59, pp. 80f., pp. 118-20; C. Stephen Evans, *Kierkegaard on Faith and the Self: Collected Essays*, Waco: Baylor University Press 2006, pp. 120-23; Richard McCombs, *The Paradoxical Rationality of Søren Kierkegaard*, Bloomington: Indiana University Press 2013.

1 See Magnús Eiríksson [Theophilus Nicolaus], *Er Troen et Paradox og "i Kraft af det Absurde"? et Spørgsmaal foranlediget ved "Frygt og Bæven, af Johannes de silentio", Besvaret ved Hjelp af en Troes-Ridders fortrolige Meddelelser, til fælles Opbyggelse for Jøder, Christne og Muhamedanere, af bemeldte Troes-Ridders Broder*, Copenhagen: Chr. Steen & Søn 1850, pp. 149-81.

2 See especially Eiríksson, *Er Troen et Paradox og "i Kraft af det Absurde"?*, pp. 13-148.

publish.[1] It seems that Kierkegaard knew that Eiríksson was behind the pseudonym Theophilus Nicolaus since he refers not just to Eiríksson's pseudonymous 1850 book but also to his signed 1846 book on rationality.[2] In this draft, Kierkegaard and his pseudonyms describe the efforts of Eiríksson (or the pseudonym Nicolaus), as sincere, honest, selfless, religious, and as having moral worth.[3] However, Kierkegaard claims that Eiríksson's 1850 book is not well-informed enough and that it lacks sharpness, and dialectical rigor.[4] Thus, Kierkegaard judges that Eiríksson's efforts are well-meant but that he lacks the necessary theoretical abilities. Kierkegaard therefore concludes that there is hardly any hope of real understanding between himself and Eiríksson. As a result, he, or rather his pseudonyms, will not deal publically with Eiríksson. This appears to be the reason why Kierkegaard never published his response to Eiríksson in his lifetime.

Still, Kierkegaard indicates that *if* he were to answer Eiríksson, then the response should be attributed to himself and Anti-Climacus.[5] But as it stands Kierkegaard's 17-page response is attributed to the pseudonyms de silentio, Climacus, and Kierkegaard himself, although he mentions that one part may be attributed to Anti-Climacus.[6] De silentio and Climacus seem to be chosen because it is these authors that Eiríksson criticizes, while Anti-Climacus could be invoked to add some Christian seriousness and authority to the response.

---

1 See *Pap.* X-6 B 68-82, pp. 72-88 / *JP* 1, 9-12 and *JP* 6, 6598-6601.

2 *Pap.* X-6 B 68, p. 74 / *JP* 6, 6598, p. 301 references Magnús Eiríksson, *Tro, Overtro og Vantro, i deres Forhold til Fornuft og Forstand, samt til hinanden indbyrdes*, Copenhagen: H.C. Klein 1846.

3 See *Pap.* X-6 B 68, pp. 75f. / *JP* 6, 6598.

4 See *Pap.* X-6 B 79, pp. 85f. / *JP* 1, 10.

5 See *Pap.* X-6 B 77, p. 84 / *JP* 6, 6600.

6 *Pap.* X-6 B 68-B 69, pp. 72-78 and *Pap.* X-6 B 72-74, pp. 80-83 is attributed to Climacus, while *Pap.* X-6, B 70-B 71, pp. 78-80 is attributed to de silentio. *Pap.* X-6 B 75-76, pp. 83f., is not explicitly attributed to a pseudonym, although *Pap.* X-6, B 75 mentions de silentio and appears to be a reworking of *Pap.* X-6 B 68 that is attributed to Climacus. *Pap.* X-6 B 77-82, pp. 84-88 is attributed to "me," something that appears to be a reference to Kierkegaard. Finally, it is said that *Pap.* X-6, B 79-82, pp. 85-88 (and possibly B 78, pp. 84f.) may best be attributed to Anti-Climacus. See Gerhard Schreiber, "Magnús Eiríksson: An Opponent of Martensen and an Unwelcome Ally of Kierkegaard," in *Kierkegaard and his Danish Contemporaries*, Tome II, *Theology*, ed. by Jon Stewart, Aldershot: Ashgate 2009 (*Kierkegaard Research: Sources, Reception and Resources*, vol. 7), pp. 49-94, here p. 81 (note).

Kierkegaard indicates two reasons for using pseudonyms: First, it makes it possible to avoid a straightforward public attack on someone one is personally acquainted with (for example, Martensen).[1] Pseudonyms make it possible to distance oneself from the persons involved and to avoid unnecessary offense or embarrassment in a small-town context where the leading figures are all personally acquainted.[2] Second, the different pseudonyms can present the matter at hand from different perspectives.[3] While de silentio and Climacus speak from the perspective of the nonbeliever, Anti-Climacus and Kierkegaard himself seem to speak from the perspective of the Christian believer.

Kierkegaard faults Eiríksson for not paying sufficient attention to this perspectival approach when he bluntly identifies Kierkegaard with his pseudonyms.[4] But even if Kierkegaard does not want to be simply identified with his pseudonyms,[5] it does not follow from this that he

---

1 See *Pap.* X-6 B 128 / *JP* 6, 6596; *Pap.* VII-1 B 88-92.

2 See Jon Stewart, *Kierkegaard's Relations to Hegel Reconsidered*, New York and Cambridge: Cambridge University Press 2003, p. 42; Schreiber, "Magnús Eiríksson," p. 88.

3 See *SKS* 23, 182f., NB17:28 / *KJN* 7, 185.

4 See *SKS* 23, 182f., NB17:28 / *KJN* 7, 185; *Pap.* X-6 B 71, p. 80; *Pap.* X-6 B 128 / *JP* 6, 6596.

5 See *SKS* 7, 571 / *CUP1*, 627. For the debate on the pseudonyms, see for example Henning Fenger, *Kierkegaard, the Myths and their Origins: Studies in the Kierkegaardian Papers and Letters*, New Haven and London: Yale University Press 1980, pp. 21f., pp. 145-7; Lars Bejerholm, "Anonymity and Pseudonymity," in *Kierkegaard Literary Miscellany*, ed. by Niels Thulstrup and Maria Mikulová Thulstrup, Copenhagen: C.A. Reitzel 1981 (*Biblioteca Kierkegaardiana*, vol. 9), 18-23; Louis Mackey, *Points of View: Readings of Kierkegaard*, Tallahassee, Florida: Florida University Press 1986, pp. 187-90; Roger Poole, *Kierkegaard: The Indirect Communication*, Charlottesville: University Press of Virginia 1993; Johannes Sløk, *Kierkegaard – humanismens tænker*, Copenhagen: Hans Reitzel 1995, pp. 134f.; Anders Kingo, *Analogiens teologi. En dogmatisk studie over dialektikken i Søren Kierkegaards opbyggelige og pseudonyme forfatterskab*, Copenhagen: Gad 1995, p. 252, pp. 279-282; Merold Westphal, *Becoming a Self: A Reading of Kierkegaard's* Concluding Unscientific Postscript, West Lafayette, Indiana: Purdue University Press 1996, pp. 8-19, p. 60, pp. 192f.; Roger Poole, " 'My wish, my prayer': Keeping the Pseudonyms Apart. Preliminary Considerations," in *Kierkegaard Revisited: Proceedings from the Conference "Kierkegaard and the Meaning of Meaning It", Copenhagen, May 5-9, 1996*, ed. by Niels Jørgen Cappelørn and Jon Stewart, Berlin and New York: Walter de Gruyter 1997 (*Kierkegaard Studies Monograph Series*, vol. 1), pp. 156-76; Michelle Kosch, *Freedom and Reason in Kant, Schelling, and Kierkegaard*, Oxford: Clarendon Press 2006, pp. 10-13; C. Stephen Evans, *Kierkegaard's Ethics of Love: Divine Commands and Moral Obligations*, Oxford: Oxford University Press 2006, pp. 37-44; C. Stephen Evans, *Kierkegaard: An Introduction*, Cambridge: Cambridge University Press 2009, pp. 27f.; Jamie Turnbull, "Kierkegaard on Emotion: A Critique

himself does not agree with much (or most) of what the pseudonyms say or that the different perspectival voices are fundamentally at odds with each other. Indeed, we will see that Kierkegaard criticizes Eiríksson's contention that de silentio and Climacus are at odds with each other.

II. Agreement and Shared Enemies

Much like Kierkegaard, Eiríksson wants to promote (what he sees as) genuine religious faith and to attack the inauthentic and complacent faith of bourgeois Christendom.[1] Both Kierkegaard and Eiríksson criticize speculative theology for confusing authentic Christianity with bourgeois Christendom.[2] Still, Eiríksson is more explicit and less polite than Kierkegaard when it comes to publicly singling out his enemies. Eiríksson identifies not just the Hegelians Heiberg and Martensen but also Hegel himself as enemies.[3] He also tries to ally himself with Danish critics of Hegelianism, including not just Kierkegaard but also Rasmus Nielsen and Peter Michael Stilling.[4] However, Eiríksson emphasizes that the Hegelians and Christendom represent the establishment, while he, Kierkegaard, and Nielsen are the underdogs. He contends that Kierkegaard and his allies have not received the attention they deserve and that the establishment is trying to use a *Totschweigetaktik* (death by silence) against their critics by ignoring them.[5]

---

of Furtak's *Wisdom in Love*, "*Religious Studies*, vol. 46, 2010, pp. 489-508, here p. 507; Phillip Schwab, *Der Rückstoß der Methode: Kierkegaard und die indirekte Mitteilung*, Berlin and New York: Walter de Gruyter 2012 (*Kierkegaard Studies Monograph Series*, vol. 25); Jon Stewart, "Søren Kierkegaard and the Problem of Pseudonymity," *Graduate Faculty Philosophy Journal*, vol. 32, 2012, pp. 407-34; *Kierkegaard's Pseudonyms*, ed. by Katalin Nun and Jon Stewart, Aldershot: Ashgate 2015 (*Kierkegaard Research: Sources, Reception and Resources*, vol. 17).

1 See Eiríksson, *Er Troen et Paradox og "i Kraft af det Absurde"?*, pp. iv and f., pp. 5f., pp. 9ff. And like Kierkegaard, Eiríksson criticizes those who believe that religious faith represents a defeated and outdated stage (p. 13).

2 See *Pap.* X-6 B 68, p. 72 / *JP* 6, 6598. Kierkegaard notes his agreement with Eiríksson at this point.

3 See Eiríksson, *Er Troen et Paradox og "i Kraft af det Absurde"?*, p. 118, p. 120, p. 122. See also Eiríksson, *Tro, Overtro og Vantro*, p. 10, pp. 17f., p. 30; *Pap.* VII-1 B 88-92.

4 See Eiríksson, *Er Troen et Paradox og "i Kraft af det Absurde"?*, p. 160 and p. 174.

5 See Schreiber, "Magnús Eiríksson," pp. 51f.

Eiríksson's critique of *Fear and Trembling* and the *Postscript* thus belongs to a larger context where Eiríksson tries to ally himself with Kierkegaard against the Hegelians and the mainstream Danish intellectuals (something Kierkegaard does *not* seem to appreciate).[1] For this reason, Eiríksson's criticism of Kierkegaard's pseudonyms is much less harsh and satirical than his criticism of Martensen. Eiríksson takes Kierkegaard much more seriously than most of his contemporaries did, and recommends *Fear and Trembling* highly to potential readers, partially because of its psychological insight. He describes Johannes de silentio as an ingenious and profound thinker and has deep respect for Johannes Climacus as well.[2] Although he tries to ally himself with Kierkegaard and to supplement *Fear and Trembling*, Eiríksson's book focuses on his disagreement with de silentio and Climacus.[3] Indeed, Eiríksson indicates that he agrees with Martensen in *principle* that Christian faith cannot possibly be grounded in absurdity (although Martensen's application of this principle is said to be false).[4]

Much like Kierkegaard, Eiríksson argues that Christendom puts too much emphasis on dogmas, confessions, ceremonies, and customs and too little emphasis on how we live our lives. However, Eiríksson goes beyond Kierkegaard by criticizing the role baptism plays in Christendom, attacking the idea that infant baptism is somehow necessary and sufficient for being a Christian and that it therefore needs to be enforced by the state. Eiríksson goes so far as to suggest that Christendom is misled by a well-paid and corrupt clergy and that it is motivated by laziness and impure motives.[5]

Eiríksson believes that authentic religiousness needs to be reintroduced in Christendom. Again, this is very similar to Kierkegaard. Like Johannes de silentio, Eiríksson appeals to Abraham in The Old

---

1 See ibid.

2 See Eiríksson, *Er Troen et Paradox og "i Kraft af det Absurde"?*, p. 1, p. 18, p. 175. Eiríksson is interested in describing the character and state of mind of authentic religious believers (p. 66). Although, Eiríksson speaks highly of de silentio's psychological insight, he nevertheless objects that de silentio's descriptions are too idealized to be quite realistic psychologically (p. 78).

3 See Eiríksson, *Er Troen et Paradox og "i Kraft af det Absurde"?*, p. 2, p. 148

4 See Schreiber, "Magnús Eiríksson," p. 65.

5 See Eiríksson, *Er Troen et Paradox og "i Kraft af det Absurde"?*, pp. 5f., pp. 9ff.

Testament, the father of faith, as a paradigmatic case of religious belief,[1] contrasting Abraham with Danish Christendom. However, Eiríksson goes beyond *Fear and Trembling* (and Kierkegaard) by emphasizing that Abraham is common not just to Judaism and Christianity but also to Islam ("Muhammadanism").[2]

Eiríksson accepts the Kierkegaardian view that authentic religious faith is about more than assenting to doctrine or dogma.[3] Faith is not just about holding correct theoretical beliefs but also about how one leads one's life. Eiríksson describes the necessary theoretical views in a minimalist manner as the belief that God is wise, good, and powerful (omnipotent). More emphasis is put on the believer's unconditional trust (*tillid*) in God as well as his obedience towards God. This trust and obedience should be expressed in the whole life of the believer, Eiríksson maintains. By being obedient and imitating God, the believer becomes not just morally good but also God's organ. This is related to the fact that, for Eiríksson, authentic religiousness involves not just belief (faith) but also neighbor-love and hope (the expectancy of good).

III. Reason, Understanding, Unbelief, and Superstition

In order to make sense of Eiríksson's work we need to look at his conceptual apparatus. Eiríksson breaks with Kierkegaard by introducing a notion of reason (*Fornuft*) as a higher faculty that is the sense (*Sands*) for the infinite and eternal.[4] Indeed, Eiríksson describes reason as the faculty (or sense) for perceiving God and his revelations inside and outside of us.[5] As such, reason is receptive (passive), involving an immediate, intuitive and non-discursive ability to make judgments

---

1 See ibid., p. 71, p. 143, p. 147.

2 By focusing on these three Abrahamic religions, Eiríksson advocates syncretism and ecumenism, see *Er Troen et Paradox og "i Kraft af det Absurde"?*, p. 8, p. 103, p. 134, p. 137, pp. 162f.

3 See Eiríksson, *Er Troen et Paradox og "i Kraft af det Absurde"?*, pp. 20ff.

4 Ibid., p. 18. Eiríksson appears to be following Mynster or Martensen as well as Jacobi by stressing the etymology of the Danish *Fornuft* from the German *vernehmen*. See Schreiber, "Magnús Eiríksson," pp. 61f. (note). See also Schreiber's contribution in this volume.

5 See Eiríksson, *Tro, Overtro, Vantro*, p. 27, p. 40.

about God, the supernatural and supersensual. The understanding (*Forstanden*), by contrast is an active, discursive, and mediating ability to make judgments that comprehend what is given from reason and sense perception.[1] While reason receives or perceives something (for example, revelation), understanding processes and analyzes it propositionally. Reason makes the judgment that something is given (or not), whereas the understanding analyzes it by asking what it is, how it is, and why it is.[2]

Eiríksson maintains that reason is certain, unless obscured by the understanding.[3] The idea seems to be that unbelief (*Vantro*) is caused by the understanding not accepting facts given to it by reason but rather relying on sense perception. The unbeliever uses the mere understanding to judge and exclude faith, something that is said to involve a partial absurdity.[4] Presumably, this is a weak absurdity where one denies what transcends understanding and the humanly possible.

Eiríksson interprets superstition (*Overtro*) as faith that is constrained by neither reason nor the understanding. Superstition involves a total (strong) absurdity where one believes something that is untrue.[5] Presumably, superstition involves believing in something logically impossible, by embracing a formal contradiction. As we will see, Eiríksson interprets faith by virtue of the absurd as a classical expression of (the principle of) superstition.[6]

Unlike most of the Western tradition, Eiríksson seems to align reason with special revelation rather than general revelation (*lumen naturale*). This involves a peculiar use of the term where reason is inherently religious and makes it possible to receive special (supernatural) revelation. Kierkegaard explicitly objects to this peculiar notion of

1 See ibid., pp. 24ff.; Carl Henrik Koch, *Den danske idealisme 1800-1880*, Copenhagen: Gyldendal 2004 (*Den danske filosofis historie*, vol. 4), pp. 295f.

2 See Eiríksson, *Tro, Overtro og Vantro*, pp. 36-43.

3 See ibid., p. 37. This is important since it indicates that unbelief is caused by an intellectual or cognitive failure rather than a volitional failure (something Kierkegaard would not accept). However, this would appear to make it very difficult, if not impossible, for Eiríksson to hold unbelievers accountable for their unbelief by blaming them.

4 See Eiríksson, *Er Troen et Paradox og "i Kraft af det Absurde"?*, pp. 51-55.

5 See ibid., pp. 54f.

6 See ibid., p. 55.

reason.[1] The closest he comes to Eiríksson's notion of reason, seems to be the notion of the condition of faith (*Troens Betingelse*) in *Philosophical Fragments*, a condition involving a criterion for receiving revelation and recognizing it as such.[2] However, Climacus presents the condition of faith as something supernaturally given directly by God to each singular individual that transcends human understanding (and rationality).

Kierkegaard's response insists that Eiríksson's rationalism is at odds with his endorsement of supernatural (special) revelation. Kierkegaard thinks that Eiríksson tries to tone down this problem by presenting supernatural revelation as natural, while ending up with an appeal to higher rationality that resembles the speculative theology of Martensen.[3] The implication is that Eiríksson must choose between rationalism and belief in supernatural revelation if he is to be consistent. As it is, Eiríksson risks that what he calls "reason" will represent not the divine but something all too human (such as confused thinking or intellectual hang-ups).

As is well-known, Kierkegaard's thought belongs to a Danish context in which rationalism and supernaturalism and Hegelian logic were at the center of a heated debate.[4] Kierkegaard generally viewed rationalism in matters of faith as incompatible with supernaturalism, denying that these terms could be mediated like the Hegelians and Eiríksson thought.[5] Although more work is needed on Eiríksson's notion of

---

[1] See *Pap.* X-6 B 68, pp. 73f. / *JP* 6, 6598; *Pap.* X-6 B 72, p. 82; *Pap.* X-6 B 75, p. 83.

[2] See *SKS* 4, 222 / *PF*, 13; *SKS* 4, 270 / *PF*, 69f.; *SKS* 4, 299 / *PF*, 92f.

[3] See *Pap.* X-6 B 68, pp. 73f. / *JP* 6, 6598.

[4] The debate started when Bishop Mynster argued that the law of excluded middle must hold true, and that the revelation of Christ is therefore either supernatural as the supernaturalists maintain or not supernatural as the rationalists maintain. Stewart, *Kierkegaard's Relations to Hegel Reconsidered*, pp. 78f.; *Mynster's "Rationalism, Supernaturalism" and the Debate about Mediation*, ed. and trans. by Jon Stewart, Copenhagen: Museum Tusculanum Press 2009 (*Texts from Golden Age Denmark*, vol. 5).

[5] However, it is not obvious that rationalism in manners of faith needs to preclude the possibility of supernatural revelation as Kierkegaard suggests. To illustrate this, a Kantian typology of religious belief would seem to suffice. Consider the distinction between (1) *denying* supernatural revelation and affirming natural religion (that is, naturalism), (2) *agnosticism* about supernatural revelation and affirmation of natural religion (that is, rationalism) (3) *affirmation* of supernatural religion without taking it to be necessary as natural religion is (that is, pure rationalism), and (4) holding supernatural revelation to be necessary (that is, pure supernaturalism), see Immanuel Kant, *Religion and Rational Theology*, ed. and trans. by Allen W. Wood and George

rationality, it nevertheless seems that he advocates a pre-Kantian notion of reason as intuitive cognition of the supernatural and supersensual that Kierkegaard does not accept. A fairly obvious difficulty with Eiríksson's notion of rationality is that it does not leave much room for critical thinking, dissent or disobedience, since reason merely receives or intuits what is given from above.

IV. Faith Only Seemingly Absurd

As indicated by the title, *Is Faith a Paradox and "By Virtue of the Absurd"?*, Eiríksson's central concern is whether religious faith is absurd, as claimed by de silentio and Climacus. Eiríksson argues that de silentio and Climacus do not offer any real proof for the alleged absurdity of faith,[1] and concludes that faith is neither absurd for religious believers nor for God, although it may appear absurd for nonbelievers (for example, de silentio and Climacus). For believers, faith is rational or reasonable, even though it transcends human understanding and knowledge.

Eiríksson starts by asking: "What is really faith? In what does it consist? What is its basis and motivating force? Is it based on reason or what is reasonable? Or is it based on the non-rational, the irrational, the absurd?"[2] As can be seen from this passage, Eiríksson—unlike Kierkegaard—equates or aligns the absurd with the irrational. Eiríksson therefore takes de silentio and Climacus to portray faith in *irrationalist*

---

di Giovanni, Cambridge: Cambridge University Press 2001 (*The Cambridge Edition of the Works of Immanuel Kant*), pp. 177f. This typology suggests that there are more conceptual options available to Eiríksson than Kierkegaard indicates. Kierkegaard tends to present a simple either/or between naturalism and supernaturalism and gives little attention to the intermediary positions (rationalism and pure rationalism). Still, Eiríksson's position hardly fits this Kantian typology, since Eiríksson wants to be a rationalist who not only affirms supernatural revelation but also take it to be necessary. Thus, Eiríksson wants to combine, or mediate between, rationalism and supernaturalism in a manner that neither Kierkegaard nor Kantians conceive of as possible.

1 See Eiríksson, *Er Troen et Paradox og "i Kraft af det Absurde"?*, p. 159.

2 Ibid., p. 14. I have not distinguished systematically between the paradox and the absurd in this article since this would only seem to complicate matters unnecessarily.

terms, something Kierkegaard does not seem to do.[1] Eiríksson claims that the Tertullian *credo quia absurdum* is pushed to the extreme by *Fear and Trembling* (and the *Postscript*).[2] Eiríksson takes this principle to prescribe believing something (only) because it is absurd, because it cannot be comprehended and proved by the understanding. He then claims that this would commit one to believe any kind of absurdity.

Eiríksson argues that the absurd is neither the motivating force nor the cause or basis of genuine religious faith.[3] Presumably, the point is that authentic religious faith cannot be motivated by absurdity as such since then any absurdity, logical contradiction, or untruth would suffice for motivating religious faith. If that were the case, there is hardly anything religious about believing absurdities. And it does not make sense to believe something just because it is absurd, irrational, or untrue. Neither can absurdity nor irrationality be the cause or basis of genuine faith; if this were the case, faith would not be genuine or true. Indeed, faith based on absurdity would be nothing less than superstition (*Overtro*), Eiríksson concludes.[4]

In his reply, Kierkegaard maintains that religious absurdity should not be confused with "the absurd in the ordinary sense."[5] Elsewhere, Kierkegaard contrasts religious absurdity with nonsense, adding that not every absurdity is the absurd or the paradox in the religious sense.[6] Kierkegaard thus tries to draw a distinction that Eiríksson appears to overlook since this distinction is already at work in the *Postscript*.[7]

Eiríksson stresses that the category of the absurd (or paradox) belongs to the understanding (something Kierkegaard would accept), but he adds that it does not belong to reason.[8] He also distinguishes between weak and strong absurdities. A strong or true absurdity is

---

1 For Kierkegaard's claim to the effect that the absurd or the paradox is above reason, not against it, see *SKS* 19, 390f., Not13:23 / *KJN* 3, 388.

2 See Eiríksson, *Er Troen et Paradox og "i Kraft af det Absurde"?*, p. 15, p. 54.

3 See ibid., p. 11.

4 Absurdity is said to be the principle of superstition. Eiríksson, *Er Troen et Paradox og "i Kraft af det Absurde"?*, p. 16.

5 *Pap.* X-6 B 68, p. 73 / *JP* 6, 6598.

6 See *SKS* 23, 23, NB15:25 / *KJN* 7, 20; *SKS* 7, 516 / *CUP1*, 567f.; Schreiber, "Magnús Eiríksson," p. 85.

7 See *SKS* 7, 516 / *CUP1*, 567f.

8 See Eiríksson, *Er Troen et Paradox og "i Kraft af det Absurde"?*, pp. 51f.

something that is neither conceivable nor reasonable.[1] Although Eiríksson does not say so, this type of absurdity seems to involve a formal logical contradiction, something it would be irrational to believe in. A weak absurdity, by contrast, represents something that is impossible for humans to think or realize, although it is possible for God.[2] This type of absurdity represents something logically possible that we cannot grasp in a clear and determinate manner, something that appears to conflict with the everyday calculations of the understanding.[3] Eiríksson then argues that authentic Abrahamic faith and original Christianity only involve absurdity in the weak sense and that de silentio and Climacus are not sufficiently clear about this since they portray Abrahamic and Christian religion as irrational.[4]

In this context, Eiríksson distinguishes between the believer's general confidence in God and his specific confidence in particular objects or events promised, or hinted at, by God.[5] While the former involves believing in providence and having hope for the future, the latter involves expecting specific things. Eiríksson is clear that Abrahamic faith must be supported or accompanied by (special) revelation, something that he aligns with miracles and wonders, hints and signs from God. Eiríksson takes these hints and signs to involve communication from God, but this communication does not consist in theoretical doctrine as much as a divine promise and covenant that make up the basis for religious hope and trust.[6] Like Kierkegaard, Eiríksson follows Paul in describing religious hope as a hope against hope. And like Kierkegaard, he takes this Pauline term to mean that religious hope (and its associated faith) transcends human understanding, since it is not based on ordinary rational inferences.[7] As a consequence, Christian and Abrahamic hope and faith *are* seemingly absurd.

---

1 See ibid., p. 164.

2 See ibid., p. 68, p. 164.

3 See ibid., p. 48.

4 Yet Eiríksson maintains that traditional Christianity involves strong absurdity, because of its dogmas; see ibid., pp. 164ff. referencing P.M. Stilling.

5 See ibid., p. 116.

6 See ibid., pp. 113-15, pp. 140ff. Eiríksson emphasizes that God's purpose will be realized through means unknown to us (see p. 32, p. 44, p. 109).

7 See ibid., p. 33.

This also becomes the central point for Kierkegaard. In his reply, Kierkegaard suggests that Eiríksson's attempt to present religious belief as reasonable has the result that he completely overlooks a central part of the Abraham story in *Fear and Trembling*.[1] Kierkegaard correctly points out that Eiríksson does not discuss the teleological suspension of the ethical or the collision between faith and ethics.[2] In this respect, Eiríksson's book differs from much of the later secondary literature on Kierkegaard since Eiríksson shows no interest in the question of whether Abraham tries to commit murder by sacrificing Isaac.

However, Kierkegaard is clear that religious faith is *not* absurd to believers, although it appears absurd to nonbelievers such as de silentio and Climacus who are offended or scandalized by it. He (Anti-Climacus) writes: "When the believer has faith, the absurd is not the absurd—faith transforms it, but in every weak moment it is again more or less absurd to him."[3] Religious absurdity consists in a veridical or truth-telling paradox in that it can be interpreted as indicating rightly (though surprisingly) that something is (divinely) possible.[4] Kierkegaard explains the absurd as a boundary concept, which indicates where the sphere of faith is negatively cut off from the operations of human understanding.[5] "The absurd is the negative criterion of that which is higher than human understanding and knowledge."[6] The point seems to be that faith supersedes rationality without violating it,[7] since the absurd is *above* reason rather than against it.[8] Kierkegaard writes: "All *Problemata* [in *Fear and Trembling*] should end as follows: This is the paradox of faith, a paradox which no reasoning is able to master—and yet it is so, or we must obliterate the story of Abraham.[9] Elsewhere he writes: "The absurd is the negative determinant [*Bestemmelse*] which assures...that I have not overlooked one or other possibility which still

---

1 See *Pap.* X-6 B 68, p. 76 / *JP* 6, 6598.

2 See *Pap.* X-6 B 68, p. 76 / *JP* 6, 6598; *Pap.* X-6 B 72, p. 82; *Pap.* X-6 B 80, p. 86 / *JP* 1, 11.

3 *Pap.* X-6 B 79, p. 86 / *JP* 1, 10.

4 See Jackson, "Kierkegaard's Metatheology," pp. 79-81.

5 See Schreiber, "Magnús Eiríksson," p. 84.

6 *Pap.* X-6 B 80, p. 87 / *JP* 1, 11.

7 Jackson, "Kierkegaard's Metatheology," p. 81.

8 See *SKS* 19, 390f., Not13:23 / *KJN* 3, 388.

9 See *Pap.* IV B 75 / *JP* 3, 3079.

lies within the human area. The absurd is the expression of despair: that humanly it is not possible—but despair is the negative sign of faith."[1] Without the category of the absurd, we can all too easily confuse the divine with something all too human.[2] The role of the absurd then is to account for why there is religious faith and not something else (such as human possibilities or human knowledge).[3]

The claim that belief only appears absurd to nonbelievers may look like a concession that Kierkegaard makes to Eiríksson. But Kierkegaard certainly does not present it as a concession. Instead, he writes as if this central point was almost obvious, as if it had been implicitly made by himself long before Eiríksson published his book. The question then is whether this is some kind of *post hoc* rationalization or whether Kierkegaard anticipated Eiríksson's central point? Did Kierkegaard give an after the fact rationalization in 1850 or was he aware of (at least some of) the problems which Eiríksson identified already in 1843 and 1846? Did he fool himself? Or did he anticipate criticism, not by having a sixth sense, but by thinking through (potential) conceptual problems and difficulties related to the category of the absurd? To the present commentator the latter seems more plausible than the former for the simple reason that Kierkegaard portrays religiousness very differently in his signed and pseudonymous writings. The pseudonyms de silentio and Climacus are nonbelievers who portray faith as absurd and paradoxical. But Kierkegaard himself does not portray faith as absurd or paradoxical for the believer in his signed writings, because these writings typically speak from the perspective of the believer.[4] Thus, Kierkegaard seems to say that Eiríksson is somewhat misled by reading the pseudonymous writings and not the signed ones.[5]

This point is also related to an important methodological issue where Eiríksson and Kierkegaard disagree. Throughout his 1850 book,

---

1 *Pap.* X-6 B 78, p. 84 / *JP* 1, 9.

2 See *Pap.* X-6 B 68, p. 74 / *JP* 6, 6598.

3 Jackson, "Kierkegaard's Metatheology," p. 82.

4 See *SKS* 23, 182f., NB17:28 / *KJN* 7, 185; *Pap.* X-6 B 68-82 / *JP* 6, 6598-6601 and *JP* 1, 9-12.

5 Kierkegaard also finds it necessary to remind Eiríksson of the motto from Hamann that suggests that *Fear and Trembling* should not be read literally (*Pap.* X-6 B 70, p. 80). However, Kierkegaard does not specify what Eiríksson misses by reading too literally.

Eiríksson argues that religious faith needs to be described from the inside and not from a third-person perspective if we are to get a true description of it.[1] Put in Paul Tillich's terms, faith should be described from within the theological circle, something that involves accepting divine revelation.[2] Kierkegaard approaches this issue differently by distinguishing systematically between the perspectives of the believer and the nonbeliever. While the former stays within the theological circle,[3] the latter describes faith from the outside. This dual approach avoids reducing the divine to the humane, while still making it possible to motivate the transition to Christianity by identifying problems with non-Christian positions that Christianity avoids.[4]

V. Fear and Trembling *and* Concluding Unscientific Postscript

Eiríksson's short chapter on the *Concluding Unscientific Postscript* (Chapter 3) starts by comparing the *Postscript* with *Fear and Trembling*. Eiríksson claims (rather plausibly) that the *Postscript* represents a partially new form and content compared to *Fear and Trembling*, notably by introducing the incarnation as a historical event and central dogma.[5] Eiríksson's general strategy in this chapter is to use the *Postscript* to criticize *Fear and Trembling* (and *vice versa*).

Eiríksson starts by noting that the *Postscript* interprets absurdity in Christological terms, as the belief that Christ was finite and infinite, temporal and eternal. He then argues that this means that there is no

---

1 See Eiríksson, *Er Troen et Paradox og "i Kraft af det Absurde"?*, p. vi, p. 11, pp. 36f., pp. 73ff., p. 101.

2 See Paul Tillich, *Reason and Revelation: Being and God*, Chicago: The University of Chicago Press 1973 (*Systematic Theology*, vol. 1), pp. 8-11.

3 See *SKS* 19, 126, 129f., Not4:3 and Not4:5 / *KJN* 3, 125-29. See also Kingo, *Analogiens teologi*, pp. 13-20, pp. 85-139, pp. 231-318; Arne Grøn, "Kierkegaards forudsætning," *Dansk teologisk tidsskrift*, vol. 58, 1995, pp. 267-90.

4 Grøn points to a similar duality in *The Sickness unto Death* in which Anti-Climacus argues that different positions fail *either* on their own terms *or* on Christian terms. See Arne Grøn, *Subjektivitet og negativitet: Kierkegaard*, Copenhagen: Gyldendal 1997, pp. 230-32, pp. 296-99, p. 364, p. 407. See also Roe Fremstedal, *Kierkegaard and Kant on Radical Evil and the Highest Good: Virtue, Happiness, and the Kingdom of God*, Basingstoke: Palgrave Macmillan 2014, Chapters 6-8.

5 See Eiríksson, *Er Troen et Paradox og "i Kraft af det Absurde"?*, p. 150.

absurdity before the birth of Christ, concluding that Abraham cannot be absurd as *Fear and Trembling* maintains.[1] Thus, Eiríksson uses the *Postscript* to support the central thesis that Abraham, and Abrahamic faith, is not absurd.[2] To the present commentator this use of the *Postscript* is not convincing. Eiríksson only shows that Abraham is not absurd in the Christological sense of the term found in the *Postscript*; but he does not show that Abraham is not absurd in another (non-Christological) sense. As we will see, this is a point that is not lost on Kierkegaard.

Eiríksson's next move is to argue that traditional Christianity, unlike the faith of Abraham, is truly absurd, because of its problematic (absurd) dogmas. To support this point, Eiríksson references P.M. Stilling's work and mentions briefly the dogmas of the trinity, the incarnation, the fall, heredity sin, vicarious atonement, and Christ's presence in the sacraments. Based on this, he concludes that traditional Christianity involves not just the Christological absurdity that Climacus stresses but also several other absurdities.[3] Christianity is absurd, because it goes against both our understanding and our reason.[4] Indeed, it is the only absurd religion known to us.[5]

Eiríksson continues by arguing that, even though these absurd dogmas are central to traditional Christianity, they are not to be found in original Christianity.[6] He suggests that the absurd dogmas belong to Christendom rather than Scripture. The idea is that original Christianity is based on Abrahamic theism, whereas traditional Christianity is corrupted by the church, creeds, and theology of Christendom.[7] Somewhat rhetorically, Eiríksson concludes that the *Postscript* does not go far enough, since Climacus is blinded by the traditional dogmas of Christendom (notably, the incarnation).[8] Kierkegaardian polemics against Christendom is inconsistent because it accepts traditional dogmas and creeds in an

---

1 See ibid., p. 152; Schreiber, "Magnús Eiríksson," p. 79.

2 See ibid., Eiríksson, *Er Troen et Paradox og "i Kraft af det Absurde"?*, pp. 154f., p. 158.

3 See ibid., pp. 162f. Kierkegaard does not accept this plurality of absurdities, see *Pap.* X-6 B 79, p. 85 / *JP* 1, 10.

4 See Eiríksson, *Er Troen et Paradox og "i Kraft af det Absurde"?*, p. 163.

5 See ibid., pp. 165f.

6 See ibid., pp. 169-78.

7 For Eiríksson's anticipation of historical-critical theology, see Schreiber, "Magnús Eiríksson," pp. 63-71.

8 See Eiríksson, *Er Troen et Paradox og "i Kraft af det Absurde"?*, pp. 175-78.

uncritical manner instead of returning to authentic Abrahamic faith. The upshot is that the genuine religious believer, or even the genuine Christian, needs to follow the Kierkegaardian spirit rather than the letter by returning to Abrahamic faith.

It is hardly surprising that Kierkegaard objects to this idea of being Christian without believing in the incarnation. Kierkegaard says that Eiríksson wants to abolish the dogmas of faith and to replace Christianity with the Old Testament. Kierkegaard thinks this shows how confused Eiríksson is.[1] Still, Eiríksson seems to have anticipated readings of Kierkegaard by later commentators who saw Kierkegaard as a somewhat inconsistent thinker who was the last Christian or the last Protestant.[2]

Eiríksson's comparison of *Fear and Trembling* and the *Concluding Unscientific Postscript* includes one of the most interesting parts of his book. In this comparison (Chapter 3), Eiríksson argues persuasively that the Kierkegaardian faces a problem.[3] Put in traditional theological terms, the question is whether Abraham's faith belongs to natural or revealed religion. Put in Kierkegaardian terms (from the *Postscript*), the question is whether it belongs to immanent or transcendent religiousness. If the Kierkegaardian opts for the latter, this basically amounts to interpreting Abraham as a Christian who believes in the incarnation, something that is not just anachronistic but also nonsensical. If he opts for the former, this appears to deny that there is any special revelation and promise available to Abraham, putting him on the same footing as the Greeks or pantheists.[4] But neither option represents Abraham's religious faith accurately. Eiríksson then concludes that Abraham does not fit into the

---

1 See *Pap.* X-6 B 68, p. 73 and p. 76 / *JP* 6, 6598; *Pap.* X-6 B 72, p. 81; *Pap.* X-6 B 74, p. 83.

2 While Eiríksson uses Kierkegaard to criticize Christendom and to defend Abraham, Georg Brandes and the cultural radicals go a step further by attacking religious faith more generally. Similar tendencies can be found in Existentialism and in the Catholic reception of Kierkegaard in Germany and Austria (in which Kierkegaard was sometimes seen as the last Protestant). See *Kierkegaard's International Reception*, Tome I, *Northern and Western Europe*, ed. by Jon Stewart, Aldershot: Ashgate 2009 (*Kierkegaard Research: Sources, Reception and Resources*, vol. 8); *Kierkegaard and Existentialism*, ed. by Jon Stewart, Aldershot: Ashgate 2011 (*Kierkegaard Research: Sources, Reception and Resources*, vol. 9).

3 See Eiríksson, *Er Troen et Paradox og "i Kraft af det Absurde"?*, pp. 154-58.

4 Eiríksson interprets religiousness A as pantheism and B as Christianity (Eiríksson, *Er Troen et Paradox og "i Kraft af det Absurde"?*, p. 150).

stages or spheres developed in the *Postscript* and that *Fear and Trembling* and the *Postscript* therefore are fundamentally at odds with each other.[1] Even though Abraham is the father of faith, or a paradigmatic case of religious belief, he cannot be considered religious if we accept the *Postscript*'s interpretation of religion.[2]

At this point Eiríksson identified a problem that has occupied and troubled commentators until the present day.[3] In his response, Kierkegaard first says that Eiríksson is quite right to distinguish between the absurd in *Fear and Trembling* and the paradox in the *Postscript*.[4] However, he goes on to say that Eiríksson does not grasp what the difference between these two works consists in. Eiríksson is wrong to suggest that these two works are fundamentally at odds with each other,[5] and he is also mistaken in identifying de silentio with Climacus[6] and with Kierkegaard himself.[7] Then comes the interesting part where Kierkegaard compares the notions of faith and absurdity in *Fear and Trembling* and the *Postscript*. This is

---

1 See ibid., p. 152, pp. 154f., p. 158.

2 See ibid., pp. 154-58.

3 Davenport says that "'the holy grail' remains finding a single consistent understanding of 'religiousness' that makes sense of what is said about resignation and faith in *Fear and Trembling* while also explaining what is said about religiousness A and B in the *Concluding Unscientific Postscript*." (John J. Davenport, "Kierkegaard's *Postscript* in light of *Fear and Trembling*: Eschatological Faith," *Revista Portuguesa de Filosofia*, vol. 64, 2008, pp. 879-908; here p. 880). Krishek points to similarities between *Fear and Trembling* and the *Postscript* but concludes that there is still need for more research on the relation between these works. Theunissen indicates that the double movement of faith belongs to Kierkegaard's Christian religiousness, whereas Davenport argues that Kierkegaard gives a single unified conception of religious belief which describes the subjective attitude of believers in *many different religions* (including religiousness A *and* B, as well as the belief of Zoroastrians and Socrates). See Sharon Krishek, *Kierkegaard on Faith and Love*, Cambridge: Cambridge University Press 2009, p. 143; Michael Theunissen, *Negative Theologie der Zeit*, Frankfurt am Main: Suhrkamp 1991, p. 346; John J. Davenport, "Faith as Eschatological Trust in *Fear and Trembling*," in *Ethics, Love, and Faith in Kierkegaard*, ed. by Edward Mooney, Indianapolis: Indiana University Press 2008, pp. 196-233; here p. 214, p. 222, p. 233; Davenport, "Kierkegaard's *Postscript* in light of *Fear and Trembling*," pp. 905-07. See also Fremstedal, *Kierkegaard and Kant on Radical Evil and the Highest Good*, Chapter 7.

4 See *Pap.* X-6 B 80, p. 86 / *JP* 1, 11. However, this does not amount to a distinction between paradox and absurdity as such but rather to a distinction between *Fear and Trembling* and the *Postscript*.

5 See *Pap.* X-6 B 81, p. 87 / *JP* 1, 12.

6 See *Pap.* X-6 B 71, p. 80.

7 See *Pap.* X-6 B 128 / *JP* 6, 6596.

perhaps the most important part in Kierkegaard's response to Eiríksson, a part that has yet to receive the attention it deserves.

In his response, Kierkegaard claims that the absurd in *Fear and Trembling* "is the mere personal definition [*Bestemmelse*—determination] of the existential belief," whereas the paradox in the *Postscript* is "belief related to a doctrine."[1] De silentio speaks of believing "by virtue of the absurd," whereas Climacus speaks of "believing the absurd."[2] The point seems to be that the *Postscript* uses absurdity (and paradox) in a Christian, Christological sense in which the absurd refers to the dogma of the incarnation (as something finite and infinite, temporal and eternal). *Fear and Trembling*, by contrast, does not use the absurd in this Christological sense. So far, Eiríksson is right. However, Kierkegaard goes on to say that "according to the New Testament Abraham is called the father of faith, and yet it is [*vel*—arguably] clear that the content of his faith cannot be Christian—that Jesus Christ has been in existence. But Abraham's faith is the formal definition [*Bestemmelse*] of faith."[3]

The idea seems to be that the faith of Abraham, as interpreted in the double movement of faith in *Fear and Trembling*, explicates the formal structure of faith rather than its content. The content of faith refers to the dogmas or objects of faith, whereas the formal definition of faith corresponds to the *act* whereby one believes (in the sense of trusting God or putting one's confidence in him).[4] The content of Judaism differs from that of Christianity, but Kierkegaard claims that they share a structure, which formally defines or determines what faith is.

The upshot is that absurdity in *Fear and Trembling* refers to an absurd (subjective) attitude or act, whereas absurdity in the *Postscript* refers (in addition) to the incarnation as an absurd object (dogma).[5] *Fear*

---

1 *Pap.* X-6 B 80, p. 86 / *JP* 1, 11.

2 *Pap.* X-6 B 80, p. 87 / *JP* 1, 11.

3 *Pap.* X-6 B 81, p. 87 / *JP* 1, 12. The Hongs' translation leaves out "*vel*," a word which can be translated "presumably," "arguably," or "certainly."

4 This is in line with the lexical meaning according to which the Danish word for movement, "*Bevægelse*," can mean (subjective) "attitude" or "state of mind." See Roe Fremstedal, "Double Movement," in *Kierkegaard's Concepts*, Tome II, *Classicism to Enthusiasm*, ed. by Steven Emmanuel, William McDonald and Jon Stewart, Aldershot: Ashgate 2014 (*Kierkegaard Research: Sources, Reception and Resources*, vol. 15), pp. 187-94.

5 Eiríksson (*Er Troen et Paradox og "i Kraft af det Absurde"?*, pp. 56f., p. 61, pp. 68f., p. 87, pp. 89f., p. 113) also presents another objection to Kierkegaard that the latter responds

and Trembling analyzes the subjective attitude of the religious believer, an attitude that is common to Judaism *and* Christianity (but probably not religiousness A). However, absurdity in the *Postscript* does not merely include the incarnation as an absurd object but also the subjective attitude of the believer. This attitude is absurd insofar as it goes against the understanding by transcending human possibilities and embracing divine grace. It is not absurd by virtue of believing something logically or objectively impossible, but only by virtue of believing something that is humanly impossible such as the absolution of sins, getting Isaac back after sacrificing him, resurrecting the dead, or realizing the kingdom of God.

This still leaves an important problem that Eiríksson identified: Do Abraham and Judaism belong to religiousness A or B? Kierkegaard does not seem to formulate an answer to this important question in his response to Eiríksson. But he does seem to sketch an answer elsewhere (even though it has not attracted much attention in the research).[1] Kierkegaard indicates that the pagan can resign only if he realizes that loss is inevitable. The piety of Judaism, by contrast, is capable of both resignation and faith (only) if the believer is put through an ordeal (as Abraham and Job were presumably). Finally, the Christian differs from

---

to. Eiríksson argues at length, with much repetition, that the example of the princess in *Fear and Trembling* is not suited for the purpose of understanding religious faith. Eiríksson makes a number of claims; the most important is possibly that the example portrays religiousness in subjectivist terms. This claim seems to be based on the fact that de silentio introduces the princess as an example of what is subjectively most valuable (see *SKS* 4, 136 / *FT*, 41f.). De silentio states that only the single individual can give himself a more precise explanation of what is subjectively perceived as the highest (see *SKS* 4, 163 / *FT*, 71). Eiríksson seems to read this as some kind of subjectivism on Kierkegaard's part. However, de silentio actually identifies what is objectively highest with eternal happiness and the human *telos* (see *SKS* 4, 148 / *FT*, 54). This means that he distinguishes what is objectively valuable (eternal happiness or salvation) from what is subjectively perceived as valuable (getting the princess). In his response, Kierkegaard (Climacus) says, that the story of the princess is only a minor illustration, a (subjective) approximation to faith, and not the chief substance as Eiríksson thinks (see *Pap.* X-6 B 68, pp. 76f. / *JP* 6, 6598; *Pap.* X-6 B 74, p. 83). He concludes that Eiríksson developed a somewhat unhealthy obsession with the parable of the princess and that he misunderstood the point (see Schreiber, "Magnús Eiríksson," pp. 83f.).

[1] For a more systematic analysis, see Fremstedal, *Kierkegaard and Kant on Radical Evil and the Highest Good*, Chapter 7.

both by being capable of *voluntary* resignation and belief.[1] The first part of the double movement of faith (that is, resignation) seems to belong to immanent (natural) religiousness, whereas the second part belongs exclusively to transcendent (revealed) religiousness (Judaism *and* Christianity). What sets Christianity apart from Judaism on this account is not divine revelation or divine assistance as such, but the ability to resign without being put through an ordeal (as Abraham and Job were).[2]

Kierkegaard thinks that whereas Christianity sees our whole life as an ordeal or examination, Judaism believes that true happiness can be realized in this world since an ordeal is something that passes.[3] Whereas Judaism interprets the highest good as this-worldly, Christianity sees this life is an ordeal that prepares for the realization of the highest good in the afterlife.[4] Kierkegaard suggests then that extreme scenarios in Judaism, such as Abraham's sacrifice of Isaac, anticipate Christianity by necessitating resignation and belief. The idea is that the extreme cases of Judaism anticipate the normal situation of Christian existence. While the extraordinary ordeals of Abraham and Job necessitate resignation and belief, the demanding nature of Christianity necessitates voluntary resignation and belief.

VI. Closing Remarks

Magnús Eiríksson's *Is Faith a Paradox and "By Virtue of the Absurd"?* represents an important book in the Kierkegaard literature. Not only was it (in all likelihood) the very first monograph published on Kierkegaard, but it also provoked Kierkegaard to draft a response that is important for understanding the category of the absurd, his use of pseudonyms, and the relation between *Fear and Trembling* and the *Postscript*. To some extent, Kierkegaard's views on these matters appears to have been poorly understood because Kierkegaard's response to Eiríksson has received very

---

1 See *SKS* 10, 189 / *CD*, 178f.; *SKS* 25, 152f., NB27:39 / *JP* 2, 1433; *SKS* 15, 268 / *BA*, 112f.

2 In addition to these formal characteristics, Christianity also has dogmas that separate it from Judaism (notably, the incarnation).

3 See *SKS* 4, 131 / *FT*, 56; *SKS* 4, 115f. / *FT*, 19f.; *SKS* 12, 183 / *PC*, 183; *SKS* 20, 392, NB5:48 / *KJN* 4, 392f.

4 See ibid.

little attention. Most discussions of Kierkegaard's alleged irrationalism, for instance, appear to overlook the fact that Kierkegaard was not only aware of the accusation of irrationalism but also that he responded to it in some detail.

Kierkegaard's unwillingness to enter into a dialogue with Eiríksson is remarkable. Kierkegaard seems to think that he has little or nothing to gain from entering a discussion with Eiríksson. Yet his comments on Eiríksson's book show that Eiríksson's critique forces him to clarify important points. One could perhaps have hoped that Kierkegaard would have been able to clarify more points if he engaged in discussions with contemporaries to a greater extent than he did. However, it seems that Kierkegaard did not want to have allies, pupils or sympathizers since he preferred to work on his own.

Kierkegaard's response to Eiríksson contains some important points that have received little attention. Presumably, one of the reasons for this is that Kierkegaard's response is difficult to understand unless one has read the 1850 book by Eiríksson that he discusses. Kierkegaard's response shows that he was a sharp reader and critic who concedes little and is quick to find problems with Eiríksson's account. It also seems that Kierkegaard is able to anticipate some of Eiríksson's critique by portraying religiousness as absurd only to non-believers. Kierkegaard was able to see in advance how the category of the absurd may lead to difficulties and problems. More specifically, he saw the need for distinguishing between plain nonsense and religious absurdity. However, Eiríksson also raises objections that Kierkegaard does not respond to. Eiríksson objects, notably, to Kierkegaard's overly dualistic interpretation of human nature.[1] This objection anticipates a central point in later scholarship that became only more relevant after Kierkegaard radicalized his position in the 1854-55 attack on the state church.[2]

---

1 See Eiríksson, *Er Troen et Paradox og "i Kraft af det Absurde"?*, p. 44, p. 59, p. 86, p. 91, p. 127, p. 130, p. 136, pp. 139f., p. 166.

2 See Johannes Sløk, *Da Kierkegaard tav. Fra forfatterskab til kirkestorm*, Copenhagen: C.A. Reitzel 1980, pp. 7f., pp. 98-113, pp. 121-27, pp. 135-37; Michael Theunissen, *Der Begriff Verzweiflung*, Frankfurt am Main: Suhrkamp 1993, p. 155; Rick Anthony Furtak, *Wisdom in Love: Kierkegaard and the Ancient Quest for Emotional Integrity*, Notre Dame: University of Notre Dame Press 2005, p. 186.

Magnús Eiríksson and Grundtvig

Carl Henrik Koch

In the brief autobiography included in the foreword of the first work of the Icelandic theologian Magnús Eiríksson (1806-81), the author mentions that when he came to Copenhagen from Iceland in 1831 to study theology, he felt that among the theological movements there were two that stood sharply opposed to each other: the "evangelical movement" led by theology professor H.N. Clausen (1793-1877) and the "Grundtvigians" or the "Catholizing divines," with N.F.S. Grundtvig (1783-1872) as the leading figure.[1]

In 1837 Eiríksson took the theological examination, but he continued his studies and in 1839 attended a part of the lectures, which the young and feted university lecturer Hans Lassen Martensen (1808-84), later professor of theology and in 1854 bishop of Zealand, gave on the age's fashionable trend in theology, the Hegel-inspired speculative theology. Like most of Martensen's young audience, Eiríksson was also carried away by the eloquent lecturer. Many years later another of his auditors wrote the following about the word "speculative":

> This mysterious word, which appeared with the sound of the "Absolutes," shone through all of our master's powerful phrases like the shimmering of the sun in a spring. Where it came from we did not know; it dashed past as if by magic. But when we came to a somewhat better understanding, it turned out to be the art of being able, with an eclectic aggregate of German

---

[1] Magnús Eiríksson, *Om Baptister og Barnedaab, samt flere Momenter af Den kirkelige og speculative Christendom*, Copenhagen: P.G. Philipsen 1844, p. IV and p. VI. Eiríksson's excessive use of italics and other forms of emphasis have not been reproduced in the quotations.

> systems, to bring the mysteries of Christianity under the daylight of the Concept, as surely as if one had put an angel in spirits for analysis.[1]

Eiríksson got over his infatuation and realized "what was fundamentally mistaken"[2] in Martensen's theology. In his first book he described the movement which Martensen stood for as a "very dangerous speculating movement not in agreement with the Gospel," which he juxtaposed to "the crass extreme ecclesial, Catholicizing, Grundtvigian"[3] movement. He considered both movements, but mostly the Martensenian one, as a menace to the simple, non-scholarly Christianity with emphasis on the message of love, which Eiríksson thought was the core of Christ's preaching.

The Baptist movement was the reason that Eiríksson appeared on the literary scene. His criticism of Martensen's and Grundtvig's contributions to the discussions about baptism became a kind of gateway to his later rejection of the scholarly theology and the majority of the traditional dogmas of the Lutheran-evangelical theology.

Grundtvig seems never to have noticed Eiríksson, judging from the book collection he left behind. Here Eiríksson is only represented by a single book in which he criticizes Martensen's *magnum opus*, *Christian Dogmatics* from 1849.[4] None of the works in which he criticized Grundtvig appears in the list of Grundtvig's books.

We know nothing about the personal relationship between Grundtvig and Eiríksson. Given how small Copenhagen and the city's intellectual upper class was, they could not have avoided meeting each other, and undoubtedly Eiríksson attended some of Grundtvig's church services. The only recorded meeting between them took place as late as in 1871 in connection with the Fourth Nordic Church Meeting in

---

[1] Johannes Fibiger, *Mit Liv og Levned som jeg selv har forstaaet det*, ed. by Karl Gjellerup, Copenhagen: Gyldendal 1898, p. 74.

[2] Eiríksson, *Om Baptister og Barnedaab*, p. XI.

[3] Ibid., p. XIII.

[4] Magnús Eiríksson, *Speculativ Rettroenhed, fremstillet efter Dr. Martensens "christelige Dogmatik," og Geistlig Retfærdighed, belyst ved en Biskops Deeltagelse i en Generalfiskal-Sag*, Copenhagen: Trykt hos J.S. Salomon 1849. This work appears as no. 1290 on p. 43 in *Fortegnelse over N.S.F. Grundtvigs Bibliotek, som bortsælges ved offentlig Auction Mandag d. 29. September 1873*, [Copenhagen:] Trykt i E.C. Løsers Bog- og Nodetrykkeri [1873].

Copenhagen. There Eiríksson spoke immediately after Grundtvig had spoken, but was ordered to sit down again since he did not touch on the meeting's topic which was neo-rationalism. Instead he asked and briefly discussed the question: "Is the Christian or religious faith which we now have the same thing as the doctrine and faith of Christ?" When he was prevented from speaking, he prayed a prayer that God would lead the participants of the meeting to true Christianity.[1] He was until the end of his days a soldier for the Lord.

I. The Arrival of the Baptists in Denmark around 1840

In the 1830s the Baptists struck root in Denmark, and in 1839 the first Baptist congregation was established in Copenhagen. The arrival of the sect in Denmark immediately attracted the attention of the church and the state authorities. Unlike the Evangelical-Lutheran faith, which was established in the Augsburg Confession of 1530, the Baptists rejected infant baptism and practiced instead adult baptism. Further, they administered the sacrament in a different way from the Danish State Church. The enforcement of church discipline was for the Baptists, moreover, an affair for the congregations and not, as in the Danish State Church, the task of the pastors.

In particular, the rejection of infant baptism based on the fact that it apparently lacks evidence in the New Testament[2] caused a stir and was also at variance with the fundamental laws for the Danish state. By the Danish Royal Law of 1665, it was stated that the Crown was charged with enforcing the Augsburg Confession and the dogmatic rules contained therein "and with keeping by force the country's citizens in these lands and kingdoms in same pure and unadulterated Christian faith and protecting them against all heretics, enthusiasts and

---

[1] See *Forhandlingerne paa Det Fjerde Nordiske Kirkemöde i Kjøbenhavn den 5., 6. og 7. September 1871, ed. by Kr. Madsen*, Copenhagen: Gyldendal 1871, pp. 46-51.

[2] This issue was controversial. For example, the great German theologian of the age Friedrich Schleiermacher, whom the leading Danish theologians H.N. Clausen and H.L. Martensen were influenced by, wrote in his main work on dogmatics that the Reformation should have abandoned infant baptism. See Friedrich Schleiermacher, *Der christliche Glaube nach den Grundsäzen der evangelischen Kirche im Zusammenhange dargestellt*, vols. 1-2, 2nd ed., Berlin: G. Reimer 1830-31; vol. 2, p. 423 (§ 138).

blasphemers."[1] In the ninth article of the Confession it is stated that the evangelical congregation's doctrine about baptism "is necessary for salvation, and God's grace is offered at baptism, and children should be baptized, since, when they are given over for God at baptism, they are received by him in grace."[2] It states further that the Anabaptists or just the Baptists should be condemned since they claimed that personal faith was a prerequisite for baptism and therefore rejected infant baptism. The article claimed thus that baptism was necessity and that only infant baptism was legitimate. In Christian V's Danish law it was further established that in addition to the Bible and the Augsburg Confession the three early Christian Symbols (the Apostles' Creed, the Nicene Creed, and the Athanasian Creed) and Luther's Small Catechism belong to the symbolic books of the Danish Church. Specifically it is stated in § 2-5-5 that if children are not baptized within eight days after birth, the parents are to be sentenced to pay a fine.[3] The possibility of withdrawing from the state church or standing outside it was thus excluded.[4]

Both the religious and the secular authorities—which were one entity—were slightly confused as to how to deal with the declared Baptists. There was no consensus in the episcopacy, and the case was submitted to the Danish Chancellery, which requested an opinion from the Danish Church Primate, Jacob Peter Mynster (1775-1854), who had been Bishop of Zealand since 1834.

Already early in the process Mynster had made his position clear. In a speech he gave on the 30th of March 1842 on the occasion of the ordination of a priest who was to be sent to Greenland, he took as his theme the words of Jesus from the Gospel of John: "I have other sheep that do not belong to this fold. I must bring them in also, and they will listen to my voice. So there will be one flock, one shepherd."[5] Here

---

1 Jens Himmelstrup and Jens Møller, *Danske Forfatningslove 1665-1953*, 2nd ed., Copenhagen: Schultz 1958 [1932], p. 16.

2 *Den lutherske Bekendelse i dag*, ed. by Johannes Langhoff, Århus: Aros 1980, p. 26.

3 *Kong Christian den Femtes Danske Lov*, ed. by Vilhelm Adolf Secher, Copenhagen: Gad 1929.

4 The legal foundation of the Danish State Church was developed in 1842 by the young Ditlev Gothard Monrad in an article that is worthy of attention even today: "Om Retten til at udtræde af Statskirken (I Anledning af Baptisterne)" in the fourth of his *Flyvende politiske Blade*, Copenhagen: C.A. Reitzel 1842, pp. 3-23.

5 John 10:16.

Mynster says that he regretted the conflict that had arisen within the Church, and that the Church's baptism was even called into question. However, the country's magistrates have the duty to maintain the unity of the Church and therefore to "enforce the Christian faith among the people," and he asks, "dare it give the people up to all delusions?"[1] Mynster in this context was obliged to maintain that the Baptists' children should be forcibly baptized against their parents' will, and the Royal Decree of December 27, 1842 decided the matter. The Baptists' children should be baptized, and those parents who failed to bring them to baptism should be fined and possibly imprisoned, and their children should be baptized by force. The reason for Mynster's position on Baptism was not least his fear that the unity between church and state, which was enshrined in the Danish Royal Law and was characteristic of the Danish Golden Age, would disintegrate.

However, the Danish clergy did not agree with the law to force something that was actually a matter of conscience. Søren Kierkegaard's brother Peter Christian Kierkegaard (1805-88), who was a pastor in Pedersborg near Sorø, a little town on Zealand, refused on grounds of conscience to baptize the children of Baptist parents who were brought to his church by the police. Others also followed suit. In § 81 of the new Danish Constitution of 1849 religious freedom was instituted in Denmark with the words: "Citizens have the right to assemble in society in order to worship God in the manner that is in accord with their convictions…."[2] On June 6, 1848 by royal decree all cases against the Baptists had been lifted. Throughout the period 1842 to 1848 the administration of the 1842 resolution had been faltering. Slightly offended, Mynster wrote in the part of his memoirs which is dated 1846:

> During negotiations in the Privy Council, the King (Christian VIII) had zealously affirmed that the Baptist children should be baptized, although his motives were not ultimately quite the same as mine. I for my part cannot abandon the conviction that the state has the right to demand that every child immediately should be reckoned among one of the recognized

---

[1] Jacob Peter Mynster, *Der skal blive een Hjord, een Hyrde. Ordinations-Tale holden den 30te Marts 1842 ved Indvielsen af en til Grønland beskikket Missionær*, Copenhagen: C.A. Reitzel 1842, p. 12.

[2] Himmelstrup and Møller, *Danske Forfatningslove 1665-1953*, p. 69.

> religious communities. Therefore, since the Baptists declare explicitly that their children do not belong to their community before they, as grown-ups, are able to declare it themselves, then our church must receive them as it does other abandoned children.[1]

After mentioning the refusal of P.C. Kierkegaard and others to follow the resolution, Mynster continues:

> I explained on this occasion to the King that it was impossible for me to see to it that the resolutions were observed if I did not get support. The King promised me this, and he had a fierce conversation with one of the noncomplying pastors who came to him, but it ended up with him saying that he would take the matter under careful deliberation; the Chancellery gave a wavering statement, and thus the case stopped there, so that everyone could do what he wanted.[2]

The authorities' proceeding against the Baptists produced several polemical works, the most important of these were authored by N.F.S. Grundtvig, the bishop of Funen Nicolai Faber (1787-1848), Hans Lassen Martensen, the philosopher Hans Brøchner (1820-75), and, last but not least, Magnús Eiríksson, whose contribution to the debate was by far the longest, over 700 pages.[3] The four first contributions to the discussion were commented upon by Eiríksson, and he criticized Grundtvig, Martensen and Faber. Here only Eiríksson's criticism of Grundtvig's view will be the subject of further examination, whereas Faber's, Martensen's and Brøchner's contributions to the discussion will only be touched upon briefly.

---

1 Jacob Peter Mynster, *Meddelelser om mit Levnet*, Copenhagen: Gyldendal 1854, p. 273

2 Ibid.

3 N.F.S. Grundtvig, *Om Religions-Forfølgelse. En Stemme*, Copenhagen: Wahlske Boghandlings Forlag 1842; Nicolai Faber, *De anabaptistiske Bevægelser i Danmark betragtede fra det christelige og kirkelige Standpunct*, Odense: S. Hempels Forlag 1842; Hans Lassen Martensen, *Den christelige Daab betragtet med Hensyn paa det baptistiske Spørgsmaal*, Copenhagen: C.A. Reitzel 1843; Hans Brøchner, *Nogle Bemærkninger om Daaben, foranledigede ved Professor Martensens Skrift: "Den christelige Daab,"* Copenhagen: P.G. Philipsen 1843, and Magnús Eiríksson, *Om Baptister og Barnedaab, samt flere Momenter af Den kirkelige og speculative Christendom*, Copenhagen: P.G. Philipsen 1844.

With regard to the Baptists' claim that baptism requires faith, Martensen maintained that "faith comes by baptism."[1] Baptism's mystery is that the baptized child is subject to Christ's selection, "because he, as head of the church, puts himself in an organic relation to the individual and thereby bestows upon him the source of all development of faith, all Christian enthusiasm and productivity."[2] Brøchner criticized Martensen's attempt to understand the dogma of baptism and described ironically the dogmatists of the time of the Reformation as "Men with an admirable courage and resignation of all reason, who must awaken our astonishment and extort us with the same esteem that we must feel for the Indian fakirs. There was not the sad indecision and cowardice of the theology of our day...."[3] Faber ascribed to the child an innate rational soul which "is able to receive impressions from both the outside world in general and from other people in particular and, through its higher faculties, from God itself. This evokes an activity in the soul of the child, which is completely natural, although the child remains unaware of it for a long time."[4] Although it was explicitly denied by both Martensen and Faber, nonetheless they both seem to confer upon baptism a magical power—to use Schleiermacher's expression.[5]

The discussion on baptism was indicative of all of Eiríksson's later, relatively extensive writings, which, from an ecclesiastical point of view, evolved in an ever more radical direction. Central dogmas like that of the divine nature of Christ and the Trinity ended up being rejected, just as he rejected the Gospel of John, regarding it as inauthentic. As early as in his first work, he claimed, like the Baptists, that infant baptism could not be justified by the New Testament and denied that baptism was a sacrament. Of the Danish theologians especially Hans Lassen Martensen was the object of his criticism.[6] He also aimed the heavy

---

1 Martensen, *Den christelige Daab betragtet med Hensyn paa det baptistiske Spørgsmaal*, p. 12.

2 Ibid., p. 13.

3 Brøchner, *Nogle Bemærkninger om Daaben*, p. 19.

4 Faber, *De anabaptistiske Bevægelser i Danmark*, p. 32.

5 See Schleiermacher, *Der christliche Glaube*, vol. 2, p. 423 (§ 138).

6 On Eiríksson's criticism of Martensen, see Gerhard Schreiber, "Magnús Eiríksson: An Opponent of Martensen and an Unwelcome Ally of Kierkegaard," in *Kierkegaard and his Danish Contemporaries*, Tome II, *Theology*, ed. by Jon Stewart, Aldershot: Ashgate 2009 (*Kierkegaard Research: Sources, Reception and Resources*, vol. 7), pp. 49-94 and

artillery at Faber. But he never received any reply. He wrote that his opponents seemed to be afraid of his writings and therefore sought to undermine them by ignoring them and leaving them to be forgotten in silence.[1] It must also be said that they succeeded in this. Today Eiríksson is only remembered for his warm defense of the young activist for woman's rights Mathilde Fibiger (1830-72), who under the pseudonym Clara Raphael, in 1851, published the book *Twelve Letters*, in which she argued that women should have the same right as men to choose their life path.[2] The vast majority of Eiríksson's many publications are forgotten and not easy to track down.

II. Grundtvig's Conception of Baptism

After having occupied himself for a number of years with world history and cultural history and with the translations of the historical work, *Heimskringla*, which is attributed to the Icelander Snorri Sturluson (ca. 1178-1241), the historical work, *Gesta Danorum* (The Deeds of the Danes) written by Saxo Grammaticus (born around 1160), and the Old English heroic epic *Beowulf*, which probably dates from the 8th century, Grundtvig in 1821 became pastor of Præstø, a small quiet town

Gerhard Schreiber, " 'Like a Voice in the Wilderness': Magnús Eiríksson's Tenacious Critique of Martensen—and Martensens 'Lofty Silence,'" in *Hans Lassen Martensen: Theologian, Philosopher and Social Critic*, ed. by Jon Stewart, Copenhagen: Museum Tusculanum Press 2012 (*Danish Golden Age Studies*, vol. 6), pp. 155-91. Schreiber's articles contain numerous useful references to the literature.

1 In several of his works he deals with the main points in his authorship and the silence that it met with, but he gave the best overview of his intentions with the individual works in a series of articles with the title, "Min Forfattervirksomhed," which he published in Vilhelm Møller's *Flyvende Blade for Literatur, Kunst og Samfundsspørgsmaal*, vol. 3, 1875, no. 11 (June 12), pp. 81-83; no. 12 (June 19), pp. 90-93, and no. 13 (June 26), pp. 100-04.

2 Clara Raphael, *Tolv Breve*, ed. by J.L. Heiberg, Copenhagen: C.A. Reitzel 1851. Under the pseudonym Theodor Immanuel, Eiríksson published in the same year his *Breve til Clara Raphael*, Copenhagen: C.A. Reitzel 1851. On the Clara Raphael controversy, which is discussed in many places, see especially Fredrik Bajer, *Klara-Rafael-Fejden*, Copenhagen: Topp 1879 and Katalin Nun, "Mathilde Fibiger and the Emancipation of Women," in her *Women of the Danish Golden Age: Literature, Theater and the Emancipation of Women*, Copenhagen: Museum Tusculanum 2013 (*Danish Golden Age Studies*, vol. 8), pp. 85-111, where a useful overview is given of the literature on Mathilde Fibiger and the controversy.

on Zealand. He dreamed of awakening the Danes to true Christianity, indeed, almost of re-Christianizing the North by, as he had tried in his youth, "awakening the Nordic people from the deep sleep of the soul on the edge of the abyss,"[1] reviving the ancient hero-spirit and calling it to fight for Christianity. But he felt his sphere of activity was too narrow in the small provincial town and wanted to come to the capital. Although he was not well regarded in church circles, in 1822 he received a position as curate at the Church of Our Savior in Christianshavn, a part of Copenhagen. But he was disheartened since he felt that although he was a sought preacher, he had likewise not been successful in Copenhagen in achieving a sufficient response. In late 1823, he experienced, however, that his courage returned, and he felt that "the night was past, and the day is at hand."[2] In the spring of 1824 in the great poem "New Year's Morning" (in 312 stanzas of 11 lines each in allegorical form) he described his development and characterized the period when he worked as a translator as a nighttime stay in the realm of the dead. But now he sensed that the hope he had cherished would come true, "and certainly must be my morning greeting, must be, at least, for myself, one morning hymn."[3]

But the period of his afflictions was, however, not over with this. After he had worked intensely and thrilled with Nordic mythology in his youth, he was struck in December 1810 by a depression that led him to the brink of insanity and caused him to feel that he was fighting for the salvation of his soul.[4] Not least of all his immersion in the Bible helped him out of the crisis. The word of the Bible was for him essential and the religious breakthrough that he lived through made him a Bible Christian.

During his work as a pastor in Copenhagen from 1822 to 1826, Grundtvig came to the view that many pastors who were trained in the

---

1 The Preface to the poem "Nyaars-Morgen," in *Nik. Fred. Sev. Grundtvigs udvalgte Skrifter*, vols. 1-10, ed. by Holger Begtrup, Copenhagen: Gyldendal 1904-9; vol. 4, p. 240. In the Grundtvig quotations I have omitted reproducing the different forms of emphasis such as italics and spacing of words.

2 *Nik. Fred. Sev. Grundtvigs udvalgte Skrifter*, ed. by Begtrup, vol. 4, p. 244.

3 Ibid., p. 245.

4 See Frederik Rønning, *N.F.S. Grundtvig. Et Bidrag til skildring af dansk åndsliv i det 19. århundrede*, vols. 1-4 in 8 parts, Copenhagen: Schønberg 1907-14; vol. 2.1, pp. 195-98.

18th century rationalist theology, according to which laymen on Sunday in the church and in confirmation classes, first and foremost, should be inculcated with the moral teachings that could be inferred from the Gospels, distorted the Christian message. The solution to this problem was that by means of a diligent reading of the Bible the laymen should seek the truth for themselves. But the laymen's reading of the Bible was not without problems. For example, the rationalist pastors tried to explain away Christ's miracles as natural events, and the objections of the Bible critics to the authenticity of all of the letters that survived in Paul's name, and especially the Gospel of John, could potentially create doubt and uncertainty in the truth-seeking layman. Even worse was the fact that a number of state-church pastors and professors of theology at the University presented their false teachings from the pulpit and in the auditoriums.

Haunted by this concern, Grundtvig made the discovery that both he himself and his followers described as "matchless." It was to become crucial for the remainder of his life and for the people who joined him and were the founders of the so-called Grundtvigianism, which especially in the latter half of the 19th century, but also up through the first half of the 20th, came to play a significant role in the church and religious life in Denmark.

Whereas Catholic theology operates with seven sacraments or means of mercy, the Lutheran theology counts only two, baptism and the Eucharist. Whereas Christ's institution of the Eucharist is found in the three Synoptic Gospels, baptism—understood as child baptism—was more controversial. For Grundtvig there was no doubt. Both means of mercy were ordained by Christ, and we hear Christ's own words of institution in the words that are part of the ritual of baptism and the Eucharist, words which—Grundtvig believed—have been used in an unbroken tradition ever since. The same applies to the Apostles' Creed, which is part of ritual of baptism; with this creed, the Church and the church of Christ have the determination of true Christianity.[1] If this

1 At the beginning Grundtvig seems only to want to trace the origin of the ritual of baptism to the time of the apostles, that is, the time after the ascension of Christ. Thus in his main theological work, the articles in *Theologisk Maanedsskrift* about the true Christianity and the truth of Christianity from 1826-27 (reprinted in *Nik. Fred. Sev. Grundtvigs udvalgte Skrifter*, ed. by Begtrup, vol. 4, pp. 443-723), he writes that the

were the case, there would be no reason to worry about the scholarly biblical criticism, from which disbelief drew its sustenance. The first time Grundtvig explained this view was in his sermon on Sunday, July 31, 1825.[1] Many years later the then over 80-year-old Grundtvig wrote about his discovery,

> if Scripture contains the rule of faith for the Christian community, then unbelief now, as almost all the scribes are hailing it, would have a much more valid and stronger evidence than the belief which only a few scribes testified, and my conclusion was then that as assuredly as Jesus Christ was God the Father's only-begotten Son, there had to be in the Church a far more valid and stronger evidence of the genuine, original, Christian faith, than the letters of the Scripture in any way might be for women and children and all the unlearned. Since I was now constantly pondering, reading and writing in this direction in prayer and supplication, behold! Then it struck me in a blessed moment that the matchless testimony, which

---

faith which comes to expression in the Apostles' Creed "from the days of the apostles in the baptism was continually transmitted from generation to generation and from one people to another" (ibid., p. 535). Later in his series of articles, he seems, however, to imply that the content of the entire baptism ritual, that is, also the Apostles' Creed, comes from Christ's institution of baptism. For example, he writes that if we do not perform "baptism in all manner after the institution of Christ…then we are false Christians" (ibid., vol. 4, pp. 616f.). He says to an imagined opponent, "Prove therefore if you can, that the renouncing the devil, the confession of faith and the forgiveness of sin do not originally belong to the Christian baptism" (ibid., p. 618). Both in the introduction to *Christenhedens Syvstjerne* from 1860 and in the postscript from 1865 to the second edition of the articles he says explicitly that the content of the baptism ritual, containing the Apostles' Creed, can be traced back to Christ's "spirit and the eternal words from his own mouth." See N.F.S. Grundtvig, *Christenhedens Syvstjerne. Et kirkeligt Sagakvad*, Copenhagen: Michaelsen og Tillge 1860, p. XI and *Nik. Fred. Sev. Grundtvigs udvalgte Skrifter*, ed. by Begtrup, vol. 4, p. 726. For how the shift in Grundtvig's view was expressed in the collection of sermons, which he published in the years 1827-31 (*Søndagsbogen*, vols. 1-3, Copenhagen: Wahl 1827-31), see Holger Begtrup, *Grundtvigs danske Kristendom. Historisk fremstillet*, vols. 1-2, Copenhagen: Gad 1936; vol. 1, pp. 132-37.

[1] The surviving part of the sermon is printed, based on Grundtvig's manuscript, in Holger Begtrup, *N.S.F. Grundtvigs kirkelige Syn 1825. En historisk Indledning*, Copenhagen: Schönberg 1901, pp. 190-97 and in *Nik. Fred. Sev. Grundtvigs udvalgte Skrifter*, ed. by Begtrup, vol. 4, pp. 387-94.

> I so diligently was looking for in the world of spirit, resounded through all times in Christianity at the baptism when the Apostles' Creed was read.[1]

Shortly after Grundtvig had made his matchless discovery, he initiated the well-known conflict with H.N. Clausen, with the short polemical work *The Church's Rejoinder*, which was published on September 5, 1825. Clausen filed a defamation suit, which Grundtvig lost. It was especially Grundtvig's claim that Clausen had put "himself at the head of the Christian Church's enemies and the despisers of God's word in Denmark,"[2] which understandably had brought the professor of theology to take up the fight. Many years later Clausen wrote in his memoirs about *The Church's Rejoinder* that the short work was a reflection of what Melanchthon had called "*rabies theologorum,*" theological fury.[3] The result was that Grundtvig in October 1826, when the verdict came down, was subject to censorship, which led him to resign his office that same year. Only in December 1837 was the censorship lifted.

In *The Church's Rejoinder* Grundtvig accused H.N. Clausen that he, in his book *Catholicism's and Protestantism's Church Constitution, Doctrine and Rite*, which was published on September 3, 1825 (and Grundtvig may have been familiar with it before its publication), let "the false, fleshly reason," which is the archenemy of the Christian Church,[4] be what determines what is true Christianity. It further claimed that for Clausen it was crucial that the written word, that is, The New Testament, be interpreted in the light of reason. Here no significance is given to the time interval between Christianity's first time and the present. But neither reason nor the dead letter is the foundation of the Church or Christianity. "[T]he only true, common (Catholic) Christian Church, which alone is based on a historical foundation, must necessarily stand

---

1 N.F.S. Grundtvig, *Kirke-Speil eller Udsigt over den christne Menigheds Levnetsløb*, Copenhagen: Schönberg 1871, p. 385.

2 N.F.S. Grundtvig, *Kirkens Gienmæle mod Professor Theologiæ Dr. H.N. Clausen*, Copenhagen: Wahlske Boghandlings Forlag 1825, p. III. (Reprinted in *Nik. Fred. Sev. Grundtvigs udvalgte Skrifter*, ed. by Begtrup, vol. 4, pp. 396-429; here p. 397.)

3 Henrik Nicolai Clausen, *Optegnelser om mit Levneds og min Tids Historie*, Copenhagen: Gad 1877, p. 109.

4 Grundtvig, *Kirkens Gienmæle mod Professor Theologiæ Dr. H.N. Clausen*, p. 7. (*Nik. Fred. Sev. Grundtvigs udvalgte Skrifter*, ed. by Begtrup, vol. 4, p. 405.)

and fall with historical testimonies."[1] The unbroken, living tradition since Christ, through which the ritual of baptism and the Apostles' Creed is orally passed on to the present, is the foundation upon which the true Christianity, which manifests itself in church life, is based. Although the Roman church, which Grundtvig sharply criticized, has distorted and falsified the true doctrine, nonetheless from generation to generation since the apostles and the early Church it has passed down the unadulterated Christianity.

Grundtvig's view could be criticized, and it was. It was objected that, regarded historically, the Apostles' Creed could not be traced back to Christ, and that Grundtvig, by building on the historically present tradition differed from the Protestant scriptural principle—the *sola scriptura* principle—and thus had approached a position that was related to Catholicism's view that the Christian dogmas built not only on the Bible's words but also on the ecclesiastical tradition. The accusation of having a tendency to Catholicism followed Grundtvig his entire life, even though he, as early as December 1825, rejected the accusation as "puerile chatter."[2] But that Grundtvig cannot quite be said to be free of such a tendency is evidenced by the fact that he and his followers, similar to Catholicism, assert the authority of the Church, Church tradition and the Church's sacraments.[3] But Catholicism's appeal to the Church's tradition is different from Grundtvig's, since his reference to church history only concerns what can be established from this as the original apostolic Christianity, which has been transmitted through the history of the Church, whereas Catholicism also lets true Christianity include decisions on Church meetings and the Pope's statements *ex cathedra*.

---

1 Ibid., p. 3. (*Nik. Fred. Sev. Grundtvigs udvalgte Skrifter*, ed. by Begtrup, vol. 4, p. 403.)

2 The rejection appears in Grundtvig's review (that appeared in the third volume from 1825 of *Theologisk Maanedskrift*, pp. 248-78) of the book by the church historian August Neander, namely, *Antignosticus, Geist des Tertullianus und Einleitung in dessen Schriften mit archäologischen und dogmenhistorischen Untersuchungen* (1825). Grundtvig writes here that when someone like him claims "that the one and only thing is the history of the Christian church, which can teach us what Christians have believed, that is, what Christianity is," then one is unfairly punished by being called "an obscurantist and a Catholic" (p. 249). There should be other and more evidence to ground such a charge "than a noble shrug of the shoulders and the puerile chatter that I have become a Catholic" (p. 274).

3 See Edvard Lehmann, *Grundtvig*, Copenhagen: Jespersen og Pio 1929, p. 173.

Since 1688 the Danish pastors had used a manual, called the Altar Book, which contained guidelines for the exercise of religious ceremonies and the texts of the rituals used in the Church. As time passed, however, a certain tolerance was shown by the ecclesiastical magistrates. From the late 1820s and for more than a decade there was a heated debate in newspapers, magazines and pamphlets about the lack of uniformity in the Danish state church. In 1825 H.N. Clausen more than implied that no cleric in Denmark adhered to the current guidelines, and suggested some revised formulations in order to establish some uniformity in the delivering of the sacraments.[1] Clausen's proposal, however, did not win any following.

The result of the discussion was that the Danish Chancellery in 1837 handed over to Bishop Mynster the task of preparing a proposal for a new alter book. Mynster immediately went to work, and in 1839 his proposals were released.[2] He suggested here several changes in the previously established rituals. For example, Mynster suggested that the ritual associated with adult baptism would differ from what was used in the christening.

Mynster was certainly a supporter of the freedom of preaching both in sermons and at funerals and weddings, and possibly also at baptisms. But he was opposed to the idea that the pastors could freely change the religious rituals associated with baptism and communion. Therefore Mynster's formulation amounted to a draft of an *ordained* altar book for the Danish State Church.[3]

In a polemical paper entitled *Freedom of Speech* from the same year Grundtvig turned against Mynster's proposal in a way that on the surface looked friendly but in reality was very sharp.[4] On the one hand,

---

[1] Henrik Nicolai Clausen, *Catholicismens og Protestantismens Kirkeforfatning, Lære og Ritus*, Copenhagen: Andreas Seidelin 1825, pp. 833-39.

[2] [Jacob Peter Mynster], *Udkast til en Alterbog og et Kirke-Ritual for Danmark*, Copenhagen: Schultz 1839. The draft consisted of three parts: "I. Proposal for an Ordained Altar Book for Denmark," "II. Proposal for Church Ritual for Denmark," and "III. Remarks on the Proposals for a new Altar Book and a new Church Ritual."

[3] An account of the entire affair about the rituals is found in Jens Rasmussen, *J.P. Mynster. Sjællands biskop 1834-1854. Kampen for en rummelig kirke. Forholdet til N.F.S. Grundtvig og Grundloven*, [Odense:] Odense Universitetsforlag 1999, pp. 145-72.

[4] N.F.S. Grundtvig, *Frisprog mod H[ans] H[øjærværdighed] Hr. Biskop Mynsters Forslag til en ny Forordnet Alterbog*, Copenhagen: Wahlske Boghandlings Forlag 1839.

he believed that there was no reason to change the rituals, and, on the other hand, he insisted on the pastors' claimed right to modify them if their conscience demanded this. "Freedom of conscience" Grundtvig had written in 1834, "is all religion's highest principle and any blameless citizen's inalienable right."[1] There is hardly any doubt that Mynster's use of the word "ordained" was very provocative for him, and, unlike the bishop, he was a staunch supporter of the possibility of dissolving the parish bonds, that is, to make it possible for citizens freely to choose the pastor they wanted to go to in ecclesiastical matters. In three articles, of which censors had banned the third from being published, Grundtvig had advocated the right of religious freedom—with some unspecified limitations. He claimed that both reason and history dictate that "freedom is the spirit's element, as compulsory force is that of the body,"[2] since "freedom of the body" always does damage, but the freedom of the spirit always does good.[3] He therefore wanted that the close ties between church and state, which characterized the Danish monarchy, be dissolved, and argued that it should be possible to quit the state church, which was something that Mynster fought against with all his power.

Grundtvig's main concern was to prevent a change in the baptism ritual. He succeeded in this since the newly crowned Christian VIII (1839-48) and especially his queen were much more positively disposed towards Grundtvig than his predecessor Frederik VI had been. Mynster's proposal was never implemented. Also in his contribution against Mynster, Grundtvig had confidently expressed that he expected that

---

(Reprinted in *Nik. Fred. Sev. Grundtvigs udvalgte Skrifter*, ed. by Begtrup, vol. 8, pp. 209-98.)

1 N.F.S. Grundtvig, *Den Danske Stats-Kirke upartisk betragtet*, Copenhagen: Wahlske Boghandlings Forlag 1834. (*Nik. Fred. Sev. Grundtvigs udvalgte Skrifter*, ed. by Begtrup, vol. 8, p. 57.)

2 N.F.S. Grundtvig, "Om Religions-Frihed," Parts 1-3, of which the first two parts appeared in *Theologisk Maanedsskrift*, January and February 1827. (Reprinted in *Nik. Fred. Sev. Grundtvigs udvalgte Skrifter*, ed. by Begtrup, vol. 5, pp. 46-153.) The quoted material is from the second article, see *Nik. Fred. Sev. Grundtvigs udvalgte Skrifter*, ed. by Begtrup, vol. 5, p. 86. Grundtvig's hesitation about complete freedom of religion is evident, for example, on p. 57, where he writes that the Protestant sea powers grant the inhabitants of the colonies "such an extensive freedom of religion that a bit less would be more than enough!"

3 See *Nik. Fred. Sev. Grundtvigs udvalgte Skrifter*, ed. by Begtrup, vol. 5, p. 69.

"His Majesty, under all circumstances, would permit us older pastors to baptize as before."[1]

That it was the word "ordained" that had disturbed Grundtvig is abundantly clear from his objections to Mynster's proposal. He says here clearly that if Mynster had suggested that it was possible to withdraw from the state church and form a Free Church, he would not have published his objections. In his refutation Grundtvig argued not for his views on the origin of the baptism ritual and the origin of the Apostolic Creed, although this particular creed plays an important role in many theologians' views of baptism as a covenant with the divine, since the person baptized in the creed for example, obliged himself "to renounce the devil and all his works." Grundtvig did not want for his criticism to engage in theological discussions, but contented himself with saying that Mynster's proposal was irresponsible, because if it became law,

> it would deprive all the children, who were subsequently born, of the State Church's baptism in its old form, the only one which can be the original one by Christ's institution, and it would impose upon us pastors what is contrary to the vow of our ordination, a vow to administer baptism in a form, which, since it is brand new, can in no way be in accordance with Christ's words of institution.[2]

Mynster answered his critics and Grundtvig in a short work, which was published in 1840.[3] Here he noted that Grundtvig's emphasis on the oral tradition as the highest instance runs counter to the general view that oral traditions that have lasted for centuries are unreliable. In his *Freedom of Speech* Grundtvig had also written—Mynster quotes—that "the Danish Church is only a fragment of the Roman Church-State from which we have received the faith, and the sacraments."[4] But Mynster fails to quote the entire sentence, which begins: "My Readers must know I'm far from being biased towards Rome in any of its tyrant-figures."

---

1 Ibid., vol. 8, p. 227.
2 Ibid., p. 229.
3 Jacob Peter Mynster, *Oplysninger angaaende Udkastet til en Alterbog og et Kirke-Ritual for Danmark*, Copenhagen: Gyldendal 1840.
4 *Nik. Fred. Sev. Grundtvigs udvalgte Skrifter*, ed. by Begtrup, vol. 8, p. 248; see Mynster, *Oplysninger angaaende Udkastet til en Alterbog og et Kirke-Ritual for Danmark*, p. 32.

Mynster also indicates that on another occasion Grundtvig without any hesitation invoked what is customary in the Catholic Church, and he then continues: "So we arrive happily at the Pope's feet."[1] In his criticism of Mynster, Grundtvig had not always been completely fair. For instance, he accused the bishop of trying to make his personal view into law.[2] However, as shown, Mynster likewise did not hold himself back.

III. Grundtvig and the Persecution of the Baptists

Even before the legal acceptance of forced baptism had taken place, Grundtvig, in a hastily written pamphlet, turned against the persecution that the Baptists were subject to.[3] It was not the Baptists' view of adult baptism versus infant baptism, which he wanted defend—here the disagreement between him and the Baptists was profound. However, as a spokesman for freedom of religion, that is, the idea that each citizen in a Christian country must cultivate the Christian God as his conscience dictates, he could not silently stand by and witness the behavior of the authorities against the Baptists, which he, like others, wrongly designated as Anabaptists. In his defense of the Baptists, Eiríksson therefore initially explained that the Baptists did not have to fight in the same boat as the Anabaptists, who were condemned by the Augsburg Confession.[4]

In his pamphlet Grundtvig posed and answered three questions. First: What is religious persecution? Second: Is religious persecution in accordance with the Danish Royal Law, the Augsburg Confession and the Christian faith? And third: Does the experience show that religious persecution has ever contributed to peace and harmony in a state? Where the first two questions are discussed in the context of Denmark, Grundtvig brings in material from the history of a number of European countries in answer to the third.

---

[1] Mynster, *Oplysninger angaaende Udkastet til en Alterbog og et Kirke-Ritual for Danmark*, p. 33.

[2] See *Nik. Fred. Sev. Grundtvigs udvalgte Skrifter*, ed. by Begtrup, vol. 8, p. 270.

[3] N.F.S. Grundtvig, *Om Religions-Forfølgelse. En Stemme*, Copenhagen: Wahlske Boghandlings Forlag 1842. (Reprinted in *Nik. Fred. Sev. Grundtvigs udvalgte Skrifter*, ed. by Begtrup, vol. 8, pp. 460-73.)

[4] See Eiríksson, *Om Baptister og Barnedaab*, pp. 3-31.

Grundtvig answers the first question by stating that it is religious persecution when the state punishes people who exercise and propagate a form of worship that differs from that of the State Church. It might be argued, he writes, that in formal terms people are not penalized for doing so, but for violating the existing laws. But from such a view the persecution is merely a legal persecution, which does not alter the fact that it makes the persecuted people martyrs for their conscience. When Luther, in opposition to Catholicism, claimed that people in religious affairs should follow their conscience, it is clear that religious persecution runs contrary to Lutheran Christianity and can be justified, Grundtvig thought, neither by the New Testament nor by true Christianity.

With regard to the second question Grundtvig's answer is that the Danish Royal Law in religious affairs refers to the Augsburg Confession and must protect both this and Christianity. Since the Confession is assumed not to be contrary to true Christianity, it cannot justify religious persecution. On the contrary, "the Augsburg Confession expressly protests against all religious persecution, this is undeniable."[1] Here Grundtvig is perhaps on thin ice a bit. It is only because the Creed is assumed to be in accordance with what Grundtvig means is true Lutheran Christianity that it can be said to reject religious persecution. Not only is religious persecution therefore both unchristian and anti-Lutheran, but is also in Denmark

> utterly unnatural, and in our disintegrated and confused State Church it would be so patently unfair and unreasonable that religious persecution nowhere and at no time (although it means a great deal) will make so great a calamity as it would do here, where it only by a miracle so far has been prevented from turning the State Church's best friends into its enemies, throwing the government's most loyal followers into the arms of the opposition and destroying the peaceful and most loving folk life that has flourished on Earth.[2]

The third question Grundtvig intends to answer with reference to the view that history shows that religious persecution does not diminish

[1] *Nik. Fred. Sev. Grundtvigs udvalgte Skrifter*, ed. by Begtrup, vol. 8, p. 463.
[2] Ibid., p. 472.

but rather promotes discord and disagreement in a state. He repeatedly stresses that it is the guild interests, which stand behind the state clergy's struggle against any form of worship that deviates from that of the State Church, and if you "want to wait for freedom, until it is entirely recommended by a State clergy on the whole, then one must probably wait until the coming of the millennium."[1]

IV. Eiríksson's Criticism of Grundtvig's Defense of the Baptists

The historical-critical exegesis of the 18th and 19th century and the theological rationalism of the 18th century, which had especially sought to convey the moral content of the Gospels, provoked in Denmark in the first half of the 19th century two major reformers and one minor one. The major ones were Grundtvig and Kierkegaard, although the latter, in 1855, rejected the idea that he was a reformer;[2] the minor one was Eiríksson, who possessed neither Grundtvig's poetic and visionary force nor Kierkegaard's dialectical sharpness and literary skills. While the first two had a great influence on the church and religious life in Denmark in second half of the 19th century and the first half of the 20th, Eiríksson's reformatory efforts remained totally ineffective.[3] So people interested in religion in the 20th century only remember him simply as "the first spokesman for Unitarianism in Denmark."[4]

Grundtvig's response to the challenge of biblical criticism has already been presented. In short, it assumes that it is not Scripture, "which can

---

1 Ibid., p. 473.

2 See *SKS* 14, 169 / *M*, 40: "As for myself, I am not what the times perhaps crave, a reformer."

3 In 1830-31 Grundtvig argued in his series of articles "Skal den Lutherske Reformation virkelig fortsættes" for a continuation of the Lutheran Reformation "in a Christian manner" (see, for example, *Nik. Fred. Sev. Grundtvigs udvalgte Skrifter*, ed. by Begtrup, vol. 5, p. 319). Kierkegaard's desire for a church reformation appears not least of all in his criticism from *The Moment* of the theology of mediation, that is, the claim for the unification of the Christian and the human, which Mynster and Martensen stood for. Eiríksson writes directly that "the Lutheran (namely, Danish) State Church is greatly in need of a Reformation" (see Eiríksson, *Om Baptister og Barnedaab*, p. XLIV).

4 See Thorvald Kierkegaard, *Magnus Eiriksson og Mary B. Westenholz. To Forkæmpere for Unitarismen i Danmark*, Copenhagen: no publisher given 1958 (an offprint from Protestantisk Tidende), pp. 3-9.

or should defend the Church, but the Church which should defend the Scriptures."[1] The words of faith, as uttered in the Church, the living word, should animate any reading of the Bible. For Kierkegaard, the answer was the belief in the incarnation and Christ's sacrificial death, and this alone redeemed the existing and therefore sinful person. A simple, childlike piety—and not the results of theological speculation—was the goal of the individual's religious development. Where Grundtvig found the Biblical exegesis' presupposition external to human beings, namely, in the ecclesiastical tradition, that is, in something objective, Kierkegaard and Eiríksson found it in something subjective, namely, in the individually achieved personal piety, the former in the belief in the incarnation and Christ's sacrificial death, and the latter in what he thought was the spirit of Christianity, namely, the love of God and love of neighbor. Eiríksson repeatedly stressed

> the necessity of a certain mental disposition, in order that there may be hope that one can understand and explain Scripture consistently with the spirit of Christianity....And what then is this mental disposition, you will ask. It is a certain piety, a bowing or directing of the mind toward God in general, or other words, religiosity.[2]

But he also found that the Church doctrines and rituals—and thus also the Church's symbols—should be reformulated from the results that the historical biblical criticism had reached, and only what was in line with reason inspired by love, that is, "the enlightened Christian understanding"[3] could be accepted. Whereas Grundtvig and Kierkegaard on a very different basis were both preachers, Eiríksson appeared primarily as a somewhat primitive and opinionated scholarly theologian, which undoubtedly was one of the reasons for his lack of clout.

As early as in *About Baptists and Baptism* we encounter the criticism of Grundtvig for Catholicism, but on a slightly dubious basis, namely,

---

1 *Nik. Fred. Sev. Grundtvigs udvalgte Skrifter*, ed. by Begtrup, vol. 4, p. 553.

2 Eiríksson, *Om Baptister og Barnedaab*, p. XXII. On this point Eiríksson was in agreement with more or less all Christian theologians.

3 Ibid., p. VIII. On Eiríksson's somewhat homemade definitions of reason and understanding and the relation between them, see my article "Magnus Eiríksson and Philosophy" in this volume.

based on a statement about the Baptists' beliefs that was demanded by the authorities from the Baptist Peter Christian Mønster (1797-1870) in 1839. Mønster was trained as an engraver and had lived in Slagelse, a town on Zealand, where he had organized pious assemblies, that is, gatherings of religiously awakened laymen. Since this activity was banned by the city council, he moved to Skælskør, a neighboring town, and later to Copenhagen, where he joined the circle around Grundtvig, but when he came to doubt that infant baptism was the baptism ordained by Christ, he went over to the Baptists. He was therefore subject to official persecution, was fined, and between 1839 and 1845 spent four years in prison because of his religious beliefs.

In his statement to the local authorities Mønster writes that Grundtvig during a conversation with him had said that "Laymen should refrain from reading the Bible and from studying it, since they did not have the Holy Spirit, which the pastors received when the bishop at the ordination lays a hand on their heads, and [he said] they were the ones who understood the Scripture."[1] This attitude of Grundtvig, Eiríksson says, shows at least the "Catholic element" in his view of the church and a "genuine Catholicism."[2]

That Grundtvig in the 1830s should have literally said what Mønster quotes, is hardly credible, since he never wanted to discourage laymen from reading the Bible. However, it is conceivable that he said something about the laying on of hands at the ordination of pastors that Mønster misinterpreted. In articles from 1826-27 about the truth of Christianity Grundtvig had written that

> now Church history bears witness that the Spirit and Life are given in the community of Christ, usually in a certain order, and only as a rare exception, as well as a great gift of grace, so that ordinarily all believers receive spirit and life through baptism and the Lord's Supper, and all believing scribes receive, by the bishop's laying his hand on them, their spiritual skill to be teachers, while the Lord and the Holy Spirit have reserved for themselves to bestow and distribute extraordinary gifts of grace to whom they want,

---

1 Eiríksson, *Om Baptister og Barnedaab*, p. 21.
2 Ibid, p. 22 (note).

in agreement with the degrees of faith and according to the needs of the communion.[1]

The content of this statement is clearly at odds with the position which Mønster and Eiríksson ascribe to Grundtvig. Moreover, Grundtvig seems, with the republication of the articles in 1865, to cast doubt on the historical background of the bishop's laying on of hands at the ordination ceremony.

Since at this stage he was a Bible Christian, Eiríksson was also outraged by Grundtvig's characterization of the Bible as "dead letters."[2] But there is a misunderstanding here, since Grundtvig believed that the Scripture's "dead letter" must be inspired by being read in the Christian spirit. This was also Eiríksson's view.

In connection with Grundtvig, Eiríksson had two issues: first, a critique of Grundtvig's short piece *About Religious Persecution*, and secondly, he wanted to emphasize that Grundtvig—like Faber and Martensen—with his emphasis on child baptism was in conflict with the New Testament.

A special section of *About Baptists and Baptism* is devoted to the criticism of Grundtvig's defense of baptism.[3] Here Eiríksson criticized Grundtvig by claiming that his defense is not an expression of religious tolerance, which stems from what Eiríksson calls "Christianity's principle of love,"[4] and is in conflict with Grundtvig's religious personality. As Grundtvig himself wrote, he did not have the slightest sympathy for the Baptists.[5] Therefore, Eiríksson thought that the defense was not sincere and genuine. It is not as if Grundtvig's desire for religious tolerance was born from a Christian disposition. Grundtvig was, Eiríksson claimed, in religious matters not at all tolerant, and he pointed out that in his *Freedom of Speech* he had briefly rejected as "fools"[6] those who had a

---

1 *Nik. Fred. Sev. Grundtvigs udvalgte Skrifter*, ed. by Begtrup, vol. 4, p. 702.

2 See, for example, *Nik. Fred. Sev. Grundtvigs udvalgte Skrifter*, ed. by Begtrup, vol. 4, p. 549 and pp. 554f.; Eiríksson, *Om Baptister og Barnedaab*, p. 28 (note).

3 Eiríksson, *Om Baptister og Barnedaab*, pp. 99-138.

4 Ibid., p. 127.

5 N.F.S. Grundtvig, "Om Religions-Forfølgelse," in *Nik. Fred. Sev. Grundtvigs udvalgte Skrifter*, ed. by Begtrup, vol. 8, p. 471.

6 *Nik. Fred. Sev. Grundtvigs udvalgte Skrifter*, ed. by Begtrup, vol. 8, p. 242; Eiríksson, *Om Baptister og Barnedaab*, p. 99 (note).

different view of the sacrament than the Lutheran one, that is, Calvin and Zwingli and their supporters.

Since Grundtvig's conception of baptism was fundamentally different from that of the Baptists, a defense of them, Eiríksson believed, was in violation of his deepest conviction, and it was therefore inconsistent of him to pursue such a defense. A true defense of them had to be imbued with Christian love and not with worldly wisdom and historical evidence.

The grounds which Grundtvig presented against religious persecution were rejected by Eiríksson as external, worldly and formal. When Grundtvig in the rejection of religious persecution refers to the Danish Royal Law, where nothing is explicitly written about this matter, it must be because the state power is legally bound to enforce the Augsburg Confession, but the Confession does not explicitly prescribe religious tolerance. On the contrary, harsh words were used against the Anabaptists who are condemned. In the Augsburg Confession, there is thus a seed of religious intolerance. It is true that Luther and his followers appealed to the tolerance of the emperor and the papacy, but downwards they did not exhibit a tolerant attitude. To refer to the Danish Royal Law is a purely formal argument. A law can be interpreted in many ways, and to refer to a law serves no useful purpose because—as Eiríksson writes—the worldly wisdom divides, whereas heavenly love unites.[1] Only if the reading of Scripture and the Augsburg Confession appealed to Christian love, can it be said that religious persecution is contrary to the Christian faith, although nothing is written about it anywhere.

Furthermore, Grundtvig's reference to historical evidence is misconceived since this is still an external reason to avoid religious persecution and only forms the basis for a rule of prudence that says that religious persecution is dangerous for the state because it creates internal discord and strife and is a source of sectarian movements. As the rule of prudence it is a product of the secular disposition and not born of Christian love. In addition, Eiríksson writes,

> this rule of prudence turns out, like most rules of prudence, to be very short-sighted and one-sided, for the danger which is envisaged, when speaking about the religious sects, consists in the movement, which it is

[1] See Eiríksson, *Om Baptister og Barnedaab*, p. 116.

> reasonable to think that these would cause; but who dares indeed assert that the movement is not quite as often, but perhaps more often, more beneficial than harmful? This may be especially likely to be assumed in the religious Domain: for Church history shows that such movements often had beneficial consequences.[1]

In his eagerness to refute Grundtvig, Eiríksson did not demonstrate that Grundtvig's rule of prudence is usually short-sighted and one-sided, but only claimed that religious diversity can be beneficial for a society, and on this score Grundtvig would have agreed with him. Eiríksson's criticism of Grundtvig also contains implicitly and in a way that is probably unintended a partial justification of religious persecution. If sect formation is one of the effects of religious persecution, and sects may beneficially affect a nation's religious life, persecution on religious grounds cannot be absolutely condemned. It is far from rare in Eiríksson's writings that his polemical temper runs away with him.

Eiríksson thought that Grundtvig's defense pamphlet in the long run harms the Baptists. In the pamphlet, Grundtvig criticizes the Danish clergy and highlights himself, which will immediately cause ill-will towards the Baptists among senior church officials and the state administration. Eiríksson apparently did not consider whether the same thing could not also be objected to his own defense, in which he sharply attacks Faber, Mynster and Martensen. He calmly realized that he could possibly harm himself. But the truth must take precedence over considerations for his own person. Overall, he concludes:

> The final result of these considerations is this: That the manner in which Pastor Grundtvig has gone forward in his defense of the Baptists' freedom of religion—even under the assumption that it results from, if not true motives, then at least well-intended motives—is just as little suited to convey the true Christianity among men, as their own way, which seeks to enforce the so-called Christianity by, in an unchristian and violent manner, eradicating and suppressing what they regard as struggling against it.[2]

---

[1] Ibid., pp. 110f.

[2] Ibid., pp. 137f.

In his criticism of Grundtvig, Eiríksson belittles all the reasons for why he had to publish his pamphlet. It had been far from Grundtvig's intention to defend the Baptists' conception of baptism or their administration of the sacrament; he only wanted to defend the Baptists' right to dissolve the parish bond, to leave the state church and to form an independent congregation. Whereas Eiríksson maintained his view of Christian baptism as an adult baptism, which requires faith, and on this point was in agreement with the Baptists without joining them,[1] Grundtvig maintained his view, according to which the child at baptism becomes a child of God. Whereas Eiríksson denied that baptism and communion are sacraments, for Grundtvig baptism and the Lord's Supper are the pillars on which his view of the church was built.[2] It seems to be shadowboxing from Eiríksson's side to demand that to be true, a defense of the right to freedom of religious expression must be based on the recognition of religious beliefs that differ from one's own. As hard as Eiríksson in his work attacks Mynster, Faber and Martensen, there are no indications that he met the requirements that he demanded from Grundtvig.

Eiríksson did not mind that what drives Grundtvig in his defense of the Baptists was the unshakable conviction that faith is a matter of conscience and that freedom of conscience—as Grundtvig wrote in 1834 in *The Danish State Church Regarded Impartially*—"is both the highest proposition of all religion and the inalienable right of every blameless citizen."[3] Although he disagreed with the Baptists, they should, according to his opinion, like other so-called heretics "have the right to pursue both theoretical and practical proofs of the truth and the beneficial nature of their religion."[4]

---

1 In his short epistemological work *Tro, Overtro og Vantro, i deres Forhold til Fornuft og Forstand, samt til hinanden indbyrdes* (Copenhagen: H.C. Klein 1846), Eiríksson discusses in the introduction his relation to the Baptists. He writes that it is a mistake to believe that he is a Baptist, for although "not only right from the beginning have I been completely satisfied with their religious views and efforts at reform" (p. XII) nevertheless "I believe that their deviations [from the doctrine of the Church] are not sufficient or fundamental enough" (p. XIII). The Baptists were not radical enough for Eiríksson.

2 Eiríksson, *Om Baptister og Barnedaab*, see, for example, p. XVII.

3 *Nik. Fred. Sev. Grundtvigs udvalgte Skrifter*, ed. by Begtrup, vol. 8, p. 57.

4 Ibid., p. 59.

In his book Eiríksson did not criticize separately Grundtvig's conception of baptism, but in his classification of the Danish theologians' doctrine about baptism he identifies Grundtvig among the class of "the extreme ecclesiastical and speculative theologians," which is the first main class "not because it is the most important, but because it contains the greatest confusion and the greatest delusions."[1] This class has four subdivisions, the first of which is constituted by Faber and Martensen, and the fourth of Grundtvig and his followers,

> which in an extreme ecclesiastical, Catholicizing way are approaching to the two great captains [Faber and Martensen], and in some parts agree with them, but Grundtvig's point of view is not as consistently and systematically carried out as theirs, and he therefore lacks several important points which, as regards to the systematic errors and delusions, implies that he stands behind Bishop Faber and Professor Martensen.[2]

A somewhat conditional praise! By the term "extreme ecclesiastical" Eiríksson understood "pronounced narrow-minded or ecclesiastical" or "traditional church." For Grundtvig, it must be assumed that his adherence to the Danish state church's traditional ritual made his conception of baptism, in Eiríksson's eyes, "extreme ecclesiastical."

V. Eiríksson's Conflict with Scripturalism

After 1844 and until 1852 Eiríksson wrote several major and minor treatises and newspaper articles. Three of his shorter treatises or diatribes were directed against Hans Lassen Martensen, who was attacked exceedingly harshly. There were in Martensen, Eiríksson claimed, numerous non-religious, unchristian and mistaken conceptions, and he should be removed from his professorship because, by influencing the students who came to his courses, he could harm them spiritually. Eiríksson's choice of words and not least of all his criticism of Mynster, which he presented at the same time, with a request to the king, Christian

1 Eiríksson, *Om Baptister og Barnedaab*, p. 528 (note).
2 Ibid., p. 529.

VIII, to dismiss Martensen, resulted in the authorities instructing the prosecutor general, the highest prosecuting instance in the state, to institute proceedings against him. The case was thrown out, however, by virtue of the general amnesty decree in connection with Frederik VII's accession to the throne in 1848.

From 1852 and for the next ten years Eiríksson was largely silent. When in 1863 he again continued his work as a writer, he was no longer a Bible theologian. Although he writes in his account from 1875 about his writing that

> when I now entered the study and path of discovery as I honestly and sincerely sought the truth without regard to material advantage, I came in this time, [that is, between 1852 and 1863] gradually to regard Scripture in a different way than before, to regard it as a book that probably contains the highest and most important truths, but nonetheless there are a great many faults and delusions, misunderstandings and contradictions (even in very important matters) and ignorance of nature and its laws; therefore, it is like a book where the chaff must be separated from the wheat, where everything must be tested and examined so that the erroneous and counterfeit might not be mixed up with, confuse, and obscure the true and just.[1]

As a theology student, Eiríksson had attended H.N. Clausen's lectures on biblical exegesis, which he later praised as "excellent exegetical courses."[2] After his theological degree in 1837, he worked for several years as a highly sought-after tutor in Old Testament and New Testament exegesis. But as his radical views on Christianity and the church became known, the number of his students shrank significantly. After the confrontation with Martensen in the latter half of the 1840s, he intensified his exegetical studies, and in 1863 he presented the outcome of his work in the book *Is the Gospel of John an Apostolic and True Gospel and Is its Doctrine about God*

---

1 Magnús Eiríksson, "Min Forfattervirksomhed," in *Flyvende Blade for Literatur, Kunst og Samfundsspørgsmål*, ed. by Vilhelm Møller, vol. 3, 1875, no. 11 (June 12), pp. 81-83; no. 12 (June 19), pp. 90-93, and no. 13 (June 26), pp. 100-04; the quoted passage is from p. 100.

2 Eiríksson, *Om Baptister og Barnedaab*, p. VII.

Becoming Human a True and Christian Doctrine? A Religious-Dogmatic, Historical-Critical Study.[1]

As early as the late 18th century and the first decade of the 19th the authority of the Gospel of John had been questioned, but the attacks on the gospel's apostolic authenticity were first given substance when the German rationalist theologian Karl Gottlieb Bretschneider (1776-1848), in 1820, published his *Probabilia de Evangelii et Epistolarum Joannis, Apostoli, indole et origine* (A Probable Thesis on the Nature and the Origin of the Apostle John's Gospel and Letters).[2] Bretschneider argued here among other things—in H.N. Clausen's words—that

> the Gospel was written in the 2nd century by a heathen-Christian, who used John's name with an apostolic-polemical intention, in order all the stronger to be able to lead the cause of the gospel against the Jews, who, after the destruction of their state, saw that they were obliged to change their weapons against the Christians, and instead of using violence and persecution they issued slanders and distortions.[3]

Bretschneider's book gave rise to a violent controversy in German theology, in which, among others, Schleiermacher and the controversial David Friedrich Strauss (1808-74) participated. Additional historical-critical reasons against the authenticity of the gospel were presented by leading German theologians such as Wilhelm Martin Leberecht de Wette (1780-1849) and Ferdinand Christian Baur (1792-1860), the leader of the so-called Tübingen School. Eiríksson studied them all and seems to have largely endorsed the view, which, for example, de Wette advocated, namely, that the Gospel of John was not written by the apostle, but possibly by a disciple of the apostle and was, compared to

---

1 Magnús Eiríksson, *Er Johannes-Evangeliet et apostolisk og ægte Evangelium og er dets Lære om Guds Menneskevorden en sand og christelig Lære? En religiøs-dogmatisk, historisk-kritisk Undersøgelse*, Copenhagen: Magnús Eiríksson 1863.

2 Karl Gottlieb Bretschneider, *Probabilia de Evangelii et Epistolarum Joannis, Apostoli, indole et origine*, Lipsiae [Leipzig]: J.A. Barth 1820.

3 Henrik Nicolai Clausen, *Johannes-Evangeliet, fortolket*, Copenhagen: Gad 1855, p. 351.

the Synoptic Gospels, a relatively late, anti-Jewish and Hellenistic work influenced by Gnostic mysticism.[1]

In the introduction to his book on John, Eiríksson wrote,

> Since I now regard it as my special life work to do what stands in my power to eradicate the dangerous and pernicious errors which have gained a footing in the Christian religion, and ranging from the oldest times have filled it with false doctrines, and since I of late have come to the conviction that the false doctrines at least in part have their ground in the illegitimate parts of Scripture, then it follows that I have felt called upon to make a start to explore and express my conviction about that Scripture in the New Testament, which was judged incorrectly, and which in my opinion is the cause of a false dogmatic system. This scripture is the Gospel of John.[2]

Many disputes, much hatred, many persecutions, atrocities and abominations, Eiríksson writes, could have been avoided if people could have realized at the right time that the accounts in the Old Testament, for instance, about the creation, the flood and Noah's ark, were unreasonable, and that passages in the New Testament, for example, about baptism did not come from Christ, but have been exploited by the church hierarchy to increase its power and assert its authority.[3]

VI. The Debate about Grundtvigianism in 1863

In 1863 Eiríksson was not only busy publishing his book on the Gospel of John, but he also came to participate in the discussion about Grundtvigianism that took place that year. The immediate cause was that Martensen on the 29th of April 1863 had held an ordination speech entitled "The Inspiration of the Apostles" on a passage in Paul's Letter to the Galatians, in which the following sentence appears: "But even if we or an angel from heaven preached to you a gospel different from what

---

1 See John W. Rogerson, *W.M.L. de Wette, Founder of Modern Biblical Criticism: An Intellectual Biography*, [Sheffield]: Sheffield Academic Press 1992, pp. 244f.

2 Eiríksson, *Er Johannes-Evangeliet et apostolisk og ægte Evangelium*, Copenhagen: Magnús Eiríksson 1863, p. XXIX.

3 See ibid., p. XIII and p. XV (note).

we preached to you, may he be accursed" (Galatians 1:8). The rumor went around in Copenhagen that Martensen with this had alluded to Grundtvig as a false prophet. When the speech was published fairly quickly after it was given,[1] Grundtvig read it, but could not see that it contained an attack on him, a fact that he mentioned in an article in the *Dansk Kirketidende*.[2]

As Grundtvigianism in time came to be seen by the leading theologians as a powerful movement of church life in Denmark, both H.N. Clausen and Martensen seized the seemingly arbitrary occasion to present to the public their objections against Grundtvig and his followers.[3] Also Magnús Eiríksson appeared in the choir.[4] Others also published their contributions to the discussion in the form of pamphlets and newspaper articles. Some attacked Grundtvig, others defended him, but these three were the main players.

But it was no coincidence that Clausen, Martensen and Eiríksson found reason to criticize Grundtvig and Grundtvigianism. Grundtvig had in his article in the *Dansk Kirketidende* provocatively expressed surprise that "the most learned Lutherans in Denmark," even after "a whole human age, [have] not grasped the crystal-clear difference between speech and writing, word and letter,"[5] although already Luther had taught

> that "the Word and Faith" accomplishes by means of the Holy Spirit the whole work of God in man, and that it is not by reading or by prayer and

---

[1] The speech is reprinted in Hans Lassen Martensen, *Taler ved Præstevielse, holdt i Aarene 1860 til 1868*, Copenhagen: Gyldendal 1868, pp. 82-97.

[2] N.F.S. Grundtvig, "Lys-Ordet og Livs-Ordet i Vorherre Jesu Christi Menighed," *Dansk Kirketidende*, 1863, no. 22, columns 347-58.

[3] Henrik Nicolai Clausen, *Skriftordet og "Det levende Ord." Bidrag til Vurdering af Grundtvigianismens Stilling til Evangelium og evangelisk Kirke*, Copenhagen: Gad 1863; Hans Lassen Martensen, *Til Forsvar mod den saakaldte Grundtvigianisme*, Copenhagen: Gyldendal 1863. With respect to dogmatics, Martensen's book is only an elaboration of what he had already written earlier in the remarks to § 23 in his *Den christelige Dogmatik* from 1849.

[4] Magnús Eiríksson, *Hvem har Ret: Grundtvigianerne eller deres Modstandere? og Hvad har Christus befalet om Daaben? Nogle orienterende Bemærkninger*, Copenhagen: E.L. Thaarup 1863.

[5] N.F.S. Grundtvig, "Lys-Ordet og Livs-Ordet I Vorherre Jesus Christi Menighed," *Dansk Kirketidende*, 1863, column 349.

> fasting, but by baptism and the sacrament of the Lord's own institution that the faithful are born again as the children of God and are prepared for an eternal life in Christ Jesus.[1]

Therefore, when Grundtvig teaches that "it is the words of institution from the Lord's own mouth, which, as a loving and omnipotent Word of God, both makes the believers reborn and in a heavenly way raises them to a spiritual and cordial community with Our Lord Jesus Christ,"[2] it cannot, he thought, be contrary to the Lutheran view.

In his account Clausen took off the gloves and tried to show that Grundtvig's view of the relationship between the "living" words that sound through the sacraments and Scripture's "dead letter" was contrary to the Lutheran Evangelical view. Based on Grundtvig's article and the series of articles that Grundtvig published from 1855 to 1861 in the journal *Kirkelig Samler. Tidsskrift til christelig Oplysning* and that in 1868 were published together under the title *Christian Childhood Teachings*, he characterized Grundtvigianism in five points: (1) Scripture is indispensable for the Christian ministry; (2), however, the spirit does not work on man through the written word, (3) but by the word of "the Lord's own mouth," which, as is clear from the New Testament, sounded at the institution of baptism and communion, (4) and in association with the Apostles' Creed, which for centuries has been the foundation of the Christian Church. Grundtvig had called this association the word of the sacrament. Only this word (5) has the living influence on the believers, which the written word is lacking. Then by way of summary Clausen states that the Grundtvigian view assumes that "Between the written word and the meaning and power of the sacrament there must be a distance as wide as heaven, a distance which approaches a contrast."[3]

After pointing out a number of quotations from the reformers and Catholic authorities, Clausen concluded that Grundtvig's view of the relationship between the words of sacrament and Scripture were

---

1 Ibid., column 355.

2 Ibid., columns 355f.

3 Clausen, *Skriftordet og "Det levende Ord,"* pp. 12ff. In his poem "Guds-Ordet til os," which was published in *Dansk Kirketidende* (1863, no. 22, column 347) immediately before his article, Grundtvig had written the following words, which were often quoted at the time: "Only with the bath and at the table / Do we make God's Word our own." ("*Kun ved Badet og ved Bordet / Hører vi Guds Ord til os.*")

contrary to the Lutheran Evangelical view of the relationship, but in full conformity with the Catholic. He polemically finishes his account with the remark that one wonders if the Catholic propaganda congregation, "which is far from abandoning the Nordic countries, should gratefully appreciate the preliminary cultivation of the Church soil, and by planting of the Roman seed will be prepared to expect a promising harvest? This one considers well and considers in due time!"[1]

Both here and in his memoirs H.N. Clausen expressed sharp criticism of Grundtvig and his followers, but he recognized fully Grundtvig's liberalism and poetic force. In a short essay in 1862 on the parish bond, he wrote about the Grundtvigians:

> And even when one has an eye for the frequent examples, which verge on parody, of tastelessness of diverse kinds, affected naiveté, mannered childishness, inflated berserk rage, one cannot fail to recognize how much of the free, fresh, appealing naturalness that, from this source, has come into Danish preaching and hymns, into church singing and youth teaching, as a salutary opposition to what is distressingly confined to an artificial regularity.[2]

In opposition to Mynster who only saw Grundtvig and his followers as a disturbance in the Danish church, Clausen, despite his initial harsh criticism, however, could also say some appreciative words about an ecclesial and personal opponent.

Martensen too in his *In Defense Against the so-called Grundtvigianism* had some nice words to say about Grundtvig as a major figure in the Danish church life, although he could not recognize him either as a theologian or as a reformer. With a metaphor, which was popular at that time, he compared Grundtvigianism, as it appears in practice, with a leaven that has brought church life much, and which had been a delight to both Martensen himself and others:

> Because I cannot acknowledge in Grundtvigianism any new church principle, that is, a new beginning, where a manifold of fertile consequences

---

[1] Clausen, *Skriftordet og "Det levende Ord,"* pp. 52f.

[2] Henrik Nicolai Clausen, *Anvendelsen af Loven om Løsning af Sognebaandet*, Copenhagen: Gad 1862, p. 43.

> can grow forth, I can very well in this acknowledge a ferment, a powerful leaven. And because in one respect I consider it a leaven which must be purged, I can very well in other respects regard it as a leaven that in a salutary manner has permeated the Danish Church.[1]

When Martensen commented on Grundtvig and Grundtvigianism it was on a different basis than H.N. Clausen. Although it does not appear in his memoirs, where the personal side is barely discussed, Martensen was, for a couple years in his youth before philosophy grabbed his interest, in close contact with a number of young people who gathered around Grundtvig, and to such an extent that, according to church historian J. Oskar Andersen, during this period of his life, he must be called a Grundtvigian.[2]

Like Clausen writing against Grundtvigianism, Martensen was also provoked by Grundtvig's criticism of the "most learned Lutherans in Denmark" for not having grasped the proper relationship between "the living word" and "the dead letter." Martensen was in response to provocation no less provocative, since he carefully showed that Grundtvig's "matchless" discovery was not as matchless as the author and his supporters claimed, since Lessing 50 years before Grundtvig had made the same discovery and had formulated the hypothesis, which Grundtvig and several of his followers maintained, namely, that Christ had taught his disciples about the Apostles' Creed in the period between the Resurrection and the Ascension. Also Grundtvig's juxtaposition of "the living word" and "the dead letter" was found in Lessing. Ironically Martensen wrote that by providing the *per se* known information about Lessing, he "by no means feared...that he was encroaching on Grundtvig's originality."[3] Martensen was obviously aware of the difference between Grundtvig and Lessing, who had developed his views on the spoken word in a polemic against a scripturalism, which considered every word

---

1 Hans Lassen Martensen, *Til Forsvar mod den saakaldte Grundtvigianisme*, Copenhagen: Gyldendal 1863, p. 91. This short work, which is one of Martensen's best, was widely read. In the year of its publication there appeared five editions, and a sixth appeared as late as in 1874.

2 J. Oskar Andersen, "Biskop H.L. Martensens Ungdom," *Kirkehistoriske Samlinger*, 6th series, vol. 1, 1933, pp. 130-237, see p. 183. On this point J. Oskar Andersen is using Frederik Hammerich, *Et Levnetsløb*, Copenhagen: Forlagsbureauet 1882, pp. 186ff.

3 Martensen, *Til Forsvar mod den saakaldte Grundtvigianisme*, p. 24.

of scripture as inspired and whose relationship to Christianity was far from the deep and heartfelt one of Grundtvig.

The argument that the Apostles' Creed had been available before the Gospels was also, Martensen believed, the same with Lessing and Grundtvig. There is no historical evidence for the case, but the argument is an *a priori* argument. If baptism is divinely ordained, the description of the terms and conditions of salvation for inclusion in the Christian church, as stated in the Apostles' Creed, has the same source. Therefore, the Apostles' Creed must have preceded the Gospels. In his *Dogmatics* from 1849 Martensen had already criticized the argument, which makes an inference about reality based on something purely conceptual.[1] Martensen also mentions in his defense the difficulty of explaining why the Apostles' Creed is not mentioned in the New Testament. Moreover, the belief in Jesus and the Triune God is a fundamental condition for salvation, but it is impossible, Martensen says, to conclude that it is the only one. Just as no one can say what it takes to live a moral life, no one can say how far the deity's demands on human beings extend.

Martensen also emphasizes that the Grundtvigians' talk about a baptismal covenant is misleading:

> In the first place it is misleading in the main to let the confession at baptism be the whole baptismal covenant, since it only is the Church's token of a part of the covenant, namely, the moment of the obligation in the pact which is also the expectant Christian's endorsement of this testimony. But the covenant of baptism is first and foremost a pact of grace that the Lord makes with us….But then it is misleading to look on the obligation as a commitment to a certain epitome of statements, and not primarily to the unity and spirit of these statements.[2]

For Martensen, Grundtvig's theology was bad theology. And the recognition which Martensen gave to Grundtvig was only moderate. Martensen ended his defense by pointing out that the great task was to unite the Christian and the human—which was what both Mynster and Martensen tried to do in their mediation of Christianity and civil

1 See Hans Lassen Martensen, *Den christelige Dogmatik*, Copenhagen: C.A. Reitzel 1849, pp. 47f.

2 Martensen, *Til Forsvar mod den saakaldte Grundtvigianisme*, pp. 32f.

life, a mediation which Kierkegaard claimed was not possible—but in Grundtvig it was only a vague and uncritical confusion of the Christian and the popular.

It was typical of Martensen both to grant and to withdraw his recognition. His position was rarely sharp, but often an ambiguous both-and. As Kierkegaard—the personification of the "either/or"—so aptly said: "I would never involve myself with Martensen without having a Notarius publicus [notary public] present, in order to have at least something that stands firm."[1]

VII. Magnús Eiríksson's Criticism of Grundtvig and Grundtvigianism

Eiríksson's opportunity to make his case against Grundtvig and his followers does not seem to have been Grundtvig's provocation in the article on "The Word of Life and the Word of Light,"[2] but rather that his favorite enemy Martensen had polemized against Grundtvigianism. Eiríksson's work against Grundtvig was therefore also a statement against Martensen. He answered the question as to whether Grundtvig or Martensen was right in their view of Christianity by trying to show that both are right on some points but wrong on others, and that both parties are subject to the same errors and distortions of the original Christianity, as it had been preached by Christ to the Apostles and was expressed in the Apostles' Creed.

Eiríksson was by far the most radical of the critics of Grundtvigianism in the 19th century. In his speech against Grundtvig and his group, Martensen had stressed that it

> should not be forgotten, but still maintained what also on several occasions has been granted from the Grundtvigian side, namely, that the entire struggle, however, is within Christianity, and by no means a conflict between Christianity and Anti-Christianity, and herein lies surely the opportunity

---

1 *SKS* 22, 187, NB12:79 / *KJN* 6, 186.

2 N.F.S. Grundtvig, "Lys-Ordet og Livs-Ordet i Vorherre Jesu Christi Menighed," *Dansk Kirketidende*, 1863, no. 22, columns 347-358.

> for a more detailed understanding, if not at present, then at least in time and after passing through times' ordeal of fire, which is the fate of everything.[1]

Neither Martensen nor Grundtvig ever replied to Eiríksson. They undoubtedly felt that he stood outside Christianity since he rejected not only infant baptism but also the dogma of the Trinity and the dogma of Christ's divine nature. With him no fellowship was possible, and therefore, any discussion with him was pointless.

Eiríksson's short work against the Grundtvigians is divided into four sections. In the first he discusses whether baptism in the name of the Holy Trinity and the Apostles' Creed can be attributed to Christ, and in the second he analyzes the relationship between the older Apostles' Creed (*Symbolum Apostolicum*), and the two later ones, the Nicene Creed (*Symbolum Nicaenum*) and the Athanasian Creed (*Symbolum Athanasianum*). This is followed by a third section, in which he discusses Grundtvigianism compared to the Lutheran Reformation, and he concludes with a section on what he sees as the main issue for the Grundtvigians, namely, the contrast between "the living word" and "the dead letter."

The Grundtvigians' view of the baptism ritual and thus also the Apostles' Creed as "the words from the Lord's own mouth" is, Eiríksson believes, their basic fallacy. According to Matthew 28:19, Christ says to his disciples: "Go therefore, and teach all nations, baptizing them in the name of the Father, and of the Son, and the Holy Spirit." Similarly, in Mark 16:15 he says: "Go away into all the world and preach the gospel to every creature." If it can be shown, Eiríksson writes, that Christ did not command or could not have commanded such a thing to his disciples, then neither baptism in the name of the Holy Trinity nor the Apostles' Creed can be attributed to him. Eiríksson believes that he can show that in Acts several examples of baptism are mentioned which were not done in the name of the Trinity (for example, Acts 8:29-37, where people are baptized because the baptized person signifies that he "believes that Jesus Christ is the Son of God," and Acts 10:48, and Acts 19:2-6, where in both cases baptism is done in the name of Christ). Furthermore, "all nations" in Matthew 28:19 and "all creation" in Mark 16:15 include both

[1] Martensen, *Til Forsvar mod den saakaldte Grundtvigianisme*, p. 4.

Jews and non-Jews, but in Acts 10 and 11 the apostle Peter is attacked by converted Jews for also associating with and baptizing non-Jews, and Peter responded that he had received a special revelation, which ordered him to do so. Did the disciples so quickly after the resurrection of Christ forget his commandments, and since Peter has previously been commanded to do so, why should it be revealed to him? It is most reasonable to assume that Christ never commanded this as claimed in the Gospels of Matthew and Mark, and that such passages are not genuine. Then Eiríksson concludes:

> If Christ has not given any charge concerning baptism, and especially not said the words found in Matthew 28:19, then it is clearer than day, first, that the Grundtvigian doctrine of "the living word from the Lord's own mouth" about "the eternal life—words of our Lord's own mouth," etc. are built on sand, and are pure fantasy, and furthermore that the Church's baptism "in the name of the Father and of the Son and the Holy Spirit" is not commanded by Christ since his own faithful and obedient apostles at every moment were prepared to sacrifice their lives to spread Christ's doctrine and follow his commandments, yet did not know the least thing about this commandment, or mention it with a single word, although they so often had occasion and invitation to apply and mention it.[1]

When Eiríksson believes that he has evidence that the command to baptize in the New Testament is false, this is a somewhat premature conclusion since he tacitly assumes that the stories in the book of Acts are genuine. The only viable conclusion he can draw is extremely familiar, namely, that there are passages in the New Testament, which are difficult to reconcile with one another.

Now Eiríksson's manipulation of "dead letters" hardly would have affected the Grundtvigians, and it was perhaps Martensen he had in mind, since Martensen may believe that the ecclesiastical tradition could illuminate the Scriptures, but not that tradition was the criterion of Scriptural truth. Rather, the situation was the other way around.

Next, the question arises about the relation of the Apostles' Creed and the two younger creeds. Whereas Martensen and his supporters

---

[1] Eiríksson, *Hvem har Ret: Grundtvigianerne eller deres Modstandere?*, pp. 19f.

traditionally considered the Nicene and the Athanasian Creed important, Grundtvig and his followers did not attribute any real weight to them. But both are part of the history of the Church and therefore, Martensen had to think, were, like the Apostles' Creed, elements of "the great acquisition process of the Christian Revelation."[1] This means that the two later creeds are only elaborations of what is contained in the Apostolic Creed. Eiríksson ascribes this "extreme spiritual Martensenian consideration of Church history" to the Hegelian element in Martensen's theology.[2] As evidence he refers to Martensen's short compendium on moral philosophy from 1841, where the author mentions "Hegel's well-known claim that one must acknowledge the actual as the rational...."[3] It gives Eiríksson rich occasion to make fun of Martensen for believing that "all the boundless mistakes and destruction, superficiality and hypocrisy, spiritual darkness and delusions, slavery and barbarism, persecution and fanaticism" with "all the terror of the Inquisition, the torture and executions of innocents in the thousands," to which church history testifies, belong to the "great acquisition process of the Christian Revelation."[4]

The Grundtvigians, Eiríksson believes, have the right to override the two younger creeds, but they have not acknowledged the real reason for doing so, and Martensen is wrong when he says that they are further developments or interpretations of the meaning of what is revealed in the first Creed. In this there is nothing about the Trinity, nothing about Christ's two natures, and Christ appears only as the Messiah, that is, as the expected king and deliverer from the Roman yoke, and not, as in the two later creeds, as a deity who has existed from eternity—all dogmas, which seem to be deemed to be contrary to the original simple

---

1 Martensen, *Til Forsvar mod den saakaldte Grundtvigianisme*, p. 79.

2 Eiríksson, *Hvem har Ret: Grundtvigianerne eller deres Modstandere?*, p. 22.

3 Hans Lassen Martensen, *Grundrids til Moralphilosophiens System. Udgivet til Brug ved academiske Forelæsninger*, Copenhagen: C.A. Reitzel 1841, § 53, p. 57 (H.L. Martensen, *Outline to a System of Moral Philosophy*, in *Between Hegel and Kierkegaard: Hans L. Martensen's Philosophy of Religion*, trans. by Curtis L. Thompson and David J. Kangas, Atlanta: Scholars Press 1997, p. 285.) See Hegel's oft-quoted words in *Grundlinien der Philosophie des Rechts*, vol. 7 in *Werke in zwanzig Bänden*, vols. 1-20, ed. by Eva Moldenhauer and Karl Markus Michel, Frankfurt am Main: Suhrkamp 1969-71, p. 24: "*Was vernünftig ist, das ist wirklich; und was wirklich ist, das ist vernünftig.*"

4 Eiríksson, *Hvem har Ret: Grundtvigianerne eller deres Modstandere?*, p. 23.

Christianity. The reason for these ungodly and false deviations from the pure doctrine is due to philosophy and dialectic and not least of all the religious strife that ensued in the early Church. Eiríksson agreed with both Grundtvig and Søren Kierkegaard that the so-called scientific theology, which attempts to understand the mysteries of the Christian religion with the help of philosophical categories, was doomed to lead to erroneous and non-Christian beliefs.

Then Eiríksson concludes:

> Those who now have such a wild imagination that they can persuade themselves to believe that the said Symbols from the 4th and 5th century, "are only interpretations and detailed explanations of the Apostolic Symbol" have surely no right to bring "illusions" and empty fantasies against the Grundtvigians. For even if the so-called "new discovery" [that the whole apostolic confession was given to the apostles of Jesus Christ in the period between the Resurrection and the Ascension] is an empty illusion—and it surely is an illusion—then is the abovementioned observation about "the subsequent confessions" and their relation to the apostolic not diminished? And if we ask: which of these two illusions or delusions is the most dangerous, then we suppose that there might be different opinions about it; but we should, however, be much mistaken if the Martensenian illusion was not the most dangerous, because surely the Apostles' Symbol receives an utterly excessive weight and importance when it is attributed to Christ himself and is considered the only "living and life-giving Word" in contradistinction to the "dead letter," but when the Apostolic Symbol contains the original simple Doctrine…then this exaggeration of its worth and importance can scarcely ever be as harmful as a half-speculative or quasi-orthodox implicit faith in the authenticity of the Symbol, which evidently contains an utterly false and unchristian doctrine, a doctrine which Christ and the apostles did not know anything about.[1]

After this bombastic conclusion, which gives an impression of Eiríksson's polemical language, he turns to H.N. Clausen's main concern, namely, Grundtvigianism compared to the Lutheran Reformation. His

[1] Ibid., pp. 40f.

conclusion here is that Grundtvig is certainly a Protestant, but in a somewhat different manner than the reformers were.

In his pamphlet Clausen had reached the conclusion that Grundtvigianism was not a continuation of the Lutheran Reformation but a reform, "a new founding of a new church."[1] A significant difference between Luther and Grundtvig was that Luther in his quest for true Christianity only went back to the teaching of the church father Augustine on sin and grace, but Augustine's theology was wrong, Grundtvig thought. Luther should have sought the solution much further back, in Irenaeus (2nd century), who through his teacher Polycarp represented a tradition that could be directly traced back to the circle around the apostle John, and therefore to the apostolic age. After Grundtvig had made his "matchless discovery" Irenaeus became important for him. Grundtvig regarded Irenaeus' book *Against Heresies* (*Adversus haereses*), that is, the Gnostics, as "the most Christian book" he knew since it testified to "the word of faith through baptism."[2]

Eiríksson also pointed out another difference between Luther and Grundtvig: the latter's return to apostolic times had reduced Scripture's effect, whereas Luther had stressed scripturalism against the Catholic Church's principle of authority. Where Grundtvig put enormous emphasis on the Apostles' Creed, Luther also featured the Nicene and Athanasian Creeds.

However, there is a similarity between Luther and Grundtvig, namely, that both shelf the dogma of the Trinity, about which nothing can be found in the Apostles' Creed, and both believe in the miraculous effect of baptism, not least of all because they have not stuck to the Synoptic Gospels. Moreover, they are also convinced of the authenticity of the Gospel of John and adhere to the theological niceties that were developed in the post-apostolic time. This is, Eiríksson believes, inconsistent for Grundtvig. Therefore, he is led to conclude that Grundtvig is in fact not a Lutheran, and that he "should reject the Lutheran (and even the church's) dogmatic system, which is built on the later ecclesiastical developments proceeding from speculations and dogmatic disputes, and which mainly

---

1 Clausen, *Skriftordet og "Det levende Ord,"* p. 9.

2 See Grundtvig's preface to the second edition of his translation from 1827 of the fifth book of Irenaeus' text, which in Grundtvig's translation bears the title *Om Kiødets Opstandelse og det evige Liv* (Copenhagen: J.R. Møller 1855).

originate from the 4th and 5th century."[1] Therefore Grundtvig and his circle should leave the Church, as they have often threatened to do. But when they have not done so and agreed to the essential elements of the traditional Lutheran dogmatic system, the entire dispute between the Grundtvigians and their opponents is dissolved "in smoke and steam":

> But so indeed it is worthwhile for the Grundtvigians to change their tune, for nothing can be more intolerable than such opposition that only rests on a supposition that is mere imagination or "illusion."...As I said, when the Grundtvigians would not follow the doctrine, which the Symbol, so idolized by them, contains, or they could not understand its contents, then it would be worthwhile for them to unite with their enemies and make common cause with them against the Church's enemies so that the religious delusions could be defended all the more loudly. If then my appearance might contribute something to them becoming friends with each other, like Herod and Pilate became friends that day when Jesus was condemned to death, then I will not have labored in vain.[2]

Eiríksson was also an accomplished ironist!

Eiríksson ends the section with some remarks on the relationship between Christianity and popular culture with respect to Grundtvig's well-known appeal to the popular and national as opposed to scholarship. If this relation is considered soberly, then one realizes that Eiríksson believes that Christianity with its general human content is more suited to support the national, which he identifies with the popular, than the national is suited to support Christianity, and he continues:

> If therefore the Grundtvigians really are convinced that the church development is mistaken and that church doctrine suffers from unchristian and dangerous delusions, then they must first seek to combat these delusions, and then try to make the correct conception of Christianity as popular and "national" as possible. But this certainly does not happen by deluding oneself and others into thinking that the Apostolic Confession was communicated to the apostles by Christ himself between the Resurrection

1 Eiríksson, *Hvem har Ret: Grundtvigianerne eller deres Modstandere?*, p. 45.
2 Ibid., pp. 48f.

> and the Ascension, by making this fable "popular" and national, and by deriving from it the baseless and mistaken assertion that this is the only word of God, the only "living and life-giving Word."[1]

In the last paragraph of Eiríksson's diatribe he discusses the contradiction between "the living word" and "the dead letter."

Eiríksson indeed ascribed to Grundtvig a certain spirituality, but this, he thought, is a case of a false spirituality, since Grundtvig's doctrine about "the living word from the Lord's own mouth" is pure fantasy, since that attribution of the Apostolic Creed to Christ is both unreasonable and inane.

First, Eiríksson points out that it is unreasonable to assume that Christ would have said about himself that he "ascended into heaven, and is seated at the omnipotent right hand of God the Father."[2] Next, Christ would have contradicted himself if he, in the Apostles' Creed, commanded belief in "the resurrection of the flesh," when he, according to Matthew 22:30, disclaims the resurrected as "a carnal body."[3] On this basis, Eiríksson concludes:

> The Symbol's doctrine of "the resurrection of the flesh" is therefore the opposite of Christ's doctrine of the gospel, which clearly bears the stamp of truth and so much more that Christ's statement here is put in touch with a very interesting condition and constitutes the answer to a very difficult question. And yet, would Jesus have communicated to the apostles this baptism confession containing quite the opposite doctrine of the resurrection! No, let us be men, that is, beings with a little thought and reason.[4]

Finally, thirdly, Eiríksson considered that it is highly unlikely that Christ announced to his apostles something so dogmatic and formal as the Apostles' Creed, which even at the time it was announced contained

---

1 Ibid., p. 50.

2 Eiríksson's formulation, see ibid., p. 52.

3 Matthew 22:30: "For in the resurrection they shall neither take to wife, nor be married, but are as angels of God in heaven."

4 Eiríksson, *Hvem har Ret: Grundtvigianerne eller deres Modstandere?*, p. 53.

information about upcoming events, and which further, from Christ's side, was intended as a formulation to be used until the end of the world.

> This is impossible to assume about Christ, when one has a fairly healthy and true conception of the whole of his conduct and manner of existing. He was as far from all formality as someone could be....His entire mission was to awaken the spiritual life of man, and to bring him closer to God, bring him to worship God in spirit and truth, but such things are achieved not by fixed formulations.[1]

Eiríksson also found unreasonable the Grundtvigian distinction between the spoken word and the dead letter. Christ's entire teaching was to love God and one's neighbor and to let this love affect the mind and will, that is, be reflected in action. The dry formulation of baptism cannot touch the human heart and seize the soul

> like so many of the other words that Jesus speaks to the disciples, the people or the Pharisees and the scribes, and which on so many occasions had a gripping effect, because the Spirit of God spoke through them, because they concerned "the kingdom of God" in particular as it appears in human beings ("the kingdom of God is within you" [Luke 17:21]) and "the righteousness of God," considered in its ideal purity and in its opposition to the profane mind. It takes more than an ordinary imagination to assume and believe that "the word of baptism" can be more effective in making man more spiritual than other words of Christ, which so often have shown their beneficent effect on the spirit of man and the heart....[2]

Eiríksson believed that man also hears the word of God addressed to him in Scripture. Many of the written words are "living words" too. Which of the words of Scripture "the Spirit of God speaks through" must as always, for Eiríksson, be a matter for reason, permeated by the love of God and the neighbor, to adjudicate.

The Grundtvig section in the book about baptism of 1844 and the polemical treatise from 1863 contain Eiríksson's principal and

---

[1] Ibid.

[2] Ibid., p. 58.

most comprehensive criticism of Grundtvig and the Grundtvigians, whose opinion he regarded as pure fantasy and a dangerous threat in contemporary Denmark against the pure evangelical doctrine, although it seemed to him not as dangerous as Martensen's scientific approach in theology on a speculative basis. But in his other works, he also criticized the Grundtvigians. Two years after Denmark's defeat by the Prussians in 1864, he published a short work entitled *God and Reformer: A Religious Idea*, in which he criticized Kierkegaard and the Danish philosopher Rasmus Nielsen (1809-84), but in which Grundtvig and the Grundtvigians also get their share of the criticism. Initially he asked the question of how the reduced Danish nation could regain a greater self-awareness and strength. Some, he writes, will point out that this must be done by means of the development of sources of material wealth, others by means of an increased development of democratic institutions. Both will help to develop a small nation's inner power and strength, but the most important and most crucial, Eiríksson thought, would be a recovery in the spiritual sphere especially in the province of religion. Some would argue that only the Grundtvigian movement could produce this: "But although Grundtvigianism in some respects can be interesting, and though one cannot deny it a certain 'freshness' and 'popular culture,' it is, however, precisely in the sphere of religion, all too hollow, flabby and erring to be able raise the nation at a higher spiritually level."[1] Similarly, Grundtvig himself could not bring about a spiritual awakening. In the humiliating and oppressive circumstances of the defeat, he falls into singing about "the glorious land, the lovely islands, 'the grove green in the spring, at the wonderful sound' and ends thus: that 'the Ancient of Days' cannot leave such a wonderful country as Denmark in the lurch."[2] Likewise he does not think about making "people aware that they would do well to stick more closely to God."[3] Eiríksson also rejected Grundtvig's

[1] Magnús Eiríksson, *Gud og Reformatoren. En religiøs Idee. Samt nogle Bemærkninger om de kirkelige Tilstande, Dr. S. Kierkegaard og Forfatteren*, Copenhagen: J.H. Schubothe 1866, p. X.

[2] Ibid. The two Grundtvig quotations come from the poem "Til Danmark," which Grundtvig published in 1848, see *Nik. Fred. Sev. Grundtvigs udvalgte Skrifter*, ed. by Begtrup, vol. 9, p. 125. The first ("the green grove," etc.) are verses 3-4 in the first strophe, and the second ("the Ancient of Days") are the concluding words of each strophe.

[3] Eiríksson, *Gud og Reformatoren*, p. XI.

"national view" for it seemed "to sound a bit too much like a kind of imaginary justice, and a certain national pretentiousness addressed to our Lord….An ultra-national enthusiast is never the salvation of his nation in the true sense of the word. Grundtvig has played out his role…."[1] Directing his critique clearly at both Grundtvig and Scandinavianism, Eiríksson concluded, "the Northern spirit is extinct."[2]

Five years later, in the book *Paul and Christ* from 1871, Eiríksson alluded to the Grundtvigians without naming names and called them "the present Pharisees and Sadducees."[3] The Grundtvigians have come so far "in great conceit, spiritual pride and self-complacency caused by self-idolization" that Eiríksson does not think that he "is able, in a worthy way, to portray such a peculiar spiritual madness."[4]

With the years Eiríksson did not became more mildly disposed towards those whom he regarded as enemies of the original, simple Christianity.

Translated by Jon Stewart

---

1 Ibid.

2 Ibid., p. XXXI.

3 Magnús Eiríksson, *Paulus og Christus eller Pauli Lære om Retfærdiggjørelsen sammenlignet med Christi Lære om Syndsforladelsen, tilligemed nogle Bemærkninger om andre paulinske Lærdomme m. M.*, Copenhagen: Magnús Eiríksson 1871, p. 68.

4 Ibid., p. 69.

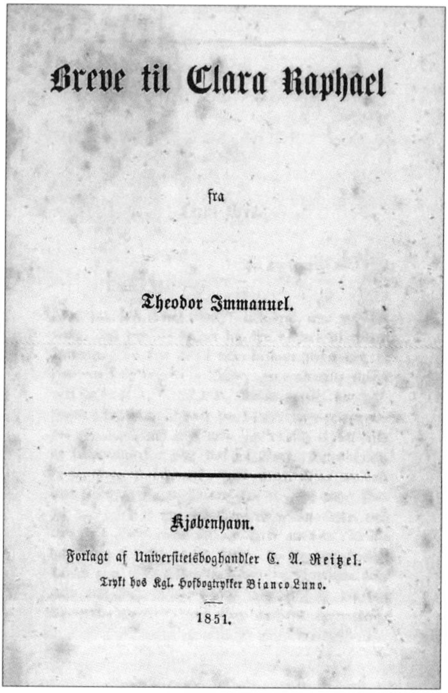

Breve til Clara Raphael

fra

Theodor Immanuel.

Kjøbenhavn.

Forlagt af Universitetsboghandler C. A. Reitzel.

Trykt hos Kgl. Hofbogtrykker Bianco Luno.

1851.

Title Page of Magnús Eiríksson's Letters to Clara Raphael
(Private collection.)

III. Eiríksson as a Defender of Women's Rights

Emancipatory and Eroticist Philosophies of Women: Magnús Eiríksson's and Søren Kierkegaard's Positions in the Controversy about Mathilde Fibiger's *Clara Raphael*

Sigridur Thorgeirsdottir

Magnús Eiríksson was a feminist thinker and an advocate of women's rights. This becomes most apparent in a book he published in 1851, *Letters to Clara Raphael*.[1] In this booklet Eiríksson responds to the ideas of *Clara Raphael*, a novel by Mathilde Fibiger that is often considered to be the first book on women's rights to be published in Denmark.[2] Eiríksson's reflections on this book display what kind of a feminist thinker he was, and what strand of feminist thought his ideas represent. At the same time the controversy that the publication of *Clara*

Thanks to Gerhard Schreiber for his manuscript of the German translation of the text (Magnús Eiríksson, *Briefe an Clara Raphael*, trans. and ed. by Gerhard Schreiber, Barnstorf: Verlag 28 Eichen 2016), and also thanks to him and Kristian Guttesen for assistance in gathering material needed for the research for this article. Jóhanna Þráinsdóttir was the first one to bring my attention to the works of Magnús Eiríksson, and Kristian Guttesen and Gerhard Schreiber initiated the first scholarly session on his work in Iceland at a conference on Kierkegaard at the University of Iceland in May 2013.

1 Magnús Eiríksson published the book under a pseudonym, *Breve til Clara Raphael fra Theodor Immanuel*, Copenhagen: C.A. Reitzel 1851.

2 Mathilde Fibiger, *Clara Raphael. Tolv Breve*, ed. by Johan Ludvig Heiberg, Copenhagen: C.A. Reitzel 1851. The book came out in December 1850, but the year of publication is 1851. References are made both to this original version and to the German translation of the text, which I have also consulted, *Clara Raphael. Zwölf Briefe*, trans. and ed. by Nadine Erler, Barnstorf: Verlag 28 Eichen 2014.

Raphael generated reveals different forms of feminist thought. The novel itself and the different responses to it represent a broad spectrum of approaches to the women's question at the time. Eiríksson's book has mostly been forgotten. His response to *Clara Raphael* as well as his stand on women's rights and emancipation have not been studied in any detail. Katalin Nun with her book on contributions of women to the cultural life of the Danish Golden Age describes his input by saying that he speaks warmly about the ideas of *Clara Raphael*, and that he "appreciates especially Clara's religious attitude and her aspiration to live for the pure idea and God."[1] This characterization only mentions one aspect of Eiríksson's multifarious response. In fact, his booklet shows Eiríksson as representing strands of feminism that have continued to be developed in 20th-century feminist thought. Jóhanna Þráinsdóttir pays tribute to this in a feuilleton article where she describes him as an early champion of women's rights.[2]

I. The Clara Raphael-Controversy

The author of *Clara Raphael*, Mathilde Fibiger (1830-72), was a young woman, only 20 years old when the novel came out. The book was published with a preface by Johan Ludvig Heiberg, a theater director and one of the best known men of letters in Copenhagen of the day. With her book Fibiger managed to spur a controversy in Danish public life on women's rights. Søren Kierkegaard read the book right after it came out and drafted a review of it that he never published.[3] His reaction is yet one example of the diversity in the reception of the novel, and it is interesting to compare it to Eiríksson's response.

Clara Raphael with the subtitle *Twelve Letters*, is an epistolary novel, consisting of 12 letters by Clara Raphael to her friend Mathilde. Clara, the storyteller and protagonist, resembles the author, Mathilde Fibiger

---

1 Katalin Nun, *Women of the Danish Golden Age. Literature, Theater and the Emancipation of Women*, Copenhagen: Museum Tusculanum Press 2013, p. 99. (See especially chapters 4 and 5 on Mathilde Fibiger and the Clara Raphael-controversy.)

2 Jóhanna Þráinsdóttir, "Gleymdur liðsmaður kvenna. Um Magnús Eiríksson, guðfræðing og rithöfund, og framlag hans til frelsisbaráttu kvenna," *Lesbók Morgunblaðsins*, May 10, 1997, pp. 4-5.

3 See *SKS* 24, 136-138, NB22:63 / *JP* 6, 6709.

who was, like Clara, working as a private tutor for children. In the following this book will be discussed in light of the philosophical ideas it conveys and not in terms of its features or qualities as a literary text. It is hard to say if Clara Raphael represents partly, largely or fully the ideas of Mathilde Fibiger, for she is a fictional character. Magnús Eiríksson, Kierkegaard and Heiberg all react to the book as the ideas of Mathilde Fibiger about women, emancipation and the authentic way of living. In terms of the ideas presented, the main content of the letters centers on the question of women's right to education because the author thinks their lack of education is a main obstacle to women's emancipation. Such ideas had already been expressed in *A Vindication of the Rights of Women* (1792)[1] by Mary Wollstonecraft (1759-97) and Olympe de Gouges' (1748-93) demands for human rights for women during the time of the French Revolution. The Danish controversy around Clara Raphael lasted only a half a year. A more widespread debate on women's rights did not take place until roughly two decades after the publication of *Clara Raphael* with the onset of the first wave of the women's rights movement with its main demand for suffrage for women. George Brandes' (1842-1927) Danish translation of John Stuart Mill's (1806-73) *The Subjection of Women*[2] that came out in 1869, is an indication of how the women's rights movement gained momentum.

During the short-lived period of the Clara Raphael debate in 1851 many of Denmark's intellectuals of the Golden Age voiced publicly their agreement or disagreement with Mathilde Fibiger's ideas. One of the issues that Kierkegaard admonishes is the fact that Clara Raphael takes sides with Eiríksson's understanding of the dogma of the Trinity and the original sin. These theological aspects of her work as they relate to Eiríksson's ideas will not be discussed here. The main goal of the following is to situate his ideas within a bourgeoning field of philosophy of women in the 19th century. Kierkegaard, Nietzsche, Schopenhauer were all mid- to late 19th-century European philosophers who wrote about women and sexual difference. Hegelian, Marxist, socialist and anarchist thinkers

[1] Mary Wollstonecraft, *A Vindication of the Rights of Women: with Strictures on Political and Moral Subject*, Boston: Peter Edes 1792.

[2] John Stuart Mill, *The Subjection of Women*, London: Longmans, Green, Reader, and Dyer 1869; *Kvindernes Underkuelse*, trans. by Georg Brandes, Copenhagen: Gyldendalske Boghandel (F. Hegel) 1869.

also discussed the woman question in sociopolitical terms. Kierkegaard's reflections on Fibiger's ideas about womanhood are based on his own theory of sexual difference that will later on be contrasted with Eiríksson's philosophy of sexual difference as presented in his book on *Clara Raphael.* Kierkegaard, Eiríksson, Heiberg and Fibiger all grapple with the question of sexual difference as it was increasingly becoming an issue for gender politics. Debates about women's contribution to culture and their rights were backed up by various philosophies of gender differences and gender identities. Eiríksson's and Kierkegaard's respective reactions to the book display a tension in the philosophy of women and sexual difference, as I will argue. This is a tension between the humanist ideas of Eiríksson and Kierkegaard's conception of the self insofar as it stands in contrast to them.

II. From Misogyny and Philosophy of Women to Feminism

It may at first sight seem odd to discuss "feminist" dimensions of Magnús Eiríksson's text on Clara Raphael. In the mid-19th century philosophies of women's rights, sexual difference and gender equality were not termed "feminism" because this concept surfaced only in the last decades of the century and did not become widespread until the 20th century. Women's rights discourses of the mid-nineteenth century, including the ideas of Mathilde Fibiger, Eiríksson, Kierkegaard and Heiberg, are, in important respects, anticipatory of different strands in 20th-century feminist thought. Debates such as the one around *Clara Raphael* are also retrospective insofar as they stand in a long tradition of philosophies and theologies of sexual difference that date back to antiquity. Such theories have mostly been misogynistic and served to legitimatize the superiority of men and the subordination of women. Women's bodies were deemed dirty or polluted, and their minds, especially their ability to reason, were regarded as deficient compared to men. In the early Church there was the belief that women could only become pure and holy by abandoning their femininity and taking on forms of masculinity. From Aristotle to Augustine and Aquinas women were considered deficient beings compared to men. In modern thought such ideas were transferred into epistemological, ethical and political consideration with claims about women's emotionality that limit them in being logical, rational, fully morally accountable and capable as political subjects. These ideas that lived on in the philosophies of Rousseau, Kant and Hegel, just to name a few, were beginning to be contested in the works of Wollstonecraft and other women thinkers, such as Mary Astell (1666-1731), of the early modern and modern periods. Descartes' idea that women and men were born with equal capacities for rational thought helped to counter the idea that women were unfit for science and politics. Yet that message was slow to undermine philosophical misogyny as evident in Kant's and Hegel's statements about women's lack of scientific and political capabilities. In the 19th century, the debates on women's abilities were mostly framed in the context of political philosophy and Enlightenment ideals of education. In the context of the Clara Raphael-debate, the issue of religion and sexual differences regarding belief is also of importance. Kierkegaard's philosophy of women is extremely important in this regard, and it continues to be debated whether he is merely misogynistic in his description of sexual difference or if he opens a new and positive view of women that counters sterile forms of masculinity, yielding a richer notion of the human being. I will argue that he is both misogynistic and that he also presents an understanding of the self that contains a critique of the humanist, rationalist ideals that Clara Raphael and Eiríksson to a somewhat lesser extent represent. Clara Raphael's rationalistic conclusion to reject erotic love for an asexual marriage for the purpose of acquiring wisdom is therefore a source of scorn by Kierkegaard. This decision of Clara Raphael is something that Eiríksson does not object to, and it is hence a point of difference between him and Kierkegaard.

In order to situate Eiríksson's reflections on the subjection and emancipation of women within the spectrum of feminist thought, it is helpful to distinguish between "liberal" feminism and feminism of "difference." Liberal feminism is based on the idea that men and women should have legally the same rights. A feminism of difference entails that there are values associated with the feminine that need to be elevated so that society is not only construed in accord with masculine values, but also in accord with feminine values. These strands were implicit in different philosophies of women and women's rights in the Clara Raphael debate. Eiríksson's review of *Clara Raphael* can also be linked to late

20th-century masculinity studies as he devotes a considerable amount of his text to describing different masculinities against a framework of a theory of sexual difference. His view was that the emancipation of women also had to go hand in hand with the emancipation of men. Men benefit in terms of power and standing from the hegemonic form of masculinity based on the idea of a duality and an opposition of the sexes. Eiríksson also views men as having created a culture that has been detrimental to gender relations, women and to culture as a whole. "We men have…not played our role so brilliantly in this world,"[1] as he says in the third letter.

III. Liberal Feminism and Difference Feminism

Magnús Eiríksson opens his letters to Clara Raphael by putting himself and his addressee on equal footing in line with the humanistic, universal idea he and she share: all men are brothers and sisters. The addressee of his text is Mathilde Fibiger, but because Eiríksson writes under a pseudonym to Clara Raphael she will be referred to as the author of the ideas he discusses with her. He localizes himself as a writer that is older than Clara Raphael but also claims that age does not necessarily guarantee more wisdom than youth although people gain with age more cleverness, cautiousness and experience. He is trying very hard to sound modest, perhaps in order to make the subsequent critique of Clara Raphael's ideas about women's emancipation as mild as possible. He is acutely aware of the fact that he is discussing with an unusually young author, and the tone of his letters is avuncular without being patronizing. Her story is about a young woman's battle to find her own way, and it is not void of the insecurity, naïve statements and soul-searching that goes along with finding one's way. Clara Raphael rebels against the bourgeois mentality and mediocrity that she feels surrounds her. Her main thesis is that the lack of education keeps women uninformed, petty and concerned with unimportant things. Being in a minority position with her views, she senses a critical attitude and rejection by the people around her. Mathilde (the namesake of the author) is therefore the

---

[1] Eiríksson, *Breve til Clara Raphael*, p. 35.

person she confides in and tells about her struggles to make women's emancipation the purpose of her life.

Eiríksson is wholeheartedly in agreement with the basic thrust of Clara Raphael's argument about the emancipation of women. He opens his remarks with the opinion that women are more advanced than men in terms of a common and a natural sense for things. It would therefore be such an advantage for mankind if women would be able to exert more influence since it would contribute to the good, the true and the just for society and human relations. The main points of Eiríksson's critique of Clara Raphael's ideas are the following: (1) Objections to her generalizations about a masculinized human ideal. (2) Objections to her idealization of wars fought for freedom.

As for the first point, Eiríksson questions how Clara Raphael adopts an ideal of reason that stands in a masculine tradition. She writes that women should strive for "the mental spirit" of men.[1] Women lack, in her view, such an ideal of freedom and truth. This is for Eiríksson a generalization that cannot hold for all men. Males are different, depending on their role in society. He therefore distinguishes between different roles that have different goals. By analyzing the goals of workers, officials, merchants, doctors, lawyers, theologians, artists, poets, soldiers, natural scientists, and so on, he comes to the conclusion that people's ideals and goals are quite different. Ergo, only a small minority of men is interested in the Enlightenment ideals of freedom and knowledge in the service of the good, the true and the beautiful that Clara Raphael advocates. On the basis of this, Eiríksson accuses Clara Raphael of regarding men more highly than women.

The second point of Eiríksson's critical remarks is tied to his first remark about the valorization of a masculine ideal of rationality. Clara Raphael is a staunch supporter of the Danish battle for independence from Germany and admires the patriotic warfare and the soldiers that sacrifice their lives for freedom. As a critic of war, Eiríksson tells her that this admiration for war is misguided, for war is always detrimental to freedom. He admits understanding her patriotic enthusiasm, but his own reflection and a Christian disposition make him abhor war. In

[1] See Fibiger, *Clara Raphael. Tolv Breve*, p. 55 (compare *Clara Raphael. Zwölf Briefe*, p. 49).

exceptional cases there may be just wars, but in general war is bad for justice, truth and humanity. This leads him in the next step to argue that Clara Raphael confuses internal and external freedom. The freedom from the oppressor that she is arguing for as a Danish patriot must be distinguished from the inner freedom, the human striving for freedom.

What is most important in assessing the feminist viewpoint of Eiríksson is his belief that Clara Raphael's alleged elevation of the masculine ideal must mean that women should strive for a masculine ideal. This is for him a great misconception because it means that women should continue to construct the world in line with the same principles men have been using throughout the ages. That cannot be the goal of emancipation. With such a viewpoint, Magnús Eiríksson shows himself as a feminist of difference. There are in his view general differences between men and women. He does not advocate a biological essentialism of sexual difference that has been the basis of the misogynistic tradition that has existed from "Plato to Proudhon"[1] as Magnús Eiríksson remarks in his third letter. In fact he says that both male and female characteristics develop and change. Yet there are differences in the outlooks and experiences of men and women that we would nowadays describe in social constructivist and phenomenological terms. In order to make the world a better place, both men and women have to become emancipated from outdated ideals that justify the superiority of men over women. That will also enable women to put their mark more strongly on public affairs, also in light of their own experiences and background that differ in important respects from men's. For that purpose they have to have the rights and the educational means that enable them to become active citizens. In this regard Eiríksson is a liberal feminist. The feminism of difference position that Eiríksson also adheres to takes the feminist agenda a step further with its basic idea that equal rights are a necessary but not a sufficient condition for women's (and men's) emancipation. The societal values also need to change. The pacifistic ideals that Eiríksson emphasizes have, for example, often been associated with feminine values rather than with masculine ideals.

In his text, Eiríksson compares men and women in light of knowledge, emotion and will. He concludes that the sexes can be equal in terms of

---

[1] Eiríksson, *Breve til Clara Raphael*, p. 41.

knowledge but that women have more emotional sensibility and men have had more opportunity to strengthen their will. These differences are based on habitual conditions that can be changed. In some of his statements, Eiríksson is quite traditional, for example, when he claims that women should do the housework. On the whole, he, however, advocates a principle of complementarity. Society would be better off if the sexes would both contribute feminine and masculine values to its further development.

IV. The Rejection of the Body and the Erotic

The thesis about the complementarity of the sexes for the purpose of creating a better society is something that Clara Raphael suggests herself. Men can, in her view, learn from women. The life affirming spirit, the enthusiasm and childlike faith that she considers to be basic to women are something that men can adopt to have more of a "unity of character."[1] When women have become conscious about themselves, the ideal of humanity can be achieved through the spiritual unification of men and women.[2] This idea relates to Eiríksson's reflection on the emotional capacities that he thinks are more advanced in women. In his third letter to Clara Raphael he refers to Kierkegaard's remarks on science and passion regarding Kierkegaard's claim that reflection alone is not enough to make scientific progress. Passion is needed for there to be made advances in science. In this context Kierkegaard is talking about passion and not emotions specifically. Eiríksson is, however, of the opinion that the passion Kierkegaard discusses is a higher level emotion. For that reason women have much to contribute to culture that has been determined by male values. He discusses how women can bring their own strengths into different professions. He does not discuss the feminine at any length, and he hardly discusses women in the roles of the mother, the wife, the lover or the like.

The physical and the erotic aspects of the sexes are absent in Eiríksson's discussion of Clara Raphael's ideas. He has nothing critical to

---

1 Fibiger, *Clara Raphael. Tolv Breve*, p. 55 (compare *Clara Raphael. Zwölf Briefe*, p. 49).
2 See ibid.

say about her decision to reject erotic love and live in a platonic relation with the man she falls in love with. He actually joins her in her idealism about brotherly and sisterly love with his own words about himself writing to her as a brother. According to Clara Raphael, she and Axel are as a couple to be married in the eyes of the world. In the eyes of God they will, however, only live in a spiritual union. She rejects erotic love, and claims she has "no need for the snake" when she refers to the story of Adam and Eve in the Old Testament.[1] With such statements Clara Raphael echoes the ancient and traditional ideas about the evil that is associated with Eve who succumbs to the snake. The feminist stand she takes also echoes old and traditional views on the purity of women that reject their erotic desires.

By entering a marriage that is a kind of a Protestant monastery, as Heiberg describes it, Clara Raphael becomes a nun of sorts. This conclusion may partly explain why the book *Clara Raphael* was controversial. This conclusion was felt as overly idealistic if not eccentric in mid-19th century Denmark. Heiberg gives a hint of this in the preface when he writes that her "resignation" reminds one of Joan of Arc (1412-31), the virgin warrior of Orleans.[2] Clara Raphael mentions her explicitly as a role model who was able to accomplish a lot by resisting earthly love.[3] Heiberg alludes to this as a youthful enthusiasm. He mentions her statement that so much has been written about young women in love, but hardly anything about idealistic women who fight for a higher cause.[4] Perhaps Mathilde Fibiger and Magnús Eiríksson are acutely aware of the fact that women have been denigrated throughout the centuries with constant remarks about their bodily nature. Yet there is a blind spot in their position. They underscore the spiritual capacities of women without realizing that if it is at the cost of the bodily and erotic it presents the impossible alternative for women of either being a saint or a slut.

---

1 Fibiger, *Clara Raphael. Tolv Breve*, p. 63 (compare *Clara Raphael. Zwölf Briefe*, p. 57).

2 See Johan Ludvig Heiberg, "Udgiveren til Læserne," in *Clara Raphael. Tolv Breve*, pp. III-X, here p. VI (compare *Clara Raphael. Zwölf Briefe*, p. 101).

3 See Fibiger, *Clara Raphael. Tolv Breve*, p. 75 (compare *Clara Raphael. Zwölf Briefe*, p. 67).

4 See Heiberg, "Udgiveren til Læserne," p. VII (compare *Clara Raphael. Zwölf Briefe*, p. 102).

Heiberg criticizes Clara Raphael for being too idealistic and too abstract. He reminds the "young girl" that in addition to the virgin, the mother is the second ideal for womanhood in Christendom.[1] With this remark Heiberg reproduces another traditional dualistic idea of women as either mothers or virgins, thus leaving little space for other alternatives for women. Clara Raphael is tied to this idea insofar she opts for the virgin and rejects motherhood in her pursuit of an emancipated way of life. It is obvious from the text that Fibiger's heroine Clara Raphael has a complicated relationship with the figure of the mother. She seems to have been raised by an aunt whom she admits not to have grieved for when she died. The aunt took good care of her, but they were not soulmates in any sense. For this reason Clara claims that God is her mother and Denmark her father.[2] By rejecting sex, she also rejects the option of being a mother by having children and chooses instead to educate children in her role as a teacher.[3]

V. Magnús Eiríksson and Clara Raphael vs. Kierkegaard

It is precisely the idea of Clara Raphael of not consummating marriage that is the main topic of Kierkegaard's unpublished and unfinished review of her letters.[4] He pokes fun at her, claiming that she yearns for nothing more than being an original thinker and the only original thought she comes up with is creating a new type of marriage where the couple lives together like sister and brother. Nun argues in her analysis of this review that Kierkegaard avoids discussing the main topic of Clara Raphael, the emancipation of women and women's rights. This was the topic that was the center of the controversy about the book. Kierkegaard was in Nun's view not interested in the question of women's emancipation. He was not

1 See ibid., p. VI (compare *Clara Raphael. Zwölf Briefe*, p. 101).

2 See Fibiger, *Clara Raphael. Tolv Breve*, p. 49 (compare *Clara Raphael. Zwölf Briefe*, p. 44).

3 It must be added that Mathilde Fibiger examines other options for women. In a novel she wrote later in her life she compares two sisters. One of them gives into love and the other one rejects having love relations with men.

4 See *SKS* 24, 136-138, NB22:63 / *JP* 6, 6709. Nun has in her analysis of this review discussed possible reasons for Kierkegaard not publishing it; see chapter five of her book, *Women of the Danish Golden Age*.

a feminist, and for many interpreters misogynistic ideas shine through his descriptions of women and the feminine, although that is contested (at least in some respects) in research on his philosophy of the masculine and the feminine.[1] He was a thinker of difference when it comes to his philosophy of the sexes. He was highly critical of liberal ideas about equality of the sexes because he was of the opinion that equal rights would diminish the difference of the sexes, and defeminize women. For this reason Kierkegaard has been accused of being an essentialist about sexual difference. He is certainly an essentialist in the sense that he believes that the sexes have different strengths and weaknesses. A biological essentialism in the Aristotelian tradition that would imply that males and females have innate attributes that are unchangeable is, however, not tenable for a protoexistentialist thinker like Kierkegaard. His essentialist remarks about the sexes are therefore descriptions of sexual differences as he views them under the conditions of a mid-19th century Danish or European Society.

As opposed to Magnús Eiríksson, who is inspired by the spirit of liberation in the wake of the democratization movements of the 19th century, Kierkegaard does not welcome ideas of gender emancipation. He is not critical of the traditional gender roles that keep women in a position where they cannot live up to their potential. He is also not critical of how men have, as a sex, used their power to organize society, as Eiríksson is. His critical remarks about men and masculinities make Eiríksson a precursor of 20th-century masculinity studies, as already said. Kierkegaard is more concerned with individual freedom as an existential question than with questions of social freedom that are the topic of political philosophy, although important strides have been made recently in Kierkegaard research to work out the political implications of his philosophy. He is certainly critical of bourgeois ideals that hinder people from being authentic and true. It therefore seems odd that he does not give Clara Raphael any credit for being a person who dares to be independent, shuns custom and tradition, with the goal of being true to herself. She prefers freedom to happiness. He could also have

[1] For a discussion of the question whether Kierkegaard's philosophy of sexual difference is misogynistic or not see *Feminist Interpretations of Søren Kierkegaard*, ed. by Céline Léon and Sylvia Walsh, University Park, Pennsylvania: Pennsylvania State University Press 1997.

understood her issue with a mother she does not connect with, given the absent mother in his own life. He could furthermore understand her wish not to enter a conventional marriage since he struggled with that himself and was unable to commit to marriage. Most importantly, it is astonishing that he takes Clara Raphael as seriously as he did, as is apparent in the scathing tone of his review, given her age and the immature character of some of her opinions. This can be read as a sign of comparable immaturity on his part. A harsh interpretation of this would be to say that since he broke up with Regine he was not confronted with women in an intimate fashion who could challenge the misogynistic aspects of his views of women. He hence took up stereotypical ideas of the misogynistic tradition about the social exclusion of women from public life. In his descriptions of feminine religiosity he, moreover, underscores their devotion which results in him contradicting himself on the issue of religious subjectivity, as will be argued later. A less *ad hominem* interpretation of his critical remarks on *Clara Raphael* would be to explain his disdain of the sexless marriage as a betrayal of something more important.

The idea of passion is, as mentioned above, central to Kierkegaard's idea of authentic existence. So a marriage without erotic passion seems to him to be missing a central component. It is a marriage that symbolizes his nightmare vision of equality as sameness. His idea of marriage would be a relation that is vibrant because of the tension sexual difference creates, as erotic, as mental and in terms of different styles and outlooks. In his unfinished review of *Clara Raphael* he therefore writes that the sexless marriage would open the way to the marriage of people of the same sex. He apparently imagined such a marriage to be an exaggerated version of the marriage Clara Raphael chooses, yet more bland in its sameness. With this remark he may be reacting to the fact that Clara Raphael alludes to the possibility of love for the same sex. She says that it is in many ways easier to fall in love with another girl, and she specifically refers to the young baroness and girlfriend she deeply admires. In the next step she describes how she has entered a relationship with Axel, the brother of the venerated girlfriend.[1] Perhaps Clara Raphael's love of the sister is

[1] See Fibiger, *Clara Raphael. Tolv Breve*, p. 84 and pp. 98-110 (compare *Clara Raphael. Zwölf Briefe*, p. 76 and pp. 88f.).

transferred into a spiritual love for the brother that is then to become her husband. From the point of view of Kierkegaard she both rejects passion and mutually enriching difference. Marriage as a heterosexual institution is of lesser importance to Kierkegaard than the feminine passion that he emphasizes in his philosophy of women. His idea of feminine passion and erotic love is central to his conception of the religious person. Clara Raphael ends up being a person deeply committed to religion, after a phase of lack of interest in it. He is therefore compelled to react to her idea of the religious woman. Her "sacrifice," to abandon erotic love, is from his point of view bound to undermine her possibility of passion. The religious person incorporates the most authentic form of existence for Kierkegaard. He discusses at length, for example in *The Sickness unto Death*, women's ability to give themselves, to surrender themselves. Alison Assiter argues, "the women who appear predominantly in the 'aesthetic' works of Kierkegaard function…as exemplary of his primarily 'religious' view of the person."[1] Kierkegaard's statements are hence highly ambiguous, if not contradictory. He adores female features he associates with passivity and vulnerability. These are features that are necessary to be able to give oneself to God. At the same time he judges these feminine features as inferior to male features. Perhaps he was afraid of or even felt inferior when confronted with this feminine ability that is for him a key to an experience of religious transcendence. This is something that comes quite naturally for women on the level of religiosity, in his view, and men have to struggle to accomplish it. Assiter rightly argues that Kierkegaard attempts "to develop an ethical and religious transubstantiation of erotic love."[2] This does not imply that the experience of erotic passion is a necessary precondition of a religious existence. What Kierkegaard is aiming at is rather a comparative model of erotic love and religious existence as a relation to oneself and god. Love of god and faith in the divine is comparable in its intensity, its unpredictability, and in its infinite possibility to erotic love.

---

[1] Alison Assiter, "Kierkegaard, Battersby and Feminism," *Women: A Cultural Review*, vol. 22, nos. 2-3, 2011, pp. 180-91, here p. 181.

[2] Ibid., p. 183. Assiter refers in this regard to George Pattison's interpretation, *Kierkegaard's Upbuilding Discourses: Philosophy, Literature and Theology*, London: Routledge 2003, p. 193.

As a relation, erotic love is sustained by difference and as a model it counteracts what Kierkegaard views as the ideal of sameness implicit in egalitarian humanism. He was not thinking of egalitarian humanism in terms of socio-political demands for equality. He was attacking the underlying philosophical, liberal idea of equal rights. Such an ideal of equal rights presupposes sameness of the agents. For him it necessarily implies that women need to strive to become similar to men. He was unable to distinguish the ontological aspect of equality as sameness and the political level of equality as equal rights. He disregards or is not sensitive to the fact that liberal principles of gender equality as stipulated in laws are a necessary precondition for battling social and political inequality of the sexes. Equal rights are a precondition for exercising one's freedom to be different. Kierkegaard may, moreover, not have been aware of the more radical demand of difference feminism to advance feminine values in a malecentric world. He was finally not critical of how men have ruled the world, as Eiríksson was. In fact, Kierkegaard was not thinking in this context about political rule and power, but worried about the individual person that he feared could become like a kingdom without a land, if the person did not stand in relation to that which is so different that it is the ultimate other. In that sense the relation of the sexes as different and other to each other is for him parallel to the relation involved in faith, in the leap of faith, in trusting that which is other. It is a relation that can be devastating, but one survives nevertheless. Such a relation is about a higher order respect than the one of legal equality. It is not a relation that is restricted to the level of rational demands for equal standing. It is a relation that is always asymmetrical in some way, for there is always difference involved. There is rarely a perfect balance of giving and taking, passivity and activity in human relations. Therefore, respect for the otherness of the other is required insofar as it challenges one and sustains one at the same time. If it is to sustain one, it is a relation that cannot be abusive. It is nevertheless at the level of relationality in which we are vulnerable, in the sense that we open ourselves to the other. Vulnerability is the risk that enables us to existentially transform ourselves. Kierkegaard offers a highly differentiated and highly contemporary model of the relational self that "challenges the liberal humanist model of selfhood," as Assiter writes.[1] It is a model that accounts for how we put ourselves at risk in any relation, also in relation to the ultimate other. The idea of the passionate self that underlies Kierkegaard's harsh refusal of Clara Raphael's idea of platonic marriage is necessarily based on his idea of the self as embodied. The embodied subject is a desiring subject, not completely in control. Kierkegaard feared Enlightenment humanism, its idea of the rational and autonomous self (such as presented in Kantian ethics) because he was sure that such an understanding of the human subject would pave the way for secularism.

Kierkegaard's review of *Clara Raphael* says more about his own reflections on gender difference and the religious disposition than about the novel since his review mainly focuses on one idea of the novel. His sarcastic remarks about the young author's ambition to be original stand in stark contrast to the encouraging and dialogical tone of Eiríksson's review. Eiríksson was highly attuned to the political demands of his day insofar as he acknowledged a crisis of a hegemonic masculine culture and the concurrent need for gender equality as a positive development for society. It was in his eyes important to welcome this book warmly. He respected the effort because it was a courageous act of a twenty-year-old woman in a patriarchal culture to publish *Clara Raphael.* He rightly saw that the book was, despite its flaws, a milestone on the road to gender awareness and gender emancipation in Denmark. Eiríksson's positive review was also well ahead of its times and is reflective of his politically progressive outlook. His review is more political than Kierkegaard's position on *Clara Raphael.* Kierkegaard's philosophy of sexual difference that has here been interpreted as feminist philosophy of difference offers, however, a richer notion of the subject than Eiríksson does in his reflections on *Clara Raphael.* Eiríksson's idea about the complementarity of the sexes represents a feminism of difference, but lacks the dimension of embodiment that is central to Kierkegaard's conception of the desiring self. The desiring subject, as a vulnerable subject that Kierkegaard presents, is not something that only women incorporate, even though he derives his conception of it from his observations about sexual difference. It is a realistic idea of what we are like, even though men have for the most part had a stronger standing in society that makes them in some

---

[1] Assiter, "Kierkegaard, Battersby and Feminism," p. 183.

respects less vulnerable than women. The reason is that we live in a world where values associated with the masculine have been prioritized. For that reason we need to emphasize values associated with the feminine as Eiríksson maintained, to make women less defenseless in comparison with men.

Reykjavik
(In Alexander Baumgartner, *Nordische Fahrten—Island und die Faröer. Skizzen und Studien*, Freiburg im Breisgau: Herder 1889, p. 105. Public domain picture, https://commons.wikimedia.org.)

IV. The Late Eiríksson

Is John John and Jesus God? On the Theological Dogfight of Magnús Eiríksson and the Catholic Church in Iceland

Gudmundur Bjorn Thorbjornsson

To anyone who has ever studied theology, arguing about God, faith or religion in general, becomes quickly problematic. It goes without saying how difficult it is to argue about what happened centuries ago in a faraway place; what to many is more of a feeling or an instinct rather than an empirical truth. Yet, such endeavors regularly take place between people of the same religion, people of different religions, and between religious people and atheists, and even among atheists and agnostics. Faith is a complex thing, and truth is subjectivity, as the Danish thinker Søren Kierkegaard famously claimed. The Icelandic theologian Magnús Eiríksson was an avid reader of Kierkegaard, an "unwelcome ally" whom Kierkegaard himself did not have much tolerance for. Eiríksson's place in the Scandinavian theological tradition of the 19th century is mostly in connection with Kierkegaard's influence on him and with his criticism of Hans Lassen Martensen's theology.[1] However, Eiríksson also wrote voluminously on theological and ecclesiological matters unconnected to Kierkegaard's or Martensen's thought. From 1863-73, Eiríksson published a number of works that are quite distinct from what he had written earlier. The main difference in his earlier works lies in his

1 On Eiríksson's relation to Kierkegaard and Martensen, see Gerhard Schreiber, "Magnús Eiríksson: An Opponent of Martensen and an Unwelcome Ally of Kierkegaard," in *Kierkegaard and His Danish Contemporaries*, Tome II, *Theology*, ed. by Jon Stewart, Aldershot: Ashgate 2009 (*Kierkegaard Research: Sources, Reception and Resources*, vol. 7), pp. 49-94.

understanding of the Bible. As time went on, his ideas became more critical and radical compared to the church's teaching. He took a stance against the Bible and questioned its validity and reliability.[1]

In this article, I will focus on Eiríksson's polemics with the so-called "Catholic Priests of Reykjavík." These theological disputes took place between the years of 1865-68 based on three books, two of them written by Eiríksson and one by the priests. At its core, this debate revolves around the ancient point of controversy regarding the divinity of Christ, on one hand, and the authenticity of the Gospel of John, on the other. What is interesting in this debate, apart from its subject, is the fact that it takes place in Icelandic, Eiríksson's native language. The priests however, came from France (and, most likely, Belgium).[2]

I will begin by taking a brief look at the Catholic setting in 19th-century Iceland (I). Then I will analyze Eiríksson's argument and why he feels it necessary to direct his attention towards his fellow countrymen, in spite living and working in Copenhagen (II). From there, I will analyze the counterargument presented by the Catholic priests, in addition to the motives for their reply (III). Lastly, I will take a look at Eiríksson's answer to their counterarguments (IV). What I hope to demonstrate is that the debate between the three men becomes highly polemical and often ends up being quite repetitive. They completely disagree on theological doctrines and on the role of the church. As often happens with people in conflict, neither side is willing to give in or admit defeat. Also, it does not help that this conflict is at its core about God himself and other central Christian doctrines, which makes the discussion highly difficult to navigate. That being said, this polemical debate is an interesting case of Eiríksson's insatiable passion for his theology and religious thinking, and a great example of his quest for truth. It also provides interesting insight into the theological setting of 19th-century Iceland. Due to the vast number of Biblical references employed by both

---

[1] See Gerhard Schreiber, "Magnús Eiríksson—Vanræktur samtímamaður Sørens Kierkegaard," trans. by Aðalsteinn Garðarsson, *Skírnir*, vol. 188, 2014, pp. 116-143; here pp. 126f.

[2] It is difficult to pinpoint clearly who actually wrote the response of the priests to Eiríksson, since their book is signed "Hinir katólsku prestar í Reykjavík" [The Catholic Priests of Reykjavík]. I will dwell more on this subject below.

Eiríksson and the priests during their argument, it is almost impossible to discuss their polemics by scrutinizing every single biblical reference. It is, as stated in the title, a *theological dogfight*, and I will therefore focus on the nature of their arguments in general, rather than attempting to determine a winner.

I. Outlining the Background

A. The Catholic Setting in 19th-Century Iceland

Before going further, it is useful to give an insight into the Catholic setting of Iceland during the time of the debates. The Reformation process in Iceland was complete in 1550 when Bishop Jón Arason (1484-1550) was beheaded at Skálholt. To make matters worse, freedom of religion was not instituted until 1874, with a new constitution.[1] At the beginning of the 19th century, the Catholic Church in Europe was in decline after years of adversity. In Protestant countries, the Catholic faith became widely prohibited.[2] Nevertheless, in 1856, the prefect of the Catholic Church in the North Atlantic, Stephan Djunkovsky (1820-70), found six missionaries willing to go to the Scandinavian countries to proclaim the Catholic faith. One of those was Bernard Bernard (1821-95), a French priest that had studied philosophy and theology in Reims.[3]

---

1 Since Christianity was made into law around the year 1000, until the later part of the 19th century the practice of any other religion than Christianity in Iceland was problematic. After the Reformation, only those who supported the evangelical Lutheran church were able to get a residence permit in Iceland, and those who did not were in danger of being punished for heresy. Ólafur Jóhannesson, *Stjórnskipun Íslands*, Reykjavík: Iðunn 1978, p. 421. It was not until the constitution about the "special matters concerning Iceland" in 1874 that freedom of religion was given the protection of law through the directive of the King of Denmark. Pétur Pétursson, "Trúarlegar hreyfingar í Reykjavík tvo fyrstu áratugi 20. aldar," *Saga*, vol. 18, 1980, pp. 179-224; here p. 183.

2 Gunnar F. Guðmundsson, *Kaþólskt trúboð á Ísland 1857-1875*, ed. by Jón Guðnason, Reykjavík: Sagnfræðistofnun Háskóla Íslands 1987, p. 9.

3 After missionary work in Norway among other missionaries, Bernard headed to Iceland along with Icelandic seminarian Ólafur Gunnlaugsson in 1857. Their trip to Iceland did not go unnoticed by the public or by the Icelandic newspapers. Gunnlaugsson only stayed for a short time in Iceland and went back to his studies in Rome in the fall of 1857. Accompanying Bernard and Gunnlaugsson on their trip to Iceland was a young

Despite general hostility towards the Catholic missionaries, Bernard was described as a "polished, kind and friendly man [*siðprúður, góðmannlegur og viðfelldinn*],"[1] and as reverend Sigurður Gunnarsson at Desjamýri noticed, nobody questioned their intentions to preach the Catholic doctrine.[2]

Bernard's first winter in Iceland, 1857-58, was rather uneventful. He lived as a hermit in the east and studied a lot. In 1858, he received, so to speak, a partner in crime when French seminarian Jean-Baptiste Baudoin (1831-75) arrived from Dunkerque, France. Baudoin had voiced his interest in serving as a missionary to the north and was granted his wish. The two of them lived together in Seyðisfjörður, sang masses, and helped the poor in neighboring villages.[3] After a brief stop in Grundarfjörður in the West of Iceland, they managed, with funding from continental Europe, to purchase land at Landakot. This land, which at the time stood on the outskirts of the capital Reykjavík, is now located in the heart of the city.[4] It would not be until 1929 that *Landakotskirkja* (formerly known as The Basilica of Christ the King [*Basilika Krists konungs*]) was consecrated. A chapel was, however, erected at the spot in 1864.

Bernard left Iceland in 1862, but Baudoin stayed until 1875. During their stay in Iceland, Baudoin and Bernard participated in public debates regarding the legitimacy of the Catholic faith. In the eyes of the locals, these were heretics of the "papal fallacy." One of the attempts to fight the influence of the Catholics in Iceland was an educational essay about the Catholic faith compared to the Lutheran faith, written by Sigurður Melsteð (1819-95). Melsteð, who was the head of the Icelandic Priest Seminary (*Prestaskólinn*), aimed to make it clear that the Catholic Church was far behind the Lutheran. It was a 304-page work called

Italian priest called Odenino. They originally planned to settle in Fárskrúðsfjörður in east Iceland, where their ship had arrived, but due to lack of housing they went to a nearby village, Seyðisfjörður, See ibid., pp. 32-39.

1 Ibid., p. 57.

2 Sigurður Gunnarsson, "Úr bréfi að austan," *Norðri*, vol. 6, 1858, nos. 7-8 (April 17), pp. 25-28.

3 See Guðmundsson, *Kapólskt trúboð á Ísland 1857-1875*, pp. 59-61.

4 Bernard purchased the land Landakot from reverend Ásmundur Jónsson for 4500 *rigsdaler*. People were in general not happy about the Catholic priests purchasing Landakot. See ibid., p. 84.

A Comparison between the Differences of the Catholic and the Protestant Church (1859).[1]

Melsteð's book was well-received in Iceland and even read by the Catholics. Even though Bernard had left Iceland a few years earlier, he showed an interest in publishing a book that expounded the Catholic doctrines in layman terms. For Baudoin, the criticism of the Catholic Church was mere "slander" [*rógburður*], and in 1861 he started writing articles in Icelandic newspapers as a way of defending the Catholic faith.[2] In 1865, he published a book as a direct answer to Melsteð's criticism.[3] The book was published by Baudoin and Emile-Marie Dekiere, a missionary from Belgium who arrived in Iceland in 1865.[4] Dekiere was the other Catholic priest at Landakot and served as an assistant to Baudoin. The book was meant to be an apologetic writing as well as an educational paper about the doctrines of the church.

In most cases, the papers and articles written by the Catholic priests during this time were replies to the criticism levied against their church. The 1867 book *Jesus Christ is God: In Spite of the Objections of Mr. Magnús Eiríksson*, a direct reply to Eiríksson's criticism of the Gospel of John and the divinity of Christ, is an exception.[5] As with the earlier book,[6] it was Dekiere (and *not* Bernard Bernard) who published the book alongside Baudoin.

---

1 Sigurður Melsteð, *Samanburður á ágreiningslærdómum katólsku og prótestantisku kirkjunnar*, Reykjavík: Egill Jónsson 1859.

2 See, for example, Jean-Baptiste Baudoin, "Til herra ritstjóra Þjóðólfs," *Þjóðólfur*, vol. 13, 1961, nos. 19-20 (April 17), p. 81.

3 [Jean-Baptiste Baudoin], *Útskýring um trú katólsku kirkjunnar í þeim trúaratriðum, þar sem ágreiningr er milli hennar og mótmælenda*, Reykjavík: Hinir katólsku prestar í Reykjavík 1865.

4 The name was either written as De Kiere or Dekiere in the sources. See Guðmundsson, *Kaþólskt trúboð á Íslandi 1857-1875*, p. 101.

5 [Jean-Baptiste Baudoin], *Jesús Kristr er Guð. Þrátt fyrir mótmæli herra Magnúsar Eiríkssonar*, Reykjavík: Hinir katólsku prestar í Reykjavík 1867.

6 Schreiber claims that Bernard and Baudoin were behind the publication of the book (see his "Magnús Eiríksson: An Opponent of Martensen and an Unwelcome Ally of Kierkegaard," p. 53; "Magnús Eiríksson—Vanræktur samtímamaður Sørens Kierkegaard," p. 119), but Gunnar F. Guðmundsson (1987) claims that it was Dekiere who published it alongside Baudoin. It appears impossible to determine who actually wrote the book since it is only signed "Hinir katólsku prestar í Reykjavík" (The Catholic Priests in Reykjavík). Bernard Bernard therefore did not publish the book alongside Baudoin, even though he kept a close eye on the situation in Iceland after his departure in 1862.

B. An Overview of the Works and its Authors

In 1863, Eiríksson published a work in Danish on the Gospel of John[1] and, two years later, published an extract of this work in Icelandic.[2] The earlier work is longer than its Icelandic version but contains the same basic material. In both works, Eiríksson argues against the authenticity of the Gospel of John, claiming 1) that the Apostle John cannot be its author, and 2) that the divinity of Jesus is questionable. Throughout the Icelandic version, Eiríksson cites the Danish publication on numerous occasions. This he does primarily to develop further clarification for his arguments; he goes deeper into the text in the Danish version, while the Icelandic version is pitched more to the laymen and those not as academically well-versed.

In the original Danish version, Eiríksson sets out to prove what he calls the "twofold lack of credibility" of the Gospel of John.[3] For Eiríksson, the idea that the gospel is written by a Palestinian Jew, John, is preposterous. He likewise attacks the idea that Jesus is God. These claims are the central point of Eiríksson's Icelandic publication and sparked the beginning of his feud with the Catholic priests at Landakot. Eiríksson's work received harsh criticism in his native Iceland, most notably from Sigurður Melsteð, who wrote, in May 1865, an unforgiving reproach of it, which was then published in the fortnightly journal *Þjóðólfur* from May until September that year.[4] It was also criticized by the Catholic

[1] Magnús Eiríksson, *Er Johannes-Evangeliet et apostolisk og ægte Evangelium og er dets Lære om Guds Menneskevorden en sand og christelig Lære? En religiøs-dogmatisk, historisk-kritisk Undersøgelse*, Copenhagen: Magnús Eiríksson 1863.

[2] Magnús Eiríksson, *Jóhannesar guðspjall og Lærdómur kirkjunnar um guð, nokkrar athugasemdir til yfirvegunar þeim Íslendíngum, sem ekki vilja svívirða og lasta guð með trú sinni*, Copenhagen: Louis Klein 1865.

[3] Eiríksson, *Johannes-Evangeliet*, p. 471.

[4] Melsteð's criticism is aimed at the Icelandic version of the book. He claims Eiríksson's attack on the foundational teaching of the Christian faith, the doctrine of the trinity and the teaching of the divinity of Christ, derives from a lack of faith in the Christian revelation. Sigurður Melsteð, "Jóhannesar guðspjall og lærdómr kirkjunnar um guð; nokkrar athugasemdir til yfirvegunar þeim Íslendingum sem ekki vilja svívirða og lasta guð með trú sinni. Eptir Magnús Elríksson cand. theol. — 8 bl. br. 1–101; tíl sölu hjá Egli Jónssyni í Rvik, 40 sk" in *Þjóðólfur*, vol. 17, 1865, no. 29 (May 23), p. 115. Melsteð finds it difficult to understand why Eiríksson has chosen to serve a "lack of faith [*vantrú*]" rather than faith; see *Þjóðólfur*, vol. 17, 1865, nos. 47-48 (October 30), p. 189. The problems do not lie with the church or its creeds and doctrines, but with its

priests in Reykjavík in their *Jesus Christ is God: In Spite of the Objections of Mr. Magnús Eiríksson*. Their writings are highly polemical, often disorganized, and overloaded with Biblical references. In his response from 1868, *A Few Remarks on the Proofs of the "Catholics Priests in Reykjavík" for the Divinity of Jesus Christ* (1868),[1] Eiríksson primarily replies to the priests, but also to Melsteð.

II. Eiríksson's The Gospel of John

For Eiríksson, numerous reasons support his claim that the apostle John cannot be regarded as the legitimate author of the Gospel of John. According to Eiríksson, great German theologians (for example, Ferdinand Christian Baur (1792-1860)) had already argued that the apostle John could not have written the Gospel of John. Despite that fact, they still find reasons to take the gospel seriously because of its *spiritual content*, and possibly because the first teachings of the apostles were not "speculative" enough.[2] What these theologians failed to see is that the main teaching of the Gospel of John about Christ cannot directly correlate with a true and simple faith in God, as was held by Christ and the apostles.[3] Philosophical influences are rich in the Gospel, according to Eiríksson, and make it into a "trickery of the mind"

---

people. The main problem of the times is, according to Melsteð, not superstition, but lack of faith, not religious passion but a lack of passion; see ibid., p. 189. For Melsteð's overall criticism, see *Þjóðólfur*, vol. 17, 1865, no. 29 (May 23), pp. 115f.; nos. 31-32 (June 3), pp. 123-125; nos. 35-36 (July 4), pp. 140f.; nos. 42-43 (September 16), pp. 168-170; nos. 45-46 (October 17), pp. 182-184; nos. 47-48 (October 30), pp. 188f.

1 Magnús Eiríksson, *Nokkrar athugasemdir um Sannanir "katólsku prestanna í Reykjavík" fyrir guðdómi Jesú Krists*, Copenhagen: Louis Klein 1868.

2 Eiríksson, *Jóhannesar guðspjall*, p. 11.

3 Rudolf Bultmann claims in his famously existential exegesis of the Gospel of John, that it is impossible to affirm anything definite about the author or the redactor of the gospel, for neither person is named in the gospel and its superscription comes from a later time. Bultmann claims that John the son of Sebedee (who was claimed as the Beloved Disciple of Jesus), was must likely killed by the Jews very early (Mark 10:39). Also, there is no claim in the gospel that it was written by an eye-witness; see Rudolf Bultmann, *The Gospel of John: A Commentary*, trans. by G. R. Beasley-Murrey, Oxford: Basil Blackwell 1971, pp. 11f.

[*heilaspuni*].[1] He is clear in his view: everything that stands against the original teachings of the apostles is unchristian. He holds the "apostolic" view that Jesus is the Messiah and that God raised him from the dead. The pinnacles of the true faith, the apostles, preached only *that* in early Christianity. For Eiríksson, the author of John makes Christ into something completely different from what the apostles thought him to be. To teach about Christ as the *logos*, as a divine *persona*, is utter nonsense to Eiríksson, and the gospel is obviously false both in regards to its origin (not being written by the apostle John), and in regards to its content (it is not in the spirit of Christ).[2] He is also highly critical of what he calls "the church" and its affinity with the gospel, but he nevertheless does not clearly distinguish which or what "church" he is talking about. Even though Icelandic and Danish ecclesiology had remained closely-knit at the time, the Icelandic church had a knack for going it own way. Ecclesiological and theological changes often arrived later in Iceland than in rest of the continent. It is safe to assume, then, that his criticism is directed towards the Danish church, but within the Icelandic church, he sees room for change, holding out hope that his countrymen are not brainwashed enough by the heresies of the church. It is his duty to point out, contrary to the church's high regard for the Gospel of John, that the Gospel does not give an accurate account of the "being" [*vera*] and acts of Christ. By pointing this out, Eiríksson hopes that laymen and priests alike will stop following the church's teachings blindly. Eiríksson claims that even after he graduated as a theologian (cand. theol) from the University of Copenhagen, he still believed in the validity of the Gospel of John, despite having had minor doubts about the first 18 verses. In the years leading up to his Danish publication (1863), he started noticing things that led him to believe otherwise. In a "divine trance" [*andleg leiðsla*][3] he starts writing against the gospel, not because he lacked faith, but precisely because he had faith. Eiríksson goes to great lengths to prove his point, as we will see below.

1 Eiríksson, *Jóhannesar guðspjall*, p. 13. Eiríksson is flabbergasted by the fact that in such a big country as Germany, the spiritual heresy of the Gospel of John had not yet been discovered, and even Luther himself had praised the gospel; see ibid., p. 13.

2 See ibid., p. 12.

3 Ibid., p. 2.

A. Jesus is Lofty

The first claim I wish to highlight in Eiríksson's criticism of the Gospel of John is his view of Christ as a lofty figure rather than a lowly one. Eiríksson points out that in the Gospel of John, Christ never turns himself to God or calls God's name in the passion narrative, contrary to what takes place in the synoptic gospels. Also, no one around Christ uses God's name. This is what initiates Eiríksson's attack on the gospel. To Eiríksson, Christ appears as someone wholly other in respect to the Christ in the synoptic gospels; his thoughts, actions and deeds are different. In the synoptic gospels, it is the humility of Christ that supports Eiríksson's theology; he gives glory to God and does not talk much about himself.[1] Miracles are made without any sense of vanity, only to help and comfort. In contrast, the Gospel of John depicts Jesus as someone who seeks his own glory and honor. It is as if Christ performs miracles out of vanity, to reveal his own glory.[2] These "vain" efforts of Christ are directly connected to Christ's eternal godly being, as the *logos*, that he in the beginning was with God and is equal to him.[3]

In the Gospel of John, Christ thereby appears to have the power to take his life back and raise himself from the dead.[4] In other places of the New Testament, the resurrection of Christ is an act of God the father, not the son.[5] Because of this lack of humility, Eiríksson sees evidence that the author of the Gospel of John considers Christ a totally different being than that of the other evangelists. Despite the fact that in many places of the New Testament, God raises Christ from the dead, theologians and clergy choose to follow the one place in John where this is different.[6] To Eiríksson this is pure heresy, and through the other evangelists, the Gospel of John thereby receives its judgment. Eiríksson underlines the utter difference between the teaching of Christ in the synoptic gospels and in John. Blinded by this heresy, the theologians and the clergy cannot see this difference.[7]

---

1 See Mark 10:13; Matthew 19:17.

2 John 2:11.

3 See Eiríksson, *Jóhannesar guðspjall*, pp. 2f.

4 John 10; John 17; John 18.

5 For example, Acts 2:24.

6 John 10:17-18

7 See Eiríksson, *Jóhannesar guðspjall*, pp. 5f.

In addition, in the Gospel of John, Christ does not say a single loving or caring word that imparts love to his disciples. Love towards god, the neighbor, or the enemy, is never demonstrated. For Eiríksson this shows that the gospel is of a totally different kind and in a different spirit, than that of Christ; and anyone who believes that this is the "Gospel of Love"[1] is a fool. The author of John also remains silent about many important events in Christ's life, such as the temptation narrative or the account of the suffering in Gethsemane. Christ is not shown in his weakness and, moreover, Christ seems contradictory on numerous occasions.[2]

B. Jesus is God

Of the criticism proclaimed by Eiríksson against the Gospel of John, none is louder than his rejection of the idea of Christ as a divine figure or as equal to God. He blames the Council of Nicaea in 325 for making Christ into God "through confession."[3] Eiríksson claims that of the 318 bishops who were at the council, not all of them agreed with the theory that Christ was the same being as God or equal to God, but they had decided to sign the creed in order to keep the peace. Because of the Arian controversy, Constantine the Great and important bishops defended Athanasius' position that Christ was one with the father.[4] Therefore, it was out of fear rather than conviction that Christ become

1 By claiming that in John 15:13, love is revealed by dying for one's friends, Eiríksson sees only a remark of love that can also be shown by pagans, and must be the creation of someone else but not the words of Christ, since no love is greater than that depicted in the Sermon on the Mount; see ibid., p. 7; see also Matthew 5:43-45.

2 The author of the gospel portrays Christ more than once as being in contradiction with himself, Eiríksson argues, See, for example, John 5:31; 8:14; 7:28; 8:19; 15:15; 16:12(19); 16:4.

3 See Eiríksson, *Jóhannesar guðspjall*, p. 15.

4 The Arian controversy was a major Christological debate between those who denied the divinity of Christ (Arians) and those who supported Athanasius of Alexandria. Arius (ca. 250-336) was a priest in Alexandria who rejected the divinity of Christ, and Athanasius (ca. 290-373) was the principal opponent of the Arian heresy. He managed to form a broad coalition of bishops to agree on the Nicene confession of the Son as *homoousios* (of the same substance) with the Father, thereby laying an important groundwork for the doctrine of the trinity; see *The Cambridge Dictionary of Christian Theology*, ed. by Ian A. McFarland, David A.S. Fergusson, Karen Kilby, and Iain R. Torrance, New York: Cambridge University Press 2011, p. 31 and p. 41.

God within the church according to Eiríksson.[1] Spiritual dominance and oppression therefore became the ruler of the church, and it was considered wicked to have an opinion different from that of the church. By losing their spiritual freedom and being forced into spiritual slavery, Christians were no longer capable of separating truth from heresy. And this is heresy to Eiríksson: Christ is God's anointed one, and thinking that can equivocate Christ with God is where theologians went astray, for it is impossible that a person can at the same time both be God and God's anointed one.[2]

Eiríksson claims that it is obvious from other writings of the New Testament, as well as extra-canonical material from the 2nd century, that ideas about the nature of Christ became more and more spiritual after the days of the apostles. Christ is not only considered as a missionary of God, or Messiah, but also as a higher being, "a heavenly Adam."[3] During the same period the thought of another godly being next to God, the *logos*, started to grow. *Logos* was seen, according to Eiríksson, as a tool of God to create himself in the world, and Christ was understood through *logos* in that manner.[4] Christ is proclaimed in John as a divine person, *logos*, that in the beginning was with God, is God, and becomes man in Jesus Christ. In the synoptic gospels, there is no depiction of Christ as a being that existed before he was born out of Mary's womb. Also, there is no knowledge of him being equal to God. However, in John, Christ's status as an eternal godly being is made known by his words and actions. Then he is glorified in the glory he had from the father.[5] This portrayal of Christ is unthinkable to Eiríksson when read in conjunction with the synoptic gospels. It is completely contrary to the nature and being of Christ depicted there.

---

1 Eiríksson's further elaboration on the Council of Nicaea can be found in his book *Hvem har Ret: Grundtvigianerne eller deres Modstandere? og Hvad har Christus befalet om Daaben? Nogle orienterende Bemærkninger*, Copenhagen: E.L. Thaarup 1863, pp. 21-41.

2 See Eiríksson, *Jóhannesar guðspjall*, p. 16.

3 See ibid., p. 18.

4 See ibid., pp. 18-22.

5 See John 17:1; 17:4; 17:24.

Eiríksson goes to great lengths to criticize gnostic influences on the gospel, which introduced the idea of the *logos*.[1]

What the apostles thought of Christ had now become something wholly other. The apostles had no knowledge of Christ being God, or that he created the world, or existed from the beginning, according to Eiríksson's understanding. Other writings of the New Testament that also supported this argument, to Eiríksson are worthless and are not written by true Christian apostles.[2] A teaching of *logos* derives from pagan thought, Gnosticism, and to Eiríksson, it supports unworthy ideas about God and his relationship to the world and cannot match the teaching of Christ and the apostles about God.

C. The Emphasis on the Atonement

Eiríksson claims that the church shows ungratefulness both to God and to Christ by not following the teachings of Christ and his predecessors about the God of mercy, the one who forgives sins through a repentance of the heart. This "new faith,"[3] as Eiríksson calls it, portrays a God who forgives sins through a payment, through the atonement of Christ's death on the cross. By allowing his son to die for humanity, an innocent man (who is God at the same time), dies. According to Eiríksson, this is a poor depiction of grace, because it requires a sacrifice on God's behalf.[4] The grace of God can only come through forgiveness, and the faith that man will benefit from God's forgiveness.[5] The faith of the church proclaims that God can only forgive through the suffering of the sinner

---

1 See Eiríksson, *Jóhannesar guðspjall*, pp. 21-24. Ernest Haenchen claims that the author of the Gospel of John was no Gnostic, despite its gnostic influences. He claims that "[g]nostic formulations in Johannine language inspired gnostics like Heracleon, of the school of Valentinus, to give the Fourth Gospel a gnostic interpretation; this delayed and complicated the recognition of the Gospel." See Ernest Haenchen, *John [Volume] 1: A Commentary on the Gospel of John, Chapters 1-6*, trans. by Robert W. Funk, Philadelphia: Fortress Press 1984, p. 90. Haenchen sees these difficulties disappear around the year 200 CE. *In toto*, the style of the Gospel of John is a combination of a diversity of styles. See ibid., p. 90.

2 See Eiríksson, *Jóhannesar guðspjall*, p. 23.

3 See ibid., p. 27.

4 See ibid., p. 28.

5 Psalms 32:1.

and by scarifying himself, God pays for what the sinner cannot pay. Is this faith, he asks? No, it is heresy and an attempt to subject reason to faith. The church does not teach that through his eternal grace and mercy, God can forgive sins without using external methods. These methods make forgiveness into business, a deal between the father and the son. This is an attempt of reason, according to Eiríksson, to find out how God is capable of forgiving sins. But to Eiríksson the answer is simple: God does forgive sins through his grace and mercy when the sinner truly repents.[1] To Eiríksson, many passages in the Old Testament depict a truer and purer faith in the forgiveness and mercy of God.[2] It is clear that the only condition of the forgiveness of sins is humble repentance and confession of sins.[3]

The prophets of the Old Testament, for example, Ezekiel, juxtapose justice and mercy. For Eiríksson, the act of forgiving cannot take place if it is done via payment, in spite of what the church teaches. The teachings of the church therefore contradict pure and true faith in God alone. The teachings about the *logos*: a godly *persona* equal to God, are teachings that the church places in the mouth of Christ and his disciples.[4] The nature of God becomes something else in the teachings of the church; grace and mercy become an abstraction, a meaningless *nothing*, since God requires a payment for sins; justice becomes injustice. Adam's sin becomes the sin of all humanity, and the death of a just man becomes required for the sake of the unjust. The power and sovereignty of God becomes a weakness.[5] Eiríksson sees this weakness as evident in the fact that God decided to create the first man, Adam, but did such a poor job that good became evil, and Eve ate from the tree. God did not have the power himself to change this, and so he waited 4000 years and then sent his son, the second person of Trinity, into this world to reclaim mankind from eternal torment. God did not seem to have been very successful at this since, after all, mankind is not much better 18 centuries later. The son therefore becomes a savior but also the creator of a new being, a new mankind, since the previous one

1 See Eiríksson, *Jóhannesar guðspjall*, p. 25 and pp. 32f.
2 See, for example, Psalm 103.
3 See Psalms 32:5; Eiríksson, *Jóhannesar guðspjall*, p. 40.
4 See ibid., p. 45 and p. 47.
5 See ibid., p. 51.

had failed. The church had made God's sovereignty into a weakness, first by making his original creation flawed, and then by him not being able to fix this problem himself. Eiríksson claims that in the eyes of the church, the son seems to be the one who has to fix this broken situation.[1]

D. Other Writings of the New Testament

At the end of his book, Eiríksson ponders the fact that many of the New Testament letters are false according to his criterion. Some letters of the New Testament include material that was written after the days of the apostles, which according to Eiríksson, is bad; it is important to distinguish between a holy truth, and letters from the past written by mere men. It would therefore be harmless if large portions of the New Testament were left out, since they are not needed.[2] Eiríksson sees contradictions in those books of the New Testament he wishes to exclude from the canon, contradictions that have caused schisms, arguments, and divisions in people of faith. If only a few books of the New Testament would have been used and selected, those which imprint clear and pure truth, "warm the hearts, enlighten the souls and place the good seed in the fields of hearts,"[3] then great sins and evils could have been avoided, and Christianity would have become something other than what it is today. A consciousness of God can only come about in people if God is in front of their eyes, and people act in accordance with their thought of him.[4] In Eiríksson's view, the prophet Jeremiah therefore shows that he had a purer and higher idea about the right relationship between God and humanity than the church ever had and ever will have as long as it acts like it does.[5]

---

[1] See ibid., pp. 52-56.
[2] See ibid., pp. 77-79.
[3] Ibid., pp. 81f.
[4] See ibid., pp. 81-82.
[5] See Jeremiah 31:32-34.

E. Eiríksson's Emphasis on Simple Faith and the End of the Church

It is not always easy to see what kind of faith Eiríksson proclaims in contrast to the one he condemns. However, he claims repeatedly in his book that the church has taught its people a pagan heresy, regarding God and his relationship to the world a new faith. Christ, however, did not introduce a new faith but only renewed and made the old faith of his ancestors and prophets better. By telling people to believe in him as God, putting himself next to God and equal to God, Jesus in the Gospel of John stands in stark contrast with the humility of his nature. In teaching this, the church turns Christ into a blasphemous individual and a heretic, and thereby a liar and a prophet of new faith—a faith that makes a lowly man, his messenger, into God.[1] Eiríksson wonders why, in light of all the fallacies he has pointed out, the church continues to profess faith in God the Father as an almighty one, and why the church persists in making fun of God and mocking him by professing faith in something it does not believe in. [2] He understands why people love Christ more than God the father, because this is how the church has portrayed him. He draws God's love towards himself, from the invisible God to the visible God. The Son is able to do something that the father could not, and so if anyone is almighty, it is the Son. The mighty theologians of the church, Eiríksson argues, have, however, not been able to explain where and how he got those powers.[3]

The faith Eiríksson himself proclaims and holds is of different nature, and he underlines the simplicity of it. During the latter stages of his book, Eiríksson speaks to his fellow countrymen. He acknowledges that many Icelanders still have what he calls "simple faith" and are therefore not as orthodox as the church wants them to be. By "simple faith," Eiríksson refers to faith in God as the father and the merciful forgiver of sins.[4] In his nature, Eiríksson claims that the individual has simple faith, but the church has disrupted that faith with its heresy. The forgiveness and mercy of God can be seen in the parable about the prodigal son.[5] Forgiveness

---

1 See Eiríksson, *Jóhannesar guðspjall*, pp. 23-27.
2 See ibid., p. 56.
3 See ibid., pp. 59-61.
4 See ibid., pp. 63-66 [*einföld trú*].
5 See Luke 16.

takes place through God's eternal love, which is true forgiveness and true love, whereas taking payment for sins requires only merciless strife and death. In this is no forgiveness, only an abstract justice that requires payment. This payment does not come from the sinner, but from Jesus, and he pays for it.[1] The teaching of the atonement and its forgiveness is therefore far from Christ's teaching, according to Eiríksson. The simple teaching of Christ is the forgiveness of sins; the sinner is forgiven by God in his repentance, and this is also the teaching of the prophets.[2]

From these remarks, we can see that the teachings of the church about God and his relationship with the world are to Eiríksson totally different than the true, simple view of God. The church has turned true worship of God and faith in him into "idolatry,"[3] and the glory of God and honor into blasphemy, because it has turned the glory of the one immortal God into the shrine of a mortal man.[4] For Eiríksson, Christ was only God's messenger, faithful and humble servant of God, who never wanted or pretended to be someone else. The church's time has come, and it, the great Babylon, has to crumble. This is necessary in order for faith in God and man's relationship to him to be made right again. He wants to abolish the church as an institution in order for the truth of God to prevail. To Eiríksson, no teaching can be more stupid and false than that God had become man. The faith of the church cannot survive except in an environment where the mistaken knowledge of God prevails. This is wrong, according to Eiríksson, because the world is dangerous for the church.[5]

Finally, Eiríksson turns to "all good and sensible Icelanders"[6] and asks them for the sake of God, truth, and themselves, to think seriously about what he has said. People should remember the words of Paul, to try everything and keep what is good, in this relation.[7] The church does not want to change its ways but only for people to follow it in blindness. He notes that he has nothing against priests, especially Icelandic priests, because they do not have the same education as priests elsewhere.

1 See Eiríksson, *Jóhannesar guðspjall*, p. 68.
2 See ibid., p. 71.
3 Ibid., p. 86.
4 See ibid., p. 86.
5 See ibid., pp. 87-91.
6 Ibid., p. 92.
7 See 1 Thessalonians 5:21.

Therefore, he also holds out the hope that they can change and will accept his reasoning.[1] He has higher hopes for the Icelandic priests and theologians than he has for the Danish ones.[2]

He therefore wishes that Grundtvig's prophecy would come true in Iceland,[3] that Icelanders will be the first men to throw away the heresy of the church, and confess the true, simple faith in the one true, invisible God (that never has become man), and follow the humble Christ. The gospel of John, preaching the incarnation of God, is simply false. Even though Icelanders are one of the smallest nations in the world, they are, according to Eiríksson, "ahead of other nations when it comes to reason and intelligence." He continues, "They can therefore, when it comes to religion, be as free and independent as other larger nations, and do not have to ask them, what they may believe, or follow them like an animal that does not go anywhere unless it is drawn or dragged."[4] The most important thing of all is to love the truth and trust God. Those who do so will somehow be able to support the victory of the truth, and cast out the wrongs and the lies.[5]

III. The Catholic Reply to Eiríksson's "Heresy"

Despite the fact that Eiríksson is a Protestant and does not directly aim his words at the Catholic Church, the priests relished the task of

---

1 See Eiríksson, *Jóhannesar guðspjall*, p. 94.

2 Eiríksson claimed that his work on the Gospel of John in Danish and about "the Grundtvigians" had not received any significant attention in Denmark, for over 15 months. He claims that people either do not have the courage to criticize him, or that they do not admit that he is right. In Sweden, however, the situation, he claims, is different. They have shown that they are better than the Danes and the Norwegians. Ekdahl, a priest in Stockholm, had translated his work into Swedish, and received good reviews in *Aftonbladet*. The Swedes know quality when they see it, according to Eiríksson. In a footnote (p. 98) he claims that it really does not matter if Icelandic priests will condemn the book, because in other places, especially Sweden, it has received good reviews. See ibid., pp. 95-98.

3 Eiríksson claims that Grundtvig's assertion that the light of the spirit should come from the north (though he was possibly speaking about himself and his followers) cannot come true because he is also "stuck in the midst of the heresy and lies of the church's teachings" (ibid., p. 100).

4 Ibid., p. 101.

5 See ibid.

correcting his heretical claims, and wondered why so few Icelandic theologians stood up against Eiríksson's arguments.[1]

They underline in their book the importance of acknowledging the fact that the Catholic Church existed prior to the writings of the New Testament. Based on the writings of the New Testament, they argue that Christ chose his apostles and ordered them to teach what he taught. So he created a *traditio*, a teaching that goes from one man to another. But in no case does his theory rely upon a single writing. This teaching comes from the word, and the word is inspired though the Holy Spirit and is in line with the needs of the church. A reliable depiction of the Catholic faith and the accurate teachings of the first centuries of Christianity can be seen from the writings of the New Testament. Therefore the church would still be indebted to keep up the teaching of Jesus through an oral tradition, even if there was no canon.[2]

The priests note that Eiríksson does not question the belief that Catholic theologians have held throughout the ages, namely, that the oral tradition about the teachings of the church should carry on from man to man. This makes them fully convinced that the faith the church proclaims, both with regards to the divinity of Christ and the writings inspired by the Holy Spirit, is accurate. To them it is quite uncanny that Protestant theologians such as Eiríksson can at one point hold the Protestant doctrine of the importance of scripture in high regard, but at the same time judge so openly individual writings of the canon, according to their own personal beliefs. With their reply, they hope to clear the schism in Eiríksson's mind and heart, so that he can come back to God and not shut his eyes to the truth. They wish not to scrutinize

---

1 They mention Einar Thorlacius as the sole opponent against the writings of Eiríksson but criticize Thorlacius for being too lenient on him. See Einar Thorlacius ["E. Th."], "Verum ekki framar börn, er hrekjumst og feykjumst af hverjum kenningarþyt. Efes. 4, 14," *Norðanfari*, vol. 3, 1864, nos. 30-31 (December 1), pp. 59-60; "Svar móti svari," *Norðanfari*, vol. 4, 1865, nos. 8-9 (March 18), pp. 15-16; "Elskanlegir, trúið ekki sjerhverjum anda, heldur reynið andana, hvort þeir sjeu frá Guði! 1, Jóh. 4,1," *Norðanfari*, vol. 4, 1865, nos. 23-24 (July 31), pp. 45f.; "Das Wort sie sollen lassen stahn, Und kein'n Dank dazu haben. Luther," *Norðanfari*, vol. 5, 1866, nos. 5-6 (February 24), pp. 9f.

2 See [Baudoin], *Jesús Kristr er Guð*, pp. 1-5.

every single argument of Eiríksson against the Gospel of John and the divinity of Christ, but only to point out why he is wrong in general.[1]

It is safe to say that they do not quite follow their own intentions since their argumentation is very detailed and addresses nearly all of Eiríksson's arguments with scriptural references. They claim that Eiríksson's methodology or system is in line with endeavors that seek to undermine all revealed faith and is in stark contrast to the essence of Christianity; it is a system that alludes to reason and prefers reason to faith. Not only does such a system cast away the holiest mysteries of the Christian faith simply because it cannot understand it, but also makes reason the only guiding light in one's conduct towards God and one's neighbors. Such an approach, or a system, denies that God can reveal to man things he cannot understand, and therefore rejects that God's eternal wisdom can go beyond the reason of man. Such a system makes man equal to God, which is a heresy. They do not deny the fact that reason is a gift from God and can teach us plenty of things (for example, about the existence of God and the immortality of the soul), but it is still limited. Without the grace of God, reason is of no use.[2]

Eiríksson is therefore a man of an unchristian and unwise faith of reason, despite the fact that he does not wish to label himself with an Enlightenment or rational faith. He is, according to the priests, just as any other Protestant in this regard. Eiríksson makes himself into a judge of the scripture and throws away the books of the canon he dislikes, despite the fact that from early Christianity these books have been considered to be the truth and word of God. The reason Eiríksson calls the author of the Gospel of John a false prophet and the material of the gospel a lie, is because his reason does not allow him to understand the divine mysteries that John proclaims in the gospel.[3] To them, Eiríksson is under direct influence of the German Enlightenment and rationalist religious thinkers. They are his gods, and he knows no other and has obviously not read Catholic theologians with a clear mind. They believe that Eiríksson is not as original in his criticism as he claims to be, for he is under influence from Baur and Albert Schwegler (1819-57) regarding the denial of the divinity of Christ, and in accordance with Baur and

---

[1] See ibid., p. 8.
[2] See ibid., pp. 10f.
[3] Ibid., pp. 12-13.

Karl Gottlieb Bretschneider (1776-1848) in rejecting the authenticity of the Gospel of John. They question Eiríksson's claim that scripture judges itself, for precisely Protestant theologians (such as Luther, Calvin, Baur and Eiríksson himself) pass judgment on it via the Holy Scripture. They have created a very inaccurate idea about the Holy Scripture. They accept some parts of it, and others they throw away. This system is sad, unreasonable and built on sand.[1]

A. Why Eiríksson is Wrong

Their book is, as stated earlier, very polemical and filled with biblical references. Their knowledge of the scripture is highly reliant upon Catholic theology, from the time of the Church Fathers and up until the Middle Ages. Regarding Eiríksson's claim that Christ cannot be considered a divine *persona*, equal to God the father, the priests distinguish five factors that prove the contrary. First, the coming of the Messiah is proclaimed in the Old Testament.[2] Second, the first three gospels prove the divinity of Christ.[3] Third, the Acts of the Apostles and the letters of Paul prove the divinity of Christ.[4] Fourth, early Christians

---

[1] See ibid., p. 18.

[2] Regarding the first argument, they claim that through a careful reading of the Old Testament, the divinity of the prophesied Messiah is obvious. From the days of Abraham, Isaac and Jacob, and the birth of God's chosen people, one continuous prophecy underlies the Old Testament: that the Glory of the Messiah will come. The Old Testament is loaded with prophecies about the Messiah; he is on everyone's lips. To them, unsurprisingly, Eiríksson did not read the Old Testament carefully. See ibid., p. 22.

[3] Regarding the second claim, the priests criticize Eiríksson's assertion that the authors of the synoptic gospels knew nothing about the pre-existence of Christ prior to him being born out of Mary's womb. This claim is false, according to their knowledge. Jesus' divinity is seen clearly in Matthew 15:17 and Mark 10:18; 18:32, despite Eiríksson's arguments. Catholics have long ago refuted the heresy of the Arians which they claim Eiríksson still seems to support. Also, how can Jesus be born out of the Holy Spirit if he is only a normal man [*réttr og sléttr maðr*]? As a child, Jesus had shown intellectual brilliance at the Passover in Jerusalem, at the age of 12. It is impossible that such a young man could have shown such maturity, without being God. The priests use numerous arguments from the synoptic gospels to prove the divinity of Christ, but their main argument is that in the synoptic gospels Jesus speaks as God, and says that he is God. And his miracles prove so as well. See ibid., pp. 42-49 and p. 73.

[4] Regarding the third claim, they argue that Eiríksson's assertion that the author of the Gospel of John makes Christ into something totally different than what the first

did believe in the divinity of Christ.[1] Finally, the view of pagans about the faith of Christians in Jesus Christ proves the divinity of Christ.[2]

Needless to say, the priests harshly criticize Eiríksson's arguments regarding the Council of Nicaea as well. It is for a valid reason that the Council of Nicea refuted Arius' heresy, and Eiríksson's claim that the council made Jesus into a God is preposterous, as well as his claim that only a small portion of the 318 bishops at the council had the conviction that Arius was wrong. Eiríksson's "divine trance" has once again led him astray and into blindness.[3] They claim that only 17 of the council members supported Arius, and they blame Eiríksson for not examining the testimonies of the past and trusting blindly the heresies of German Protestants. Eiríksson's "divine trance" has led him on a crusade against all real Christian thinkers. He is confused and does not know what he is talking about. They claimed to have already proved that Jesus is God by quoting the Holy Scripture and the writings of the Church Fathers. They claim that Eiríksson would probably defend himself by denying their proofs, and he should be careful in doing so. The freedom that Luther has given the individual to interpret the scripture by his own means has led Christian theology astray and placed all emphasis on the Holy Spirit and the individual's own religious conviction.[4]

---

apostles believed is plainly false. From the Acts of the Apostles and through the letters of Paul, this is proven otherwise. Through the words of Peter in Acts, the divinity of Christ becomes clear. See Acts 11:14. God raises a man from the dead and makes him into a god. The apostles teach in the name of Jesus, perform miracles in his name, and spread his glory around all the world, relieve sufferings and forgive sins in his name. Despite this, Eiríksson has the temerity to argue that one should not pray in Jesus' name. Did the apostles not know as well as Eiríksson, they ask? Did Paul not know better? See ibid., pp. 81-88.

1 Regarding the fourth claim, they argue that in early Christianity, people believed in the divinity of Christ. They claim this through the writings of second century thinkers such as Irenaeus and Clement of Alexandria. See ibid., p. 99 and p. 101.

2 Regarding the fifth and final claim, the priests go to Pliny the Younger and point out his testimony that early Christians praised Jesus as God. The writings of other early pagan thinkers support the claim that people in early Christianity believed in the divinity of Jesus. See ibid., pp. 101-104.

3 See ibid., p. 105.

4 The priests claim that Catholics can always prove their point. See ibid., pp. 107-109.

B. The Priests Reply to Eiríksson's Critique of the Gospel of John

The Catholic priests devote 20 odd pages to respond generally to Eiríksson's criticism of the Gospel of John. They claim to have already proven the divinity of Christ, and it is therefore easy to prove that Eiríksson is completely wrong when he questions the nature and authenticity of the Gospel of John. John is not the only evangelist that speaks about Christ's divinity, and, according to them, Eiríksson's biggest contradiction is that he claims that the Gospel of John makes Jesus Christ into God, and the other gospels do not. Regarding Eiríksson's claim that the love proclaimed in the gospel is comparable to pagan love, the priests criticize Eiríksson's translation of the text. For them, it means that nobody can show their friends more love than by giving their life for them, but not that the greatest love is to give one's life for one's friends. This is backed up by their knowledge of Koine Greek.[1] They refute Eiríksson's claim that the author of the gospel is silent about certain events in Christ's life. For them, when the author says that the word became flesh, it proves that Jesus of Nazareth is the son of God and that is the main talking point of the fourth gospel. They claim that even where there are no contradictions in the Gospel, Eiríksson goes a long way to find one.[2]

Regarding the "authenticity" of the Gospel, or of the apostle John being the author of it, the priests claim that Eiríksson's attempts to prove such a thing are futile, and nothing but his own creation. Only a few "unworthy heretics"[3] have questioned the authenticity of the fourth gospel. In this case, they speak of German theologians such as Baur, but these kinds of attacks have only made stronger their belief that the authenticity of the Gospel cannot be questioned.[4] They claim that Eiríksson sees early Christian theologians only as men that add to the Scripture, edit it and change it according to their own taste. They agree that those men existed, but that they were the heretics of the day, the

---

[1] See ibid., pp. 125f.

[2] They disagree that there is a contradiction between John 5:30 and 8:14; John 15:15 and 16:12; John 13:36 and 16:5. See ibid., p. 130.

[3] Ibid., p. 134.

[4] See ibid., pp. 134f.

Eiríkssons of their time. The priests protect the Church Fathers against Eiríksson's claims and their efforts to rise up and stand against heretics.

They speak of John the apostle (St. John) as the author of the Gospel, since all his thought and the events of his life are evident from it. Many of the things that happen are witnessed by him,[1] and many things could only have taken place in John. The author does not name John the apostle but hints at his presence.[2] This is for the priests a sound proof that John is the author of the gospel. How can Eiríksson argue against "everybody," against the church fathers and Christian writers? These proofs suggest that John the apostle is the author of the Gospel of John. The priests cite church fathers such as Irenaeus, Clement of Alexandria, Tertullian and later writers such as Origen, Eusebius, Gregory of Nazianzus and Epiphanius of Salamis, to support their arguments.[3]

Eiríksson is to be rebuked for thinking that he is greater and smarter than the Church Fathers, the writers of church history, the heretics and the pagan philosophers. Is he more familiar than they are with the Christian doctrine of the first century, they ask. Is he smarter, better read, more honest and pious than the Church Fathers and historians? Will he simply understand their words with his own arbitrary decision or through a "divine trance"? They advise him, whatever he does, to be careful. The sarcasm in the priests' speech is evident. Eiríksson is dishonest; he casts away every proof about Christianity handed to him and argues that the faith of so many Christians is both without reason and good proof. Instead, he offers up extremes and false lies, as holy truths.[4]

Eiríksson's work is poorly written and not by a knowledgeable author. It is written with an independent thought because Eiríksson does not care about the fact that he tells his readers nonsense and presents horrible

---

1 John 1:14.

2 John 13:23; 21:20.

3 They claim that Tatian the Assyrian is among those writers who do not name the author of the gospel, but nonetheless testify of it, as are Justin Martyr and Ignatius of Antioch. They explain the *logos* as it is explained in the Gospel of John. The same goes for Polycarp and Papias. See ibid., p. 138. On this note, Bultmann claims that Papias refers not only to John the son of Zebedee, but also to the Presbyter John (a presumed author of the Book of Revelation). He claims that Irenaeus and the whole later tradition might have confused the Ephesian Presbyter with the son of Zebedee of the same name. However, Bultmann claims that the author of the gospel is still a mystery. See Bultmann, *The Gospel of John: A Commentary*, p. 12.

4 See [Baudoin], *Jesús Kristr er Guð*, pp. 141f.

untruths as holy truths. It is surely written with passionate interest, but that is the same kind of passion that can be seen in "extremists in religious matters, against the truth."[1]

If Eiríksson finds the need to reject the divinity of Christ, he should not confront the "cleansed" reformed church about this. The reformed church has long since accepted that each and every person can translate and interpret the Holy Scripture as that person sees fit, as Eiríksson did. Eiríksson should rather speak to the Catholic Church, the one that has always taught what Christ asked her to teach, that is, his divinity and the teaching of the Christian faith. Before Eiríksson can explain the Holy Scripture with his own head, before he can receive the authority to deny all of the main Christian doctrines, he has to prove either that Jesus Christ did not establish a church and asked it to teach or that the church is finished and dead, because the Catholic Church is not finished, and not dead. He therefore has to prove the invalidity of the arguments of the church. And he also has to make it absolutely clear, which chapters are the holy word of God and which ones are not. The priests urge him to reply to their comments: it is his duty. They pray that he can use his reason to find the truth.[2]

IV. Eiríksson's Reply

Eiríksson's reply to the Catholic priests was published in 1868, a year after the publication of the priests, and almost three years after his Icelandic publication on the Gospel of John. It is safe to say that not much new comes across in Eiríksson's book; but naturally he refutes every single argument the priests make. However, he gives credit to the priests for writing their book, and criticizes Icelandic theologians for not doing likewise. He is not surprised that the Catholics have replied to his initial book since they hold the same basic beliefs as Protestants regarding the Trinity, about the incarnation of God and the divinity of Christ. He would actually have been more surprised if the priests with their arguments had not managed to make the Icelandic public even more

---

[1] Ibid., p. 143.

[2] See ibid., pp. 144-146.

convinced about the authenticity of the Gospel of John, and that Christ is God. Eiríksson will, however, not run away from his responsibility to refute their response; he is "more firm in his opinion than that."[1]

Regarding Sigurður Melsteð's criticism of Eiríksson's book in *Þjóðólfur*, Eiríksson provides only two footnotes to answer it. He claims that he cannot properly address his criticism because it simply is not worth answering. He claims to have originally meant to answer it, but it took him so long to finish the final version of his answer (it was published from May-September), so he lacked the patience to do so. To Eiríksson, Melsteð is no better than the Catholic priests; no better than the Catholic priests: a slave of the church, who considers everything that is contrary to its teaching a heresy and a lie. This is the spiritual freedom Eiríksson talks about repeatedly. In a lengthy footnote, Eiríksson unleashes his anger at Melsteð.[2]

Eiríksson intends to focus only on the main points of the priests' arguments, for he promised his publisher not to dig too deep with his criticism. It is safe to say that Eiríksson does not quite fulfill his promise; at least he is not very organized. His reply has no chapters, it is a 120 pages of logorrhea. It is far from being the small paper he says it is.[3] He denies the claim that he is under the influence of German rationalists, and asserts that he is far from being in agreement with F.C. Baur as they proclaim.[4]

---

1 Eiríksson, *Nokkrar athugasemdir*, p. 2.

2 On Melsteð's (and Thorlacius') criticism of his work, Eiríksson is very harsh. He claims that Melsteð is not ashamed of throwing at him all the lies and accusations he can find, and he holds him in no higher regard that the Catholic priests. Melsteð tries to depict Eiríksson as a liar and wants him to be hated and despised among Icelanders. No educated and intelligent men can argue with Melsteð, and Eiríksson claims that bishop Pétur Pétursson (1808-91) is in agreement with him when it comes to this point. On Eiríksson's detailed criticism of Melsteð's critique, see ibid., pp. 14-18 (note).

3 Eiríksson, *Nokkrar athugasemdir*, p. 3.

4 The priests display both thoughtlessness and stupidity when they criticize rationalist and Enlightenment thought. At the same time as they condemn it, they use reason to complicate matters, to the advantage of the Catholic faith (see ibid., p. 6). Eiríksson, however, also claims to have enough courage and conviction to criticize the church with reason as his weapon (See ibid., pp. 8-10). He claims that he is not as fascinated with F.C. Baur as the priests proclaim. He disagrees with him on the issue of whether the Gospel of John is a good gospel or not, and overall he is not in agreement with any German theologian, as far as he knows, and they are not his gods, as the

At first, Eiríksson turns to the proofs for the divinity of Christ they get from the Old Testament. It is obvious that they have no clue about how vivid the imagination of the authors of the Old Testament was, and read it as if it were written with the stoic calmness of a Northerner, without any poetic depth or ideas.[1] All of the scriptural references they make to argue for the divinity of Christ from the Old Testament are either misunderstood or misplaced.[2] Eiríksson's response is overall very Christocentric. Jesus Christ came to reform the faith of Jews but not to create or teach a new faith. The teachings of the church have made it hard for the nations of the world to listen to these words of Christ. It will not happen until they have torn themselves away from the slavery and the lies of the church, and reached the simple faith in God that Christ truly proclaimed.[3]

In their references to the Old Testament, Eiríksson claims that the priests overlook the obvious, namely, that God and God's anointed one, cannot be one and the same. That is, however, what they read from the prophets and Psalms. By doing so Eiríksson claims that the priests are trying to use the prophets and Psalms to make a wall so high around the divinity of Christ that it cannot be taken down.[4] Eiríksson's arguments are rarely supported by anything other than his own conviction, even though he quotes German theologians from time to time. He criticizes their misreading of the prophet Isaiah and the Psalms when it comes to

---

priests proclaim. The priests have no idea what rational faith is. For Eiríksson it is to believe that which is invisible and spiritual (Hebrews 11:1) and not try to explain it scientifically, but also not to be in opposition to the spiritual guidance, understanding, or reason, that God has given us (see ibid., p. 19).

1 See Eiríksson, *Nokkrar athugasemdir*, p. 22.

2 Eiríksson's method of argumentation is similar to that of the priests. He is also in harmony with his earlier writings. He holds his own view of the scripture, and they have another one. The passages in the Old Testament that the priests discuss in connection to the divine nature of Christ and that Eiríksson refutes are the following: Genesis 3; 12:3; 22:18; Malachi 2:17; Micah 5:1; Hosea 3:5; Isaiah 4:2; 7:1-16; 9:5-6; Psalms 2; 45:7-8; 97:7; 102:26-28; 104:4; 110:1.

3 See Eiríksson, *Nokkrar athugasemdir*, p. 22.

4 He points out that the priests' interpretation of the prophecy of Isaiah about Immanuel (God is with us; Isaiah 8:2), does not (as they claim), point towards the divinity of Christ since the name "is a symbolic one and only means that God is with the king and his men and wanted to protect them from the attacks of their enemies, but it does not have the meaning that, the boy, that would be born, was God" (Eiríksson, *Nokkrar athugasemdir*, p. 26).

Messianic interpretations. No Jew at that time would have had any idea about the incarnation of God in a man.[1]

After that, Eiríksson shifts his focus to the proofs the priests make for the divinity of Christ in the synoptic gospels. He criticizes them for splitting Christ up into two parts, with the result that he is not one person with two natures, but two persons in Christ. For Eiríksson, it is completely unthinkable that one and the same person can at the same time be all-knowing and not all-knowing, holy and unholy, just and unjust, etc.[2] The priests are "sly foxes"[3] who seek to distort his words. He takes their criticism and insinuations against him very personally, and claims never before to have seen any examples of such insolence and impertinence from the educated who have written about the Holy Scripture. In addition, they lie in the name of Christ, his apostles and the evangelists. He even goes as far as to say that it would have been better for them, if they never would have been born.[4] The review of the priests' different usage of concepts in relation to the son of God is nonsense,[5] according to Eiríksson. They wish to prove that Christ is the son of God in a totally different manner than others: God's natural son. Eiríksson claims that thereby they make all other children of god unnatural.[6]

The idea that God, like a man, can have a son with a woman, is the "poisonous seed"[7] which has sown itself into the fields of the simple faith, and has begotten the academic system of the "great whore."[8] Eiríksson, however, proclaims that we are all children of God, which is something that the priests cannot see.[9] The fact that Christ forgave sins is not a proof of his divinity either,[10] claims Eiríksson, and he asks if all good priests have not forgiven sins for hundreds of years. Even though Peter claims that Christ is the son of the living God,[11] Peter is only speaking of

1 See ibid., p. 42.
2 See ibid., pp. 49f.
3 Ibid., p. 54.
4 See ibid., pp. 56-58.
5 See [Baudoin], *Jesús Kristr er Guð*, pp. 50-57.
6 Eiríksson, *Nokkrar athugasemdir*, p. 82.
7 Ibid., p. 83.
8 Ibid.
9 See ibid., p. 83.
10 See [Baudoin], *Jesús Kristr er Guð*, p. 53.
11 See Matthew 16:16.

a man who is invested with God's spirit and power, and he would never have thought that that same man would have been God. He goes so far as to say that Peter would have been an idiot if he would have thought that the man Jesus was God.[1]

He blames the priests for not answering his remarks about whether the authors of the synoptic gospels considered Christ to be an eternal spiritual being before he was begotten by the holy spirit in the womb of Mary. The synoptic gospels say nothing about this, and therefore their teaching is something wholly different from what is taught in the Gospel of John, which proclaims that he had been an eternal godly being who in time became man.[2]

Regarding the claims the priests make about proofs for the divinity of Christ from the Acts of the Apostles and in the Pauline letters, Eiríksson asserts that neither Peter nor Paul considered Christ to be God, as the priests proclaim.[3] It is contrary to the teachings of Paul since it is God who raises Christ from the dead.[4] Paul also claims that there is only one God, the Father, and therefore he could not have believed that Jesus was also God.[5] Eiríksson states that when it comes to Christ's teachings, men should only turn themselves directly to God's love and grace and hope for everything good from him, instead of thinking about it in relation to the death of Christ or of his accomplishments.[6] Eiríksson goes back to the "simple faith" he proclaimed in his earlier work, and claims that in it one can think about a relationship with God that is built on eternal love. It involves the hope for all good things, despite the fact that the church wants to bind this hope to Christ's death and accomplishments.[7] What truly matters is to pray humbly in Jesus' name, to Christ the role model, and also to turn to God the father.

Eiríksson harshly criticizes the priests for their affinity with the Church Fathers. He claims that Irenaeus did not know the gospels properly and had only been a supporter of the oral tradition the Catholic

---

1 Eiríksson, *Nokkrar athugasemdir*, p. 87.
2 See John 1:1; 14; see ibid., p. 96.
3 See [Baudoin], *Jesús Kristr er Guð*, pp. 87-98.
4 See Romans 6:4; 8:11; 1 Corinthians 6:14; 15:15; 2 Corinthians 3:13; Galatians 1:1; Ephesians 2:5-6.
5 See 1 Corinthians 8:6 as well as Eiríksson, *Nokkrar athugasemdir*, p. 104.
6 Ibid., p. 99.
7 Ibid.

priests (and Sigurður Melsteð) are constantly referring to as a Christian truth.[1] Likewise, Athenagoras of Athens, Justin and Clement are not reliable and argue that the church has given Clement credit for works he did not even write. He also returns to his criticism of the Council of Nicaea and refutes the theory that the teaching of the divinity of Christ has come from the apostles, since so much had been changed and so many new opinions had arrived between the time of the apostles and the Council of Nicaea in 325. He stands firm on his conviction that it was a power struggle, rather than a holy conviction, that decided that Christ should be considered divine.[2]

Only very briefly at the end does Eiríksson go back to the Gospel of John specifically. This is interesting in light of the weight he gave it in his first book. Eiríksson claims that lack of space and time is the reason for this, which might give us reasons to think that this work was written in haste and not very well edited. He claims that some of what the priests say about the gospels simply is not worth answering. It should be obvious that when one cannot defend the divinity of Christ, one also cannot defend the gospel. These two things go hand in hand. Eiríksson claims to have proven the priests wrong and wishes that Icelanders will now open their eyes to the truth and finally realize how heretical such teaching is. People should never believe in any society, any book, or any man, in spite of how good he might have been. All of it is idolatry. They should rather believe in the one and only living God, the everlasting *evangelium* (Revelation 14:6).[3] It is worth noting that Eiríksson's attack on the scripture did not end here. He went further and attacked, in his work *Paul and Christ* (1871),[4] the credibility of the entire Bible.[5]

---

1 See ibid., pp. 109-11.

2 See ibid., p. 112.

3 See ibid., p. 118.

4 See *Paulus og Christus eller Pauli Lære om Retfærdiggjørelsen sammenlignet med Christi Lære om Syndsforladelsen, tilligemed nogle Bemærkninger om andre paulinske Lærdomme m. M.*, Copenhagen: Magnús Eiríksson 1871.

5 Gerhard Schreiber notes that in *Paul and Christ*, Eiríksson seeks to "demonstrate the radical incommensurability of Paul's doctrine of justification with the teaching of Jesus Christ." See Gerhard Schreiber, "Magnús Eiríksson: An Opponent of Martensen and an Unwelcome Ally of Kierkegaard," p. 69. To Eiríksson, Paul wants to restore an ancient Jewish idea of the scapegoat, which makes Christ's death into a sacrifice in order to pay for the sins of humanity. With this in mind, he attacks the credibility of the Bible *in toto*. See ibid., pp. 69f.

V. Conclusion

The saying "old habits die hard" is fitting in relation to Eiríksson's debate with the Catholic priests in Reykjavík. He has an opinion, a conviction, and he will not back down. The priests consider themselves apologists for the Catholic faith and will not back down either. They disagree on important Christian doctrines, but what they have in common is their Christian faith. Eiríksson's arguments are bold for a Scandinavian theologian at the time, and there is no wonder that his writings were not well received. However, despite what one might think about his view of the Scripture, Eiríksson's struggle for the truth and conviction in his own understanding of the Word of God and proclamation of Jesus reminds us of the Lutheran tradition he himself is deeply rooted in; according to this tradition, men and women of faith possess the freedom to interpret the Scripture. Eiríksson's "simple faith" [*einföld trú*] seeks only to underline the importance of God's mercy and forgiveness in contrast with the God of the atonement and suffering God on the cross. He does not deny the importance of Jesus Christ, but he focuses on him as a role model and a teacher rather than a divine *persona*. Such proclamations are not only in stark contrast with the Catholic faith, but also with his very own Protestant faith. The same applies to his radical claim that the church needs to come to an end and be dissolved. It is a conviction that is awakened through a careful reading of the Gospel of John, a reading that leads him eventually to reject large portions of the New Testament and the church as an establishment.

One can understand the Catholic priests' harsh reply to Eiríksson's teachings. It is in stark contrast with what the church proclaims, its confessions and doctrines. The priests certainly do their utmost to refute Eiríksson's "heresy." Their Catholic passion and need to write against Eiríksson no doubt derived from the hostile situation they encountered in remote Iceland. Eiríksson's book provided them with a golden opportunity, not only to refute his "heresy," but also to gain the attention of the Icelandic public. In reading their work, one can see that they are not overly critical of the Protestant doctrine, but rather focus on the ecumenical "truths" that Eiríksson refutes.

As I mentioned in the introduction, it is rare that men in a dogfight can settle on one opinion, let alone when religious matters are at issue.

Even though the debate between Eiríksson and the Catholic priests in Reykjavík might not give any answers, it still remains an important historical proof of lively theological exchanges in 19th-century Iceland. It is a debate between a radical theologian who lived and worked in Denmark most of his life and priests from the European continent. Both parties care about the words and deeds of Jesus Christ and the everlasting glory of God. They disagree on major issues, but *in toto*, they share the passion for the religious upbringing of a young and theologically confused nation and its pathway towards the word of God.

Magnús Eiríksson's Understanding of Christian Love for Our Neighbor

Friedrich Hauschildt

In Copenhagen in 1870 the Icelandic theologian Magnús Eiríksson published a pamphlet entitled *Can We Love Our Neighbor As Ourselves?*[1] In his writing he presents his interpretation of Christian love for the neighbor. From the very outset he is careful to distinguish between the idea of "love for our neighbor" as such from the wording generally used to express this idea. He asks, "What are the words used and what is the nature of the commandment that gives the precept of Christian love its true and right expression?"[2] So the essential questions he raises are summarized in the very wording of the title of his work: "Can we love our neighbor as ourselves?"[3]

Eiríksson develops his point of view in an elaborate discussion of the biblical accounts on the subject of love for our neighbor. However, he makes it clear—already mentioning it in the foreword—that his own account stems also from explicitly examining Søren Kierkegaard's writings.[4] Eiríksson mainly refers to Kierkegaard's *Works of Love* and

---

1 Magnús Eiríksson, *Kunne vi elske Næsten som os selv? Nogle tildeels nye Tanker om Kjærligheden samt flere derhen hørende Skriftsteder*, Copenhagen: Paa Forfatterens Forlag 1870.

2 Eiríksson, *Kunne vi elske Næsten som os selv?*, p. 2. It is striking that Eiríksson semantically distinguishes between love *command* and love *principle* (for example, ibid., p. 6 and pp. 87f.). On this distinction see Hermann Ringeling, "Liebe IX. Ethisch," in *Theologische Realenzyklopädie*, vols. 1-36, ed. by Gerhard Müller et al., Berlin and New York: Walter de Gruyter 1976-2004; vol. 21, pp. 177-187, here pp. 182f.

3 Eiríksson, *Kunne vi elske Næsten som os selv?*, p. 3.

4 See ibid., p. V and pp. VIIIff.

occasionally also the pamphlet *The Moment*.[1] In the past he had considered Kierkegaard's thoughts rather favorably,[2] but in this instance he was clearly taking a critical standpoint. Eiríksson now speaks of a fundamental "difference"[3] between Kierkegaard's and his own view. Several times Kierkegaard is quoted at great length.[4]

In his argument, which is relatively broad and sometimes has a somewhat cumbersome character,[5] Eiríksson makes remarkably highminded claims. In fact, he claims to present an interpretation of the Christian idea of love which earlier had never been thought of in the way he presents it now.[6] According to Eiríksson, the common view of the Church on this subject[7] as well as Kierkegaard's interpretation are incorrect, while his own interpretation is surely included "in the teachings of Christ,"[8] and furthermore he claims it reaches new heights of clarity.

In the following, I will first refer to Eiríksson's concept as well as the interpretation of the precept of love deriving mainly from his exposition of the biblical evidence (Part I). I will then elaborate Eiríksson's view insofar as it is focused as criticism on Kierkegaard's interpretation of the precept of love (Part II). Finally, I will discuss the question as to why Eiríksson and Kierkegaard come to such different understandings and where possibly the reasons for their different concepts can be found (Part III).

---

1 See ibid., p. VIII and p. 67.

2 See ibid., p. IX. In the beginning Eiríksson was close to Kierkegaard, concerning important religious questions (as stated by Michael Theunissen and Wilfried Greve, "Ist der Glaube ein Paradox oder 'in kraft des Absurden'?" in *Materialien zur Philosophie Søren Kierkegaards*, ed. by Michael Theunissen and Wilfried Greve, Frankfurt am Main: Suhrkamp 1979 (*suhrkamp taschenbuch wissenschaft*, vol. 241), pp. 147-160, here p. 147).

3 Eiríksson, *Kunne vi elske Næsten som os selv?*, p. VIII.

4 See ibid., pp. 24-40 and pp. 74-81.

5 The evaluation by Wilfried Greve and Michael Theunissen of Eiríksson's discussion of *Fear and Trembling* (see Theunissen and Greve, "Ist der Glaube ein Paradox oder 'in kraft des Absurden'?," pp. 147f.) applies *mutatis mutandis* also to Eiríksson's text dealt with in this effort.

6 Eiríksson, *Kunne vi elske Næsten som os selv?*, p. 110.

7 See ibid., p. 85 and p. 109.

8 Ibid., p. 110.

I. Eiríksson's Concept of the Christian Idea of Love with the Hindsight of his Interpretation of the Biblical Accounts

"Love is a life ever lived in its essential principle, emerging out in all its abundance and perfection as it is rooted in God himself";[1] Eiríksson starts his reflections with this seemingly defining sentence. Love so defined is then said to be "eternal, endless and all-embracing as God himself."[2] For Eiríksson two questions arise immediately, namely, (a) whether the "Christian precept of love,"[3] which is commonly understood to be the *greatest commandment*, really confirms correspondence to the lives of Christ and the Apostles as they encounter us in the New Testament,[4] and (b) whether this commandment can be fulfilled at all or not.

Eiríksson's argument tends to relativize the importance of the wording of the Christian command to love in Matthew 22:39 that reads, "You shall love your neighbor as yourself" which represents a quotation from Leviticus 19:18. He points out repeatedly that this commandment originates from the Mosaic Law.[5] With this hint Eiríksson apparently wants to underline that he considers this wording of the command to love to be obsolete in some ways, and he certainly does not regard it as being specifically Christian.

Yet, Eiríksson has to admit that this is the exact wording that Jesus adopts in Matthew 22:35-39 to express the commandment to love.[6] However, according to Eiríksson, this wording does not really express Jesus' point of view in all its depth, because Jesus went way beyond the thought of loving one's neighbor as oneself when he asked us to love our enemies and sacrificed himself on the cross.[7] He puts forward two reasons against a love based on the principle of equality[8]—which is Eiríksson's description of the commandment to love one's neighbor: First, a love based on the principle of equality would only be a restricted form of love, falling well short of the decidedly Christian conception, the

---

[1] Ibid., p. 1.

[2] Ibid., p. 2. A similar wording is used by Kierkegaard in *SKS* 9, 180 / *WL*, 180.

[3] Eiríksson, *Kunne vi elske Næsten som os selv?*, p. 2.

[4] See ibid., p. 3.

[5] See, for example, ibid., p. 67, p. 77 and p. 109.

[6] See, for example, ibid., p. 63.

[7] Ibid.

[8] See ibid., p. 74 and p. 77.

principles of self-sacrifice and love of the enemy that Christ himself had lived. And, secondly, he believes a love based on the principle of equality, on closer inspection, to be unfeasible.[1] You can only love you neighbor either more or less than yourself.[2] He who tries to maintain a balance between love of self and love for the neighbor, is actually—according to Eiríksson—prioritizing love of self.[3]

But why does Jesus in Matthew 22 express the idea of love by adopting this wording which—in Eriksson's view—is incomplete? Eiríksson explains this as follows: In Matthew 22 Jesus, in a way, limits himself to the horizon of the inquiring Pharisee[4] and, to be true to the tradition, holds on to the obsolete wording. However, in his actual behavior Jesus goes beyond this limited conception of the command to love. It belongs to times past and falls short of "the uppermost spiritual point of view."[5] Eiríksson does not try to conceal the fact that the command to love expressed as a love based on equality is not restricted to Matthew 22 in the New Testament, but is taken up in other passages as well.[6] Yet, according to him, the true New Testament understanding of love—different from what is phrased in Matthew 22—does not command us to love our neighbor as ourselves but precisely to love him *more* than ourselves,[7] because true love for the neighbor is actually a self-sacrificing love.[8] Love commanded by Christian faith does not take love of self as the standard of measure;[9] on the contrary, it strongly contradicts the love of self and egoism.

Eiríksson gives the example of moral education given to children and adolescents to illustrate that love of self is an inappropriate measure of love for the neighbor.[10] Education pointedly aims at overcoming love of self and egoism. This becomes impossible if love of self is made the

---

1 See ibid., pp. 64f. and p. 73.
2 See ibid., p. 74.
3 See ibid., p. 71 and pp. 73f.
4 See ibid., p. 63.
5 Ibid., p. 64.
6 See ibid., p. 4 and p. 62. Eiríksson refers to Romans 13:9; Galatians 5:14 and James 2:8. In view of this fact, it is surprising that elsewhere (p. 85) Eiríksson can state that in the New Testament love of self is never inculcated.
7 See ibid., p. 7, p. 13, p. 62 and p. 77.
8 See ibid., p. 41 and p. 77.
9 See ibid., p. 82.
10 See ibid., pp. 82f.

measure of love for the neighbor. Eiríksson states that education is first and foremost about breaking children's self will[1] and thus overcoming their love of self. In this regard the Church has often acted wrongly.[2]

As to formulating the Christian precept of love as a commandment, Eiríksson emphasizes that acts of love must not be understood as fulfillment of a commandment. In his opinion, this is an obsolete form of expression. In contrast, he makes a point by insisting that true love naturally springs from a childlike belief in God.[3]

The idea of love of one's enemy is of particular importance to the New Testament. It is generally believed that love of one's enemy is a specifically Christian form of love. Eiríksson describes the reasons for love of the enemy as follows: We humans feel humble and grateful in the face of God. We need God's forgiveness and therefore we ourselves are willing to forgive one another.[4] His understanding of love of one's enemy, in his unique manner of speaking, is a two-level process. Through forgiveness, the guilt and the evil—which have led to the enmity in the first place—are removed. Once the relationship has thus been brought "back to normal," it is then possible to love the former enemy. Eiríksson emphasizes that love of one's enemy "naturally" springs from our relationship with God and is not to be understood as an obligation.[5]

II. Eiríksson's Concept of Love for the Neighbor in Contrast to Kierkegaard's Understanding of Love

Eiríksson unfolds central points of his understanding of the Christian commandment to love in a strikingly broad as well as a polemic confrontation against the writings of Søren Kierkegaard and thus shapes his own ideas in sharp contrast to those of Kierkegaard. The result of his study of Kierkegaard's ideas can be summarized in the following six aspects of the theme under consideration.

---

1 See ibid., p. 91.
2 See ibid., pp. 85f.
3 See ibid., p. 6, p. 58 and pp. 77f.
4 See ibid., p. 55.
5 See ibid., pp. 57f.

A. Love Your Neighbor as Yourself: A Uniquely Christian Concept or a Mosaic Law?

In Kierkegaard's interpretation of the Christian commandment of love for our neighbor the paraphrase "you shall love your neighbor as yourself" plays a very important and decisive role. In Kierkegaard's opinion this thought contains the essence of the Christian understanding of the commandment to love, and this unique Christian paraphrasing surpasses all former paraphrases of the idea of love.[1] For Eiríksson this is virtually impossible to actualize since the paraphrase originates from the Old Testament. He repeatedly calls this paraphrase a Mosaic commandment.[2] For Eiríksson the origin of the paraphrase proves that it cannot be specifically Christian but can only be an obsolete paraphrase of the commandment to love.

Eiríksson quotes Kierkegaard's statement, wherein it is precisely this "as yourself" that excludes the otherwise misguided love of the self.[3] However, he forcefully rejects this claim as being unfounded[4] and points out that this Kierkegaardian thought can never be true in human experience.[5] According to Kierkegaard, interpreting the paraphrase—as Eiríksson prefers to do—as meaning that we should love our neighbor more than ourselves is just poetical exaggeration.[6] Eiríksson objects energetically, as for him, it is exactly this interpretation that expresses the truly Christian understanding of love. Christian love, according to Eiríksson, is self-abandonment in which the neighbor shall be loved more than I love myself.[7] For Eiríksson the notion of self-abandonment is the key-term for the interpretation of the phenomenon of love for our neighbor.

---

1 For example *SKS* 9, 26 / *WL*, 18: "Christianity presupposes that a person loves himself and then adds to this only the phrase about the neighbor as yourself. And yet, there is the change of eternity between the former and the latter."

2 See Eiríksson, *Kunne vi elske Næsten som os selv?*, p. 67, p. 69, p. 77 and p. 81.

3 See ibid., pp. 74f.

4 See ibid., p. 77.

5 See ibid., p. 77, note.

6 See ibid., p. 76.

7 See ibid., p. 74 and pp. 79f.

B. Impracticability

Kierkegaard explicitly agrees with a paraphrase of the commandment to love which, according to Eiríksson, not only wrongly passes off an Old Testament wording as specifically Christian but also defines the precept of love in a way that is actually impractical. Even putting aside the question as to whether the principle of equity is considered an authentic Old-Testament reminiscence or a specifically Christian feature, Eiríksson is convinced that the precept is not feasible. He claims that it lies in the very nature of things that it is impossible to achieve such a balance. Even if one tried to keep the balance between the love of self and the love for our neighbor, according to Eiríksson, love of self would, *de facto*, be given priority.[1] However, Eiríksson does not probe any further into the question or seek what might be the deeper reason as to why Kierkegaard ascribes such great importance to a thought that Eiríksson himself considers unsustainable, even problematic. Though he does not consider even the possibility that Kierkegaard could be right, had Eiríksson given it more thought, he might have concluded that while Kierkegaard and he obviously interpret the paraphrase differently, their interpretations only seemingly contradict each other.

C. Love as a Duty?

Kierkegaard's understanding of Christian love is mainly influenced by his conviction that love is a duty. Further, according to Kierkegaard, it is also specifically characterized by Christian understanding.[2] Such a claim is resolutely rejected by Eiríksson. For him, the assertion that the love is a duty is no more than the continuation of the Mosaic commandment,[3] which is an obsolete thought falling short of the "uppermost spiritual

---

1 See ibid., p. 65; see also pp. 71f.
2 See *SKS* 9, 31 / *WL*, 24 ("this is the very mark of Christian love and is its distinctive characteristic—that it contains this apparent contradiction: to love is a duty") and *SKS* 9, 33 / *WL*, 25 ("Love had existed also in paganism, but this obligation to love is a change of eternity").
3 See Eiríksson, *Kunne vi elske Næsten som os selv?*, p. 60, p. 69 and p. 77.

point of view."[1] True Christian love springs from a childlike belief and confidence in God.[2] To Eiríksson, love and duty seem irreconcilable.

D. The Neighbor

Kierkegaard argues that the category of neighbor applies to all human beings without exception.[3] The Christian concept of love does not permit dividing people into good and bad, friend and enemy.[4] Eiríksson vehemently objects to this interpretation of the Christian idea of neighbor.[5] Love for our neighbor—as love in all its forms of expression—must be "love for that which is good and true."[6] It is therefore unacceptable to erase the "distinctions between objects of love."[7] Of course, love is not exclusively aimed at those who are good in every sense but also at those who have certain weaknesses.[8] However, the very truly evil, that is, those who are unfathomably evil and obdurate, cannot be a direct object of Christian love.[9]

Eiríksson gives an elaborate justification for his point of view by quoting the Bible: Christ did not treat the Pharisees and Scribes with love but he unmasked and rebuked them for their attitudes.[10] In his denunciation of scribes and Pharisees in Matthew 23 Christ talks about punishment and condemns malice and sin. Christ has never commanded us to love obstinate sinners.[11] The New Testament speaks of an unpardonable sin against the Holy Spirit;[12] there are obstinate people for whom we shall not pray (1 John 5:16), and they are excluded from

---

1 Ibid., p. 64.
2 See ibid., p. 6, p. 58 and pp. 77f.
3 See, for example, *SKS* 9, 28f. / *WL*, 21; *SKS* 9, 56 / *WL*, 49; *SKS* 9, 62 / *WL*, 55; *SKS* 9, 68 / *WL*, 61; *SKS* 9, 73 / *WL*, 66.
4 See, for example, *SKS* 9, 74 / *WL*, 67f.
5 See, for example, Eiríksson, *Kunne vi elske Næsten som os selv?*, p. 31.
6 Ibid., p. 42; see also pp. 40f.
7 Ibid., p. 40; see also p. 51.
8 See ibid., p. 43.
9 See ibid.
10 See ibid.
11 See ibid., p. 44.
12 See ibid., p. 45.

the community (Matthew 18:15-17). There are those who are so evil that even God cannot forgive them.[1]

Though Eiríksson states two possible biblical arguments against his own interpretation, he does not attribute much significance to these arguments and finds them to be of lesser importance. Thus, the Good Samaritan might have helped a distressed person, but would not have helped an unfathomable evil person.[2] God making his sun rise on the evil and on the good (Matthew 5:45) simply means that God provides everyone's essential needs, but it does not mean that he offers his love to everybody.[3] As Eiríksson says, Jesus did not die on the cross for all people.[4]

Eiríksson interprets Kierkegaard's universal extension of the notion of neighbor to all men to be an arbitrary approach for dealing with the biblical tradition.[5] He accuses Kierkegaard of wanting to surpass the Apostles and Jesus[6] and thus even God with this "exaggerated" definition of love.[7]

Eiríksson, in a tone tinged with derision, objects to Kierkegaard's claiming that whoever really loves his enemy, closes his eyes and thus perceives the neighbor in his enemy[8] and that true love, in a certain respect, does not need an object to be directed at.[9] Love cannot close its eyes to reality; rather it is always directed at an "object"—a beloved person.

---

1 See ibid., p. 46 and p. 48.

2 See ibid., p. 47. Kierkegaard cites the Good Samaritan as an example for love of the neighbor; see *SKS* 9, 30 / *WL*, 22.

3 See Eiríksson, *Kunne vi elske Næsten som os selv?*, p. 47.

4 See ibid., p. 48.

5 See ibid., p. 49.

6 See ibid., p. 30.

7 See ibid., p. 44 and p. 48.

8 *SKS* 9, 74 / *WL*, 68: "shut your eyes—then the enemy looks just like the neighbor. Shut your eyes and remember the commandment that *you* shall love; then you love—your enemy—no, then you love the neighbor, because you do not see that he is your enemy."

9 *SKS* 9, 73 / *WL*, 66: "love for the neighbor is the most perfect love. Therefore, all other love has the imperfection that there are two questions and for that matter also a certain duplicity: first there is a question about the object and then a question about the love....But concerning love for the neighbor there is only one question, the question about love."

E. "Eccentric"

Eiríksson's criticism of Kierkegaard is not aimed solely at specific lines of his argument but is generally directed towards Kierkegaard's way of thinking. Eiríksson, though he feels that Kierkegaard's interpretation of the precept of love is ingenious as a whole, calls it paradoxical and eccentric,[1] to a certain extent vain and narcissist[2] as well as thoroughly theoretical and merely idealistic,[3] and thus taking all things to extremes.[4] Unquestionably, Kierkegaard's thinking is highly complex and characterized by a strong inner dialectic. Kierkegaard is aware of the fact that others consider his interpretation of love to be eccentric.[5] Certainly, the precept of love appears to be friendlier and more harmonized in Eiríksson's thought, in which the love for our neighbor arises from deep belief and confidence.

F. "Contradictory"

Seen from Eiríksson's perspective, Kierkegaard becomes embroiled in a series of contradictions. The critical attitude adopted by Eiríksson makes him detect contradictions in Kierkegaard's writings and point them out. Here are some examples: Kierkegaard claims that the commandment to love one's neighbor as a duty, which is peculiar to Christianity, redefines the concept of love. The truth is, according to Eiríksson, the duty to love dates back to Mosaic times, and therefore it is not to be considered a specifically Christian feature but something obsolete. Kierkegaard, on the one hand, speaks of duty—Eiríksson seems to associate an external impulse—but, on the other hand, he also speaks of an inner urge, which is to be loved.[6] Kierkegaard claims everything became new on account of Christian experience, but in his pamphlets *The Moment* he speaks of Christianity as not yet having come into this world at all.[7] In

---

[1] See Eiríksson, *Kunne vi elske Næsten som os selv?*, p. IX.
[2] See ibid., p. XI.
[3] See ibid., p. 32.
[4] See ibid., p. 37.
[5] *SKS* 9, 129f. / *WL*, 127.
[6] See Eiríksson, *Kunne vi elske Næsten som os selv?*, pp. 68f.
[7] See ibid., p. 67 and p. 69.

Kierkegaard's understanding, the term "Neighbor" is a relatively abstract and spiritual term,[1] yet our neighbor is to be loved in a concrete manner.[2] In light of these contradictions, Eiríksson claims his interpretation of Christian thinking concerning love is consistent with the true sense of the biblical tradition.[3]

III. How Could Such Divergent Interpretations Develop?

Eiríksson develops his interpretation of the Christian thought of love in the form of a sharp critique of Kierkegaard's interpretation. However, he does not sufficiently clarify what causes the differences between the two interpretations, where exactly "a fork in the road" leading to their different understandings can be found. Clarification will be attempted in this section.

A. The Neighbor

It is obvious that Eiríksson and Kierkegaard have variant understandings concerning the term "Neighbor." For Eiríksson, the neighbor is a term referring to particular, empirically identifiable facts. A person must meet certain empirical requirements in order to be perceived as a neighbor worthy of our love. The person must be a good individual, worthy-of-love and at the most may suffer from some weaknesses. Eiríksson explicitly excludes the truly evil person from the category of neighbors to be loved.[4] He understands the words "neighbor" and "enemy" as two

---

1 *SKS* 9, 63 / *WL*, 56.

2 See Eiríksson, *Kunne vi elske Næsten som os selv?*, p. 36.

3 About a 100 years after Eiríksson's argument with Kierkegaard's account of love, Løgstrup brings forward arguments, partly identical to that of Eiríksson, to criticize Kierkegaard: Kierkegaard's account is self-contradictory; his account is incompatible with reality, therefore impracticable and does not conform to Jesus' teachings (see Kirsten Marie Schmidt, "Et bidrag til diskussionen af Løgstrups opgør med Kierkegaard," *Kierkegaardiana*, vol. 14, 1988, p. 80).

4 See Eiríksson, *Kunne vi elske Næsten som os selv?*, p. 43.

different categories of people on the same level.[1] The categorizing of every person as neighbor, as Kierkegaard does, is considered too abstract by Eiríksson.[2] As we have seen, he even justifies his point of view referring to the Bible: "Thus Christ made a difference between the love of the 'neighbor' and the love of enemies."[3] Even God cannot love an obstinate and evil person.[4] For Eiríksson, the term "Neighbor" is a term for marking the difference among all people. There are people to whom this term can be applied, and there are people to whom it cannot be applied.

Not so with Kierkegaard. For him, the term "Neighbor" does not designate a group of people beside other groups, for Kierkegaard, in principle, all people come under this term. Whoever really loves "loves every human being."[5] Kierkegaard uses the term, so to speak, as a transcendental category;[6] he himself speaks of a "spiritual"[7] use. Correspondingly, love for our neighbor is the basic form underlying all possible forms of love. Kierkegaard applies the term in a universal and in an egalitarian way. These different points of views of the term by Eiríksson and Kierkegaard have far-reaching consequences.

---

1 See ibid., p. 29. Eiríksson uses this term and claims that this distinction can be found in Jesus' usage.

2 The reproach of abstractness is repeated by Adorno and Løgstrup; see Ingolf U. Dalferth, " '...der Christ muß alles anders verstehen als der Nicht-Christ....' Kierkegaards Ethik des Unterscheidens," in *Ethik der Liebe. Studien zu Kierkegaards "Taten der Liebe,"* ed. by Ingolf U. Dalferth, Tübingen: Mohr Siebeck 2002, pp. 19-46, here p. 40.

3 Eiríksson, *Kunne vi elske Næsten som os selv?*, p. 30.

4 See ibid., p. 46.

5 *SKS* 9, 269 / *WL*, 270; see *SKS* 9, 56 / *WL*, 49: "Christian love teaches us to love all people, unconditionally all"; *SKS* 9, 58 / *WL*, 52: "since the neighbor, to be sure, is all people"; similarly *SKS* 9, 62 / *WL*, 55.

6 In Kierkegaard's thinking the term "Love for the neighbor" does not compete with other forms of love, it is not on the same level as these; it is rather at the basis of all of them (*SKS* 9, 68 / *WL*, 61). Kierkegaard has also expressed: the love for the neighbor is the sanctifying element (*SKS* 9, 69 / *WL*, 62) in all types of love; "this love for the neighbor is not related as a type to other types of love" (*SKS* 9, 73 / *WL*, 66). See also Dalferth, "'...der Christ muß alles anders verstehen als der Nicht-Christ....,'" p. 41: "The specification 'neighbor' is not a characterizing or classifying note but a *locating attribute.* It places the human being in an ethical horizon within which it is understood and can be expected that he is treated in a certain way *without needing further reasons*" (my translation).

7 See *SKS* 9, 63 / *WL*, 56f.

B. Christian Love is Love of Self-Renunciation

The fact that Kierkegaard so strongly emphasizes the thought of loving *as yourself* to which Eiríksson juxtaposes his own understanding of love as self-sacrifice is the reason why Eiríksson does not sufficiently realize how much Kierkegaard sees Christian love—regardless of qualifying it with the phrase "as yourself"—at the core, as a love of self-denial.[1] True love is not readily available but can only be achieved through self-denial. Love is coming into the mode of existence through the renunciation of instinct and inclination.[2] It is "the task and requirement of love to deny oneself and to give up self-love or erotic love."[3] "To love the neighbor, however, is extending love arising out of self denial, and self-denial simply drives out all preferential love, just as it drives out all self-love."[4] Kierkegaard, in a certain way, starts from the assumption of love of the self,[5] yet he does not consider it as such to be normative but states that natural love of self requires a deeper "revolution" (*Omvæltning*)[6] if it is to become true love, which is not seeking its own.[7] For Kierkegaard, true love is very much a "self-sacrificing love,"[8] "Love is giving of oneself."[9] Indeed, he speaks of "self-annihilation,"[10] for "it is self-denial that discovers that God is."[11] Therefore, it cannot be stated that Kierkegaard propagates a type of love which is simply characterized by traits of egoistical self-love. It is true that Kierkegaard deliberately connects this clear accentuation of self-

---

1 See *SKS* 9, 15 / *WL*, 7 and *SKS* 9, 62 / *WL*, 56; see also *SKS* 9, 59 / *WL*, 52 ("Christian love is self-denial's love") and *SKS* 9, 62 / *WL*, 56 ("Wherever the essentially Christian is, there also is self-denial, which is Christianity's essential form").

2 Concerning the two preceding sentences see Friedrich Hauschildt, *Die Ethik Sören Kierkegaards*, Gütersloh: Gütersloher Verlagshaus Mohn 1982 (*Studien zur evangelischen Ethik*, vol. 15), p. 156.

3 *SKS* 9, 15 / *WL*, 7.

4 *SKS* 9, 61 / *WL*, 55.

5 See *SKS* 9, 82 / *WL*, 76.

6 *SKS* 9, 266 / *WL*, 267.

7 See *SKS* 9, 268 / *WL*, 269.

8 *SKS* 9, 272 / *WL*, 274; similarly *SKS* 9, 359 / *WL*, 365.

9 *SKS* 9, 263 / *WL*, 264. There are, admittedly, types of devotion which in truth are self-love (*SKS* 9, 60f. / *WL*, 53f.). Merely claiming sacrifice is therefore insufficient. Eiríksson's thinking is not sufficiently dialectical.

10 *SKS* 9, 276 / *WL*, 278.

11 *SKS* 9, 356 / *WL*, 362.

denial by the emphasis of the phrase "as yourself." Kierkegaard explicitly states that he does not see any contradiction in doing so.

C. "As Yourself"

For Kierkegaard, the expression "love as yourself" plays a key role, and Eiríksson, in a vehement manner, objects to ascribing such undue importance to it. This fact requires a closer examination of the meaning they respectively attribute to this phrase.

Eiríksson holds that by this phrase love of the self becomes the measure of, the comparative standard for love for our neighbor, but for him love of the self is equivalent to egoism;[1] thus it is merely an affirmation of the capabilities and interests of the self. Thus it stands to reason that he rejects the thought of turning love of one's self (so understood) into the measure of love for our neighbor. If by the phrase "as yourself" egoism is made the yardstick for love for our neighbor, then this interpretation must surely be rejected. For his interpretation of Christian love, Eiríksson starts from the assumption that the alternative to egoistic love of oneself is love as sacrifice. Against the background of this alternative, he cannot deduce any positive non-egoist meaning from the phrase "as yourself." According to him, the phrase "as yourself" clearly belongs on the side of the self-love that is to be rejected. If Eiríksson's presupposed distinction is applied to Kierkegaard's interpretation of love, Kierkegaard inevitably appears as someone who abets pure egoism, and it remains invisible to Kierkegaard as to what really matters. It does not occur to Eiríksson that it could be inappropriate to apply the distinction he takes as given to Kierkegaard's thinking and that for Kierkegaard the phrase "as yourself" might mean something distinct from pure egoism.

So what could be the interpretation of the phrase "as yourself" as truly understood by Kierkegaard? It is true that the idea of selfhood that holds love plays an important role in Kierkegaard's thought.[2] But this idea is only *one* aspect in a dialectical context, and it is not to be isolated,

---

[1] See, for example, Eiríksson, *Kunne vi elske Næsten som os selv?*, p. 82.

[2] To this compare Hauschildt, *Die Ethik Sören Kierkegaards*, pp. 158-160.

and it is inappropriate simply to declare love of self and egoism to be the same.

In order to understand Kierkegaard's interpretation of the phrase "love as yourself" it is necessary to take a wider approach. The one measure for all types of love is, according to Kierkegaard, not natural love but God's love, and it is the primacy of God's love for humanity from which human love for God springs: "the only true object of a human being's love is love, which is God."[1] As we have seen, Kierkegaard inseparably relates the love directed towards God with the aspect of self-renunciation.[2] Therefore, one cannot speak of a dominance of love of the self.

In order to understand Kierkegaard's account of love correctly, it must be made clear that, for him, God's love of us and our love of Him are the fundamental bases on which the respective meanings of self-renunciation and selfhood are conferred and must be dialectically thought together; in order not to be misinterpreted as contradictions, they must not to be separated from each other.

D. Existence

How Kierkegaard is able to attribute a positive meaning to the phrase "as yourself," in this general context, distinct from pure egoism, is not obvious unless his understanding of human existence is brought to mind.[3] However, this can only be briefly outlined here.

For Kierkegaard, a human being is characterized by being a synthesis of polar elements (the finite and the infinite, the temporal and the eternal, freedom and necessity).[4] It is the essential calling, given by

---

1 *SKS* 9, 264 / *WL*, 264f.

2 Later interpreters of Kierkegaard such as Løgstrup and Adorno reproached him for the contrary, viz., laying excessive emphasis on the aspect of self-denial. Kierkegaard defines the relation between selfhood and self-denial dialectically. However, he does not always make it easy for his readers to see this as he tends to give one-sided formulations, see *SKS* 20, 86, NB:118 / *KJN* 4, 86.

3 In the following I subscribe to "Kierkegaard's essential definition of what a human being is" such as the one he has formulated in *The Sickness until Death* (see Arne Grøn, "Der Begriff Verzweiflung," *Kierkegaardiana*, vol. 17, 1994, p. 38).

4 See *SKS* 11,129 / *SUD*, 13; *SKS* 7, 81 / *CUP1*, 92; *SKS* 7, 274 / *CUP1*, 302

human existence itself, to keep these aspects together[1] and to relate itself to this synthesis. That means, a human being cannot perceive himself as exemplary and anchored, but has to see his existence as a calling not yet fulfilled.[2] The human being must repeatedly realize himself;[3] it is a continuous active relation to himself. Human existence is essentially a self-relation in the sense that it has its origins in God and has to be lived "before God." Such a complex self-relation is never finished but should always be defined anew. Human existence is in permanent danger; it is always exposed to success and failure. Kierkegaard outlines the dimension of this danger using the following schematization.[4] The human being seeks a successful existence between the two states of being "in despair to will to be oneself" and "in despair not to will to be oneself."[5] From this description it can be deduced that successful existence is understood as the willingness of the self to be oneself humbly receiving oneself from God's hands and thus a humble self-acceptance,[6] namely, a lasting self-relation. The human being is and remains not only a self-relation, even if he sacrifices himself or, to be more precise, sacrifices his egoism. The human being is asked to accept himself as such and—in this sense—to love himself.

E. Love of Self versus Self-Sacrifice

Eiríksson assumes that self-sacrifice and self-love constitute irreconcilable differences.[7] In reading Kierkegaard, all he sees is the momentum of love of self, which he rejects, and in doing so he misses—as shown above—the

---

1 See, for example, *SKS* 7, 275 / *CUP1*, 302.

2 Arne Grøn (in *Subjektivitet og Negativitet: Kierkegaard*, Copenhagen: Gyldendal 1997, pp. 89-91) shows that the nature of existence represents a normative structure.

3 See *SKS* 7, 302 / *CUP1*, 332: Human existence is not being "in the same sense as a potato is, but not in the same sense as the idea is, either."

4 See *SKS* 20, 365, NB4:160 / *KJN* 4, 365: "excellent outline."

5 *SKS* 11, 129 et passim / *SUD*, 13 et passim. A similar wording referring to self-love can be found in *SKS* 9, 31 / *WL*, 23: "selfishly loving oneself" or "selfishly not willing to love oneself in the right way."

6 To this compare Grøn, "Der Begriff Verzweiflung," pp. 28f.; compare also Gunnar M. Karlsen, "Løgstrup's Criticism of Kierkegaard—Epistemological and Anthropological Dimension," *Kierkegaardiana*, vol. 17, 1994, p. 103.

7 See, for example, Eiríksson, *Kunne vi elske Næsten som os selv?*, p. 70.

aspect of self-sacrifice or renunciation. But unlike Eiríksson, Kierkegaard does not believe these two aspects to be contradictory to each other. For him they constitute a dialectical relationship. Much as true love for God presupposes self-denial of the human being, self-denial does not erase human existence as being a self-actualization but confirms it. Self-sacrifice and self-relation mutually preserve each other, developing towards their true sense.

Kierkegaard can only think such thoughts because he holds that self-denial as well as self-love are not defined one-dimensional parameters (following the pattern: "self-love is negative"—"sacrifice is positive") but should be assessed after they are further differentiated: "Actual life is too complex merely to point out abstract contrasts...."[1]

There is a self-denial or a devotion with which the individual abandons any distortions of his own (see above). However, there are also forms of self-denial, appearing to be sacrificial, which, in truth, are hidden types of love of the self.[2] And, by contrast, naturally, there are forms of love of the self that may be interpreted as egoistic and have to be rejected. But there are also types of humble self-acceptance, of standing by oneself, of accepting oneself as created by God.[3] There is a legitimate—and necessary—self-esteem one ought to possess. These positive types are called "proper self-love" by Kierkegaard,[4] and he makes them shine against a negative background.

> When the bustler wastes his time and powers in the service of futile, inconsequential pursuits, is this not because he has not learned rightly to love himself? When the light-minded person throws himself almost like a nonentity into the folly of the moment and makes nothing of it, is this not because he does not know how to love himself rightly? When the depressed person desires to be rid of life, indeed, of himself, is this not because he is unwilling to learn earnestly and rigorously to love himself? ...When someone self-tormentingly thinks to do God a service by torturing himself;

---

1 *SKS* 11, 163 / *SUD*, 48.

2 See *SKS* 9, 62 / *WL*, 55: "devoted self-love"; *SKS* 9, 61 / *WL*, 55.

3 It is questionable whether the term "self-*love*" is misleading or appropriate for these types.

4 See *SKS* 9, 26 / *WL*, 18 and *SKS* 9, 30f. / *WL*, 22f.; see also Eiríksson, *Kunne vi elske Næsten som os selv?*, p. 70.

> what is his sin, except not willing to love himself in the right way? Alas! If a person presumptuously lays violent hands upon himself, is not his sin precisely this, that he does not rightly love himself in the sense in which a person *ought* to love himself?[1]

Thus Kierkegaard not only recognizes the alternative of self-love and devotion but distinguishes further between unacceptable and acceptable self-love.[2] Accordingly, sacrifice and devotion can renounce a problematic egoism, but there are also forms of sacrifice and devotion which are actually forms of self-love which must be rejected.

Given these highly differentiated definitions of self-sacrifice and of self-love, the simple alternative: sacrifice versus self-love, as Eiríksson puts it, falls short of a sound argument.

For Eiríksson, love for our neighbor and a self-love defined by the phrase "as yourself" are competing types of love.[3] Therefore, he holds that a balance between these two is impossible. In Kierkegaard's understanding of proper self-love, self-love and love for our neighbor go very well together, and they even mutually define each other.[4]

Eiríksson argues—as we have seen—that a love based on the principle of equality is impossible and that true love is always loving the other more than oneself. Actually Kierkegaard considers the line of thinking, maintained by Eiríksson, that it might be morally superior to love the other "*more than oneself*."[5] However, he does not elaborate on this. Already linguistically, love is set in a comparative horizon by talking of loving someone with a "more than..." point of view.[6] Thus the universality of love is restricted since one will never love everybody more than oneself. "Exceptions…of preference 'or' of aversion"[7] then arise. To love another more than loving oneself is a preferential love, a love that selects;[8] therefore, it is exclusive and thus represents a kind of "secret

---

1 *SKS* 9, 30f. / *WL*, 23.
2 See, for example, *SKS* 9, 30 / *WL*, 22.
3 See Eiríksson, *Kunne vi elske Næsten som os selv?*, p. 86.
4 For Kierkegaard, relation to God, selfhood and self-denial mutually refer to one another; see Hauschildt, *Die Ethik Sören Kierkegaards*, pp. 133-135.
5 See *SKS* 9, 26 / *WL*, 18 and *SKS* 9, 28 / *WL*, 20.
6 See *SKS* 9, 28 / *WL*, 20.
7 *SKS* 9, 27 / *WL*, 19.
8 See *SKS* 9, 62 / *WL*, 55.

self-love."[1] With a poetic effusion this kind of love might be sung about as a higher kind of love, but actually it falls short of Christian love. Love of this kind, despite its altruistic appearances ("more than yourself"), actually is a "secret self-love."[2]

As for Kierkegaard the thought of God is closely linked with the thought of the equality of all human beings; he correlates "to love a person *more than oneself*" with "to love a person more than God."[3] God is the horizon of eternity and thus represents equality. To love more than oneself does not apply to love of other human beings, but is reserved for one's love only of God[4]—and as such is rightly exclusive.

F. Love as Feeling or Respect

It has to be unequivocally emphasized once more that the different meanings of love for our neighbor, of self-love and also—as will be shown later—of duty influence Kierkegaard's and Eiríksson's respective understandings of love. If love is thought of, in the first place, as a feeling, as an "immediate inner relation,"[5] as an enrapturing emotion,[6] then, indeed, it is not very plausible to love *all* human beings; such a love can never be *commanded*, for then self-love and neighborly love would really become *conflicting* notions. The difference between Eiríksson's and Kierkegaard's understanding arises from the fact that, when it comes to the notion of love, Eiríksson rather thinks of an emotional enrapturing whereas Kierkegaard understands love in the sense of respect and esteem,[7] which might include emotions of affection but surely is not limited to them. The idea of feeling committed to respect all human beings can

1 *SKS* 9, 27 / *WL*, 19.

2 For the theologian Kierkegaard, trained in Lutheran thinking, it does not come as a surprise that there are attitudes hidden under the contrary (*sub contrario*).

3 *SKS* 9, 26f. / *WL*, 18f. (emphasis removed).

4 See ibid.

5 See Christoph Schrempf, afterword to *Sören Kierkegaard. Leben und Walten der Liebe*, trans. by Albert Dorner and Christoph Schrempf, Jena: Diederichs 1924 (*Erbauliche Reden*, ed. by Christoph Schrempf, Jena: Diederichs 1924-29, vol. 3), pp. 398-400.

6 See *SKS* 9, 265 / *WL*, 266.

7 It would be interesting to examine more closely the question of whether there is an objective point of contact between Kierkegaard's understanding of love and Kant's idea of respect as a "moral feeling."

definitely claim plausibility, regardless of which view one may take. The same holds true for the idea that a person duly accepts one's own self and rightly should do so, and further should be at peace with oneself.[1]

Eiríksson thus perceives Kierkegaard's description of the Christian concept of love as contradictory. If one understands Kierkegaard's interpretation in the light of its intellectual presuppositions, it is characterized by a great inner tension, but there are no contradictions. Rather the opposite is true, since for Kierkegaard the thoughts that God is love, that we shall love him, that we shall love our neighbor and that we shall "love" ourselves form a remarkably consistent concept, admittedly a rather complex but nevertheless coherent one.[2] Kierkegaard himself compares the teachings of Christianity with a "circular motion"[3] in which every thought is related to all others.

G. *"You Shall Love"*

In Kierkegaard's interpretation of the precept of Christian love, great importance is attributed to the fact that true love is to be understood as a duty.[4] Eiríksson sharply criticizes this idea. How can a feeling be commanded? It is incomprehensible for Eiríksson as to why Kierkegaard carries this idea to such extremes that he even claims that the duty to

---

1 For a high esteem of self-love in current philosophy see Harry G. Frankfurt, *The Reasons of Love*, Princeton: Princeton University Press 2004. For a differentiated description of a positive self-relation with balanced self-confidence, self-respect and self-esteem in the framework of a contemporary social and philosophical recognition theory, see, for example, Axel Honneth, *Das Ich im Wir. Studien zur Anerkennungstheorie*, Berlin: Suhrkamp 2010, p. 266.

2 See *SKS* 9, 30 / *WL*, 22 ("To love yourself in the right way and to love the neighbor correspond perfectly to one another; fundamentally they are one and the same thing"); *SKS* 9, 65 / *WL*, 57 (love for the neighbor originates in love for God); *SKS* 9, 64 / *WL*, 58 ("Only by loving God above all else can one love the neighbor in the other human being"); *SKS* 9, 111 / *WL*, 107 ("To love God is to love oneself truly; to help another person to love God is to love another person; to be helped by another person to love God is to be loved," emphasis removed); see also *SKS* 9, 118 et passim / *WL*, 114 et passim. With these definitions, one type of love is defined by another.

3 *SKS* 9, 142 / *WL*, 140.

4 On the duty to love in Kierkegaard's thinking, see *SKS* 9, 30 / *WL*, 22; *SKS* 9, 95 / *WL*, 90 et passim.

love is genuinely new and specifically Christian.[1] Love, for Eiríksson, does not arise from duty but, on the contrary, naturally from a childlike confidence in God.[2] He regards duty as an inappropriate and imposed constraint on love, which thus enslaves it. He considers "duty as the enemy of love"[3]—a formulation Kierkegaard uses to characterize the aesthetic in his *Either/Or*. If love is primarily thought of as erotic love or friendship, that is, as spontaneous emotions, then—and here Kierkegaard easily agrees with Eiríksson—it is senseless to talk of commanding love.[4] Such a love is preferential; it selects; it is exclusive; it is directed towards the likable characteristics and is conditioned by them. It does not follow a "you shall," but it is a love of instincts and inclinations.[5] However, Kierkegaard, when thinking of love, primarily thinks—as we have seen—of another type of love, namely, love of our neighbor, or, to put it more explicitly, of the love which is fundamental to all other types of love, namely, love of our neighbor. This love is not attracted by likable characteristics; it does not compare human beings, selecting those worthy to be preferred and rejecting those who are unappealing. It is the love of esteem and respect for the other. This love construes love itself as something of value and therefore compelling for every individual. From this point of view Kierkegaard can say: duty is "a friend"[6] of love, and it is conducive to it, "for he [sc. the human being] does not have duty outside himself but within himself."[7]

This understanding is related to Kierkegaard's conception of the nature of existence and the nature of self as have been presented above. Since human existence is a relationship of tension between different and even contradictory poles, it is our enduring task to attain the fullness of existence.[8] In this respect, the "you shall" is inherent in human existence itself; it is not a passive state but an endless active task, namely, a never

---

1 Eiríksson, *Kunne vi elske Næsten som os selv?*, p. 68; compare *SKS* 9, 32f. / *WL*, 24f.
2 Eiríksson, *Kunne vi elske Næsten som os selv?*, pp. 78f.
3 *SKS* 3, 144 / *EO2*, 146.
4 *SKS* 9, 58 / *WL*, 50.
5 See *SKS* 9, 51 / *WL*, 44.
6 *SKS* 3, 144 / *EO2*, 146.
7 *SKS* 3, 243 / *EO2*, 254; see also *SKS* 3, 244 / *EO2*, 256.
8 See Hans Friemond, *Existenz in Liebe nach Sören Kierkegaard*, Salzburg and Munich: Pustet 1965, p. 14.

ending "you shall." Therefore, there is such a thing as a "fundamental 'you shall' of human existence."[1]

Accordingly, the "you shall" is inherent in love because love is particularly an eminent way of bringing existence into its fullness. The duty to love does not impose anything on existence that is not already inherent to it since it does not command anything else "than what love itself has always been longing for."[2]

Love is not something found outside the human heart nor does love enter the human heart through the deity. God rooted love in the human heart; it underlies all that mankind does on earth, that is, it is always to be presupposed. The urge to love is "rooted in human nature," it belongs "*essentially*...to being human."[3] Duty ties in with such an already existent urge. Duty exists "in embryo"[4] in love; it is also the lasting companion, a friend, and a confidant. It unmasks wrong types of selfish love, even if these are disguised as devotion,[5] and thus it holds on to the urge to love against all selfish instincts.[6] Duty commands what love itself desires, since duty is "only a more majestic, a more elevated, a divine way of expressing that their wish can be realized."[7] He, for whom love is "supreme,"[8] feels the duty to remain in it,[9] to preserve it. For Kierkegaard this duty is not felt as being a matter of compulsion; for him, duty and voluntary assent belong together.[10] "Christianity begins immediately with

---

1 Ibid., p. 14. See also Romano Guardini, "Der Ausgangspunkt der Denkbewegung Sören Kierkegaards" in *Sören Kierkegaard*, ed. by Heinz-Horst Schrey, Darmstadt: Wissenschaftliche Buchgesellschaft 1971, pp. 52-80, here p. 55, pp. 57f. and p. 68. The notion of existence, of self is defined by Kierkegaard in such a way that it includes the aspect of the normative, of measure.

2 Friemond, *Existenz in Liebe nach Sören Kierkegaard*, p. 99.

3 *SKS* 9, 156 / *WL*, 155; for the motive of love as a need see also *SKS* 9, 19 / *WL*, 10 and *SKS* 9, 75 / *WL*, 66f.

4 *SKS* 3, 144 / *EO2*, 146.

5 See *SKS* 9, 61f. / *WL*, 55.

6 See Kresten Nordentoft, *Søren Kierkegaard. Bidrag til kritikken af den borgerlige selvoptagethed*, Copenhagen: Dansk Universitets Presse 1977, p. 181.

7 *SKS* 3, 144 / *EO2*, 146.

8 *SKS* 3, 143 / *EO2*, 145. See also *SKS* 9, 65f. / *WL*, 58f.: In seeking the supreme there is an inherent repulsion against the offensive.

9 On the special relationship between love and "remaining" see 1 John 4:16: "God is love; and those who remain in love remain in God and God remains in them."

10 See *SKS* 3, 257 / *EO2*, 270: "duty is the expression of his [sc. a person's] absolute dependence and his absolute freedom in their identity with each other."

what *every* person *should become*...if he *himself wants*"[1] this. Kierkegaard's way of reasoning in this instance is evocative of Kant's moral philosophy.

Love that depends on preferences, on the lovability of its object, is insecure and is not free. Love is truly free when it is duty-bound. As long as one's love depends on whether the person who is loved reciprocates or not, as long as it is seen as a kind of barter exchange, love is not free.[2] True love feels an inner necessity; it knows it is placed under a norm; it knows it is a duty.[3] Unless love is a duty, the significance of the neighbor cannot be understood: "If it were not a duty to love, the concept 'neighbor' would not exist either."[4] Against this background Kierkegaard is able to write: "only when it is a duty to love, only then is love eternally made free in blessed independence."[5]

To what extent true love can and shall be understood as a duty is highlighted by Kierkegaard's interpretation of the parable of the Good Samaritan in Luke 10.[6] It is not about knowing the neighbor, not about pondering on the question of who might eventually be my neighbor (possibly so extensively that it will keep me from actual action), but, quite the contrary, it is accepting the demands of the situation put on oneself, about perceiving the obligation and accepting the inherent "you shall."

Again, the crucial argument whether love and duty are irreconcilable or not appears in a different light if one admits Kierkegaard's thought that the Gospel appears to be severe only for the hard-hearted—those who see it from the outside of the true experience of loving—but for those who live in it, that is, for the people who truly love, it is mild.[7] Since "only then do I in truth know the truth, when it becomes a life in me."[8]

---

1 *SKS* 9, 180 / *WL*, 180 ("*himself*" is my emphasis).

2 A love understanding itself to be a sacrifice remains in danger of secretly "compelling" the other for reciprocation.

3 See Dalferth, "'...der Christ muß alles anders verstehen als der Nicht-Christ....,'" p. 36.

4 *SKS* 9, 51 / *WL*, 44 (emphasis removed).

5 *SKS* 9, 45 / *WL*, 37 (emphasis removed).

6 *SKS* 9, 30 / *WL*, 22.

7 See *SKS* 9, 369-372 / *WL*, 376-379.

8 *SKS* 12, 203 / *PC*, 206.

H. The Strenuousness

Eiríksson calls Kierkegaard's reasoning eccentric,[1] morbid and paradoxical. And indeed, one can say that Kierkegaard's thinking has a strenuous character.[2] This might be particularly odd and disconcerting when the topic is love. However, there is a reason for this, and it is not simply due to the author's mental condition, but it is on account of his philosophy. For Kierkegaard a person is not just—as we have seen—something simple, some existing thing, some stationary fact but a relation, a relation to itself.[3] This relation has to be constantly established anew, for it is in danger of failure. This failure is not always obvious; it might be hidden even from the individual itself. Starting from this position, the human concept of being a person and the reflection on it become very complex and therefore add a rather strained character to them. In Kierkegaard's opinion this is to a certain extent inevitable since "without this exertion, one's thinking becomes superficial."[4]

IV. Conclusion

With his pamphlet *Can We Love Our Neighbor As Ourselves?*, published in 1870, Magnús Eiríksson launched a serious debate on Kierkegaard's concept of love.[5] Eiríksson deploys his own point of view in the course of a critical as well as a polemical discussion with Kierkegaard. Essential lines in Kierkegaard's argumentation remain incomprehensible to Eiríksson since his own understanding starts from different assumptions. Yet, the fact that certain aspects of Eiríksson's critique of Kierkegaard's

---

1 To this compare Theodor W. Adorno, "Kierkegaards Lehre von der Liebe," in his *Kierkegaard. Konstruktion des Ästhetischen*, 3rd enlarged edition, Frankfurt: Suhrkamp 1966, pp. 265-291, here p. 276.

2 See Guardini, "Der Ausgangspunkt der Denkbewegung Sören Kierkegaards," p. 56, p. 58 and p. 68.

3 See ibid., p. 55.

4 *SKS* 9, 356 / *WL*, 362.

5 See Theunissen and Greve, "Ist der Glaube ein Paradox oder 'in kraft des Absurden'?," p. 148: "Due to his intense efforts in interpreting, Eiríksson may be considered the precursor to today's Kierkegaard studies, though, in a formal way, they were initiated much later" (my translation).

concept of love reappear *mutatis mutandis* in Theodor W. Adorno's[1] and Knud Ejler Løgstrup's[2] interpretations of Kierkegaard's writings might hint at the possibility that Kierkegaard's interpretation is embedded in a specific structure of thought—a particular kind of Christian-idealist understanding of the individual—which is not shared by all. Outside this structure of thought, the plausibility of Kierkegaard's concept of love seems to be restricted. This was obvious very early because of Eiríksson's critique of Kierkegaard's understanding of love.

1 See Adorno, "Kierkegaards Lehre von der Liebe" as well as Michael Theunissen, "Das Kierkegaardbild in der neueren Forschung und Deutung (1945-1957)," in *Sören Kierkegaard*, ed. by Heinz-Horst Schrey, pp. 324-384, here pp. 357f.

2 See p. 277, note 3 and p. 282 note 6 above.

Copenhagen
(Illustration from Hermann Achenbach, *Skizzen aus dem Norden, oder: Erinnerungen eines Ausruhenden*, Part 2: *Reise nach Dänemark und Schweden im Sommer 1835*, Düsseldorf, gedruckt auf Kosten des Verfassers, bei Jos. Wolf 1836. Public domain picture, https://commons.wikimedia.org.)

V. History of Reception

Magnús Eiríksson: The First Icelandic Unitarian

Ágúst H. Bjarnason

Transcribed from the original manuscript,
edited and introduced by Stefan M. Jonasson

Introduction

"Magnús Eiríksson: The First Icelandic Unitarian," by Ágúst H. Bjarnason (1875-1952), was delivered as an address at Harvard University in May of 1923; later the same month at Meadville Theological School, then located in Meadville, Pennsylvania; and again, in Icelandic, at the founding convention of *Hins sameinaða kirkjufjelags Íslendinga í Norður-Amerika* (The United Conference of Unitarian Churches) at Winnipeg, Manitoba, on June 25, 1923. The lecture was subsequently published in Icelandic as "Um Magnús Eiríksson,"[1] but the complete English version never made it into print.

Several copies of Ágúst H. Bjarnason's manuscript are extant, including his own handwritten original, which is in the possession of the Archives of the Unitarian Universalist Association at Harvard Divinity School.[2] Several years ago, I took it upon myself to transcribe a copy of the original that had been in the possession of the Rev. Dr. V. Emil Gudmundson (1924-82), a Unitarian minister and historian who had included a short chapter about Magnús Eiríksson in his book *The*

[1] Ágúst Hákonarson Bjarnason, "Um Magnús Eiríksson," *Skírnir*, vol. 98, 1924, pp. 39-73.

[2] Andover-Harvard Theological Library, Cambridge, MA (bMS 103/5-15).

Icelandic Unitarian Connection.[1] Since Bjarnason was writing in a second language, this transcription has undergone some very minor editing for punctuation and vocabulary. For instance, Bjarnason's use of "childish" has been rendered as "childlike," since the author was unaware of the negative connotations of the former; he clearly intended this word to evoke a positive understanding. Otherwise, this transcription offers a precise account of Bjarnason's public addresses about Magnús Eiríksson during his 1923 North American lecture tour.

The convention at Winnipeg marked the amalgamation of the Icelandic Unitarian and New Theology movements in North America, and Bjarnason had been invited to address the convention in order to bolster the credibility of this merger by adding the voice of a distinguished Icelandic academic to the list of speakers. Bjarnason was professor of philosophy at the University of Iceland, where he taught from 1911 until 1928. He served as rector of the university from 1917 to 1918 and again from 1927 until 1928, when he became principal of the Reykjavik Lower Secondary School, a position he held until his retirement in 1944. Bjarnason matriculated from *Efterslægtselskabets Skole* in Copenhagen in 1894 and earned Master of Philosophy (1901) and Doctor of Philosophy (1911) degrees from the University of Copenhagen. He was a member of the British Society of Psychological Research, the British Psychological Society and the *Deutsche Philosophische Gesellschaft.* A prolific writer, he published numerous articles and six books, including volumes on ethics and logic, as well as *Almenn sálarfræði* (General Psychology), the first original text on human psychology written in the Icelandic language. Bjarnason was married to Sigríður Jónsdóttir (1883-1971), the daughter of Jón Ólafsson (1850-1916), an Icelandic journalist and parliamentarian who was the second president of the First Icelandic Unitarian Society of Winnipeg and brother-in-law to its founding minister, Rev. Björn Pétursson. Ágúst and Sigríður had five children.

Although Magnús Eiríksson was a familiar figure to the liberal religious leaders among the Icelanders in North America, his influence on the emigrant community was largely an indirect one. The Icelandic Unitarian movement was more directly influenced by American sources

[1] Valtýr Emil Gudmundson, *The Icelandic Unitarian Connection: Beginnings of Icelandic Unitarianism in North America, 1885-1900*, completed posthumously by Barbara J.R. Gudmundson, Winnipeg, Manitoba: Wheatfield Press 1984, pp. 6-10.

in its early years, although the inspiration of Magnús Eiríksson and Rev. Matthías Jochumsson (1835-1920) certainly had some bearing on creating the conditions whereby Icelandic emigrants in North America proved receptive to Unitarian missionary activity. In a sense, Ágúst H. Bjarnason was making the case for Magnús Eiríksson as a retroactive inspiration for Icelandic Unitarianism. Alongside Magnús Eiríksson, the Icelandic Unitarians also came to see Chief Justice Magnús Stephensen (1763-1833) and the mathematician and poet Björn Gunnlaugsson (1788-1876) as having paved the way for the emergence of Unitarianism among the Icelandic emigrants. Moreover, there was a deep fondness for Rev. Matthías Jochumsson among the Icelandic Unitarians, although their affection was largely unrequited, since Jochumsson found the brand of Unitarianism represented by North American Icelanders to be excessively rationalistic, in contrast to his own romanticism.

So Magnús Eiríksson's influence upon the Icelandic Unitarian movement was essentially one that was grafted onto this religious movement once it was already underway. In hindsight, he was seen as a figure who could help to unite the major streams of liberal religious thought that had developed among the Icelandic emigrants—Unitarianism and the New Theology—when these two movements had grown close enough together to consider merging. As the liberal religious leaders moved towards establishing the United Conference of Icelandic Churches, Magnús Eiríksson proved to be the historical figure with whom all strands of Icelandic religious liberalism could identify themselves: the rationalistic Unitarianism of Rev. Björn Pétursson (1826-93), who had deconstructed the doctrines of Icelandic Lutheranism; the romantic Unitarianism of Rev. Rögnvaldur Pétursson (1877-1940), who celebrated what he called "[t]he sacred Triad" of saga times—wisdom, fortitude, and justice;[1] the Universalism of Rev. Magnús J. Skaptason (1850-1932), who taught that eternal damnation was contrary to the nature of a God who was the "eternal source of love";[2] and the New Theology of Rev. Friðrik J. Bergmann (1858-1918), who had stressed that, "the thought is eternal, not the letter," that the creeds were only

---

[1] Rögnvaldur Pétursson, "The Development of Liberal Religion in Iceland," *The Proceedings of the Unitarian Historical Society*, vol. 2, part 2, 1932, pp. 1-13, here p. 2.

[2] See Magnús J. Skaptason, "Easter Sermon" (1891); published as *Ræða*, Gimli, Manitoba: G.M. Thompson 1892.

historic milestones marking the church's development, and that "[t]ruth withers in the possession of those who think they have a monopoly on it."[1] In the teachings of Magnús Eiríksson, each of these strains saw themselves represented, and Bjarnason masterfully painted a portrait of a historical figure who could bind the religious liberals together in unity, liberty, and charity. In the aftermath of his address, the United Conference of Icelandic Churches prospered for a generation before assimilation and secularization led to its inevitable decline.

Magnús Eiríksson: The First Icelandic Unitarian (1923)

Ladies and Gentlemen!

With your kind permission I'm going to speak to you about the very first Icelandic Unitarian, perhaps the first determined Unitarian in all Scandinavia, telling you about his life, his strife and his works, in the hope that you will find him a remarkable man of a great religious genius.

This man is Magnús Eiríksson.

But kindly allow one some introductory remarks.

The Renaissance was the dawning of a new era of Free Thought, and the Reformation was a revolution against the authority and the traditions of the Medieval Church. The Reformation was the true child of the Renaissance. It was the interest for the old classic literature, which brought the learned men of that time to study their classics and classic languages; and the Seventy Interpreters, the Evangelists, St. Paul and the Fathers of the Church had just written in those languages. Now it seemed nearer to hand to study the Christian classics than the pagan classics, as the readers themselves were Christians and only few of them had heard anything about the pagan classics, which had fallen into oblivion. So the learned men of that time were especially eager to study the Bible: Zwingli, Calvin, Luther and Melanchthon, as well as their predecessors, Valdez, Wycliff and Hus were industrious students of the Holy Scripture.

---

[1] Wilhelm Kristjanson, *The Icelandic People in Manitoba: A Manitoba Saga,* Winnipeg, Manitoba: Wallingford Press 1965, p. 352; see pp. 351-56.

It was no ordinary scientific interest which drove these men to the study of the Bible, it was something more; it was their heart's desire to reach the very fountains of the Christian faith, to know something about the Christian religion as it was at the very beginnings to the Christian era. It was a kind of spiritual crusade to the Holy Land.

Ladies and gentlemen, you know as well as I that a crude supernaturalism of traditional Christianity was then holding its sway throughout the Christian world. In every Catholic church throughout the world you could, in the mist of theological dogmas, see the image of Christ the only begotten, Christ the crucified and Christ the glorified with a halo around his head. And you were told that the only way to him and to your own salvation led through the Church and the sacraments of the Church. *Nulla salus extra ecclesiam!*—And the Pope was the supreme authority.

But the Reformers longed for the Jesus of the Gospel, to see the real man behind the deified man and how he led his simple life among simple folk. And they were eager to listen to his message, so deep and warm and so human. But they did not get far enough; they could not get beyond St. Paul, the real founder of the Christian doctrine and the Christian Church. They only founded a new church and renewed the theology, the dogmatics.

But you cannot still the hunger of a longing heart and a clear, dissatisfied thought with—dogmatics. And the Protestant thought, once awake, never wholly falls asleep to gain. We have in our own time got the New Protestantism in Germany, the Liberalism in France, the Free Theology in Holland, the New Theology in England and the Unitarianism in America. My hero was one of the forerunners of this liberated thought, of the New Theology and Unitarianism.

I. The Man

Magnús Eiríksson was born on the northernmost farm of Iceland, close to the polar circle, on a delightful summer night, the longest day of the year, the 21st of June 1806, when the midnight sun was lingering above the horizon. He was the son of the farmer there and his wife, a worthy couple. Eiríksson lost his father already in his sixth year, and his mother married a second time another farmer, Björn Sigurðsson by name,[1] who proved a real father to his little stepson. He was also a good child to his parents, an obedient and industrious boy. He was of that sort of young people who have an absolute faith in their elders and think it is a sin to act against their will and command. His first private instructor, a clever and educated man, declared, when his pupil left him, that he parted with him "with a real feeling of regret."[2] And when he left college as the foremost in his class, you read in the certificate that "he never with a word has offended or hurt the feelings of his masters and has been gentle and modest towards all."[3] His stepfather and his schoolmaster had, therefore, great confidence in him: he assisted his father with the farming and the schoolmaster as a superintendent of school. And he was as capable of bodily as mental labor. In the winter he was at school from the beginning of October to the end of June. In the summer he either stayed at the school farm as a farm laborer or he went home to the north, doing all kinds of work, tending the sheep or the cattle, fishing trout or salmon in the brooks and rivers, making hay, sailing, fishing, or gathering drift timber on the coast, always gay and cheerful and never giving in at a hard job. It must have been delightful for his fellow workers to be with him, for he was always at the top of his spirits.

In 1829 he got his certificate for the University; but his parents, who in the meantime had many children, were too poor to be able to sustain him at the University of Copenhagen. Then he became the clerk of the provincial governor of Iceland, who soon turned out to be his benefactor. Although Eiríksson, as he himself relates, proved but a moderate clerk, Krieger the governor,[4] a man of great experience, soon became favorably disposed towards him and encouraged him to go to Copenhagen. As Eiríksson expressed his fear that he might not be able to sustain himself in a foreign country, Krieger offered to assist him with money until he had taken his degrees, which promise he faithfully kept.

His mother, whom he dearly loved and who herself was the daughter of a clergyman, had often expressed the wish that her firstborn should

---

1 Björn Sigurðsson (1778-1852).

2 Þorsteinn Erlendsson Hjálmarsson (1794-1871), who was later a priest in Hítardalur. Reference unknown.

3 Examination certificate (*prófskjalinu*) from Bessastaðaskóli, 1829.

4 Lorentz Angel Krieger (1797-1838), Governor of Iceland from 1829 until 1836.

become a servant of God. And as he himself had always been very religious, he made up his mind to study theology.

In the year 1831 he went to Copenhagen, got a scholarship for four years, showed great ardor in his studies and passed with distinction his final examination in 1837. He then went on a short summer trip to Iceland to visit his parents. His parents had hoped that he had come to stay in Iceland, for as a university graduate he could now apply for any of the best benefices in Iceland. But his thoughts were never bent on secular benefits, and he went back to Copenhagen, never to return. Then his stepfather wrote to him a letter which he ever since remembered with emotion.[1] It concluded: "It is enough; Joseph my son is yet alive" (Genesis 45:28).

In older times it was very usual in Iceland that ordinary people read the Bible and become very familiar with it. Eiríksson had, from the time he was quite young, read his Bible and had already at school got a sort of theological training, to which were now added his studies at the University; he, therefore, grew a very clever exegetist and, as such, was in great demand as a tutor for the young students of theology. Thus he, for several years, was able to gain a fair livelihood by teaching at Copenhagen.

But Eiríksson never felt satisfied with the drudgery of daily life. He always felt the need of some intellectual interests and, by and by, the religious problem became the ruling passion of his life.

II. The Spiritual Atmosphere

Now we must know something about the spiritual atmosphere in Denmark at that time in order to understand Eiríksson's life and strife and his relations to his contemporaries.

Grundtvig (1783-1872), the priest and the poet, and the founder of the Danish "People's High Schools," had already in 1810 and again in 1825 made a great stir in Denmark, first as an orthodox Lutheran, maintaining strict belief in the dogmas, in a personal devil, etc.; but after he had been sentenced for his sharp controversies and after a sort

[1] Letter from Björn Sigurðsson to Magnús Eiríksson, circa 1837.

of conversion, he grew more liberal and his faith a sort of "rejoicing Christianity," especially after he, as he himself expressed it, had made a matchless discovery, that Christ in the time between the resurrection and the ascension must have taught his disciples the "Apostles' Creed" or, as he himself called it, "the little word from the lips of our Lord."[1] You can express his whole trend of thought in the dictum: *Credo quia revelatum,* "I believe because it is revealed."

In 1837, the same year in which Eiríksson had taken his degrees in divinity, a new trend of theological teaching found its way to the University. Hegel became *à la mode.* A young doctor in divinity, *Dr. H.L. Martensen* (1808-84) introduced a sort of Hegelian theology at the University of Copenhagen. It was of a rather poetical and speculative nature and tried to rationalize the dogmas so that he could say, *credo ut intelligam,* "I believe in order to understand." He soon grew a popular lecturer, and all the young theologians began to speculate. But Eiríksson did not like these "speculative theologians," and, expert as he was in the Scripture, he taught students to read and interpret it conscientiously, contrary to the somewhat fantastic interpretations of the favorite lecturer. At last he could not endure the speculations any longer and attacked Dr. Martensen several times, in his first work with great vehemence, later on more moderately and with impressive arguments.

Then there was the religious thinker *Søren Kierkegaard* (1813-55), who about the middle of the 19th-century made a great sensation in Denmark. He too revolted against the teachings of Grundtvig and especially against Martensen. He said: *Credo quia absurdum,* "I believe because I cannot understand." It is the veriest crux for my understanding that God could become a man, but I believe it, and I throw myself into the bottomless abyss of faith like a man throwing himself into a 70,000 fathoms depth of water.

Against all these men Magnús Eiríksson rose and remonstrated with them about their absurdities. As a Viking of old, he steered his war-galley into their midst and slew and struck on both hands, relying on God and his own reason. *Intelligo ut credam,* "I try to understand in order

---

1 See N.F.S Grundtvig, "Kirkelige Oplysninger især for Lutherske Christne," *Nordisk Tidsskrift for christelig Theologi*, ed. by Theodor Wilhelm Oldenburg and Peter Christian Kierkegaard, Copenhagen: P. Chr. Kierkegaard/C.A. Reitzel 1840-42; vol. 1, pp. 1-48, vol. 2, pp. 171-207, vol. 4, pp. 15-42.

to believe," he might have said, "and I believe only such things as I find reasonable and worthy of God. The rest I throw overboard."

Still Eiríksson was for some years too occupied with his teaching to be able to appear in public. It was first when his indignation was *aroused* that he rushed to the battlefield, eager to fight and well armed, although perhaps with somewhat heavy and ponderous weapons.

Our hero waged two wars in his life. The former he made in order to defend a little sect, the Baptists, from persecution; and because Dr. Martensen had raised his voice against them he turned his chief attack upon him and his teachings. This campaign took five years of Eiríksson's life, from 1844 to 1849. Then there came the great silence of his life, with an amiable intermezzo, from 1851 to 1863, during which he conscientiously prepared himself for the great campaign against the church as a *whole* and its teachings. This campaign lasted ten years, from 1863 to 1873.

And what was he fighting for? you will ask. This may be promptly answered: for a pure and untainted Christianity; or to be more distinct: for the teachings, which it was his conviction according to his biblical research, that Christ *himself* had taught, and *against* everything which he thought to be human invention and additions of later date.

III. The First Campaign

About the year 1840, a little sect—the Baptists—made itself conspicuous in Denmark. As soon as they began to protest against having their babies baptized, a good old-fashioned Christian persecution broke out, in which the highest ecclesiastical authorities took the lead against these peaceful people: fines, distraining and arrests followed in rapid succession, and bishops and professors of the University—such as the said Dr. Martensen—came forward as persecutors of the sect as well as advocates of this intolerance. Then it was that Eiríksson could not restrain himself any longer. His indignation reached the boiling point, and he wrote a voluminous book entitled *On the Baptists and Baptism,* published in 1844 at his own expense, as there was no publisher who would risk his reputation and his money in such a dubious enterprise.

With a lack of regard, which only a good cause can justify, he declared that the line of actions, which the ecclesiastical authorities had adopted against these people, was unworthy of the church as well as a witness to its spiritual wretchedness. Would you like, ladies and gentlemen, to hear the words of Magnús Eiríksson himself on this matter?

> To use any other than the intellectual weapons against anybody in the intellectual, particularly the spiritual, domain, shows that the Christian spirit is falsified and spurious in those who do or exhort to do such things; no doubt, an aggressive spiritual contest can be consistent with the supreme Law of Love, but external constraint, oppression, deprivation of property, liberty or life can in no way be compatible with this; he who fights according to the principles of Christian charity will therefore *never, can never* deprive anybody of such things, not even those against whom he has most vehemently fought or will fight with his intellectual weapons. But what a Christian individual will not and cannot do, without breaking the fundamental law of Christianity, neither the church nor a whole community will be able to do without committing the same transgression. Here no proofs will avail to prove the right of the church to external constraint or persecution; a heap of such proofs would only lead to such an absurd conclusion that you should be allowed *to lose sight of the chief purpose*, whence all the subordinate ends obtain their value, in order to realize some of the subordinate ends. When, therefore, the church *in order to be Christian*, transgresses and annihilates as much as possible the Law of Charity, which is the very essence and foundation of the Christian faith, then, I say, it manifestly works *its own destruction as a Christian Commonwealth*; and the more it has been capable of establishing the principle of intolerance and unfriendliness, the more it has already proven that it *is not* a Christian Commonwealth except in name. But, besides that, *the church proves its own impotence in its persecutions* of the sects. If it were conscious of an inner spiritual force, which at least animated the majority of its members, there would be no valid reason for fearing that it should sustain any injury or damage from a small, proportionately insignificant group, unless it should happen to be spiritually stronger; for then you can understand that a spiritually weaker, but materially stronger and more numerous community will use external force, as it has not enough of the spiritual one. The church, therefore, resorting to this line of action,

> proves its own spiritual weakness and wretchedness while it is feigning might and power.[1]

These were his words against the church.

As to the baptism of infants, he came, after a laborious exploration of the New Testament, to the conclusion that infant baptism *was not* apostolic, having been brought into practice later and then accepted by the Church. He therefore maintained the right of the Baptists to retain the apostolic baptism as the only genuine one and to refuse the baptism of their infants, who could not make their own confession. Such a baptism, he said, was also incompatible with the religious conviction and conscience of the adults, and everything which was not in accordance with this might be considered by them a sin.

In the last copious section of the book he attacks the then prevailing conception of baptism and its mystical effects, described as "an immersion into the grace of God" or as "a passing over to a new nature,"[2] etc., but especially Martensen's assertion that "Christ gives himself and the Holy Spirit, whole and undivided, to every child at its baptism,"[3] so that it becomes a kind of "Christophoros" who does not seem to need any further improvement. Still more absurd he found the older conception thereof, that the newly born was possessed by the devil, who should be cast out by the act of baptism.

In the conclusion of his book Eiríksson draws his more broad and general inferences as to the position of the Church and its task in modern life. One of the most remarkable of these is perhaps the one where he insists upon its continued evolution of a freer, more evangelical conception of the dogmas.[4] And another, that it should show tolerance to all dissenters, especially to those who embrace a more evangelical conception. And he closes with these words: "Within the church—if it will be the *Church of Christ*—you should more than in any other

---

1 Bjarnason's note. Magnús Eiríksson, *Om Baptister og Barnedaab, samt flere Momenter af Den kirkelige og speculative Christendom*, Copenhagen: P.G. Philipsen 1844, pp. 19f. (trans. by Ágúst H. Bjarnason).

2 See Hans Lassen Martensen, *Den christelige Daab betragtet med Hensyn paa det baptistiske Spørgsmaal*, Copenhagen: C.A. Reitzel 1843, pp. 57f.

3 Ibid., p. 59.

4 Bjarnason's note. See Eiríksson, *Om Baptister og Barnedaab*, p. 565.

community observe the rule: '*Unity in the essentials, liberty in the dubious* and *charity in all.*'"[1]

Eiríksson's frank and weighty work attracted no small attention. It was honorably mentioned and reviewed in the liberal journals and was not unfavorably received in the more conservative periodicals. But the clergy took care not to mention it with a word. All the more was the influence it had on his own position and way of thinking: it excited his inclination for thoroughgoing, independent investigations, and he resolved to pursue the way, upon which his sense of justice and love of truth had brought him.

But then it would first of all be necessary to examine his own religious conception, and this led him (in 1846) to write a little pamphlet, entitled *Belief, Disbelief and Superstition.*[2] Already here his conception is a liberal one or what he himself describes as a "rational belief," as far from disbelief as from superstition. He describes reason as a sort of incense, giving you the idea of God, the Infinite and the Eternal, in contradistinction to the intellect, which gives you the empirical scientific conception of the outer things, and superstition, which either springs from coarse ignorance or from an unbridled speculative imagination. Reason in connection with the intellect is the only sound basis to build a belief upon, and our author concludes his meditations in the following words:

> Therefore, everybody should honestly and conscientiously use the talents and gifts which God has given him unselfishly and without worldly considerations. He is to "test everything and keep to the good"; have a firm conviction "in his own mind" and "be not the slave of man." How can Christ say these words: "Truth shall make you free,." how can these words have any sense, if Christians are destined to be led by others and believe on account of the beliefs of others and dare not accept or decline anything except that which is accepted or declined by others? Is this *spiritual freedom*? And any other kind of freedom cannot be meant by the Savior.[3]

[1] Bjarnason's note. Ibid., p. 571 (trans. by Ágúst H. Bjarnason).

[2] Magnús Eiríksson, *Tro, Overtro, Vantro, i deres Forhold til Fornuft og Forstand, samt til hinanden indbyrdes,* Copenhagen: H.C. Klein 1846.

[3] Bjarnason's note. Eiríksson, *Tro, Overtro og Vantro*, p. 110 (trans. by Ágúst H. Bjarnason).

Already in this pamphlet Eiríksson begins to keep aloof from Søren Kierkegaard, who had said: *credo quia absurdum*. Eiríksson reproves this and maintains that it will lead to superstition. Still more outspoken is his contempt for the speculative theologians, especially Dr. Martensen, the Hegelian. If you should like to know some of his opinions and Eiríksson's scornful remarks about them, they are as follows.

Dr. Martensen thinks that God, in the beginning, was some sort of an unconscious, physical cause of the world. In order to become conscious of Himself, he was obliged to objectify himself in the Son, His antithesis. Then the Son created the world as an antithesis to Himself in order to vanquish sin. In the end, Father and Son will be united, as a sort of synthesis, in the Holy Spirit as the supreme Unity. To this Eiríksson remarks:

> It is the characteristic conception of the God of these theologians that they make the Godhead's so-called First Person, the Father, pass away into the Second Person of the Trinity, the Son, and Father and Son into the third, the Holy Spirit. Christ, then, seems to have swallowed up the Father, who then—let us be sincere!—after he has *transformed himself* into the Son, *does not exist anymore*, except as a divine essence in the Son, who has succeeded him. This, in short, is Dr. Martensen's concept of the Deity. This is the teaching of the man who wants people to believe that he is an orthodox Christian teacher.[1]

Against such conceptions of the Father and the Son, Eiríksson now entered upon an enraged controversy, in which he combated the whole speculative theology and through which he came to his own simple Unitarian conviction, that God, the Father, was the only God, and the Son and the Spirit only his temporary servants.

We shall not enter into the details of this controversy. Eiríksson spends three volumes and the four following years (1846-1850) on it.[2]

---

1 Bjarnason's note. Ibid., pp. 61f. (trans. by Ágúst H. Bjarnason).

2 Bjarnason's note. The three volumes were *Dr. Martensen's Published Moral Paragraphs* (1846) [*Dr. Martensens trykte moralske Paragrapher, eller det saakaldte "Grundrids til Moralphilosophiens System af Dr. Hans Martensen", i dets forvirrede, idealistisk-metaphysiske og phantastisk-speculative, Religion og Christendom undergravende, fatalistiske, pantheistiske og selvforguderske Væsen*, Copenhagen: H.C. Klein 1846], *Speculative Orthodoxy* (1849) [*Speculativ Rettroenhed, fremstillet efter Dr. Martensens*

Dr. Martensen only replied to his adversary once, just in the beginning. As the mighty and influential man he was, he did not think it necessary to enter upon a discussion with a man he thought inferior to himself and who got his whole livelihood from coaching theology into the young theologians. He could be brought to silence in another way, by depriving him of his pupils. And before long things went so far that no pupil knocked at the door of the once so-much-sought-after tutor, and he was totally bereaved of his former large income. But this did not bring Eiríksson to silence.

Certainly his situation was a miserable one. Because of his generosity and his kind-heartedness towards others, for whom he had endorsed some drafts, he too got into the claws of usurers. And he went so far during his controversy with Martensen that he, in a private application to the King, requested Dr. Martinson's removal from office, at the same time frankly criticizing some of the measures of the government itself. Therefore, he found himself with a public charge on his hands. The Attorney General was ordered to bring an action against him, and all the many friends of Eiríksson thought that he was lost. But he himself, who firmly believed in the righteousness of his cause, was of good cheer, and he wished for the action. But then the King died (in 1848) and the new Sovereign, who was of a more liberal mind, issued a general amnesty, whereby the action against Eiríksson was suspended. About the same time, or some years later, his usurers were arrested, convicted and condemned and his debts to them reduced to no value. You would have deemed our hero lucky to get out of the stipulations so well. Nevertheless, he regretted that the action against him was not decided upon, and it took him almost his *whole* life to pay his debts. And he was now so poor that he was lacking the very necessities of life.

In this desperate situation the Bishop of Iceland, Helgi Thordersen,[1] went to Copenhagen (in 1856) and, when he heard of his compatriot's precarious situation, he kindly proposed to him that he apply for a

"christelige Dogmatik", og Geistlig Retfærdighed, belyst ved en Biskops Deeltagelse i en Generalfiskal-Sag, Copenhagen: Trykt hos J.S. Salomon 1849] and *The Cardinal Virtues of the New Danish Theology* (1850) [*Den nydanske Theologies Cardinaldyder belyste ved Hjelp af Dr. Martensens Skrifter samt Modskrifterne, tilligemed 75 theologiske Spørgsmaal, rettede til Dr. H. Martensen*, Copenhagen: Chr. Steen & Søn 1850].

[1] Helgi Thordersen (1794-1867).

benefice in Iceland. His conception of baptism would not disqualify him for this—and he was not known until then to have uttered any other heterodox opinions. Eiríksson applied for and got one of the best benefices in his native country. But a few days later he applied for a release from this office, as he thought he was not qualified to enter the church.—What was the matter?

Eiríksson had gone through a moral crisis. Conscientious as he was, he saw that he already had gone so far in his criticism of the Christian dogmas that it would not beseem him to become a servant of the Church. On the contrary, if he wished to see this very church reformed, he ought to continue his criticism and express the whole truth. Now his opinions had long since, through the study of the Bible and his own meditations, grown so radical, that he for twelve whole years (1851-1863) hesitated in making them public.

IV. An Intermezzo

Ladies and gentlemen, in the great silence of his life—in the dead calm before the tempest, in which Eiríksson was making up his mind for his long decisive battle—there was a little amiable intermezzo, of which I am now going to tell you.

In 1850 a Danish lady, Miss M.L. Fibiger,[1] whose *nom de plume* was Clara Raphael, wrote *Twelve Letters* about the subjection and emancipation of women,[2] which letters were much debated and combated by men of distinction. With his *Letters to Clara Raphael* by "Theodor Immanuel," from 1851,[3] Eiríksson became her chief champion, chivalrous and liberal as he was. He uses similar arguments to those that John Stuart Mill used eighteen years later in his *Subjection of Women*.[4]

Clara Raphael began her letters by postulating that men usually have a higher aim of life, tending to liberty, humanity and unity. This

---

[1] Mathilde Lucie Fibiger (1830-72).

[2] Mathilde Fibiger, *Clara Raphael. Tolv Breve*, ed. by Johan Ludvig Heiberg, Copenhagen: C.A. Reitzel 1851.

[3] [Theodor Immanuel], *Breve til Clara Raphael*, Copenhagen: C.A. Reitzel 1851.

[4] John Stuart Mill, *The Subjection of Women*, London: Longmans, Green, Reader and Dyer 1869.

Eiríksson, after mustering the different classes of men, does not admit, contending that they usually pursued narrow selfish aims and thus were in need of emancipation themselves. There were only a few extraordinary personalities in each generation who showed themselves willing and disinterested enough to fight for the higher universal aims of life.

As for women, they were no doubt in possession of essentially the same mental faculties as men; they possessed reason, sentiments and will. The only question is whether women have received an equal opportunity to develop their abilities. This they had not, since they usually live their whole life within the narrow limits of domestic circles, but if they had the same opportunity as men to develop their faculties, you would have a conclusive proof of their equality or their disparity to men.

Beforehand you only can say as much as this, that when girls get the same intellectual training as boys, they show themselves as able and often possess a quicker and sounder judgment than boys. Their feelings are usually more delicate and often more impulsive, more unreflected, whereby women should be particularly fitted to promote the evolution of life.

But, it is said, they usually have no will or a weaker one than man, or they have ten desires for one, for which reason the woman's will is most fickle. But give her a sound intellectual and moral basis to build will upon, and she will show as much fidelity to her ideals as any man, and even more, as the life of Joan of Arc and other great women shows.

After mentioning the significant part women play in domestic and public life in the new world—especially in the United States—our author maintains that women should be admitted to the universities and allowed to become ministers, judges and especially doctors and, on the whole, be allowed "to play their part in the world development" and attain their own ideal of perfection.[1]

There was a mental kinship between Clara Raphael and Theodor Immanuel, and therefore it is no wonder that he already, in his second letter, addresses her as his sister. Their religious conceptions were very much akin. Miss Raphael had in her letters had a great deal to remark about baptism, Original Sin, the Atonement, the Trinity and the Divinity

[1] Magnús Eiríksson, *Breve til Clara Raphael*, Copenhagen: C.A. Reitzel 1851, page reference unknown.

of Christ. Her relation to God was a childlike confidence in him, and her confession ran as follows: "I have never had the feeling that there was any need for a mediator between God and me."[1]—"There is one God, the father of all; I cannot think he is divided into three. I believe in the holy Unity, not in the holy Trinity."[2]

If I am not much mistaken, I should think that just such utterings of Clara Raphael brought our hero to take up the cudgels for her. He heartily subscribes to all her opinions and undertakes to prove them singly. He lays special stress on the fact that Christ never designated himself nor behaved as God, but only as a son (a child) of God with just the same confidence and humility towards God his Father as any other religious mortal. And his conception of God's fatherliness and mercy, his message to the world in regard to the love of God, was just to be found in the parable of the prodigal son. Repentance, conversion and the bettering of life is the way to God's forgiveness, and it is God's charity, not his righteousness, which is the core of Christ's message. Jesus was a son of God, a God-sent man like the prophets; his life and his message is just the supreme [example of] the highest gospel of God the Father. Jesus is only God's emissary and, if you like, the Lord's anointed, His Messiah. Thus was the prelude to the great religious fugue, begun in 1863 but now, in the year 1851, only fluted in an amiable low voice by Eiríksson, under the disguise of the God-sent Theodore Immanuel.

V. The Great Quest

Above the altar in Our Lady's Church in Copenhagen there is a sublime statue of Christ, made by our countrymen Albert [that is, Bertel] Thorvaldsen,[3] expressing the words: "Come to me all ye who are laden with sorrow, I will give you rest." Eiríksson, who was so religious, no doubt often admired this work of art and its mild, charitable expression. But like most religious geniuses, he had a mystic vein, and he certainly more than once felt that this place above the altar was reserved only for the most High—God Himself.

---

[1] Ibid.
[2] Ibid.
[3] Bertel Thorvaldsen (1770-1844).

In 1844 and again in 1845, Eiríksson had a dream, which he relates as follows: "It seemed to me that I was in Our Lady's Church, where there were only a few people besides me. I was near the altar, facing it. Then I became aware of an enormous pillar to the left of the altar....It reached to the dome of the church and seemed abutted to it. Astonished I gazed at the pillar, for I remembered quite well that I had never seen it there before. But while I am standing there and gazing at the pillar, it becomes detached from the dome, grows lower and lower, and, when it was not more than 2 to 3 yards in height, it becomes transformed into a human figure, and then I see that this figure is the same image of Christ as is standing above the altar in Our Lady's Church (and at the same time I observed that the statue was not there)....Now this white marble figure moves, walks a few paces along the floor, then turns round so as to face the altar...and lies down, face forward, two to three yards in front of the altar."[1]

This dream Eiríksson dreamt in the month of July 1844, but about thirteen months later he dreamt the same dream with the following addition: "As the figure of Christ walked along the floor and turned round to the altar and knelt, I heard a voice (but saw no one) saying to me: 'The pillar, you see, denotes the prodigy that the Church has made of Christ. He himself wants to show you that he worships God, but no one who worships God is God.'"[2]

The modern interpretation of this dream would be that Eiríksson had repressed his skeptical thoughts to the subconscious; but now through a sort of upheaval they broke loose from his subconscious in this vision, which he himself took as a hint from Christ for the right conception of him. This dream vision no doubt had great influence on Eiríksson's *whole* way of thinking during the following years, for he believed in dreams, and it at last brought him straight to the Unitarian standpoint. This standpoint he had, as we have already seen, reached in his letters to Miss Raphael in 1857; but there were still two great obstacles in the Holy Scripture itself against this conception, to wit the Gospel of St. John and the doctrine of St. Paul, and, as you remember, none of the recognized Reformers had, in their quest for the true message of Christ,

[1] Hafsteinn Pjetursson, "Magnús Eiríksson," *Teologisk Tidsskrift for den danske Folkekirke*, Ny Række, vol. 3, 1901-1902, pp. 116-143; here pp. 129f.

[2] Ibid., p. 130.

reached beyond these two venerated spur-posts of the Church. Now Eiríksson himself undertook the hard task of undermining by a patient thoroughgoing criticism these two spur-posts in order to get to the very fountain of the Christian message.

Suffering wants and privations and sacrificing all his future prospects, but with full confidence in God, he sits year after year in his garret—in Hotel Stadt Hamburg in Copenhagen—bent over the scripture and his theological books and patiently works his way through the theological jungle of the centuries in the firm assurance that he someday or other shall reach the lighted fountain of unsophisticated Christianity.

Eiríksson began his quest by asking which of his contemporaries was nearest to the truth, his old adversary, Dr. Martensen, who had now become the primate of the Danish Church, or Grundtvig, the old Lutheran, who now was going even farther back in his faith than Luther. This is discussed in a little pamphlet from 1863, entitled *Who is Right*?[1] The answer runs: Neither is right, neither Dr. Martensen nor Grundtvig. Bishop Dr. Martensen maintains that the Christian truths have been evolving in the Christian church from the Apostles' Creed through the Nicene Creed into the Athanasian Creed; while Grundtvig thought that the Apostles' Creed was "the living word from the lips of our Lord himself."[2] Eiríksson strictly denied both these assertions. Against Bishop Martensen he maintained that the faith had been deteriorating from the days of the Apostles downward. The worst of the creeds is the Athanasian, treating of the two natures of Christ, the next worst the Nicene, making a God of Christ, the best is the Apostles' Creed, describing Jesus only as Messiah. Thus Grundtvig is nearer to the truth. And yet this creed is by no means "the word from the lips of the Lord himself," no more than the words on the baptism, which have been interpolated later into the texts (Matthew 28:19-20, Mark 16:15). Christ's own teachings, Christianity pure and simple, were to be found in the first three Gospels, especially in the parable of the prodigal son, and Christ did not demand any creed, only the love of God and your neighbor. Therefore, study what you deem to be Christ's own teachings and omit all other additions.

---

[1] Magnús Eiríksson, *Hvem har Ret: Grundtvigianerne eller deres Modstandere? og Hvad har Christus befalet om Daaben? Nogle orienterende Bemærkninger*, Copenhagen: E.L. Thaarup 1863.

[2] See p. 302 above, note 1.

Eiríksson had always valued the Holy Scripture highly; although he did not consider it an inspired book, it was the sole tradition on which the Christian Church could build. But there were, as he thought, incommensurable things in the Bible, not only in the Old but also in the New Testament, and therefore the Bible had to be subjected to a thoroughgoing conscientious criticism, and this Eiríksson now, in all his poverty and tribulations, resolved to undertake.

This criticism he laid down in four books, published between 1863 and 1873: *The Gospel of St. John, God and the Reformer, St. Paul and Christ,* and *Jews and Christians.*[1] Of the four books we have especially to do with two—*The Gospel of St. John* and *St. Paul and Christ*—because they include Eiríksson's criticism of his main stumbling blocks. In this criticism he not only seeks to resolve all manifest contradictions by the standard laid down in the first three synoptic Gospels, containing as he thought Christ's real teachings, but he also uses his own highly developed religious feeling as a touchstone, contending that there is no God but one, the Most High, or to use the words of Christ himself: "There is none good but one, that is, God."[2]

Eiríksson's weighty treatise on the Gospel of St. John (1863) contains a vigorous criticism of the same. As everybody knows, Christ in this gospel is identified with the Greek *Logos*, a sort of Godhead, a second God, emanating in the very beginning of time from the Supreme, creating and maintaining the world and, in the fullness of time, incarnated in Jesus Christ for the redemption of the world. Thus Christ should be the incarnate *Logos*. And this Gospel is said to be written by the beloved disciple of Jesus, who had rested at his master's breast.

---

[1] Magnús Eiríksson, *Er Johannes-Evangeliet et apostolisk og ægte Evangelium og er dets Lære om Guds Menneskevorden en sand og christelig Lære? En religiøs-dogmatisk, historisk-kritisk Undersøgelse*, Copenhagen: Magnús Eiríksson 1863; *Gud og Reformatoren. En religiøs Idee. Samt nogle Bemærkninger om de kirkelige Tilstande, Dr. S. Kierkegaard og Forfatteren*, Copenhagen: J.H. Schubothe 1866; *Paulus og Christus eller Pauli Lære om Retfærdiggjørelsen sammenlignet med Christi Lære om Syndsforladelsen, tilligemed nogle Bemærkninger om andre paulinske Lærdomme m. M.*, Copenhagen: Magnús Eiríksson 1871; *Jøder og Christne eller Hvorledes blev Jesus fra Nazareth betragtet i den ældste Kirke og hvorledes blev han senere betragtet? En populær, historisk-kritisk Undersøgelse, tilegnet de Sandhedskjærlige*, Copenhagen: Magnús Eiríksson 1873.

[2] Matthew 19:17, Mark 10:18, Luke 18:19.

Now Eiríksson shows by a host of facts that this gospel cannot have been written by a Palestinian Jew and still less by St. John, the beloved disciple. His arguments are chiefly the following: (1) The Evangelist ascribes to Christ, John the Baptist and the Jews opinions and words which they cannot have expressed. (2) The sermons of Christ, which are related in this Gospel and he is said to have held, stand in such marked contrast to the teachings and parables in the first three Gospels that they seem to have been held by a quite different person. (3) Christ's last sermons in this Gospel stand in absolute *contrast* to the description of his suffering in Gethsemane, as it is related in the Synoptic Gospels. And (4) even his passion is related in quite another way: Christ's own merits are emphasized by Christ himself, and the name of God is not mentioned, not even in the last words of the cross. Then we have the dogmatic improbabilities, such as (5) that Christ is able to resurrect himself from the dead, (6) that the love of our fellow men in the love of our enemies is not mentioned throughout the whole Gospel. (7) The narration of the call of the disciples is highly fantastic and improbable, as the presumed author does not mention his own brother, and (8) the miracles related are of the most extraordinary kind. Lastly, it is a historical fact that (9) the disciples of St. John did not know anything about this Gospel seventy to ninety years after it is alleged to have been written. And finally (10), this Gospel so abounds with errors and mistakes about the Jews in the Jewish mode of living that it seems an impossibility that it was written by a Palestinian Jew. Still less can we for a moment assume that it was written by St. John, son of Zebedee. It seems to have been written by a Gnostic Christian in the middle of the 2nd century of our era.

The image of Christ, which this gospel gives us, is wholly different from the image of the first three Gospels: the Christ of the fourth Gospel is constantly glorifying himself, while the Christ of the first three Gospels is constantly emphasizing the love of God and the love of men towards each other. The fourth gospel therefore must be said to be unworthy of Jesus Christ, such as he and his teachings have been described in the Synoptic Gospels, and it gives us a glorified but nevertheless a distorted image of Christ in his teachings. In reality it is a dogmatic statement of the Godhead of Christ, nowhere warranted in the first three Gospels, where Christ only calls himself the Son of

Man and he is at most designated as the Lord's anointed or Messiah, he himself constantly venerating God the Father, the Most High, even with the last words on the cross. The Gospel of St. John is, therefore, neither historically nor dogmatically to be regarded as a genuine source of Christian faith.

This *weighty* criticism was received with silence in Denmark, with scorn in Iceland, but honorably mentioned in Sweden, where a clergyman, the Reverend Pastor Ekdahl in Stockholm,[1] translated his book into Swedish and where our author ever since had a sort of sympathetic stronghold, while he in Denmark was killed by silence.

In his next work, *God and the Reformer: A Religious Idea* (1866), where our author expresses his admiration for Theodore Parker, he maintains that a founder of a religion or a reformer has only to shape the right conception of God and to establish a direct relation of childlike confidence between man and God, even as Jesus Christ so admirably did. But the reformer and his followers should beware of placing him between man and God, for that would only lead to the distortion of religion. This the apostles, especially St. Paul, have done with Christ, and the Gospel of St. John has even deified him, the Church finishing the work by establishing the dogma of Trinity, so that God the Father has passed into the background. The gospel of Jesus is thereby transformed into the faith in Christ. This placing of a mediator between man and God and making a second God of the mediator annihilates man's direct connection with God. And thus deifying a reformer, even if he be as good and sinless as Jesus Christ himself, is a sort of serpentine theology, practicing to the uttermost the precept, *Eritis sicut deus.*—It is a sort of religious crime and even this the Christian Church has committed.

St. Paul does not go so far; he only regards Christ as "the Lord from Heaven" (1 Corinthians 15:17) and as the Redeemer. But even St. Paul's doctrine of reconciliation has distorted the idea of God and cast the teachings of Jesus into the shadow. St. Paul is the real founder of Christian Faith, but thereby he has overshadowed and injured the teachings of Jesus. This assertion our author has tried to prove in his chief work, *St. Paul and Christ* (1871), which may be regarded as his chief criticism of the "historic-dogmatic Christian religion."

---

1 Nils Johan Ekdahl (1799-1870).

Our author thinks that the core of Christ's own teachings is to be found in the parable of the prodigal son (Luke 15), that the relation of man to God is as that of a son to his loving father; and if the son, as in the parable, sins and becomes guilty, he has only to repent, better his life, go to his father and confess his sins, and the loving father will take him in his arms and rejoice that a son who was lost is found again. Thus Jesus himself describes man's relation to God, and God as the loving, compassionate father of all men, and he does not demand any ransom or atonement for their sins.

But how unlike this simple teaching is not the doctrine of St. Paul, who maintains that men because of the sin of Adam are quite lost and become the children of wrath and can only be redeemed and made righteous through the blood and death of Christ, whom God himself has sent to reconcile man with Him, that His righteousness may be satisfied!

This is just the old doctrine of sacrifice in a new guise. This is the old God of wrath and anger, and not the loving Father of Christ. And what a "righteous" God to make a guiltless man a victim for the sins of others! And such morality! How can men be made better through the sufferings of another? And how can faith alone make men better, if they do not repent their sins and better their own lives?—All this doctrine is so immoral and so far from Christ's own that one cannot but wonder that the Church has been able to maintain it so long.

But by far the worst drawback of this faith is the fact that it places Christ himself between God and man and demands the belief in him and his crucifixion as essential to salvation. Instead of the direct relation to God as the loving Father in the parable, you have to believe in Christ, his crucifixion and resurrection in order to be sure of your own salvation. But are you then, according to St. Paul's teachings, sure of your own salvation?

The core of St. Paul's teachings is to be found in these words of his: "For I determined not to know anything among you, save Jesus Christ, and him crucified" (1 Corinthians 2:2). How can this enhance our own hope of resurrection? Let us admit that Christ himself did rise from the dead, how can this help us?—St. Paul himself teaches that he who is sinless lives and that death is the consequence of sin. Now Christ was sinless, and therefore he may have been able to rise from the dead. But we are sinful, and therefore we cannot rise from the dead. You say that

Christ's atonement has made us sinless? That is an absurdity: how can another's blood and death make us sinless?! But if you are sinful, you have to die, according to St. Paul's own teachings. Therefore, the death and resurrection of Christ does not afford you any hope of your own resurrection.

So St. Paul gainsays himself in his own teachings. But besides that, his teaching is as irreligious as it is immoral. It is irreligious to teach the incessant wrath of God because of the First Sin. And it is immoral to teach that another's death can make you better, if you only believe in his atonement. Lastly, it is no real atonement for the sins of men that God himself sent his Son to atone for them. It is a mock performance! A real sacrifice and atonement for the sins of men should come from themselves. It makes them neither better nor more righteous that God sends them the sacrifice, which is to satisfy his own sense of justice. And, what "sense of justice," to make an innocent victim suffer for the sins of men!

No, let us abandon all this theology, so unworthy of God, the gracious Father of the parable, and go back to the admirable and simple teachings of Christ himself about God, the loving Father of all men, and let us believe that repentance and moral improvement is the only and direct way to our salvation. Let us, instead of teaching our children Pauline or other theology, teach them the simple, elevating Gospel of Christ himself, such as it is revealed in his own parables and his loving life. For it is not faith nor hope, but only unfailing charity, which will bring us unto God our Father.

VI. The Climax

In 1871, our poet laureate, Matthías Jochumsson,[1] who died much regretted in the autumn of 1920, went from England to Copenhagen, and the very first of his countrymen he met there was—Magnús Eiríksson. He [that is, Magnús Eiríksson] told him [that is, Matthías Jochumsson] that the fourth Scandinavian church conference was just then being held in the festival hall of the University; this was the second day and *the*

[1] Matthías Jochumsson (1835-1920).

new rationalism was to be debated; there was a great stir, and he himself intended to speak. Our beloved poet got a ticket to the conference, and now let he himself relate what he witnessed:

> The hall was overcrowded, mostly by Danes, but there were also many noted men, laymen and scholars from Norway and from Sweden. Dr. Kalkar,[1] a renowned Christian Jew, was in the chair, alternating with Professor F. Hammerich.[2] There I saw the learned excellent author, Bishop Martensen, and old Grundtvig; this gigantic old man attracted my attention; he was then eighty-five [that is, eighty-eight] years old, bent with age, still in a way the imposing [figure]. He was the first to speak. As this Nestor of the North walked supported to the pulpit, I felt touched, and it seemed to one as if he bore a whole century and the joys and sorrows, wisdom and folly of a whole nation on his shoulders. His voice sounded as if coming out of a mound, so dull and low. He said he had not expected to hear that rationalism was again the order of the day: "I did not know better," he said, "than that I had made away with that hobgoblin sixty years ago." He had nothing else remarkable to say and was then helped to his seat; but what he said was greatly applauded. (Here I wish to remark that the following winter I never neglected any opportunity to attend Grundtvig's church, for his imposing appearance had long before won my admiration, in spite of his antiquated language, poetry and doctrines. But more of him later.)
>
> Next to Grundtvig, Magnús Eiríksson mounted the pulpit and commenced speaking. He began by saying that it was now inevitable to investigate the origin and the authority of the old doctrines of the church and begin with the Apostles' Creed, which could not be proved to date from the days of the Apostles; the so-called symbolic books from the time of the Reformation were much less to be tolerated; he said it was the duty of every teacher of dogmatics and especially the duty of such a select meeting to investigate and to explain their own sources and those of others for everything which was taught as a matter of salvation; the synoptic gospels, which might be regarded as the best historical records of Jesus and his teachings, required special investigation. The speaker said that he had long felt convinced that an unusual amount of dust had from one

[1] Christian Andreas Herman Kalkar (1802-86).
[2] Peter Frederik Adolph Hammerich (1809-77).

century to another fallen on all the traditions of the Church, from the time of the oldest and most simple Christianity downwards.

Already at the beginning of Eiríksson's brave and eloquent speech, there was a stir and uneasiness among the assembly and the tumult increased so that at last not a word was to be heard, the chairman, ringing the bell and shouting loudly, asked the speaker to confine himself to the order of the day, as such investigations were far away from the subjects to be discussed here. (Shouts in the hall): "Down with the speaker!" (and others cried): "We know in whom we believe!" But Eiríksson did not flinch; and when there was a short silence he tried to go on: "The teachings of Jesus have been put under a bushel—that is shown and proved by history—the confessions of the Church are works of man!" (Enormous shouts.) Now Eiríksson called out and received a hearing: "Even if it was at the price of my eternal salvation, I cannot hush the voice of my conscience and conviction!"—more of what he said was not to be heard on account of the shouts and the ringing of the bell. Still Eiríksson stood in the pulpit. I became excited and recollected the words of my poem on Luther: "And the crowd stared in awe; / They shuddered at his daring / In defending life and light / With vigorous faith and might."

It is not every day that one listens to great spirits. I had listened to the great speech of our national hero, President Jón Sigurðsson,[1] in 1867, when all the members of the House were awed by his boldness, and his chief adversary cried: "I wish such a man to live eternally!" Thus I felt now at the conduct and demeanor of Eiríksson—this childlike, modest and poor man, my only countryman in this great university hall, filled with all the most noted members of the Scandinavian clergy. Yes, I became excited and I thought of our president and Luther: "Alone he stood against all / In the awe-inspiring hall; / Alone he rushed against all / To the triumphant of the soul."—"God be praised," I thought, "the Icelandic spirit is not yet extinct." But now to the end of my story:

After a great clamor there was a short silence and Eiríksson, who still stood in the pulpit, lifted up his hands and cried: "As I get no hearing, I cry to Thee in my distress, Thou eternal Father of All, who holds out Thy hand all day over the stubborn people." I've forgotten the words of his prayer, save these, but the contents were a heartfelt prayer to God to forgive the

---

[1] Jón Sigurðsson (1811-79).

> Church its sleep, its lacking love of truth and courage in its faith: "Let the servants of Thy Word seek truth without dissimulation, that it may make them free—free and willing to follow the example of Thy holy and modest servant, Jesus."
>
> (Note: Moreover, I find these words written down from Eiríksson's prayer: "Heavenly Father, to Thee I commit my heart's cause; let it come to Thy ears and judge my heart and mind.…If I have conscientiously testified to the truth, be my spokesman and lead these people to the recognition of truth!")
>
> During this prayer there was a dead silence in the hall, and the women began to weep, and I saw that some of those who stood nearest to me were deeply touched and others trembled. And as Eiríksson descended from the pulpit, some of the prelates tried to speak to him, and one of them embraced him weeping in the throng, and I heard him say: "Let me embrace you! Your candor and frankness overwhelms me, and yet Jesus, my redeemer, has never been more precious to me than while you denied him thrice!" This clergyman was Sven Brun,[1] a tall and imposing Norwegian; he had preached that morning in Our Lady's Church and was evidently of an impetuous temper and ardent in the old-fashioned way. But Magnús Eiríksson answered neither him nor anyone else, but hurried out of the hall and never came to this church conference again.[2]

Thus he, the real defender of pure Christianity, was drowned out by the multitude, at the same time as he excited the fear and gained the respect of his adversaries. But he did not yield. In the following years he wrote his last great work, *Jews and Christians*,[3] published in 1873, a history of the evolution of the Christian dogmas in the first three Christian centuries to the time of the Church Council at Nicaea in 325, where the dogma of the Trinity was finally settled.

The Christian Jew, Dr. Kalkar, who had been the president of the conference in Copenhagen had, in 1868, written a sort of apology for

---

1 Sven Brun (1812-94).

2 Bjarnason's note. Matthías Jochumsson, "Dvöl mín í Danmörku 1871-1872," *Iðunn*, vol. 1, 1916, no. 3 (January), pp. 258ff. (trans. by Ágúst H. Bjarnason).

3 Magnús Eiríksson, *Jøder og Christne eller Hvorledes blev Jesus fra Nazareth betragtet i den ældste Kirke og hvorledes blev han senere betragtet? En populær, historisk-kritisk Undersøgelse, tilegnet de Sandhedskjærlige*, Copenhagen: Magnús Eiríksson 1873.

the Christian Church, entitled: *The Mission among the Jews.*[1] Prompted by this book, Eiríksson took the occasion to show that it was the Jewish Christians, who, in the first two centuries, had maintained the essential teachings of Christ and pure Christianity, believing in him as the expected Messiah, but neither as *Logos* nor as God. It was the Gospel of St. John, written in the middle of the 2nd century, which originated the heathen *Logos* doctrine, distorted the original Christianity, and finally, by the imperative command of Constantine the Great, brought about the resolution that Christ was a real God, similar to God the Father, and that the Godhead was a Trinity. With the assistance of the Tübingen School, whose scientific results Eiríksson now made use of for the first and last time, he strictly demonstrated that (1) the Jewish Christians only believed in Jesus as Messiah; (2) the doctrine of the *Logos* first came forward in the middle of the 2nd century; (3) at the end of that century and throughout the whole 3rd century there came a period of transition, in which so-called Monarchians and Subordinatians quarreled about the nature of Christ; until (4), the Arian doctrine was finally subdued at Nicaea in 325 and the dogma of Trinity accepted.

Nobody had anything to remark to this strict historical proof, and our hero had reason to think that silence meant consent. But—oh, no!—he himself was silently branded as a heretic, the man who all his life had fought for the reformation of the Church and tried to bring it back to Christ's own teachings. And so hard was the sentence that he, one of the best educated men of his time, could not obtain a teaching post at a public school, unless he was willing to abjure all his "heresies." But Eiríksson was too proud a man for that, and he preferred to starve in his old age. Then some friends of his provided him with a small annuity, on which he, with his great thrift, could live. To this the Government of Denmark added $100 a year the last two years of his life, as "an acknowledgement for his unselfish and idealistic strivings";[2] but fortunately for him, he did not need this "gratuity" too long. He died in 1881, the third of July, "a child of light" in birth and death.

Like all prophets, Eiríksson has got his monument in the following generation, at the same time as it was killing its own. And now he is

---

[1] Christian Andreas Hermann Kalkar, *Missionen iblandt Jøderne*, Copenhagen: O.H. Delbanco 1868.

[2] No reference available.

acknowledged as one of the most clear-minded and by far the most voracious man of his time. And we Icelanders, his compatriots, ought to be proud of him. For it is so seldom that one of the smallest nations in the world has a son who, so heroically through his whole life, bears witness to the truth and brings all the noted men of a larger nation to silence. For it is not the case that they would not refute him, they simply—*could not*!

Therefore, Eiríksson will stand as a luminous model for all lovers of truth, and he will be one of the pillars, if not the "tried stone," the "precious cornerstone," "the stone which the builders rejected" in the final building of God.

A Man of Polemics and Principles: The Reception of Magnús Eiríksson in Iceland

Vilhjálmur Árnason and Jón Bragi Pálsson

Magnús Eiríksson was twenty-five years old when he went to Denmark for his University studies. He lived there for fifty years and never returned to Iceland. Although he had a quite remarkable intellectual career in Denmark, the history of the reception of his works in Iceland is rather poor. In this article we have divided this history into eight main periods. The first period spans the first thirty years (1831-63) of Eiríksson's stay in Denmark which were colorful but largely went unnoticed in Iceland. Several sources, however, tell about his interaction with his countrymen in Denmark. The second period covers the next five years (1864-69) which was characterized by fierce and hostile reactions in Iceland to Eiríksson's book on the Gospel of John. The third period is the last decade of his life (1870-80) which was uneventful from our point of view, culminating in news about celebration of his seventieth birthday in Copenhagen. In the fourth period (1881-90) a very critical article about Eiríksson's work by Hafsteinn Pjetursson is in focus, while in the fifth period (1890-1930) he gains special attention from Unitarians, and two prominent Icelanders, the minister and poet Matthías Jochumsson and the professor of philosophy and psychology Ágúst H. Bjarnason, write favorably about him. In the sixth period (1930-40) a doctoral thesis about Eiríksson's work is defended at the University of Iceland and is widely discussed. After this there was a long period of silence (1940-97), which was followed in the eighth and last period by a renewed interest where Eiríksson's intellectual contribution, both to theology and to the battle for the rights of women, seems finally to be recognized as it deserves.

I. The First Years: Studies in Denmark and Disputes with the Danes (1831-63)

In this first section we discuss the period between 1831, when Eiríksson started his studies in Copenhagen, and 1863, when he published his book *The Gospel of John*. Even though Eiríksson's intellectual life was rather eventful, very little is written about him in Iceland during these years. This period was characterized by difficulties and struggles. He defended a group of Baptists which were persecuted by the Danish church at the time. He thought that this attack on the Baptists was unfair and unchristian, and he wrote a book in their defense.[1] He also undertook a fierce polemic against a major religious thinker in Denmark, Hans Lassen Martensen, whose religious doctrines were highly popular in Denmark at the time. Martensen's theology was based on Hegelian philosophy which Eiríksson opposed relentlessly, and the bulk of his writings in the period 1844-50 consisted of writings against Martensen. He even wrote a letter to the Danish king where he demanded that Martensen be dismissed from his post for heresy. This affair turned into a prosecution against Eiríksson, but luckily for him a new and more liberal king came to power in Denmark and decided to disallow the case.[2] Last but not least, Eiríksson wrote against the views of Søren Kierkegaard and criticized him for his concept of faith as "by virtue of the absurd," annulling the role of reason which Eiríksson regarded as the basis of true faith.[3]

All of this should have been a reason for awakening interest in Iceland about this vigilant man, but very little appeared in public about Eiríksson during this period. The single exception was a short article in

1 Magnús Eiríksson, *Om Baptister og Barnedaab, samt flere Momenter af Den kirkelige og speculative Christendom*, Copenhagen: P.G. Philipsen 1844. This was later discussed by Ágúst H. Bjarnason in his article, "Um Magnús Eiríksson," *Skírnir*, vol. 98, 1924, pp. 39-73; see pp. 47f.

2 Gerhard Schreiber, "Magnús Eiríksson—Vanræktur samtímamaður Sørens Kierkegaard," trans. by Aðalsteinn Garðarsson, *Skírnir*, vol. 188, 2014, pp. 116-43; see p. 117; see Bjarnason, "Um Magnús Eiríksson," p. 58.

3 Magnús Eiríksson [Theophilus Nicolaus], *Er Troen et Paradox og "i Kraft af det Absurde"? et Spørgsmaal foranlediget ved "Frygt og Bæven, af Johannes de silentio", besvaret ved Hjelp af en Troes-Ridders fortrolige Meddelelser, til fælles Opbyggelse for Jøder, Christne og Muhamedanere, af bemeldte Troes-Ridders Broder*, Copenhagen: Chr. Steen & Søn 1850. On this see Schreiber, "Magnús Eiríksson," p. 134.

Skírnir, News of the Icelandic Literary Society, describing his defense of the Baptists and his criticism of Martensen.[1] In this period, *Skírnir* brought news from Denmark to Iceland. By contrast, Icelanders in Copenhagen showed interest in Eiríksson's affairs and were generally supportive of him. In 1844, the poet and public official, Grímur Thomsen (1820-96), wrote a short piece to support him in the Baptist dispute.[2] A letter dated 1844 from Jón Sigurðsson (1811-79) to Páll Melsteð (1791-1861), a regional leader in Iceland (*amtmaður*), shows that Sigurðsson admired Eiríksson for his campaign.[3] Sigurðsson writes: "Our brother, Magnús Eiríksson, is fighting for God's Christianity, but the wretched watchdogs of Christianity in Denmark neither bark nor bay as Magnús has knocked them out. I hope that you obtain the book by Magnús, especially if you are going to be a clergyman."[4] Sigurðsson is probably referring to Eiríksson's book *On Baptists and Infant Baptism* (1844) and to the fact that the clergy in Denmark ignored it and never responded to it in print.[5]

Jón Sigurðsson was a *primus inter pares* among Icelanders in Copenhagen and the leader in the battle of independence from Denmark. Icelanders met regularly in his house, and Eiríksson was a popular companion. He was referred to as "Magnús frater" because he was like a loving brother to his fellowmen and greeted them as "frater."[6] According to Benedikt Gröndal (1826-1907), who was studying in Copenhagen around 1847-50, Eiríksson "was loved by everyone, both Danes and Icelanders."[7] He is said to have been "a heavy eater and merrymaker,"[8] an aesthete who was fond of singing and played the guitar.[9] These laudatory character descriptions were not available to Icelanders until 1914 when

1 Anonymous, "Frá Norðurlöndum. 1. Frá Dönum," *Skírnir*, vol. 21, 1847, pp. 144-60.

2 Grímur Thomsen [anonymous], *En Privatskrivelse til den anden gamle Landsbypræst, fra hans gamle Ven, den første gamle Candidat, som Commentar over Herr Pastors Epistola til Sr. Magnus Eiriksson*, Copenhagen: P.G. Philipsen 1844.

3 Jón Sigurðsson, obtained from R.P., [No title], *Heimir*, vol. 8, 1912, no. 9 (May 1), pp. 205-07.

4 Ibid., p. 206.

5 Eiríkur Albertsson, *Magnús Eiríksson. Guðfræði hans og trúarlíf*, Doctoral Dissertation, Háskóli Íslands, Reykjavik 1938, p. 65.

6 Páll Valsson, *Jónas Hallgrímsson: Ævisaga*, Reykjavík: Mál og Menning 1999, p. 34.

7 Benedikt Gröndal, *Dægradvöl*, Reykjavík: Forlagið 2014, p. 199.

8 Valsson, *Jónas Hallgrímsson*, p. 395.

9 Gröndal, *Dægradvöl*, p. 200; see also Albertsson, *Magnús Eiríksson*, p. 134.

Gröndal's posthumous memoirs were first published. Even stronger praise of Eiríksson was written by Matthías Jochumsson (1835-1920) in an autobiography (posthumously published 1922): "he was sheer goodness and piety and as a holy man in disguise among the secularists, whom he ate and drank with, as the lord long ago..., and was always glad and just as entertaining as he was learned and knowledgeable."[1]

Eiríksson is reported to have been generous to his countrymen when they needed assistance, but after the debate with Martensen it became difficult for him to provide for himself. His friends and relatives tried to persuade him to apply for a parish in Iceland so as to gain financial security and make practical use of his theological education. Already in 1839 he was offered a good parish in East Iceland after his brother had applied for it in his name without asking Eiríksson, who refused to take the offer.[2] But in 1856 he agreed to apply for a prosperous parish in Iceland, not least of all due to the incentive of Helgi Guðmundsson Thordersen (1794-1867), Bishop of Iceland 1846-66. The Bishop had been in Copenhagen in 1855-56 and become aware of the financial difficulties that Eiríksson was in. Eiríksson was offered the parish, but he declined at the last minute, probably because of the radical changes that were taking place in his theological outlook.[3] The letter he wrote with his refusal was published in the Icelandic fortnightly review *Þjóðólfur* in 1857, entitled "To the Icelanders."[4] Eiríksson writes that God has led him onto another path of faith and that he intends to stay on that path and strengthen his faith. The letter demonstrates that Eiríksson was already at that this time in conflict with the Icelandic church which was only to escalate later in his career. The letter reveals a deep character trait in Eiríksson, which was often mentioned when other people referred to him. He saw it as a matter of conscience not to join the church, which he disagreed with, in order to meet his financial needs. Eiríksson writes:

---

1 Matthías Jochumsson, *Sögukaflar af sjálfum mér,* 2nd ed., Reykjavík: Ísafold 1959 [1922], p. 109.

2 Valsson, *Jónas Hallgrímsson*, p. 395. See also Jón Helgason, *Kristnisaga Íslands: Frá öndverðu til vorra tíma*, Tome II, *Kristnihald þjóðar vorrar eftir siðaskipti*, Reykjavík: Félagsprentsmiðjan 1927, p. 330.

3 Albertsson, *Magnús Eiríksson*, p. 135.

4 Magnús Eiríksson, "Til Íslendínga," *Þjóðólfur*, vol. 9, 1857, nos. 34–35 (September 14), p. 140.

> It is not the first and foremost duty of a man, who has been given opportunity by God, to sell it for the highest prize or try to get the most out of it, but to use it as best he can and in the most truthful way in accordance with his conscience and conviction, regardless of whether it will benefit him or not....This is, in fact, my duty, and I will try to fulfill it as well as I can....On the other hand, the authorities have done what they and many others have considered their duty; they have done what lies in their power to enable me to become a pastor in Iceland...where I could expect that not only my many acquaintances and friends but also most good people would embrace me...where I could have hoped to escape from my debts sooner than otherwise and in all likelihood be more unconcerned in old age. But now this temptation has with God's help been overcome and the oversight is in my opinion less than had I done something that I could not do with good conscience.[1]

Both his supporters and opponents respected Eiríksson for this principled standpoint. He would not sell his soul or conscience for personal gain.

II. Polemics with Icelanders (1864-69)

In 1863, Eiríksson published his book *Is the Gospel of John an Apostolic and True Gospel* (1863).[2] Two years later an excerpt of the book was also published in Icelandic, entitled *The Gospel of John and the Doctrines of the Church about God, a few Observations for Reflection of those Icelanders who do not want to Disgrace and Slur God with their Faith.*[3] In these publications, Eiríksson criticizes the Gospel of John and argues that it is of a different kind than the other three gospels of the Bible. In his view, the Gospel of John is a fabrication written after the death of the apostle John. He also argues that the gospel conveys the message that Jesus is the son of God or even God in human form. Eiríksson's view is that this

---

[1] Ibid.

[2] Magnús Eiríksson, *Er Johannes-Evangeliet et apostolisk og ægte Evangelium og er dets Lære om Guds Menneskevorden en sand og christelig Lære? En religiøs-dogmatisk, historisk-kritisk Undersøgelse*, Copenhagen: Magnús Eiríksson 1863.

[3] Magnús Eiríksson, *Jóhannesar guðspjall og Lærdómur kirkjunnar um guð, nokkrar athugasemdir til yfirvegunar þeim Íslendíngum, sem ekki vilja svívirða og lasta guð með trú sinni*, Copenhagen: Louis Klein 1865.

is false because there is only one God and that Jesus is only his servant and *prophet.*

To say the least, these ideas were not well received in Iceland and many wrote against them. First, even before the publication of the Icelandic short version of the book, two anonymous authors[1] harshly criticized Eiríksson's book about the Gospel of John.[2] Eiríksson guessed that these were Icelandic theologians and responded in a similarly harsh tone.[3] After the short Icelandic version of the book was published, the criticism reached new heights. This time it was no anonymous author who attacked him, but a well-respected teacher at the Icelandic Seminary (*Prestaskólinn*) and a member of the city council, Sigurður Melsteð (1819-95), who a year later became the director of the seminary. The criticism appeared in six parts in the fortnightly review *Þjóðólfur* in the period February 1865 to January 1866, consisting of about fifteen pages total.[4]

The review is extremely critical of Eiríksson and his doctrines about the Gospel of John. It is full of insults, and the author is clearly angry and offended by Eiríksson's writing, which he says has "desecrated the most sublime and the holiest."[5] Melsteð argues that the Gospel of John is authentic and that Eiríksson's reasoning to the contrary does not hold. He also argues that since the other gospels of the Bible have much in common with the Gospel of John it is not possible to deny it without denying them all.

The next round for Eiríksson was when the Catholic priests in Iceland attacked his theories about the Gospel of John. In 1867, Jean-

---

[1] One of them signed as E.Th. (sc. Einar Thorlacius, a priest) and the other is fully anonymous.

[2] [E.Th.], "Verum ekki framar börn, er hrekjumst og feykjumst af hverjum kenningar-þyt. Efes. 4, 14," *Norðanfari*, vol. 3, 1864, nos. 30-31 (December 1), pp. 59f.; Anonymous, "Hálfyrði um Jóhannesar guðspjall. (Úr brèfi frá presti)," *Þjóðólfur*, vol. 17, 1864, nos. 1-2 (October 28), pp. 2f.

[3] Magnús Eiríksson, "Svar til 'E.Th.'," *Norðanfari*, vol. 4, 1865, nos. 4-5 (February 13), p. 7; nos. 25-26 (August 15), p. 49; nos. 31-32 (October 7), pp. 61f.; nos. 33-34 (November 15), p. 67; vol. 5, 1866, nos. 3-4 (January 29), p. 5; Magnús Eiríksson, *Svar uppá "hálfyrði" "Prestsins" í "Þjóðólfi"*, Akureyri: B.M. Stephánsson 1865.

[4] Sigurður Melsteð, "(Aðsent)," *Þjóðólfur*, vol. 17, 1865, no. 29 (May 23), pp. 115f.; nos. 31-32 (June 3), pp. 123-25; nos. 35-36 (July 4), pp. 140f.; nos. 42-43 (September 16), pp. 168-70; nos. 45-46 (October 17), pp. 182-84; nos. 47-48 (October 30), pp. 188f.

[5] Sigurður Melsteð, "(Aðsent)," *Þjóðólfur*, vol. 17, 1865, no. 29 (May 23), p. 116.

Baptiste Baudoin (1831-75), one of the first Catholic priests in Iceland after the Reformation, published the book *Jesus Christ is God: In spite of the Objections of Mr. Magnús Eiríksson.*[1] In 146 pages the priest criticizes Eiríksson's views severely, however, not in the rude and angry manner that characterizes some of the writings of Icelanders about Eiríksson. Baudoin's critique is also more substantial and scholarly; instead of personal attacks he tries to demonstrate the divinity of Christ by references to the scriptures. He mentions several examples, both in the Old and the New Testament, including all the gospels, which he takes to prove the holiness of Christ. The argument is that if Eiríksson is to renounce the holiness of Jesus Christ, he would also have to renounce the entire Bible as false. Baudoin also refers to other ancient Christian writings that Eiríksson had used to support his view and argues that Eiríksson has twisted them.

In 1868 Eiríksson responded to the criticism of the Catholic priests in a small book.[2] In a footnote at the beginning of the book, he also responds to the criticism of Sigurður Melsteð. Eiríksson meets the criticism of his views rather viciously and accuses Melsteð of being prejudiced against everything which is not in accordance with the message of the church. His views are, therefore, dogmatically based on his pre-established opinions and not on scholarly research of the scriptures. Eiríksson writes about Melsteð (that is, S.M.): "He knows in advance that everything that 'the heretics' say is wrong and unchristian, even though it is as a rule the most rational and godly. S.M. has in any event become a slave of the Church…and therefore he must regard everything as error and lie which is not according to its teachings, but everything which is accepted by the Church as true and correct."[3]

In the same year that Baudoin launched his criticism, 1867, a farmer on the islands Skáleyjar, Magnús Einarsson (1795-1876), published a pamphlet with a few critical observations against Eiríksson's interpretation of the Gospel of John.[4] This is a curious piece of writing

---

1 [Jean-Baptiste Baudoin], *Jesús Kristr er Guð. Þrátt fyrir mótmæli herra Magnúsar Eiríkssonar*, Reykjavík: Hinir katólsku prestar í Reykjavík 1867.

2 Magnús Eiríksson, *Nokkrar athugasemdir um Sannanir "katólsku prestanna í Reykjavík" fyrir guðdómi Jesú Krists*, Copenhagen: Louis Klein 1868.

3 Eiríksson, *Nokkrar athugasemdir*, p. 2.

4 Magnús Einarsson, *Nokkrar Athugasemdir, gegn Magnúsi Eiríkssyni m. fl.*, Akureyri: Jónas Sveinsson 1867.

with strange arguments. Einarsson's text is vitriolic, emphasizing Eiríksson's insolence to write such mockery (*spott*) of Jesus Christ and God, without considering Eiríksson's arguments for his views. The farmer from Skáleyjar repeatedly refers to Eiríksson as Satan's messenger. In this context he even talks about Eiríksson as an agent of secret corruption, Satan's device to debauch Christianity. And there were other articles of this kind. For example, in an article written by an author who called himself an old clergyman from the Westfjords it is stated that Eiríksson is Satan incarnated and tries to quell his effects by references to the Bible.[1] The following chapter from the old clergyman's article shows the kind of "arguments" that Eiríksson was confronted with in this debate:

> It is obvious that...we are not only fighting Eiríksson's flesh and blood but the evil spirits of darkness, a whole legion of which has embodied Magnús Eiríksson and used him as a blind tool against the gospel that they dislike the most, in the joyful hope that with Eiríksson's help they might succeed in refuting the truth of that gospel, ...after which it will not be difficult to reject the truth of the entire New Testament, and thereby ruin the church of Christ and his salvific teaching on earth.[2]

But the reception among Icelanders in this period was not entirely negative. Before the wave of criticism that has been described above, two brief news reports about the publication of Eiríksson's interpretation of the Gospel of John appeared, where the book is briefly described in a rather positive way.[3] Also, in the midst of the fierce criticism that Eiríksson met with in Iceland, twenty-one of his countrymen in Copenhagen signed a declaration in his support, stating that he was being unfairly treated by the Icelandic clergy.[4] Moreover, a few Icelanders

---

1 Anonymous ["Gamall klerkur á Vesturströndum"], "Vaktið yður fyrir fallskennöndum, sem koma til yðar í sauðaklæðum, en hið innra eru þeir glepsandi vargar. Matt. 7," *Íslendingur*, vol. 4, 1865, no. 9 (March 10), pp. 70-72.

2 Ibid., p. 71.

3 Anonymous, "Bókafregn" *Norðanfari*, vol. 3, 1864, nos. 24-25 (October 20), p. 47; Anonymous, "Frjettir: Danmörk," *Skírnir*, vol. 38, 1864, p. 117.

4 Konráð Gíslason et al., "Herra ritstjóri!," *Norðanfari*, vol. 4, 1865, nos. 31-32 (October 7), p. 61.

in Copenhagen translated a positive review of Eiríksson's work that had been published in the German review *Hamburger Nachrichten*.[1]

These attempts to come to Eiríksson's defense did not have significant impact compared to the strong and widespread opposition that he met with from Icelanders of various professions: theologians, pastors, Catholics, district magistrates, farmers and poets joined hands in criticism of Eiríksson's interpretation of the Gospel of John. From the viewpoint of reception history, this criticism had a double effect. Before that Eiríksson was not given much attention. In fact, the five years during which the polemics lasted, 1864–69, is the only period when Eiríksson's ideas received major attention in Iceland. Neither before nor after the criticism of his views of the Gospel of John did there appear as many writings about him. His views came like a bomb into Icelandic theological discussions and shook up a still religious world with sharp polemics and criticism of the church.

In this way, these religious disputes put Eiríksson on the map in Iceland, so to speak. Although they were undoubtedly difficult for him personally, the polemics had the positive effect of bringing him to the attention of the people in his native country. Surely that was partly because his views were regarded as scandalous, but the attention is also due to the fact that during this period his first and only books were published in Icelandic. These are his book about the Gospel of John and his response to the proofs of the Catholic priests for the divinity of Christ.[2] According to his critics, Sigurður Melsteð and Magnús Einarsson, Eiríksson personally sent his book on the Gospel of John to some Icelanders in 1864, so that they could get acquainted with his theological interpretation.[3]

---

1 Anonymous ["Nokkrir Íslendingar í Kaupmannahöfn"], "Dómur um Magnús Eiríksson," *Norðanfari*, vol. 5, 1866, nos. 21-22 (September 27), pp. 41f.

2 Eiríksson, *Nokkrar athugasemdir*, p. 2.

3 See Melsteð, "(Aðsent)," *Þjóðólfur*, vol. 17, 1865, no. 29 (May 23), p. 115 and Einarsson, *Nokkrar athugasemdir*, pp. 11f.

III. The Last Years: New Writings, Events and Silence (1870-80)

In this last decade of Eiríksson's life, there was not much discussion about him in Iceland. Apparently, Icelandic theologians and ministers no longer wrote about him. With the exception of the periodical *Skírnir*, which brought news about his writings, reviews of his works, and a report about his seventieth birthday in 1876, this period was characterized by silence about him and his views. The news briefs are generally positive, and no one in Iceland or Denmark disputed his writings publicly. For Eiríksson, it was either difficult dispute or deadly silence.

During this period there was one event, however, that brought Eiríksson again to public attention. This occurred at the fourth Nordic synod held in Copenhagen 1871. After Eiríksson had been booed by the audience when giving a speech, he responded with a touching, pious prayer. Not much was written about this incident in Iceland; it was only mentioned briefly in the journals *Gangleri* and *Skírnir* 1871. The poet and minister Matthías Jochumsson (1835-1920) witnessed the incident and wrote a detailed and vivid description of it in an article which was not published until 1916[1] and later reappeared in his autobiography in 1922.[2]

Seen from Iceland, the most conspicuous event in Eiríksson's life in this period was a party in Copenhagen on June 22, 1876, to celebrate his seventieth birthday on June 5. It was reported in the Icelandic media that almost all Icelanders living in Copenhagen at the time attended the celebration which showed how popular Eiríksson was among his countrymen in Denmark. Jón Sigurðsson honored him with a speech and Gísli Brynjúlfsson (1827-88) had written poetry which he read at the party. The media coverage of the celebration was mostly positive and Eiríksson was praised.[3]

Nevertheless, this stirred some discontent in Iceland. Not everyone was pleased by the fact that Eiríksson was being praised in the media. The polemics about the Gospel of John were deep-seated in the Icelandic

---

1 Matthías Jochumsson, "Dvöl mín í Danmörku 1871-1872," *Iðunn*, vol. 1, 1916, no. 3 (January), pp. 258-65.

2 Matthías Jochumsson, *Sögukaflar af sjálfum mér*, Reykjavik: Þorsteinn Gíslason 1922.

3 See, for example, Anonymous ["Reykvíkingur"], "Magnús Eiríksson," *Þjóðólfur*, vol. 28, 1876, no. 27 (September 6), p. 114; Anonymous, "Aðsent frá Kaupmannahøfn," *Norðanfari*, vol. 10, 1871, nos. 42-43 (October 28), p. 88.

psyche. An anonymous author wrote a short piece in the journal *Útsynningur* complaining that he had seen Eiríksson characterized as "one of the most distinguished theologians in the Nordic countries."[1] The author's point is that, in light of the vulgarity which Eiríksson had displayed against the holy gospels, such a statement could not be substantiated. This indicates the division that seems to have existed between the Icelanders in Copenhagen, who generally liked him, not least because they knew him personally as a man of integrity, and in Iceland, where he was disliked for his controversial views.

IV. After his Death (1881-90)

Eiríksson died on July 3, 1881, and after his death four articles in his memory appeared in Icelandic journals. The authors of these articles discussed the main events in Eiríksson's life, his works and religious disputes. By far the longest and most substantial of these articles was also the most critical. It was published in the *Journal of the Icelandic Literary Society* in 1887 and written by cand. theol. Hafsteinn Pjetursson (1858-1929).[2] This article also appeared in Danish in *Teologisk Tidsskrift for den danske Folkekirke* 1902[3] and was republished in Icelandic in 1951, in a collection on distinguished Icelanders.[4] It is likely to have had an important impact on the views of Icelanders of Magnús Eiríksson in the first decades of the 20th century, and it remained the main source on his life and writings in Icelandic until Ágúst H. Bjarnason (1875-1952) wrote his article in *Skírnir* 1924 which is discussed below.

The article by Pjetursson is positive with regard to Eiríksson as a person but very critical of him as an author and scholar. Even though it is written as a biographical overview, it is far from providing an objective

[1] Anonymous ["Einn af kaupendum Þjóðólfs"], "Sá sem ekki er með mér hann er á móti mer," *Útsynningur*, vol. 1, 1876, no. 3 (October 19), columns 23-24.

[2] Hafsteinn Pjetursson, "Magnús Eiríksson," *Tímarit hins íslenzka bókmenntafélags*, vol. 8, 1887, pp. 1-33.

[3] Hafsteinn Pjetursson, "Magnús Eiríksson," *Teologisk Tidsskrift for den danske Folkekirke*, Ny Række, vol. 3, 1901-2, pp. 116-43.

[4] Hafsteinn Pjetursson, "Magnús Eiríksson," in *Merkir Íslendingar: ævisögur og minningargreinar*, ed. by Þorkell Jóhannesson, vols. 1-5, Reykjavík: Bókfellsútgáfan 1947-57, vol. 5, pp. 314-44.

account of Eiríksson's writings. The author is obviously in opposition to his theoretical views, and his critical appraisal is framed in a questionable psychological model. Pjetursson argues that both Eiríksson's life and writings were characterized by "the major opposition" (*hinni miklu mótsetning[u]*) or "the great division"[1] (*hinn[i] miklu tvískipting[u]*) between rationalistic and providential faith. With this interpretive tool, Hafsteinn twists the sources he is analyzing and comes up with a rather curious reading of Eiríksson's works. Hafsteinn writes:

> [Eiríksson] starts by rejecting the foundation of Christian faith: Christ. The retrogression in his intellectual and emotional life becomes ever more terrible. His rationalistic faith becomes skepticism, his providential faith turns into superstitious idealism [*draumtrú*]. Because of this dualism [*tvídeiling*], Magnús is constantly struggling with himself in all his works....This dualism in his spiritual life makes all his works practically insignificant. They are all born with this lethal paradox which resides in his own thought.[2]

The other three articles are much more positive. One anonymous author is most laudatory and speaks of Eiríksson as a very important scholar and a fierce advocate of his views.[3] All four authors of the articles that appeared in Iceland after Eiríksson's death agree that he was an admirable man, while his theological writings were controversial.

V. The First Unitarian (1890–1930)

At the turn of the last century and the first decades of the 20th century, major changes were taking place in the religious life of Iceland. Icelanders who had immigrated to Canada became acquainted with Unitarianism, and Unitarian congregations were founded. Unitarians denounced the divinity of Christ and thus the holy trinity and argued that there was only one God. These doctrines were in accordance with the views

1 Pjetursson, "Magnús Eiríksson," 1887, p. 4.
2 Ibid., pp. 28f.
3 Anonymous, "Magnús Eiríksson," *Þjóðólfur*, vol. 34, 1882, no. 29 (December 6), pp. 87f. and pp. 116f.

of Eiríksson who caught the attention of his countrymen in Canada who even called him "the first Unitarian." Two prominent figures in intellectual life in Iceland, the minister and poet Matthías Jochumsson and Ágúst H. Bjarnason, a professor of philosophy and a prolific writer on the history of ideas, had connections to Unitarian congregations in Canada. These two influential figures can be said to be the first real spokesmen for Eiríksson in Iceland.

Unitarian doctrines were most controversial in Iceland in this period, and some Icelandic clergymen wrote against them. For example, the minister Niels Steingrímur Þorláksson (1857-1943) gave a substantial presentation in 1891 about the divinity of Jesus Christ and tried to demonstrate the falsity of the Unitarian doctrines about his unholiness.[1] In this lecture it is maintained that Magnús Eiríksson is the main culprit behind the dissemination of this "anti-Christian position" among the Icelandic nation.[2] This statement is the first confirmation of the fact that Eiríksson's views directly influenced religious life in Iceland.

Later, there are clear indications that Icelandic Unitarians in Canada regarded Eiríksson as a predecessor of their school of thought. A clear example of this is that in 1912 the 9th edition of *Heimir*, the journal of The Unitarian Church of West Icelanders in Winnipeg, was largely devoted to the memory of Magnús Eiríksson.[3] A few years later, in 1923, Ágúst H. Bjarnason gave a lecture at the inaugural meeting of The United Conference of Unitarian Churches in North America (*Hið sameinaða kirkjufjelag Íslendinga í Norður-Amerika*) entitled "Magnús Eiríksson: The First Icelandic Unitarian." The lecture had previously been delivered as an address at Harvard University in May of 1923 and at Meadville Theological School, Pennsylvania. The lecture was published in *Skírnir* 1924, but the English version was never published.[4]

Bjarnason's article is no doubt the most important source from this period. It is interesting to compare it to the article it replaced as the

---

1 Niels Steingrímur Þorláksson, "Guðdómr drottins vors Jesú Krists," *Aldamót*, vol. 1, 1891, pp. 76-116.

2 Ibid., p. 78.

3 Frederik Clemens Bendtsen Dahl, "Um Magnús Eiríksson: Nokkrar endurminningar," trans. by Jón Helgason, *Heimir*, vol. 8, 1912, no. 9 (May 1), pp. 197-203; R.P., [No title], *Heimir*, vol. 8, 1912, no. 9 (May 1), pp. 205-07.

4 Ágúst H. Bjarnason, "Um Magnús Eiríksson," *Skírnir*, vol. 98, 1924, pp. 39-73. See the transcription of the original manuscript by Stefan M. Jonasson in this volume.

major discussion about Eiríksson in Icelandic, namely, the one written by Pjetursson in 1887. The article by Bjarnason shows much more respect for Eiríksson and discusses the arguments he presented for his views in a fair and substantial manner. Bjarnason goes systematically through the life, works and views of Eiríksson, the main causes he fought for and the fierce disputes he engaged in to defend his views. Contrary to Pjetursson earlier, Bjarnason's article clearly demonstrates the author's enthusiasm for the writings of Eiríksson. While Pjetursson ridiculed Eiríksson's views and twisted them rhetorically to paint a negative picture of him, Bjarnason evaluates Eiríksson's reasoning, and his positive approach is substantiated with arguments. This article by a respected professor at the University of Iceland played a major role in correcting the misleading discussion that had characterized the Icelandic reception of his works. Bjarnason concludes his article by encouraging scholars of theology to seriously study Eiríksson's works.

The contribution of the other main spokesman for Eiríksson in this period, the revered minister and poet Matthías Jochumsson, consisted mainly in telling the aforementioned story of the incident from the fourth Nordic synod which Jochumsson attended in Copenhagen in 1871. In response to the shouts and boos of his speech, Eiríksson is reported to have said: "Even at the cost of my own salvation, I cannot silence the voice of my conscience and conviction."[1] When he was further attacked by the audience, he responded with a heart-rending prayer. Jochumsson talks about Eiríksson as a "spiritual giant" (*andlegt stórmenni*), likening him to Jón Sigurðsson the undisputed leader of Icelanders in the 19th century. Jochumsson writes in admiration: "I was overcome by the behavior of M. Eiríksson—this childlike and humble pauper, my only countryman in this magnificent aula of the university, full with the distinguished figures of the Nordic clergy."[2] This description caught the attention of Bjarnason who refers to it at the start of his article about Eiríksson in *Skírnir*.[3] The story appeared in Jochumsson's memoirs,[4] but was also published in a few journals, and Bjarnason includes a large part of it in his *Skírnir* article about Eiríksson. Eiríksson's behavior in this

---

1 Jochumsson, "Dvöl mín í Danmörku," p. 261.
2 Ibid.
3 Bjarnason, "Um Magnús Eiríksson," p. 39.
4 See Jochumsson, "Dvöl mín í Danmörku 1871-1872," pp. 259-64.

incident was generally regarded as admirable and contributed to a more positive view of him among Icelanders.

In 1894 Jochumsson also wrote an article, which appeared both in Iceland and in Canada, where he likened Magnús Eiríksson to Leo Tolstoy. The article is mainly about Tolstoy's book *The Kingdom of God Is Within You*, but in the beginning and at the end he compares the teachings of Tolstoy to Eiríksson. Jochumsson writes:

> It is remarkable how similar [Tolstoy] is to Magnús Eiríksson in his last books...especially as regards Christ's teachings and following....Both are strong enemies of all denominations within the church, both criticize the church for a radical misunderstanding of the "Christendom of Christ" and with its dogmas and ecclesiastical belief steer people onto the path of pagan error. Both say that the main error of the church is not to follow the words of Christ, especially in the sermon on the mount.[1]

Jochumsson adds that the main difference between Tolstoy and Eiríksson is that the latter wrote in a language that was not understood by people in the world at large, while Tolstoy was read by all nations.

In 1912 a philosophically minded farmer published a book in Iceland entitled *The Story of my Thought about Myself and my Existence*. The author mentions Eiríksson's works as one of the main reasons why he started thinking about religion. He had not read anything by Eiríksson but heard of his writings and how dangerous his doctrine would be, "unless it would be refuted with convincing arguments."[2] In this way, Eiríksson's writings indirectly contributed to one of the first philosophical treatises in Iceland.

The final contribution to the reception of Eiríksson in Iceland in this period came in 1922 when Bishop Jón Helgason (1866-1942) published a major work in Danish about the history of Christianity in Iceland in two volumes,[3] and an Icelandic version appeared a few

---

1 Matthías Jochumsson, "Tolstoi og Magnús Eiríksson," Lögberg, vol. 7, no. 74, 1894, p. 1.

2 Brynjúlfur Jónsson frá Minna-Núpi, *Saga hugsunar minnar: um sjálfan mig og tilveruna*, 2nd ed., Reykjavík: Hið íslenska bókmenntafélag 1997 [1914], p. 18.

3 Jón Helgason, *Islands kirke fra dens grundlæggelse til reformationen. En historisk Fremstilling*, Copenhagen: Gad 1925; *Islands kirke fra reformationen til vore dage. En historisk Fremstilling*, Copenhagen: Gad 1922.

years later.[1] In both the Danish and the Icelandic editions, Magnús Eiríksson is discussed in a few pages and is thereby formally recognized as a significant contributor to Christian thought, worthy of having a place in the history of Icelandic Christianity.[2] On the other hand, much of Bishop Helgason's discussion of Eiríksson is very critical, stating in effect that his doctrines are badly written and obsolete. His description of the Icelandic reception of Eiríksson's book on the Gospel of John is striking:

> Here in the motherland of Magnús people shivered with cold when this book was published in Iceland. This was indeed the first work of disbelief [*vantrúarrit*] to appear in Icelandic. People expressed amazement over the fact that a man of this sort would be at liberty instead of being put in jail like any other renegade [*trúníðingur*] and a hater of god [*guð-hatari*]. One of the district magistrates [sc. Jón Thoroddsen (1818-66)] in Iceland inquired among his superiors what could be done to prevent the spreading of such a dangerous book. He would have preferred that the sale of the book be prohibited and the whole print run be burned.[3]

Bishop Helgason's evaluation of this reception is clear: "About almost everything that was written in this country against Magnús, one can say that it was an offence to the printer's ink to print it. It was a pitiable witness of immaturity and lack of understanding of a proper Christian theodicy. There was no indication of an attempt to understand the nature of Eiríksson's writings."[4]

These forty years of the history of the Icelandic reception of Magnús Eiríksson show an interesting development. To begin with, members of the Icelandic clergy found Eiríksson's doctrines threatening, and he was criticized for being the pioneer of Unitarianism among Icelanders. Next, we learned that Icelandic Unitarians, both in Iceland and North America, admired Eiríksson as the first Icelandic Unitarian. Finally,

---

1 Jón Helgason, *Kristnisaga Íslands frá öndverðu til vorra tíma*, Tome I, *Kristnihald þjóðar vorrar fyrir siðaskipti*; Tome II, *Kristnihald þjóðar vorrar eftir siðaskipti*, Reykjavík: Félagsprentsmiðjan 1927.

2 Helgason, *Islands kirke fra reformationen til vore dage*, pp. 188-90; Helgason, *Kristnihald þjóðar vorrar eftir siðaskipti*, pp. 327-30.

3 Helgason, *Kristnihald þjóðar vorrar eftir siðaskipti*, p. 329.

4 Ibid., p. 330.

Magnús Eiríksson gained recognition by his countrymen; first through two important intellectuals, Jochumsson and Bjarnason, and secondly through the writings of minister Þorláksson and bishop Helgason who, although both were critical of him, confirmed that Eiríksson had become an influential figure in the history of the Icelandic church.

VI. A Doctoral Thesis about Magnús Eiríksson (1930-40)

In the decade 1930-40 the discussion about Magnús Eiríksson in Iceland centered exclusively around a doctoral thesis by Eiríkur Albertsson (1887-1972), defended at The Theological Faculty of the University of Iceland in 1938, and reactions to this thesis. Before 1938, nothing of significance was written about Eiríksson, and he is only briefly mentioned in different contexts. One example is an article entitled "The Crusade against Bolshevism" in a labor journal where the story about Eiríksson's battle with the Icelandic clergy is used to exemplify the insolence of the conservatives in Iceland.[1] The main spokesman of the communist party in Iceland, Einar Olgeirsson (1902-93), had previously used this comparison in an article about Icelanders' reactions to new cultural movements.[2] In this context, Eiríksson is presented as a radical thinker whose ideas are rejected by his reactionary countrymen.

The doctoral thesis by Albertsson, *Magnús Eiríksson: His Theology and Religious Life*,[3] was the first dissertation to be defended at The Faculty of Theology at the University of Iceland. It is no doubt by far the most substantial and significant event in the history of the reception of Magnús Eiríksson in Iceland. The thesis, which is almost 400 pages long, discusses Eiríksson's life and doctrines in detail. Not only was it published as a dissertation in a few copies before the defense in 1938, but also as a book the same year before Christmas when most Icelanders buy books for presents. Albertsson also gave a few talks on the subject on

1 Anonymous, "Krossferðin gegn bolshevismanum," *Verkamaðurinn*, vol. 13, 1930, no. 24 (March 15), p. 3.
2 Einar Olgeirsson, "Erlendir menningarstraumar og Íslendingar," *Réttur*, vol. 11, 1926, pp. 9-24.
3 Eiríkur Albertsson, *Magnús Eiríksson: Guðfræði hans og trúarlíf*, Reykjavík: Doctoral Dissertation, Háskóli Íslands 1938.

the public radio in December 1937. His thesis was thus far from being confined to narrow academic circles; it was disseminated widely among the general public.

There were many reactions to Albertsson's thesis in the years after it was published, and in most of them Eiríksson is positively referred to. The general judgment about Albertsson's book is that in spite of being an academic work, it is entertaining and accessible. The book is generally praised, but those who criticize it argue that it lacks scientific objectivity and is biased in favor of Eiríksson. Bjarnason, who had earlier encouraged some "learned, truthful theologian" to research Eiríksson's work,[1] wrote a review of Albertsson's book in *Skírnir* in 1939.[2] Bjarnason is not of the opinion that Albertsson had managed to respond to this challenge adequately, but he writes that it is a "respectable attempt" even though it lacks "an impartial assessment of Magnús and his work from a modern standpoint."[3]

VII. A Long Period of Silence (1940-97)

After the last review of Albertsson's doctoral thesis appeared in 1940, there was almost no mention of Eiríksson for decades in Iceland. Surprisingly, the lively and critical discussion about the thesis did not engender further research or academic debate about Eiríksson's work. Instead, Albertsson's book seems eventually to have closed the discussion, as if the final word had been said about Eiríksson in Iceland. Eiríksson was only mentioned in passing when other of his contemporary writers, such as J.-B. Baudoin,[4] and Brynjúlfur Jónsson,[5] were being discussed.

The only exception to this lack of interest is a chapter about Eiríksson in a book by Jón Helgason (1914-81), a journalist and popular writer about ethnological matters. Helgason traces the history of

---

1 Ágúst H. Bjarnason, "Um Magnús Eiríksson," *Skírnir*, vol. 98, 1924, p. 73.

2 Ágúst H. Bjarnason, "Eiríkur Albertsson: Magnús Eiríksson, guðfræði hans og trúarlíf," *Skírnir*, vol. 113, 1939, pp. 211-17.

3 Ibid., p. 211 and p. 217.

4 Gunnar F. Guðmundsson, *Kaþólskt trúboð á Íslandi 1857–1875*, ed. by Jón Guðnason, Reykjavík: Sagnfræðistofnun Háskóla Íslands 1987, pp. 103f. and p. 109.

5 Atli Harðarson, "Heimspekingurinn Brynjúlfur frá Minna Núpi," *Lesbók Morgunblaðsins*, 1992, no. 44 (December 21), pp. 30-32.

Eiríksson's family and discusses his personality. This text is not a product of theoretical research but is primarily a rather poetic narrative about Eiríksson and his family.[1]

VIII. Renewed Interest at the Turn of the Century

At the end of the 20th century, Magnús Eiríksson finally caught the attention of Icelanders anew after a long period of silence about his works. This was not due to a renewed interest in his theology but because of his stance in the battle for the rights of women. In the earlier reactions to Eiríksson's works in Iceland, this aspect of his thought had certainly not been in focus. When a new Icelandic edition of the epoch-making book, *On the Subjection of Women* by John Stuart Mill,[2] was published in 1997, the political scientist Auður Styrkársdóttir (b. 1951) wrote a comprehensive introduction about the history of the battle for women's rights in Iceland.[3] Styrkársdóttir calls Magnús Eiríksson one of the first champions in this battle and tells about his correspondence with the women's rights activist Mathilde Fibiger, which was published as *Letters to Clara Raphael* in 1851.[4]

The theologian Jóhanna Þráinsdóttir (1940-2005) also wrote about this correspondence between Eiríksson and Mathilde Fibiger in an article which appeared in the cultural section of the main Icelandic newspaper in 1997. The article is entitled "A Forgotten Supporter of Women: On the Theologian and Writer Magnús Eiríksson and his Contribution to the Struggle for the Emancipation of Women."[5] Þráinsdóttir's article

---

1 Jón Helgason, *Vér Íslands börn*, vols. 1-3, Reykjavík: Iðunn 1970, vol. 3, pp. 7-124.

2 John Stuart Mill, *The Subjection of Women*, London: Longmans, Green, Reader, and Dyer 1869.

3 John Stuart Mill's *On the Subjection of Women* first appeared in Icelandic in 1900, but the Icelandic translation was revised and republished in the Theoretical Series of The Icelandic Literary Society in 1997: John Stuart Mill, *Kúgun kvenna*, with an introduction ("Forspjall") by Auður Styrkársdóttir. The discussion about Eiríksson is on pp. 37f.

4 Magnús Eiríksson [Theodor Immanuel], *Breve til Clara Raphael*, Copenhagen: C.A. Reitzel 1851.

5 Jóhanna Þráinsdóttir, "Gleymdur liðsmaður kvenna. Um Magnús Eiríksson guðfræðing og rithöfund, og framlag hans til frelsisbaráttu kvenna," *Lesbók Morgunblaðsins*, 1997, May 10, pp. 4f.

is a rather substantial discussion of Eiríksson's arguments in support of women's rights, and she points out that Bjarnason had already written in his *Skírnir* article from 1924 that Eiríksson employed many of the same arguments that were later used by Mill in *On the Subjection of Women.* She also quotes and agrees with a chapter from Albertson's doctoral thesis where he argues that Eiríksson in fact provided the argumentative basis for the women's rights movement in Denmark, although his part in that had never been appreciated. In a four-volume work on Christianity in Iceland, published in the year 2000, however, Eiríksson is only mentioned as a leading figure in the struggle for women's rights.[1]

In the 21st century the history of the reception of Magnús Eiríksson in Iceland took a new turn when scholars started examining his relationship to the religious and philosophical thinker, Søren Kierkegaard, but this had gone largely unnoticed before. In the last years, three articles have been published about this topic which comprises the last theme of Eiríksson's reception history in Iceland. All these articles discuss how Eiríksson admired Kierkegaard's battle against the main theologians in Denmark but also criticized some of the main arguments Kierkegaard used to criticize their ideas.

The first of these was written by the aforementioned theologian Jóhanna Þráinsdóttir and is about Eiríksson's criticism of Kierkegaard's religious views, especially Christian faith as a paradox, as they appear in *Fear and Trembling.*[2] The second article is about the reception of Kierkegaard in Iceland by Vilhjálmur Árnason (b. 1953), professor of philosophy at the University of Iceland, who briefly discusses Eiríksson's criticism of Kierkegaard.[3] Árnason also organized a special session about Magnús Eiríksson at a conference of The Nordic Network of Kierkegaard

---

1 Inga Huld Hákonardóttir, "Konur og Kristur á 19. öld," in *Kristni á Íslandi,* vol. 4, *Til móts við nútímann*, ed. by Þórunn Valdimarsdóttir and Pétur Pétursson, Reykjavík: Alþingi 2000, p. 126.

2 Jóhanna Þráinsdóttir, "Er trúin þverstæða: Gagnrýni Magnúsar Eiríkssonar á trúarskoðunum Kierkegaards í Ugg og ótta," *Tímarit Máls og menningar*, vol. 61, 2000, pp. 35-45.

3 Vilhjálmur Árnason, "Iceland: 'Neglect and Misunderstanding': The Reception of Kierkegaard in Iceland," in *Kierkegaard's International Reception*, Tome I, *Northern and Western Europe*, ed. by Jon Stewart, Aldershot: Ashgate 2009 (*Kierkegaard Research: Sources, Reception and Resources*, vol. 8), pp. 219-34, especially pp. 221f.

Research in Reykjavik on May 24, 2013.[1] The session consisted of short introductions and a panel discussion by Icelandic scholars, followed by a presentation by Gerhard Schreiber, "Eiríksson's Relation to Kierkegaard Reconsidered."

Last but not least, the theologian Gerhard Schreiber (b. 1978), who can be labeled a Magnús Eiríksson scholar, published an article in *Skírnir* in 2014, entitled "Magnús Eiríksson: A Neglected Contemporary of Søren Kierkegaard."[2] Schreiber's article is divided into two main parts. In the first part, he discusses Eiríksson's life and works and in the second part he scrutinizes the debate between Eiríksson and Kierkegaard. This article squarely places Eiríksson into contemporary scholarly discussion, where his arguments are carefully examined and interpreted. Schreiber's contribution, which appropriately appeared in *Skírnir*, the same journal as the influential article by Bjarnason in 1924, will become a valuable source for Icelanders who want to become acquainted with the thought of Eiríksson and exchange points of view about his scholarship.

---

1 The network is funded by NordForsk and operated by The Søren Kierkegaard Research Centre at the University of Copenhagen, under the chairmanship of Professor Jon Stewart.

2 Gerhard Schreiber, "Magnús Eiríksson—Vanræktur samtímamaður Sørens Kierkegaard," trans. by Aðalsteinn Garðarsson, *Skírnir*, vol. 188, 2014, pp. 116-43. See also Gerhard Schreiber, "Magnús Eiríksson: An Opponent of Martensen and an Unwelcome Ally of Kierkegaard," in *Kierkegaard and His Danish Contemporaries*, Tome II, *Theology*, ed. by Jon Stewart, Aldershot: Ashgate 2009 (*Kierkegaard Research: Sources, Reception and Resources*, vol. 7), pp. 49-94, as well as Schreiber's article "'Like a Voice in the Wilderness': Magnús Eiríksson's Tenacious Critique of Martensen—and Martensen's 'Lofty Silence,'" in *Hans Lassen Martensen. Theologian, Philosopher and Social Critic*, ed. by Jon Stewart, Copenhagen: Museum Tusculanum Press 2012 (*Danish Golden Age Studies*, vol. 6), pp. 155-91.

VI. Appendix

International Bibliography on Magnús Eiríksson

Gerhard Schreiber

I. Eiríksson's Works

“Hinar helztu bækr útkomnar í Kaupmannahöfn, árið 1834,” *Skírnir*, vol. 9, 1835, pp. 96-103.

(trans. with Ólafur Indriðason, Konráð Gíslason and Ólafur Pálsson), Gerhard Peter Brammer, *Lýsing Landsins helga á Krists dögum, gefin út af enu íslenzka Bókmenntafélagi. Með steinprentaðri landsmynd*, Copenhagen: Hið íslenska bókmenntafélag 1842.

“Præsterne paa Island,” *Den Berlingske Tidendes Søndagsblad*, 1842, nos. 11-12.

[Necrologue on Þorbjörg Stefánsdóttir], *Skírnir*, vol. 16, 1842, pp. 132-133.

(ed. et al.), *Ný Félagsrit, gefin út af nokkrum Íslendíngum*, vols. 2-16, Copenhagen: Salomon and L. Klein 1842-56.

(ed. et al.), *Fjórir þættir um alþíng og önnur málefni Íslendínga*, Copenhagen: J.D. Quist 1843.

Om Baptister og Barnedaab, samt flere Momenter af Den kirkelige og speculative Christendom, Copenhagen: P.G. Philipsen 1844.

“Academisk Væsen,” *Berlingske politiske og Avertissements-Tidende*, 1844, no. 124 (May 9).

“Geistlig Stændervirksomhed eller Bidrag til Bedømmelsen af den mynsterske Logik, den mynsterske Billighed og Retfærdighed med specielt Hensyn til Skolelærer-Brevdrageriet,” *Kjøbenhavnsposten*, 1845, nos. 17-18.

"Det Almeen Menneskelige og det Nationale," *Kjøbenhavnsposten*, 1845, nos. 203-206 (September 2-5).

"Nogle Ord om Nutidens kirkelige Tilstande og religiøse Bevægelser," *Kjøbenhavnsposten*, 1845, nos. 222-223, 226, 232-234.

Tro, Overtro og Vantro, i deres Forhold til Fornuft og Forstand, samt til hinanden indbyrdes, Copenhagen: H.C. Klein 1846.

[Replies to reviews of *Tro, Overtro og Vantro* (1846)], *Kjøbenhavnsposten*, 1846, nos. 225-226; *Nyt Aftenblad*, 1846, nos. 213 and 230.

Dr. Martensens trykte moralske Paragrapher, eller det saakaldte "Grundrids til Moralphilosophiens System af Dr. Hans Martensen", i dets forvirrede, idealistisk-metaphysiske og phantastisk-speculative, Religion og Christendom undergravende, fatalistiske, pantheistiske og selvforguderske Væsen, Copenhagen: H.C. Klein 1846.

[Reply to a review of *Dr. Martensens trykte moralske Paragrapher* (1846)], *Fædrelandet*, 1846, nos. 303-304.

"En Præst i Danmark," *Kjøbenhavnsposten*, 1846, nos. 17-18, 20, 23, 25, 28-29.

[Gottlieb], "Oplysningen stiger!," *Kjøbenhavnsposten*, 1846, no. 43.

[Anonymous review of Johann Hinrich Röben, *Der souveraine christliche Staat, das Ende aller Zeitwirren*, Leipzig: F.A. Brockhaus 1846], *Kjøbenhavnsposten*, 1846, no. 140 (June 20), pp. 557-558; no. 141 (June 23), pp. 561-563 and no. 143 (June 27), pp. 569-570.

["Anmelderen af Senator Röbens Skrift"], "Et Par Ord til Kirkemanden i 'Aftenbladet,'" *Kjøbenhavnsposten*, 1846, no. 145 (June 26), pp. 577-579.

[Preface and Afterword], in Ólafur Indriðason, *Nokkrar Athugasemdir um Dóm þann, er herra "J. S." hefir lagt á "sjø føstuprédikanir, samdar af Olafi Indridasyni, presti til Kolfreyustadar,"* Copenhagen: S.L. Møller 1847, pp. 3-4 and 37-44.

(ed. with Sally B. Salomon), *Forhandlinger i det offentlige Møde i Hippodromet, Mandagen den 14. August 1848*, Copenhagen: Sally B. Salomon 1848.

(ed.), *Forhandlinger i det offentlige Møde i Hippodromet, Onsdagen den 16. August 1848*, Copenhagen: Sally B. Salomon 1848.

Speculativ Rettroenhed, fremstillet efter Dr. Martensens "christelige Dogmatik", og Geistlig Retfærdighed, belyst ved en Biskops Deeltagelse i en Generalfiskal-Sag, Copenhagen: Trykt hos J.S. Salomon 1849.
[Replies to reviews of *Speculativ Rettroenhed* (1849)], *Kjøbenhavnsposten*, 1849, no. 253; *Flyve-Posten*, 1849, no. 262.
["Af en Theolog"], "Nogle Bemærkninger til Orientering i de nærværende kirkelige Tilstande," *Den Nordiske Folkeskole*, vol. 10, 1849, no. 5 (February 9), columns 65-72; no. 8 (March 2), columns 113-119; no. 22 (June 8), columns 337-344; no. 47 (December 21), columns 681-691.
Den nydanske Theologies Cardinaldyder belyste ved Hjelp af Dr. Martensens Skrifter samt Modskrifterne, tilligemed 75 theologiske Spørgsmaal, rettede til Dr. H. Martensen, Copenhagen: Chr. Steen & Søn 1850.
[Theophilus Nicolaus], *Er Troen et Paradox og "i Kraft af det Absurde"? et Spørgsmaal foranlediget ved "Frygt og Bæven, af Johannes de silentio", besvaret ved Hjelp af en Troes-Ridders fortrolige Meddelelser, til fælles Opbyggelse for Jøder, Christne og Muhamedanere, af bemeldte Troes-Ridders Broder*, Copenhagen: Chr. Steen & Søn 1850.
[Theodor Immanuel], *Breve til Clara Raphael*, Copenhagen: C.A. Reitzel 1851.
"Brigham Joung," *Illustreret Magazin*, vol. 2, 1854, no. 36 (September 2), pp. 281-283 and no. 37 (September 9), pp. 290-292.
"Wartburg," *Illustreret Magazin*, vol. 2, 1854, no. 36 (September 2), pp. 283-284 and no. 38 (September 16), p. 301.
"Endnu et Indlæg i Sagen: Dr. S. Kierkegaard contra Biskop Martensen m. Fl.," *Kongeriget Danmarks Avertissements-Tidende*, 1855, no. 82 (April 10), columns 16-17; no. 83 (April 11), columns 16-17; no. 84 (April 12), columns 16-17; no. 85 (April 13), columns 16-17; no. 86 (April 14), column 16; no. 89 (April 18), column 16; no. 91 (April 20), columns 16-17; no. 92 (April 21), column 16; no. 93 (April 23), column 16.
(trans.), "Brudstykker af den islandske Elucidarius," *Annaler for nordisk Oldkyndighed og Historie*, [vol. 17], 1857, pp. 238-308.
"Til Íslendínga," *Þjóðólfur*, vol. 9, 1857, nos. 34-35 (September 14), p. 140.

Hvem har Ret: Grundtvigianerne eller deres Modstandere? og Hvad har Christus befalet om Daaben? Nogle orienterende Bemærkninger, Copenhagen: E.L. Thaarup 1863 (2nd edition, 1863).

Er Johannes-Evangeliet et apostolisk og ægte Evangelium og er dets Lære om Guds Menneskevorden en sand og christelig Lære? En religiøs-dogmatisk, historisk-kritisk Undersøgelse, Copenhagen: Magnús Eiríksson 1863.

Jóhannesar guðspjall og Lærdómur kirkjunnar um guð, nokkrar athugasemdir til yfirvegunar þeim Íslendíngum, sem ekki vilja svívirða og lasta guð með trú sinni, Copenhagen: Louis Klein 1865.

Svar uppá "hálfyrði" "Prestsins" í "Þjóðólfi," Akureyri: B.M. Stephánsson 1865.

"Svar til [Herra] 'E. Th.,'" *Norðanfari*, vol. 4, 1865, nos. 4-5 (February 13), p. 7; nos. 25-26 (August 15), p. 49; nos. 31-32 (October 7), pp. 61-62; nos. 33-34 (November 15), p. 67; vol. 5, 1866, nos. 3-4 (January 29), p. 5.

[Reply to "Útaf 'bókafregn' í Norðanfara," (1865)], *Þjóðólfur*, vol. 17, 1865, nos. 45-46 (October 17), p. 185.

Gud og Reformatoren. En religiøs Idee. Samt nogle Bemærkninger om de kirkelige Tilstande, Dr. S. Kierkegaard og Forfatteren, Copenhagen: J.H. Schubothe 1866.

Nokkrar athugasemdir um Sannanir "katólsku prestanna í Reykjavík" fyrir guðdómi Jesú Krists, Copenhagen: Louis Klein 1868.

[Necrologue on Árni Jónsson], *Norðanfari*, vol. 7, 1868, nos. 3-4 (Aukablað), pp. 1-2.

Kunne vi elske Næsten som os selv? Nogle tildeels nye Tanker om Kjærligheden samt flere derhen hørende Skriftsteder, Copenhagen: Magnús Eiríksson 1870.

Om Bønnens Virkning og dens Forhold til Guds Uforanderlighed. Nogle Oplysninger og Bemærkninger, nærmest byggede paa andelig Erfaring og et umiddelbart Gudsforhold, Copenhagen: Magnús Eiríksson 1870.

Paulus og Christus eller Pauli Lære om Retfærdiggjørelsen sammenlignet med Christi Lære om Syndsforladelsen, tilligemed nogle Bemærkninger om andre paulinske Lærdomme m. M., Copenhagen: Magnús Eiríksson 1871.

[Reply to a remark by Konsul Olsson], *Fædrelandet*, 1871, no. 213 (September 14).

"Svar til Hr. 'Ab.,'" *Folkets Avis*, 1871, no. 243 (September 26).

[Reply to a review of *Paulus og Christus* (1871) in *Dagbladet*, 1872, no. 8 (January 9)], *Dagbladet*, 1872, no. 54, Annex, (February 29).

Jøder og Christne eller Hvorledes blev Jesus fra Nazareth betragtet i den ældste Kirke og hvorledes blev han senere betragtet? En populær, historisk-kritisk Undersøgelse, tilegnet de Sandhedskjærlige, Copenhagen: Magnús Eiríksson 1873.

Herr A. Pedrin og Christendommen. Nogle Oplysninger om hans Skrift: "Vor Herres og Frelsers Jesu Christi nye Testament og Magnus Eirikssons reformeerte Jødedom," Copenhagen: no publisher given 1874.

"Min Forfattervirksomhed," *Flyvende Blade for Literatur, Kunst og Samfundsspørgsmaal*, ed. by Vilhelm Møller, vol. 3, no. 11 (June 12, 1875), pp. 81-83; no. 12 (June 19, 1875), pp. 90-93, and no. 13 (June 26, 1875), pp. 100-104.

(ed.), *Borðsálmur Íslendinga í Kaupmannahöfn á Þorláksmessu*, [Copenhagen] [1876].

"Förnuftstro och kyrkolära," *Sanningsökaren. Nordisk månadskrift för förnuftstro och praktisk kristendom*, vol. 1, 1877, no. 2, pp. 41-47.

"Förtröstan på Gud," *Sanningsökaren. Nordisk månadskrift för förnuftstro och praktisk kristendom*, vol. 1, 1877, no. 4, pp. 113-121.

"Kierkegaard och kristendomen," *Sanningsökaren. Nordisk månadskrift för förnuftstro och praktisk kristendom*, vol. 1, 1877, nos. 7-8, pp. 203-239.

"Ortodoxe teologer och kritiske filosofer," *Sanningsökaren. Nordisk månadskrift för förnuftstro och praktisk kristendom*, vol. 1, 1877, nos. 9-10, pp. 289-305.

"Kristi religion och kristna religionen. Svar till Robinson," *Sanningsökaren. Nordisk månadskrift för förnuftstro och praktisk kristendom*, vol. 2, 1878, nos. 1-2, pp. 11-34.

"Död och odödlighet," *Sanningsökaren. Nordisk månadskrift för förnuftstro och praktisk kristendom*, vol. 2, 1878, no. 9, pp. 259-267.

"Om Johannesevangeliets Kristus," *Sanningsökaren. Nordisk månadskrift för förnuftstro och praktisk kristendom*, vol. 3, 1879, no. 4, pp. 104-121.

"Striden om Johannesevangeliet," *Sanningsökaren. Nordisk månadskrift för förnuftstro och praktisk kristendom*, vol. 4, 1880, nos. 1-2, pp. 39-49.

II. Further Works ascribed to Magnús Eiríksson[1]

[Adam Homo], *Epistel eller Sendebrev til Den Herre "Intrepidus" (?) angaaende H. M. Kongens Ægteskab og Reise i Jydernes Land*, Copenhagen: Zuschlags Boghandling 1852.

[Lars Maagensen], *En liden Epistel til Hvidtølsbrygger Hans Mikkelsen, i Kallundborg, indeholdende en chemisk Undersøgelse af hans "Hvidtøl,"* Copenhagen: Møllers Boghandel 1852 (2nd edition, 1852).

III. Letters[2]

A. Letters from Magnús Eiríksson

To Søren Kierkegaard (October 14, 1847), in *SKS* 28, 370-372, Brev 245 (Kierkegaard Archive at the Royal Library in Copenhagen, D pk. 2 læg 8).

[1] See Edvard Collin, *Anonymer og Pseudonymer i den danske, norske og islandske Literatur samt i fremmede Literaturer, forsaavidt disse omhandle nordiske Forhold, fra de ældste Tider indtil Aaret 1860*, Copenhagen: J. Lund 1869, p. 135; Emil Ottokar Weller, *Lexicon Pseudonymorum. Wörterbuch der Pseudonymen aller Zeiten und Völker, oder Verzeichniss jener Autoren, die sich falscher Namen bedienten*, 2nd revised and enlarged edition, Regensburg: Coppenrath 1886, p. 4 and p. 336; Balder Vermund Aage Erichsen and Alfred Krarup, *Dansk historisk bibliografi. Systematisk fortegnelse over bidrag til Danmarks historie til udgangen af 1912*, vols. 1-3, Copenhagen: Gad 1917-27, vol. 1, p. 265 (no. 4546) and p. 266 (no. 4569); *Index bio-bibliographicus notorum hominum*, ed. by Jean-Pierre Lobies et al., Pars C, Corpus alphabeticum, I. Sectio generalis, Supplementum vol. 99,7, ed. by Susanna Wand, Osnabrück: Biblio-Verlag 2003, p. 618.

[2] Letters *not* contained in the Department of Manuscripts at The National and University Library of Iceland (*Handritadeild Landsbókasafns Íslands*). See the letters from and to Magnús Eiríksson in Lbs. 302 a/b, fol. (ID 282); Lbs. 303 a/b, fol. (ID 283); Lbs. 304 a/b, fol. (ID 284); Lbs. 305 a-c, fol. (ID 285); Lbs. 1238, 4to (ID 1561); Lbs. 1464, 4to (ID 1791); Lbs. 387, fol. (ID 7954); Lbs. 2174, 4to (ID 8157); Lbs. 2561 (ID i 142); Lbs. 2755 (ID i 336-337); Lbs. 3672 (ID iii 222) and Lbs. 4271 (ID iii 821).

B. Letters to Magnús Eiríksson

From Søren Kierkegaard (October 1847) (copy), in *SKS* 28, 372, Brev 246 (Kierkegaard Archive at the Royal Library in Copenhagen, D pk. 2 læg 8).

From Hans Lassen Martensen (April 21, 1873), reprinted in Hafsteinn Pjetursson, "Magnús Eiríksson," *Teologisk Tidsskrift for den danske Folkekirke*, Ny Række, vol. 3, 1901-1902, pp. 138-139 (NKS 1867 4°, New Royal Collection at the Royal Library in Copenhagen).

IV. Translations of Eiríksson's Works

A. French Translation

Gud og Reformatoren. En religiøs Idee (1866), trans. by Olivier Cauly, in *Encyclopédie philosophique universelle*, vol. 4, *Le discours philosophique*, ed. by Jean-François Mattéi, Paris: Presses Universitaires de France 1998, pp. 651-652 [excerpts].

B. German Translations

"Ist der Glaube ein Paradox oder 'in kraft des Absurden'?" [a translation of *Er Troen et Paradox og "i Kraft af det Absurde"?* (1850)], trans. by Wilfried Greve, in *Materialien zur Philosophie Søren Kierkegaards*, ed. and introduced by Michael Theunissen and Wilfried Greve, Frankfurt: Suhrkamp 1979 (*suhrkamp taschenbuch wissenschaft*, vol. 241), pp. 147-160 [excerpts].

Briefe an Clara Raphael, trans. and ed. by Gerhard Schreiber, Barnstorf: Verlag 28 Eichen 2016.

C. Swedish Translations

Johannis Evangelium. Är det en äkta apostolisk Bok och är dess Lära: att Gud är vorden Menniska, en sann och kristlig Lära? En Religiös-Dogmatisk Historisk-Kritisk Undersökning, trans. by Nils Johan Ekdahl, Stockholm: L.J. Hiertas Forläg 1864.

Läran om dopet [a translation of *Hvem har Ret: Grundtvigianerne eller deres Modstandere?* (1863)], trans. by Nils Johan Ekdahl, Stockholm: L.J. Hiertas Forläg 1865.

Om bönens verkan och dess förhållande till Guds oföränderlighet. Några upplysningar och anmärkningar, närmast byggda på andlig erfarenhet och ett omedelbart gudsförhållande, trans. by Eric Carsten, with a preface by G. Halfdan Liander, Stockholm: no publisher given 1936.

V. Bibliographies of Eiríksson's Works

Erslew, Thomas Hansen, *Supplement til Almindeligt Forfatter-Lexicon for Kongeriget Danmark med tilhørende Bilande 1841 til efter 1858*, vols. 1-3, Copenhagen: Rosenkilde og Bagger 1963-64 [1858-68], vol. 1, pp. 406-408.

Gudmundson, Valtýr Emil, *The Icelandic Unitarian Connection*, completed posthumously by Barbara J.R. Gudmundson, with a foreword by Conrad Wright, Winnipeg, Manitoba: Wheatfield Press 1984, pp. 91-92 ("Magnús Eiríksson Bibliography").

Schreiber, Gerhard, "Eiríksson, Magnús," *Biographisch-Bibliographisches Kirchenlexikon*, vols. 1-30, ed. by Friedrich Wilhelm Bautz and Traugott Bautz, Nordhausen: Verlag Traugott Bautz 1975-2009, vol. 28, 2007, columns 517-538.

— "Ritaskrá Magnúsar Eiríkssonar," *Skírnir*, vol. 189, 2015, pp. 519-531.

VI. Reviews of Eiríksson's Works

Review of *Fjórir þættir um alþíng og önnur málefni Íslendínga* (1843):

— *Fjölnir*, vol. 7, 1844, pp. 74-85 (by Gísli Magnússon).

Reviews of *Om Baptister og Barnedaab* (1844):

— *Kjøbenhavnsposten*, 1844, no. 92 (April 20) (by "Th. G. R.");

— *Kjøbenhavnsposten*, 1844, no. 104 (May 6) (by "En Lægmand i den angrebne danske Statskirke");

— *Aarhuus Stifts-Tidende*, 1844, no. 89 (May 21) (by anonymous);

— *Fædrelandet*, 1844, no. 1572 and nos 1590-1591 (by anonymous);

— *For Literatur og Kritik*, vol. 2, 1844, pp. 305-314 (by Ludvig Nicolaus Helveg);
— *Theologisk Tidsskrift*, vol. 8, 1844, pp. 399-404 (by Carl Emil Scharling and Christian Thorning Engelstoft);
— "Die Baptisten-Frage in Dänemark," *Allgemeine Literatur-Zeitung*, 1845, vol. 2, no. 246 (November), columns 777-784; no. 247 (November), columns 785-792; no. 248 (November), columns 795-800 (by anonymous).

Reviews of *Tro, Overtro og Vantro* (1846):
— *Dansk Kirketidende*, vol. 2, 1846, columns 14-16 (by Carl Joakim Brandt);
— *Nordisk Literatur-Tidende*, 1846, no. 42 (by anonymous);
— *Berlingske politiske og Avertissements-Tidende*, 1846, no. 208 (by anonymous);
— *Kjøbenhavnsposten*, 1846, no. 257 (by anonymous);
— *Nyt Aftenblad*, 1846, no. 213 and 230 (by anonymous).

Reviews of *Dr. Martensens trykte moralske Paragrapher* (1846):
— *Fædrelandet*, 1846, no. 287 (by Johannes Georg Fog Steenberg);
— *Nyt Aftenblad*, 1846, no. 287 (by anonymous);
— *Berlingske politiske og Avertissements-Tidende*, 1846, no. 290 (by anonymous);
— *Kjøbenhavnsposten*, 1846, nos. 286 and 295 (by anonymous).

Reviews of *Speculativ Rettroenhed* (1849):
— *Kjøbenhavnsposten*, 1849, no. 249 (October 24) (by anonymous);
— *Flyve-Posten*, 1849, no. 249 (October 24) (by anonymous).

Review of *Den nydanske Theologies Cardinaldyder* (1850)
— *Flyve-Posten*, 1850, nos. 301-302 (by Magnús Eiríksson).

Reviews of *Er Troen et Paradox og "i Kraft af det Absurde"?* (1850):
— *Dansk Kirketidende*, vol. 5, 1850, no. 25, columns 423-424 (by anonymous);
— *Flyve-Posten*, 1850, no. 80 (by anonymous).

Reviews of *Breve til Clara Raphael* (1851):
— *Berlingske politiske og Avertissements-Tidende*, 1851, no. 66 (by anonymous);
— *Kjøbenhavnsposten*, 1851, no. 95 (by anonymous).

Reviews of *Er Johannes-Evangeliet et apostolisk og ægte Evangelium* (1863) / *Johannis Evangelium* (1864) / *Jóhannesar guðspjall* (1865):

— *Flyve-Posten*, 1863, no. 289 (December 12) (by anonymous);
— *Norðanfari*, vol. 3, 1864, nos. 24-25 (October 20), p. 47 [erroneously numbered "43"] (by anonymous);
— *Skírnir*, vol. 38, 1864, no. 1, p. 117 (by anonymous);
— *Theologisk Tidskrift* [Uppsala], vol. 4, 1864, pp. 290-303 (by "R—g");
— *Þjóðólfur*, vol. 17, 1865, no. 29 (May 23), pp. 115-116; nos. 31-32 (June 3), pp. 123-125; nos. 35-36 (July 4), pp. 140-141; nos. 42-43 (September 16), pp. 168-170; nos. 45-46 (October 17), pp. 182-184; nos. 47-48 (October 30), pp. 188-189 (by Sigurður Melsteð).

Reviews of *Hvem har Ret: Grundtvigianerne eller deres Modstandere?* (1863):
— *Evangelisk Ugeskrift*, Anden Række, vol. 10, 1863, no. 52 (December 18), p. 411 (by anonymous);
— *Flyve-Posten*, 1864, no. 4 (January 6) (by anonymous);
— *Aftonbladet* [Stockholm], 1865 (January 29) (by anonymous).

Reviews of *Gud og Reformatoren* (1866):
— *Fædrelandet*, 1866, no. 73 (by anonymous);
— *Dagbladet*, 1866, no. 147 (June 28) (by "R.V.");
— *Hamburger Nachrichten*, 1866, no. 140 (by anonymous).

Reviews of *Om Bønnens Virkning* (1870) and *Kunne vi elske Næsten som os selv?* (1870):
— *Berlingske politiske og Avertissements-Tidende*, 1870, no. 66 (March 19) (by "C.M.");
— *Dagbladet*, 1870, no. 187 (August 12) (by anonymous);
— *Heimdal*, 1870, no. 44 (by anonymous);
— *Dagens Nyheder*, 1870, no. 289 (by anonymous).

Reviews of *Paulus og Christus* (1871):
— *Folkets Avis*, 1871, no. 234 (September 17) (by anonymous);
— *Folkets Avis*, 1871, no. 237 (September 20) (by "Ab.");
— *Fædrelandet*, 1871, no. 249 (October 26) (by anonymous);
— *Dagbladet*, 1872, no. 8 (January 9) (by anonymous);
— "Kristi religion och kristna religionen. Paulus och Christus," *Sanningsökaren. Nordisk månadskrift för förnuftstro och praktisk kristendom*, vol. 1, 1877, no. 6, pp. 187-202 (by Axel Frithiof Åkerberg).

Reviews of *Jøder og Christne* (1873):
— *Dansk Arbejder-Tidende, Ugeblad for "Dansk Arbejder-Samfund,"* 1873, no. 14 (April 5) (by "A-Ø");
— *Dagens Nyheder*, 1873, no. 113 (April 28) (by anonymous).

VII. Reactions to Eiríksson by his Contemporaries

Anonymous, *Epistola eller Sende-Brev til Sr. Magnus Eiriksson fra en anden gammel Landsbypræst. Til Publici videre Nytte og Fornøielse nu til Trykken befordret*, Copenhagen: H.C. Klein 1844.
Anonymous, "*Kjøbenhavnspostens* Theologi," *Nyt Aftenblad*, 1846, no. 142.
Anonymous, "Frjettir, er ná til nýárs 1847," *Skírnir*, vol. 21, 1847, pp. 3-176, here pp. 144-160 ("Frá Norðurlöndum. 1. Frá Dönum").
Anonymous, "Danmark" [with regard to Eiríksson's letter to King Christian VIII], *Den Norske Rigstidende*, 1847, no. 157 (July 28).
Anonymous, "Udenlandske Efterretninger" [with regard to Eiríksson's letter to King Christian VIII], *Morgenbladet*, 1847, no. 209 (July 28).
Anonymous, [with regard to the Public Prosecutor's Action against Eiríksson], *Nyt Aftenblad*, 1848, no. 36; *Berlingske politiske og Avertissements-Tidende*, 1848, no. 37.
Anonymous, "Hálfyrði um Jóhannesar guðspjall. (Úr brèfi frá presti)," *Þjóðólfur*, vol. 17, 1864, nos. 1-2 (October 28), pp. 2-3.
Anonymous ["Gamall klerkur á Vesturströndum"], "Vaktið yður fyrir fallskennöndum, sem koma til yðar í sauðaklæðum, en hið innra eru þeir glepsandi vargar. Matt. 7," *Íslendingur*, vol. 4, 1865, no. 9 (March 10), pp. 70-72.
Anonymous, "Útlendar frèttir," *Þjóðólfur*, vol. 17, 1865, no. 38 (August 7), pp. 151-152.
Anonymous, [with regard to Eiríksson's "Svar til 'E. Th.'" (1865)], *Norðanfari*, vol. 4, 1865, nos. 35-36 (December 23), p. 69.
Anonymous ["Nokkrir Íslendingar í Kaupmannahöfn"], "Dómur um Magnús Eiríksson," *Norðanfari*, vol. 5, 1866, nos. 21-22 (September 27), pp. 41-42.
Anonymous, "(Aðsent)," *Þjóðólfur*, vol. 20, 1867, nos. 5-6 (December 13), p. 22.

Anonymous, "Úr brèfi," *Þjóðólfur*, vol. 21, 1868, nos. 1-2 (November 13), pp. 6-7.
Anonymus ["Austanvjeri"], "Fiskiveiðafjelagið danska," *Norðanfari*, vol. 7, 1868, nos. 29-30 (October 22), p. 57.
Anonymous, "Ávarp til M. E.," *Norðanfari*, vol. 7, 1868, nos. 35-36 (December 18), pp. 70-71.
Anonymous, [On Eiríksson at the "Nordiske Kirkemøde" (1871)], *Berlingske politiske og Avertissements-Tidende*, 1871, no. 212 (September 6).
Anonymous, [On Eiríksson at the "Nordiske Kirkemøde" (1871)], *Dagbladet*, 1871, no. 215 (September 6).
Anonymous, [On Eiríksson at the "Nordiske Kirkemøde" (1871)], *Bergens Adressecontoirs Efterretninger*, 1871, no. 220 (September 18).
Anonymous, [On Eiríksson at the "Nordiske Kirkemøde" (1871)], *Dagbladet*, 1871, no. 232 (September 26).
Anonymous, [On Eiríksson at the "Nordiske Kirkemøde" (1871)], *Dagbladet*, 1871, no. 233 (September 27).
Anonymous, "Literatur," *Dagbladet*, 1871, no. 233 (September 27).
Anonymous, [On Eiríksson at the "Nordiske Kirkemøde" (1871)], *Dagbladet*, 1871, no. 234 (September 28).
Anonymous, [On Eiríksson at the "Nordiske Kirkemøde" (1871)], *Folkets Avis*, 1871, no. 234 (September 28).
Anonymous, "Aðsent frá Kaupmannahøfn," *Norðanfari*, vol. 10, 1871, nos. 42-43 (October 28), p. 88 (erroneously numbered "42").
Anonymous, "Kaili úr brjeíi frá Kaupmannahöfn," *Gangleri*, vol. 2, 1871, nos. 19-20 (December 5), pp. 73-74.
Anonymous ["R."], [Review of Theodor Faber's *Aabent Brev til Danmarks Theologer om Nyrationalismens Forhold til den kristne Tro* (1871)], *Dagbladet*, no. 13, 1872.
Anonymous, "En Aands-Arbejder," *Dansk Arbejder-Tidende, Ugeblad for "Dansk Arbejder-Samfund,"* 1873, no. 10 (March 8) and no. 11 (March 15).
Anonymous ["G. f. G."], "Útlendar frjettir," *Norðanfari*, vol. 15, 1876, nos. 35-36 (August 18), p. 72.
Anonymous ["Reykvíkingur"], "Magnús Eiríksson," *Þjóðólfur*, vol. 28, 1876, no. 27 (September 6), p. 114.

Anonymous [“Einn af kaupendum Þjóðólfs”], “Sá sem ekki er með mér hann er á móti mer,” *Útsynningur*, vol. 1, 1876, no. 3 (October 19), columns 23-24.

Anonymous, “Sundrlausar hugsanir um prestamálið og laun embættismanna,” *Skuld*, vol. 2, 1878, no. 36 (November 30), columns 421-429, here columns 427-429.

Anonymous, “Landi vor herra Magnús Eiríksson,” *Norðanfari*, vol. 18, 1879, nos. 43-44 (September 9), p. 88.

Anonymous [“H.”], [Necrologue on Magnús Eiríksson], *Norðanfari*, vol. 20, 1881, nos. 53-54 (August 17), pp. 105-106.

Anonymous, “Magnús Eiríksson,” *Þjóðólfur*, vol. 34, 1882, no. 22 [erroneously numbered “23”] (September 23), pp. 87-88; no. 29 (December 6), pp. 116-117.

Åkerberg, Axel Frithiof and Arnoldson, Klas Pontus, “Om Magnus Eiriksson,” *Sanningsökaren. Nordisk månadskrift för förnuftstro och praktisk kristendom*, vol. 5, 1881, no. 1, p. 95.

— “Magnus Eiriksson,” *Sanningsökaren. Nordisk månadskrift för förnuftstro och praktisk kristendom*, vol. 5, 1881, nos. 7-8, pp. 193-203.

Andersen, Carl et al., *Indbydelse til at bidrage til at understøtte Magn. Eiriksson, Kbh. d. 11. Nov. 1872*, Copenhagen: no publisher given 1872.

Bárðdal, Jónas Fr., “Úr brjefi frá Jónasi Fr. Bárðdal,” *Norðanfari*, vol. 13, 1874, nos. 5-6 (February 6), p. 12.

Baudoin, Jean-Baptiste [“Hinir katólsku prestar í Reykjavík”], *Útskýring um trú katólsku Kirkjunnar í þeim trúaratriðum, þar sem ágreisningr er milli hennar og mótmælanda*, Reykjavík: Hinir katólsku prestar í Reykjavík 1865.

— [“Hinir katólsku prestar í Reykjavík”], *Jesús Kristr er Guð. Þrátt fyrir mótmæli herra Magnúsar Eiríkssonar*, Reykjavík: Hinir katólsku prestar í Reykjavík 1867.

— [anonymously], *Er það satt eðr ósatt, sem hra Jónas Guðmundsson segir um bækling vorn: “Jesús Kristr er Guð” o. s. frv.?*, Reykjavík: Einar Þórðarson 1867.

Borgfirðingur, Sighvatur Grímsson, “Höfundur Skírnis og M. Eyríksson,” *Norðanfari*, vol. 10, 1871, nos. 44-45 (November 7), pp. 93-94 (erroneously numbered “89-90”).

Bøgh, Erik [anonymously], *Søren Kierkegaard og St. Erik og St. Magnus Dyrkelsen. Et Bidrag til Bedømmelsen af S. Kierkegaards Virksomhed item Erik Bøghs og Magnus Eiriksons Productivitet*, Copenhagen: V. Pio 1870.

Brynjúlfsson, Gisli, *Til Magnúsar Eiríkssonar á 71. afmælisdag hans, 22. júní 1876. Flutt í samsæti Íslendinga í Kaupmannahöfn*, [Copenhagen] [1876].

— "Til Magnúsar Eiríkssonar á 71. afmælisdag hans, 22. júní 1876. Flutt í samsæti Íslendinga í Khöfn," *Norðanfari*, vol. 15, 1876, nos. 51-52 (October 31), p. 102.

Einarsson, Magnús, *Nokkrar Athugasemdir, gegn Magnúsi Eiríkssyni m. fl.*, Akureyri: Jónas Sveinsson 1867.

— "(Aðsent)," *Þjóðólfur*, vol. 20, 1868, nos. 34-35 (July 10), p. 139.

— "Svar til Dr. J. Hjaltalíns," *Norðanfari*, vol. 7, 1868, nos. 25-26 (September 22), pp. 49-50.

Faber, Theodor, *Aabent Brev til Danmarks Theologer om Nyrationalismens Forhold til den kristne Tro*, Copenhagen: Gad 1871.

Gíslason, Konráð et al., "Herra ritstjóri!," *Norðanfari*, vol. 4, 1865, nos. 31-32 (October 7), p. 61.

Guðmundsson, Jónas, "Útaf 'bókafregn' í Norðanfara," *Þjóðólfur*, vol. 17, 1865, nos. 18-19 (March 13), pp. 72-73.

— [with regard to "E. Th.," *Norðanfari*, vol. 3, 1864, nos. 30-31 (December 1), pp. 59-60], *Þjóðólfur*, vol. 18, 1865, no. 3 (November 4), pp. 10-11.

— *Hvaða trú hafa hinir svo nefndu kath. prestar, eptir því sem þeir koma fram í riti sínu, Jesús Kristur er guð, þrátt fyrir mótmæli hr. Magnúsar Eiríkssonar?*, Reykjavík: Einar Þórðarson 1867.

— "Svar til pápisku prestanna í Reykjavík," *Norðanfari*, vol. 7, 1868, nos. 15-16 (July 4), pp. 29-30.

Hallgrímsson, Jónas, *Ritverk Jónasar Hallgrímssonar*, ed. by Haukur Hannesson, Páll Valsson and Sveinn Yngvi Egilsson, vols. 1-4 Reykvavík: Svart á Hvítu 1989; vol. 1, *Ljóð og Lausanal*, p. 265; vol. 2, *Bréf og dagbækur*, p. 11, p. 129, p. 208; vol. 4, *Skýringar og skrár*, p. 6, p. 108, p. 230, p. 246, p. 274, p. 383, p. 403.

Helveg, Hans Friedrich, "Om Ankerne over det Nordiske Kirkemøde," *Dansk Kirketidende*, 1871, no. 42 (October 15), columns 659-666.

— "Gammel- og Ny-Rationalisme," *Dansk Kirketidende*, 1876, no. 37 (September 17), columns 601-610.

Helveg, Ludvig Nicolaus, "Prof. Martensens Dogmatik og dens Angribere (Slutning)," *Dansk Kirketidende*, vol. 5, 1850, no. 22 (March 3), columns 369-373.

Hjaltalín, Jón, "Fáein orð til Magnúsar Einarssonar í Skáleyjum," *Þjóðólfur*, vol. 20, 1868, nos. 20-21 (April 8), p. 81.

Jónsson, Björn, "Landi vor herra Magnús Eiríksson," *Norðanfari*, vol. 18, 1879, nos. 43-44 (September 9), p. 88.

Jensen, Jens Laurits ["Leonard Philolalos"], *Er det Noget, eller er det ikke Noget? Ærbødigst Forespørgsel til de ærede Theologer, Troesriddere og Paradoxmagere, Troens og Theologiens nyeste Kamp vedrørende*, Aalborg: Rée'ske Boghandel 1850, p. 6.

Levinssøn, M. Chr., *Magnus Eirikssons "Restancer" i "Folkets Avis" og paa det nordiske Kirkemøde*, Copenhagen: no publisher given 1872.

Lindberg, Niels, [On Eiríksson at the "Nordiske Kirkemøde" (1871)], *Dansk Kirketidende*, 1871, no. 36 (September 10), columns 565-576 and nos. 38-39 (September 24), columns 593-624.

— [Review of Theodor Faber's *Aabent Brev til Danmarks Theologer om Nyrationalismens Forhold til den kristne Tro* (1871)], *Dansk Kirketidende*, 1871, no. 50 (December 10), columns 794-799.

Madsen, Kr. (ed.), *Forhandlingerne paa Det Fjerde Nordiske Kirkemöde i Kjøbenhavn den 5., 6. og 7. September 1871*, Copenhagen: Gyldendal 1871, pp. 46-51.

Magnússon, Eiríkur, "Herra Ritstjóri 'Þjóðólfs'!," *Þjóðólfur*, vol. 25, 1873, no. 46 (October 6), pp. 185-186.

Martensen, Hans Lassen, "Litterairt Uvæsen," *Berlingske politiske og Avertissements-Tidende*, 1844, no. 115 (April 29).

— *Dogmatiske Oplysninger. Et Leilighedsskrift*, Copenhagen: C.A. Reitzel 1850, p. 4.

— Letter to Ludvig Jacob Mendel Gude (November 26, 1850), in *Biskop H. Martensens Breve*, ed. by Selskabet for Danmarks Kirkehistorie ved Bjørn Kornerup, vols. 1-3, Copenhagen: Gad 1955-57; vol. 1, 1955, p. 14 (no. 10).

— Letter to Ludvig Jacob Mendel Gude (April 21, 1873), in *Biskop H. Martensens Breve*, ed. by Selskabet for Danmarks Kirkehistorie ved

Bjørn Kornerup, vols. 1-3, Copenhagen: Gad 1955-57; vol. 3, 1957, p. 75 (no. 360).

Kierkegaard, Søren Aabye, *SKS* 21, 301-302, NB10:87 / *KJN* 5, 312; *SKS* 22, 325-328, NB13:86 / *KJN* 6, 329-332; *SKS* 23, 176-177, NB17:19 / *KJN* 7, 178-179; *SKS* 23, 177-178, NB17:21 / *KJN* 7, 180; *SKS* 23, 182-183, NB17:28 / *KJN* 7, 185; *SKS* 23, 197-198, NB17:50 / *KJN* 7, 200-201; *Pap*. VII-1 B 87, pp. 284-286 / *CUP2*, 125-127; *Pap*. VII-1 B 88, pp. 287-298 / *CUP2*, 127-137; *Pap*. VII-1 B 89-91; *Pap*. VIII-2 B 175-176; *Pap*. X-6 B 68-69 / *JP* 6, 6598-6599; *Pap*. X-6 B 70-71; *Pap*. X-6 B 72-76; *Pap*. X-6 B 77 / *JP* 6, 6600; *Pap*. X-6 B 78-81 / *JP* 1, 9-12; *Pap*. X-6 B 82 / *JP* 6, 6601; *Pap*. X-6 B 128, pp. 170-171 / *CUP2*, 161-163 (*JP* 6, 6596); *Pap*. X-6 B 129, pp. 171-172.

Paijkull, Carl Wilhelm, *En Sommer i Island. Reiseskildring*, Copenhagen: Forlagsbureauet 1867, pp. 81-84.

Pedrin, Andreas Daniel, *Vor Herres og Frelsers Jesu Christi nye Testament og Magnus Eirikssons reformeerte Jødedom*, Copenhagen: no publisher given 1874.

Sigurðsson, Jón, *Bréf Jóns Sigurðssonar. Úrval*, Reykjavík: Prentað í Ísafoldarprentsmiðju 1911, p. 30, p. 42, p. 52, p. 71, p. 76, p. 82, p. 103, p. 126, p. 131, p. 175, p. 231, p. 252, p. 305, p. 374, p. 492, p. 553.

Thorlacius, Einar ["E. Th."], "Verum ekki framar börn, er hrekjumst og feykjumst af hverjum kenningar-þyt. Efes. 4, 14," *Norðanfari*, vol. 3, 1864, nos. 30-31 (December 1), pp. 59-60.

— "Svar móti svari," *Norðanfari*, vol. 4, 1865, nos. 8-9 (March 18), pp. 15-16.

— "Elskanlegir, trúið ekki sjerhverjum anda, heldur reynið andana, hvort þeir sjeu frá Guði! 1, Jóh. 4,1," *Norðanfari*, vol. 4, 1865, nos. 23-24 (July 31), pp. 45-46.

— "Das Wort sie sollen lassen stahn, Und kein'n Dank dazu haben. Luther," *Norðanfari*, vol. 5, 1866, nos. 5-6 (February 24), pp. 9-10.

Thomsen, Grímur [anonymously], *En Privatskrivelse til den anden gamle Landsbypræst, fra hans gamle Ven, den første gamle Candidat, som Commentar over Herr Pastors Epistola til Sr. Magnus Eiriksson*, Copenhagen: P.G. Philipsen 1844.

Thorkilsen, C.[hristen], *Bibelens Lære om den christelige Daab nærmest i Anledning af de baptistiske Bevægelser og Eirikssons ubeføiede Angreb*, Copenhagen: no publisher given 1845.

Thóroddsen, Jón Þórðarson ["J. Þ. Th."], "NOKKUR ORÐ um Magnús Eiríksson og stóru bókina," *Íslendingur*, vol. 4, 1865, no. 12 (June 22), pp. 89-90.

VIII. Works on Eiríksson

Albertsson, Eiríkur, *Magnús Eiríksson. Guðfræði hans og trúarlíf*, Doctoral Dissertation, University of Iceland, Reykjavik 1938.

Árnason, Vilhjálmur and Pálsson, Jón Bragi, "Falskennandi eða einherji sannleikans? Um viðtökur Magnúsar Eiríkssonar meðal Íslendinga," *Skírnir*, vol. 189, 2015, pp. 491-518.

Bjarnason, Ágúst Hákonarson, "Magnus Eiriksson, the first Icelandic Unitarian" (handwritten manuscript, address at Harvard Divinity School, May 21, 1923), Andover-Harvard Theological Library, Cambridge, MA (bMS 103/5-15).

— "Um Magnús Eiríksson," *Skírnir*, vol. 98, 1924, pp. 39-73.

Bjarnarson, Björn, "Magnús Eiríksson," *Heimdallur*, vol. 1, 1884, no. 7 (July), pp. 97-100.

Cauly, Olivier, "La foi est-elle un paradoxe ou 'une vertu de l'absurde'? À propos d'une critique de Magnus Eiriksson (Theophilus Nicolaus)," *Kairos. Revue de la Faculté de Philosophie de l'Université de Toulouse*, vol. 10, 1997, pp. 99-114.

Elberling, Emil, "Eiríksson, Magnús," in *Nordisk familjebok. Konversationslexikon och realencyklopedi*, 2nd edition, vols. 1-38, ed. by Theodor Westrin, Stockholm: Nordisk familjeboks förlags aktiebolag 1904-26; vol. 7, 1907, columns 63-66.

Fritchman, Stephen Hole, *Men of Liberty. Ten Unitarian Pioneers*, Boston: Beacon Press 1944, pp. 163-180 ("X. Magnus Eiriksson").

Gudmundson, Valtýr Emil, *The Icelandic Unitarian Connection: Beginnings of Icelandic Unitarianism in North America, 1885-1900*, completed posthumously by Barbara J.R. Gudmundson, with a foreword by Conrad Wright, Winnipeg, Manitoba: Wheatfield Press 1984, pp. 6-10 ("The Soul of Icelandic Religious Liberalism—Magnús Eiríksson").

Helgason, Jón (ed.), "Um Magnús Eiríksson. Nokkrar endurminningar eftir prófessor Fredr. C. B. Dahl i Khöfn.," *Óðinn*, vol. 8, 1912, no. 2 (May), pp. 14-16; *Heimir*, vol. 8, 1912, no. 9 (May 1), pp. 197-203.

Jochumsson, Matthías ["M."], "Tolstoi og Magnús Eiríksson," *Austri*, vol. 4, 1894, no. 21 (July 21), pp. 82-83; *Lögberg*, vol. 7, 1894, no. 74 (September 22), p. 1.

Johansen, August, *Bibel-Rensning* [*Om Magnus Eirikssons Værk*]. *Et Bidrag. Efter flere Forfattere, ordnet og fremstillet af August Johansen. Buenos Aires, i Argentina, 1923* (119 p.), The Royal Library in Copenhagen, Additamenta 468, 2°folio.

Jonsson, Finnur, "Eiríksson, Magnús," in *Salmonsens Konversations Leksikon*, 2nd edition, vols. 1-26, ed. by Christian Blangstrup, Copenhagen: J.H. Schultz 1915-30; vol. 6, 1917, pp. 796-797.

Kierkegaard, Thorvald, *Magnus Eiriksson og Mary B. Westenholz. To Forkæmpere for Unitarismen i Danmark*, Copenhagen: no publisher given 1958 (an offprint from *Protestantisk Tidende*, 1957), pp. 3-9 ("Magnus Eiriksson. Den første Forkynder af Unitarisme i Danmark").

Koch, Carl Henrik, "En ihærdig kritiker: Magnús Eiríksson," in his *Den danske idealisme. 1800-1880*, Copenhagen: Gyldendal 2004, pp. 292-298.

Linder, Nils et al. (ed.), "Eiríksson, Magnús," in *Nordisk Familjebok. Konversationslexikon och Realencyklopedi*, vols. 1-20, Stockholm: Gernandts boktryckeri-aktiebolag 1876-99; vol. 4, 1881, columns 281-284.

Neiiendam, Michael, "Eiríksson, Magnús," in *Dansk biographisk Leksikon*, vols. 1-27, ed. by Povl Engelstoft, Copenhagen: J.H. Schultz 1933-44; vol. 4, 1935, pp. 275-276.

Nielsen, Frederik, "Eiriksson, Magnus," in *Kirke-Leksikon for Norden*, vols. 1-4, ed. by Frederik Nielsen, Aarhus: Jydsk Forlags-Forretning 1900-29, vol. 1, p. 733.

Pálsson, Jón Bragi, and Árnason, Vilhjálmur, "Falskennandi eða einherji sannleikans? Um viðtökur Magnúsar Eiríkssonar meðal Íslendinga,“ *Skírnir*, vol. 189, 2015, pp. 491-518.

Pjetursson, Hafsteinn, "Magnús Eiríksson," *Tímarit hins íslenska bókmenntafjélags*, vol. 8, 1887, pp. 1-33.

— "Magnús Eiríksson," *Teologisk Tidsskrift for den danske Folkekirke*, Ny Række, vol. 3, 1901-1902, pp. 116-143.

— "Magnús Eiríksson," in *Merkir Íslendingar: ævisögur og minningargreinar*, ed. by Þorkell Jóhannesson, vols. 1-5, Reykjavík: Bókfellsútgáfan 1947-57; vol. 5, pp. 314-344.

R.P., "[No title]," *Heimir*, vol. 8, 1912, no. 9 (May 1), pp. 205-207.

Schreiber, Gerhard, "Eiríksson, Magnús," *Biographisch-Bibliographisches Kirchenlexikon*, vols. 1-35, ed. by Friedrich Wilhelm Bautz and Traugott Bautz, Nordhausen: Verlag Traugott Bautz 1975-2014; vol. 28, 2007, columns 517-538.

— "Ist der Glaube ein Paradox und 'kraft des Absurden'? – Kierkegaards Auseinandersetzung mit Magnús Eiríksson," in *Kierkegaard and Faith*, ed. by Roman Králik et al., Šaľa and Mexico City: Sociedad Iberoamericana de Estudios Kierkegaardianos 2008, pp. 34-47.

— "Magnús Eiríksson: An Opponent of Martensen and an Unwelcome Ally of Kierkegaard," in *Kierkegaard and His Danish Contemporaries*, Tome II, *Theology*, ed. by Jon Stewart, Aldershot: Ashgate 2009 (*Kierkegaard Research: Sources, Reception and Resources*, vol. 7), pp. 49-94.

— "Je viera paradoxom a 'cestou absurda'? Názorový rozpor S. Kierkegaarda s Magnúsom Eiríkssonom," in *Kierkegaardovo zrkadlo pre súcasnost*, ed. by Roman Králik et al., Toronto: Kierkegaard Circle, University of Toronto 2010 (*Acta Kierkegaardiana. Series and Supplements*, vol. 1), pp. 160-171.

— "'Like a Voice in the Wilderness': Magnús Eiríksson's Tenacious Critique of Martensen—and Martensen's 'Lofty Silence,'" in *Hans Lassen Martensen. Theologian, Philosopher and Social Critic*, ed. by Jon Stewart, Copenhagen: Museum Tusculanum Press 2012 (*Danish Golden Age Studies*, vol. 6), pp. 155-191.

— "Magnús Eiríksson—Vanræktur samtímamaður Sørens Kierkegaard," trans. by Aðalsteinn Garðarsson, *Skírnir*, vol. 188, 2014, pp. 116-143.

Schwanenflügel, Hermann Heinrich Louis, "Magnus Eirikson," [sic!] *Det nittende Aarhundrede. Maanedskrift for Literatur og Kritik*, vols. 1-6, ed. by Georg Brandes and Edvard Brandes, Copenhagen: Gyldendal 1875-77; vol. 6, 1877, pp. 266-294.

— "Magnus Eiriksson" [necrologue], *Morgenbladet*, 1881, no. 156 (July 9).
— ["H."], "Magnús Eiríksson, látinn 3. dag júnímánaðar 1881," [necrologue], *Norðanfari*, vol. 20, 1881, nos. 53-54 (August 17), pp. 105-106.
— "Eiríksson, Magnus," in *Dansk biographisk Lexikon, tillige omfattende Norge for Tidsrummet 1537-1814*, vols. 1-19, ed. by Carl Frederik Bricka, Copenhagen: Gyldendalske Boghandels Forlag (F. Hegel & Søn) 1887-1905; vol. 4, 1890, pp. 479-482.
Skjoldager, Emanuel, "An Unwanted Ally: Magnus Eiriksson," in *Kierkegaard as a Person*, ed. by Niels Thulstrup and Marie Mikulová Thulstrup, Copenhagen: C.A. Reitzel 1983 (*Bibliotheca Kierkegaardiana*, vol. 12), pp. 102-108.
Þorleifsson, Bertel E. Ó., "Magnús Eiríksson" [poem], *Heimdallur*, vol. 1, 1884, no. 12, pp. 181-182; *Heimir*, vol. 8, 1912, no. 9 (May 1), pp. 204-205.
Þráinsdóttir, Jóhanna, "Gleymdur liðsmaður kvenna. Um Magnús Eiríksson, guðfræðing og rithöfund, og framlag hans til frelsisbaráttu kvenna," *Menningarblað. Lesbók Morgunblaðsins*, 1997, May 10, pp. 4-5.
— "Er trúin þverstæða? Gagnrýni Magnúsar Eiríkssonar á trúarskoðunum Kierkegaards í 'Ugg og ótta,'" *Tímarit Máls og menningar*, vol. 61, 2000, pp. 35-45.
Watkin, Julia, "Eiríksson, Magnus" in her *Historical Dictionary of Kierkegaard's Philosophy*, Lanham and London: Scarecrow Press 2001, pp. 69-72.

IX. Works that Discuss Eiríksson

Anonymous, "Bálkestir og vitfirringahæli," *Verkamaðurinn*, vol. 13, 1930, no. 24 (March 15), pp. 2-3
Arildsen, Skat, *Biskop Hans Lassen Martensen. Hans Liv, Udvikling og Arbejde. I. Studier i det 19. Aarhundredes danske Aandsliv*, Copenhagen: Gad 1932, especially pp. 206-211; pp. 274-275; pp. 288-289.
Árnason, Vilhjálmur, "Iceland: 'Neglect and Misunderstanding': The Reception of Kierkegaard in Iceland," in *Kierkegaard's International*

Reception, Tome I, *Northern and Western Europe*, ed. by Jon Stewart, Aldershot: Ashgate 2009 (*Kierkegaard Research: Sources, Reception and Resources*, vol. 8), pp. 219-236, especially pp. 221-230.

Bjarnason, Ágúst Hákonarson, "Eiríkur Albertsson: Magnús Eiríksson, guðfræði hans og trúarlíf. Á kostnað höfundar. Ísafoldarprentsm. Rvík 1938. 381 bls.," *Skírnir*, vol. 113, 1939, pp. 211-217.

Brandes, Georg Morris Cohen, *Søren Kierkegaard. En kritisk Fremstilling i Grundrids*, Copenhagen: Gyldendal 1877, p. 268.

Cauly, Olivier, "La philosophie dans les pays du Nord," in *Encyclopédie philosophique universelle*, vol. 4, *Le discours philosophique*, ed. by Jean-François Mattéi, Paris: Presses Universitaires de France 1998, pp. 617-653, especially pp. 637-638.

Fabro, Cornelio, "Faith and Reason in Kierkegaard's Dialectic," in *A Kierkegaard Critique: An International Selection of Essays Interpreting Kierkegaard*, ed. by Howard Albert Johnson and Niels Thulstrup, New York: Harper and Brothers 1962, pp. 156-206; especially pp. 174-185.

Fix, Hans, "Edition im Altnordischen am Beispiel des Elucidarius,'" in *Maschinelle Verarbeitung altdeutscher Texte*, vol. 4, *Beiträge zum Vierten Internationalen Symposion Trier 28. Februar bis 2. März*, ed. by Kurt Gärtner et al., Tübingen: Max Niemeyer 1991, pp. 155-167, especially p. 161 (note).

Garff, Joakim, *Søren Kierkegaard: A Biography*, translated by Bruce H. Kirmmse, Princeton: Princeton University Press 2005, pp. 425-427; p. 534; p. 638; p. 646.

Gröndal, Benedikt, *Dægradvöl*, Reykjavík: Forlagið 2014, pp. 199-200.

Guðmundsson, Gunnar F., *Kaþólskt trúboð á Íslandi 1857–1875*, ed. by Jón Guðnason, Reykjavík: Sagnfræðistofnun Háskóla Íslands 1987, pp. 103-104 and p. 109.

Hákonardóttir, Inga Huld, "Konur og Kristur á 19.öld," in *Kristni á Íslandi*, vol. 4, *Til móts við nútímann*, ed. by Hjalti Hugason, Pétur Pétursson and Þórunn Valdimarsdóttir, Reykjavík: Alþingi 2000, p. 126.

Harðarson, Atli, "Heimspekingurinn Brynjúlfur frá Minna Núpi," *Lesbók Morgunblaðsins*, 1992, no. 44 (December 21), pp. 30-32.

Helgason, Jón (1866-1942), *Islands kirke fra reformationen til vore dage. En historisk Fremstilling*, Copenhagen: Gad 1922 (*Islands Kirke. En historisk Fremstilling*, vol. 2), pp. 188-190.

— *Kristnisaga Íslands: Frá öndverðu til vorra tíma*, Tome II, *Kristnihald þjóðar vorrar eftir siðaskifti*, Reykjavík: Félagsprentsmiðjan 1927, pp. 327-330.

— *Íslendingar í Danmörku fyr og síðar*, Reykjavík: Íslandsdeild Dansk-íslenzka félagsins 1931.

Helgason, Jón (1914-81), *Vér Íslands börn*, vols. 1-3, Reykjavík: Iðunn 1968-70; vol. 3, *Heimur á við hálft kálfskinn*, pp. 7-123.

Jochumsson, Matthías, "Dvöl mín í Danmörku 1871-1872," *Iðunn*, vol. 1, 1916, no. 3 (January), pp. 258-265 ("I. Um Magnús Eiríksson o. fl.").

— *Sögukaflar af sjálfum mér*, Reykjavik: Þorsteinn Gíslason 1922, pp. 184-188 et passim.

— [Letter to Steingríms Þorsteinssonar from April 1865], in *Bréf Matthíasar Jochumssonar*, ed. by Steingrímur Matthíasson, Akureyri: Bókadeild Menningarsjóðs 1935, p. 22 et passim.

Jónsson, Eirík, "Danmörk," *Skírnir*, vol. 44, 1870, pp. 171-195, especially pp. 194-195.

— "Danmörk," *Skírnir*, vol. 46, 1872, pp. 137-154, especially pp. 141-142 and p. 152

— "Danmörk," *Skírnir*, vol. 56, 1882, pp. 108-118, especially pp. 116-117.

Jónsson frá Minna-Núpi, Brynjúlfur, *Saga hugsunar minnar um sjálfan mig og tilveruna*, Reykjavík: Hið íslenzka bókmenntafélag 1997 [1912], p. 18.

Jørgensen, Alfred Theodor, "Nogle Træk af Martensens Dogmatiks Historie. Et Afsnit af den danske Teologis Historie," in Hans Lassen Martensen, *Den christelige Dogmatik*, 5th edition, ed. and with an introduction by Alfred Theodor Jørgensen, Copenhagen: Gad 1904, pp. I-XXII, especially p. XV.

Kabell, Aage, *Kierkegaardstudiet i Norden*, Copenhagen: Hagerup 1948, pp. 81-82; p. 125; p. 179; p. 214.

Koch, Hal and Kornerup, Bjørn (eds.), *Den Danske Kirkes Historie*, vols. 1-8, Copenhagen: Gyldendalske Boghandel, Nordisk Forlag 1950-

66; vol. 6, *Tiden 1800-1848*, by Hal Koch, 1954, p. 322; vol. 7, *Tiden 1849-1901*, by Poul Georg Lindhardt, 1958, pp. 188-189.

Nielsen, Rasmus, *Regensen. Erindringer fra 1858-62*, Copenhagen: H. Hagerups Boghandel 1906, pp. 64-65.

Nielsen, Svend Aage, *Kierkegaard og Regensen. Kierkegaards forhold til F.C. Petersen, Poul Martin Møller, D.G. Monrad, Magnus Eiriksson, Carl Ploug, P.L. Møller, Hans Brøchner og J.C. Hostrup*, Copenhagen: Graabrødre Torv's Forlag V. Severin Petersen 1965, pp. 70-75 and p. 144.

Law, David R., *Kierkegaard's Kenotic Christology*, Oxford: Oxford University Press 2013, p. 120 (note).

Olgeirsson, Einar, "Erlendir menningarstraumar og Íslendingar," *Réttur*, vol. 11, 1926, nos. 1-2, pp. 9-24, especially pp. 15-16.

Olesen, Tonny Aagaard, "The Obscure Kierkegaard: One Hundred Years of *Postscript* Commentary," *Kierkegaard Studies Yearbook*, 2005, pp. 314-338; especially pp. 318-319.

Petersen, Carl S. and Andersen, Vilhelm, *Illustreret dansk Litteraturhistorie*, vol. 4, Copenhagen: Gyldendal 1925, p. 32 and p. 875.

Possen, David D., "On Kierkegaard's Copenhagen Pagans," in *'Christian Discourses' and 'The Crisis and a Crisis in the Life of an Actress'*, ed. by Robert L. Perkins, Macon: Mercer University Press 2008 (*International Kierkegaard Commentary*, vol. 17), pp. 35-59; especially pp. 42-47.

— *Søren Kierkegaard and the Very Idea of Advance Beyond Socrates*, vol. 1, Dissertation, University of Chicago, 2009, pp. 386-393 and p. 417.

Rubow, Paul Victor, *Kierkegaard og hans Samtidige*, Copenhagen: Gyldendalske Boghandel Nordisk Forlag 1950, pp. 23-29.

Schreiber, Gerhard, "Glaube und 'Unmittelbarkeit' bei Kierkegaard," *Kierkegaard Studies Yearbook*, 2010, pp. 391-426, especially pp. 412-417.

— "Kierkegaard's Account of Faith as 'The New Immediacy,'" *Filozofia*, vol. 68, 2013, pp. 27-37, especially pp. 32-34.

— *Apriorische Gewissheit. Das Glaubensverständnis des jungen Kierkegaard und seine philosophisch-theologischen Voraussetzungen*, Berlin and Boston: Walter de Gruyter 2014 (*Kierkegaard Studies Monograph Series*, vol. 30), especially pp. 117-118 and pp. 330-332.

Schröer, Henning, "Paradox II. Theologisch," in *Theologische Realenzyklopädie*, vols. 1-36, ed. by Gerhard Müller et al., Berlin and New York 1976-2004; vol. 25, 1995, pp. 731-737.

Sigurðardóttir, Sigurbjörg, "Útlendar frjettir," *Norðanfari*, vol. 15, 1876, nos. 35-36 (August 18), p. 72.

Sigurðardóttir, Vilborg, *Um kvenréttindi á Íslandi til 1915*, Unpublished BA Thesis, University of Iceland, 1967.

Sigurjónsson, Arnór, *Einars saga Ásmundssonar*, vols. 1-3, Reykjavík: Bókaútg. Menningarsjóðs 1957-70; vol. 1, *Bóndinn í nesi*, pp. 37-38 and pp. 258-316 (Section XIII).

Stewart, Jon, *Kierkegaard's Relations to Hegel Reconsidered*, New York: Cambridge University Press 2003, p. 454.

Styrkársdóttir, Auður, "Forspjall," in John Stuart Mill, *Kúgun kvenna*, trans. by Sigurð Jónasson, ed. by Vilhjálmur Árnason, Reykjavik: Hið íslenska bókmenntafélag 1997, pp. 9-65, especially pp. 37-38.

Søe, Niels H., "Kierkegaard's Doctrine of the Paradox," in *A Kierkegaard Critique: An International Selection of Essays Interpreting Kierkegaard*, ed. by Howard Albert Johnson and Niels Thulstrup, New York: Harper and Brothers 1962, pp. 207-227; especially pp. 207-210.

Swatos Jr., William H. and Gissurarson, Loftur Reimar, *Icelandic Spiritualism: Mediumship and Modernity in Iceland*, New Brunswick, NJ: Transaction Publisher 1997, pp. 44-45, p. 75, p. 110.

Thomas, John Heywood, "Christianity as Absurd," in *The Sources and Depths of Faith in Kierkegaard*, ed. by Niels Thulstrup and Marie Mikulová Thulstrup, Copenhagen: C.A. Reitzel 1978 (*Bibliotheca Kierkegaardiana*, vol. 2), pp. 58-62.

Thompson, Curtis L., *Following the Cultured Public's Chosen One: Why Martensen Mattered to Kierkegaard*, Copenhagen: Museum Tusculanum Press 2008 (*Danish Golden Age Studies*, vol. 4), especially p. 46 and p. 152.

Þorláksson, Niels Steingrímur, "Guðdómr drottins vors Jesú Krists," *Aldamót*, vol. 1, 1891, pp. 76-116, especially pp. 78f.

Thulstrup, Niels, "Martensen's *Dogmatics* and its Reception," in *Kierkegaard and His Contemporaries: The Culture of Golden Age Denmark*, ed. by Jon Stewart, Berlin and New York 2003 (*Kierkegaard Studies Monograph Series*, vol. 10), pp. 181-202, especially pp. 194-195.

Valsson, Páll, *Jónas Hallgrímsson. Ævisaga*, Reykjavík: Mál og menning 1999, pp. 34-35, p. 55, pp. 68-69, p. 141, p. 339, pp. 395-396, p. 484.

Vodskov, Hans Sofus, "Magnus Eiriksson," in his *Spredte Studier*, Copenhagen: Gyldendalske Boghandels Forlag (F. Hegel & Søn) 1884, pp. 31-40 (reprinted in Vodskov, Hans Sofus, *Litteraturkritik i udvalg*, ed. by Erik Reitzel-Nielsen, vol. 1, Copenhagen: C.A. Reitzel 1992, pp. 204-209).

Walsh, Sylvia, "Echoes of Absurdity: The Offended Consciousness and the Absolute Paradox in Kierkegaard's *Philosophical Fragments*," in *Philosophical Fragments and Johannes Climacus*, ed. by Robert L. Perkins, Macon: Mercer University Press 1994 (*International Kierkegaard Commentary*, vol. 7), pp. 33-46, especially p. 34 and p. 39.

— *Living Christianly: Kierkegaard's Dialectic of Christian Existence*, University Park: Pennsylvania State University Press 2005, especially pp. 58-60 and p. 173.

X. Miscellaneous

Hee, Christian Peter (ed.), *Fortegnelse over endel forskjellige gode og velconditionerede Bogsamlinger, bestaaende af theologiske, juridiske, medicinske, historiske, æsthetiske, sprog- og naturvidenskabelige Værker samt Restoplagene af forskjellige theologiske Bøger, tilhørende Boerne efter afdøde Overlærer Nielsen, Districtslæge Wilhjelm, Pastor Krogh, Cand. theol. Magnus Eiriksson, Krigsraad Juul m.fl.*, Copenhagen: J.D. Qvist 1881, pp. 138-170.

The Auction Catalogue of Eiríksson's Library

edited by Gerhard Schreiber
in collaboration with Jón Bragi Pálsson and Silvia Vignati

Introduction

After Eiríksson's death on July 3, 1881, it was decided that his extensive personal library with more than 1,200 different books (more than 3,000 volumes altogether) would be sold at auction. This public auction began on September 27, 1881 and continued during the subsequent days at Niels Juelsgade 6 (close to Kongens Nytorv) in Copenhagen, which was where the auction house of the auctioneer Christian Peter Hee (1838-97) was located.[1] It was also Hee who prepared a catalogue of the works of Eiríksson and of other personal libraries to be sold at this auction. Since it was intended for use in the context of an auction and was never conceived to be the object of scholarly study, the original edition of the catalogue, published in September 1881,[2] contained incomplete, inaccurate, and/or unclear bibliographical information about the works in the auction.

The following is a revised edition of the original auction catalogue of Eiríksson's private library. The goal was to get hold of copies of all the books and check the bibliographical information first-hand. The titles

1 See Station Dødeblade; Filmrulle 0008; Registerblad 8307 (ID 3333113), issued May 1, 1892; Københavns Stadsarkiv (Copenhagen City Archives).

2 Christian Hee (ed.), *Fortegnelse over endel forskjellige gode og velconditionerede Bogsamlinger, bestaaende af theologiske, juridiske, medicinske, historiske, æsthetiske, sprog- og naturvidenskabelige Værker samt Restoplagene af forskjellige theologiske Bøger, tilhørende Boerne efter afdøde Overlærer Nielsen, Districtslæge Wilhjelm, Pastor Krogh, Cand. theol. Magnus Eiriksson, Krigsraad Juul m.fl.*, Copenhagen: J.D. Qvist 1881, pp. 138-170.

of the individual works have been given in italics in the form in which they appear on the title pages of the individual books. Only in rare cases of highly unusual orthography have these been modified with the use of square brackets. In addition to the full names of the authors of the books, the place of publication, publishing house and year of publication have also been given in their standard English form. Other editorial information such as "ed. by" or "trans. by" has been given in English and not as it appears on the title pages. The division of the collection into the categories: "History and Literature of Iceland" (nos. 1-396), "Theology and Philosophy" (nos. 397-980), "History, Literature, etc." (nos. 981-1177), and "Publisher" (nos. 1178-1220), which contains mostly copies of Eiríksson's own books,[1] belongs to the original edition of the catalogue and is thus retained.

With the catalogue in hand, one can determine with some degree of probability what books Eiríksson read and what editions he used for his information about specific authors. This is not to say that the presence or absence of the listing of a book in the auction catalogue can be the sole criterion for answering the question of whether or not Eiríksson knew that text at a particular time. From the beginning of his student days Eiríksson had access for example to the University Library, and it cannot be ruled out that Eiríksson himself at some earlier point got rid of some of his books. In the case of the books, for example, of Søren Kierkegaard, to whom Eiríksson refers throughout his work, this is even highly probable, since only a few of Kierkegaard's works were found in the library at the time of Eiríksson's death.[2] Finally, and most importantly, the mere fact that Eiríksson possessed a specific book cannot be taken as proof that he ever read it.

Despite these caveats, the information provided by the auction catalogue can at least be interpreted as an indication of Eiríksson's probable familiarity with a certain work. It is my hope that this catalogue will represent a useful point of departure for any deeper understanding of Eiríksson and his sources.

1 But see also nos. 193-212, 474, 494-511, 519-520 of the catalogue.

2 See nos. 593-595 as well as no. 596 of the catalogue.

History and Literature of Iceland

1 Ýngvaldsson [i.e., Ingjaldsson], Jón, *Aldaskrá*, Akureyri: no publisher given 1856.

2 *Almanak Hins íslenska þjóðvinafélags*, Copenhagen: Hið íslenzka þjóðvinafélag 1875-1881.

3 Schjellerup, Hans Carl Frederik Christian, *Almanak um ár eptir Krists fæðing*, ed. by Jón Sigurðsson, Copenhagen: Schultz 1867-1879 and 1881. (Bound copy)

4 Oddsson, Gunnlaugur, *Almenn jarðarfræði og landaskipun eður, Geographia*, [vol. 1], Copenhagen: Hið íslenzka bókmenntafélag 1821 [vol. 2, 1822]. (Bound copy)

5 Guðmundsson, Sigurður, *Alþingisstaður hinn forni við Öxará. Með uppdráttum eptir Sigurð Guðmundsson málara*, Copenhagen: S.L. Møller 1878.

6 Indriðason, Ólafur, *Andlegt Sálmasafn*, Akureyri: H. Helgason 1857. (Bound copy)

7 *Andvari. Tímarit hins íslenska Þjóðvinafélags*, vol. 2, ed. by Björn Magnússon Ólsen, Eiríkur Jónsson, Jón Sigurðsson, Kristján Jónsson and Sigurður L. Jónasson, Copenhagen: L. Klein 1875.

8 *Andvari. Tímarit hins íslenska Þjóðvinafélags*, vol. 3, ed. by Jón Sigurðsson, Sigurður L. Jónasson, Eiríkur Jónsson, Eðvald Johnsen and Guðmundur Þorláksson, Copenhagen: L. Klein 1876.

9 *Andvari. Tímarit hins íslenska Þjóðvinafélags*, vol. 4, ed. by Björn Magnússon Ólsen, Eiríkur Jónsson, Guðmundur Þorláksson, Jón Sigurðsson and Sigurður L. Jónasson, Copenhagen: L. Klein 1877.

10 *Andvari. Tímarit hins íslenska Þjóðvinafélags*, vol. 6, ed. by Anonymous, Copenhagen: S.L. Møller 1880.

11 Pjétursson, Pjétur and Melsteð, Sigurdur Pálsson, *Árrit prestaskólans*, vol. 1, Reykjavík: no publisher given 1850.

12 Anonymous ["Prestar og Aðstoðarprestar í Þórnesþingi"], *Ársrit samið og gefið út af prestum og aðstoðarprestum í Þórnesþingi*, vol. 2, Reykjavík: Helgi Helgason 1847.

13 *Årsritið Gestur Vestfirðíngur*, vol. 1, ed. by Ólafur Sívertsen, Brynjúlfur Benedictsen, Eiríkur Kúld and Guðmundur Einarsson, Reykjavík: Flateyar framfara stofnfélag bréflegt félag 1847.

14 Krabbe, Harald, *Athugasemdir handa Íslendingum um sullaveikina og varnir móti henni*, trans. by Anonymous ["Dómsmálastjórnin"], Copenhagen: J.H. Schultz 1864.

15-16 Halldórsson, Björn, *Atlí eður rádagjørdir ýngismanns um búnad sinn. Helzt um jarðar- og kvikfjár-rækt, adferð og ágóda, med andsvari gamals bónda. Åsamt Búa-Lögum*, Copenhagen: P.N. Jørgensen 1834. (2 copies)

17 Ólafsson, Arnljótur, *Auðfræði*, Copenhagen: Hið íslenska bókmenntafélag 1880.

18 Johnsson, Vigfús, *Barna-Liood. Med Ljuflings-Lag*, Copenhagen: N. Möller 1780.

19 Bastholm, Christian, *Kristilegra Trúarbragda Høfud-Lærdómar, til almennilegrar uppbyggíngar*, vols. 1-2, trans. by Guðmundur Jónsson, Leirárgørdum við Leirá: Forlag Islands almennu Upp-frædíngar Stiptunar 1799. (Bound copy)

20 *Biblia: Það er Heløg Ritning*, Videyar Klaustri: Hið íslenska Biblíu-félag 1841. (Bound copy)

21-26 Anonymous, *Biskupa sögur*, vols. 1-2, Copenhagen: S.L. Møller 1858-1878.

27 Gunnlaugsson, Björn, *Regulas quasdam simpliciores ad computandum motum lunae*, Videyar Klaustri: Guðmundur Jónsson Skagfjörð 1828. (2 copies)

28 Gunnlaugsson, Björn, *De mensura et delineatione Islandiæ interioris cura societatis litterariæ Islandaicæ his temporibus facienda*, Videyar Klaustri: H. Helgason 1834. (2 copies)

29 *Bragða-Mágus Saga*, transcripted by Gunnlaugur Þórðarson, Copenhagen: Páll Sveinsson 1858. (2 copies)

30 Polycarpus, *Brjef Polýkarpusar til Filippíborgarmanna, ásamt ingangi og ágripi af æfi hans*, trans. by Anonymous, Copenhagen: S.B. Sívertsen 1863.

31 Egilsson, Sveinbjörn, *Brot af Placidus-drápu*, Videyar Klaustri: no publisher given 1833. (2 copies)

32 Brynjúlfsson, Gílsi, *Bemærkinger om Haarvard Isfiirdings saga. Med forklaring over viserne*, Copenhagen: N.H. Stenderup 1860.

33 Anonymous, *Búnaðar-Rít Suður-Amtsins Húss- og Bú-stjórnar Félags*, vol. 1, no. 1, Videyar Klaustur: Helgi Helgason 1839.

34 Lord Byron [George Gordon Byron], *Bandinginn í Chillon og Draumurinn*, trans. by Steingrímur Thorsteinsson, Copenhagen: Páll Sveinsson 1866. (2 copies)

35 Lord Byron [George Gordon Byron], *Manfred (sorgarleikur) og nokkur kvæði*, trans. by Matthías Jochúmsson, Copenhagen: S. Trier 1875.

36 Indriðason, Ólafur, *Nýtt bæna- og sálmakver*, Reykjavík: E. Þórðarson 1853.

37 Arngrímsson, Bjarni, *Sálma- og bæna-kver. Haldandi Tvennar Viku-Bænr og Eina Viku-Sállma, ásamt Hátída-Missiraskipta- Sakramentis- og Ferda-bænum og Bæn um gódann afgáng*, Videyar Klaustur: M. Stephensen 1832.

38 Pétursson, Pétur, *Bænakver*, Reykjavík: Egill Jónsson 1860. (4 copies)

39-42 *Diplomatarium Islandicum = Íslenzkt fornbréfasafn Sem hefir inni að halda bréf og gjörninga, dóma og máldaga og aðrar skrár, er snerta Ísland eða íslenzka menn*, vol. 1, Copenhagen: Hið íslenzka bókmenntafélag 1857-1876. (4 copies)

43 Sturluson, Snorri, *Edda Snorra Sturlusonar*, Copenhagen: Þorleifur Jónsson 1875.

44 *Eðlisfræði, eptir J[ohann] G[eorg] Fischer*, trans. by Magnús Grímsson, Copenhagen: Hið íslenska bókmenntafélag 1852. (Bound copy)

45 Anonymous, *Eitt Æfentyr, er kallast Johohønu Rauner*, trans. by Snorri Björnsson, Hrappsey: Guðmundur Jónsson 1784.

46 Balle, Nicolai Edinger, *Evangelísk-kristileg Lærdóms Bók handa Unglingum*, trans. by Einar Guðmundsson and Hannes Finnson, 6th edition, Leirárgarðar: Islands konúnglega Uppfrædíngar Stiptun 1811.

47 *Evangelisk-kristileg Messu-Saungs og Sálma-Bók, ad Konúnglegri tilhlutun samantekin til almennilegrar brúkunar*

í Kirkjum og heima-Húsum, 4th edition, Videyar Klaustri: Hið konúnglega íslendska Lands-uppfrædíngar Félag 1825. (Bound copy)

48 *Evangelisk-kristileg Messu-Saungs og Sálma-Bók, ad Konúnglegri tilhlutun samantekin til almennilegrar brúkunar í Kirkjum og heima-Húsum*, 8th edition, Videyar Klaustri: Hið konúnglega íslendska Lands-uppfrædíngar Félag 1837. (Bound copy)

49 Espólín, Jón, *Íslands Árbækr í sögu-formi*, vols. 11-12, Copenhagen: Hið íslenska bókmenntafélag 1854-1855. (Bound copy)

50-56 *Fjölnir. Árs-rit handa Íslendíngum*, vol. 1, ed. by Brynjólfur Pétursson, Jónas Hallgrímsson, Konráð Gjíslason and Tómas Sæmundsson, Copenhagen: J.D. Qvist 1835.
Fjölnir. Árs-rit handa Íslendíngum, vols. 2-4, ed. by Brynjólfur Pétursson, Jónas Hallgrímsson, Konráð Gjíslason and Tómas Sæmundsson, Copenhagen: J.D. Qvist 1836-1838.
Fjölnir. Árs-rit handa Íslendíngum, vol. 5, ed. by Tómas Sæmundsson, Copenhagen: J.D. Qvist 1839.
Fjölnir. Árs-rit handa Íslendíngum, vol. 6, ed. by Anonymous ["Nokkrir Íslendingar"], Copenhagen: J.D. Qvist 1843.
Fjölnir. Árs-rit handa Íslendíngum, vol. 9, ed. by Anonymous ["Nokkrir Íslendingar"], Copenhagen: J.D. Qvist 1847.

57 *Fjölnir. Árs-rit handa Íslendíngum*, vol. 3, ed. by Brynjólfur Pétursson, Jónas Hallgrímsson, Konráð Gjíslason and Tómas Sæmundsson, Copenhagen: J.D. Qvist 1837. (3 copies)

58-60 Anonymous, *Fornmanna Sögur, eptir gömlum handritum*, vols. 2-3 and vol. 11, Copenhagen: Hið norræna fornfræða félag 1826-1828.

61 Anonymous, *Forspjallsliób*, Videyar Klaustur: Hallgrímur Scheving 1837.

62-63 *Fréttir frá Fulltrúa-þínginu í Hróarskeldu, viðvíkjandi málefnum Íslendinga*, ed. by Anonymous ["Nokkrir Íslendingar"], Copenhagen: S.L. Møller 1840. (2 copies)

64-76 *Fréttir frá Fulltrúaþínginu í Hróarskeldu 1842, viðvíkjandi málefnum Íslendinga*, ed. by Anonymous ["Nokkrir Íslendingar"], Copenhagen: S.L. Møller 1843. (13 copies)

77 Friðriksson, Halldór Kristján, *Íslenzk málmyndalýsing*, Copenhagen: Hið íslenzka bókmenntafélag 1861.

78 Friðriksson, Halldór Kristján, *Dönsk málfræði*, Copenhagen: Egill Jónsson 1857.

79-80 Friðriksson, Halldór Kristján, *Islandsk læsebog*, Copenhagen: Jæger 1846.

81-87 Briem, Valdimar, *Frjettir frá Íslandi*, vols. 1-7, Reykjavík: Hið íslenska bókmenntafélag 1873-1879.

88 Gröndal, Benedikt Sveinbjarnarson, *Gandreiðin, sorgarleikr í mörgun þáttum,* Copenhagen: L. Klein 1866. (2 copies)

89 Geikie, Archibald, *Eðlislýsing jarðarinnar*, Reykjavík: Hið íslenzka bókmenntafélag 1879. (Bound copy)

90 Gíslason, Jón, *Einføld meining til frekari eptirþánka um haganlegustu Kyrkna byggíngar á Islandi einkum í fjalldala regna-plázum*, Copenhagen: Jón Gíslason 1837.

91 Gíslason, Konráð, *Um frumparta íslenzkrar túngu í fornöld*, Copenhagen: Hið íslenska bókmenntafélag 1846.

92 Gíslason, Konráð, *De ældste runeindskrifters sproglige stilling*, vols. 1-2, Copenhagen: Thieles Bogtrykkeri 1869-1871. [Offprint]

93 Gíslason, Konráð, *Om helrim i første og tredje linie af regelmæssigt "dróttkvætt" og "hrynhenda"*, Copenhagen: Schultz 1877. (2 copies)

94 Gíslason, Konráð, *Småbemærkninger til udgaverne af den Arnamagnæanske membran nr. 674 A, 4to*, Copenhagen: Thieles Bogtrykkeri 1870. [Offprint]

95 Gíslason, Konráð, *Hljóðstafr, hljóðfyllandi (-hljóðfyllendr), hljóðfylling; Rímhenda eller runhenda?*, Copenhagen: Thieles Bogtrykkeri 1875. [Offprint]

96 Gíslason, Konráð, *Kuett, et Forklaringsforsög*, Copenhagen: no publisher given 1866. [Offprint]

97 Gíslason, Konráð, *Tillægsbemærkninger om -ríðr. Småbemærkninger til de tvende udgaver af den arnamagnæanske* *membran nr. 674 A, 4to*, Copenhagen: no publisher given 1866. [Offprint]

98 Gíslason, Konráð, *Bemærkninger til nogle Steder i Skáldskaparmál*, Copenhagen: Thiele 1879. [Offprint]

99 Gíslason, Konráð, *Et Par Bemærkninger til et Vers af Arnórr Jarlaskáld*, Copenhagen: Thiele 1879. [Offprint]

100 Gíslason, Konráð, *Nogle bemærkninger om Skjaldedigtenes beskaffenhed i formel henseende*, Copenhagen: B. Lunos bogtrykkeri 1872.

101 Gíslason, Konráð, *Om navnet Ýmir*, Copenhagen: B. Lunos bogtrykkeri 1874.

102 Anonymous, *Graduale, Ein Almenneleg Messusaugns Bok*, 19th edition, Hoolar i Hialltadal: Pétur Jónsson 1779. (Bound copy)

103 Gunnlaugsson, Björn, *Töblur yfir sólarinnar sýnilega gáng á Íslandi*, Viðeyjar Klaustur: Bessastaða Skóli 1836. (2 copies)

104 Gunnlaugsson, Björn, *Leiðarvísir til að þekkja stjörnur*, vols. 1-2, Reykjavík: Bessastaða Skóli 1845-1846.

105 Anonymous, *Hallfreds Saga Öfversä från Isländskan jemte Anmärkingar*, trans. by Sven Herman Benjamin Svensson, Lund: Håkan Ohlasons Boktryckeri 1864.

106 Helgason, Árni, *Helgidaga predikanir, árid um kring*, Videyar Klaustri: O.M. Stephensen 1839. (Bound copy)

107 Helgason, Árni, *Stutt Æfi-Minníng Sáluga Stiptprófastsins Marcusar Magnussonar flutt vid hans Jardarför þann 31ta Aug. 1825*, Videyar Klaustri: Jón Jónsson 1826.

108 Hjaltelin, Jón Jónsson, *Docent Paijkulls "En Sommer i Island,"* Reykavík: no publisher given 1867. (6 copies)

109 Homer, *Ilíons-kvæði, I.-XII. Kviða*, trans by Benedikt Sveinbjarnarson Gröndal, Reykjavík: Hið íslenska bókmenntafélag 1856.

110 Homer, *Odyssea 1-12*, trans. by Sveinbjörn Egilsson, Viðeyjarklaustur: no publisher given 1829-1838.

111 Flaccus, Horatius, *Þýðing brjefa Hórazar*, no. 1, trans. by Gísli Magnússon and Jón Þorkelsson, ed. by Íslenzka bókmenntafjelag, Reykjavík: no publisher given 1864. (2 copies)

112 Horster, Joachim Fredrik, *Ágrip af Historium Heilagrar Ritningar*, trans. by Hálfdán Einarsson, Videyar Klaustri: O.M. Stephensen 1837. (Bound copy)

113 Anonymous, *Hugvinns-mál ásamt þeirra látínska frumriti*, Viðeyjar Klaustur: Bessastaða Skóli 1831. (4 copies)

114 *Ingólfur. Tímarit frá 12. jan 1853 til 30. maí 1855*, ed. by Sveinbjörn Hallgrímsson, Reykjavík: no publisher given 1855. (Bound copy)

115 Irwing, Washington, *Pílagrímur ástarinnar eða Sagan af Ahmed al Kamel,* trans. by Steingrímur Thorsteinsson, Copenhagen: Páll Sveinsson 1860. (3 copies)

116 *Ísafold*, vols. 1-8, no. 7, ed. by Björn Jónsson, Reykjavík: E. Þórðarson 1874-1881 (vol. 3, no. 18 and vol. 4, nos. 20-22 are missing).

117 Magnússon, Finnur, *Íslands bergmál af Danmerkur hátídargledi vid hid konúnglega brúdkaup í Kaupmannahøfn, ár ása ok goð-þjóðar tímatølu 1866. Eptir Krists burd 1828*, Copenhagen: Schultz 1828.

118 Map of Iceland, printed by Pacht & Crone, Copenhagen. (6 copies)

119 Sigurðson, Jón, *Hið íslenzka bókmentafélag. Stofnan félagsins og athafnir um fyrstu fimmtíu árin 1816-1866*, Copenhagen: Hið íslenska bókmenntafélag 1867.

120 Guðjónsson, Pétur, *Íslenzk sálmasaungs- og messubók með nótum*, Copenhagen: Hið íslenska bókmenntafélag 1861.

121 *Íslenzkar þjóðsögur og æfintýri,* collected by Jón Árnason, vol. 1, Leipzig: J.C. Hinrichs 1862.

122 *Íslenzkar fornsögur*, vol. 1, ed. by Finnur Jónsson, Copenhagen: S.L. Møller 1880.

123 Icelandic dictionary of foreign words. Title page and first leaf are missing.

124 Icelandic Evangelical treatises. One bunch.

125 Kålund, Kristian, *Bidrag til en historisk-topografisk Beskrivelse af Island*, vols. 1-2, Copenhagen: Gyldendal 1877-1882.

126-127 Stoll, Heinrich Wilhelm, *Kennslubók í goðafræði Grikkja og Rómverja*, trans. by Steingrímur Thorsteinson, Copenhagen: S.L. Møller 1871. (2 copies)

128	Stoll, Heinrich Wilhelm, *Myndir með goðafræði Grikkja og Rómverja*, trans. by Steingrímur Thorsteinson, Copenhagen: S.L. Møller 1873.
129-134	Briem, Halldór, *Kennslubók í enskri tungu. Vasabók fyrir Vesturfara og aðra, er eiga viðskipti við Englendinga, eða læra vilja ensku*, Akureyri: no publisher given 1873. (6 copies)
135-136	*Kirkjutíðindi fyrir Ísland*, vols. 1-2, ed. by Þórarinn Böðvarsson and Hallgrímur Sveinsson, Reykjavík: no publisher given 1878-1879.
137	*Konráðs saga keisarasonar, er fór til Ormalands*, transcripted by Gunnlaugur Þórðarson, Copenhagen: Páll Sveinsson 1859. (7 copies)
138	*Krókarefssaga, Gunnars saga Keldugnúpsfífls og Ölkofra þáttr*, ed. by Thorvaldur Bjarnarson, Copenhagen: L. Klein 1866. (6 copies)
139	Thóroddsen, Jón, *Kvæði*, ed. by Steingrímur Thorsteinsson, Jón Sigurðsson and Eiríkur Jónsson, Copenhagen: Hið íslenska bókmenntafélag 1871. (Bound copy)
140	Grímsson, Magnús, *Kvöldvaka í sveit*, Reykjavík: Egill Jónsson 1848.
141	Gunnlaugsson, Björn, *Einföld landmælíng til að kenna að semja afstöðu uppdrætti með auðfengnum verkfærum*, Copenhagen: no publisher given 1868.
142	*Lanztíðindi*, vol. 1, Reykjavík: Pretsmiðja landsins 1850.
143-144	*Den islandske Forfatningssag i Landsthinget 1868-69*, ed. by Orla Lehmann, Copenhagen: G.E.C. Gad 1869. (2 copies)
145	Gíslason, Oddur Vigfús, *Leiðarvísir í enskri tungu*, Reykjavík: E. Þórðarson 1863.
146	Gebauer, Johan Christian, *Leiðarvísir til þekkingar á saunglistinni*, trans. by Pétur Guðjónsson, Reykavík: E. Þórðarson 1870.
147	Sveinsson, Sveinn, *Leiðarvísir til að þekkja og búa til hin almennustu landbúnaðar verkfæri*, Copenhagen: S. Trier 1875.
148	Pétursson, Sigurður, *Leikrit og Nokkur ljódmæli. Agrip æfisøgu Sigurdar Sýslumanns Péturssonar*, vol. 2, Reykjavík: Egill Jónsson 1846 [vol. 1, 1844].

149-150 Böðvarsson, Þórarinn, *Lestrarbók handa alþýðu á Íslandi*, Copenhagen: H. Klein 1874. (2 copies)

151 Asgrímsson, Eystein, *Lilja (The Lily). An Icelandic Religious Poem of The Fourteenth Century*, ed. by Eirikr Magnusson, London: Williams and Norgate 1870. (Elegant bound copy)

152 Sigurðsson, Jón, *Lítil Fiskibók, með uppdráttum og útskýríngum, handa fiskimönnum á Íslandi. Samin eptir fiskiveiðabókum W. Heins*, Copenhagen: Thiele 1859.

153-154 Þorláksson, Jón, *Íslenzk ljódabók Jóns Þorlákssonar prests að Bægisá*, vols. 1-2, Copenhagen: J.D. Quist 1842-1843.

155 Hallgrímsson, Jónas, *Ljóðmæli*, ed. by Brynjólf Pétursson and Konrað Gíslason, Copenhagen: J.D. Quist 1847. (Bound copy)

156 Oddsson, Brynjúlfur, *Nokkur ljóðmæli*, Reykjavík: Brynjúlfur Oddson 1869.

157-158 Þorleifsson, Jón, *Ljóðmæli og ýmislegt fleira*, Copenhagen: L. Klein 1868. (2 copies)

159 *Lodbrokar-Quida*, trans. by Nils Henrik Sjöborg, Parts 3-5, Lund: Berling 1802.

160 Friðriksson, Halldór Kristján, *Lýsing Íslands*, Reykjavík: E. Þórðarson 1880.

161-162 Anonymous ["Members of the Icelandic Literary Society"], *Lög hins íslenzka bókmentafélags*, 1st and 3rd edition, Copenhagen: Hið íslenska bókmenntafélag 1818 and 1851.

163 Thoroddsen, Jón, *Maður og kona*, ed. by Jón Sigurðsson, Eiríkr Jónsson and Sigurður L. Jónasson, Copenhagen: Hið íslenzka bókmenntafjelag 1876.

164-170 Melsteð, Páll, *Fornaldarsagan, íslenzkuð og aukin eptir sögubók H.G. Bóhrs*, ed. by Íslenzka bókmentafélag, Reykjavík: E. Thórðarson 1864; Melsteð, Páll, *Miðaldasagan*, ed. by Íslenzka bókmentafélag, Reykjavík: E. Thórðarson 1866; Melsteð, Páll, *Nýjasagan*, vol. 1, ed. by Íslenzka bókmentafélag, Reykjavík: E. Thórðarson 1868.

171 Hallgrímsson, Sveinbjörn, *Minnilegur fermingardagur*, Reykjavík: Prensmiðja Íslands 1851.

172 *Minning Consistoríal-Assessors Síra Gunnlaugs Oddssonar Dómkyrkjuprests í Reykjavík*, ed. by Þorgeir Guðmundsson and Þorsteinn Helgason, Copenhagen: S.L. Møller 1838.

173 Anonymous, *Myndabók handa börnum*, Copenhagen: E. Jónsson 1853. (7 copies)

174 Gunnlaugsson, Björn, *Njóla*, Videyar Klaustri: Bessastaða Skóli 1842.

175 Gunnlaugsson, Björn, *Njóla eða Hugmynd um alheimsáformið*, 2nd edition, Reykjavík: E. Þórðarson 1853. (3 copies)

176 *Nockrer Marg-Rrooder Søgu-Þætter Islendinga*, ed. by Gísli Magnússon and Bjørn Markússon, Hoolum i Hialltadal: no publisher given 1756. (Bound copy)

177 Breiðfjörð, Sigurður, *Nokkrir smákveðlíngar*, Copenhagen: Páll Sveinsson 1862. (7 copies)

178 *Nokkur blöð úr Hauksbók og brot úr Guðmundarsögu*, ed. by Jón Þorkelsson, Reykjavík: E. Þórðarson 1865.

179 Hjaltalín, Jón Andrésson, *Nokkur orð um hreinlæti*, Copenhagen: L. Klein 1867.

180-191 *Nordiske oldskrifter*, vols. 3, 5, 15, 21-24, 26-28, 30-31, Copenhagen: Nordiske Literatur-Samfund 1847-1862.

192 *Ný félagsrit*, vol. 1, ed. by Bjarni Sívertsen, Jón Hjaltalín, Jón Sigurðsson, Oddgeir Stephensen and Ólafur Pálsson, Copenhagen: S.L. Møller 1841.

193 *Ný félagsrit*, vol. 2, ed. by Bjarni Sívertsen, Jón Hjaltalín, Jón Sigurðsson, Magnús Eiríksson and Sigurður Melsteð, Copenhagen: Salomon 1842.

194-196 *Ný félagsrit*, vols. 3-5, ed. by Jón Hjaltalín, Jón Sigurðsson, Magnús Eiríksson, Oddgeir Stephensen and Sigurður Melsteð, Copenhagen: Salomon (vols. 3-4) / L. Klein (vol. 5) 1843-1845.

197 *Ný félagsrit*, vol. 6, ed. by Grímur Þorgrímsson, Jón Sigurðsson, Magnús Eiríksson, Oddgeir Stephensen and Þorsteinn Jónsson, Copenhagen: L. Klein 1846.

198 *Ný félagsrit*, vol. 7, ed. by Brynjólfur Snorrason, Jón Sigurðsson, Magnús Eiríksson, Oddgeir Stephensen and Vilhjálmur Finsen, Copenhagen: L. Klein 1847.

199 *Ný félagsrit*, vol. 8, ed. by Gísli Brynjúlfsson, Jón Sigurðsson, Magnús Eiríksson, Oddgeir Stephensen and Vilhjálmur Finsen, Copenhagen: L. Klein 1848.

200 *Ný félagsrit*, vol. 9, ed. by Gísli Brynjúlfsson, Jón Guðmundsson, Jón Sigurðsson, Magnús Eiríksson and Vilhjálmur Finsen, Copenhagen: L. Klein 1849.

201 *Ný félagsrit*, vol. 10, ed. by Brynjólfur Snorrason, Gísli Brynjúlfsson, Jón Sigurðsson, Magnús Eiríksson and Vilhjálmur Finsen, Copenhagen: L. Klein 1850.

202 *Ný félagsrit*, vol. 11, ed. by Gísli Brynjúlfsson, Jón Guðmundsson, Jón Sigurðsson, Magnús Eiríksson and Vilhjálmur Finsen, Copenhagen: L. Klein 1851.

203 *Ný félagsrit*, vol. 12, ed. by Bogi Thorarensen, Gísli Brynjúlfsson, Jón Guðmundsson, Jón Sigurðsson, Magnús Eiríksson, Copenhagen: L. Klein 1852.

204 *Ný félagsrit*, vol. 13, ed. by Gísli Brynjúlfsson, Grímur Þorgrímsson, Jón Hjaltalín, Jón Sigurðsson, Magnús Eiríksson, Copenhagen: L. Klein 1853.

205 *Ný félagsrit*, vol. 14, ed. by Bogi Thorarensen, Gísli Brynjúlfsson, Grímur Þorgrímsson, Jón Sigurðsson, Magnús Eiríksson, Copenhagen: L. Klein 1854.

206 *Ný félagsrit*, vol. 16, ed. by Arnljótur Ólafsson, Gísli Brynjúlfsson, Grímur Þorgrímsson, Jón Sigurðsson, Magnús Eiríksson, Copenhagen: L. Klein 1856.

207 *Ný félagsrit*, vol. 22, ed. by Guðrandr Vigfússon, Gunnlaugur Blöndal, Jón Sigurðsson, Sigurður L. Jónasson and Steingrímur Thorsteinsson, Copenhagen: L. Klein 1862.

208 *Ný félagsrit*, vol. 29, ed. by Guðrandr Vigfússon, Jón Sigurðsson, Magnús Stephensen, Sigurður L. Jónasson and Þorvaldur Björnsson, Copenhagen: L. Klein 1864.

209 *Ný félagsrit*, vol. 30, ed. by Björn Jónsson, Björn Magnússon Ólsen, Eiríkur Jónsson, Jón Sigurðsson, Sigurður L. Jónasson, Copenhagen: L. Klein 1873.

210 *Ný félagsrit*, vol. 10, ed. by Brynjólfur Snorrason, Gísli Brynjúlfsson, Jón Sigurðsson, Magnús Eiríksson and Vilhjálmur Finsen, Copenhagen: L. Klein 1850. (2 copies)

211 *Ný félagsrit*, vol. 11, ed. by Gísli Brynjúlfsson, Jón Guðmundsson, Jón Sigurðsson, Magnús Eiríksson and Vilhjálmur Finsen, Copenhagen: L. Klein 1851. (4 copies)

212 *Ný félagsrit*, vol. 13, ed. by Gísli Brynjúlfsson, Grímur Þorgrímsson, Jón Hjaltalín, Jón Sigurðsson, Magnús Eiríksson, Copenhagen: L. Klein 1853. (19 copies)

213 *Ný jarðabók fyrir Ísland*, Copenhagen: J. H. Schultz 1861.

214-218 *Ný sumargjöf*, vols. 1-4 and vol. 7, ed. by Páll Sveinsson, Copenhagen: Páll Sveinsson 1859-1862 and 1865.

219-222 *Ný sumargjöf*, vols. 1-3 and vol. 7, ed. by Páll Sveinsson, Copenhagen: Páll Sveinsson 1859-1861 and 1865.

223 Einarsson, Indriði, *Nýársnóttin*, Akureyri: B.M. Stephánsson 1872. (5 copies)

224 Haldórsson, Jóhann, *Nýársgjöf handa Børnum*, Copenhagen: S.L. Møller 1841. (2 copies)

225 Haldórsson, Jóhann, *Nýársgjöf handa Børnum*, Copenhagen: S.L. Møller 1841.

226 Óttarsson, Hallfreður, *Ólafs drápa Tryggvasonar*, ed. by Sveinbjörn Egilsson, Viðeyjar Klaustur: Bessastaða Skóli 1832. (4 copies)

227 Pétursson, Pétur, *Historia Ecclesiastica Islandiæ. Ab anno 1740, ad annum 1840*, Copenhagen: no publisher given 1841.

228 Pétursson, Pétur, *Prjedikanir, ætlaðar til helgidaga lestra í heimahúsum*, 2nd edition, Reykjavík: Egill Jónsson 1864.

229-231 Pétursson, Pétur, *Hugvekjur til kvöldlestra, frá veturnóttum til langaföstu*, Reykjavík: Egill Jónsson 1858. (3 copies)

232-234 Pétursson, Pétur, *Fimtíu hugvekjur út af pínu og dauða Drottins vors Jesú Krits*, Reykjavík: Egill Jónsson 1859. (3 copies)

235 Pétursson, Pétur, *Hugvekjur til kvöldlestra, frá páskum til hvítasunnu*, Copenhagen: S.L. Møller 1871. (Bound copy)

236 Pétursson, Pétur, *Stutt Rædusnid, eda Fáeinar Hugvekjur, ætladar Prédikurum*, Videyar Klaustur: Pétur Pétursson 1839.

237 Pétursson, Pétur, *Commentatio de jure ecclesiarum in Islandia ante et post reformationem*, Copenhagen: J.D. Quist 1844. (2 copies)

238 Níelsson, Sveinn, *Presta tal og prófasta á Íslandi*, Copenhagen: Hið íslenzka bókmenntafélag 1869.

239 Magnússon, Finnur (ed.), *Qvæþi i rúnom á krýningardag Fridreks Konungs ok Mariu Drottningar i Danmörko 1815*, Copenhagen: J.F. Schultz 1815.

240 Gröndal, Benedict, *Ragnarökkur kvæði um Norðurlanda guði*, Copenhagen: L. Klein 1868.

241 Rask, Rasmus Kristian, *Kortfattet Vejledning til det oldnordiske eller gamle islandske Sprog*, 2nd edition, Copenhagen: Schubothe 1844. (Bound copy)

242 *Reykjavíkurpósturinn*, vols. 1-3, ed. by Þórður Jónassen, Sigurður Melsteð and Páll Melsteð, Reykjavík: Prentsmiðja landsins 1847-1849.

243 Breiðfjörð, Sigurður Eiríksson, *Rímur af Gísla Súrssyni*, ed. by J. B. Breiðfjörð, Copenhagen: S.L. Møller 1857. (6 copies)

244 Böðvarsson, Árni, *Rímur af Þorsteini Uxafæti*, 2nd edition, Copenhagen: Páll Sveinsson 1858.

245 Ólafsson, Guðmundur, *Ritgjörð um ætlunarverk bóndans, sem jarðyrkjumanns*, Chapter 1, Part 1, Copenhagen: S.L. Møller 1853.

246 Roscoe, Henry Enfield, *Efnafræði*, trans. by Benedikt Gröndal, Reykjavík: Hið íslenzka bókmenntafjelag 1879. (Bound copy)

247-253 *Safn til sögu Íslands og íslenzkra bókmenta að fornu og nýju*, vols. 1-2, ed. by Íslenzka Bókmenntafélag, Copenhagen: S.L. Møller 1853-1876.

254 Sturluson, Snorri, *Sagan af Agli Skallagrímssyni*, Reykjavík: E. Þórðarson 1856. (Bound copy)

255 *Saga Játvarðar konúngs hins helga*, ed. by Carl Christian Rafn and Jón Sigurðsson, Copenhagen: Det kongelige nordiske oldskrift-selskab 1852.

256 *Sagan af Hrafni ok Gunnlaugi Ormstúngu*, ed. by Carl Christian Rafn and Jón Sigurðsson, Copenhagen: Det kongelige nordiske oldskrift-selskab 1847.

257 *Sagan af Hrafnkeli Freysgoða*, ed. by Peder Goth Thorsen and Konrað Gíslason, Copenhagen: no publisher given 1839.

258 Gröndal, Benedict, *Sagan af Heljarslóðarorrustu*, Copenhagen: Páll Sveinsson 1861. (2 copies)

259-260 *Hervarar saga og Heiðreks konungs*, ed. by Niels Matthias Petersen, trans. by Gísli Thorarensen, Copenhagen: no publisher given 1847; *Bjarnar saga Hitdœlakappa*, ed. and trans. by Halldór Kristján Friðriksson, Copenhagen: no publisher given 1847; *Vapnfirdinga Saga*, ed. and trans. by Gunnlaugur Þórðarson, Copenhagen: no publisher given 1848.

261 *Hervarar saga og Heiðreks konungs*, ed. by Niels Matthias Petersen, trans. by Gísli Thorarensen, Copenhagen: no publisher given 1847.

262 Hymn-book (no title page). Copenhagen 1835.
[It is possible that this work is Hjaltalín, Jón Oddsson, *Níutíu og þrír Hugvekju Sálmar útaf [Christoph Christian] Stúrms Hugvekna 1sta parti frá Veturnóttum til Lángaføstu og til vissra tíma*, Copenhagen: S.L. Møller 1835.]

263 Balfour, Stewart, *Eðlisfræði*, Reykjavík: Hið íslenzka bókmenntafjelag 1880.

264-265 Schleisner, Peter Anton, *Forsög til en Nosographie af Island*, Copenhagen: no publisher given 1849. (2 copies)

266 Indriðason, Ólafur, *Sjö Føstu-prédikanir*, Videyjar Klaustur: Ólafur Indriðason 1844.

267 Sigurðsson, Jón, *Om Islands statsretlige forhold*, Copenhagen: Gyldendal 1855.

268 Sigurðsson, Jón, *Lítil varníngsbók, handa bændum og búmönnum á Íslandi*, Copenhagen: Thiele 1861.

269-270 Anonymous, *Hin Þriðja Makkabeabók*, trans. by Sigurður Brynjólfsson Sivertsen, Copenhagen: Sivertsen 1869. (2 bound copies)

271-283 *Skírnir*, vols. 8-15, 19-20, 22, 24, 25, 27, Copenhagen: S.L. Møller 1834-1853.

283-308 *Skírnir*, vols. 29-34 and 36-54, Copenhagen: S.L. Møller 1855-1860 and 1862-1880.

309 Jónsson frá Minna-Núpi, Brynjúlfur, *Skuggsjá og ráðgáta eða Hugmynd um Guð og verk hans*, Reykjavík: Anonymous ["Nokkrir menn í Reykjavík"] 1875.

310-311 Sigurðsson, Jón, *Skýrsla og lög Hins íslenzka þjóðvinafélags 1869-1873*, Reykjavík: no publisher given 1873.
Sigurðsson, Jón, *Skýrsla og lög Hins íslenzka þjóðvinafélags 1873-1875*, Copenhagen: no publisher given 1876.

312 Jónasson, Sigurður Lárentíus, *Skýrsla um handritasafn Hins íslenzka bókmenntafélags*, vol. 1, Copenhagen: Hið íslenzka bókmenntafjelag 1869.

313-314 Guðmundsson, Sigurður, *Skýrsla um Forngripasafn Íslands í Reykjavík*, vols. 1-2, Copenhagen: Hið íslenzka bókmenntafjelag 1868-1874.

315 *Skýrslur og reikníngar Hins íslenzka bókmentafélags*, Copenhagen: Hið íslenzka bókmenntafjelag 1858-1880.

316-334 *Skýrslur um landshagi á Íslandi*, vols. 1-5, Copenhagen: Hið íslenzka bókmenntafélag 1858-1875.

335 Friðriksson, Halldór Kristján, *Skýring hinna almennu málfræðislegu hugmynda*, 2nd edition, Reykjavík: E. Þórðarson 1864. (2 copies)

336 *Hið nýa testamenti drottins vors Jesú Krists, ásamt með Davíðs sálmum*, Oxford: Hið brezka og erlenda Biblíufélag 1863. (Bound copy)

337-338 Pétursson, Pétur und Melsteð, Sigurður, *Skýringar yfir nokkra staði í Nýja testamentinu*, vols. 1-2, Reykjavík: E. Þórðarson 1861-1862. (Bound copy)

339 Magnússon, Gísli and Thóroddsen, Jón Þórðarson, *Snót, nokkur kvæði eptir ýmis skáld*, Copenhagen: J.D. Quist 1850.

340 Magnússon, Gísli and Thóroddsen, Jón Þórðarson, *Snót, nokkur kvæði eptir ýmis skáld*, 3rd edition, Akureyri: no publisher given 1877.

341 Stephensen, Magnús, *Minníng Sálugu Frúar Sígrídar Stephánsdóttir Stephensen*, Videyar Klaustri: G.J. Schagfjord 1828.

342 Jónsson, Magnús, *Stuttur leiðarvísir fyrir alþýðu til þess að skrifa íslenzku rjett og greinilega*, Reykjavík: E. Þórðarson 1856.

343-348 Swedenborg, Emanuel, *Vísdómur englanna um hina guðdómlegu elsku og hina guðdómlegu speki*, trans. by Jón Hjaltalín, Copenhagen: J. Cohen and L. Klein 1869. (2 copies)

349 Björnsson á Húsafelli, Snorri, *Rímur af Arnljóti Upplendínga-Kappa*, Copenhagen: Þ. Sveinsson 1833.

350 *Nockur Gaman-Kvædi orkt af Ymsum Skáldum á 18du Øld*, ed. by Þórarinn Sveinsson, Copenhagen: Þ. Sveinsson 1832.

351-352 Anonymous, *Udvalgte sagastykker*, vol. 1, trans. by Grimur Thomsen, Copenhagen: L. Klein 1846; vol. 2, trans. by Grimur Thomsen, Copenhagen: C. G. Iversen 1854.

353-354 Þorkelsson, Jón, *Supplement til islandske Ordbøger*, nos. 1-2, Reykjavík: E. Þórdarson 1876.

355 Þorkelsson, Jón, *Um r og ur í niðrlagi orða og orðstofna í íslenzku*, Reykjavík: E. Þórðarson 1863.

356 Þorkelsson, Jón, *Nogle bemærkninger om adjuct C. Iversens islandske formlære*, Reykavík: Anonymous 1862.

357 Thorlacius, Børge Riisbrigh, *Undersøgelse over en i det 12te Aarhundrede skreven islandsk Historie, kaldet Fliotsdælernes, eller, Dropløgs sønners Helges og Grims saga*, Copenhagen: Beeken 1828.

358 Tegnér, Esaias, *Axel*, trans. by Steingrímur Thorsteinsson, Copenhagen: Páll Sveinsson 1857. (6 copies)

359 Tegnér, Esaias, *Axel*, trans. by Steingrímur Thorsteinsson, Copenhagen: Páll Sveinsson 1857. (7 copies)

360-365 *Tíðindi frá Alþíngi Íslendínga 1849*, ed. by Th. Gudmundsen and Haldór Jónsson, Reykjavík: Alþíngi 1850.

366-368 *Tíðindi um stjórnarmálefni Íslands*, vols. 1-3, ed. by Íslenzka bókmenntafélag, Copenhagen: S.L. Møller 1864-1875.

369-371 *Tímarit Hins íslenzka bókmenntafélags*, vol[s]. 1[-2], Reykjavík: Hið íslenzka bókmenntafélag 1880-1881.

372 *Þjóðólfur*, vols. 2-7 and 15-17 (vol. 2, nos. 30-33 and vol. 3, nos. 49-59 are missing), ed. by Sveinbjörn Hallgrímsson (vols. 2-4) and Jón Guðmundsson (vols. 5-7 and 15-17), Reykjavík: Prentaður í prentsmiðju Íslands 1850-1855 and 1863-1865.

373-374 *Þúsund og ein nótt. Arabiskar sögur*, vols. 1-2, trans. by Steingrímur Thorsteinsson, Copenhagen: Páll Sveinsson 1857-1859. (Bound copy)

375 *Þúsund og ein nótt*, trans. by Steingrímur Thorsteinsson, vol. 1, Copenhagen: Páll Sveinsson 1857.

376 Tullin, Christian Braunman, *Nogle, af den velbekiændte danske Pöet Salig Herr Christ. Br. Tullins Vers, tilligemed et Anhang af andre Materier / Nockur, þess alþeckta danska Skálds Sál. Herr Christ. Br. Tullins Kvæde, med litlum Vidbæter añars efnes*, trans. by Jón Þorláksson, Hrappsøe [Hrappsey]: no publisher given 1774.

377 Musäus, Johann Carl August and Motte-Fouqué, Friedrich Heinrich Karl de la, *Tvær smásögur*, trans. by Steingrímur Thorsteinsson, Copenhagen: S.L. Møller 1861.

378 Sivertsen, Sigurður, *Tvær ræður*, Copenhagen: Trier 1875. (2 copies)

379 Jónassen, Jónas, *Um eðli og heilbrigði mannlegs líkama*, Reykjavík: no publisher given 1879.

380 Sigurðsson, Jón, *Um fjárhagsmálið og meðferð þess á alþingi 1865*, Reykjavík: E. Þórðarson 1867.

381 Ásmundsson, Einar, *Um framfarir Íslands*, Copenhagen: F.S. Muhle 1871. (3 copies)

382 Lock, Alfred George, *Um jarðrækt og garðyrkju á Íslandi*, Copenhagen: Valentin og Lund 1876.

383 Bjarnason, Þorkell, *Um siðbótina á Íslandi*, Reykjavík: Prentað í Ísafoldar-prentsmiðju 1878.

384 *Útfararminning Jóns Thorstensen, Landlæknis Íslands, Jústizráðs og Doctors í heimspeki d. 15. dag febrúarm. 1855*, ed. by Jón Sigurðsson, Copenhagen: N.H. Stenderup 1856.

385 Jochumsson, Matthías, *Útilegumennirnir, leikur í fimm þáttum*, Reykjavík: E. Þórðarson 1864.

386 Bødvarson, Þorvaldur, *Utleggíngar Tilraun af [Christian Fürchtegott] Gellerts Qvædi, er kallast Sá Kristni*, Leirárgørdum vid Leirá: G.J. Schagfjord 1800.

387 Vídalín, Jón, *Húss-postilla innihaldandí Predikanir yfir øll Hátida og Sunnudaga Gudspjøll árid um kring*, 12th edition, Copenhagen: no publisher given 1829; *Húss-Postilla innihaldandi Prédikanir yfir øll Hátída og Sunnudaga Gudspjøll árid um kring*, 13th edition, Copenhagen: S.L. Møller 1838. (Bound copy)

388 Songs, 1 bunch of Icelandic occasional Songs and funeral songs.

389 Wimmer, Ludvig Frands Adalbert, *Oldnordisk læsebog med tilhørende Ordsamling*, Copenhagen: Chr. Steen & Søn 1870.

390 *Tvær Æfisøgur útlendra merkismanna*, ed. by Íslenzka bókmenntafélag, Copenhagen: S.L. Møller 1839.

391 Thiele, Just Matthias, *Alberts Thorvaldsens æfisaga*, ed. by Íslenzka bókmenntafélag, Copenhagen: S.L. Møller 1841.

392 Pálsson, Sveinn, *Æfisaga Gísla Þórarinssonar, fyrrum prófasts í Rangárþingi*, revised and ed. by Gísli Thorarensen, Copenhagen: S.L. Møller 1845.

393 Jónsson, Jón, *Ágrip af Æfisögu Gunnlaugs Guðbrandssonar Briems, kammerráðs og sýslumanns í Eyafjarðar sýslu*, Copenhagen: no publisher given 1838.

394 Sigurðson, Øgmundur, *Øgmundar-Géta eda Ø. Sivertsens andligu Sálmar og Kvædi*, Copenhagen: Popp 1832.

395 One bundle of Icelandic magazines.

396 One bundle of Icelandic books.

Theology and Philosophy

397 Adams, William, *Passionsbetragtninger eller hvad lægger den stille Uge os paa Hjerte?*, trans. by Betty Salomon, Copenhagen: Jacob Lund 1860.

398 Adler, Adolph Peter, *Den isolerede Subjectivitet i dens vigtigste Skikkelser. Første Deel*, Copenhagen: Trykt i det Berlingske Bogtrykkeri 1840.

399 Adler, Adolph Peter, *Studier og Exempler*, Copenhagen: Trykt paa Forfatterens Forlag hos L. Klein. I Commission hos Universitets-Boghandler C.A. Reitzel 1846.

400 Adler, Adolph Peter, *Christelige Afhandlinger*, Copenhagen: C.A. Reitzel 1852.

401 Adler, Adolph Peter, *Momenter med Hensyn til Forløsningsværket i Jesu, logisk fremstillede*, Copenhagen: Trykt paa Forfatterens Forlag hos L. Klein. I Commission hos Universitets-Boghandler C.A. Reitzel 1853.

402 Adler, Adolph Peter, *To Afhandlinger*, Copenhagen: I Commission hos C.A. Reitzels Bo og Arvinger. Forfatterens Forlag 1855.

403 Agardh, Carl Adolph, *Om Propheterne og Essæerne hos det jødiske Folk. Dansk Bearbejdelse*, Odense: Milos 1866.

404 *Allgemeines Gesangbuch, auf Königlichen Allergnädigsten Befehl zum öffentlichen und häuslichen Gebrauche in den Gemeinen des Herzogthums Schleswig, des Herzogthums Hollstein, der Herrschaft Pinneberg, der Stadt Altona, und der Grafschaft Ranzau gewidmet und mit Königlichem Allerhöchsten Privilegio herausgegeben*, ed. by Johann Andreas Cramer, Altona: Eckhardt and Glückstadt: Augustin 1781.

405 [Antoninus, Marcus Aurelius], *Den Romerske Keisers Mark. Aurel. Antonins Leveregler for sig selv*, trans. by Christian Bastholm, Copenhagen: Trykt paa den Gyldendalske boghandlings forlag hos Johan Rudolph Thiele 1805.

406 *Anvendelse af Livet. Et kort og fyndigt Moral-System i Østerlandsk Stiil. Med et Chemitypi efter Rafaello d'Urbino*, ed. and trans. by Malthe Christian Hoff, Copenhagen: Gyldendal 1846.

407 [Arndt, Johann], *Johann Arnd's Sechs Bücher vom wahren Christenthume und dessen Paradiesgärtlein*, ed. by Friedrich Wilhelm Krummacher, Leipzig: Philipp Reclam jun. 1842.

408 [Arndt, Johann], *Des Hocherleuchteten Johann Arndts, weiland General-Superintendenten des Fürstentuhms Lüneburg,* *u. Paradies-Gärtlein | Voller Christlicher Tugenden, Wie solche, Zur Ubung des wahren Christenthums, Durch Andächtige, lehrhaffte und trostreiche Gebete in die Seele zu pflantzen; Wozu jetzo kommen I. Vierzehen Wunder-Geschichte, welche sich mit diesem Büchlein, und dieses Mannes andern Schriften begeben. II. Bernhardi verteutschtes Jubel- und Jesus-Lied. III. Ein dreyfaches Register, so den Nutz und Gebrauch dieses Gebet-Büchleins weiset*, Frankfurt am Main: Möller 1756. (Bound copy)

409 Arnoldson, Klas Pontus, *Verkligheten. En lifsåsigt*, Upsala: Edquist 1877.

410 Augusti, Johann Wilhelm Christian, *Lehrbuch der christlichen Dogmengeschichte*, 2nd enlarged and revised ed., Leipzig: Dyk 1811 [1805]. (Bound copy)

411-412 Baird, Robert, *Afholdenheds-Selskabernes Historie i de forenede Stater i Nordamerika*, trans. by Adolph Frederik Mønster, Copenhagen: Klein 1841. (2 copies)

413 Ballum, Niels, *Forklarende Omskrivning af Jesu Christi Lidelses-Historie efter de fire Evangelisters Beretninger, med Anmærkninger*, Copenhagen: Gyldendal 1781. (Bound copy)

414-415 Barclay, Robert, *Forsvar for den Sande Christelige Theologi, Som den Kundgiøris og Prædikis af det Folk som, af Foragt, kaldis Quækere: DET ER, En Fuld Forklaring og Forsvar paa deris Lærdomme og Hovedstykker, ved mange Beviisninger, uddragne af Skriften og Sund Fornuft, og Berømmelige Authorers Vidnisbyrd, baade Gamle og Nye: Med et fuldt Svar til de sterkiste Modsigelfer, som gemeenligen giøris imod DEM. Skreven paa Latin og Engelsk...Og siden oversat paa Tydsk, Hollandsk, Fransk, Spansk, og nu paa Dansk...til Fremmedis Underviisning*, trans. by Christopher Gertsen Meidel, London: Trykt hos T. Sowle Raylton 1738. (2 copies)

416 [Basedow, Johann Bernhard], *Johann Bernhard Basedows theoretisches System der gesunden Vernunft, ein akademisches Lehrbuch*, Altona: David Iversen 1765. (Bound copy)

417 Bastholm, Christian, *Alle Jesu Christi Taler, oversatte efter Grundsproget og oplyste ved Forerindringer og Omskrivninger*, Copenhagen: Gyldendal 1797. (Bound copy)

418 Bastholm, Christian, *Andagtsøvelser for Communicantere*, Copenhagen: Gyldendal 1788. (Bound copy)

419 Bastholm, Christian, *Andagts-Øvelser for Syge og Sengeliggende, indeholdende 64 Betragtninger til christelig Opbyggelse og Trøst i Livets forskjellige Forfatninger*, Copenhagen: Gyldendal 1785. (Bound copy)

420 Bastholm, Christian, *Den geistlige Talekonst, tilligemed en Bedømmelse over en af Saurins Taler*, Copenhagen: Gyldendal 1775. (Bound copy)

421-423 Bastholm, Christian, *Den jødiske Historie fra Verdens Skabelse til Jerusalems sidste Ødelæggelse, med historiske, geographiske, chronologiske og critiske Oplysninger*, vols. 1-3, Copenhagen: Gyldendal 1777-1782. (Bound copy)

424 Bastholm, Christian, *Den naturlige Religion saaledes som den findes i de hedenske Philosophers Skrifter*, Copenhagen: Gyldendal 1784. (Bound copy)

425-426 Bastholm, Christian, *Det nye Testamente, oversat efter Grundsproget og oplyst med Anmerkninger*, vols. 1-2, Copenhagen: Gyldendal 1780. (Bound copy)

427 Bastholm, Christian, *Kort Udsigt over den aabenbarede Religions Historie*, Copenhagen: Gyldendal 1789. (Bound copy)

428 Bastholm, Christian, *Korte Tanker til nærmere Eftertanke over Den geistlige Stand*, Copenhagen: Gyldendal 1794.

429 Bastholm, Christian, *Philosophiske Breve over Sielens Tilstand efter Legemets Død*, Copenhagen: Gyldendal 1790.

430 Bastholm, Christian, *Religions-Bog for Ungdommen, tilligemed Betragtninger over saadan en Bogs nyttigste Indretning*, Copenhagen: Gyldendal 1785; *De fire Evangelisters Efterretninger om Christo ordnede efter Tidsfølgen*, Copenhagen: Gyldendal 1786; *Betragtninger over Selvmord*, Copenhagen: Gyldendal 1787. (Bound copy)

431 Bates, Elisha, *The Doctrines of Friends: or, the Principles of the Christian Religion, as held by The Society of Friends, commonly called Quakers,* York: W. Alexander & Son 1829. (Bound copy)

432 Baur, Ferdinand Christian, *Das Christenthum und die christliche Kirche der drei ersten Jahrhunderte*, 2nd revised edition, Tübingen: Ludwig Friedrich Fues 1860 [1853].

433 Baur, Ferdinand Christian, *Die christliche Kirche vom Anfang des vierten bis zum Ende des sechsten Jahrhunderts in den Hauptmomenten ihrer Entwicklung*, Tübingen: Ludwig Friedrich Fues 1859.

434 Baur, Ferdinand Christian, *Die christliche Kirche des Mittelalters in den Hauptmomenten ihrer Entwicklung*, posthumously ed. by Ferdinand Friedrich Baur, Tübingen: Ludwig Friedrich Fues 1861.

435 Baur, Ferdinand Christian, *Kirchengeschichte der neueren Zeit, von der Reformation bis zum Ende des achtzehnten Jahrhunderts*, posthumously ed. by Ferdinand Friedrich Baur, Tübingen: Ludwig Friedrich Fues 1863.

436 Baur, Ferdinand Christian, *Kirchengeschichte des neunzehnten Jahrhunderts*, posthumously ed. by Eduard Zeller, Tübingen: Ludwig Friedrich Fues 1862 (*Geschichte der christlichen Kirche*, vol. 5).

437 Baur, Ferdinand Christian, *Lehrbuch der christlichen Dogmengeschichte*, Stuttgart: Becher's Verlag 1847.

438 Baur, Ferdinand Christian, *Paulus, der Apostel Jesu Christi. Sein Leben und Wirken, seine Briefe und seine Lehre. Ein Beitrag zu einer kritischen Geschichte des Urchristenthums*, Stuttgart: Becher & Müller 1845.

439 Beck, Christian Daniel, *Commentarii historici decretorum religionis Christianae et formulae Lutheriae*, Leipzig: Dyck 1801. (Bound copy)

440 Beda den Ærværdige [Beda Venerabilis], *Angler-Folkets Kirkehistorie*, trans. by Christian Malta Kragballe, Copenhagen: E.L. Thaarup 1864.

441 *Biblia Hebraica manualia ad praestantiores editiones accurata*, ed. by Johann Simonis, 3rd revised edition, Halle: Orphanotropheum 1822. (Bound copy)

442 *Biblia Sacra sive Testamentum Vetus et Novum ex linguis originalibus in linguam latinam translatum, additis capitum summariis et partitionibus*, trans. and ed. by Sebastian Schmidt, Argentorati (Strasbourg): J.F. Spoor 1697. (Bound copy)

443 *Biblia sacra ex Sebastiani Castellionis interpretatione eiusque postrema recognitione praecipue in usum studiosae iuventutis denuo evulgata*, Leipzig: Bernhard Christoph Breitkopf 1750.

444 *Biblia Sacra vulgatæ editionis Sixti Quinti Pont. Max. jussu recognita atque edita Romæ ex typographia apostolica vaticana MDXCIII*, new edition, Frankfurt am Main: Andreae 1826. (Bound copy)

445 *The Holy Bible, Containing the Old and New Testaments. Translated out of the original tongues; and with the former translations, diligently compared and revised*, Cambridge: The British and Foreign Bible Soc. 1830. (Bound copy)

446 *Biblia, Das ist: Die gantze Heilige Schrifft, Altes und Neues Testaments. Verteutscht von Doctor Martin Luther: Und auf gnädigste Verordnung Des...Herrn Ernsts / Hertzogen zu Sachsen...Von etlichen reinen Theologen dem eigentlichen Wort-Verstand nach erkläret...Ist auch zu End / neben den Christlichen Haupt-Symbolis / mit beygedruckt worden / ein kurtzer und nützlicher Bericht / von der Augspurgischen Confession / samt den Artickeln der Augspurgischen Confession selbsten wie sie in dem rechten Original / so im Jahr 1530*, Nuremberg: In Verlegung Johann Andreä Endters Seel. Söhne 1700. (Bound copy)

447 *Biblia, Das ist: Die gantze Heil. Schrift Altes und Neues Testaments, Nach der Teutschen Uebersetzung D. Martin Luthers: Mit iedes Capitels kurtzen Summarien, auch beygefügten vielen und richtigen Parallelen; Mit Fleiß übersehen...und von...Druckfehlern gesaubert. Nebst der*

Vorrede Des S. Hn. Baron Carl Hildebrands von Canstein, 25th edition, Halle: Wäysenhause 1731. (Bound copy)

448 *La Sainte Bible qui contient le Vieux et le Nouveau Testament*, 2nd revised edition, Basel: E. Tourneisen 1818. (Bound copy)

449 *Biblia, det er: den ganske Hellige Skrifts Bøger, med Flid efterseete og rettede efter Grundtexten, saa og med mange Parallelsteder og udførlige Indholdsfortegnelser forsynede*, 18th edition, Copenhagen: Kongelige Vaisenhuses Forlag 1830. (Bound copy)

450 *Bibelen eller den hellige Skrift, paany oversat af Grundtexten og ledsaget med Indledninger og oplysende Anmærkninger*, installments containing Leviticus 1-16 and Leviticus 18-45, ed. in collaboration with H.F. Helweg, Chr. Hermansen and C. Levinsen by Christian Hermann Kalkar, Copenhagen: Bing & Søn and P.G. Philipsen 1845-1846 [this work was published in installments from 1844 until 1847].

451-453 [Scherer, Johann Ludwig Wilhelm], *Bibelcommentar, zum Handgebrauch für Prediger, Schullehrer und Layen, nach den jetzigen Interpretationsgrundsätzen, ausgearbeitet von einer Gesellschaft von Gelehrten*, vol. 1, Altenburg: Carl Heinrich Richter 1799, vol. 2, Altenburg and Erfurt: Rinck und Schnuphase 1800, vol. 3, Altenburg and Erfurt: Rinck und Schnuphase 1801 (vols. 4-5, 1804-1805). (Bound copy)

454 Billroth, Johann Gustav Friedrich, *Commentar zu den Briefen des Paulus an die Corinther*, Leipzig: Weidmann'sche Buchhandlung 1833. (Bound copy)

455 Birch, Hans Jørgen, *Haandbog for Præster og unge Geistlige*, Copenhagen: Trykt paa Forfatterens Forlag hos P.H. Höecke 1791.

456 Birkedal, Vilhelm, *De syv Folke-Menigheder i Lyset af Herrens Spaadoms-Ord (Aab. 2.3). Et Forsøg*, Odense: Miloske Boghandel 1877. (together with 4 (other) works)

457 Bornemann, Johann Christian August, *Trostgründe gegen den Tod*, Stendal: D.C. Franzen und Grosse 1786.

458 Bossard, Heinrich, *Psychologische Erkenntnisse der göttlichen Wahrheit*, Frankfurt am Main: no publisher given 1853.

459 Brammer, Gerhard Peter, *Præsten og Menigheden. En Samling af Taler ved Præste- og Kirke-Indvielser*, Copenhagen: C.A. Reitzel 1859.

460 Brorson, Christian, *Underholdning og Beroligelse i mørke og sorgfulde Timer*, Copenhagen: Beeken 1828.

461-462 Brøchner, Hans, *Om det Religiøse i dets Enhed med det Humane. Et positivt Supplement til "Problemet om Tro og Viden,"* Copenhagen: P.G. Philipsen 1869. (2 copies)

463 Buchholtz, Friedrich, *Moses og Jesus eller om Jødernes og de Christnes intellektuelle og moralske Forhold, en historisk-politisk Afhandling*, trans. by Thomas Thaarup, 2nd edition, Copenhagen: Fr. Brummer 1813.

464 Bugge, Peter Olivarius, *Pauli Breve til Korintherne og Brevet til Ebræerne, oversatte med Anmærkninger. Et Forsøg*, Fredericia: Trykt paa Udgiverens Bekostning, af Søren Elmenhoff 1803.

465 Bugge, Peter Olivarius, *Johannes's Evangelium, oversat med Anmærkninger. Et Forsøg*, Fredericia: Trykt hos Søren Elmenhoff, paa Forfatterens Bekostning 1803. (Bound copy)

466 Caird, John, *Om religion i alldagliga lifvet*, trans. by E.G. Munck, preface by C.C.J. Bunsen, Norrköping: M.W. Walberg 1860.

467 Campe, Joachim Heinrich, *Theophron oder der erfahrene Rathgeber für die unerfahrene Jugend*, Braunschweig: Schulbuchhandlung 1806. (Bound copy)

468 *Canones et Decreta Sacrosancti Oecumenici Concilii Tridentini Sub Paulo III. Iulio III. et Paulo IV. Pontificibus Maximis*, 2nd stereotyp edition, Leipzig: Tauchnitz 1842.

469 Channing, William Ellery, *Religionstal*, trans. by Nils Ignell, Stockholm: L.J. Hjerta 1845.

470 Christlieb, Theodor F., *Den moderne Vantroes Bekæmpelse. Et Foredrag*, Copenhagen: A.F. Høst & Søn 1876.

471 *Christelig Samler. Tidsskrift til opbyggelig Underholdning for Christne af alle Stænder*, ed. by Lars Nannestad Boisen and Carl Christian Boisen, nos. 1-11, Copenhagen: E. Mau 1835-1838.

472 Christiani, Christoph Johann Rudolph, *Beiträge zur Veredlung der Menschheit, herausgegeben aus dem Erziehungsinstitut bei Kopenhagen*, vols. 1-2, Copenhagen and Lübeck: no publisher given 1796 (vol. 1), Copenhagen and Leipzig: Johann Heinrich Schubothe 1797 (vol. 2.1), Copenhagen and Leipzig: Johann Heinrich Schubothe 1799 (vol. 2.2).

473 [Fibiger, Mathilde Lucie], *Clara Raphael. Tolv Breve*, ed. by Johan Ludvig Heiberg, Copenhagen: C.A. Reitzel 1851; [Fibiger, Mathilde Lucie], *"Et Besøg." Nye Breve af Forfatterinden til Clara Raphael*, Copenhagen: C.A. Reitzel 1851. (Bound copy)

474 Theodor Immanuel [i.e., Magnús Eiríksson], *Breve til Clara Raphael*, Copenhagen: C.A. Reitzel 1851. (4 copies)

475 Bajer, Fredrik, *Klara-Rafael-Fejden*, Copenhagen: C.A. Topp 1879.

476 Clasen, Joachim Friedrich, *Die christlichen Grund- und Glaubenslehren der Orthodoxen und Rationalisten, oder der Blind- und Denkgläubigen in der evangelisch-protestantischen Kirche*, Itzehoe: Nissen 1841.

477 Clausen, Henrik Nikolai, *Udvikling af de christelige Hovedlærdomme*, Copenhagen: C.A. Reitzel 1844.

478 Clemens, Gerke Friedrich, *Das Manifest der Vernunft; eine Stimme der Zeit in Briefen an eine schöne Mystikerin*, Altona: J.F. Hammerich 1836. (Bound copy)

479 Cockburn, Patrick, *An Enquiry into the Truth and Certainty of the Mosaic Deluge. Wherein the Arguments of the Learned Isaac Vossius, and others, for a Topical Deluge are examined; and Some Vulgar Errors, relating to that Grand Catastrophe, are discover'd*, London: C. Hitch and M. Bryson 1750. (Bound copy)

480-481 [Cölln, Daniel Georg Conrad von], *Dr. Daniel Georg Conrad von Cölln's...biblische Theologie mit einer Nachricht über des Verfassers Leben und Wirken*, vols. 1-2, ed. by David Schulz, Leipzig: Johann Ambrosius Barth 1836. (Bound copy)

482 Dahl, Frederik Clemens Bendtsen, *Om Forskjellen imellem Platos og Aristotelesses Naturphilosophie, forsaavidt samme kan antages grundet i disse to Philosophers forskjellige Opfattelse af "Ideen,"* Copenhagen: P.G. Philipsen 1854.

483 Dahl, Frederik Clemens Bendtsen, *Om Naturbegrebets Grundmomenter. Et philosophiskt Forsøg*, Copenhagen: P.G. Philipsen 1859.

484 *Danmarks og Norges Kirke-Ritual*, 2nd edition, Copenhagen: Trykt hos E. H. Berling 1738 [1685]. (Bound copy)

485 *Dansk Nykirke-Tidende*, vols. 1-2, ed. by Alfred Hellemann, Copenhagen: J.P. Hvidbergs Bogtrykkeri 1877-1879.

486 [Dathe, Johann August], *Psalmi ex recensione Textus Hebraei et Versionum Antiquarum Latine versi notisque philologicis et criticis illustrati*, Halle: Orphanotropheum 1787. (Bound copy)

487 Dedekind, Gustav Ernst Wilhelm, *Ueber Geisternähe und Geisterwirkung oder über die Wahrscheinlichkeit daß die Geister der Verstorbenen den Lebenden sowohl nahe seyn, als auch auf sie wirken können. Einige Versuche*, 2nd revised edition, Hannover: Gebrüder Hahn 1793.

488 Bauer, Georg Lorenz, *Dicta Classica Veteris Testamenti post Georgii Laurentii Baueri curas notis perpetuis et philologicis et historico-criticis illustravit*, ed. by Karl Friedrich Stegmann, Leipzig: Weygand 1838. (Bound copy)

489 Dreier, Frederik, *Aandetroen og den frie Tænkning*, Copenhagen: Trykt hos J.D. Quist 1852. (2 copies)

490 Drechsler, Adolph, *Kirchenlehre und Ketzerglaube. Eine Umschau über Religion und Christenthum, Gerechtigkeit und Gnade, Diesseits und Jenseits*, Leipzig: Theile's Buchhandlung 1844.

491 Döllinger, Johann Joseph Ignaz von, *Morten Luther. En Skitze*, Copenhagen: I Commission hos Andr. Fred. Høst & Søn. I Cohens Bogtrykkeri 1875. [Offprint from *Nordisk Kirketidende for katholske Christne*]

492-493 Ebert, Samuel, *Homiletisches Magazin über die evangelischen Texte des ganzen Jahres*, vols. 1-2, 2nd revised edition, Leipzig: A.F. Böhme 1788-1789. (Bound copy)

494 Eiríksson, Magnús, *Om Baptister og Barnedaab, samt flere Momenter af Den kirkelige og speculative Christendom*, Copenhagen: P.G. Philipsen 1844.

495 Eiríksson, Magnús, *Speculativ Rettroenhed, fremstillet efter Dr. Martensens "christelige Dogmatik", og Geistlig Retfærdighed, belyst ved en Biskops Deeltagelse i en Generalfiskal-Sag*, Copenhagen: Trykt hos J.S. Salomon 1849. (Bound copy with gilt edges)

496 Eiríksson, Magnús, *Tro, Overtro og Vantro, i deres Forhold til Fornuft og Forstand, samt til hinanden indbyrdes*, Copenhagen: H.C. Klein 1846.

497 Eiríksson, Magnús, *Tro, Overtro og Vantro, i deres Forhold til Fornuft og Forstand, samt til hinanden indbyrdes*, Copenhagen: H.C. Klein 1846. (Bound copy with gilt edges)

498 Eiríksson, Magnús, *Hvem har Ret: Grundtvigianerne eller deres Modstandere? og Hvad har Christus befalet om Daaben? Nogle orienterende Bemærkninger*, 2nd edition, Copenhagen: E.L. Thaarup 1863.

499 Eiríksson, Magnús, *Er Johannes-Evangeliet et apostolisk og ægte Evangelium og er dets Lære om Guds Menneskevorden en sand og christelig Lære? En religiøs-dogmatisk, historisk-kritisk Undersøgelse*, Copenhagen: Udgivet og forlagt af Forfatteren 1863.

500-501 Eiríksson, Magnús, *Johannis Evangelium. Är det en äkta apostolisk Bok och är dess Lära: att Gud är vorden Menniska, en sann och kristlig Lära? En Religiös-Dogmatisk Historisk-Kritisk Undersökning*, trans. by Nils Johan Ekdahl, Stockholm: L.J. Hierta 1864. (2 copies)

502 Eiríksson, Magnús, *Den nydanske Theologies Cardinaldyder belyste ved Hjelp af Dr. Martensens Skrifter samt Modskrifterne, tilligemed 75 theologiske Spørgsmaal, rettede til Dr. H. Martensen*, Copenhagen: Chr. Steen & Søn 1850.

503 Eiríksson, Magnús, *Jóhannesar guðspjall og Lærdómur kirkjunnar um guð, nokkrar athugasemdir til yfirvegunar þeim Íslendíngum, sem ekki vilja svívirða og lasta guð með trú sinni*, Copenhagen: L. Klein 1865.

504 Eiríksson, Magnús, *Gud og Reformatoren. En religiøs Idee. Samt nogle Bemærkninger om de kirkelige Tilstande, Dr. S. Kierkegaard og Forfatteren*, Copenhagen: J.H. Schubothe 1866. (Bound copy)

505 Eiríksson, Magnús, *Nokkrar athugasemdir um Sannanir "katólsku prestanna í Reykjavík" fyrir guðdómi Jesú Krists*, Copenhagen: L. Klein 1868. (Bound copy)

506 Eiríksson, Magnús, *Paulus og Christus eller Pauli Lære om Retfærdiggjørelsen sammenlignet med Christi Lære om Syndsforladelsen, tilligemed nogle Bemærkninger om andre paulinske Lærdomme m. M.*, Copenhagen: Udgivet og forlagt af Forfatteren 1871. (Bound copy)

507-508 Theophilus Nicolaus [i.e., Magnús Eiríksson], *Er Troen et Paradox og "i Kraft af det Absurde"? et Spørgsmaal foranlediget ved "Frygt og Bæven, af Johannes de silentio", besvaret ved Hjelp af en Troes-Ridders fortrolige Meddelelser, til fælles Opbyggelse for Jøder, Christne og Muhamedanere, af bemeldte Troes-Ridders Broder*, Copenhagen: Chr. Steen & Søn 1850. (2 copies)

509-510 Theophilus Nicolaus [i.e., Magnús Eiríksson], *Er Troen et Paradox og "i Kraft af det Absurde"? et Spørgsmaal foranlediget ved "Frygt og Bæven, af Johannes de silentio", besvaret ved Hjelp af en Troes-Ridders fortrolige Meddelelser, til fælles Opbyggelse for Jøder, Christne og Muhamedanere, af bemeldte Troes-Ridders Broder*, Copenhagen: Chr. Steen & Søn 1850. (2 copies with gilt edges)

511 Eiríksson, Magnús, *Läran om dopet*, trans. by Nils Johan Ekdahl, Stockholm: L.J. Hiertas Forläg 1865.

512 Anonymous, *Epistola eller Sende-Brev til Sr. Magnus Eiriksson fra en anden gammel Landsbypræst. Til Publici videre Nytte og Fornøielse nu til Trykken befordret*, Copenhagen: H.C. Klein 1844.

513 Levinssøn, M. Chr., *Magnus Eirikssons "Restancer" i "Folkets Avis" og paa det nordiske Kirkemøde*, Copenhagen: no publisher given 1872.

514 Baudoin, Jean-Baptiste ["Hinir katólsku prestar í Reykjavík"], *Útskýring um trú katólsku Kirkjunnar í* *þeim trúaratriðum, þar sem ágreisningr er milli hennar og mótmælanda*, Reykjavík: Hinir katólsku prestar í Reykjavík 1865.

515 Baudoin, Jean-Baptiste ["Hinir katólsku prestar í Reykjavík"], *Svar hinna katólsku presta upp á I. Brèfið frá París eptir Herra Eirík Magnússon. Hvað segir Sagan um Parísarbrèfið?*, Reykjavík: Hinir katólsku prestar 1866. (3 copies)

516-517 Baudoin, Jean-Baptiste ["Hinir katólsku prestar í Reykjavík"], *Jesús Kristr er Guð. Þrátt fyrir mótmæli herra Magnúsar Eiríkssonar*, Reykjavík: Hinir katólsku prestar í Reykjavík 1867. (2 copies)

518 Einarsson, Magnús, *Nokkrar Athugasemdir, gegn Magnúsi Eiríkssyni m. fl.*, Akureyri: Jónas Sveinsson 1867.

519 Eiríksson, Magnús, "Min Forfattervirksomhed," *Flyvende Blade for Literatur, Kunst og Samfundsspørgsmaal*, ed. by Vilhelm Møller, vol. 3, no. 11 (June 12, 1875), pp. 81-83; no. 12 (June 19, 1875), pp. 90-93, and no. 13 (June 26, 1875), pp. 100-104. [Offprint]

520 Eiríksson, Magnús, *Herr A. Pedrin og Christendommen. Nogle Oplysninger om hans Skrift: "Vor Herres og Frelsers Jesu Christi nye Testament og Magnus Eirikssons reformeerte Jødedom,"* Copenhagen: Sally B. Salomons Tryk 1874.

521 Engelstoft, Christian Thorning, *Liturgiens eller Alterbogens og Kirkeritualets Historie i Danmark, udarbeidet med stadigt Hensyn til det efter allerhøieste Befaling forfattede Udkast til en Alterbog og et Kirkeritual for Danmark*, Copenhagen: C.A. Reitzel 1840.

522 Engelstoft, Christian Thorning, *Om den academiske Borgerrets Betydning, Hæder og Pligter i Særdeleshed med Hensyn til Kjøbenhavns Universitet, Tale holden den 8. Nov. 1808 i Anl. af Reformationsfesten og de nye academiske Borgeres Optagelse*, Copenhagen: Trykt hos Johan Frederik Schultz 1809.

523 Engstrand, Carl Johan Henrik, *Kritik af Realismen. En indirect bevisning för den absoluta Idealismens sanning och nödvändighet*, Upsala: Edquist & Berglund 1863.

524 [Eusebius of Caesarea], *Eusebs Kirkehistorie indtil Aar 305, med Tillæg*, trans. by Carl Augustin Høffding Muus, 2nd edition, Copenhagen: Karl Schønberg 1865 [1832].

525 Faber, Nicolai, *Katechetik eller den practiske Theologies andet Hovedstykke*, Copenhagen: Wahlske Boghandel 1845.

526 Faber, Nicolai, *De anabaptistiske Bevægelser i Danmark betragtede fra det christelige og kirkelige Standpunct*, Odense: G. Hempel 1842.

527 Faber, Theodor, *Fantasiens Ret i Virkelighedens Rige*, Copenhagen: G.E.C. Gad 1876.

528 Faber, Theodor, *Livskampens Frugter og Visdommen i Verdensplanen*, Copenhagen: G.E.C. Gad 1880.

529 Fabricius, Johann Albert, *Centifolium Lutheranum sive Notitia Litteraria Scriptorum Omnis Generis de B. D. Luthero*, Hamburg: C. König & G. Richter 1728. (Bound copy)

530 *Forhandlingerne paa Det Første Skandinaviske Kirkemøde. Kjøbenhavn Juli 1857*, ed. by Frederik Hammerich, Copenhagen: C.G. Iversen 1857.

531 *Forhandlingerne paa Det Fjerde Nordiske Kirkemöde i Kjøbenhavn den 5., 6. og 7. September 1871*, ed. by Kr. Madsen, Copenhagen: Gyldendal 1871.

532-535 Fritsch, Johann Heinrich, *Handbuch für Prediger zur praktischen Behandlung der Sonn- und Festtägigen Evangelien*, vols. 1-4, 3rd revised and enlarged edition, ed. by Karl Gerhard Haupt, Magdeburg: Wilhelm Heinrichshofen 1831. (Bound copy)

536 Frost, Peter Nicolai, *Oversættelse af det Gamle Testamentes apocryphiske Bøger*, Haderslev: Trykt hos H. Seneberg 1835. (Bound copy)

537 Frost, Peter Nicolai, *Oversættelse af det Gamle Testamentes historisk-canoniske Bøger*, vols. 1-2, Haderslev: Trykt hos H. Seneberg 1836-1837.

538 Gad, Ole Christian Lund, *Efterladte Prædikener*, Copenhagen: G.E.C. Gad 1859.

539 Galle, Friedrich, *Versuch einer Charakteristik Melanchthons als Theologen und einer Entwickelung seines Lehrbegriffs*, Halle: Johann Friedrich Lippert 1840. (Bound copy)

540-541 Hess, Johann Jakob, *Geschichte der drey letzten Lebensjahre Jesu. Nebst einer Einleitung welche die Beschreibung von Palæstina und die Jugendgeschichte Jesu enthält*, vols. 1-2, 4th revised edition, Zürich: Orell, Geßner, Füeßlin u. Comp. 1774. (Bound copy)

542 Goulburn, Edward Meyrick, *Betragtninger over personlig Religiøsitet*, trans. by Christian Carl August Gosch, Copenhagen: Otto Schwartz's Efterfølger 1868.

543 Graul, Karl, *De forskjellige christelige Troesbekjendelser i deres indbyrdes Afvigelser i Læren, belyste af Guds Ord. Samt Efterviisning af den rene Læres høie Betydning for det christelige Liv, og et Afrids af de vigtigste falske religiøse Retninger*, trans. by Adolf Enkebølle, 2nd edition, Copenhagen: Wøldike 1861.

544 Gretsch, Adrian, *Fastenpredigten*, vols. 1-2, new edition, Mainz: Simon Müller'sche Buchhandlung and Vienna: Franz Tendler 1829. (Bound copy)

545 Grüder, Herman, *Det protestantiske og det katholske Troesprincip, i Anledning af Biskop Martensens Lejlighedsskrift: "Katholicisme og Protestantisme," critisk belyst*, Copenhagen: A.F. Høst & Søn 1875.

546 Gude, Ludvig Jacob Mendel, *Den hellige Nadvere*, vol. 1, *Forberedelsen og Indstiftelsen*, Copenhagen: Gyldendalske Boghandel (F. Hegel) 1874.

547 Gäbler, Bernhard, *Die vollständige Liturgie und die 39 Artikel der Kirche von England nebst einer Einleitung*, Altenburg: H.A. Bierer 1843.

548 Hagenbach, Karl Rudolph, *Enzyklopädie und Methodologie der theologischen Wissenschaften*, Leipzig: Weidmann'sche Buchhandlung 1833. (Bound copy)

549 Hahn, August, *Lehrbuch des christlichen Glaubens*, 2nd revised edition, Leipzig: Friedrich Christian Wilhelm Vogel 1857 [1828].

550 Harless, Gottlieb Christoph Adolph von, *Christliche Ethik*, 2nd printing, Stuttgart: S.G. Liesching 1842. (Bound copy)

551 Harless, Gottlieb Christoph Adolph, *Christi Reich und Christi Kraft. Zwanzig Predigten*, Stuttgart: S.G. Liesching 1840.

552 Hase, Karl, *Kirkehistorie. Lærebog nærmest for akademiske Forelæsninger*, trans. by Christian Winther and Theodor Schorn, Copenhagen: C.A. Reitzel 1837. (Bound copy)

553 Haupt, Karl Gerhard, *Biblisches Casual-Text-Lexikon. Enthaltend: Auserwählte Aussprüche der heiligen Schrift, die Predigten und Reden zum Grunde zu legen sind, welche Geistliche vortragen bei besonderen, außerordentlichen Fällen, merkwürdigen Begebenheiten und ungewöhnlichen Veranlassungen, mit Hinzufügung solcher Bibelstellen...Für Geistliche aller Confessionen*, Quedlinburg and Leipzig: Gottfried Basse 1826. (Bound copy)

554 Hebel, Johann Peter, *Biblische Geschichten. Für die Jugend*, vols. 1-2, new edition, Stuttgart and Tübingen: J.G. Cotta'sche Buchhandlung 1830. (Bound copy)

555 Heegaard, Sophus, *Bidrag til Spörgsmålet om Filosofiens Betydning og Værd*, Stockholm: P.A. Nordstedt & Söner 1878. [Offprint]

556 Heegaard, Sophus, *Om Intolerance, især i Henseende til religiøs Overbevisning*, Copenhagen: Gyldendal 1878.

557 Heiberg, Johan Ludvig (ed.), *Perseus, Journal for den speculative Idee*, vol. 1, Copenhagen: C.A. Reitzel 1837 (vol. 2, 1838).

558 Heinicke, Samuel, *Scheingötterei der Naturalisten, Deisten und Atheisten*, Köthen: Glandenbergische Buchhandlung 1788.

559 Heise, Victor, *Om Opfatningen af Høisangen* [part of *Indbydelsesskrift til den offentlige Examen i Sorø Akademis Skole i Juni og Juli 1864*], Sorø: V. Røhrs Bogtrykkeri 1864.

560 Herbart, Johann Friedrich, *Kurze Encyclopädie der Philosophie aus praktischen Gesichtspuncten*, 2nd revised and enlarged edition, Halle: C.A. Schwetschke und Sohn 1841 [1831].

561 Hermas, *Hyrde-Bogen*, trans. by P.W. Christensen, Copenhagen: C.G. Iversen 1856.

562 Hermann, Wilhelm, *Geschichte der protestantischen Dogmatik von Melanchthon bis Schleiermacher*, Leipzig: Breitkopf und Härtel 1842.

563 Hess, Jean Gaspard, *Lebensbeschreibung M. Ulrich Zwingli's*, Zurich: Gessnerische Buchhandlung 1811. (Bound copy)

564 Hilgenfeld, Adolph, *Der Kanon und die Kritik des Neuen Testaments in ihrer geschichtlichen Ausbildung und Gestaltung, nebst Herstellung und Beleuchtung des Muratorischen Bruchstücks*, Halle: C.E.M. Pfeffer 1863.

565 Hindmarsh, Robert, *The Church of England Weighed in the Balance of the Sanctuary, and found Wanting. Being an Examination of the Thirty-nine Articles of Religion, the Three Creeds, and the Book of Common Prayer*, London: J.S. Hodson 1846. (Bound copy)

566 Holberg, Ludvig, *Jødiske Historie*, vols. 1-2; vol. 1, *Fra Verdens Begyndelse, Fortsatt til disse Tider*, Copenhagen: Trykt paa Autoris Bekostning 1742; vol. 2, *Fra Maccabæernes souveraine Regimente indtil denne Tid*, Copenhagen: Trykt hos Ernst Heinrich Berling 1742. (Bound copy)

567 Holstein-Ledreborg, Johan Ludvig Carl, *Evangelisk-Luthersk (en negativ Bestemmelse)*, Copenhagen: A.F. Høst 1872.

568 [Hase, Karl August von], *Hutterus redivivus eller den Evangelisk-Lutherske Kirkes Dogmatik. Et dogmatisk Repertorium for Studerende*, trans. from the 4th revised edition by A.L.C. Listow, Copenhagen: C.A. Reitzel 1841.

569 Ignell, Nils, *Jesu Christi och hans Apostlars Lära, enligt Nya Testamentets kanoniska Skrifter kritiskt framställd*, Stockholm: Zacharias Haeggström 1864.

570 Ignell, Nils, *Den ursprungliga Christna Tron och Dogmtron. Sändebref till svensk Kyrkotidning*, Stockholm: J. & A. Riis 1861.

571 [Saint Irenaeus], *Irenæus om den ægte Christendom. Udvalgte Steder af første og anden Bog, samt hele tredie og fjerde Bog af ovennævntes Værk mod Kjætterne, fordanskede og forsynede med Anmærkninger og Indledning*, trans. by P.W. Christensen, Copenhagen: C.G. Iversen 1854.

572-573 Ivimey, Joseph, *A History of the English Baptists*, vols. 1-2, London: Wightman and Cramp 1827.

574 Johannsen, Johann Christian Gottberg, *Allseitige wissenschaftliche und historische Untersuchung der Rechtmäßigkeit der Verpflichtung auf symbolische Bücher überhaupt und die Augsburgische Konfession insbesondere*, Altona: J.F. Hammerich 1833. (Bound copy)

575 Johannsen, Karl Theodor, *Die kosmogonischen Ansichten der Juden und Hebräer durch Zusammenstellung der Maurischen und Mosaischen Kosmogonie erläutert*, Altona: J.F. Hammerich 1833.

576 Josef, Karl, *Weltgericht der Philosophen von Thales bis zu Fichte*, new edition, Leipzig: Sommersche Buchhandlung 1807 [1801]. (Bound copy)

577-578 [Flavius Josephus], *Flavii Josephi Jødiske Historie*, vols. 1-2, trans. by Andreas Reyersen, Copenhagen: Trykt og bekostet af Deres Kongelige Majestæts Hof-Bogtrykker, Ernst Henrich Berling 1750-1751 (vol. 3, *Flavii Josephi Beskrivelse om Jødernes Krig med Romerne*, 1757). (Bound copy)

579 Jungersen, Frederik, *Miraklet, Videnskaben og Troen. Et Stridsskrift*, Copenhagen: Karl Schønberg 1875.

580-581 Kalkar, Christian Andreas Hermann, *Forelæsninger over den bibelske Historie*, vols. 1-2, Odense: S. Hempel 1837-1839.

582 Kalkar, Christian Andreas Hermann, *Betragtninger over "Missionen blandt Jøderne" samt nogle historiske Bemærkninger*, Copenhagen: Chr. Steen & Søn 1868.

583-584 Kanne, Johann Arnold, *Leben und aus dem Leben merkwürdiger und erweckter Christen aus der protestantischen Kirche*, vols. 1-2, 2nd edition, Leipzig: F.A. Brockhaus 1842.

585 Kant, Immanuel, *Anthropologie udi pragmatisk Hensigt*, trans. from the 2nd revised edition by Christian Carl Pflueg, Copenhagen: K.H. Seidelin 1802. (Bound copy)

586 [Kant, Immanuel], *Immanuel Kants Logik. En Haandbog til Forelæsninger*, trans. by Christian Carl Pflueg, Copenhagen: K.H. Seidelin 1803. (Bound copy)

587 Kardec, Allan [i.e., Rivail, Hippolyte Léon Denizard], *Aandeverdenen. Spiritismens Principer om Sjælens Udødelighed, Aandernes Natur og deres Forbindelser med Menneskene; de moralske Love, det nuærende Liv, det tilkommende Liv og Menneskehedens Fremtid. Efter de af de højere Aander givne Forskrifter, ved Hjælp af forskjellige Medier*, Copenhagen: Chr. Steen & Søn 1865.

588 Kardec, Allan [i.e., Rivail, Hippolyte Léon Denizard], *Den experimentale Spiritisme. Mediernes Bog eller Anvisning for Medierne og de Paakaldende. En Fortsættelse af Aandeverdenen*, Copenhagen: Chr. Steen & Søn 1866.

589 Kardec, Allan [i.e., Rivail, Hippolyte Léon Denizard], *Evangeliet forklaret efter Spiritismen, indeholdende Udtydningen af Christi moralske Læresætninger, deres Overenstemmelse med Spiritismen og Anvendelse i de forskjellige Forhold i Livet*, Copenhagen: Hagerup 1868.

590 Karup, Wilhelm Ignatius, *Christendommen, Prostestantismen og Freden. Otte practiske Afhandlinger i Dr. Søren Kierkegaards, Pastor Østergaards og alle andre ærlige og gudfrygtige Protestanters gode Villie og Aand*, Christiania: Berlingske Bogtrykkeri ved A. H. Stenderup 1859.

591 [Kempis, Thomas à], *Thomas a Kempis, om Christi Efterfølgelse, fire Bøger*, trans. and ed. by Andreas Gottlob Rudelbach, Copenhagen: Wahlske Boghandlings Forlag 1826. (Bound copy)

592 [Kempis, Thomas à], *Den lille Kempis eller Korte Tankesprog og Bønner af fordetmeste ubekjendte Skrifter*, trans. from the 10th edition, by A.W. [Adolf Enkebølle], Copenhagen: Fr. Wøldikes Forlagsboghandel 1860.

593 Kierkegaard, Søren, *Kjerlighedens Gjerninger. Nogle christelige Overveielser i Talers Form*, vols. 1-2, 3rd edition, Copenhagen: C.A. Reitzel 1862 [1847]. (Bound copy)

594 [Kierkegaard, Søren], *Frygt og Bæven. Dialektisk Lyrik af Johannes de silentio*, Copenhagen: C.A. Reitzel 1843.

595 Kierkegaard, Søren, *Synspunktet for min Forfatter-Virksomhed. En ligefrem Meddelelse, Rapport til Historien*, posthumously ed. by Peter Christian Kierkegaard, Copenhagen: C.A. Reitzel 1859.

596 [Kierkegaard, Søren], *Søren Kierkegaards Efterladte Papirer 1833-1843*, ed. by Hans Peter Barfod, Copenhagen: C.A. Reitzel 1869.

597 Bøgh, Erik, *Søren Kierkegaard og St. Sørens-Dyrkelsen. Feuilletoner*, Copenhagen: Th. Gandrup 1870.

598 Klötzner, Christian Wilhelm, *Reden vor Gebildeten bei besonderen Gelegenheiten nebst zwei Gelegenheitspredigten*, vols. 1-3, Altenburg: Schnuphase'sche Buchhandlung 1837-1844 [vol. 1, *Reden vor Gebildeten bei besonderen Gelegenheiten nebst zwei Gelegenheitspredigten*, Altenburg: Schnuphase'sche Buchhandlung 1837; vol. 2, *Reden vor Gebildeten bei Taufen, Trauungen, Communionen und am Grabe*, Altenburg: Schnuphase'sche Buchhandlung 1842; vol. 3, *Reden vor Gebildeten bei Taufen, Trauungen, Communionen und am Grabe*, Altenburg: Schnuphase'sche Buchhandlung 1844].

599 [Knapp, Georg Christian], *D. Georg Christian Knapp's Biblische Glaubenslehre vornehmlich für den praktischen Gebrauch*, ed. by Heinrich Ernst Ferdinand Guericke, Halle: C.A. Kümmel 1840. (Bound copy)

600 Knigge, Adolph von, *Om Egennytte og Utaknemmelighed. Et Sidestykke til Bogen: Om Omgang med Mennesker*, trans. by Lauritz Hasse, Copenhagen: Trykt hos Directeur Joh. Fred. Schultz 1799. (Bound copy)

601 Knudsen, Hans, *Grundtvigianismen, Papismen og Kirke-Unionen. Bidrag til en kirkelig Tidsbetragtning*, Copenhagen: A.F. Høst 1854.

602 *Der Koran oder Das Gesetz der Moslemen durch Muhammed den Sohn Abdallahs*, new trans. (on the basis of the translation by Friedrich Eberhard Boysen) by Samuel Friedrich Günther Wahl, Halle: Gebauersche Buchhandlung 1828. (Bound copy)

603 Krehl, August Ludwig Gottlob, *Neu-Testamentliches Handwörterbuch zur Darstellung der christlichen Glaubens-*

und Sittenlehre für Prediger der evangelischen Kirche, Leipzig: Carl Heinrich Reclam sen. 1843. (Bound copy)

604 Kromm, Johann Jacob, *Der Beichtvater. Ideen und Andeutungen zu Beicht- und Communion-Reden in extemporirbaren Entwürfen. Ein praktisches Handbuch für alle Prediger*, Mainz: Kupferberg 1836. (Bound copy)

605 Kronblad, Samuel Johan, *Om det allmänna Prestadömet och dess Werksamhet inom Kyrkan*, Lund: Ohlssons Boktrykkeri 1863.

606 Krummacher, Friedrich Wilhelm, *Elisa. Atten Betragtninger over 2 Kong. 2, 19.-5, 27*, trans. by Hans Holmboe, Bergen: F.D. Beyer 1846. (Bound copy)

607-609 Kühnöl, Christian Gottlieb, *Commentarius in libros Novi Testamenti historicos*, vols. 1-3, Leipzig: J.A. Barth 1807-1812 (vol. 4, 1818). (Bound copy)

610 Kühnöl, Christian Gottlieb, *Commentarius in libros Novi Testamenti historicos*, vol. 1, *Evangelium Matthaei*, 3rd revised and enlarged edition, Leipzig: J.A. Barth 1823. (Bound copy)

611 Lang, Heinrich, *Det Nye Testamente og Fremtidens Kirke*, ed. by Literaturselskabet, Copenhagen: Gyldendal 1872. (2 copies)

612 Larsen, Alfred Christian, *Pauli første Brev til Menigheden i Korinth fortolket*, Copenhagen: C.A. Reitzel 1872.

613 Larsen, Alfred Christian, *Johannes's Breve fortolkede*, Copenhagen: C.A. Reitzel 1873.

614 Larsen, Alfred Christian, *Samvittighed og Videnskab*, Copenhagen: C.A. Reitzel 1865; *Theologiske Smuler*, Copenhagen: C.W. Stinck 1872; *Om det Theologiske Facultet. Et Foredrag holdt i Studenterforeningen d. 14de Marts 1874*, Copenhagen: Jacob Erslev 1874.

615 Lasserre, Henri, *Notre Dame de Lourdes*, Paris: V. Palmé 1869.

616 Leander, Pehr Johan Herman, *Om Substansbegreppet hos Cartesius, Spinoza och Leibnitz*, Lund: Tryckt uti Berlingska Bogtryckeriet 1862; *Om Substansbegreppet hos Kant och* *de tänkare, som fran honom utgått*, Lund: H. Ohlssons Boktryckeri 1863.

617 Less, Gottfried, *Christliche Religions-Theorie fürs gemeine Leben, oder Versuch einer praktischen Dogmatik*, 2nd revised and enlarged edition, Göttingen: Vandenhoeksche Buchhandlung 1780. (Bound copy)

618 Less, Gottfried, *Den christelige Religions Sandhed*, trans. from the 2nd revised and enlarged edition by Hans Jørgen Birch, Copenhagen: A.H. Godiches Efterleverskes Forlag 1774. (Bound copy)

619 Lessing, Gotthold Ephraim (ed.), *Von dem Zwecke Jesu und seiner Jünger. Noch ein Fragment des Wolfenbüttelschen Ungenannten*, new edition, Berlin: Arnold Wever 1788 [1778]. (Bound copy)

620 Lilja, Nils, *Kristendomen, dess uppkomst, dess lära, dess historia och dess utveckling jemte judendomens historia och litteratur*, Stockholm: På författarens förlag 1860.

621 Lindberg, Jacob Christian, *Hebraisk Grammatik*, 2nd enlarged edition, Copenhagen: Wahlske Boghandling 1828 [1822]. (Bound copy)

622 Listov, Andreas Laurits Carl, *Om Brødrene Wesley og Methodismen. En kort historisk Fremstilling*, Copenhagen: Methodisternes Forlag 1861. (2 copies)

623 Llorente, Juan Antonio, *Geschichte der Inquisition. Nebst der Lebensbeschreibung von Llorente und seinem Bildnisse*, trans. by Gottfried Wilhelm Becker, Leipzig: Voß 1823. (Bound copy)

624 Lorentzen, Simon, *Forklaring over Mosis første Bog, tilligemed Oplysninger af nyere moralske, physiske og historiske Skrivter*, vol. 1, Copenhagen: Gyldendal 1781. (Bound copy)

625 Lund, John Christian, *Grammaticalsk Analyse af første Mosebog. Udarbejdet med stadigt Hensyn til Professor [Jens Lassen] Rasmussens hebraiske Sproglære, til Brug for de første Begyndere*, Copenhagen: Schultz 1819. (Bound copy)

626 Lund, Troels, *Om Sokrates's Lære og Personlighed*, Copenhagen: Bianco Lunos Bogtrykkeri ved F.S. Muhle 1871.

627 [Luther, Martin], *Dr. Martin Luthers kristelige Betragtninger til hver Dag i Aaret. Udvalgte Steder af hans samlede Skrifter*, trans. by Hans Peter Møller, 2nd edition, Copenhagen: L.A. Jørgensen 1866 [1861].

628 Luther, Martin, *Bibelske Sprog- og Skat-Kiste i tre Dele, hvori over 400 Sprog af den hellige Skrift, med aanderige og eftertrykkelige Ord, blive forklarede*, ed. by Johann Christoph Schinmeier, Christiansand: Moe 1832. (Bound copy)

629 Hjort, H. Smith, *Lys og Mørke eller Om Drømme, Somnambulisme, Anelser, Spaadomme, Varsler o.s.v., med 156 Fortællinger, der vise Exempler paa Tilværelsen af den menneskelige Anelsesevne*, Christiania: Nissen 1850.

630 Madsen, Peder, *De Christnes aandelige Præstedømme. Afhandling for den theologiske Doctorgrad ved Universitetets Firehundredaars-Fest*, Copenhagen: G.E.C. Gad 1879.

631 *Magazin von Leichen-Reden. Herausgegeben von einer Gesellschaft evangelischer Prediger. Zugleich auch zum Gebrauche bei Leseleichen bestimmt*, vols. 1-2, Bayreuth: Grau'sche Buchhandlung 1835-1837. (Bound copy)

632 Martensen, Hans Lassen, *Prædikener, holdte i Aarene 1859 til 1863*, Copenhagen: Gyldendalske Boghandling (F. Hegel) 1863. (Bound copy)

633 Martensen, Hans Lassen, *Katholicisme og Protestantisme. Et Leilighedsskrift*, Copenhagen: Gyldendal 1874.

634 Martensen, Hans Lassen, *Grundrids til Moralphilosophiens System. Udgivet til Brug ved academiske Forelæsninger*, Copenhagen: C.A. Reitzel 1841.

635 Martensen, Hans Lassen, *Om Tro og Viden. Et Leilighedsskrift*, 2nd edition, Copenhagen: C.A. Reitzel 1867 [1867].

636 Martensen, Hans Lassen, *Den christelige Daab, betragtet med Hensyn paa det baptistiske Spørgsmaal*, Copenhagen: C.A. Reitzel 1843; *Dogmatiske Oplysninger. Et Leilighedsskrift*, Copenhagen: C.A. Reitzel 1850. (together with 4 (other) works)

637 Matthies, Konrad Stephan, *Baptismatis expositio biblica historica dogmatica*, new edition, Berlin: E.H. Schröder 1840 [1831].

638 Maudsley, Henry, *Om Forholdet mellem Sjæl og Legeme samt mellem Sindssygdomme og andre Lidelser af Nervesystemet. Tre Foredrag*, Copenhagen: C.A. Reitzel 1870.

639 Maurer, Franz Joseph Valentin Dominik, *Practischer Cursus über die Formenlehre der hebräischen Sprache oder Analysirübungen zur methodischen Einführung des Scholars in die hebräische Formenlehre nebst einem etymologischen Wortregister*, Leipzig: F. Volckmar 1837.

640 Maurer, Franz Joseph Valentin Dominik, *Commentarius grammaticus criticus in Vetus Testamentum in usum maxime gymnasiorum et academiarum adornatus*, vols. 1-2, Leipzig: F. Volckmar 1835-1838.

641 Maurer, Franz Joseph Valentin Dominik, *Commentarius grammaticus historicus criticus in psalmos in usum maxime academiarum adornatus*, Leipzig: F. Volckmar 1838. (Bound copy)

642 Maurer, Franz Joseph Valentin Dominik, *Commentarius grammaticus historicus criticus in Prophetas Minores in usum maxime academiarum adornatus*, Leipzig: F. Volckmar 1840. (Bound copy)

643 Maurer, Franz Joseph Valentin Dominik, *Commentarius grammaticus criticus in Proverbia, in usum academiarum adornatus*, Leipzig: F. Volckmar 1841.

644 Scharling, Carl Emil, *Methodistiske Lægpræster*, Slagelse: Trykt hos Peter Magnus 1832 [Offprint from *Blandninger fra Sorøe*]. (2 copies)

645 Meyer, Heinrich August Wilhelm, *Kritisch exegetisches Handbuch über die Evangelien des Matthäus, Markus und Lukas*, Göttingen: Vandenhoeck und Ruprecht 1832; *Kritisch exegetisches Handbuch über das Evangelium des Johannes*, Göttingen: Vandenhoeck und Ruprecht 1834; *Kritisch exegetisches Handbuch über den Römerbrief*, Göttingen: Vandenhoeck und Ruprecht 1836; *Kritisch exegetisches Handbuch über den ersten Brief an die Korinther*,

Göttingen: Vandenhoeck und Ruprecht 1839. (Bound copy)

646 Düsterdieck, Friedrich, *Kritisch exegetisches Handbuch über die Offenbarung Johannis*, Göttingen: Vandenhoeck und Ruprecht 1859 (*Kritisch exegetischer Kommentar über das Neue Testament*, vol. 16).

647 Meyer, Heinrich August Wilhelm, *Kritisk exegetisk Haandbog til Pauli Brev til de Philippenser*, trans. by W. Skram, Copenhagen: Michaelsen & Tillge 1859.

648-658 [Michaelis, Johann David], *Johann David Michaelis Oversættelse af det Gamle Testament, med Anmærkninger*, vols. 1-4, trans. and ed. by Jens Bech, Copenhagen: Gyldendal 1785-1790; *Johann David Michaelis Oversættelse af det Nye Testament, med Anmærkninger*, vols. 1-4, trans. and ed. by Jens Bech, Copenhagen: Gyldendal 1793-1797. (Bound copy)

659-661 Michaelis, Johann David, *Mosaiske Ret*, vols. 1-3, trans. from the 2nd revised edition by Jakob Wolf, Copenhagen: Gyldendal 1780-1783. (Bound copy)

662 Mignet, François Auguste Marie Alexis, *Die Einführung der Reformation und die Verfassung des Calvinismus zu Genf*, trans. by Johann Jakob Stolz, Leipzig: Köhler & Tauchnitz 1843.

663 Monod, Adolphe, *La femme. Deux Discours*, 9th edition, Paris: Librairie de Ch. Meyrueis 1871.

664 Monod, Adolphe, *Prædikener*, Collections 1-2, trans. by M. Th. Becher, Copenhagen: P. G. Philipsen 1856-1858.

665 Monrad, Ditlev Gothard, *Politiske Breve Nr. 14-18. Liberalismens Gjenmæle til Biskop Martensens sociale Ethik*, 2nd edition, Copenhagen: C.A. Reitzel 1878 [1878].

666 Monrad, Marcus Jacobus, *En Episode under Forhandlingerne mellem Tro og Viden*, Christiania: J. Chr. Abelsted 1869.

667 Monrad, Marcus Jacobus, *Tankeretninger i den nyere Tid. Et kritisk Rundskue*, Christiania: H. Aschehoug & Co. 1874.

668 Moritz, Karl Philipp, *Götterlehre oder mythologische Dichtungen der Alten. Mit fünf und sechzig in Kupfer gestochenen Abbildungen, nach antiken geschnittenen Steinen* *und andern Denkmälern des Alterthums*, 5th revised edition, Berlin: A.W. Schade 1819. (Bound copy)

669 A bundle of books on Mormons.

670 [Mosheim, Johann Lorenz von], *Johann Lorenz von Mosheim allgemeines Kirchenrecht der Protestanten*, posthumously ed. by Christian Ernst von Windheim, Helmstädt: Christian Friedrich Weygand 1760. (Bound copy)

671 Mosheim, Johann Lorenz von, *Pastoral-Theologie von denen Pflichten und Lehramt eines Dieners des Evangelii*, Frankfurt and Leipzig: no publisher given 1754.

672-674 Mosheim, Johan[n] Lorenz von, and Miller, Johan Peter, *Den hellige Skrifts Sædelære. Tilligemed den christelige Sædelæres Historie*, vols. 1-3, Copenhagen: Gyldendal 1780-1782. (Bound copy)

675 Müller, Peter Erasmus, *System i den christelige Dogmatik til Brug ved academiske Forelæsninger*, Copenhagen: Fr. Brummer 1826. (Bound copy)

676 Müller, Peter Erasmus, *Christeligt Moralsystem til Brug ved Academiske Forelæsninger*, 2nd revised edition, Copenhagen: Fr. Brummer 1827 [1808]. (Bound copy)

677 [Münscher, Wilhelm], *Dr. Wilhelm Münschers Lærebog i den christelige Kirkehistorie, til Brug ved Forelæsninger*, trans. by Frederik Münter, revised and ed. by Jens Møller, new edition, Copenhagen: Fr. Brummer 1831 [1805]. (Bound copy)

678-679 Münter, Frederik, *Den Danske Reformationshistorie*, vols. 1-2, Copenhagen: J.F. Schultz 1802. (Bound copy)

680-681 Münter, Frederik, *Haandbog i den ældste Christelige Kirkes Dogmehistorie*, vols. 1-2, Copenhagen: Fr. Brummer 1801-1804. (Bound copy)

682 Mynster, Jakob Peter, *Udkast til en Alterbog og et Kirke-Ritual for Danmark*, Copenhagen: Trykt hos Directeur Jens Hostrup Schultz, Kongelig og Universitets-Bogtrykker 1839; "Second printing", Copenhagen: Trykt hos Directeur Jens Hostrup Schultz, Kongelig og Universitets-Bogtrykker 1840.

683-685 *Det Gamle Testaments poetiske og prophetiske Skrifter, efter Grundtexten paa ny oversatte og med Indholdsfortegnelse samt Anmærkninger forsynede*, vols. 1-2.2, trans. by Jens Møller and Rasmus Møller, Copenhagen: Andreas Seidelin 1828-1830.

686 Neander, August, *Allgemeine Geschichte der christlichen Religion und Kirche*, vols. 1-4 (in 8 vols.), Hamburg: Friedrich Perthes 1826-1836.

687 Newton, Thomas, *Afhandlinger over Prophetierne, hvilke mærkværdig ere opfyldte, og paa denne Tid blive opfyldte i Verden*, vols. 1-3, trans. by Diderik de Thurah, 2nd edition, Copenhagen: Trykt i det Kongelige Waysenhuses Bogtrykkerie, ved Gerhard Giese Salikath, paa Oversætterens Bekostning 1770 [1765]. (Bound copy)

688 Nielsen, Fredrik Kristian, *Tertullians Ethik. Afhandling for den theologiske Doktorgrad ved Universitetets Firehundredaars-Fest*, Copenhagen: Schønberg 1879.

689 Nielsen, Gotfred, *Troen og Tvivlen. Religiøse Betragtninger*, Copenhagen: A.F. Høst 1870.

690 Nielsen, Rasmus, *Grundideernes Logik*, vol. 1, Copenhagen: Gyldendalske Boghandel (F. Hegel) 1864. (Bound copy)

691 Nielsen, Rasmus, *Om Theologiens Naturbegreb* [part of *Indbydelsesskrift til Kjøbenhavns Universitets Aarsfest til Erindring om Kirkens Reformation*], Copenhagen: Trykt i det Schultziske Officin 1855. (2 copies)

692 Nielsen, Rasmus, *Om det oprindelige Forhold mellem Religion og Videnskab* [part of *Indbydelsesskrift til Kjøbenhavns Universitets Fest i Anledning af Majestæts Kongens Fødselsdag den 8de April 1881*], Copenhagen: Trykt hos J.H. Schultz 1881.

693 Nielsen, Rasmus, *Forelæsningsparagrapher til Kirkehistoriens Philosophie. Et Schema for Tilhørere*, Copenhagen: P.G. Philipsen 1843.

694 Nielsen, Rasmus, *Om Hindringer og Betingelser for det aandelige Liv i Nutiden. Sexten Forelæsninger, holdte ved Universitetet i Christiania September-Oktober 1867*, Copenhagen: Gyldendalske Boghandel (F. Hegel) 1868.

695 Nielsen, Rasmus, *Om Phantasiens Magt. Sex Forelæsninger*, Copenhagen: Gyldendal 1876.

696 Nielsen, Rasmus, *Evangelietroen og Theologien. Tolv Forelæsninger, holdte ved Universitetet i Kjøbenhavn i Vinteren 1849–50*, Copenhagen: C.A. Reitzel 1850.

697 Nielsen, Rasmus, *Pauli Brev til Romerne*, Copenhagen: Trykt paa Forfatterens Forlag i Bianco Lunos Bogtrykkeri 1841.

698 Nielsen, Rasmus, *Om "Den gode Villie" som Magt i Videnskaben*, Copenhagen: Gyldendalske Boghandel (F. Hegel) 1867.

699 Nielsen, Rasmus, *Paa Kierkegaardske "Stadier", et Livsbillede*, Copenhagen: Gyldendalske Boghandling (F. Hegel) 1860.

700 Nielsen, [Rasmus], 6 various books.

701 [Niemeyer, August Hermann], *D. August Hermann Niemeyers Haandbog for christelige Religions-Lærere*, vols. 1-2, translated from the German on the basis of the 3rd edition, Copenhagen: Gyldendal 1798. (Bound copy)

702 Nyblæus, Axel, *Är en practisk Philosophi möjlig efter Hegels Verldsåsigt? Critisk Betraktelse*, 2nd edition, Lund: Tryckt uti Berlingska Bogtrykkeriet 1856 [1855].

703 Nyblæus, Axel, *Om den religiösa Tron och Vetandet. Theodor Parker och den religiösa Frågan. Tvenne religionsfilosofiska Uppsatser*, Lund: Fr. Berling 1868.

704 [Öhmann, Adolph], *Om Religion och Religiositet uti deras Forhållande till Kyrkans Dogmer alla Samvetsfrihetens verklige vänner vördsamt tillegnad*, Stockholm: Tryckt hos N. Marcus 1862.

705 Orchard, George H., *A Concise History of Foreign Baptists*, London: George Wightman 1838. (Bound copy)

706 Orelli, Conrad von, *Spinoza's Leben und Lehre. Nebst einem Abrisse der Schelling'schen und Hegel'schen Philosophie*, Aarau: H.R. Sauerländer 1843.

707 Anonymous, *Papstthum und Hierarchie gegenüber der Religion des neuen Bundes*, trans. from English and ed. by W.A. Lampadius, Leipzig: Köhler 1843.

708 Paine, Thomas, *Förnuftets tidehvarf*, trans. by Olof Bergstedt, Gefle: A.P. Landin 1865.

709 Parker, Theodore, *Sermons of Theism, Atheism, and the Popular Theology*, 2nd edition, London: N. Trübner & Co. 1867 [1853] (*The Collected Works of Theodore Parker*, ed. by Frances Power Cobbe, vol. 11). (Bound copy)

710 Parker, Theodore, *En Afhandling om Religionen*, trans. by Albert Réville, Stockholm: Axel Hellsten 1862.

711 Parker, Theodore, *Tio Predikningar om Religiositeten*, anonymous translation, Stockholm: Axel Hellsten 1864.

712 Parker, Theodore, *Teism, Ateism och kyrklig Teologi afhandlade i Tio Predikningar*, anonymous translation, Stockholm: Axel Hellsten 1865.

713 Réville, Albert, *En amerikansk Reformators, Theodor Parkers Lære og Levnet*, Copenhagen: Chr. Steen og Søn 1868.

714 Paulli, Just Henrik Voltelen, *Prædikener om Kirken og Sacramenterne*, Copenhagen: C.A. Reitzel 1844.

715 Paying, Walther [i.e., Nielsen, Rasmus], *Et Levnetsløb i Underverdenen*, Copenhagen: Otto Schwartz 1853.

716 Pétur Pétursson, *Symbolæ ad fidem et studia tyrannii Rufini presbyteri aquileiensis illustranda, e scriptis ipsius petitæ, quas pro gradu licentiati Theologiæ rite impetrando, Respondente M. Eyriksen*, Copenhagen: Tengnagel 1840. (2 copies)

717 Pfaff, Emil Richard, *Om Drømmelivet og dets Udtydning*, Copenhagen: Chr. Steen og Søn 1868.

718 Philippson, Ludwig, *Die Entwickelung der religiösen Idee im Judenthume, Christenhume und Islam. In zwölf Vorlesungen über Geschichte und Inhalt des Judenthumes dargestellt*, Leipzig: Baumgärtners Buchhandlung 1847.

719 [Plato], *Platons Theaitetos*, trans. by Bendt Treschow Dahl and Frederik Clemens Bendtsen Dahl, Copenhagen: C.A. Reitzel 1869.

720 Pontopiddan, Erik, *Troens Speil, eller Guds Børns Kiendetegn*, trans. by Vesti Egeberg, Copenhagen: N.E. Ditlewsen 1834. (Bound copy)

721 [Nerses Snorhali, Monastero di San Lazzaro], *Preces Sancti Nersetis Clajensis Armeniorum Patriarchae, viginti quatuor* *linguis editae*, Venice: In Insula S. Lazari 1837. (Bound copy with gilt edges)

722 Priedemann, J., *Uranus. Die mythologischen Dichtungen der alten Griechen und Römer*, Berlin: Hugo Kastner & Co. 1862.

723 *Evangelisk-kristelig Psalmebog, til Brug ved Kirke- og Huus-Andagt*, Copenhagen: Trykt udi det Kongl. Vaisenhuses Bogtrykkerie og paa dets Forlag, af Carl Frid. Schubart 1823. (Bound copy with gilt edges).

724 Anonymous [G.V.E.], *Leben Des Weltberühmten Pater Quesnel, Nebst einer curieusen Historie des zwischen dem Pabst und Franckreich noch währenden Kirchen-Streits: Samt dessen aller-accuratesten Portrait*, Hamburg: Thomas von Wierings Erben 1718.

725 [Gerke, Friedrich], *Rabbi Jeschua ben Josef hanootzri, kaldet Jesus Kristus. En kritisk og historisk Skildring*, Copenhagen: S.J. Lorias Forlag 1863.

726 Ralston, Thomas N., *Grundrids til Theologien eller en Række af Forelæsninger, indeholdende en klar og concis Oversigt over Theologiens Hovedlærdomme, saaledes som de læres i den hellige Skrift, med passende Spørgsmaal knyttede til hver Forelæsning*, trans. by C. Willerup, Copenhagen: Paa Methodisternes Forlag 1858.

727 Ralston, Thomas N., *Grundrids til Theologien eller en Række af Forelæsninger, indeholdende en klar og concis Oversigt over Theologiens Hovedlærdomme, saaledes som de læres i den hellige Skrift, med passende Spørgsmaal knyttede til hver Forelæsning*, trans. by C. Willerup, Copenhagen: Paa Methodisternes Forlag 1858.

728 Rambach, August Jakob, *Entwürfe der über die evangelischen Texte gehaltenen Predigten*, Collections 20-23 and 25-26, Hamburg: Johann August Meissner 1858-1861 and 1865-1866.

729 Redslob, Gustav Moritz, *Das Mysterium oder der geheime Sinn der Stelle 2. Kor. 12, 1-10*, vols. 1-2, Hamburg: Wilhelm Jowien 1860-1864.

730 Reinbeck, Emil, *Tilværelsen efter Døden, Vidnesbyrd om Sjælens Udødelighed og et Gjensyn hinsides Graven*, trans. from the 3rd edition, Copenhagen: Emil Bergmann 1881.

731-734 Reinhard, Franz Volkmar, *System i den Kristelige Moral*, vols. 1-5, on the basis of the 4th revised and enlarged edition, trans. by Andreas Krag Holm, Copenhagen: Boghandler Hegelunds Forlag 1803-1821. (Bound copy)

735 Reinhold, Ernst, *Lehrbuch der Geschichte der Philosophie*, 2nd enlarged and revised edition, Jena: Friedrich Mauke 1839. (Bound copy)

736 Paludan-Müller, Charite, *Religiøse Studier. Uddrag af en Dagbog*, Copenhagen: Gyldendal 1863.

737 Paludan-Müller, Charite, *Religiøse Studier. Uddrag af en Dagbog*, Copenhagen: Gyldendal 1863. (Bound copy)

738 Schmid, Jacob, *La religion chrétienne. Précis d'instruction religieuse*, Genève: no publisher given 1872.

739 Renan, Joseph Ernest, *Jesu Levnet*, trans. from the 7th edition, Copenhagen: Fr. Wøldikes Forlagsboghandel 1864.

740 Renan, Joseph Ernest, *Rom och Kristendomen*, trans. by Axel Frithiof Åkerberg, Stockholm: Looström 1880.

741 Réville, Albert, *Dogmen om Kristi Guddom till sin historiska Utveckling*, trans. by O.W. Ålund, Stockholm: Albert Bonnier 1870.

742 Réville, [Albert], 3 works in Danish.

743 Rheinwald, Friedrich Heinrich, *Die kirchliche Archäologie*, Berlin: Theod. Chr. Friedr. Enslin 1830. (Bound copy)

744 Rosenmüller, Ernst Friedrich Karl, *Scholia in Pentateuchum in compendium redacta*, Leipzig: J.A. Barth 1828. (Bound copy)

745 Rosenmüller, Ernst Friedrich Karl, *Scholia in prophetas minores*, posthumously ed. by Johann Christoph Sigmund Lechner, Leipzig: J.A. Barth 1836. (Bound copy)

746-749 [Rosenmüller, Johann Georg], *Io. Georgii Rosenmülleri Scholia in Novum Testamentum*, vol. 1, *Continens Evangelia Matthaei et Marci*, 5th revised and enlarged edition, Nuremberg: Felsecker 1801; vol. 2, *Evangelia Lucae et Joannis*, 5th revised and enlarged edition, Nuremberg:

Felsecker 1803; vol. 3, *Acta Apostolorum et epistola Pauli ad Romanos*, 5th revised and enlarged edition, Nuremberg: Felsecker 1804; vol. 5, *Continens Pavli Epistolas Ad Timotheum, Titum, Philemonem, Et Hebraeos; Epistolam Iacobi, Utramque Petri, Epistolas Ioannis, Epistolam Iudae Et Apocalypsin Ioannis*, 4th enlarged and revised edition, Nuremberg: Felsecker 1794. (Bound copy)

750 Rosenmüller, Johann Georg, *Abhandlung über die Stufenfolgen der göttlichen Offenbarungen. Nebst einem Anhang über einige Gedanken in Leßings Erziehung des Menschengeschlechts*, Hildburghausen: Johann Gottfried Hanisch 1784. (Bound copy)

751 Rudelbach, Andreas Gottlob, *Den evangeliske Kirkeforfatnings Oprindelse og Princip, dens Udartning og dens mulige Gjenreisning fornemmelig i Danmark. Et udførligt kirkeretligt og kirkehistorisk Votum for virkelig Religionsfrihed*, Copenhagen: P.G. Philipsen 1849.

752 [Melanchthon, Philipp], *Den rette uforandrede Augsburgske Troesbekjendelse med sammes, af Ph. Melanchthon forfattede, Apologie, med en historisk Indledning og oplysende Anmærkninger til de vanskeligste Steder*, trans. and ed. by Andreas Gottlob Rudelbach, Copenhagen: Trykt i C. Græbes Officin 1825. (Bound copy)

753 Rudelbach, [Andreas Gottlob], three different books.

754 Rydberg, Victor, *Bibelns Lära om Kristus. Samvetsgrann Undersökning*, Göteborg: Handelstidningens bolags tryckeri 1862 [2nd edition, 1862].

755 Rydberg, Victor, *Bibelns Lära om Kristus. Samvetsgrann Undersökning*, 3rd edition, Stockholm: Albert Bonnier 1868 [1862].

756 Rydberg, Victor, *Middelalderens Magi*, translated from Swedish, Copenhagen: Wilhelm Prior 1873.

757 Röben, Johann Hinrich, *Der souveraine christliche Staat, das Ende aller Zeitwirren*, Leipzig: F.A. Brockhaus 1846.

758 Rønne, Bone Falch, *Anden Aargang af Prædikener over de til Søndagene og Festerne anordnede Texter, holdne og udgivne til*

Brug ved Huus-Andagt, vols. 1-2, Copenhagen: Trykt hos Christopher Græbe 1824. (Bound copy)

759 Rørdam, Thomas Skat, *Historisk Oplysning om Den Hellige Skrift*, Copenhagen: G.E.C. Gad 1866.

760 *Salomons Denksprüche*, trans. from Danish and ed. by Johann Christian Schønheider, Flensburg and Leipzig: Rortensche Buchhandlung 1784.

761 Sandberg, P., *Haandbog ved den kateketiske og dialogiske Underviisningsmaade*, Ribe: Paa Forfatterens Bekostning. Trykt hos Niels Siersted Hyphoff 1812.

762-765 *Sanningsökaren. Nordisk månadskrift för förnuftstro och praktisk kristendom*, vols. 1-5 (no. 6), ed. by Axel Frithiof Åkerberg, Upsala and Stockholm: Esaias Edquist 1877-1881 (vol. 2, nos. 10-11 are missing).

766 Scharling, Carl Emil, *Paastanden om den christelige Kirkes Ebionitisme gjennem de tvende förste Aarhundreder, historisk og kritisk oplyst* [part of *Indbydelses-Skrift til Kjöbenhavns Universitets Fest i Anledning af Hans Majestæt Kongens Fødselsdag den 18de September 1843*], Copenhagen: Trykt hos Directeur Jens Hostrup Schultz 1843. (2 copies)

767 Scharling, Carl Emil, *Muratoris Kanon, den ældste Fortegnelse over den christelige Kirkes nytestamentlige Skrifter*, Copenhagen: Trykt i Bianco Lunos Bogtrykkeri ved F.S. Muhle 1865. [Offprint from *Oversigt over det Kgl. danske Videnskabernes Selskabs Forhandlinger og dets Medlemmers Arbeider i Aaret 1865*, ed. by G. Forchhammer, Copenhagen: Trykt i Bianco Lunos Bogtrykkeri ved F.S. Muhle]

768 Scharling, Carl Emil, *Hvad er Hensigten, Betydningen og Resultaterne af Theologernes videnskabelige Undersøgelser om det Nye Testamentes Skrifter? Tolv indledende Forelæsninger til det Nye Testamente for dannede Christne*, Copenhagen: C.A. Reitzel 1833.

769 Scharling, Carl Henrik, *Den nyere hollandske Theologi*, Copenhagen: C.A. Reitzel 1865.

770 Scharling, Carl Henrik, *Jakob Bøhmes Theosophi. En religionsphilosophisk og dogmatisk Undersøgelse*, Copenhagen: G.E.C. Gad 1879.

771 Schatter, Carl Gottfried, *Predigten für den christlichen Landmann auf alle zwei und funfzig Wochen des Jahres*, Neustadt an der Orla: Wagner 1834. (Bound copy)

772 Schleiermacher, Friedrich, *Dialektik. Aus Schleiermachers handschriftlichem Nachlasse*, ed. by Ludwig Jonas, Berlin: G. Reimer 1839. (Bound copy)

773 [Schleiermacher, Friedrich], *Dr. Friedrich Schleiermachers Prædikener om det christelige Huusliv*, trans. by Christian Winther, Copenhagen: P.G. Philipsen 1839.

774 Schmid, Gotthelf Johannes, *Hielpebog til rigtig at forstaae, og med Nytte at catechisere, over den nye Catechismus*, Schlesvig: Trykt hos Johann Wilhelm Serringhausen 1788. (Bound copy)

775 Schott, Heinrich August, *Isagoge historico-critica in libros Novi Foederis sacros*, Jena: C.H. Walz 1830. (Bound copy)

776 Schwarz, Carl, *Zur Geschichte der neuesten Theologie*, 3rd enlarged and revised edition, Leipzig: F.A. Brockhaus 1864.

777 Schweizer, Alexander, *Das Evangelium Johannes nach seinem innern Werthe und seiner Bedeutung für das Leben Jesu kritisch untersucht*, Leipzig: Weidmann'sche Buchhandlung 1841. (Bound copy)

778-779 Schwengler, Albert, *Das nachapostolische Zeitalter in den Hauptmomenten seiner Entwicklung*, vols. 1-2, Tübingen: Ludwig Friedrich Fues 1846. (Bound copy)

780 Seiler, Georg Friedrich, *Kurze Geschichte der geoffenbarten Religion. Vornehmlich zum gemeinen Gebrauche für solche Christen, die keine Theologen sind*, 5th edition, Erlangen: Wolfgang Walther 1777 [1772]. (Bound copy)

781 [Semler, Johann Salomo], *D. Joh. Salomo Semlers... umständliche Untersuchung der dämonischen Leute oder so genan[n]ten Besessenen, nebst Beantwortung einiger Angriffe*, Halle: Johann Immanuel Gebauer 1762.

782 Sibbern, Frederik Christian, *Psychologie, indledet ved almindelig Biologie, i sammentrængt Fremstilling*, new edition, Copenhagen: Paa eget Forlag trykt hos Directeur Jens Hostrup Schultz 1843. (Bound copy)

783 Sibbern, Frederik Christian, *Moralphilosophie som Retsindigheds- og Tilbørlighedslære. Et efterladt Skrift*, posthumously ed. by Gabriel Sibbern, Copenhagen: C.A. Reitzel 1878.

784 Sibbern, Frederik Christian, *Speculativ Kosmologie med Grundlag til en speculativ Theologie*, Copenhagen: Paa Forfatterens eget Forlag trykt hos Directeur Jens Hostrup Schultz 1846.

785 Sibbern, Gabriel, *Den stoiske og epikuræiske Moral. En philosophisk-historisk Sammenligning. Et akademisk Prøveskrift*, Copenhagen: P.G. Philipsen 1853.

786 *Skandinaviens Stjerne. Organ for de Sidste Dages Hellige*, vol. 1 and vol. 3, Copenhagen: F.E. Bording 1851 and 1854 (together with a damaged copy of vol. 2, 1852).

787 Sommer, Mogens Abraham, *Stadier paa Livets Vei. Et kortfattet Levnetsløb*, vol. 1, Aalborg: Trykt i det Bechske Bogtrykkeri ved Bech & Møller 1868 (vol. 2, 1891). (Bound copy)

788 Sommer, Mogens Abraham, *Hvem har Ret? Dr. Søren Kierkegaard eller Præsten. Samtaler i Præstens Huus over Dr. S. Kierkegaards "Øieblikke,"* Aalborg: Paa Udgiverens forlag 1869. (Bound copy)

789-790 Southey, Robert, *John Wesley's Leben, die Entstehung und Verbreitung des Methodismus*, ed. by Friedrich Adolph Krummacher, new inexpensive edition, vols. 1-2, Hamburg: Herold'sche Buchhandlung 1841 [1828].

791 Spencer, Herbert, *Om Opdragelse*, trans. by Harald Høffding, Copenhagen: A.F. Høst & Søn 1876.

792 Spurgeon, Charles Haddon, *Sex nye Prædikener*, Copenhagen: Boghandler B. Pio's Forlag 1868.

793 Statius, Martin, *Lutherus Redivivus, Det er: Lutheri Christendom hvorudi den sande levende Troe, dens Oprindelse og Natur, samt Kraft og Virkning; item, en sand Christens Majestæt, Herlighed, Hellighed og Foreening med Christo, samt og hans usminkede Kjerlighed og Christelige Levnet, Lutheri ganske Christelige og aanderige Ord stilles for Øjne. Sammendraget med stor Flid og Arbeide af alle Lutheri tydske* *til Wittenberg og Jena trykte Skrifter*, Copenhagen: N.C. Ditlewsen 1832.

794 Steele, Richard, *Beviis, at intet uden Religionen kan danne en stor Mand*, trans. by Paul Danchel Bast, Copenhagen: Trykt hos Nicolaus Møller 1782. (Bound copy)

795 Steenberg, Georg, *Om Synspunktet for Opfattelsen af Philos Gudserkjendelse. Et Bidrag til at oplyse den theosophiske Erkjendelses Natur, skrevet for den theologiske Licentiatgrad*, Copenhagen: Thiele 1849.

796 Stickel, Johann Gustav, *Das Buch Hiob, rhythmisch gegliedert und übersetzt, mit exegetischen und kritischen Bemerkungen*, Leipzig: Weidmann'sche Buchhandlung 1842. (Bound copy)

History, Literature etc.

797 4 books by [Peter Michael] Stilling.

798 Strauß, David Friedrich, *Das Leben Jesu für das deutsche Volk bearbeitet*, 2nd edition, Leipzig: F.A. Brockhaus 1864.

799-800 Strauß, David Friedrich, *Jesu Levnet, kritisk bearbejdet*, vols. 1-2, trans. from the 4th edition by Frederik Julius Schaldemose, Copenhagen: Steen 1842-1843. (Bound copy)

801 Strauß, David Friedrich, *Den gamle og den ny[e] Tro. En Bekjendelse*, Copenhagen: Erslev 1875.

802-803 Strauß, David Friedrich, *Fremstilling af den christelige Troeslære i dens historiske Udvikling og i dens Kamp med den moderne Videnskab*, vols. 1-2, trans. by Hans Brøchner, Copenhagen: H.C. Klein 1842-1843. (Bound copy)

804 Swedenborg, Emanuel, *True Christian Religion; Containing the Universal Theology of the New Church, which was Foretold by the Lord, in Daniel, Chap. vii. 13, 14; and in the Apocalypse, Chap. xxi. 1, 2.*, trans. from the original Latin, 2nd edition, London: R. Hindmarsh 1786. (Bound copy)

805 Swedenborg, Emanuel, *The Apocalypse revealed, wherein are disclosed the Arcana there foretold, which have hitherto* *remained concealed*, St. Clairsville, Ohio: J.H. Williams 1848. (Bound copy)

806 Swedenborg, Emanuel, *Den sanna Christna Religion innehållande den nya Församlingens hela Gudalära som af Herren for Daniel Cap. 7, 13.14, samt uti Uppanbarelse-boken Cap. 21, 1.2 blifvit företsagt*, vol. 1, Copenhagen: Johan Rudolph Thiele 1795.

807 Swedenborg, Emanuel, *Ängla-visheten om den gudomliga Kärleken*, vol. 1, trans. by Pehr Falck, Copenhagen: Johan Rudolph Thiele 1795.

808 Swedenborg, Emanuel, *Angelic Wisdom Concerning the Divine Love and the Divine Wisdom*, Boston: Otis Clapp 1852.

809 Swedenborg, Emanuel, *Aandelige Værker*, vols. 1-5, trans. by Constant Dirckinck-Holmfeld, Copenhagen: F. Thaarup 1856.

810 Swedenborg, Emanuel, *The Doctrine of Life for the New Jerusalem. From the Commandments of the Decalogue*, Boston: Otis Clapp 1838.

811 Swedenborg, Emanuel, *Om Himlen og dens Undere og om Helvede, overensstemmende med hørt og seet*, trans. by Adolph Theodor Boyesen, Christiania: J. Dybwad 1868. (Bound copy)

812-813 Atterbom, Per Daniel Amadeus, *Emanuel Swedenborgs Lære om Liv, Kjærlighed og Skjønhed, efter P. D. A. Atterboms: "Svenska siare och skaldere,"* anonymous translation, Copenhagen: G.E.C. Gad 1863. (2 copies)

814 Spear, William, *Emanuel Swedenborg, den aandelige Columbus. En Skitse af U.S.E.*, trans. by Marie Brynjulfson and Wilhelm Winsløw, Copenhagen: C. G. Iversen 1879.

815-817 Süßmilch, Johann Peter, *Die göttliche Ordnung in den Veränderungen des menschlichen Geschlechts, aus der Geburt, dem Tode und der Fortpflanzung desselben erwiesen*, vols. 1-3, 3rd edition, Berlin: Im Verlag des Buchladens der Realschule 1765-1776. (Bound copy)

818 Tauler, Johann, *Betragtninger over vor Frelsers Jesu Christi Liv og Lidelse, udgivne paa Dansk med*

Forord og Anmærkninger, trans. by Christian Malta Kragballe, Copenhagen: Wilhelm Prior 1860.

819-820 Teller, Wilhelm Abraham, *Predigten an den Sonn- und Festtagen des ganzen Jahrs. Ueber die gewöhnlichen Abschnitte aus den Lebensgeschichten Jesu Christi*, vols. 1-2, Berlin: Siegismund Friedrich Hesse 1785. (Paperback)

821 Terson, Jean, *Das Ende der alten und das Aufleben einer neuen Welt. Streifzüge durch rationalistische Gebiete*, anonymous translation, Weimar: Bernhard Friedrich Voigt 1838.

822-823 *Η ΠΑΛΑΙΑ ΔΙΑΘΗΚΗ ΚΑΤΑ ΤΟΥΣ ΕΒΔΟΜΗΚΟΝΤΑ. I.E. Vetus Testamentum Graecum ex versione Septuaginta interpretum una cum Libris Apocryphis[.] Secundum exemplar Vaticanum Romæ editum et aliquoties recognitum*, vols. 1-2, 2nd edition, ed. by Christian Reneccius, Leipzig: Breitkopf 1757. (Bound copy)

824 *Jesu Christi D.N. Novum testamentum, sive Novum fœdus. Cuis Græco contextui respondent interpretationes duæ: una, vetus: altera, nova, Theodori Bezę [Théodore de Bèza], diligenter ab eo recognita. Eiusdem Th. Bezae Annotationes, quas itidem hac tertia editione recognovit, & acceßione non parva*, vols. 1-2, Geneva: Stephanus 1582. (Old wooden boards)

825 *Novum Testamentum Graece secundum editiones probatissimas expressum; nova versione Latina illustratum, praecipuae lectionum et interpretationum diversitatis indice instructum*, ed. by Heinrich August Schott, 4th edition, Leipzig: Barth 1839. (Bound copy)

826 *Novum Testamentum Graece. Textum ad fidem antiquorum testium recensuit brevem apparatum criticum una cum variis lectionibus Elzeviriorum, Knappii, Scholzii, Lachmanni subiunxit argumenta et locos parallelos indicavit commentationem isagogicam notatis propriis lectionibus edd. Stephanicae tertiae atque Millianae, Matthaeianae, Griesbachianae praemisit A. Frid. Constantin Tischendorf [Konstantin von Tischendorf]*, Leipzig: C.F. Köhler 1841. (Bound copy)

827-828 *Domini nostri Jesu Christi Novum Testamentum, duce et autore Sebastiano Castellione dilucidata interpretatione Latine* *reddidit, suis pariter ac recentioribus variorum exegeticis et philologicis notis illustravit, in usum studiosæ juventutis hunc laborum suorum academicorum fructum*, vols. 1-2, ed. by Laurits Sahl, Copenhagen: P. Horrebowius 1780. (Bound copy)

829 *Le Nouveau Testament De Notre Seigneur Jésus-Christ*, ed. by Jean Frédéric Ostervald, London: Société pour l'Impression de la Bible en Langue Anglaise et en Langues Etrangères 1855. (Bound copy)

830 *The New Testament of Our Lord and Saviour Jesus Christ. Newly Translated Out of the Original Greek and with the Former Translations Diligently Compared and Revised by His Majesties Special Command; Appointed to be Read in Churches*, Oxford: Printed at the Theater 1675. (Bound copy)

831 *Vor HErres og Frelsers JEsu Christi Nye Testamente / The new Testament of our Lord and Saviour Jesus Christ*, New York: Amerikanske Bibel Selskab / American Bible Society 1856. (Bound copy)

832 *Vor Herres og Frelsers Jesu Christi Nye Testament, ved Kong Frederik den Siettes christelige Omsorg med Fliid efterseet, og rettet efter Grundtexten, saa og med mange Parallelsteder og udførlige Indholdsfortegnelser forsynet*, Copenhagen: Kongelige Vaisenhuses Forlag 1825. (Bound copy)

833 *Vor Herres og Frelsers Jesu Christi Nye Testament, ved Kong Frederik den Siettes christelige Omsorg med Fliid efterseet, og rettet efter Grundtexten, saa og med mange Parallelsteder og udførlige Indholdsfortegnelser forsynet*, Copenhagen: Kongelige Vaisenhuses Forlag 1864. (Bound copy)

834 Theile, Karl Gottfried Wilhelm, *Zur Biographie Jesu*, Leipzig: Eisenach 1837.

835 Theodorus [i.e., Alfred Christian Larsen], *Breve til en Landsbypræst fra hans Ven Theodorus*, Copenhagen: Hoffensberg Jespersen & Fr. Traps Etabl. 1876; Møller, Christian Vilhelm Victor, *Breve til den religiøse Fritænker Theodorus fra hans Ven, Landsbypræsten*, Copenhagen: Hoffensberg Jespersen 1877; *Død og Udødelighed. Tre Foredrag*, ed. by Theodorus [i.e., Alfred Christian Larsen],

Copenhagen: no publisher given 1878; Simonsen, Carl Cederfeld de, *Nogle Bemærkninger til Theodorus's Brevvexling i Anledning af den kirkelige Vielse*, Copenhagen: no publisher given 1878; Theodorus [i.e., Alfred Christian Larsen], *Religionen og Børnene*, Copenhagen: no publisher given 1880.

836-872 *Theologisk Bibliothek*, vols. 1-20, ed. by Jens Møller, Copenhagen: Andreas Seidelin 1811-1821; *Nyt theologisk Bibliothek*, vols. 1-20, ed. by Jens Møller, Copenhagen: Andreas Seidelin 1821-1832. (Bound in 37 volumes)

873-878 Eckermann, Jacob Christoph Rudolph, *Theologische Beyträge*, vols. 1-6, Altona: Johann Friederich Hammerich 1791-1799. (Bound copy)

879-888 *Theologische Jahrbücher*, vols. 1-10, ed. by Eduard Zeller, Tübingen: Ludwig Friedrich Fues 1842-1851. (Bound copy)

889-900 *Theologisk Tidsskrift*, vols. 1-12, ed. by Carl Emil Scharling and Christian Thorning Engelstoft, Copenhagen: C.A. Reitzel 1837-1849 [*Nyt Theologisk Tidsskrift*, vols. 1-3, ed. by Carl Emil Scharling and Christian Thorning Engelstoft, Copenhagen: C.A. Reitzel 1850-1852].

901-904 *Nordisk Tidskrift for christelig Theologi*, vols. 1-4, ed. by Theodor Vilhelm Oldenburg and Peter Christian Kierkegaard, Copenhagen: P. Chr. Kierkegaard/C.A. Reitzel 1840-1842.

905-927 *Tidsskrift for udenlandsk theologisk Litteratur*, vols. 1-20, ed. by Henrik Nicolai Clausen and Martin Hagen Hohlenberg, Copenhagen: C.A. Reitzel 1833-1852; *Nyt Tidsskrift for udenlandsk theologisk Litteratur*, vols. 1-13, ed. by Henrik Nicolai Clausen, Copenhagen: C.A. Reitzels Bo og Arvinger / Gyldendal 1853-1865.

928 Thiersch, Heinrich Wilhelm Josias, *Die Geschichte der christlichen Kirche im Alterthum*, vol. 1, *Die Kirche im apostolischen Zeitalter und die Entstehung der neutestamentlichen Schriften*, Frankfurt am Main and Erlangen: Heyder und Zimmer 1852. (Bound copy)

929 Treschow, Niels, *Indledning til den hele Philosophie og de vigtigste Lærebygninger af samme*, Copenhagen: Fr. Brummer 1805.

930 Treschow, Niels, *Om den menneskelige Natur i Almindelighed, især dens aandelige Side*, Copenhagen: Fr. Brummer 1812. (Bound copy)

931 Treschow, Niels, *Elementer til Historiens Philosophie i Forelæsninger holdne Vinteren 1806-1807*, vols. 1-2 [in one volume], Copenhagen: Fr. Brummer 1811. (Bound copy)

932 Treschow, Niels, *Om Philosophiens Natur og Dele. [E]n dogmatisk og historisk Indledning til denne Videnskab*, Copenhagen: Fr. Brummer 1811. (Bound copy)

933 Treschow, Niels, *Moral for Folk og Stat*, vols. 1-2 [in one volume], Copenhagen: Fr. Brummer 1810-1811.

934 Treschow, Niels, *Oratio habita in Universitate Hauniensi d. 16to Junii 1808, cum rectoratum deponeret Nicolaus Treschow, de quibusdam ex ingenio nostrorum temporum repetitis rationibus metuendi, ne nova barbaries iterum ingruat, Tale holden ved Kiøbenhavns Universitet den 16de Juni 1808 i Anledning af Rectoratets Nedlæggelse...om nogle Grunde, tagne af vor Tids Aand, til at frygte for et nyt Barbarie*, Copenhagen: Andreas Seidelin 1808.

935-936 Ullman, Carl, *Reformatoren vor der Reformation, vornehmlich in Deutschland und den Niederlanden*, vols. 1-2, Hamburg: Friedrich Perthes 1841-1842. (Bound copy)

937 *Ungdommens Veiledning til sand Gudsfrygt*, ed. by Johan Frederik Felberg, Copenhagen: no publisher given 1850. (Bound copy)

938 Usteri, Leonhard, *Commentar über den Brief Pauli an die Galater*, Zurich: Orell, Füßlin und Compagne 1833. (Bound copy)

939 Vatke, Wilhelm, *Die menschliche Freiheit in ihrem Verhältniß zur Sünde und zur göttlichen Gnade*, Berlin: Bethge 1841. (Bound copy)

940 Vierthaler, Franz Michael, *Geist der Sokratik. Ein Versuch, den Freunden des Sokrates und der Sokratik geweiht*, 2nd edition, Salzburg: Mayr'sche Buchhandlung 1798.

941 Voltaire [i.e., François-Marie Arouet], *Voltaires Domme om Religion og Bibel, tilligemed hans Levnet ved Condorcet*, Part 1, trans. by Otto Horrebow, Copenhagen: A. Soldin 1798.

942 Wahl, Christian Abraham, *Clavis Novi Testamenti philologica. Usibus scholarum et juvenum theologiae studiosorum accommodata*, 2nd revised and enlarged edition, Leipzig: Barth 1829. (Bound copy)

943 Walden, Frederik, *Blandede Tanker i Breve til en Ven over Religionen, Ordet og Jesus Christus*, vols. 1-5 (vol. 6 with the title *Asessor Swedenborgs Levnet, adskillige Udtog af hans Skrifter, nogle blandede Tanker, tilligemed Swedenborgs System i Kort Udtog*) Copenhagen: Thiele 1804-1806.

944-946 Wette, Wilhelm Martin Leberecht de (trans.), *Die Heilige Schrift des Alten und Neuen Testaments*, vols. 1-3, 3rd edition, Heidelberg: J.C.B. Mohr 1839. (Bound copy)

947 Wette, Wilhelm Martin Leberecht de, *Lehrbuch der hebräisch-jüdischen Archäologie. Nebst einem Grundrisse der hebräisch-jüdischen Geschichte*, 2nd revised edition, Leipzig: Vogel 1830. (Bound copy)

948-949 Wette, Wilhelm Martin Leberecht de, *Lehrbuch der historisch-kritischen Einleitung in die kanonischen und apokryphischen Bücher des Alten Testamentes*, vols. 1-2, 4th revised and enlarged edition, Berlin: G. Reimer 1833-1834. (Bound copy)

950 Wette, Wilhelm Martin Leberecht de, *Über die Religion, ihr Wesen, ihre Erscheinungsformen und ihren Einfluss auf das Leben. Vorlesungen*, Berlin: G. Reimer 1827.

951 Wette, Wilhelm Martin Leberecht de, *Lehrbuch der christlichen Dogmatik, in ihrer historischen Entwickelung dargestellt*, vol. 1, 3rd revised edition, Berlin: G. Reimer [1831]; vol. 2, [1st edition], Berlin: In der Realschulbuchhandlung 1816. (Bound copy)

952 Wette, Wilhelm Martin Leberecht de, *Kurzgefasstes exegetisches Handbuch zum Neuen Testament*, vol. 1.1-4, 2nd revised and enlarged edition, vol. 2.1-5, 2nd revised and enlarged edition, Leipzig: Weidmann 1838-1854.

953 Whately, Richard, *The Kingdom of Christ delineated, in Two Essays on Our Lord's own Account of His person and of the Nature of His Kingdom, and on the Constitution, Powers, and Ministry of a Christian Church, as Appointed by Himself*, 2nd edition, London: B. Fellowes 1842. (Bound copy)

954 Wikner, Pontus, *Tankar och Frågor inför Menniskones Son*, Stockholm: Hæggström 1872.

955-956 Winer, Georg Benedikt, *Biblisches Realwörterbuch zum Handgebrauch für Studirende, Kandidaten, Gymnasiallehrer und Prediger*, vols. 1-2, Leipzig: Reclam 1820. (Bound copy)

957 Wieland, Christoph Martin, *Empfindungen eines Christen. Lobe den Herrn du meine Seele*, Zurich: Orell 1757. (Bound copy)

958 Holm, Andreas Krag, *Jesuiternes Historie efter Peter Philip Wolf*, Copenhagen: Gyldendal 1815.

959 Zahle, Peter Christian, *Aposteltiden og det nye Testamentes Historie. En almeenfattelig Fremstilling tildeels med de historiske Kilders egne Ord, med en Indledning om det gamle Testamente samt et autograferet Kort*, Copenhagen: Th. Lind 1858.

960 Zeller, Eduard, *Urchristendommen. En Afhandling*, anonymous translation, Copenhagen: C. Steen 1868.

961 Zeuthen, Frederik Ludvig Bang, *Humanitet betragtet fra et christeligt Standpunkt, med stadigt Hensyn til den nærværende Tid*, Copenhagen: Gyldendal 1846; *Philosophiske Afhandlinger til Orientering i den schellingske Verdensbetragtning*, Copenhagen: Fr. Wøldikes Forlagsboghandel 1860.

962 Zerrenner, Heinrich Gottlieb, *Predigten, ganz und stückweise, für die lieben Landleute*, Magdeburg and Leipzig: Scheidhauer 1785. (Bound copy)

963 Zimmermann, Ernst, *Om det protestantiske Princip i den christelige Kirke*, trans. and with an introduction by Henrik Nicolai Clausen, Copenhagen: C.A. Reitzel 1830.

964 Zollikofer, Georg Joachim, *Predigten*, [vol. 1], Leipzig: Weidmanns Erben und Reich 1769. (Bound copy)

965 1 bundle of Danish and German theological treatises.
966 1 bundle of theological treatises (31 works).
967 1 bundle of philosophical treatises (18 works).
968-969 2 bundles of sermons (21 works).
970-971 2 bundles of bibles and explanations on the bible (36 works).
972-980 9 bundles of theological books and short works (ca. 550 works).

History, Literature etc.

981 Allen, Carl Ferdinand, *De rebus Christiani Secundi Daniæ, Norvegiæ, Sueciæ regis exsulis commentatio*, Part 1, Copenhagen: L. Klein 1844.
982 *Allgemeine homöopathische Zeitung*, ed. by Veit Meyer, vol. 56, Leipzig: Baumgärtners Buchhandlung 1858. (Bound copy)
983 *Allgemeine musikalische Zeitung*, vol. 42, Leipzig: Breitkopf & Härtel 1840.
984 *Annaler for nordisk Oldkyndighed og Historie*, [vol. 17], published by Det Kongelige Nordiske Oldskrift-Selskab, Copenhagen: Trykt i L. Levins Bogtrykkeri 1857.
985 *Antiquarisk Tidsskrift*, published by Det Kongelige Nordiske Oldskrift-Selskab, [vol. 2], *1846-1848*, Copenhagen: J.D. Quist 1847; [vol. 3], *1849-1851*, Copenhagen: Berling 1852.
986 Arnesen, Paul, *Græsk-Dansk Ordbog til Brug for den studerende Ungdom, under de fortrinligste Hielpemidlers stadige Sammenligning med de vigtigste græske Forfattere*, Copenhagen: Gyldendal 1830. (Bound copy)
987 *Ars memoriæ latino danico germanica comprehendens usitatissima primitiva et derivativa una cum appendice grammaticæ germanicæ et danicæ. Eller kort Anviisning til det latine, danske og tydske Sprog...afdeelt ordentlig i 42 Capitler tillige med et curieus Tilleg og Begrif paa en Dansk og Tydsk*

Grammatica, som tilforn aldrig er seet, for Lærde og U-Lærde, [Copenhagen:] Johann Melchior Lieben [1700].

988 Autenrieth, Albert, *The English Reader. A Selection of Prose and Poetry from the Best British Authors*, 3rd edition, Christiania: Peter Tidemand Malling 1859. (Bound copy)

989 Plato, *Axiochus graece recensuit notis illustravit indicemq[ue] verborum locupletis[simum] cum Hier. Volfii [Hieronimus Wolf] versione latina notisq[ue]*, ed. by Johann Friedrich Fischer, Leipzig: Langenheim 1758. (Bound copy)

990-992 Baden, Jacob, *Fuldstændig tydsk og dansk Ordbog*, vols. 1-3, Copenhagen: Gyldendal 1787-1880. (Bound copy)

993-994 Baden, Jacob, *Latinsk-dansk Lexicon eller Ordbog*, vols. 1-2, 2nd revised and enlarged edition by Torkel Baden, Copenhagen: Gyldendal 1815. (Bound copy); Baden, Jacob, *Dansk-Latinsk Ordbog, som indeholder de brugeligste danske Ord og Talemaader, med deres latinske Navne og Oversættelser*, 3rd revised and enlarged edition, Copenhagen: Gyldendal 1831. (Bound copy)

995 Bailey, Nathan, *Mr. Nathan Bailey's English dictionary. Shewing both the orthography and the orthoepia of that tongue, by I. Accents placed on each word, directing to their true pronunciation. II. Distinguishing those words of approved authority from those that are not. III. Their various senses and significations, in English, and also French, Latin and German. IV. The idiom, phrases and proverbial sentences belonging to it. V. A short pointing at the French and Latin etymology. A work useful for such as would speak what they mean in a proper and pure diction; and write true English*, trans. by Theodore Arnold, Leipzig: Groß 1736; *Neues deutsch-englisches Wörter-Buch, worinnen nicht nur die Wörter, und dererselben verschiedene Bedeutung; sondern auch die nöthigsten Redens-Arten nach der reinsten deutschen und englischen Mund- und Schreib-Art*, collected by Theodor Arnold, Leipzig: Groß 1739. (Bound copy)

996 Bajer, Fredrik, *Frøken Rudenschöld. Tidsbillede fra Gustav III.s og Hertug Karls Hof*, Copenhagen: O. Prieme 1873.

997 A bunch of older and newer Danish ballets.

998 Pio, Jean and Brøchner-Larsen, Christian, *Beretning om Forhandlingerne paa det 3die nordiske Skolemøde i Kjøbenhavn, den 9de, 10de og 11te Avgust 1877*, Copenhagen: C.A. Reitzel 1877.

999 Le Lorrain de Vallemont, Pierre, *Der Heimliche und unerforschliche Natur-Kündiger, Oder: Accurate Beschreibung Von der Wünschel-Ruthe, Darinnen enthalten Der besondere Nutz bey Entdeckung der Wasser-Quellen, Metallen, vergrabenen Schätze, flüchtiger Diebe und Mörder. Dabey Solche Lehrsätze mit eingebracht, welche die allerdunckelsten Phaenomena der Natur erklären, und die abgehandelte Materi mit unhintertreiblichen Beweiß-Gründen bewähren*, trans. and ed. by Matthes Wille, Nuremberg: Andreas Otto 1694. (Bound copy)

1000 Blicher, P. B., *Biographisk Galerie*, nos. 1-5, Copenhagen: no publisher given 1843.

1001-1004 Birckner, Michael Gottlieb, *M. G. Birckners Samlede Skrifter*, vols. 1-4 [vol. 4 ed. by Anders Sandøe Ørsted], Copenhagen: Soldin and Schubothe 1798-1800. (Bound copy)

1005 Borring, Lauritz Stephan, *Dictionnaire danois-français et français-danois*, Copenhagen: F.V. Soldenfeldt 1856. (Bound copy)

1006 Gregersen, E., and Borring, Lauritz Stephan, *Fransk-dansk og dansk-fransk Haandordbog til brug for begge nationer*, Copenhagen: Steen 1861. (Bound copy)

1007-1018 *Allgemeine deutsche Real-Encyklopädie für die gebildeten Stände (Conversations-Lexikon)*, vols. 1-12, 8th original edition, Leipzig: F.A. Brockhaus 1833-1837. (Bound copy)

1019-1034 *Allgemeine deutsche Real-Encyklopädie für die gebildeten Stände. Conversations-Lexikon*, vols. 1-15, 10th revised and enlarged edition, Leipzig: F.A. Brockhaus 1851-1855. (Bound copy)

1035 Bruzelius, Nils Gustaf, *Svenska fornlemningar, aftecknade och beskrifna*, vol. 1, Lund: Berlingska Boktryckeriet 1853.

1036 Buhl, Frants, *Sproglige og historiske Bidrag til den arabiske Grammatik med udvalgte tekststykker af Ibn-Al-Hâgibs As-Sâfya*, Leipzig: G. Kreysing 1878.

1037 Bulwer, Edward Lytton, *Athens. Its Rise and Fall*, [vols. 1-2] Paris: Baudry 1837.

1038 Bulwer, Edward Lytton, *Athen, seine Erhebung und sein Fall*, vols. 1-4, trans. by Gustav Pfizer, Stuttgart: Metzler 1837-1838.

1039 Bøgh, Erik, *Dit og Dat fra 1871*, Copenhagen: Gandrup 1872.

1040 Christensen, Christen, *Hørsholms Historie fra 1305 til 1875*, new edition, Copenhagen: R. Levin 1879.

1041 [Cicero, Marcus Tullius], *M.T. Ciceronis Opera rhetorica et orationes quae supersunt omnes*, ed. by Johann Peter Miller, Berlin: Haude 1748. (Bound copy)

1042-1043 Claëson, Kristian Theodor, *Skrifter. Samlade och utgifna efter författarens död*, vols. 1-2, Stockholm: Z. Hæggström 1860.

1044 Schmidt, Valdemar, *Congres international d'anthropologie et d'archéologie préhistoriques. Compte-rendu de la 4e session*, Copenhagen: Thiele 1875.

1045 Crowe, Catherine, *The Night Side of Nature: Or, Ghosts & Ghost Seers*, vols. 1-2, 3rd edition, London: Routledge 1852-1853.

1046 Crowe, Catherine, *Die Nachtseite der Natur, oder Geister und Geisterseher*, trans. by Carl Kolb, vols. 1-2, Stuttgart: Scheible 1849. (Bound copy)

1047 *Deutsche Jugendzeitung*, vol. 4, Hamburg: J.G.H. Hüter 1856. (Bound copy)

1048 *Diplomatarium Norvegicum*, vols. 1.1, ed. by Christian Lange and Carl Richard Unger, Christiania: P.T. Mallings Forlagshandel 1847.

1049 Dunker, Bernhard, *Om Revision af Foreningsakten mellem Sverige og Norge*, Copenhagen: Gyldendal 1866.

1050 Eibe, Niels Julius, *Cursus paa 100 Timer i Fransk*, 4th edition, Copenhagen: Chr. Steen & Søn 1875. (Bound copy)

1051 Ferrall, James Stephen and Repp, Þorleifur Guðmundsson, *Dansk-Engelsk Ordbog*, revised by W. Mariboe, Copenhagen: Gyldendal 1861. (Bound copy)

1052 *Populær homøopatisk tidende*, vol. 1, ed. by Den Homøopatiske Forening, Rendsborg: no publisher given 1861.

1053 Fistaine, Gustav, *Saggi di prose e di poesie italiane per uso degli studiosi della toscana favella*, Copenhagen: no publisher given 1861. (Bound copy)

1054 Fistaine, Gustav, *Dansk-Italiensk Tolk, en Veiledning for Enhver, der i kort Tid ved Selvstudium ønsker at tilegne sig den fornødne Sprogfærdighed for at kunne gjøre sig forstaaelig i Italiensk*, Copenhagen: no publisher given 1863.

1055 Flamand, Ludvig Joseph, *Christian den Syvendes Hof, eller Struensee og Caroline Mathilde. En sand Fremstilling af de vigtigste Begivenheder under Christian den Syvende, efter de nyeste Kilder og mundtlige Beretninger af Samtidige*, Copenhagen: J. G. Salomon 1854.

1056 Stokfleth, Thomas Rosing de, *Forsøg til originale danske Fortællinger, efter Hr. Fontaines Maade*, Copenhagen: N. Møller 1772.

1057 *Fortegnelsen over de ved det Kongelige Akademie for de skjönne Kunster offentligt udstillede Kunstværker*, Copenhagen: Thiele 1832-1834, 1836-1838, 1840-1846, 1849, 1851, 1852, 1854-1855, 1857, 1861, 1863, 1869, 1880.

1058 [Gellert, Christian Fürchtegott], *Christian Fürchtegott Gellerts Briefe*, ed. by Johann Adolph Schlegel and Gottlieb Leberecht Heyer, Leipzig: Weidmanns Erben und Reich 1774; Cramer, Johann Andreas, *Christian Fürchtegott Gellerts Leben*, Leipzig: Weidmanns Erben und Reich 1774. (Bound copy)

1059-1063 [Goethe, Johann Wolfgang von], *Johann Wolfgang v. Göthe's Udvalgte Skrifter*, vols. 1-4, trans. by S. Meisling (vols. 1-2) and Frederik Schaldemose (vols. 3-4), Copenhagen: Martin 1832-1834 (vols. 5-6, 1834-1835). (Beautiful binding)

1064-1065 Grönberg [Grønberg], Bendt Christian, *Tydsk-Dansk og Dansk-Tydsk Haand-Ordbog*, vols. 1-2, 2nd enlarged and revised edition, Copenhagen: Gyldendal 1836-1839. (Bound copy)

1066 3 books by A.[rtur] Hazilius, Stockholm 1869-1871.

1067 Holm Hansen, Johan, *Vikingeblod. En Nutidssaga*, Copenhagen: C.A. Reitzel 1879.

1068 Hederich, Benjamin, *Graecum lexicon manuale, tribus partibus constans tribus partibus constans hermeneutica, analytica synthetica*, 3rd enlarged and revised edition, ed. by Johann August Ernesti, Leipzig: Gleditsch 1788. (Bound copy)

1069 Homer, *Homeri Ilias*, vols. 1-2, ed. by Friedrich August Wolf, Leipzig: Göschen 1817. (Bound copy)

1070-1072 Montesquieu, Charles de Sécondat, *Om Lovenes Natur og Aarsag, eller om det Forhold, som Lovene bør have til hver Regierings Forfatning, til dens Sæder, Clima, Religion Handel o.s.v., hvortil Forfatteren har lagt ny Undersøgninger over de Romerske Love angaaende Arvefølgen, over de Franske Love og Lehnslovene*, vols. 1-3, trans. by Jens Madsen Hvas, Copenhagen: no publisher given 1770-1771. (Bound copy)

1073 Høst, Jens Kragh, *Lommebog for Fruentimmer. En Nytaarsgave*, Copenhagen: P. Liunge 1796.

1074 *Illustreret Folkeven. Bibliothek til Underholdning og Belæring for Alle*, vol. 1, Copenhagen 1863 (vol. 2, 1866).

1075 Ingemann, Bernhard Severin, *Blanca. Trauerspiel*, trans. by Dieterich Wilhelm von Levetzow, Copenhagen: Bonnier 1815.

1076 Palm, Georg Friedrich, *Interessante Scenen aus der Geschichte der Menschheit*, vols. 1-3, Hannover: Ritscher 1798. (Bound copy)

1077 Jenisch, Daniel, *Philosophisch-kritische Vergleichung und Würdigung von vierzehn ältern und neuern Sprachen Europens, namentlich: Der griechischen, lateinischen, italienischen, spanischen, portugiesischen, französischen, englischen, deutschen, holländischen, dänischen, schwedischen, polnischen, russischen, litthauischen Preisschrift*, Berlin: Maurer 1796.

1078 [Juvenal, i.e., Decimus Junius Juvenalis], *D. J. Juvenal's Ottende, trettende og fjortende Satire, Fordanskede og med en*

Commentar oplyst, trans. by Oluf Worm, Copenhagen: F. Brummer 1801.

1079 Kaltschmidt, Jacob Heinrich, *Vollständiges Taschen-Wörterbuch der französischen und deutschen Sprache / Petit dictionnaire complet français-allemand et allemand-français*, vols. 1-2, Leipzig: F.A. Brockhaus 1844.

1080 Kønigsfeldt, Johannes Peter Frederik, *De catholske erkebiskopper og biskopper i Danmark / De evangeliske biskopper i kongeriget Danmark, og paa Island*, Copenhagen: J.H. Schultz 1851 [Offprint from Molbech, Christian (ed.), *Historiske aarbøger, Til Oplysning og Veiledning i Nordens, særdeles Danmarks Historie*, vol. 3, Copenhagen: Schultz 1851, pp. 1-72 and pp. 73-272]. (Bound copy)

1081 [Johannes Peter Frederik] Kønigsfeldt, 3 books from 1857-1865.

1082 [Lactantius, Lucius Caecilius Firmianus], *Lactantii Firmiani opera, quae extant omnia*, ed. by Christoph Cellarius, Leipzig: Fritsch 1698.

1083 Lassen, Axel Frederik, *Lægen Axel Frederik Lassen's Anke over tre Fyenske Embedsmænd*, Copenhagen: Axel Frederick Lassen 1827. (Bound copy)

1084 Anonymous, *Ledetraad til Nordisk Oldkyndighed*, ed. by Det kongelige Nordiske Oldskrift-Selskab, Copenhagen: S.L. Møller 1836. (2 copies)

1085 Lindfors, Anders Otto, *Handbok i de Romerska Antiqviteterna*, Lund: Lindfors 1814. (Bound copy)

1086 *Literært Maanedsskrift*, [vol. 2], ed. by Kristian Arentzen and G. Fistaine, Copenhagen: Chr. Steen & Søn 1851.

1087 Lund, Laurentius, *Compendium bibliothecæ Græcæ ex prælectionibus Vindingianis compositum*, Copenhagen: Bockenhoffer 1704.

1088 Adlersparre, G., *Läsning i blandade Ämnen*, vols. 1-4, Stockholm: Hendrick A. Nordström 1797-1800 (vol. 5, 1801).

1089 [Johan Nikolai] Madvig, 14 Latin treatises, Copenhagen.

1090 Mayer, Carl Emil Louis, *Die Beziehungen der krankhaften Zustände und Vorgänge in den Sexual-Organen des Weibes zu Geistesstörungen*, Berlin: Hirschwald 1870.

1091 *Melodier fra alle Lande. Danske og fremmede Folkemelodier, Romancer og Operasange, arrangeret for Pianoforte med Text*, vols. 1-3, Copenhagen: Wilhelm Hansen 1877-1882. (Paperback)

1092 Meyer, Ludvig, *Fremmedord-Bog, eller Kortfattet Lexikon over fremmede, i det danske Skrift- og Omgangs-Sprog forekommende Ord, Konstudtryk og Talemaader; tilligemed de i danske Skrifter mest brugelige, fremmede Ordforkortelser*, 2nd enlarged and revised edition, Copenhagen: J.H. Schubothes Boghandling 1844. (Bound copy)

1093 Michelsen, Conrad, *Kasuslehre der Lateinischen Sprache vom kausal-lokalen Standpunkte aus,* Berlin: T. Trautwein 1843. (Bound copy)

1094-1095 Mignet, François Auguste Marie Alexis, *Histoire de la révolution française, depuis 1789 jusqu'en 1814*, vols. 1-2, 6th edition, Paris: Firmin Didot Frères 1836.

1096 Mignet, François Auguste Marie Alexis, *Den franske Revolutions Historie fra 1789 til 1814*, vols. 1-2, trans. by Knud Lyne Rahbek, Copenhagen: Brummer 1826-1827.

1097-1098 Ramsay, Anders Vilhelm, *Persiens berømmelige Monark Cyrus, i hans Ungdom, og paa hans Reiser, Hvor han forhverver sig den dybeste Indsigt i Religionerne, Philosophien, Naturvidenskaben, Lovene, Stats- og Krigskonsten. Efter Ridder Ramsays Maade*, vols. 1-2, trans. by Christian Gran Molberg, Copenhagen: M. Hallager 1784-1785. (Bound copy)

1099 Molière [i.e., Jean-Baptiste Poquelin], *Misanthropen. Komedie i fem Akter. Med en Indledning efter Louis Moland og Kommentarer efter Aimé-Martin*, trans. by Peter Hansen, Copenhagen: C.A. Reitzel 1880.

1100 Montesquieu [Charles-Louis de Secondat, Baron de La Brède et de Montesquieu], *De l'Esprit des Lois*, vols. 1-5, stereotype edition, Paris: Didot 1803.

1101 Ollendorff, Heinrich Gottfried, *Nouvelle méthode pour apprendre a lire, a écrire et a parler une langue en six mois appliquée au latin*, 5th edition, Frankfurt am Main: Charles Jugel 1870. (Bound copy)

1102 Ovid [i.e., Publius Ovidius Naso], *Publii Ovidii Nasonis Klage-Breve over sin ulyksalige Landflygtighed til Keyser Augustum, Hustru og andre Venner, forfattede udi fem Bøger*, trans. by Christian Falster, Copenhagen: O. Lynow 1719. (Bound copy)

1103-1104 [Schneider, Johann Gottlob], *Johann Gottlob Schneiders Handwörterbuch der Griechischen Sprache. Nach der dritten Ausgabe des größern Griechischdeutschen Wörterbuchs mit besondrer Berücksichtigung des Homerischen und Hesiodischen Sprachgebrauchs und mit genauer Angabe der Sylbenlängen*, vols. 1-2, ed. by Franz Ludwig Carl Friedrich Passow, Leipzig: Vogel 1819-1823. (Bound copy)

1105 Borgaard, Carl, *Portefeuillen for 1840*, vol. 4, ed. by Georg Carstensen, Copenhagen: Georg Carstensen 1840; Borgaard, Carl, *Portefeuillen for 1841*, vol. 1, ed. by Georg Carstensen, Copenhagen: Georg Carstensen 1841.

1106 Rask, Rasmus Christian Nielsen, *Engelsk Formlære, udarbejdet efter en ny Plan*, Copenhagen: Gyldendal 1832.

1107 Richter, Johann Christian, *Miniatur-Ariebog for Dame og Herrer*, vols. 2-4, Copenhagen: Richter 1837-1838; *Supplement for 1839*, Copenhagen: Richter 1839; *Supplement for 1840*, Copenhagen: Richter 1840. (Bound copy)

1108 Rosing, Svend, *Engelsk-Dansk Ordbog*, Copenhagen: Gyldendal 1853. (Bound copy)

1109-1114 Rousseau, Jean-Jacques, *Emil eller om Opdragelsen*, vols. 1-6, trans. by Johan Werfel, Copenhagen: Sebastian Popp 1796-1799. (Bound copy)

1115 Rydberg, Viktor, *Romerske Dage*, trans. by Otto Borchsenius, Copenhagen: Schou 1877.

1116 Salzmann, Christian Gotthilf, *Om Ungdommens hemmelige Synder. Tilligemed et Tillæg Om Lægemaaden i de Sygdomme, som ere Følger af samme af S.A.D. Tissot*, anonymous translation, Copenhagen: Trykt hos P. H. Höecke 1786.

1117 *Samlingar*, ed. by Svenska Fornskrift-Sällskapet, vol. 2.1-4 and nos. 11, 16, 19-21, 24, 32-33, Stockholm: P.A. Norstedt & Söner 1845-1860.

1118 *Sarsena eller den fuldkomne Bygmester, indeholdende: Underretning om Frimurerordenens Oprindelse og Historie, Meningerne om hvad den kunde være i vore Tider, hvad en Loge er, hvorledes Lemmerne optages i Ordenen, Logernes Aabning og Slutning i den første samt Befordringen i den anden og tredie St. Johannesgrad, de høiere Skotske Grader og Andreasridderne,* trans. by C. P. F. Knudsen, Copenhagen: Knudsen 1823.

1119 [Scapula, Johann], *Scapulae lexicon Graeco-latinum*, ed. by Henri Stephanus, Basel: Hervag 1557. (Folio. Perg[ament])

1120 Schaldemose, Frederik Julius (trans. and ed.), *Beo-Wulf og Scopes Widsið, to angelsaxiske Digte,* Copenhagen: Steen 1847.

1121 Anonymous ["Lose" and/or Wolke, Christian Heinrich], *Schattenrisse edler Teutschen. Aus dem Tagebuche eines physiognomischen Reisenden*, vols. 1-3, Halle: Chr. Hendel 1783-1784. (Bound copy)

1122 Schiller, Johann Christoph Friedrich von, *Kleinere prosaische Schriften*, vols. 1-2, Leipzig: S.L. Crusius 1792-1800 (vols. 3-4, 1801-1802). (Bound copy)

1123 [Schiller, Johann Christoph Friedrich von], *Friedrich von Schillers Udvalgte Skrifter,* vols. 2-5, trans. by Frederik Julius Schaldemose, Copenhagen: Martin 1833-1834 (vol. 1, 1832).

1124 Schneider, Johann Gottlob, *Griechisch-Deutsches Wörterbuch*, vols. 1-2, 3rd revised and enlarged edition, Leipzig: Hahn 1819; *Griechisch-deutsches Wörterbuch. Supplement-Band zu allen drey Auflagen*, Leipzig: Hahn 1821. (Bound copy)

1125-1126 [Shakespeare, William], *The Dramatic Works of William Shakespeare, From the Correct Edition of Isaac Reed*, vols. 1-2, London: J. Walker 1834. (Bound copy)

1127 Drama. 1 bunch of works including theater repertoire and older dramatic works.

1128 Souvestre, Émile, *Au coin du feu. Nouvelle Édition*, Paris: Michel Lévy frères 1861. (Bound copy)

1129 Sporon, Benjamin Georg, *Eenstydige danske Ords Bemærkelse, oplyst ved Betragtninger og exempler*, vols. 1-2, Copenhagen: Gyldendal 1778-1786.

1130 Stang, Friederich [Frederik], *Systematisk Fremtilling af Kongeriget Norges constitutionelle eller grundlov-bestemte Ret*, Christiania: P.J. Hoppe 1833.

1131 *Neues Taschen-Wörterbuch der dänischen und deutschen Sprache / Dansk-Tydsk og Tydsk-Dansk Lomme-Ordbog*, Part 1-2, 2nd revised stereotyp edition, Leipzig: Holtze 1871 [Leipzig: Karl Tauchnitz 1841]. (Bound copy)

1132 Tegnér, Esaias, *Frithiofs saga*, 6th edition, Stockholm: P.A. Norstedt & Söner 1840. (Bound copy)

1133 Tegnér, Esaias, *Frithiofs saga*, trans. by Adolph Engelbert Boye, Copenhagen: Schubothe 1838. (Bound copy)

1134-1135 [Terence, i.e., Publius Terentius Afer], *P. Terentii Afri Comoediæ sex, secundum Editionem Westerhovianam, cum notis veterum scholiastarum, item Westerhovii et aliorum, selectis*, vols. 1-2, ed. by Gudmundus Magnaeus, Copenhagen: Gyldendal 1780-1782. (Bound copy)

1136 Thieme, Friedrich Wilhelm, *Neues und vollständiges Handwörterbuch der Englischen und Deutschen Sprache / A new and complete English and German dictionary*, Part 1-2, 7th stereotyp edition, Braunschweig: Vieweg 1860. (Bound copy)

1137 Thiers, Adolphe, *Om Eiendommen*, trans. by Christian Georg Nathan David, Copenhagen: H. J. Bing & Søn 1849.

1138 Thomsen, Grímur, *Om den nyfranske Poesi, et Forsøg til Besvarelse af Universitetets æsthetiske Priisspørgsmaal for 1841: "Har Smag og Sands for Poesi gjort Frem- eller Tilbageskridt i Frankrig i de sidste Tider og hvilken er Aarsagen?,"* Copenhagen: Wahlske Boghandlings Forlag 1843. (Bound copy)

1139 Thorsen, Peder Goth (ed.), *Valdemar den Andens jydske Lov - efter den Flensborgske Codex - tilligemed den 1590* *foranstaltede ny Udgave af Loven og den af Ekenberger 1593 besørgede plattydske Oversættelse af samme,* Copenhagen: A.F. Høst 1853.

1140 Wielandt, Joachim (ed.), *En Samling udaf smukke og udvalde danske Vers og Miscellane, Nationen til Ære og Sproget til Ziir befordrede*, vols. 1-2, Copenhagen: no publisher given 1725. (Bound copy)

1141 *Tidsskrift for populære Fremstillinger af Naturvidenskaben*, ed. by Carl Fogh, Christian Frederik Lütken and Christian Theodor Vaupell / Eugenius Warming, 2nd series, vol. 1; 3rd series, vol. 1; 4th series, vol. 1, Copenhagen: P.G. Philipsen 1859-1870.

1142 Lee, Florence S., *Veiledning til Konsten at pleie Syge efter Florence S. Lees' Handbook for Hospitals Sisters*, trans. by S. Lüttichau, preface by S. Engelsted, Copenhagen: C.A. Reitzel 1876.

1143 Veneroni, Giovanni and Placardi, Carlo, *Das Kaiserliche Sprach- und Wörterbuch, darinnen die vier Europäischen Hauptsprachen, als nämlich: I. Die Italiänische, mit der Französisch-Teutsch- und Lateinischen, II. Die Französische, mit der Italiänisch-Teutsch- und Lateinischen, III. Die Teutsche, mit der Französisch-Lateinisch und Italiänischen, IV. Die Lateinische, mit der Italiänisch-Französisch- und Teutschen Sprache erkläret und vorgetragen werden*, Cologne: F.W.J. Metternich 1766. (Bound copy)

1144 [Virgil, i.e., Publius Vergilius Maro], *P. Virgilii Maronis opera perpetua adnotatione illustrata a Chr. Gottl. Heyne* [on the basis of the commented edition of Christian Gottlob Heyne], vols. 1-2, ed. by Jacob Baden, Copenhagen: Gyldendal 1778-1780. (Bound copy)

1145 One bundle of Danish songs and occasional songs.

1146 Voltaire [i.e, François-Marie Arouet], *Histoire de Charles XII*, Paris: Librairie De Pougin 1836. (Bound copy)

1147 Voltaire [i.e, François-Marie Arouet], *Gengiskan i China*, trans. by Christen Henriksen Pram, Copenhagen: Andreas Seidelin 1815.

1148 Voltaire [i.e, François-Marie Arouet], *Keiser Peter den Stores Liv og Levnet, som indbefatter det Russiske Riges Historie udi hans Regierings-Tid*, vols. 1-2, Copenhagen: no publisher given 1766-1769. (Bound copy)

1149 Walker, John, *A Critical Pronouncing Dictionary, and Expositor of the English Language...To which are prefixed, Principles of English Pronunciation...Likewise, Rules to be observed by the Natives of Scotland, Ireland and London, for avoiding their respective peculiarities; and Directions to Foreigners...The whole interspersed with Observations, etymological, critical, and grammatical*, London and Leipzig: E. Fleischer 1826. (Bound copy)

1150 Watt, Robert, *Hinsides Atlanterhavet. Skildringer fra Amerika*, vol. 3, *Religieuse Sekter*, Copenhagen: P. Bloch 1874 (vols. 1-2, 1872-1873).

1151 Formey, Jean Henri Samuel, *Begyndelsesgrunde til de skiönne Videnskaber*, trans. by Niels H. Weinrich, Copenhagen: no publisher given 1787.

1152 Welander, Peter Olof, *Norskt- (och danskt-) svenskt hand-lexikon*, ed. by C. A. Guldberg, Christiania: Guldberg & Dzwonkowski 1846.

1153 Welander, Peter Olof, *Svensk-dansk-norsk Lommeordbog*, ed. by Svante Ströhm, Copenhagen: G.H. Jægers skandinaviske Forlagshandel 1846.

1154 Wieland, Christoph Martin, *Poetische Schriften*, vols. 1-3, 3rd revised edition, Zurich: Orell, Geßner 1770. (Bound copy)

1155 Woltersdorf, K. von, *Der Lebenspunkt, oder Grund und Ursache aller Krankheiten und Mittel zur gründlichen Heilung derselben. Ein Buch in Briefen für jeden denkenden Leser*, Berlin: Voß 1841. (Bound copy)

1156-1157 Worm, Jens, *Forsøg til et Lexicon over danske, norske og islandske lærde Mænd, som ved trykte Skrifter have giort sig bekiendte, saavelsom andre Ustuderede, som noget have skrevet, hvorudi deres Fødsel, betydeligste Levnets Omstændigheder og Død ved Aarstal kortelig erindres, og deres Skrifter, saavidt mueligt, fuldstændig anføres*, vol. 1, Helsingør: Trykt i det Kongelig allene privilegerede Bogtrykkerie 1771; vol.

2, Copenhagen: Trykt paa det typographiske Selskabs Bekostning hos August Frieder. Stein 1773 (vol. 3, 1784). (Bound copy)

1158 Zahle, Peter Christian, *Folkesaga især om Nordboens Liv, Daad og Idræt ude og hjemme, I, De tolv første Aarhundreder efter vor Tidsregning, Udarbeidet nærmest til Brug for Landboerne*, Copenhagen: Trykt hos C.G. Schiellerup 1866-1868. (together with 2 (other) works)

1159-1160 Zeh, Philipp, *Nuovo Dizionario italiano-tedesco e tedesco-italiano. Composto su i migliori e piu recenti dizionari delle due lingue / Vollständiges deutsch-italienisches und italienisch-deutsches Wörterbuch. Verfaßt nach den vorzüglichsten über beide Sprachen bisher erschienenen Wörterbüchern*, vols. 1-2, Nuremberg and Leipzig: Zeh 1825. (Bound copy)

1161-1175 15 bundles of books.

1176 A large role of maps and engravings.

1177 A carved rune stick.

Publisher

1178 Eiríksson, Magnús, *Dr. Martensens trykte moralske Paragrapher, eller det saakaldte "Grundrids til Moralphilosophiens System af Dr. Hans Martensen", i dets forvirrede, idealistisk-metaphysiske og phantastisk-speculative, Religion og Christendom undergravende, fatalistiske, pantheistiske og selvforguderske Væsen*, Copenhagen: H.C. Klein 1846. (2 copies)

1179 Eiríksson, Magnús, *Speculativ Rettroenhed, fremstillet efter Dr. Martensens "christelige Dogmatik", og Geistlig Retfærdighed, belyst ved en Biskops Deeltagelse i en Generalfiskal-Sag*, Copenhagen: Trykt hos J.S. Salomon 1849.

1180 Eiríksson, Magnús, *Hvem har Ret: Grundtvigianerne eller deres Modstandere? og Hvad har Christus befalet om Daaben? Nogle orienterende Bemærkninger*, Copenhagen: E.L. Thaarup 1863.

1181 Eiríksson, Magnús, *Hvem har Ret: Grundtvigianerne eller deres Modstandere? og Hvad har Christus befalet om Daaben? Nogle orienterende Bemærkninger*, 2nd edition, Copenhagen: E.L. Thaarup 1863.

1182 Eiríksson, Magnús, *Gud og Reformatoren. En religiøs Idee. Samt nogle Bemærkninger om de kirkelige Tilstande, Dr. S. Kierkegaard og Forfatteren*, Copenhagen: J.H. Schubothe 1866.

1183 Eiríksson, Magnús, *Nokkrar athugasemdir um Sannanir "katólsku prestanna í Reykjavík" fyrir guðdómi Jesú Krists*, Copenhagen: L. Klein 1868. (9 copies)

1184 Eiríksson, Magnús, *Kunne vi elske Næsten som os selv? Nogle tildeels nye Tanker om Kjærligheden samt flere derhen hørende Skriftsteder*, Copenhagen: Paa Forfatterens Forlag 1870. (91 copies and 2 copies with beautiful bindings)

1185 Eiríksson, Magnús, *Om Bønnens Virkning og dens Forhold til Guds Uforanderlighed. Nogle Oplysninger og Bemærkninger, nærmest byggede paa andelig Erfaring og et umiddelbart Gudsforhold*, Copenhagen: Paa Forfatterens Forlag 1870. (76 copies and 2 copies with beautiful binding)

1186 Eiríksson, Magnús, *Paulus og Christus eller Pauli Lære om Retfærdiggjørelsen sammenlignet med Christi Lære om Syndsforladelsen, tilligemed nogle Bemærkninger om andre paulinske Lærdomme m. M.*, Copenhagen: Udgivet og forlagt af Forfatteren 1871. (69 copies and 5 elegant bound copies)

1187 Eiríksson, Magnús, *Jøder og Christne eller Hvorledes blev Jesus fra Nazareth betragtet i den ældste Kirke og hvorledes blev han senere betragtet? En populær, historisk-kritisk Undersøgelse, tilegnet de Sandhedskjærlige*, Copenhagen: Udgivet og forlagt af Forfatteren 1873. (80 copies and 1 bound copy)

1188 Eiríksson, Magnús, *Herr A. Pedrin og Christendommen. Nogle Oplysninger om hans Skrift: "Vor Herres og Frelsers Jesu Christi nye Testament og Magnus Eirikssons reformeerte Jødedom,"* Copenhagen: Sally B. Salomons Tryk 1874. (387 copies)

1189 Anonymous [Grímur Thomsen], *En Privatskrivelse til den anden gamle Landsbypræst, fra hans gamle Ven, den første gamle Candidat, som Commentar over Herr Pastors Epistola til Sr. Magnus Eiriksson*, Copenhagen: P.G. Philipsen 1844. (227 copies)

1190 Eiríksson, Magnús (ed. et al.), *Fjórir þættir um alþíng og önnur málefni Íslendínga*, Copenhagen: J.D. Quist 1843. (52 copies)

1191-1196 Eiríksson, Magnús, *Om Baptister og Barnedaab, samt flere Momenter af Den kirkelige og speculative Christendom*, Copenhagen: P.G. Philipsen 1844. (83 copies and 1 bound copy)

1197-1213 Eiríksson, Magnús, *Er Johannes-Evangeliet et apostolisk og ægte Evangelium og er dets Lære om Guds Menneskevorden en sand og christelig Lære? En religiøs-dogmatisk, historisk-kritisk Undersøgelse*, Copenhagen: Udgivet og forlagt af Forfatteren 1863. (552 copies, 1 bound copy and one bundle of damaged copies)

1214 Eiríksson, Magnús, *Jóhannesar guðspjall og Lærdómur kirkjunnar um guð, nokkrar athugasemdir til yfirvegunar þeim Íslendíngum, sem ekki vilja svívirða og lasta guð með trú sinni*, Copenhagen: L. Klein 1865. (4 copies and 1 bound copy)

1215 Benedikt Gröndal, Gísla Brynjúlfson and Steingrímur Thorsteinsson, *Svava. Ýmisleg kvæði*, Copenhagen: Á kostnað P. Sveinssonar 1860. (53 copies and one bundle of damaged copies)

1216 Anonymous [Axel Frederik Lassen], *Om Aarsagen til Cholera. Af en dansk Naturforsker*, Copenhagen: Printed for the Author by Qvist and Co. 1866.

1217 Anonymous [Axel Frederik Lassen], *Origine du Choléra. Par un Naturaliste Danois*, Copenhagen: Printed for the Author by Qvist and Co. 1866. (20 copies)

1218 Anonymous [Axel Frederik Lassen], *De causa Cholerae. Scripsit Investigator Naturae Danus*, Copenhagen: Printed for the Author by Qvist and Co. 1866.

1219 Anonymous [Axel Frederik Lassen], *The Cause of Cholera. By a Danish naturalist*, Copenhagen: Printed for the Author by Qvist and Co. 1866. (24 copies)

1220 One bundle of portraits of various Icelanders.

Index to the Auction Catalogue of Eiríksson's Library

Gerhard Schreiber

The index includes the names of the authors and editors appearing in the original printed edition of the auction catalogue along with those names that have been added to the catalogue in the present edition. The numbers refer to the entry numbers of the books.

Index of Persons

Martensen, Hans Lassen (1808-84), Danish theologian, 2-6, 8, 10, 17-18, 20-21, 23-24, 26-29, 31, 35, 39-40, 43, 47, 51-54, 59-73, 76, 80-94, 100-105, 107-111, 113, 115-144, 147-151, 153, 167-169, 172-174, 185, 188, 190-193, 195-196, 198-204, 210, 235, 239, 263, 302-303, 305, 307-308, 313, 319, 326-328, 345.
Mary, 245, 254, 262.
Maudsley, Henry (1835-1918), English psychologist, 19.
Melanchthon, Philipp (1497-1560), German theologian, 178, 298.
Melsteð, Páll (1791-1861), regional leader in Iceland, 327.
Melsteð, Sigurður (1819-95), Icelandic theologian, 238-241, 259, 263, 330-331, 333.
Mill, John Stuart (1806-73), English philosopher, 11, 95, 217, 309, 343-344.
Minna-Núpi, Brynjúlfur Jónsson frá (1838-1914), Icelandic farmer, 339.
Monrad, Ditlev Gothard (1811-87), Danish politician and bishop, 63, 170.
Mønster, Peter Christian (1797-1870), Danish Baptist, 187-188.
Mynster, Jacob Peter (1775-1854), Danish bishop, 47, 50-51, 54, 65, 80-81, 85-89, 100-102, 151, 153, 170-172, 180-183, 185, 190-192, 198, 200.
Nielsen, Rasmus (1809-84), Danish philosopher, 24, 29-32, 92-93, 110, 149, 210.

Ólafsson, Jón (1850-1916), Icelandic journalist and parliamentarian, 296.
Olgeirsson, Einar (1902-93), Icelandic politician, 341.
Origen (ca. 184-254), church father, 257.
Ørsted, Hans Christian (1777-1851), Danish natural scientist, 37-38.
Overbeck, Franz Camille (1837-1905), German Protestant theologian, 11, 104.

Papias of Hierapolis (2nd century), Christian author, 257.
Paludan-Müller, Jens (1813-99), Danish pastor, 20, 92, 110.
Paul the Apostle (ca. 5-67), 3-4, 7, 9, 30, 94, 98, 156, 176, 195, 211, 250, 254-255, 262-163, 298-299, 312, 314, 316-318.
Pedrin, Andreas Daniel (1823-91), Danish religious author, 7, 100, 112.
Pétursson, Björn (1826-93), Unitarian minister, 296-297.
Pétursson, Pétur (1808-91), Icelandic bishop, 237, 259, 344.
Pétursson, Rögnvaldur (1877-1940), Unitarian minister, 297.
Pjetursson, Hafsteinn (1858-1929), Icelandic theologian, 76, 86, 98-

Sturluson, Snorri (ca. 1178-1241), Icelandic historian and politician, 174.
Styrkársdóttir, Auður (b. 1951), Icelandic political scientist, 95, 343.

Theunissen, Michael (1932-2015), German philosopher, 10, 162, 166, 268, 290-291.
Thomas Aquinas (1225-74), Catholic theologian, 218.
Thomsen, Grímur (1820-96), Icelandic poet, 66, 327.
Thordersen, Helgi Guðmundsson (1794-1867), Icelandic bishop, 3, 308, 328.
Thorlacius, Einar (1816-72), Icelandic priest, 252, 259, 330.
Þorláksson, Niels Steingrímur (1857-1943), Icelandic minister, 337, 341.
Thoroddsen, Jón (1818-66), Icelandic district magistrate, 5, 340.
Þráinsdóttir, Jóhanna (1940-2005), Icelandic theologian, 10-11, 72, 343-344.
Thulstrup, Niels (1924-88), Danish theologian, 2, 10, 76, 99, 109, 146, 148.
Tillich, Paul (1886-1965), German theologian, 159.
Tolstoy, Leo (1828-1910), Russian writer, 339.
Treschow, Niels (1751-1833), Danish philosopher, 34-36.

Vodskov, Hans Sofus (1846-1910), Danish literary critic, 7-8, 76, 99.

Wette, Wilhelm Martin Leberecht de (1780-1849), German theologian, 21, 53, 97, 118, 194-195.
Whately, Richard (1787-1863), Irish theologian, 36-37.
Winther, Christian (1796-1876), Danish poet, 20.
Wolff, Christian (1679-1754), German philosopher, 34.
Wollstonecraft, Mary (1759-97), English writer and philosopher, 217, 219.
Wycliff, John (ca. 1320-84), English philosopher and theologian, 298.

Zeuthen, Frederik Ludvig Bang (1805-74), Danish philosopher, 22.
Zwingli, Ulrich (1484-1531), Swiss theologian, 189, 298.

Index of Subjects

Previously Published Titles in the Series
Danish Golden Age Studies and *Texts from Golden Age Denmark*

Danish Golden Age Studies

Volume 1
K. Brian Soderquist, *The Isolated Self: Truth and Untruth in Søren Kierkegaard's On the Concept of Irony* (2007). Hardback. viii+247pp. ISBN 978-87-635-3090-3. Paperback edition: 2013. ISBN 978-87-635-4065-0.

Volume 2
Robert Leslie Horn, *Positivity and Dialectic: A Study of the Theological Method of Hans Lassen Martensen* (2007). Hardback. xviii+246pp. ISBN 978-87-635-3089-7.

Volume 3
Jon Stewart, *A History of Hegelianism in Golden Age Denmark*
Tome I: *The Heiberg Period: 1824-1836* (2007). Hardback. xxi+629pp.
ISBN 978-87-635-3086-6.
Tome II: *The Martensen Period: 1837-1842* (2007). Hardback. xx+775pp.
ISBN 978-87-635-3101-6.

Volume 4
Curtis L. Thompson, *Following the Cultured Public's Chosen One: Why Martensen Mattered to Kierkegaard* (2008). Hardback. xvi+216pp. ISBN 978-87-635-1097-4.

Volume 5
Jon Stewart (editor), *Johan Ludvig Heiberg: Philosopher, Littérateur, Dramaturge, and Political Thinker* (2008). Hardback. xxii+548pp. ISBN 978-87-635-1096-7.

Volume 6
Jon Stewart (editor), *Hans Lassen Martensen: Theologian, Philosopher and Social Critic* (2012). Hardback. xv+351pp. ISBN 978-87-635-3169-6.

Volume 7
Jon Stewart (editor), *The Heibergs and the Theater: Between Vaudeville, Romantic Comedy and National Drama* (2012). Hardback. xi+267pp. ISBN 978-87-635-3897-8.

Volume 8
Katalin Nun, *Women of the Danish Golden Age: Literature, Theater and the Emancipation of Women* (2013). Hardback. xvi+180pp. ISBN 978-87-635-3913-5.

Volume 9
Jon Stewart, *The Cultural Crisis of the Danish Golden Age: Heiberg, Martensen and Kierkegaard* (2015). Hardback. xvi+180pp. ISBN 978-87-635-4269-2.

Texts from Golden Age Denmark

Volume 1
Heiberg's On the Significance of Philosophy for the Present Age and Other Texts, trans. and ed. by Jon Stewart (2005). Hardback. xxii+46pp. ISBN 978-87-635-3084-2.

Volume 2
Heiberg's Speculative Logic and Other Texts, trans. and ed. by Jon Stewart (2006). Hardback. xviii+387pp. ISBN 978-87-635-3091-0.

Volume 3
Heiberg's Introductory Lecture to the Logic Course and Other Texts, trans. and ed. by Jon Stewart (2007). Hardback. xvii+33pp. ISBN 978-87-635-3085-9.

Volume 4
Heiberg's Contingency Regarded from the Point of View of Logic and Other Texts, trans. and ed. by Jon Stewart (2008). Hardback. vxi+457pp. ISBN 978-87-635-1099-8.

Volume 5
Mynster's "Rationalism, Supernaturalism" and the Debate about Mediation, trans. and ed. by Jon Stewart (2009). Hardback. vxi+683pp. ISBN 978-87-635-3096-5.

Volume 6
Heiberg's Perseus and Other Texts, trans. and ed. by Jon Stewart (2011). Hardback. xiii+406pp. ISBN 978-87-635-3170-2.

Both series are published by
Museum Tusculanum Press
University of Copenhagen, Birketinget 6, DK-2300 Copenhagen S.
Tel. +45 32 34 14 14. E-mail: info@mtp.dk. www.mtp.dk.